Taking Sides: Clashing Views
on Educational Issues, 20/e

Glenn L. Koonce

http://create.mheducation.com

This McGraw-Hill Create text may include materials submitted to
McGraw-Hill for publication by the instructor of this course.
The instructor is solely responsible for the editorial content of such
materials. Instructors retain copyright of these additional materials.

ISBN-10: 1260494241   ISBN-13: 9781260494242

2 3 4 5 6 7 8 9 LOV 24 23 22 21 20

Contents

Detailed Table of Contents

Unit 1: Basic Theoretical Issues

Issue: Should the Curriculum Be Standardized for All?
YES: Ervin Sparapani and David Pérez, from "A Perspective on the Standardized Curriculum and Its Effect on Teaching and Learning," *Journal of Education and Social Policy* (2015)
NO: John Holt, from "Escape from Childhood," *E.P. Dutton* (1974)

Saginaw Valley State University Professor Ervin Sparapuni and Associate Provost at Saginaw Valley State University, David Perez contend that even though a curriculum may be standard, teachers need to use a variety of teaching approaches to meet the needs of diverse student populations. Educator John Holt argues that an imposed curriculum damages the individual and usurps a basic human right to select one's own path of development.

Issue: Should "Public Schooling" Be Redefined?
YES: Stephanie T. Scott, from "An Argument for Redefining Public Schools," *Pawley Learning Institute* (2008)
NO: Linda Nathan et al., from "A Response to Frederick Hess," *Phi Delta Kappan* (2004)

Researcher Stephanie Scott explains that the purpose of public schools must be clarified at a minimum and redefined at a maximum in this era where parents have increased choices for the education of their children. Linda Nathan, Joe Nathan, Ray Bacchetti, and Evans Clinchy express a variety of concerns about the conceptual expansion that Hess proposes.

Unit 2: Current Fundamental Issues

Issue: Are Truly Democratic Classrooms Possible?
YES: Lina Bell Soares, from "The Education Students Deserve: Building a Democratic Classroom in Teacher Education," *Critical Literacy: Theories and Practices* (2013)
NO: Gary K. Clabaugh, from "Second Thoughts about Democratic Classrooms," *Educational Horizons* (2008)

Lina Soares, Associate Professor of Education, draws from John Dewey and literature related to social justice and critical multicultural education as a way to practice democracy in the classroom. Gary K. Clabaugh, Professor of Education, examines such factors as top-down management, compulsory attendance, business world influences, and federal mandates to declare Morrison's ideas to be "out of touch" with reality.

Issue: Do Public Schools Have Grounds to Punish Students for Their Off-Campus Online Speech?
YES: Theodore A. McKee, from *J.S. v. Blue Mountain School District*, United States Court of Appeals (2011)
NO: Theodore A. McKee, from *Layshock v. Hermitage School District*, United States Court of Appeals (2011)

On February 11, 2010, a panel of judges from the Third Circuit Court of Appeals heard the *J.S. v. Blue Mountain District* case ruling against a suspended junior high school student who ridiculed her principal online using MySpace with a computer that was accessed off-campus. The student had been suspended by her school district. On the previous day, February 10, 2010, another panel of three judges from the same Third Circuit Court of Appeals heard *Layshock v. Hermitage School District* and ruled on June 3, 2010 that the school district had violated high school senior Justin Layshock's First Amendments free speech rights. A local Pennsylvania school official suspended Layshock for10 days. He was also placed in an alternative education setting and banned from extracurricular activities and graduation ceremonies for mocking his principal with a fake MySpace profile that he accessed off-campus. Both the *J.S.* and *Layshock* cases were later heard on June 3, 2011 by the Full Third Circuit Court of Appeals, with a twist and changes to the earlier ruling in J.S. due to application of a 1969 U.S. Supreme Court ruling. Chief Judge Theodore McKee wrote the court's opinion for both the Layshock & J.S. cases. In 2012, the U.S. Supreme Court declined to hear either of these social media cases.

With a focus on the new math standards, Michigan State University researchers William Schmidt and Nathan Burroughs indicate the Common Core State Standards will address two tenacious problems in U.S. education: the mediocrity quality of mathematics learning and unequal opportunity in U.S. schools. Tom Loveless, a senior fellow at the Brookings Institute, takes the position that chances for the Common Core Standards to be successful are "slim at best" when compared to the claims on how well similar policies have worked in the past.

Policy Analyst and Director of preK-12 Educator Quality with the Education Policy Program at New America, Roxanne Garza and Melissa Tooley, author of *From Frenzied to Focused: How School Staffing Models Can Support Principals in Instructional Leadership*, discuss how three districts divvy up principals' duties so they can devote time to instructional leadership. Media contact, Laura Hoxworth interviews Coby Meyer, research associate professor at the University of Virginia and co-editor Marlene Darwin of the American Institutes for Research advocate addressing in their book, *Enduring Myths that Inhibit School Turnaround*, the myths that inhibit school turnaround, so that policy makers and school leaders can address them head on.

Unit 3: Current Specific Issues

Arvin Campbell, in a White Paper in partial fulfillment required for graduation from the Leadership Command College, Benbrook Police Department, supports arming teachers and administrators to serve as a deterrent because time is a big factor in confronting a shooter. Led by President Kenneth Trump, the National School Safety and Security Services asserts that teachers want to be armed with "textbooks and computers, not guns."

Dr. Sara Vecchiotti, Esq., Chief Program Officer at the Foundation for Child Development, in her support for early learning environments notes that children can receive benefits from early care and education if early childhood education professionals are adequately prepared, competent, supported, and well compensated. Erika Christakis from *The Atlantic* posits that the same educational policies that are pushing academic goals down to ever earlier levels seem to be contributing to—while at the same time obscuring—the fact that young children are gaining fewer skills, not more.

Council for the Accreditation of Educator Preparation President Jim Cibulka states that tightening government licensure regulation is needed to assure candidate and program quality that can result in a more favorable learning environment for Pre-K–12 students. David Chard indicates that current state control of teacher preparation and licensing does not ensure that teachers will be of high quality.

Issue: <u>Does Funding Improve Student Achievement?</u>
YES: Jesse Rothstein, Julien Lafortune, and Diane Whitmore Schanzenbach, from "Can School Finance Reforms Improve Student Achievement?" *Washington Center for Equitable Growth* (2016)
NO: Caitlin Emma, from "Here's Why $7 Billion Didn't Help America's Worst Schools," *Politico* (2015)

Jesse Rothstein, a Ph.D. candidate at the University of California, Berkley Economics Department, Julien Lafortune, Professor of Public Policy and Economics at the University of California, and Diane Whitmore Schanzenbach, Chair of the Program on Child, Adolescent, and Family Studies at Northwestern's Institute for Policy Research and senior fellow at the Brookings Institute, find that "money matters for student achievement" and through a new strand of research have found positive effects of additional funding on student achievement. Caitlin Emma, Politico reporter covering education, inquires as to why the government pumped $3 billion dollars of economic stimulus money into School Improvement Grants when six years later the program failed to produce only modest or no gains in student achievement.

Issue: <u>Should Charter Schools Be Expanded?</u>
YES: Derrell Bradford, from "Strengthening the Roots of the Charter-School Movement," *Education Next* (2018)
NO: Robin Lake, et al., from "Why Is Charter Growth Slowing?" *Education Next* (2018)

Derrell Bradford, executive vice-president of 50CAN, a national non-profit that advocates for equal opportunity in K-12 education and senior visiting fellow at the Thomas B. Fordham Institute, notes that we would be better advised to provide leaders of charter schools with more support because they allow the autonomy and flexibility to do what some districts can't or won't. Robin Lake, director of the Center on Reinventing Public Education at the University of Washington Bothell, where Roohi Sharma is research coordinator and Alice Opalka is special assistant to the director, Trey Cobb, a graduate student at the University of Notre Dame and a middle school math teacher, share their study of charter school growth and decline in the San Francisco Bay area of charter schools over the last five years and they note that districts have become skilled at limiting charter growth.

Issue: <u>Is the Use of Technology Changing How Teachers Teach and Students Learn?</u>
YES: Joanne Jacobs, from "Beyond the Factory Model," *Education Next* (2014)
NO: Benjamin Herold, from "Why Ed Tech Is Not Transforming How Teachers Teach: Student-Centered, Technology-Driven Instruction Remains Elusive for Most," *Education Week* (2015)

Former San Jose Mercury News editorial writer and columnist for K-12 education, Joanne Jacobs, provides evidence from the field that technology use through Blended Learning strategies has a positive effect on student learning outcomes even though she acknowledges it is not "transformational" right now. Benjamin Herold posits that a mountain of evidence indicates that teachers have been painfully slow to transform the way they teach despite the massive influx of new technology into their classrooms.

Issue: <u>Should Students Be Allowed to Opt Out?</u>
YES: Kristina Rizga, from "Sorry, I'm Not Taking This Test," *Mother Jones* (2015)
NO: Jonah Edelman, from "This Issue Is Bigger Than Just Testing," *Education Next* (2016)

Kristina Rizga, a former education correspondent at *Mother Jones* and author of *Mission High,* argues that with so much controversy revolving around the effects of testing on struggling students and schools, it's hard to remember that the movement's original goal was to level the educational playing field. Jonah Edelman, an American advocate for public education and the co-founder and Chief Executive Officer of Stand for Children deeply values teachers' perspective on how students are progressing academically, but he also wants a more objective gauge of whether students are on grade level in math, reading, and writing.

Issue: <u>Does Homework Matter?</u>
YES: Lee Walk and Marshall Lassak, from "Making Homework Matter to Students: More Meaningful Homework Is an Easily Achievable Goal," *Mathematics Teaching in the Middle School* (2017)
NO: Cory A. Bennette, from "'Most Won't Do It!' Examining Homework as a Structure for Learning in a Diverse Middle School," *American Secondary Education* (2017)

Lee Walk who teaches eighth-grade math and science at Cumberland Middle School in Toledo, Illinois and Marshall Lassak who teaches at Eastern Illinois University in Charleston believe that with an appropriate level of demand and timely feedback will allow students to learn from their homework and be confident that the work they do outside of class is meaningful.
Cory Bennett, an Associate Professor of Education at Idaho State University, provides recommendations for homework policy and practice that requires critical examination of practices and beliefs.

Speaking to the U.S. House Committee on Education and the Workforce, Jane Robbins is opposed to using technology to track student social emotional behavior because she feels the government will have enormous leeway to disclose personal information on individual students without their consent. Benjamin Herold comments on both sides of the issue, but identifies school districts that have already implemented SEL assessment and comments favorable on the growing push to use educational technology to measure, monitor, and modify students' emotions, mindsets, and ways of thinking.

Ty Pierce, Manager of Education and Multimedia Services at the Ohio History Connection states that electronic textbooks are quickly becoming the norm for K12 education, and the use of myriad electronic resources is now standard practice in the modern classroom. The Paper and Packaging Board support print books noting that current research shows people are still more likely to have read a print book than a digital one.

Preface

This book presents opposing or sharply varying viewpoints on educational issues of current concerns. Unit 1 offers consideration of two basic theoretical issues that have been discussed by scholars and practitioners in the past century and are still debated today: curriculum content and its imposition upon the young and the philosophical underpinning of the purpose and process of public education. Unit 2 features four issues that are fundamental to understanding the present circumstances that shape American education: democratic classrooms for citizenship preparation; student First Amendment rights; common curriculum considerations, including policy and the Common Core standards; and the challenges of *turning around* schools with poor school performance. Unit 3 examines more specific issues currently being discussed and debated: arming teachers, universal preschool, teacher preparation and federal government policies, no-zero grading practices, twenty-first century skills movement, flipped learning and flipped classrooms, class size and student achievement, school funding and student achievement, charter school expansion, impact of technology on teaching and learning, opting out of testing, homework, technology and tracing student social–emotional learning, electronic versus print textbooks, and K–12 school accreditation.

Every effort has been made to select views from a wide range of thinkers—philosophers, psychologists, sociologists, professional educators, political leaders, historians, researchers, and, at times, gadflies who want to have their voices heard. Time-honored stances in education are being disputed. All K–12 students are affected in the discussions to improve the outcomes for their career and college readiness. A special effort has been made to include the new Federal law, Every Student Succeeds Act (ESSA), and its effect on many of the issues.

By combining the material in this volume with the informational background provided by a good introductory textbook, students should be prepared to address the problems confronting schools today. My hope is that students will find challenges in the material presented here in Taking Sides—provocations that will inspire them to better understand the roots of educational controversy, to attain a greater awareness of possible alternatives in dealing with the various issues, and to stretch their personal powers of creative thinking in the search for more promising resolutions to the problems.

Changes to This Edition

This 20th edition continues with *enhanced pedagogy*: Expanded Introduction; Learning Outcomes; Exploring the Issue featuring Critical Thinking and Reflection Questions; Is There Common Ground?; Additional Resources; and Internet References relevant to each issue. With the publication of this 20th edition of *Taking Sides: Clashing Views on Educational Issues*, readers should stay attuned to changes in the literature because as the debate continues, so do the issues and their outcomes.

Acknowledgments

I am thankful for the kind and efficient assistance given to me by Jill Meloy and the other members of the editorial staff at McGraw-Hill Create®/Contemporary Learning Series, and appreciation to my wife, Suzanne, for love, support, and assistance in completing this edition.

Glenn L. Koonce
Regent University

Editor of This Volume

Glenn L. Koonce is chair of the Educational Leadership Programs in the School of Education at Regent University. A Vietnam combat veteran and 30 teacher, principal, and assistant superintendent veteran in the public schools, Dr. Koonce has been recognized as Principal of the Year for the State of Virginia, President of the Virginia Association of Secondary School Principals, President of the Virginia Education Coalition, President of the Virginia Professors of Educational Leadership, President of the Virginia Education Research Association, Boss of the Year several times in the public schools, Education Professor of the Year for Regent University School of Education, Distinguished Service Award from Regent University, and Distinguished Service Award from the Virginia Professors of Educational Leadership. Research, consulting, publications, teaching, and service from the local level to international levels, and serving on the editorial review board for publications from the National Council of Professors of Educational Administration (NCPEA) and the *European Journal of Education Sciences* round out his extensive experiences. His personal interests include spiritual, family, community, and wellness activities of all kinds. He loves music, travel, and adventures, in no particular order. He is married to Suzanne, has four children, and nine grandchildren.

Academic Advisory Board Members

Members of the Academic Advisory Board are instrumental in the final selection of articles for Taking Sides books. Their review of the articles for content, level, and appropriateness provides critical direction to the editor and staff. We think that you will find their careful consideration reflected in this book.

Paul G. Fitchett
University of North Carolina, Charlotte

Kathleen E. Fite
Texas State University – San Marcos

Betty Jane Fratzke
Indiana Wesleyan University

Josephine Fritts
Ozarks Technical Community College

Shelly Furuness
Butler University

George Georgiou
Towson University

Lois Gilchrist
Georgia Military College

Gina Giuliano
University at Albany, SUNY

Francis Godwyll
Ohio University

Vella Goebel
University of Southern Indiana

Rose Gong
Eastern Illinois University

Denise Greene
Roanoke College

Charles Grindstaff
Concord University

Jason Helfer
Knox College

Sharon Hirschy
Collin College-Frisco

Michael Hohn
Portland Community College

Jennifer Holleran
Community College of Allegheny County

Wanda Hutchison
Athens State University

Charles Jackson
Augusta State University

Mary Alice Jennings
Mississippi Valley State University

Leslie Jones
Nicholls State University

Kevin Jones
Lincoln Memorial University

Tanya Judd Pucella
Marietta College

Steven Kaatz
Bethel University

Jeffrey Kaplan
University of Central Florida

Linda Karges-Bone
Charleston Southern University

Alan Karns
Wilkes University/Edinboro University

Harvey Karron
Stony Brook University

Amy Kavanaugh
Ferris State University

Barbara Kawulich
University of West Georgia

Susan Kelewae
Kent State University

Janna Kellinger
University of Massachusetts Boston

Richard Kennedy
North Carolina Wesleyan College

Walter Klar
Cape Cod Community College

Ellie Kunkel
Peru State College

Patricia Lanzon
Henry Ford Community College

Aaron J. Lawler
Benedictine University

Sandra L. Leslie
Shorter College

Joslen Letscher
University of Detroit Mercy

Ronald E. Lewis
Grand Canyon University

Lawanna M. Lewis
Grand Canyon University

Dennis A. Lichty
Wayne State College

Lennie Little
Jackson State University

Harold London
DePaul University

Alfred Longo
Ocean County College

Arthur Maloney
Pace University NYC

Roosevelt Martin, Jr.
Chicago State University

Carmen McCrink
Barry University

John W. McNeeley
Daytona State College

Joanne Milke
Southern Connecticut State University

Greg Morris
Grand Rapids Community College

Thalia Mulvihill
Ball State University

Paul Nelson
Pacific Lutheran University

Susan J. Nix
West Texas A&M University

Myron Oglesby-Pitts
Belmont University

Jessie Panko
Saint Xavier University

Robert Parrish
University of North Florida, COEHS

Lynn Patterson
Murray State University

Graham Patterson
Grambling State University

Roy R. Pellicano
St. Joseph's College, New York

Peter Phipps
Dutchess Community College

Mary Pickard
East Carolina University

Monte Piliawsky
Wayne State University

Dawn Lydia Piper
Brown Mackie College

Ernest Pratt
Mount Union College

Patrice Preston-Grimes
University of Virginia

Guillermina Raffo Magnasco

Broward College

Anne Marie Rakip
South Carolina State University

Cynthia Rand-Johnson
Albany State University

Doug Rice
California State University, Sacramento

Timothy Richards
McKendree University

Kathryn Righter
Ashland University

Linda Mattern Ritts
Western Nebraska Community College – Alliance

Thomas R. Scheira
Buffalo State College

Carol Schmid
Guilford Technical Community College

Lisa Schoer
Converse College

Stephen T. Schroth
Knox College

Jill Schurr
Austin College

Kathleen Scott
Ashland University, Elyria

Jan Seiter
Texas A & M Central Texas

Melanie Shaw
North central University

Ralph Shibley
University of Rio Grande

Nicholas Shudak
Mount Marty College

Michael V. Smith
The Catholic University of America

Pamela Smith
Eastern Michigan University

Leone Snyder
University of St. Thomas Capella University

Harvey Solganick
LeTourneau University

Shirley Sommers
Nazareth College

Theresa Stahler
Kutztown University

Robert Stennett
University of North Georgia, Gainesville

Robert Stevens
The University of Texas at Tyler

Tricia Stewart
University of Rochester

Terri Suico
Saint Mary's College

Mona Thompson
California State University, Channel Islands

Sandra M. Todaro
Bossier Parish Community College

Kristopher Treat
Arizona State University

Introduction

Ways of Thinking about Educational Issues

Society needs a forum where philosophers, politicians, legislators, policy makers, practitioners, parents, students, and the community can freely deliberate educational issues. History has often chronicled these issues as problems to be fixed rather than issues to be debated. Problems were often resolved without dispute by strong willed leaders. Others chose to dispute first and fix later. The term *problem* seems to be disappearing from the conversations about schooling. Rather than to admit to perceiving problems, writers and speakers now frame their positions in terms of issues. Issues better lend themselves to taking sides often with clashing viewpoints.

If educators never take a stand, then issues are in constant flux and ever wavering on the brink of discourse. There has been a perpetual and unresolved dialogue regarding the definition of education and what is expected of educators. There should be a relationship between schooling and society, and the distribution of decision-making powers. Options are formulated by deliberating pros and cons of an issue. Individuals can be very persuasive and should be provided the opportunity to do so.

The twenty-first century education system looks different today because the needs of students and the society they are growing up in are different. Many times the needs of students become a part of the issues that are debated, such as democratic classrooms, free speech, preschool, inclusive classrooms, virtual schooling, zero-tolerance, and twenty-first century skills. Changes are necessary to help our youth reach their full potential and be college and career ready after 12 years of education. For change to occur, education issues must be clearly identified and deliberated by both educators and other members of society.

Ways of thinking about educational issues include a review of historical perspectives, examining viewpoints, philosophical considerations, and power and control. Three areas of focus for debating are basic theoretical issues, current fundamental issues, and current specific issues.

Historical Perspectives

In recent decades, the growing influence of thinking drawn from the humanities and the behavioral and social sciences has brought about the development of interpretive, normative, and critical perspectives, which have sharpened the focus on educational concerns. These perspectives allowed scholars and researchers to closely examine the contextual variables, value orientations, and philosophical and political assumptions that shape both the status quo and reform efforts.

The study of education involves the application of many perspectives to the analysis of "what is and how it got that way" and "what can be and how we can get there." Central to such study are the prevailing philosophical assumptions, theories, and visions that find their way into real-life educational situations. The application situation, with its attendant political pressures, sociocultural differences, community expectations, parental influence, and professional problems, provides a testing ground for contending theories and ideals.

This "testing ground" image applies only insofar as the status quo is malleable enough to allow the examination and trial of alternative views. Historically, institutionalized education has been characteristically rigid. As a testing ground of ideas, it has often lacked an orientation encouraging innovation and futuristic thinking. Its political grounding has usually been conservative.

As social psychologist Allen Wheelis points out in The Quest for Identity (1958), social institutions by definition tend toward solidification and protectionism. His depiction of the dialectical development of civilizations centers on the tension between the security and authoritarianism of "institutional processes" and the dynamism and change-orientation of "instrumental processes."

The field of education seems to graphically illustrate this observation. Educational practices are primarily tradition bound. The twentieth-century reform movement, spurred by the ideas of John Dewey, A. S. Neill, and a host of critics who campaigned for change in the 1960s, challenged the structural rigidity of schooling. In more recent decades, reformers have either attempted to restore uniformity in the curriculum and in assessment of results or campaigned for the support of alternatives to the public school monopoly. The latter group comes from both the right and the left of the political spectrum.

We are left with the abiding questions: What is an "educated" person? What should be the primary purpose of organized education? Who should control the decisions influencing the educational process? Should the schools follow society or lead it toward change? Should schooling be compulsory?

Long-standing forces have molded a wide variety of responses to these fundamental questions. The religious impetus, nationalistic fervor, philosophical ideas, the march of science and technology, varied interpretations of "societal needs," and the desire to use the schools as a means for social reform have been historically influential. In recent times, other factors have emerged to contribute to the complexity of the search for answers—social class differences, demographic shifts, increasing bureaucratization and federal; imprint into public education, the growth of the textbook and now electronic textbook industry, the changing financial base for schooling, teacher unionization, and strengthening of parental and community pressure groups.

The struggle to find the most appropriate answers to these questions now involves, as in the past, an interplay of societal aims, educational purposes, and individual intentions. Moral development, the quest for wisdom, citizenship training, socioeconomic improvement, mental discipline, the rational control of life, job preparation, liberation of the individual, freedom of inquiry, and many others continue to be the topics of discourse on education.

A detailed historical perspective on these questions and topics may be gained by reading the interpretations of noted scholars in the field. R. Freeman Butts has written a brief but effective summary portrayal in "Search for Freedom—The Story of American Education," *NEA Journal* (March 1960). A partial listing of other sources includes R. Freeman Butts and Lawrence Cremin, *A History of Education in American Culture;* S. E. Frost, Jr., *Historical and Philosophical Foundations of Western Education;* Harry Good and Edwin Teller, *A History of Education;* Adolphe Meyer, *An Educational History of the American People;* Robert L. Church and Michael W. Sedlak, *Education in the United States: An Interpretive History;* Merle Curti, *The Social Ideas of American Educators;* Henry J. Perkinson, *The Imperfect Panacea: American Faith in Education, 1865–1965;* Clarence Karier, *Man, Society, and Education;* V. T. Thayer, *Formative Ideas in American Education;* H. Warren Button and Eugene F. Provenzo, Jr., *History of Education and Culture in America;* David Tyack and Elisabeth Hansot, *Managers of Virtue: Public School Leadership in America, 1820–1980;* Joel Spring, *The American School, 1642–1990;* S. Alexander Rippa, *Education in a*

Free Society: An American History; John D. Pulliam, *History of Education in America;* Edward Stevens and George H. Wood, *Justice, Ideology, and Education;* and Walter Feinberg and Jonas F. Soltis, *School and Society.*

These and other historical accounts of the development of schooling demonstrate the continuing need to address educational questions in terms of cultural and social dynamics. A careful analysis of contemporary education demands attention not only to the historical interpretation of developmental influences but also to the philosophical forces that define formal education and the social and cultural factors that form the basis of informal education.

Examining Viewpoints

In his book *A New Public Education* (1976), Seymour Itzkoff examines the interplay between informal and formal education, concluding that economic and technological expansion have pulled people away from the informal culture by placing a premium on success in formal education. This has brought about a reactive search for less artificial educational contexts within the informal cultural community, which recognizes the impact of individual personality in shaping educational experiences.

This search for a reconstructed philosophical base for education has produced a barrage of critical commentary. Those who seek radical change in education characterize the present schools as mindless, manipulative, factory-like, bureaucratic institutions that offer little sense of community, pay scant attention to personal meaning, fail to achieve curricular integration, and maintain a psychological atmosphere of competitiveness, tension, fear, and alienation. Others deplore the ideological movement away from the formal organization of education, fearing an abandonment of standards, a dilution of the curriculum, an erosion of intellectual and behavioral discipline, and a decline in adult and institutional authority.

Students of education (whether prospective teachers and school leaders, practicing professionals, or interested laypeople) must examine closely the assumptions and values underlying alternative positions in order to clarify their own view points. This tri-level task may best be organized around the basic themes of purpose, power, and reform. These themes offer access to the theoretical grounding of actions in the field of education, to the political grounding of such actions, and to the future orientation of action decisions.

A general model for the examination of positions on educational issues includes the following dimensions: identification of the viewpoint, recognition of the stated or implied assumptions underlying the viewpoint, analysis of the validity of the supporting argument, and evaluation of the conclusions and action-suggestions of the originator of the position. The stated or implied assumptions may be derived from a philosophical or religious orientation, from scientific theory, from social or personal values, or from accumulated experience. Acceptance by the reader of an author's assumptions opens the way for a receptive attitude regarding the specific viewpoint expressed and its implications for action. The argument offered in justification of the viewpoint may be based on logic, common experience, controlled experiments, information and data, legal precedents, emotional appeals, and a host of other persuasive devices.

Holding the basic model in mind, readers of the positions presented in this volume (or anywhere else, for that matter) can examine the constituent elements of arguments—basic assumptions, viewpoint statements, supporting evidence, conclusions, and suggestions for action. The careful reader will accept or reject the individual elements of the total position. One might see reasonableness in a viewpoint and its justification but be unable to accept the assumptions on which it is based. Or one might accept the flow of argument from assumptions to viewpoint to evidence but find illogic or impracticality in the stated conclusions and suggestions for action. In any event, the reader's personal view is tested and honed through the process of analyzing the views of others.

Philosophical Considerations

Historically, organized education has been initiated and instituted to serve many purposes—spiritual salvation, political socialization, moral uplift, societal stability, social mobility, mental discipline, vocational efficiency, social reform, among others. The various purposes have usually reflected the dominant philosophical conception of human nature and the prevailing assumptions about the relationship between the individual and society. At any given time, competing conceptions may vie for dominance—social conceptions, economic conceptions, conceptions that emphasize spirituality, or conceptions that stress the uniqueness and dignity of the individual, for example.

These considerations of human nature and individual–society relationships are grounded in philosophical assumptions, and these assumptions find their way to such practical domains as schooling. In Western civilization, there has been an identifiable (but far from consistent and clear-cut) historical trend in the basic assumptions about reality, knowledge, values, and the human condition. This trend may manifest itself in the philosophical positions of idealism, realism, pragmatism, and existentialism. There has been a shift in emphasis from the spiritual world to nature to human behavior to the social individual to the free individual, and from eternal ideas to fixed natural laws to social interaction to the inner person.

The idealist tradition, which dominated much of philosophical and educational thought until the eighteenth and nineteenth centuries, separates the changing, imperfect, material world and the permanent, perfect, spiritual or mental world. As Plato saw it, for example, human beings and all other physical entities are particular manifestations of an ideal reality that in material existence humans can never fully know. The purpose of education is to bring us closer to the absolute ideals, pure forms, and universal standards that exist spiritually, by awakening and strengthening our rational powers. For Plato, a curriculum based on mathematics, logic, and music would serve this purpose, especially in the training of leaders whose rationality must exert control over emotionality and basic instincts.

Against this tradition, which shaped the liberal arts curriculum in schools for centuries, the realism of Aristotle, with its finding of the "forms" of things *within* the material world, brought an emphasis on scientific investigation and on environmental factors in the development of human potential. This fundamental view has influenced two philosophical movements in education: naturalism, based on following or gently assisting nature (as in the approaches of John Amos Comenius, Jean-Jacques Rousseau, and Johann Heinrich Pestalozzi), and scientific realism, based on uncovering the natural laws of human behavior and shaping the educational environment to maximize their effectiveness (as in the approaches of John Locke, Johann Friedrich Herbart, and Edward Thorndike).

In the twentieth century, two philosophical forces (pragmatism and existentialism) have challenged these traditions. Each has moved the primary attention away from fixed spiritual or natural influences and toward the individual as a shaper of knowledge and values. The pragmatic position, articulated in America by Charles Sanders Peirce, William James, and John Dewey, turns from metaphysical abstractions toward concrete results of action. In a world of change and relativity, human beings must forge their own truths and values as they interact with their environments and each other. The European-based philosophy of existentialism, emerging from such thinkers as Gabriel Marcel, Martin Buber, Martin Heidegger, and Jean-Paul Sartre, has more recently influenced education here. Existentialism places the burdens of freedom, choice, and responsibility squarely on the individual, viewing the current encroachment of external forces and the tendency of people to "escape from freedom" as a serious diminishment of our human possibilities.

These many theoretical slants contend for recognition and acceptance as we continue the search for broad purposes in education and as we attempt to create curricula, methodologies, accountability, and learning environments that fulfill our stated purposes. This is carried out, of course, in the real world of the public schools in which social, political, and economic forces often predominate.

Power and Control

Plato, in the fourth century B.C., found existing education manipulative and confining and, in the *Republic,* described a meritocratic approach designed to nurture intellectual powers as to form and sustain a rational society. Reform oriented as Plato's suggestions were he nevertheless insisted on certain restrictions and controls, so that his particular version of the ideal could be met.

The ways and means of education have been fertile grounds for power struggles throughout history. Many educational efforts have been initiated by religious bodies, often creating a conflict situation when secular authorities have moved into the field. Schools have usually been seen as repositories of culture and social values and, as such, have been overseen by the more conservative forces in society. To others, bent on social reform, the schools have been treated as a spawning ground for change. Given these basic political forces, conflict is inevitable.

When one speaks of the control of education, the range of influence is indeed wide. Political influences, governmental actions, court decisions, professional militancy, parental power, and student assertion all contribute to the phenomenon of control. And the domain of control is equally broad—school finances, curriculum, instructional means and objectives, teacher certification, accountability, student discipline, censorship of school materials, school safety, determination of access and opportunity, and determination of inclusion and exclusion.

The general topic of power and control leads to a multitude of questions: Who should make policy decisions? Must the schools be puppets of the government? Can the schools function in the vanguard of social change? Can cultural indoctrination be avoided? Can the schools lead the way to full social integration? Can the effects of social class be eradicated? Can and should the schools teach values? Dealing with such questions is complicated by the increasing power of the federal government in educational matters. Congressional legislation has broadened substantially from the early land grants and aid to

agricultural and vocational programs to more recent laws covering aid to federally impacted areas, school construction aid, student loans and fellowships, support for several academic areas of the curriculum, work–study programs, compensatory education, employment opportunities for youth, adult education, aid to libraries, teacher preparation, educational research, career education, education of the handicapped, and equal opportunity for females. This proliferation of areas of influence has caused the federal administrative bureaucracy to blossom from its meager beginnings in 1867 into a cabinet-level Department of Education in 1979. The U.S. Department of Education has grown substantially since 1979, which includes a very large footprint into the control and accreditation of schools across the nation.

State legislatures and state departments of education have also grown in power, handling greater percentages of school appropriations and controlling basic curricular decisions, special education, attendance laws, accreditation, research, and so on. Local school boards, once the sole authorities in policy-making, now share the role with higher governmental echelons as the financial support sources shift away from the local scene. Simultaneously, strengthened teacher organizations and increasingly vocal pressure groups at the local, state, and national levels have forced a widening of the base for policy decisions. Now, almost through the second decade of the 21st century, there are discussions and policy changes taking place to reverse the large federal imprint into schools returning more of the power and autonomy back to the states.

Concluding Remarks

Schools often seem to be either facing backward or completely absorbed in the tribulations of the present, lacking a vision of possible futures that might guide current decisions. The present is inescapable, obviously, and certainly the historical and philosophical underpinnings of the present situation must be understood, but true improvement often requires a break with conventionality— a surge toward a desired future.

The radical reform critique of government-sponsored compulsory schooling has depicted organized education as a form of cultural or political imprisonment that traps young people in an artificial and mainly irrelevant environment and rewards conformity and docility while inhibiting curiosity and creativity. Constructive reform ideas that have come from this critique include the creation of open classrooms, the de-emphasis of external motivators, the diversification of educational experience, the rise of accountability for student outcomes, and the building of a true sense of community within the instructional environment.

Starting with Francis Wayland Parker's schools in Quincy, MA, and John Dewey's Laboratory School at the University of Chicago around the turn of the twentieth century, the campaign to make schools into more productive and humane places has been relentless. The duplication of A. S. Neill's Summerhill model in the free school movement in the 1960s, the open classroom/open space experiments, the several curricular variations, and the emergence of schools without walls, charter schools, privatization of management, escalating federal involvement and accountability, home schooling across the country, and new technologies like online schools testify to the desire to reform the present system or to build alternatives to it.

The progressive education movement, the development of "life adjustment" goals and curricula, and the "whole person" theories of educational psychology moved the schools toward an expanded concept of schooling that embraced new subject matters and new approaches to discipline during the first half of the twentieth century. Since the 1950s, however, pressure for a return to a narrower concept of schooling as intellectual training has sparked new waves of debate. Schools in the twenty-first century wrestle with more federal involvement that now is in hot debate on determining regulations and implementation for the Every Student Succeeds Act (ESSA) and the future of the Common Core State Standards (CCSS). Out of this situation have come attempts by educators and academicians to design new curricular approaches in the basic subject matter areas, efforts by private foundations to stimulate organizational innovations and to improve the training of teachers and school leaders, and federal government support of educational technology. Yet criticism of schools abounds. The schools, according to many who use their services, remain too factory-like, too age-segregated, and too custodial. Alternative paths are still sought—paths that would allow action learning, work study, and a diversity of ways to achieve success.

H. G. Wells has told us that human history becomes more and more a race between education and catastrophe. What is needed in order to win this race is the generation of new ideas regarding cultural change, human relationships, ethical norms, the uses of technology, and the quality of life. These new ideas, of course, may be old ideas newly applied. One could do worse, in thinking through the problem of improving the quality of education, than to turn to the third-century philosopher Plotinus, who called for an education directed to "the outer, the inner, and the whole." For Plotinus, "the outer" represented the public person, or the socioeconomic dimension of the total human being; "the inner" reflected the subjective dimension, the uniquely experiencing individual, or the "I"; and "the whole" signified the universe of meaning and relatedness, or the realm of human, natural, and spiritual connectedness. It would seem that education must address all of these dimensions if it is to truly help people in the lifelong struggle to shape a meaningful existence. If educational experiences can be improved in these directions, the end result might be people who are not just filling space, filling time, or filling a social role, but who are capable of saying something worthwhile with their lives.

The argument presented sets the stage for debate about educational issues that often result in clashing views. Healthy discourse will assure change comes to the field of education that results in higher student success/achievement and more democratic actions to improve the American education system.

Glenn L. Koonce
Regent University

Unit 1

UNIT

Basic Theoretical Issues

*W*hat is the basic purpose of education? How should the curriculum be organized and how much control should students have over their own development? What is the best way to teach and motivate students to learn? What philosophy of education should guide the process of education? These questions have been discussed throughout the history of American education and continue to be debated today. In this section, a major figure from the twentieth century—John Holt is highlighted, and newer reflections from twenty-first century scholars Ervin Sparapani, David Perez, Linda Nathan, and Stephanie Scott.

Selected, Edited, and with Issue Framing Material by:
Glenn L. Koonce, *Regent University*

ISSUE

Should the Curriculum Be Standardized for All?

YES: Ervin Sparapani and David Pérez, from "A Perspective on the Standardized Curriculum and Its Effect on Teaching and Learning," *Journal of Education & Social Policy* (2015)

NO: John Holt, from "Escape from Childhood," *E. P. Dutton* (1974)

Learning Outcomes

After reading this issue, you will be able to:

- Compare and contrast reasons why public schools need a uniform curriculum for all students.
- Evaluate how a standardized curriculum may be adversarial to the human rights of students.
- Understand The Paideia Curriculum and expand on the justification to implement it in public schools.
- Define the concept "the barbarism of speculation."
- Critique how the quality of life depends on the quality of schooling.

ISSUE SUMMARY

YES: Saginaw Valley State University Professor Ervin Sparapani and Associate Provost at Saginaw Valley State University, David Pérez contend that even though a curriculum may be standard, teachers need to use a variety of teaching approaches to meet the needs of diverse student populations.

NO: Educator John Holt argues that an imposed curriculum damages the individual and usurps a basic human right to select one's own path of development.

Controversy over the curriculum content in education has been particularly keen since the 1950s and is still viewed as a basic theoretical issue. The pendulum has swung from learner-centered progressive education to an emphasis on a structured intellectual discipline that calls for radical reform in the direction of "openness" as opposed to the recent rally to go "back to basics." Simply stated, standardizing the curriculum is a way to organize the content in different subject areas so that the activities are not repetitive, but sequential, founded on knowledge previously presented and learned. Students then demonstrate the acquisition of knowledge on their performance on standardized tests. Standards become the basis for what

is assessed and what value will be placed on the level(s) of mastery for each standard measured. The standards then become the measure of the quality of the curriculum whereby the State can hold schools and school districts accountable for what teachers are expected to teach and students to learn.

The conservative viewpoint, articulated by such writers as Robert M. Hutchins, Clifton Fadiman, Jacques Barzun, Arthur Bestor, Mortimer J. Adler, Ervin Sparapani, and David Pérez arises from concerns about the drift toward informalism and the decline in academic achievement in recent decades. Taking philosophical cues from Plato's contention that certain subject matters have universal qualities that prompt mental and characterological development, the "basics" advocates argue against incidental learning, student choice, and diminution of structure and standards. Barzun summarizes the viewpoint succinctly: "Nonsense is at the heart of those proposals that would replace definable subject matters with vague activities copied from 'life' or with courses organized around 'problems' or 'attitudes.'"

The reform viewpoint, represented by John Holt, Paul Goodman, Ivan Illich, Charles Silberman, Edgar Friedenberg, and others, portrays the typical traditional school as a mindless, indifferent, social institution dedicated to producing fear, docility, and conformity. In such an atmosphere, the viewpoint holds, learners either become alienated from the established curriculum or learn to play the school "game," and thus achieve a hollow success. Taking cues from the ideas of John Dewey and A. S. Neill, the "radical reformers" have given rise to a flurry of alternatives to regular schooling during recent decades. Among these are free schools, which follow the Summerhill model; urban storefront schools, which attempt to develop a true sense of "community"; "schools without walls," which follow the Philadelphia Parkway Program model; "Commonwealth" schools, in which students, parents, and teachers share responsibility; and various "humanistic education" projects within regular school systems, which emphasize students' self-concept development and choice-making ability.

The utilitarian tradition that has descended from Benjamin Franklin, Horace Mann, and Herbert Spencer; Dewey's theory of active experiencing; and Neill's insistence on free and natural development support the reform position. The ideology rejects the factory model of schooling with its rigidly set curriculum, its neglect of individual differences, its social engineering function, and its pervasive formalism. "Basics" advocates, on the other hand, express deep concern over the erosion of authority and the watering down of demands upon students that result from the reform ideology.

Arguments for a more standardized curriculum have been embodied most recently in Theodore R. Sizer's Coalition of Essential Schools and the Core Knowledge Schools of E. D. Hirsch, Jr., whose 1996 book *The Schools We Need and Why We Don't Have Them* summarizes the basic points of this view. An interview with Hirsch by Mark F. Goldberg titled "Doing What Works" appeared in the September 1997 issue of *Phi Delta Kappan*. A thorough critique of Hirsch's position is presented by Kristen L. Buras in "Questioning Core Assumptions," *Harvard Educational Review* (Spring 1999). In 1998, Terry Roberts and the staff of the National Paideia Center at The University of North Carolina released *The Power of Paideia Schools: Defining Lives through Learning*. Mortimer J. Adler (1982) outlines his "Paideia Proposal," which calls for a uniform and unified curriculum and methodological approach—a common schooling for the development of a truly democratic society.

A broad spectrum of ideas on the curriculum may be found in John I. Goodlad's *A Place Called School* (1984), Maxine Green's *The Dialectic of Freedom* (1987), Theodore R. Sizer's *Horace trilogy*, and Ernest L. Boyer's *The Basic School* (1995). Some provocative ideas on this and related issues may be found in *"The Goals of Education"* by Richard Rothstein and Rebecca Jacobsen in *Phi Delta Kappan* (December 2006).

In the following YES selection, Sparapani and Perez (2015) outline their views on curriculum design, specifically standardized curriculum and its impact on teaching and learning. Their focus is primarily on how to deal with standardized curriculum and the relationship between education, teaching, curriculum, and learning. Additionally, why standardized curriculum is addressed, as well as, is there a place for standardized curriculum, and approaches for sustainability for a standardized curriculum in a school? In the NO selection, John Holt goes beyond his earlier concerns about the oppressiveness of the school curriculum to propose complete freedom for the learner to determine all aspects of his or her educational development. The two opposing perspectives on the issue is reflected in the thought that the most basic *standard* is that all knowledge must be measured, which immerses students into a world of competitiveness and ultimately categorized standardization as if they were merely a part of a quality control process.

YES

Ervin Sparapani and David Pérez

A Perspective on the Standardized Curriculum and Its Effect on Teaching and Learning

That education should be regulated by law and should be an affair of state is not to be denied, but what should the character of this public education, and how young person's should be educated, are questions which remain to be considered . . . . The existing practice is perplexing, no one knows on what principles we should proceed [should the useful life, or should virtue, or should the higher knowledge, be the aim of our training] all three opinions have been entertained. Again, about the means there is no agreement: for different persons, starting with different ideas about the nature of virtue, naturally disagree about the practice of it. There can be no doubt that children should be taught those useful things that are really necessary, but not all useful things (Aristotle, as quoted in Westbury, 2008).

Introduction

This paper focuses on curriculum design, specifically standardized curriculum and its impact on teaching and learning. In this paper, we will discuss some of the issues related to standardized curriculum and provide some suggestions for practice that can address teaching and learning. When we think about a standardized curriculum, three key perspectives emerge when addressing the role of standardized curriculum. First, and primarily, the issue is political. Second is the issue of whether a standardized curriculum is appropriate for everyone and meets the educational needs of different persons with different ideas. Third is the pragmatic notion of how teaching practices can meet both the needs of the learners and those of the policy makers. We contend, not disregarding governmental mandates, that even though a curriculum may be standard, teachers need to use a variety of teaching approaches to meet the needs of diverse student populations.

It is not our intention to provide a history of or rationale for curriculum design or development, but to provide a dialogue to address how to deal with standardized curriculum. This article will focus on the curriculum (specifically in K–12 schools) and how curriculum decisions affect the teachers who teach the curriculum and the students who experience the curriculum by understanding the relationship between curriculum, educators, and students through the interactions occurring within the environment in which those interactions occur. We look at four such relationships. First, for the students that come to our schools, we need to know where they come from and where they are going, their history, their beliefs, and so on. We have to utilize techniques that help us understand where to meet students in terms of the curriculum and the school. Second, teachers need to self-reflect on their practice, writing about education, teaching, curriculum, and learning. Third, curriculum needs to reflect our philosophy and that of our place. The last aspect is that the relationship between these three (learner, teacher, and curriculum) needs to be lived out in the school/classroom through understanding of place, a critical pedagogy where we learn from our students, their future students, current teachers, and our own institutions (Carini, 2001).

The reality of how teachers and students experience the curriculum and the standardization culture came immediately to our attention, when one of us (Sparapani) had a surreal experience in a doctor's office.

When visiting doctor's offices, I typically have a book with me so that I can read something while I am waiting. On this day, the book I had with me was Integrating Differentiated Instruction and Understanding by Design: Connecting Content and Kids by Carol Ann Tomlinson and Jay McTighe (Tomlinson & McTighe, 2006). Actually, I was reading the book not only because I am interested in differentiating instruction, but mainly to help inform my thinking about this article.

When I was called into the examining room, I continued reading the book while I was waiting for the doctor to arrive. When the doctor entered the room, he saw that I was reading a book and asked what I was reading. I have been seeing this doctor for several years. He already knew that I was a teacher educator, and over the years we have had a number of discussions about issues related to education. It was not a surprise to him when I told him that I was interested in something called differentiated instruction, and was reading a book about differentiating instruction and curriculum design. This piqued his interest. He asked me what differentiated instruction was. I tried to explain differentiated instruction to him as clearly and succinctly as I could, and its relationship to curriculum design.

His response to my explanation was typical of many people, and gives insight to the point of this article. He, casually, but in all seriousness, said something like,

"You know, I don't understand why teachers don't just tell students what they need to learn and then give them a test to make sure they've learned it. That's what my teachers did with me, and that's the way I want my kids' teachers to teach them and the way I expect my kids to learn. In my opinion, teachers waste too much time with all this other stuff, and it doesn't help learning anyway."

This doctor's comment brings to the surface the belief of a lot of people (educators and non-educators alike), and generally when people say things like this to me, I don't say anything. This time, however, I asked him how he treated his patients.

He asked me what I meant, and I said, "How do you treat your patients? Do you treat them all the same?"

He said, "Basically, yes, I do. I try to listen, to be respectful, and to treat each patient with dignity."

I responded, "Don't you think teachers do the same thing with their students?"

He said, "Hmm. I never thought of that, but, yes, I suppose they do."

Then I said, "And do you prescribe identical medications for every patient?"

He responded, "Well, yes. There are standard kinds of treatments."

I said, "I realize that, but don't you sort of customize the treatment depending on the patient's condition?" He responded, "Well, yes, but it depends on the patient's age, severity of the condition, and the patient's general health."

"Don't you think teachers should try to do the same kind of thing when they teach?" By that I meant that each student is unique, and then I asked, "Don't you think teachers should try to meet the needs of each student, as best they can, depending on their age and intellectual ability?"

He continued, "Well, yes, they should. Isn't that what they do?" I said, "Typically, they want to. That's what this differentiated instruction idea is about."

He said, "If they want to, why don't they?" I replied, "Because of what you said initially. The public wants teachers to tell students what they need to learn and then test them against some standard, and if the student doesn't perform well on the standard, based on the test that's used, the teacher is at fault."

He then asked, "Isn't that the way it should be? Shouldn't the teacher be held accountable?" I responded, "If a patient comes back to you after you've prescribed something, and says the treatment didn't work and says it's your fault, what do you say to the patient?"

Well [sic] "I ask the patient if they followed the treatment appropriately?"

"So, you're placing responsibility on the patient."

"Well, not exactly." I responded to him about what he meant with "not exactly?"

He then said, "So, you're saying that teachers shouldn't be held accountable for how their students perform."

To this, I kind of grimaced because he just wasn't getting it. I responded,

"No, I'm not saying that. I believe teachers should be held accountable for how their students perform; however, I am saying that I don't think teachers are any different than you. A lot of times accountability has to do with whether the patient (or in this case the student) does what they're supposed to do based on what the teacher has taught and prescribed. We don't live in a one size fits all world. Each person is unique, and we need to provide them with a variety of opportunities to learn, not just tell them something and expect them to know it. There are many ways of knowing and demonstrating understanding. That's what differentiation is about."

At this point, I was finished with my appointment, and I went on my way; however, even though my appointment was finished, the discussion stayed with me, particularly as we began writing this article. The comment the doctor made about teachers just telling students what they need to learn and then testing them kept coming back to us again and again, and cemented the direction of our thinking and, as a result, the focus of this article.

The conversation with the doctor made us realize that anyone who has been an educator for any length of time realizes that their lives are spent dealing in some way with curriculum; and when dealing with curriculum, there are three overriding issues that need to be considered, which are articulated by Aristotle. Issues we emphasize in our paper are (1) people are unique, (2) what works in one place may not work in another place, at least not in the same way, and (3) governments will have a lot to say about the design and implementation of curricula.

Defining Curriculum

Although most educators dislike the notion that their profession is instrumental, the reality of this rationality sits at the forefront of teacher innovation and inclusion in the curriculum process. Practitioners cordon behind ontological excuses of time constraints and curricular rigidity to avoid direct contact with theory. Indeed, it appears that when curriculum moved from the realm of the practical to that of the possible, teachers were left at the curriculum crossroads. The deprofessionalization of the teaching profession has historical origins and today continues to be dominated by (a) accountability issues that handcuff teachers and administrators, (b) societal and parental expectations of what schooling should be, and (c) educational textbook writers grounded in the subject-matter approach to teaching (Klein, 1994, p. 22).

As is the case with much reform, we need to remain grounded in the conversation about measureable outcomes that Washington, DC, has continued to pursue since Lyndon Johnson's administration. Educators need to ask the following questions: (a) How can the evaluation of students, teachers, administrators, and even our communities improve our community schools?, (b) How can that evaluation be used for strategic planning?, and (c) What constitutes evidence of thinking for our students, teachers, administrators, and communities? We suggest that school leaders look inward and reassess how they measure learning. As educators, what we have to keep in mind is that the impetus, planning, and budgetary support for the subject-centered and test-driven curriculum revision taking place comes from outside the state and local school districts.

Student work is more than merely a benchmark; it is the foundation of growth toward learning. Significance of learning cannot be determined by the size of the quantitative measurement (statistical) but by what it represents. Worthy artifacts can show breakthroughs such as instances where skills or strategies that were confused are now performed well. Under NCLB, parents became disconnected from their children's schools. This is one reason many choose alternative options for their children such as charter schools, home schools, or private schools (Apple, 2004). This practice continues currently in many school districts. Historically, schools and teachers have had adversarial relationships with parents, mainly over moral and religious content. Schools should invite parents to invest in the common cause that is the education of their children. School leaders need to think about data as a living and dynamic history of their schools. As Dahl (1970) notes, revolutions emerge from individual solutions to common problems. We need to consider all solutions. We need to search for multiple ways to measure thinking.

Diversity and Curriculum

Diverse populations require diverse evaluation systems. Looking at the merit and worth (absolute and relative) of a particular person is much more difficult than an automobile or a coffee maker. With an automobile or a coffee maker, you can easily measure its specifications and performance. A social or educational program is much more complex and includes many elements. If we agree about the complexity of educational programs, then we have to agree that there are also many different ways to evaluate them. Thus, why do we only use one type of measurement to measure these diverse activities that make up learning? Any democratic action taken to change and transform schools must begin by asking how schools define reform, and educational programs should require the use of dialogical and conscious approaches to open-ended dialogue that encompass the transformational language of democracy and action. A position that is often overlooked is that a sustainable definition of leadership can be realized through inquiry and reflection, rather than through the management-controlled approaches schools are currently experiencing.

Freire (1970/1997, p. 36) declares, "Pedagogy of the oppressed must be animated by authentic, humanistic (not humanitarian) generosity and present itself as pedagogy of human kind." Concurrently, transactional leadership functions on a system that exchanges performance for rewards or punishment; however, the exchange could be social, political, philosophical, economic, or psychological. The relationship among people remains as long as the common interest is maintained—goods, such as votes or money, are bargained though participants have no investment other than an understanding that they need each other. Once the arrangement is over, participants may choose to go their separate ways. In education, this relationship is mistakenly seen as transformative—although not unique to education as seen by the current debate on health care where disparate groups are attempting to exchange goods for votes—we use transformative language to describe these simple acts of transactional leadership. Burns (1978/1982) clearly uses transformative leadership and transactional leadership to differentiate between management as method, and leadership as art. What is ironic is that we continue to use transformative leadership to describe and justify any action we label reform. What needs to occur in public places is a deep discussion of curriculum as politics.

Curriculum as Transformative Leadership

Currently, we are experiencing a management approach to schools that treats subjects as objects (Freire, 1970/1997). Curriculum design and evaluation provide a set of standards based on short-term goals that seek to respond to predetermined skill- and content-based subject learning. The dominance of such curriculum pervasive in schools is based on narrowly defined ideas of change and reform—seeking to align performance on mathematics and reading (i.e., the achievement gap) to the larger social issues of poverty and race.

With apologies to Charles Dickens, it is the best of times; it is the worst of times. It is an age of unprecedented spending for program growth; it is an age of record budget deficits and cutbacks. In countless school districts across America, new programs have risen to replace traditional ones and accommodate a growing number of students. Yet, a faltering economy has put the squeeze on operating budgets and has made constituents less likely to support ambitious construction proposals. So, as programs and alternatives open at record pace, new graduates are falling behind because they are taught in programs that are inadequate and unsupported. The push for improving the quality in education is more than just a question of aesthetics. According to Darling-Hammond (1999), Darling-Hammond, Berry, and Thorenson (2001), and Constantine et al. (2009), students in traditional schools, who are taught by teachers who are certified through alternative means still do better than their counterparts (this includes comparisons with children of high poverty and minorities). Currently, the debate rages over Common Core Standards (CCS) policy and implementation focusing on control of education (federal or state), fast-tracking of unreliable measurements, research demonstrating no connection between international benchmarks and U.S. economic growth, implementation and impact, and limiting curriculum (lack of teacher input, creativity, and literature within state-adopted CCS curricula).

More broadly, critique has been focused on the suitability of lower grade standards because the development of the standards has focused on what high school graduates should know and then working backward, causing them to not take into account how younger students learn. Advocates, who have evidence and data that demonstrate the impact of national benchmarks and who include bipartisan political groups, teacher, and administrator groups, and industry, government, and foundation entities, state that supporting the adoption of the CCS by the states will allow them to articulate to all stakeholders the expectations for students; align curriculum, texts, and other educational media to international standards; provide professional development for teachers based on student needs and best practices; develop and implement student performance assessment process aligned to the common core across the nation; and create policy that helps schools and students meet CCS and high school graduation requirements.

In the arguments made by educational reformers, assessment has been cited as the key to educational change; however, little to no discussion is articulated as to the purpose of curriculum leadership. The idea that emerged from school leaders and their formal and informal educations is that one model will materialize as the dominant form to articulate and prepare future democratic citizens (Levine, 2005). This articulation has emerged from management literature that seeks to create a single process for change that can easily be measured and readjusted to deal with the changing contexts (Levine, 2005; Robinson, 2001). We propose that this single process model—which has led American manufacturing to its full collapse—is based on the ability to grow and profit from change (Egan, 2008). Robinson (2001) writes that this Industrial Revolution model has driven education, and training is hampered by archaic ideas of intelligence and creativity that, according to Eisner (1997/2008), has wasted the potential of countless numbers of human beings.

Why Standardized Curriculum

As Aristotle says in the beginning quote, education is a political issue, and in recent times, countries have had the tendency to take more and more control of the curriculum, resulting in standardized education. This has become problematic, mainly because times have changed, and, as times change, people's needs change. People's needs are different. Believing that all people need the same things and they need those things in the same way causes problems for curriculum design and how the curriculum is delivered. In education, we do not like to think about it, but curriculum is politics (Breault, 1999) and somewhere in the middle are teachers and students. In the process of thinking about and reading literature about the standardized curriculum, two thoughts keep emerging. The first thought is how political curriculum is and the second thought is that everybody has attended school and has an opinion about education and what people should be taught. Sparapani came face-to-face with these same attitudes that day in the doctor's office.

Concerning the politics of curriculum, Westbury (2008) writes that over the past two decades, the practice and operation of curriculum making by national or state governments or boards of education has become basic to designing and assessing curricula. In his paper, Westbury examines what has happened in a variety of countries, specifically England, the United States, and Norway. Regarding England, Westbury says that the British Education Reform Act of 1988, with its National Curriculum, signaled a radical departure in the design of and implementation of curriculum in schools in England and Wales. He writes that in the United States, in the 1990s, virtually all states developed curriculum standards, in many cases as their first-ever state curricula. And in societies, like Norway, where state-based curriculum making has been a long-standing institution, new curricula are appearing more frequently. Westbury further says that the form of such curriculum making varies by country and can change over time. At one time, or in one country, the curriculum may be content specific. In another country or at another time, the curriculum may address achievement standards. In another country, the curriculum may be highly prescriptive or presented as frameworks. Wherever the country or whatever the time, such curriculum making plays a similar role within the educational systems of the country.

Government-determined curriculum mandates spell out what schools should be doing and how schools should be doing what they do. Whatever the format or intention (Westbury, 2008), government-mandated curricula present authoritative statements about the knowledge, attitudes, and competencies seen as appropriate to populations of students. In addition, these government-mandated curricula can authorize or recommend programs of study and/or methods of instruction that reflect, for example, an understanding of science as inquiry, specific mathematics or civics standards, as well as what are effective, or "best," practices. As such, it becomes obvious that such government-mandated curriculum documents spell out standards for the work of schools, teachers, and students (Hill & Johnston, 2010; Mehta & Spillane, 2010) The second thought, concerning the politics surrounding curriculum, is that everyone has gone to school, so just about everyone has a feeling of being knowledgeable about and has a personal response to educational issues (Levin, 2008).

This is central to what the doctor was saying in the story at the beginning of this article, and it is obvious that the doctor's own school experiences influenced his views about education and educational policy. It is very true that a person's own school experiences deeply affect their views about education. In the late twentieth century and here in the twenty-first century, governments around the world have become more and more involved with making educational policies that regulate curriculum. This regulation has resulted in government-mandated standards and benchmarks, measured by some form of government-mandated assessments, which has resulted in educational systems designing standardized curricula.

Is There a place for Standardized Curriculum?

It goes without saying that we live in a global society, and because of recent trends in immigration and other factors, the demographics of the world have changed dramatically. Here, in the twenty-first century, this is especially true (Futrell, Gomez, & Bedden, 2003; Hodgkinson, 2000/2001). The United Nations Educational, Scientific and Cultural Organization (UNESCO), for example, documents that the world landscape is becoming increasingly multicultural and multilingual as international migration rates grow each year (He, Phillion, Chan, & Xu, 2008). UNESCO reports that in 2000, more than 6,809 languages were in use, including 114 sign languages, in 228 countries. Additionally, UNESCO reports that approximately 185 million people worldwide live outside their countries of birth, up from 80 million three decades ago. Population data from 1999 show that the foreign-born population in Australia is 23.6 percent; in Canada, the foreign-born population is 18.4 percent; in Sweden, it is 11.8 percent; in the United States, it is 11.1 percent; in the Netherlands, it is 9.8 percent; and the foreign-born population of Norway is 6.5 percent (He et al., 2008).

The cultural and language diversity in the United States (Daniel, 2007) further demonstrates this world phenomenon. In 2000, for example, the foreign-born population of the United States is 31.1 million, which, as we have already said, represents 11.1 percent of the total population. Of that 11.1 percent foreign-born population, Latin Americans represent 52 percent, Asians 26 percent, Europeans 16 percent, and other countries of the world 6.0 percent (He et al., 2008).

All this diversity in culture and language means that each person is different, with different needs and understandings, which are brought into the classroom. In addition to bringing differences in culture and language into the classroom, students learn at different rates. Students have different aptitudes. They have different levels of motivation. They have different learning styles. Further, differences in aptitude, motivation, and learning style tend to increase as a student progresses through the educational system. Beyond this, students learn in a remarkable variety of organizational arrangements (Weiner & Oakes, 2008).

Introduced into this diversity is the government-mandated curriculum with its standards and benchmarks. As educators, we have to say that the idea of a standardized curriculum is a good one. We believe this because the idea, in and of itself, solves many issues in education and teacher performance. For one thing, as the doctor in our story says, with a standardized curriculum, it is much easier to assess student performance and, supposedly, measure teacher accountability; however, as standardized curricula are evaluated, there is a general fallacy that cannot be resolved. It is the idea of standardized education. There is the assumption in standardized curricula that with this one lesson and these specific examples, using something commonly referred to as "best practice," each student in each classroom can be reached and educated about the topic of the lesson. The conceit of this assumption is astonishing, especially since each person is completely unique, from their brain down to their DNA.

The assurance that somehow the establishment of standards will serve as an adequate guide for reforming curricula may be misplaced. Even given the considerable efforts that have gone into writing them, standards are unlikely to fulfill their proponents' intentions. Rather, they are often symbolic accomplishments. That being said, it is doubtful that government-mandated standards and benchmarks and the standardized curriculum will disappear any time soon.

Teaching Practices for the Standardized Curriculum

As has already been explained, the people of the world live in a complex, multifaceted society, and that societal complexity brings a variety of learners into the classroom (Daniel, 2007; VanSciver, 2005). The challenge to help all students succeed in such a diverse society is present for teachers every day in every classroom at every educational level. Mastering the art of bringing variety to the curriculum according to the needs of any given set of students is the challenge that such diversity can bring. We believe that the most appropriate way to address the diverse composition of learners in the classroom is by using the instructional concept of differentiated instruction (Tomlinson, 1999).

Before discussing differentiated instruction and instructional practices that differentiate instruction, we will discuss what is clearly the most common way in which curricula are planned and made available in most nations. Textbooks, both required and supplemental, accompanied by lecture, are the key here. In most nations, textbooks are the key element of the curriculum for a number of reasons. First, textbooks are essential parts of the curriculum in most schools. Indeed, it has been estimated that 80 percent of teachers use textbooks in their classrooms as the primary curricular device. Further, it is believed (Apple, 2008) that nearly 50 percent of student's time in public schools is related to textbook use. Other data suggest that in many classrooms 80–90 percent of classroom and homework assignments are textbook-driven or textbook-centered. Although fully testing accuracy of these claims may need further analyses inside classrooms and at home, nearly all the research on textbooks documents their central location as the primary curricular item, and in many places, in essence, the curriculum.

Often teachers have the belief that focusing on the diversity of the learner, by attempting to differentiate instruction, brings chaos and instability to the classroom. Relying solely on the textbook brings stability to the classroom and an easy focus on the government-mandated standards and benchmarks, in other words, the standardized curriculum. Teachers want order and continuity, not complexity and uncertainty, and teachers believe that relying on the textbook leads not only to order and continuity but to order and stability as well. Relying heavily on the textbook and lecture as the primary pedagogical devices bring tedium to the classroom, for both the teacher and the student.

As we have already suggested, a better way (a more appropriate way) to deliver the curriculum, a more interesting way for both teachers and students, and a way that still maintains classroom order is by using instructional practices that differentiate instruction.

Traditional methods of teaching in the form of textbooks, lecturing, and teaching to the test have benefited teachers' comfort levels by not adapting to change, but have hindered students in their learning process. Teachers struggle with doing an adequate job presenting the curriculum that they teach. Where resources and training are not available, teachers revert back to traditional methods of teaching (Vega & Tayler, 2005; Johnston, 2001; Weitz, 1995). Also, most teachers tend to emulate the traditional methods of teaching, having been trained with the instructor being the center of attention. Unfortunately, this does not assist the students in their learning, as it may be the least effective way in helping students to both recall and apply new information (Apple, 2008; Green, 1999).

Students who truly understand concepts, ideas, and information will naturally perform higher on assessments of achievement (Faulkner & Cook, 2006). More importantly, students who truly understand concepts, ideas, and information will experience academic success, which encourages them to continue to succeed academically (Tomlinson, 2006; Dreher, 1997). The major point here is that by using differentiated instruction all students can learn.

The key to learning in a differentiated classroom is that all students are regularly offered choices, and students are matched as closely as possible with tasks compatible with their interests as learners. The curriculum in such a classroom should be differentiated in three areas, (1) content [The teacher provides multiple options to students for taking in information], (2) process [The teacher provides multiple options to students to make sense out of the ideas being presented], and (3) product [The teacher provides multiple options to students for expressing what they know about what they have learned] (Willis & Mann, 2000; Tomlinson, 1999).

Approaches to Sustainability for Schools in a Culture of Knowledge Transfer

In rethinking our curriculum for change, we should ask questions such as *what practical experiences could our students' experiences bring to their own development?* Eisner (1979/2008) claims that evaluation of learning is best determined by the individual. Eisner (1979/2008, pp. 203–210) suggests that:

1. Tasks used to evaluate what the students know and can do need to reflect the tasks they will encounter in the world outside schools, not those limited to schools themselves. Evaluation tasks should think about more than one possible solution and one possible answer to a problem.
2. Tasks should have curricular relevance, but not be limited by the curriculum itself.
3. Tasks should require students to display sensitivity to configurations or wholes, not simply discrete elements.
4. Tasks should permit the student to select a form of representation they choose to use to display what has been learned.
5. The tasks used to evaluate students should reveal how students go about solving a problem, not only the solutions they formulated.
6. Tasks should reflect the values of the intellectual community from which they are derived.
7. Tasks need not be limited to solo performance. Many of the most important tasks we undertake require group efforts.

The predicament in creating change is that society is suffering from an inertia born out of a helpless marriage to economic utility. Schools' reliance on the capitalist sphere has not only tainted the curriculum but also reoriented students to accept a new kind of reward, "economic utility," and, as such, graduates are told to study not for knowledge sake but to get "well-paying jobs" in the future (Postman, 1996, p. 27).

Concluding Thoughts

It probably is no secret that we are not advocates of a standardized curriculum. Around 2300 years ago, Aristotle, as suggested in the quote by him at the beginning of this paper, seems to have understood this. He understood that issues related to curriculum are political. We understand that too. He also seems to have believed that people are different and not everyone needs the same thing, at least not in the same way. We believe that too. Here, in the twenty-first century, we live in a global society. In that global society, countries are very competitive. Countries want their people to be productive citizens. Countries also want their citizens to think critically and creatively. It is the responsibility of education to teach people what they need to know in order to be productive citizens.

In order to make sure that educators do what the country wants them to do, governments have mandated standards and benchmarks that, in the educational systems, have evolved into standardized curricula. We do not believe that traditional instructional practices that are conducive to standardized learning environments spawn productive citizens or produce critical and creative thinkers.

Our possibilities for change are endless, but these must emerge from our imagination—where we reinvent our resources for teachers and administrators and treat curriculum through a new culture of evaluation (Eisner, 1979/2008). We must also examine how to move beyond the industrial model to an idea of curriculum change for academic sustainability—a new idea of what is meant by a competitive advantage. The approach lies in enhancing interactions between the schools and the community to form strategies for transfer of knowledge that develop the local community through intellectual sustainability. Schools need to operate as "complex systems," where state of affairs and their processes are not necessarily placed within traditional structures of particular disciplines. Instead, they are allowed to be a representation of a slice of life, conceptualized as an organized totality, in which elements are not separable, and therefore cannot be separately studied. In this environment, education is constantly occurring and evolving. Schooling must strike a balance between methodology and curriculum (accountability) and interpretation and curriculum (curiosity) as driving forces. Eisner (1979/2008; 1998) is not concerned with methods or approach but with the notion of seeing. His notion of the educational experience encompasses any situation that involves interactions between groups of people where learning leads to changes in one's outlook (1979/2008). Given Eisner's challenge to leadership, we believe we need to examine practice and what can be done to change how transformative leadership is realized.

Educators are no longer involved in self-determination, allowing fear to dominate how we run our schools (Carini, 2001). In the preface to *A Reassessment of the Curriculum,* Huebner (1964) explained that the curriculum field was bourgeoning. He observed that "ideas are rampant, innovation is encouraged, and the pressure to change is sometimes uncomfortably great . . . the curriculum worker wishes to act constructively and responsibly" (p. v). Further, Robert J. Schaefer concluded (as stated by Huebner, 1964) that "to regain the sense of excitement which has so long been characteristic of educators interested in curriculum, we need to develop new analytical skills and a new faith in the relevance and power of classroom research" (p. 7). The curriculum leader in schools has historically had two choices, like Robert Frost (1920): (1) continue along the traditional path or (2) choose the one less traveled.

To accomplish this, transformative leadership is needed. Transformative leadership is, ultimately, political change and must begin in common moral relationships with others. Stakeholders need to value an open community based upon ideals in which freedom of expression is protected, civility is affirmed, appreciation and understanding of individual differences are honored, and stakeholders value a caring community in which the wellbeing of each person is important.

Curriculum needs to (1) engage in an active process of questioning that examines what is visible and hidden in an aesthetic method, intended to foster close links between theory and practice, (2) develop leadership skills to affect change, and (3) prepare learners for a wider understanding of learners and learning, confronting the complexity of diversity in traditional and nontraditional educational settings.

Most teachers are not involved in policy making, nor are most teachers involved in designing curricula.

All teachers, however, are involved in delivering the curriculum. The identified curriculum, whether designed by governments or schools, sets down the beliefs about what should be taught. In that sense, any curriculum document should be viewed as a guide. The curriculum is not dogma (Fryshman, 2008). We have forgotten that and have created an educational structure that is convenient for government, convenient for teachers, and convenient for society, but seemingly highly unsuitable for many young people.

References

Apple, M. W. (2004). Away with all teachers: The cultural politics of home schooling. In D. Callejo Perez, S. M. Fain, & J. J. Slater (Eds.), *Pedagogy of place: Seeing space as cultural education.* New York, NY: Peter Lang.

Apple, M. W. (2008). Curriculum planning: Content, form, and the politics of accountability. In *The SAGE handbook of curriculum and development.* SAGE Publications. Retrieved from http://www.sage-ereference. comlhdbk_curriculumlArtic1e_n2.html.

Breault, R. A. (1999). The sound-bite curriculum. *The Teacher Educator, 35* (l), 1–7.

Burns, J. M. (1978/1982). *Leadership.* New York, NY: Harper.

Carini, P. (2001). *Starting strong: A different look at children, schools, and standards.* New York, NY: Teachers College Press.

Constantine, J., Player D., Silva, T., Hallgren, K., Grider, M., & Deke, J. (2009). *An evaluation of teachers trained through different routes to certification, final report* (NCEE 2009-4043). U.S. Department of Education, Washington, DC: National Center for Education Evaluation and Regional Assistance, Institute of Education Sciences.

Dahl, R. A. (1970). *After the revolution.* New Haven, CT: Yale University Press.

Daniel, M. C. (2007). Authentic literacy practices for English Language Learners: A balanced curriculum design. *Journal of Reading Education, 32* (2), 18–25.

Darling-Hammond, L. (1999). *Teacher quality and student achievement: A review of state policy evidence.* Seattle, WA: University of Washington Center for the Study of Teaching and Policy.

Darling-Hammond, L., Berry, B., & Thorenson, A. (2001). Does teacher education matter? Evaluating the evidence. *Educational Evaluation and Policy Analysis, 23* (1), 57–77.

Dreher, S. (1997). Learning styles: Implications for learning & teaching. *Rural Educator, 19* (2), 26–29.

Egan, K. (2008). *The future of education: Reimagining our schools from the ground up.* New Haven, CT: Yale University Press.

Eisner, E. (1979/2008). *The educational imagination: On the design and evaluation of school programs.* Upper Saddle River, NJ: Prentice Hall.

Eisner, E. (1998). *The enlightened eye: Qualitative inquiry and the enhancement of educational practice.* Upper Saddle River, NJ: Prentice Hall.

Faulkner, S. & Cook, C. (2006). Testing vs. teaching: The perceived impact of four assessment demands on middle grades instructional practices. *Research in Middle Level Education Online, 29* (7). Retrieved from www.nmsa.org/Publications/RMLEOnline/Articles.

Freire, P. (1970/1997). *Pedagogy of the oppressed.* New York, NY: Continuum.

Frost, R. (1920). *Mountain interval.* New York, NY: Holt.

Fryshman, B. (2008, August 27). Curriculum is not dogma. *Education Week, 52,* p. 28.

Futrell, M. H., Gomez, J., & Bedden, D. (2003). Teaching the children of a new America: The challenge of diversity. *Phi Delta Kappan, 84* (5), 381–385.

Green, F. (1999). Brain and learning research: Implications for meeting the needs of diverse learners. *Education, 119,* 682–688.

He, M. F., Phillion, J., Chan, E., & Xu, S. (2008). Immigrant students experience of curriculum. In *The SAGE handbook of curriculum and development.* SAGE Publications. Retrieved from http://www.sage-ereference.comlhdbk_curriculum!Article_nII.html.

Hill, P., & Johnston, M. (2010). In the future, diverse approaches to schooling. *Phi Delta Kappan, 92* (3), 43–47.

Hodgkinson, H. (2000/2001). Educational demographics: What teachers should know. *Educational Leadership, 58* (4), 6–11.

Huebner, D. (1964). *A reassessment of the curriculum.* New York, NY: Teachers College Press.

Johnston, F. (2001). Exploring classroom teachers spelling practices and beliefs. *Reading Research and Instruction, 40,* 143–156.

Klein, M. F. (1994). The toll for curriculum design. *Peabody Journal of Education, 69* (3), 19–35.

Levin, B. (2008). Curriculum policy and the politics of what should be learned in schools. In *The SAGE handbook of curriculum and development.* SAGE Publications. Retrieved from http://www.sage-ereference.comlhdbk_curriculum!Article_nl.html.

Levine, A. (2005). *Educating school leaders.* Washington, DC: Education Schools Project. Retrieved from www.edschools.org/pdf/Final313.pdf.

Mehta, J., & Spillane, J. (2010). Unbounding promises and problems. *Phi Delta Kappan, 92* (3), 48–52.

Postman , N. (1996). *The end of education: Redefining the value of school.* New York, NY: Knopf.

Robinson, K. (2001). *Out of our minds: Learning to be creative.* New York, NY: John Wiley and Sons.

Tomlinson, C. A. (1999). *The differentiated classroom: Responding to the needs of all learners.* Alexandria, VA: Association for Supervision and Curriculum Development.

Tomlinson, C. A. (2006). An alternative to ability grouping. *Principal Leadership* (Middle School Edition), *6* (8), 31–32.

Tomlinson, C. A., & McTighe, J. (2006). *Integrating differentiating instruction + understanding by design.* Alexandria, VA: Association for Supervision and Curriculum Development.

Vansciver, J. H. (2005). Motherhood, apple pie, and differentiated instruction. *Phi Delta Kappan, 86,* 534–535.

Vega, Q., & Tayler, M. (2005). Incorporating course content while fostering a more learner-centered environment. *College Teaching, 53* (2), 83–86.

Weiner, K. G., & Oakes, J. (2008). Structuring curriculum: Technical, normative, and political considerations. In *The SAGE handbook of curriculum and development.* SAGE Publications. Retrieved from http://www.sage-ereference.comlhdbk_curriculum!Article_n5.html.

Weitz, A. (1995). Change how to remove the fear, resentment, and resistance. *Hospital Material Management Quarterly, 17* (2), 75–80.

Westbury, 1. (2008). Making curricula: Why do states make curricula, and how? In *The SAGE handbook of curriculum and development*. SAGE Publications. Retrieved from http://www.sage-ereference.comlhdbk_curriculum!Article_n3.html.

Willis, S., & Mann, L. (2000). Differentiating instruction: Finding manageable ways to meet individual needs. In *Curriculum Update*, Winter, pp. 1–8. Alexandria, VA: Association for Supervision and Curriculum Development.

ERVIN F. SPARAPANI is a professor at Saginaw Valley State University in the Department of Middle School and Secondary Teacher Education, having taught there for twenty-four years. He earned his Ph.D. at the University of Michigan, AN, in 1983.

DAVID M. CALLEJO PÉREZ earned an Ed.D. from Florida International University. He is currently the Carl A. Gerstacker Endowed Chair in Education at Saginaw Valley State University, President of the American Association for Teaching and Curriculum, and a member of the Society for Professors of Curriculum.

John Holt

 **NO**

Escape from Childhood

Young people should have the right to control and direct their own learning, that is, to decide what they want to learn, and when, where, how, how much, how fast, and with what help they want to learn it. To be still more specific, I want them to have the right to decide if, when, how much, and by whom they want to be *taught* and the right to decide whether they want to learn in a school and if so which one and for how much of the time.

No human right, except the right to life itself, is more fundamental than this. A person's freedom of learning is part of his freedom of thought, even more basic than his freedom of speech. If we take from someone his right to decide what he will be curious about, we destroy his freedom of thought. We say, in effect, you must think not about what interests and concerns you, but about what interests and concerns *us*.

We might call this the right of curiosity, the right to ask whatever questions are most important to us. As adults, we assume that we have the right to decide what does or does not interest us, what we will look into and what we will leave alone. We take this right for granted, cannot imagine that it might be taken away from us. Indeed, as far as I know, it has never been written into any body of law. Even the writers of our Constitution did not mention it. They thought it was enough to guarantee citizens the freedom of speech and the freedom to spread their ideas as widely as they wished and could. It did not occur to them that even the most tyrannical government would try to control people's minds, what they thought and knew. That idea was to come later, under the benevolent guise of compulsory universal education.

This right to each of us to control our own learning is now in danger. When we put into our laws the highly authoritarian notion that someone should and could decide what all young people were to learn and, beyond that, could do whatever might seem necessary (which now includes dosing them with drugs) to compel them to learn it, we took a long step down a very steep and dangerous path. The requirement that a child go to school, for about six hours a day, 180 days a year, for about ten years, whether or not he learns anything there, whether or not he already knows it or could learn it faster or better somewhere else, is such gross violation of civil liberties that few adults would stand for it. But the child who resists is treated as a criminal. With this requirement we created an industry, an army of people whose whole work was to tell young people what they had to learn and to try to make them learn it. Some of these people, wanting to exercise even more power over others, to be even more "helpful," or simply because the industry is not growing fast enough to hold all the people who want to get into it, are now beginning to say, "If it is good for children for us to decide what they shall learn and to make them learn it, why wouldn't it be good for everyone? If compulsory education is a good thing, how can there be too much of it? Why should we allow anyone, of any age, to decide that he has had enough of it? Why should we allow older people, any more than young, not to know what we know when their ignorance may have bad consequences for all of us? Why should we not *make* them know what they *ought* to know?"

They are beginning to talk, as one man did on a nationwide TV show, about "womb-to-tomb" schooling. If hours of homework every night are good for the young, why wouldn't they be good for us all—they would keep us away from the TV set and other frivolous pursuits. Some group of experts, somewhere, would be glad to decide what we all ought to know and then every so often check up on us to make sure we knew it—with, of course, appropriate penalties if we did not.

I am very serious in saying that I think this is coming unless we prepare against it and take steps to prevent it. The right I ask for the young is a right that I want to preserve for the rest of us, the right *to decide what goes into our minds*. This is much more than the right to decide whether or when or how much to go to school or what school you want to go to. That right is important, but it is only part of a much larger and more fundamental right, which I might call the right to learn, as opposed to being educated, i.e., made to learn what someone else thinks would be good for you. It is not just compulsory schooling but compulsory education that I oppose and want to do away with.

That children might have the control of their own learning, including the right to decide if, when, how much, and where they wanted to go to school, frightens and angers many people. They ask me, "Are you saying that if the parents wanted the child to go to school, and the child didn't want to go, that he wouldn't have to go? Are you saying that if the parents wanted the child to go to one school, and the child wanted to go to another, that the child would have the right to decide?" Yes, that is what I say. Some people ask, "If school wasn't compulsory, wouldn't many parents take their children out of school to exploit their labors in one way or another?" Such questions are often both snobbish and hypocritical. The questioner assumes and implies (though rarely says) that these bad parents are people poorer and less schooled than he. Also, though he appears to be defending the right of children to go to school, what he really is defending is the right of the state to compel them to go whether they want to or not. What he wants, in short, is that children should be in school, not that they should have any choice about going.

But saying that children should have the right to choose to go or not to go to school does not mean that the ideas and wishes of the parents would have no weight. Unless he is estranged from his parents and rebelling against them, a child cares very much about what they think and want. Most of the time, he doesn't want to anger or worry or disappoint them. Right now, in families where the parents feel that they have some choice about their children's schooling, there is much bargaining about schools. Such parents, when their children are little, often ask them whether they want to go to nursery school or kindergarten. Or they may take them to school for a while to try it out. Or, if they have a choice of schools, they may take them to several to see which they think they will like the best. Later, they care whether the child likes his school. If he does not, they try to do something about it, get him out of it, find a school he will like.

I know some parents who for years had a running bargain with their children. "If on a given day you just can't stand the thought of school, you don't feel well, you are afraid of something that may happen, you have something of your own that you very much want to do—well, you can stay home." Needless to say, the schools, with their supporting experts, fight it with all their might— Don't Give in to Your Child, Make Him Go to School, He's Got to Learn. Some parents, when their own plans make it possible for them to take an interesting trip, take their children with them. They don't ask the schools' permission, they just go. If the child doesn't want to make the trip and would rather stay in school, they work out a way for him to do that. Some parents, when their child is frightened,

unhappy, and suffering in school, as many children are, just take him out. Hal Bennett, in his excellent book *No More Public School*, talks about ways to do this.

A friend of mine told me that when her boy was in third grade, he had a bad teacher, bullying, contemptuous, sarcastic, cruel. Many of the class switched to another section, but this eight-year-old, being tough, defiant, and stubborn, hung on. One day—his parents did not learn this until about two years later—having had enough of the teacher's meanness, he just got up from his desk and without saying a word, walked out of the room and went home. But for all his toughness and resiliency of spirit, the experience was hard on him. He grew more timid and quarrelsome, less outgoing and confident. He lost his ordinary good humor. Even his handwriting began to go to pieces—it was much worse in the spring of the school year than in the previous fall. One spring day he sat at breakfast, eating his cereal. After a while he stopped eating and sat silently thinking about the day ahead. His eyes filled up with tears, and two big ones slowly rolled down his cheeks. His mother, who ordinarily stays out of the school life of her children, saw this and knew what it was about. "Listen," she said to him, "we don't have to go on with this. If you've had enough of that teacher, if she's making school so bad for you that you don't want to go any more, I'll be perfectly happy just to pull you right out. We can manage it. Just say the word." He was horrified and indignant. "No!" he said, "I couldn't do that." "Okay," she said, "whatever you want is fine. Just let me know." And so they left it. He had decided that he was going to tough it out, and he did. But I am sure knowing that he had the support of his mother and the chance to give it up if it got too much for him gave him the strength he needed to go on.

To say that children should have the right to control and direct their own learning, to go to school or not as they choose, does not mean that the law would forbid the parents to express an opinion or wish or strong desire on the matter. It only means that if their natural authority is not strong enough the parents can't call in the cops to make the child do what they are not able to persuade him to do. And the law may say that there is no limit to the amount of pressure or coercion the parents can apply to the child to deny him a choice that he has a legal right to make.

When I urge that children should control their learning, there is one argument that people bring up so often that I feel I must anticipate and meet it here. It says that schools are a place where children can for a while be protected against the bad influences of the world outside, particularly from its greed, dishonesty, and commercialism. It says that in school children may have a glimpse of a higher way of life, of people acting from other and better motives than greed and fear. People say, "We know that society is bad enough as it is and that if children go out into the larger world as soon as they wanted, they would be tempted and corrupted just that much sooner."

They seem to believe that schools are better, more honorable places than the world outside—what a friend of mine at Harvard once called "museums of virtue." Or that people in school, both children and adults, act from higher and better motives than people outside. In this they are mistaken. There are, of course, some good schools. But on the whole, far from being the opposite of, or an antidote to, the world outside, with all its envy, fear, greed, and obsessive competitiveness, the schools are very much like it. If anything, they are worse, a terrible, abstract, simplified caricature of it. In the world outside the school, some work, at least, is done honestly and well, for its own sake, not just to get ahead of others; people are not everywhere and always being set in competition against each other; people are not (or not yet) in every minute of their lives subject to the arbitrary, irrevocable orders and judgement of others. But in most schools, a student is every minute doing what others tell him, subject to their judgement, in situations in which he can only win at the expense of other students.

This is a harsh judgement. Let me say again, as I have before, that schools are worse than most of the people in them and that many of these people do many harmful things they would rather not do, and a great many other harmful things that they do not even see as harmful. The whole of school is much worse than the sum of its parts. There are very few people in the U.S. today (or perhaps anywhere, any time) in *any* occupation, who could be trusted with the kind of power that schools give most teachers over their students. Schools seem to me among the most anti-democratic, most authoritarian, most destructive, and most dangerous institutions of modern society. No other institution does more harm or more lasting harm to more people or destroys so much of their curiosity, independence, trust, dignity, and sense of identity and worth. Even quite kindly schools are inhibited and corrupted by the knowledge of children and teachers alike that they are *performing* for the judgement and approval of others—the children for the teachers; the teachers for the parents, supervisors, school board, or the state. No one is ever free from feeling that he is being judged all the time, or soon may be. Even after the best class experiences teachers must ask themselves, "Were we right to do that? Can we prove we were right? Will it get us in trouble?"

What corrupts the school, and makes it so much worse than most of the people in it, or than they would like it to be, is its power—just as their powerlessness corrupts the students. The school is corrupted by the endless anxious demand of the parents to know how their child is doing—meaning is he ahead of the other kids—and their demand that he be kept ahead. Schools do not protect children from the badness of the world outside. They are at least as bad as the world outside, and the harm they do to the children in their power creates much of the badness of the world outside. The sickness of the modern world is in many ways a school-induced sickness. It is in school that most people learn to expect and accept that some expert can always place them in some sort of rank or hierarchy. It is in school that we meet, become used to, and learn to believe in the totally controlled society. We do not learn much science, but we learn to worship "scientists" and to believe that anything we might conceivably need or want can only come, and someday will come, from them. The school is the closest we have yet been able to come to Huxley's *Brave New World*, with its alphas and betas, deltas and epsilons—and now it even has its soma. Everyone, including children, should have the right to say "No!" to it.

JOHN HOLT (1923–1985) was an educator and a critic of public schooling who authored several influential books on education and promoted homeschooling.

EXPLORING THE ISSUE

Should the Curriculum Be Standardized for All?

Critical Thinking and Reflection

1. Is the Paideia Curriculum a feasible choice for public schools? If so, how would it be implemented for all students?
2. Do John Holt's educational views address the question of standardized curriculum?
3. How would a teacher or principal fully address the question of public educational systems need for or against a standardized curriculum?
4. Should young people have the right to choose and direct their own learning and are they really knowledgeable enough to be making those choices?
5. What is the nexus between standardized curriculum and the Common Core State Standards?

Is There Common Ground?

The free/open school movement values small, personalized educational settings in which students engage in activities that have personal meaning. One of the movement's ideological assumptions, emanating from the philosophy of Jean-Jacques Rousseau, is that given a reasonably unrestrictive atmosphere, the learner will pursue avenues of creative and intellectual self-development. This confidence in self-motivation is the cornerstone of Holt's advocacy of freedom for the learner, a position he elaborates upon in his books *Instead of Education* (1988) and *Teach Your Own* (1982). The argument has gained some potency with recent developments in home-based computer-assisted instruction.

Mortimer Adler's proposal for a unified curricular and methodological approach, released in 1982 by the Institute for Philosophical Research, was fashioned by a group of distinguished scholars and practitioners and has its roots in such earlier works as Arthur Bestor's *Educational Wastelands* (1953), Mortimer Smith's *The Diminished Mind* (1954), and Paul Copperman's *The Literacy Hoax* (1978). The proposal has widely been discussed since its release, and it has been implemented in a number of school systems. See, for example, "Launching Paideia in Chattanooga," by Cynthia M. Gettys and Anne Wheelock, *Educational Leadership* (September 1994) and Terry Roberts and Audrey Trainor, "Performing for Yourself and Others: The Paideia Coached Project," *Phi Delta Kappan* (March 2004). Sparapani and Perez (2015) support a standardized curriculum because children should be taught those useful things that are really necessary making it a pragmatic gesture to meet the needs of learners, while at the same time, the needs of policy makers.

Holt's plea for freedom from an imposed curriculum has a champion in John Taylor Gatto, New York City and New York State Teacher of the Year. Gatto has produced two provocative books, *Dumbing Us Down: The Hidden Curriculum of Compulsory Schooling* (1992) and *Confederacy of Dunces: The Tyranny of Compulsory Schooling* (1992). Two other works that build upon Holt's basic views are Lewis J. Perelman's *School's Out: The New Technology and the End of Education* (1992) and George Leonard's "Notes: The End of School," *The Atlantic Monthly* (May 1992).

A final word on the issue relates to a key standardization effort, the Common Core (standards), which was developed to hold American students to a high level of expectation for academic success while moving, at the same time, away from a culture of testing, test preparation, and deep learning. But the Common Core is facing a lot of criticism, even backlash, that it is creating a national curriculum focused on a one-size-fits-all approach to student learning that maintains a strong emphasis on testing and undermining teacher autonomy.

Additional Resources

Mortimer, A. (1982). *The Paideia proposal: An educational manifesto*. Institute for Philosophical Research. New York: Touchstone-Simon & Shuster.

Berlau, J. (2001). What happened to the great ideas? *Insight on the News*. Retrieved from https://

www.questia.com/magazine/1G1-77812349/what-happened-to-the-great-ideas

Eisner, E. (2002). The kind of schools we need. *Phi Delta Kappan. 83/8*. Retrieved from https://eric.ed.gov/?id=EJ644873

Kohn, A. (2001). One-Size-Fits-All education doesn't work. *The Boston Globe*. Retrieved from https://www.alfiekohn.org/article/one-size-fits-education-doesnt-work/

Ohanian, S. (2001). *Caught in the middle: Nonstandard kids and a killing curriculum*. Portsmouth, NH: Heinemann-Reed Elsevier, Inc.

Roberts, T., & Billings, L. (2008). Thinking is literacy, literacy thinking. *Educational Leadership. 65/5*. Retrieved from http://www.ascd.org/publications/educational-leadership/feb08/vol65/num05/Thinking-Is-Literacy,-Literacy-Thinking.aspx

Internet References . . .

Education Standardization: Essential or Harmful?

http://www.gettingsmart.com/2013/04/education-standardization-essential-or-harmful/

Five Reasons to Have a Standardized Curriculum

http://www.borgenmagazine.com/5-reasons-to-have-a-standardized-curriculum/

Standardized Curriculum and Loss of Creativity

https://www.tandfonline.com/doi/abs/10.1080/00405841.2013.804315?journalCode=htip20

Should the United States Education System Standardize the Curriculum?

http://www.debate.org/opinions/should-the-united-states-education-system-standardize-the-curriculum

Teach: A one-size-fits-all approach to instruction to instruction is stifling our classroom

https://www.washingtonpost.com/news/answer-sheet/wp/2016/12/23/teacher-a-one-size-fits-all-approach-to-instruction-is-stifling-our-classrooms/?noredirect=on&utm_term=.8be4f740abd1

Selected, Edited, and with Issue Framing Material by:
Glenn L. Koonce, *Regent University*

ISSUE

Should "Public Schooling" Be Redefined?

YES: Stephanie T. Scott, from "An Argument for Redefining Public Schools," *Pawley Learning Institute* (2008)

NO: Linda Nathan, Joe Nathan, Ray Bacchetti, and Evans Clinchy, from "A Response to Frederick Hess," *Phi Delta Kappan* (February 2004)

Learning Outcomes

After reading this issue, you will be able to:

- Contrast varying meanings for the term "public schooling."
- Define who should be permitted to provide public schooling.
- Compare and contrast politicizing verses.
- Analyze the four responses to Hess's view of a public school.
- Identify how new technologies complicate the definition of public schooling.

ISSUE SUMMARY

YES: Researcher Stephanie Scott explains that the purpose of public schools must be clarified at a minimum and redefined at a maximum in this era where parents have increased choices for the education of their children.

NO: Linda Nathan, Joe Nathan, Ray Bacchetti, and Evans Clinchy express a variety of concerns about the conceptual expansion that Hess proposes.

The original public school crusade, led by Massachusetts education official Horace Mann (1796–1859) and other activists, built on the growing sentiment among citizens, politicians, and business leaders that public schools were needed to deal with the increase in immigration, urbanization, and industrialism, as well as to bind together the American population and to prepare everyone for participatory democracy. For the most part, the right of the government to compel school attendance, dating from Massachusetts legislation in 1852, went unchallenged, although Catholics formed their own private school system in reaction to the predominant Protestantism of public schools in certain areas. In the 1920s there were efforts to eliminate all alternatives to government-run public schools to ensure attendance compliance and curricular standardization. Such an effort in Oregon was challenged in court, and the U.S.

Supreme Court ultimately ruled, in *Pierce v. Society of Sisters* (1925), that such legislation unreasonably interferes with parental rights. While this ruling preserved the private school option, it did not alter the governmental prerogative to compel school attendance.

This governmental authority met with sharp criticism from liberal writers in the 1950s and beyond, in works such as Paul Goodman's "Compulsory Mis-education" (1964), Ivan Illich's "Deschooling Society" (1971), John Holt's "Instead of Education" (1976), and John Taylor Gatto's "Dumbing Us Down: The Hidden Curriculum of Compulsory Schooling" (1992). Gatto condemned the public school system for its emphasis on obedience and subordination rather than the unleashing of the intellectual and creative powers of the individual. Since the 1980s, a parallel attack has come from conservatives, such as William J. Bennett, E. D. Hirsch, Jr., Chester E. Finn, Jr., Charles J. Sykes, Grover Norquist, and

Cal Thomas, and conservative groups such as Parents for School Choice, the Cato Institute, and the Alliance for Separation of School and State. Building on the findings of the 1983 *A Nation at Risk* report, a significant segment of the American population continues to express disdain for the public education "establishment" (the U.S. Department of Education, the National Education Association, and teacher-training institutions) for its inability or unwillingness to improve public school performance. Their basic contention is that only choice-driven competition will bring about lasting improvement. William J. Bennett, in "A Nation Still at Risk," *Policy Review* (July/August 1998), has stated that although choices are spreading, charter schools are proliferating, privately managed public schools have long waiting lists, and home schooling is expanding, "the elephant still has most of the power." He concludes that "we must never again assume that the education system will respond to good advice. It will change only when power relationships change, particularly when all parents gain the power to decide where their children go to school."

Educator-reformer Deborah Meier, in "The Road to Trust," *American School Board Journal* (September 2003), argues that we must make public education feel like a public enterprise again. Hers is a call for the rebuilding of trust between public schools and the communities they directly serve. "Our school boards need to turn their eyes to their constituencies—not just to following the dictates of state and federal government micromanagers."

In the following articles, Stephanie Scott makes the case that the time to examine the most fundamental issues in public education is now. Linda Nathan, Joe Nathan, Ray Bacchetti, and Evans Clincy, in response to Fredrick Hess' 2004 *Education Next* article defending public schools, challenge what they perceive to be an unproductive assault on public schooling.

YES ⤶

Stephanie T. Scott

An Argument for Redefining Public Schools

The nation's problems have shifted significantly since the founding of public schools in the 18th century. At that time the nation was immersed with huge influxes of immigrants, planning the development of great urban centers and gearing up for the production demands of industrialization. Since that time, the information age has come forth and the world has become significantly smaller with the increased use and invention of innovative technology. So, now public schools must consider their purpose in current times and determine if there is a need to redefine public schools.

The Impact of NCLB on the Purpose of Schools

The purpose of public schools must be redefined in the information age where parents have increased choices for the education of their children. The importance of creating shared understandings of the essential ideas driving the mission of public schools cannot be underestimated. If the mission of public schools, driven by the mandates of NCLB, is askew, confounded or irrelevant in these times, then it is critical to redefine that mission in order to ensure the core operation of schools is not mired in waste. In clarifying the essential idea of what the purpose of schools is, it is possible to focus resources for maximum effectiveness. By developing shared thinking about the purpose of schools is, innovation can be fostered and a climate for continuous improvement realized.

According to Webster's Dictionary, the definition of public is "pertaining to or affecting the people or community, for everyone's use," and the definition of pertain is "to be appropriate or fitting." Following these definitions, I believe public schools are not fitting the needs of the community. The need for schools to carry forth the metric of relevance in the most fundamental aspects of mission fulfillment are at the heart of the position presented here.

The federal government, namely President George W. Bush, instituted a band-aid to fix student achievement problems. According to the "No Child Left Behind Act" (NCLB), by 2014 all students must be proficient in both reading and mathematics. While the program is highly publicized for its intent, the community-at-large is not privy to all the details of how NCLB standards are measured. NCLB requires students from grades 3–8 to take standardized tests and schools who fail to meet the standards or show progress are considered "failing schools." The federal government offers no incentive and has shown little regard for the financial burden NCLB has piled on to the individual states to create and administer these standardized tests.

Beyond financial implications, the standardized testing program of NCLB sets up a climate for teaching and learning that is focused on teaching to the test. Teaches are intimidated into teaching toward a single assessment. Creativity, innovation, and content depth are now replaced with a quick-paced and lower-level thinking curriculum. Students have become test-taking robots, and the needs of the community to produce productive members of society are lost as the new purpose of public schools is implicitly defined as a place where students take tests to prove that their school is meeting minimum standards.

The Essential Idea of the Purpose of Schools

Hess (2004) argues that the purpose of public schools should be to provide for productive citizenship development by teaching skills, instilling knowledge and encouraging dispositions that honor the tenets of constitutional freedoms and responsibilities. Nathan (2004) offers a more liberal purpose of public schools. Public schools should:

- be open to all kinds of students and not use admission tests
- follow due process procedures with regard to students and educators

---

- use state-approved, standardized, and other measures to help monitor student progress or lack thereof
- close the achievement gap between white students and racial minority and low-income students as an explicit, measurable goal; and be actively chosen by faculty, families, and students

I offer a more progressive purpose that puts the power of learning back into the hands of the community. Putting the standardized tests on the back burner, but not forgetting about them, is the first step in redefining the purpose of public schools. If we really are to fit the needs of the community, districts and states should be actively involved in providing funds for cutting-edge research to improve student progress through new technology, with better resources, innovative teaching styles, and effective teaching practices. The funds tied up through these standardized assessments would more than benefit the state and nation if put to better use to support improvement. Allowing the states to choose how to assess minimum progress of schools would put this power back into the community.

The purpose of schools could then be focused on:

- creating productive members of society who are critical thinkers
- meeting the needs of a diverse population of students, including students with disabilities, gifted and talented students, students from a variety of cultures students from different income levels, and other backgrounds
- creating learners with a profound understanding of foundational content
- teaching the standards set by the states through innovative instructional techniques that make learning student-centered
- involving the community in student success and their progress

Clarifying the Essential Idea: Refuting the Opponents' Views

Opponents of redefining public schooling hold to several beliefs. I argue against three of these common arguments.

1. There is a larger and more democratic purpose to public schools than private and parochial schools.

The argument that all students are served in public schools is not supported, and is evidenced by the increasing number of parents choosing charter school education for their children. There still remain public schools that

have minimum IQ scores for entrance. In districts such as the Paradise Valley Unified School District in Arizona, a student with a cognitive score too low will not be placed in the general education classroom. There are more districts across the nation whose policies are the same. NCLB expects all students to pass minimum requirements, and all students with disabilities are expected to meet these standards, as well. Public schools are not meeting these students' needs when the standardized assessments are driving the curriculum. Rather than meeting student needs through individualized or differentiated learning, the public schools are now prescribing a one-size- fits-all education to pass these assessments. They are essentially shutting the door on our students who cannot meet these minimum requirements.

2. Public schools provide choice in public education.

Perhaps schools are providing some choices for education geographically, but schools are not providing choice that allows the community to have input into what ideals and values will be taught in the classroom, what big ideas are most important. If public schools are intended to meet the needs of a community, then presently communities have no choice in how their schools are led. Parents have more say about how schools are run when they send their child to a parochial, or private school. These schools receive funding from the parents, who have expectations. When these needs or expectations are not met, the parents voice their concerns. Private schools that do not meet parent approval will be forced to change to meet these needs, or face losing their student population. If public schools expect the public to believe they have a choice in education, they have created hypocrisy. Those in the community do not make the major decisions that affect the communities' children; unfortunately bureaucrats at the district, state, and federal levels make them.

3. Increased funding will decrease the achievement gap across the nation.

To argue that funding reduces the gap in achievement in inner-city schools is contrary to research conducted in schools around the country. The 90/90/90 case study by Reeves (2000), according to the Leadership and Learning Center (formerly the Center for Performance Assessments), found that the mental model of poverty and minority status as correlated to low test scores is not supported. Instead, Reeves found that schools with a shared essential idea that the purpose of the school is to help students achieve and when that mission was clearly operationalized in the school, high achievement at a 90% success rate does occur. According to Reeves (2000), in the 228 buildings of the 90/90/90 cases studied:

- More than 90 percent of the students are eligible for free and reduced lunch, a commonly used surrogate for low-income families
- More than 90 percent of the students are from ethnic minorities
- More than 90 percent of the students met or achieved high academic standards, according to independently conducted tests of academic achievement

The study found five characteristics common to these schools, despite their obvious economical disadvantages:

- A focus on academic achievement
- Clear curriculum choices
- Frequent assessment of student progress and multiple opportunities for improvement
- An emphasis on nonfiction writing
- Collaborative scoring of student work

To argue that socioeconomic status is a reason for failure is putting the blame on the community. Schools and teachers must be prepared and informed about practices that will help these students succeed, not make excuses that impede their academic success. When held to high standards with clear and consistent expectations, students will rise to the challenges as seen in the 90/90/90 schools.

Conclusion

If the purpose of schools is not explicitly redefined and its expectations made clear, we can expect to produce students who will be unable to look at problems from different perspectives, and unable to solve problems that require higher level thinking. Our schools must be future-focused on creating leaders to ensure that all students' needs are met. We must stop putting blame on the community for the achievement gap and instead look to them for resources and guidance. If we don't tap into the communities' needs, the achievement gap will only become greater and the exclusion of students will increase to the detriment of education and society.

References

Hess, F. (2004). What is a 'public school?' Principles for a new century. In J. Noll (Ed.), *Taking sides: Clashing views on educational issues* (pp. 152–160). Dubuque, Iowa: McGraw-Hill.

Nathan, J. (2004). A response to Frederick Hess: Some questions for advocates of public education. In J. Noll (Ed.), *Taking sides: Clashing of views on educational issues* (pp. 164–165). Dubuque, Iowa: McGraw-Hill.

Reeves, D. B. (2000). *Accountability in action: A blueprint for learning organizations, 2nd edition.* [Electronic version]. (pp. 185–208). In Barnes, C. A. & Schumacher, A. W. (Eds.) Denver: CO: Advanced Learning Press. Retrieved July 2008 from: http://208.112.40.253/resources/custom/articles/AinA%20Ch19.pdf

Reeves, D. B. (2000). High performance in high poverty schools: 90/90/90 and beyond. [Electronic version]. The Leadership and Learning Center. Retrieved July 2008 from: http://www.sabine.k12.la.us/online/leadershipacademy/high%20perfor mance%2090%2090%2090%20and%20beyond.pdf

STEPHANIE T. SCOTT is an assistant principal at Gendale Elementary School District in Phoenix, Arizona.

Linda Nathan et al.

A Response to Frederick Hess

Linda Nathan, The Larger Purpose of Public Schools

At times I want to cheer for Frederick Hess's words in "What Is a 'Public School'? Principles for a New Century." How true it is that many reformers "regard public schooling as a politicized obstacle rather than a shared ideal." How true that "those of us committed to the promise of public education are obliged to see that the idea does not become a tool of vested interests."

Yet there is also something chilling about his article that stops the cheer in my throat. His use of innuendo in place of evidence, his sloppy logic, and his attacks on some of the most effective public school reformers—painting them as the enemy—suggest that his real agenda is not strengthening public education but privatizing it through vouchers and for-profit takeover schemes.

Hess's labored analysis obscures a simple fact: public schools have a larger and more democratic purpose than private and parochial schools (although this is not to say that these schools contribute nothing to public life). Public school systems are open to everyone regardless of disability, wealth, status, race, or religion. Private and parochial schools are not. While some are more open than others, they can have entrance exams and can explicitly exclude students with disabilities or those who otherwise don't fit a preferred profile. And of course they can also exclude those who can't pay. They can expel students who cause trouble, at their sole discretion, without recourse.

Hess himself acknowledges this core principle of universal access, conceding that public schooling "implies an obligation to ensure that all students are appropriately served." But he seems indifferent to the inequities inherent in his "more expansive" notion of what makes a school public.

Hess makes a false analogy when he equates schools that buy textbooks from for-profit companies with schools that are managed by for-profit firms. Basic educational

decisions should be made by citizens of the local school community—not by distant shareholders looking only at a corporate balance sheet. (It's ironic that Hess picks as his exemplar Edison Schools, Inc., which sold off the textbooks, computers, lab supplies, and musical instruments of the Philadelphia public schools it had been hired to manage just days before school was to open in 2002 in order to pay down the company's mounting debt.)

Hess objects to teaching "tolerance" and affirming "diversity" because, he says, these words are open to multiple interpretations. Then he states that "public schools should teach children the essential skills and knowledge that make for productive citizens" and "teach them to respect our constitutional order," as if these were absolute truths *not* open to interpretation. The example of tolerance he cites, wherein a radical Muslim is calling for jihad, slyly exploits a hot-button issue to imply that the "professional community" of educators condones terrorism. Similarly, he smears the notion of defending tolerance as "uniformly teaching students to accept teen pregnancy as normal" and implies that liberals equate these activities with their definition of "public schooling." Nonsense.

His attack on Deborah Meier, Alfie Kohn, and others is equally baseless. It's the classic straw man fallacy: he attributes a position to them—that they oppose the teaching of basic academic mastery in favor of promoting "preferred social values"—that they have in fact never espoused. Meier's argument, with which Hess is surely familiar, is that such a tradeoff is unnecessary and that strong academic habits and mastery of literacy are essential and are furthered by an intellectually open and challenging spirit of inquiry.

The Coalition of Essential Schools, another of Hess's targets, gets similar treatment. Without offering a single example or other evidence of any kind, he asserts that faculty members at Coalition schools routinely promote partisan political views and are determined to "stamp out 'improper' thoughts." Of course, he's right that some teachers and schools—including many private and religious schools—do have a "party line," whether they're conscious of it or not. But he wants to have it both ways. While he attacks Coalition teachers for promoting values he dislikes, he argues at the same time that there should be choice in education so that parents can select schools that reflect their values.

Hess's argument with regard to the personal views and political leanings of educators is simply a red herring. The underlying issue is his fear that his own preferred values are being "stamped out." He uses that phrase again in making the absurd claim that the goal of liberal educators is to subvert the influence of families on their children. If he were serious about the rights of parents, Hess would be attacking the idea of a federalized education system—with or without vouchers—in which the *state* defines which values, priorities, intellectual habits, and performance standards will dominate and in which schools must accept intrusive guidelines to receive a stamp of approval and public funding. It seems to me that his scorn should fall not on Deborah Meier and Ted Sizer but on George W. Bush and the other proponents of top-down standardization.

Hess wants teachers to promote respect for the law—unless the laws in question are those that guarantee equal rights to people regardless of sexual orientation. When I began teaching in the late 1970s, it was dangerous for a teacher to be homosexual, not because of students' or parents' reactions but because of administrative reprisals. And it was dangerous in those days to talk about the threat of nuclear war or to suggest that the U.S.-sponsored war in El Salvador was unjust or even to imply that there was another view of these issues than the government's. My colleagues daily taught their students that might was right and homosexuality was a sin. I had my tires slashed by colleagues who felt that desegregation had ruined the Boston Public Schools. That we have created schools in which more open dialogue is possible indeed represents progress.

In calling for more innovation and choice in public education, Hess is absolutely right. In diversity, after all, there is strength. The U.S. has tried many experiments in public schooling over the past two centuries. We are in the midst of yet another experiment with our charter schools. In many ways, this kind of exploration is healthy. It allows us to look at different models and seek out best practices. Yet the charter school experiment has largely ignored issues of equity. In Boston and many other districts, charter schools often make no provision for accepting students who require special educational services or facilities, while traditional public schools are required to do so. This is one reason that some see charter schools as less "public" than other public schools. The same inequities exist in many parochial schools.

We need schools that help young people and adults learn and practice the skills necessary to be participants in a vibrant democracy. Such schools will be messy places that must balance the public interest with America's pluralist tradition. In their classrooms everyone learns to ask probing questions, to use evidence well, to make legitimate arguments, and to recognize fallacies and lies. I invite Frederick Hess to come to the Boston Arts Academy, where we will be happy to give him the opportunity to practice these skills with our students.

Joe Nathan, Some Questions for Advocates of Public Education

Three very specific questions for advocates of public education came to my mind as I read Frederick Hess's argument that we need to "reappraise our assumptions as to what constitutes 'public schooling.'" Let me pose them to *Kappan* readers, who no doubt are advocates for public education.

What is public about a suburban district in which the price of admission to the local public schools is the ability to purchase a home for more than one million dollars (and to pay tax-deductible property taxes on that home)?

What is public about an inner-city school with an admissions test that screens out all students with mental disabilities and more than 95% of the students in the surrounding district and so proclaims that it serves only the "cream of the crop"?

What is public about preventing some inner-city students from attending a magnet school just a few blocks from their homes that receives $1,500 per pupil more than the neighborhood school they attend? At the same time, in the name of integration, white students from wealthy suburbs are transported to this school—some via taxi.

These three questions form the basis for two larger questions that continue to trouble me even after being involved with public education for 33 years. I don't have definitive answers to these larger questions. But I share them with readers in the hope that they, too, will find them worth pondering. . . .

❧

. . . 1. *Since all public schools are not open to all kinds of students, what admissions standards should be acceptable for schools supported by public funds?* When my teachers in the Wichita public schools talked about public education, they stressed that a key difference between public and private schools was that public schools were open to all. Many of the authorities I read while I was at Carleton College, preparing to become a teacher, said the same thing.

This idea of "open to all" makes great sense to me. It seems like the right and just way to operate. Hess writes that he thinks it "appropriate" for some public schools to select some children and exclude others. I've disagreed with this position for more than 30 years. But lately, I'm not so sure.

When I began teaching I learned that many public schools were *not* open to all students. As I traveled the country, I learned that there were more than a thousand magnet schools and programs that have admissions tests. A study some years ago found that more than half of the nation's secondary magnet schools have admissions tests, as do about a quarter of the elementary magnets.[1]

Wisconsin Rep. Polly Williams, a Democrat and an African American state legislator, was enraged because most of the youngsters in her inner-city Milwaukee district were not able to get into exclusive magnet schools in the neighborhood, which brought in affluent, white, suburban students. Her frustration led her to fight successfully for the nation's first formal voucher plan.

Some opponents of vouchers insist that a level playing field isn't available when private schools can cherry-pick their students. I agree. But many educators, including me, have the same frustration about elite magnet schools: they have an unfair advantage over neighborhood public schools that are open to all in that they can screen out students with whom they don't wish to work.

I also learned that the country's single biggest choice system is called the suburbs. Millions of youngsters attend schools in the suburbs, and these schools clearly are *not* open to all students. They are open only to those whose families can afford to live in suburban communities.

A few years ago, I visited a school district on the northern coast of Long Island. Administrators there told me that the least expensive home in the district sold for $1,000,000. None of the district's teachers could afford to live there.

Today, some people argue that there should be publicly funded schools that are open only to young women. Two such schools have opened—one in New York, the other in Chicago. Even though I was not fond of this type of school, I visited the New York City district school, Young Women's Leadership Academy. I was impressed. The young women reported that, without boys around, they felt much more comfortable raising their hands in class and much more comfortable doing well on tests.

Should public funds go to some schools of choice that are only open to women? Or only to men? Five years ago, I would have said emphatically not. Today, I don't know.

2. *Shouldn't schools we describe as public accept and use some of the country's basic ideas to help improve education?* Americans generally endorse a number of ideas:

- choice of religion, job, neighborhood, places to obtain services, and so on;
- the provision of opportunities to try new ideas and approaches;
- the shared belief that this is a country not just of rights, but of responsibilities; and
- the notions that our cherished freedoms are not unlimited.

However, for three decades I've watched major public education groups vigorously oppose school choice programs, including public school choice programs, that are built on these principles. For example, there was intense opposition from educators in 1970 to the creation of the St. Paul Open School.

These organized groups ignore the professional and pedagogical rationales for public school choice, expressed best by veteran educator Deborah Meier:

Choice is an essential tool in the effort to create . . . good public education. . . . We'll have to allow those most involved (teachers, administrators, parents) to exercise greater on-site power to put their collective wisdom into practice. Once we do all this, however, school X and school Y are going to start doing things differently. . . . Creating a school different from what any of those who work in the system are familiar with, one that runs counter to the experiences of most families, is possible only if teachers, parents, and students have time to agree on changes and a choice on whether or not they want to go along with them.[2]

Colleagues involved in other efforts to create new options over the last three decades have had similar experiences. During his tenure as president of the American Federation of Teachers, Al Shanker described what happened to teachers who proposed schools-within-schools:

> Many schools-within-schools were or are treated like traitors or outlaws for daring to move out of the lockstep and do something different. Their initiators had to move Heaven and Earth to get school officials to authorize them, and if they managed that, often they could look forward to insecurity, obscurity, or outright hostility.[3]

Over the past decade, with help from the Gates, Blandin, and Annenberg Foundations, the Center for School Change at the University of Minnesota has tried to help educators create new schools-within-schools in a number of communities. Shanker's words have often proved to be very accurate. The most intense, vigorous critics of offering a different kind of school—whether in a single building or in a district—have often been other educators.

Many educators have argued over the past 30 years that public, district schools serving racial minorities and students from low-income families are doing the best job they can with existing funds. According to the most recent Phi Delta Kappa/Gallup poll, 80% of the public thinks the achievement gap between white children and minority children is mostly related to factors other than the quality of schooling.[4]

Perhaps in part because some educators have helped to convince the public that inner-city schools are mostly not responsible for the achievement gap, 58% of the nation and 62% of public school parents think it is possible to narrow the achievement gap *without* spending more money than is currently being spent on these students.[5] Unfortunately, many state legislators are opting not to raise taxes and not to give more to schools serving low-income, limited-English-speaking students.

Some of us vigorously disagree with these legislative actions and think that both more public school choice and more funding would help reduce the achievement gap. We have seen—and in some cases have worked in—schools that have served the public interest by helping all

youngsters achieve their potential and have done much to close the gap between students of different races.

Despite encouragement from such strong public school supporters as former President Bill Clinton, former Secretary of Education Richard Riley, and the late Sen. Paul Wellstone (D-Minn.), efforts to create independent charter public schools still face huge opposition from state teacher, school board, and superintendent groups. The opposition uses the same arguments used in 1970 against the St. Paul Open School: new options take away our money.

But it isn't their money. Legislatures allocate money for the education of children, not for the preservation of a system. If 50 students move from a city to a suburb or from a suburb to a city, the dollars follow them. The money doesn't belong to "the system."

Thousands of parents and educators are voting with their feet. The number of states with a charter law has gone from one in 1991 to 40 in 2003. The number of charter schools has gone from one school in 1991 to more than 3,000 in 2003. Federal statistics show that low-income students and racial minorities are overrepresented in charter schools. While the evidence is mixed—and almost certainly will be so when charter and district schools are compared—some charters are clearly producing major achievement gains. Shouldn't we learn from and replicate their best practices?

Starting new schools is extremely difficult work. But whether it's a Pilot School in the Boston Public Schools or a New Visions option in New York City or a charter school in any of 40 states, the opportunity to try new approaches is as vital for education as it is for medicine, business, or technology.

Some Tentative Conclusions

So Frederick Hess wants to "discern what . . . makes schooling public and accept diverse arrangements that are consistent with those tenets." I'm not sure what standards all publicly supported schools should meet. But after 33 years, I offer these as minimum requirements for schools that serve the public interest and are thus eligible to receive public funds. Public schools should:

- be open to all kinds of students and not use admissions tests;
- follow due process procedures with regard to students and educators;
- use state-approved, standardized, and other measures to help monitor student progress or lack thereof;

- have closing the achievement gap between white students and racial minority and low-income students as an explicit, measurable goal;[6] and
- be actively chosen by faculty, families, and students.

Thanks to Hess and to the *Kappan* for urging a timely reconsideration of the basic principles of public education. As social justice activist Leonard Fein states it:

The future is not something we discover around the next corner. It is something we shape, we create, we invent. To hold otherwise would be to view ourselves as an audience to history, and not its authors. History, and even our own lives, cannot always be turned and twisted to make them go exactly where we should like. But there is, for people of energy and purpose, more freedom of movement than most ever exercise.[7]

Notes

1. Lauri Steel and Roger Levine, *Educational Innovation in Multiracial Contexts: The Growth of Magnet Schools in American Education* (Palo Alto, Calif.: American Institutes for Research, 1994). This study was prepared for the U.S. Department of Education under Contract No. LC 90043001.

2. Deborah Meier, "Choice Can Save Public Education," *The Nation,* 4 March 1991.

3. Al Shanker, "Where We Stand: Convention Plots New Course—A Charter for Change," *New York Times* (paid advertisement), 10 July 1988, p. E-7.

4. Lowell C. Rose and Alec M. Gallup, "The 35th Annual Phi Delta Kappa/Gallup Poll of the Public's Attitudes Toward the Public Schools," *Phi Delta Kappan,* September 2003, p. 48.

5. Ibid.

6. Student progress should be monitored using various measures, not just standardized tests. If there is not major improvement in narrowing the achievement gap in most areas over a five-year period, the school should be "reconstituted."

7. Leonard Fein et al., *Reform Is a Verb: Notes on Reform and Reforming Jews* (New York: Union of American Hebrew Congregations, 1972), p. 152.

Ray Bacchetti, An Ongoing Conversation

We don't look at the big issues of the principles and purposes of public schools often or carefully enough. Sadly, the political and philosophical conversation seems increasingly polarized. In Venn diagram terms, the two circles—labeled right/left, basics/constructivist, academic/child-centered, etc.—reveal at best a vanishingly thin region of overlap. When the true believers on either side look in the mirror, they see Dumbledore. Over their shoulders and gaining, they see Voldemort.

Frederick Hess's beefy rhetoric stakes out a position that reflects a more conservative world view than my own. In essence, he argues that the purposes of public education will be better served if we narrow the number of principles that define its publicness and expand the number of ways those principles can be implemented. In that expanded universe, religious schools, vouchers, for-profit ventures, and other alternatives would be welcome.

The principles advertised in Hess's title are woven through his essay, making it difficult to distinguish his main point from his subsidiary concerns. Here is what I take to be the core of his definition of what makes a school public. In addition to teaching skills and content, public schools should:

- prepare students to be "productive members of the social order";
- enable students to "become aware of their societal responsibilities," including the "principles, habits, and obligations of citizenship"; and
- educate students to be "respectful of constitutional strictures," including laws, process, and individual rights.

In carrying out these functions, public school systems should also:

- not "deny access to students for reasons unrelated to [a school's] educational focus"; and
- "provide an appropriate placement for each student" in every community.

Asserting by implication that the meanings of his key terms are inherently obvious, Hess goes on to argue that the terms others might use to set forth other principles are not. For example, he observes that "diversity" and "tolerance" are "umbrella terms with multiple interpretations." Therefore, they lie outside his cluster of principles because, when we try to define them more precisely, "it becomes clear that we must privilege some values at the expense of others." If he believes that a similar privileging of certain values might color his own key terms, such as "obligations of citizenship," "productive members of the social order," "societal responsibilities," "individual rights," and the like, he gives no indication.

Hess seems to arrive at his position partly for affirmative reasons (e.g., an emphasis on academic learning) and partly because of a surprisingly bitter view of educators (some of whom he names, but most of whom he only characterizes). In his view, these educators:

- "explicitly promote a particular world view and endorse a particular social ethos";
- "promote partisan attitudes toward American foreign policy, the propriety of affirmative action, or the morality of redistributive social policies";
- teach students to "accept teen pregnancy or homosexuality as normal and morally unobjectionable";
- attempt to "stamp out familial views and impress children with socially approved beliefs"; and
- treat public institutions as their personal playthings.

To illustrate his more general points, Hess portrays the "meaningful questions" asked in the classrooms of the Coalition of Essential Schools as a herd of Trojan ponies surreptitiously unloading the teachers' agendas. It's not clear what "meaningful questions" might be in the classrooms he approves of, though readers might infer that they would be limited to the rational analysis of topics that arise from well-developed and authoritatively taught subject matter. There is nothing wrong with such questions, of course. But anyone who thinks that they—or the answers to them—would be value-free is likely to have slept through his or her undergraduate philosophy classes.

More to the point, however, a narrow and academic definition of such questions would exclude from the public school universe those who think students should also wrestle with forming habits of the heart as well as the mind, should learn to use critical inquiry to amend and expand values and understandings as well as to confirm them, and should go beyond "my country, right or wrong" to embrace the rest of Carl Schurz's famous phrase, "if right, to be kept right; and if wrong, to be set right."

I have spent a fair amount of time in schools of late, witnessing heroic efforts of underfinanced and overregulated teachers to enact both the academic preparation and the democracy-building ethos that our schools were meant to embody. If Hess is suggesting that generally left-leaning personal agendas have dominated public school instruction for a generation or more, then we should be able to see around us a widely shared value system that reflects those views. However, when I survey newspapers, polls, elections, and even school reform debates at national and local levels, I see instead an enormous variety of values and priorities. Some may find that diversity of views troubling. What troubles me is not that people disagree but that we seem increasingly incapable of working through our differences to embed public school policies and practices in a conception of the common good that can transcend political perspectives without disrespecting them.

The sort of public conversations about public education that would open minds to a critical look at new ideas would be, as I'm sure Hess would agree, tough to structure and to conduct. Where he and I are likely to disagree is on whether the topic of those conversations will ever be settled and, more important, whether it ever should be. Teaching skills and developing in each generation the social cohesion on which so much else depends will be easier (though never easy) to approach than will matters of values, educational philosophies, social goals, and civic priorities. Moreover, balancing the relative claims of the student, family, community, nation, and the wider world on how and what schools teach is a democratic journey, not a settled destination.

From the start, Hess acknowledges the powerful resonance of the concept of public education. What seems to make him impatient, even exasperated, is that the people who lead what he and some others pejoratively call "government-run schools" aren't listening to him. Not listening can be a stance or a reaction. Seeing it as a *stance*, I join him in his exasperation. The habit of "reflexively shrinking" from a consideration of alternatives hardens the democratic arteries. Seeing it as a *reaction*, I worry that world views (a term I prefer to "ideology") too often appear as righteous opposites, leaving all but the most robust listeners wondering what's the point.

Finding areas of overlap in our views under such conditions isn't easy. Developing the skills of measured and thoughtful dialogue needed to create such overlap is even harder. The challenge of doing so, however, demonstrates why a free nation needs public schools that are set up to make public decision making meaningful at the daily, close-to-home levels, as well as at higher levels. Such deliberative procedures force us to ask not only what we want our own children to learn but also what we want all children to learn. Children are, after all, collectively as well as individually the next generation, and the education we bequeath to them is communal as well as personal.

We need to talk and listen our way into more overlap in our political/philosophical Venn diagrams. Having

that running conversation looms large in my definition of what makes the public schools public. Hess seems to argue that, through a few principles and a multitude of entities all claiming the mantle of public education, we can make the need for that conversation go away. I would argue instead that getting better at it should be our number-one priority.

Evans Clinchy, Reimagining Public Education

I heartily agree with Frederick Hess that we need to rethink and reimagine our antiquated American system of public education. But not for the reasons he sets forth.

I also agree with his broad definition of the purposes of public schooling: "that public schools are . . . defined by their commitment to preparing students to be productive members of the social order" (and therefore active citizens of a democratic society) who are able to think and use their minds well and are "aware of their societal responsibilities and respectful of constitutional strictures" (including an understanding of the Constitution and especially the Bill of Rights); "that such schools cannot deny access to students for reasons unrelated to their educational focus" (i.e., no racially, ethnically, or economically segregated schools); "and that the system of public schools available in any community must provide an appropriate placement for each student" (all students and their parents must be offered the kind of schooling they believe is most suitable). But I do not agree that we should seek to create the kind of reimagined system Hess appears to be proposing.

Questions of Definition, Control, and Funding

Throughout most of the history of the U.S., a public school has been defined as a school created, operated, and largely paid for by the citizens of each community through a locally elected board of education. While the Constitution leaves the basic authority for education in the hands of the individual states, and even though such locally controlled schools have, over the past century, received increased funding from both state and federal sources, this tradition of local control has managed to endure more or less intact—at least until the past 25 or so years.

The continued importance of this tradition was underscored in 1973 by the U.S. Supreme Court in its *Rodriguez* decision. The majority opinion put the matter this way:

In an era that has witnessed a consistent trend toward centralization of the functions of government, local sharing of responsibility for public education has survived. The merit of local control was recognized in both the majority and dissenting opinions in *Wright v. Council of the City of Emporia.* Mr. Justice Stewart stated there that "direct control over decisions vitally affecting the education of one's children is a need that is strongly felt in our society." The Chief Justice in his dissent agreed that local control is not only vital to continued public support of the schools, but it is of overriding importance from an educational standpoint as well.

The persistence of attachment to government at its lowest level where education is concerned reflects the depth of commitment of its supporters. In part local control means . . . the freedom to devote more money to the education of one's children. Equally important, however, is the opportunity it offers for participation in the decision-making process that determines how those local dollars will be spent. Each locality is free to tailor local programs to local needs. Pluralism also affords some opportunity for experimentation, innovation, and a healthy competition for educational excellence. An analogy to the Nation–State relationship in our federal system seems uniquely appropriate. Mr. Justice Brandeis identified as one of the peculiar strengths of our form of government each state's freedom to "serve as a laboratory; to try novel social and economic experiments." No area of social concern stands to profit more from a multiplicity of viewpoints and from a diversity of approaches than does public education.

Further, Justice William Brennan found in his dissent that "Here, there can be no doubt that education is inextricably linked to the right to participate in the electoral process and to the rights of free speech and association guaranteed by the First Amendment."[1]

During the past quarter century, however, the "consistent trend toward centralization of the functions of government" has run rampant in the field of public schooling. In the name of public school "reform," the states have usurped local control by imposing uniform, authoritarian, "high," "rigorous," one-size-fits-all academic standards and punitive high-stakes standardized testing on all students, all schools, and all school systems.

The federal education establishment, through its No Child Left Behind Act, has carried this intrusive, antidemocratic curricular control and standardized testing program to ludicrous extremes, requiring the testing of all students in grades 3 through 8 and insisting on annual progress in test scores with severe sanctions for schools that fail to show such progress. However, neither the federal government nor the states have provided the financial resources to pay for all this "reform" or to remedy the gross inequities that exist between those school systems that serve the wealthy and those that serve our poor and minority students and parents. I find these events distressing, but none of them appear to worry Hess very much.

If the powerful democratic tradition of local control is to be maintained and if we are to genuinely reimagine our public education system, we will need to do several things. First, we will have to abandon the authoritarian standards and high-stakes testing agenda that currently afflict our public schools and return to the citizens of our local communities the control over what is taught, how it will be taught, and who will teach it. State and federal interference should be limited to ensuring minimum competency in the basic skills of reading, writing, and mathematics.

Second, we will simultaneously need both state and federal governments to guarantee that all of the nation's public schools are fully and equitably funded and that the civil rights of all students and parents—but especially our poor and minority students and parents—are fully protected. Hess does not appear to recommend any of these policies.

The Threat of Vouchers and Privatization

We will also have to erect strong safeguards against the threat of vouchers and any further encroachment of the private corporate sector into the field of public schooling.

Now that the Supreme Court has permitted the use of public funds to finance vouchers that can be used to pay tuition at nonpublic, including religious, schools, Hess appears to be saying that we should aim to create a system of public education similar to that of many European countries, where public funding is given directly to all nonpublic schools. Such a proposal would still violate both the First Amendment's separation of church and state and the democratic commitment to local public citizen control.

In addition, Hess proposes that we permit the private, for-profit sector to run both schools and school systems so long as those schools are monitored by some public body—despite the fact that the track record of Edison and other corporate EMOs (education management organizations) is educationally and economically dismal. Hess appears to believe that it is morally legitimate for private corporations to profit from the education of children, rather than being required to plow "profits" back into our chronically underfunded public schools. This thinking parallels the already-established view that it is somehow morally legitimate for corporate HMOs to make a profit out of caring for the sick, rather than being required to plow that money back into the health-care system. Neither of these policies is morally acceptable in any fair, just, and equitable system of democratic government.

A Truly Reimagined, Genuinely Democratic Public System of Diversity and Choice

Hess does raise an issue of fundamental importance when he points out that "there are many ways to provide legitimate public education." I assume that he means that there is no single kind of school—be it rigidly "traditional," wildly "progressive," or something in between—that could possibly serve the diverse educational beliefs of this nation's parents, the equally diverse professional philosophies of our public school educators, and most especially the enormously varied educational needs of our children and young people.

Strangely, however, Hess believes that many "prominent educational thinkers" (among others, he names Frank Smith, Susan Ohanian, Deborah Meier, and Alfie Kohn) have encouraged the public schools to promote "preferred social values" to the American public rather than advocating that all public schools limit themselves to teaching children "the essential skills and knowledge that make for productive citizens." He asserts that the "public schools should teach children . . . to respect our constitutional order and instruct them in the framework of rights and obligations that secure our democracy and protect our liberty." He argues this point as if this educational prescription were not itself an ideology—even if it is one that may be widely shared and one that in its main outlines is most certainly shared by his list of misguided thinkers.

Hess then goes on to advocate not just his own ideological prescription but the basic rule of what I would see as that truly reimagined public system we should be attempting to create. In order to encompass those diverse educational beliefs of parents and professional educators and to meet the varied educational needs of our children and young people, he says that we should "allow families to avail themselves of a range of schools with diverse perspectives, so long as each teaches respect for our democratic and liberal tradition." Thus we need that wide diversity of public schools—ranging from traditional to progressive—from which parents, teachers, administrators, and older students can choose the type of schooling they believe will most benefit each child and young person. As Hess puts it, such strictly public school choice would create "heightened family involvement" and produce "a shared sense of commitment" that would tend to make such "self-selected schools more participatory and democratic."

It is, I believe, the job of our local public school systems, assisted and encouraged by state and federal governments, to provide that diversity of options. But the basic control of what goes on in all of our public schools must always remain solely in the public domain and solidly anchored in the will of the citizens of our local communities.

Note

1. *San Antonio Independent School District* v. *Rodriguez,* U.S. Supreme Court, 411 U.S. 1 (1973).

LINDA NATHAN is Headmaster of the Boston Arts Academy, a public high school for the visual and performing arts.

JOE NATHAN is Director of the Center for School Change in the Hubert H. Humphrey Institute of Public Affairs at the University of Minnesota, Minneapolis.

RAY BACCHETTI is former Vice President for Planning and Management at Stanford University and is a scholar at the Carnegie Foundation for the Advancement of Teaching.

EVANS CLINCHY is Senior Consultant at the Institute for Responsive Education at Northeastern University in Boston and Editor of *Transforming Public Education.*

EXPLORING THE ISSUE

Should "Public Schooling" Be Redefined?

Critical Thinking and Reflection

1. How many ways are there to provide legitimate public schooling?
2. Is the word "choice" a part of public schooling?
3. Are schools underfinanced and teachers overregulated?
4. Why is the Coalition of Essential Schools one of Hess's targets in his article?
5. Has public schooling strayed from its purpose and been captured by self-interested parties?

Is There Common Ground?

In the February 2004 issue of *Phi Delta Kappan*, Frederick M. Hess put forth a rejoinder to his four critics in an article titled "Debating Principles for Public Schooling in a New Century." He lists some significant points of agreement, including that it is necessary and useful to reconsider the essence of "public schooling" in an age marked by radical changes in how education is being provided. However, these critics, Hess contends, attack reforms as "anti-public education" for permitting the same practices that some "public schools" already engage in—for example, schools that are not open to all students when located in an affluent community. He feels that some critics allow the notion of public schooling to become a rhetorical banner for bolstering partisan positions and delegitimatizing opposing ideas. Hess further states that "there is a real danger to the rhetorical strategy of branding objectionable reforms as de facto 'assaults on public schooling.' This device is fruitless and divisive. Perhaps more forebodingly, it excommunicates many who honor public education because they fail to endorse the 'right kind' of public schooling."

John C. Lundt, a professor of educational leadership, says that education is leaving the schoolhouse as technology increasingly makes it an anytime-anywhere activity. In a provocative article in the December 2004 issue of *The Futurist* titled "Learning for Ourselves: A New Paradigm for Education," Lundt concludes that the antiquated structure of today's school was designed to meet the needs of a world that no longer exists, that public schools will not change as long as they monopolize educational funding, and that growing numbers of parents find the activities and values of public schools inappropriate for their children. This basic concern about funding is echoed by reporter Joe Williams in his book *Cheating Our Kids: How Politics and Greed Ruin Education* (2005). Williams examines the impact of special-interest groups on local public school systems (especially in New York and Milwaukee), finding that most "reform" money only expands already bloated district bureaucracies. He calls for a concerted effort by concerned parents to reclaim power.

Additional Resources

F. Hess. "What Is a Public School? Principles for a New Century," *Phi Delta Kappan* (2009)

Ross Hubbard, "Tinkering Change Vs. System Change," *Phi Delta Kappan* (June 2009)

Hannah Lobel, "Putting the Public Back in Public Education," *Utne* (January–February 2009)

Susan Ohanian, "Refrains of the School Critics," *The School Administrator* (August 2005)

James Schuls, "It is Time We Redefine Public Education," *Re-define Ed* (August 1, 2013)

Paul A. Zoch, *Doomed to Fail: The Built-in Defects of American Education* (2004)

Internet References . . .

Center for Education Reform

www.edreform.com

Inner City Education Foundation

www.icefla.org

National Alliance for Civic Education

www.civnet.net

Rethinking Schools

www.rethinkingschools.org

Turnaround for Children

http://turnaroundusa.org

Unit 2

UNIT

Current Fundamental Issues

*T*he issues discussed in this unit cover a number of fundamental social, cultural, legal, and political questions currently under consideration by education experts, social scientists, court judges, and politicians, as well as by parents, teachers, and the media. Positions on these issues are expressed by Lina Bell Soares, Gary K. Clabaugh, Chief Judge Honorable Theodore A. McKee, William H. Schmidt, Nathan Burroughs, Tom Loveless, Roxanne Garza, Melissa Tooley, and Laura Hoxworth.

Selected, Edited, and with Issue Framing Material by:
Glenn L. Koonce, *Regent University*

ISSUE

Are Truly Democratic Classrooms Possible?

YES: Lina Bell Soares, from "The Education Students Deserve: Building a Democratic Classroom in Teacher Education," *Critical Literacy: Theories and Practices* (2013)

NO: Gary K. Clabaugh, from "Second Thoughts about Democratic Classrooms," *Educational Horizons* (2008)

Learning Outcomes

After reading this issue, you will be able to:

- Define and describe a democratic classroom.
- Analyze and describe internal and external factors that shape democratic classrooms.
- Explore how schools are a reflection of society.
- Identify the closest challenges to democratic education.
- Gain an understanding of the role of federal government in democratic education.

ISSUE SUMMARY

YES: Lina Soares, Associate Professor of Education, draws from John Dewey and literature related to social justice and critical multicultural education as a way to practice democracy in the classroom.

NO: Gary K. Clabaugh, Professor of Education, examines such factors as top-down management, compulsory attendance, business world influences, and federal mandates to declare Morrison's ideas to be "out of touch" with reality.

Certainly everyone would agree that one of the primary aims of education is to produce citizens capable of effectively participating in their society. The controversial aspect of this aim resides in determining the best way of carrying it out. In recent years educators and theorists have renewed a basic question that has been discussed for over a hundred years, namely "Is it possible to produce democratic citizens if the schooling the young are subjected to is clearly undemocratic?"

As Charles C. Haynes, in "Schools of Conscience," *Educational Leadership* (May 2009), states, "We need schools that actually practice what their civics classes are supposed to teach. . . . At a time when the United States faces unprecedented challenges at home and abroad, public schools must do far more to prepare young people to be engaged, ethical advocates of 'liberty and justice for all.'" Haynes contends that education's highest aim is to create moral and civic habits of the heart. This central purpose was articulated by the early leaders of American education. Thomas Jefferson made the principles of democratic government an essential element in the free public education of the general citizenry. Horace Mann's common school was dedicated to producing people able to critically judge the political and social needs of the nation. Waves of European immigrants in the nineteenth century prompted a new emphasis on socialization strategies and the development of patriotism. As Joel Spring has pointed out in his book *Conflict of Interests*, "In a totalitarian society it is possible to teach a single interpretation of the laws and government in the public schools, but in a society such as that of the United States, which fosters a variety of political beliefs . . . , attempts to teach principles of government can result in major political battles."

In "Civic Education and Political Participation," *Phi Delta Kappan* (September 2003), William A. Galston declares that school-based civic education has been in decline over recent decades. He claims that every significant indicator of political engagement among the young has fallen. Community service programs in high schools are on the increase, but there is no evidence that such "mandatory volunteerism" leads to wider civic participation. He states that "the surge of patriotic sentiment among young people in the immediate wake of September 11th has not yielded a comparable surge in engaged, active citizenship."

If the school atmosphere is by design, by tradition, or by habit undemocratic, can truly democratic citizens emerge? Haynes states that "to prepare students to be ethical, engaged citizens we must give them . . . meaningful opportunities to practice freedom responsibly in a school culture that encourages shared decision-making. . . . In short we need schools that actually practice . . . freedom and democracy, not censorship and repression."

Similarly, Marion Brady, in "Cover the Material—Or Teach Students to Think?" *Educational Leadership* (February 2008), claims that students need to tackle issues straight out of the complex world in which they live. "A focus on real-world issues . . . enables students and teachers to experience the 'meatiness' of the direct study of reality. . . . It shows respect for students, who become more than mere candidates for the next higher grade. . . . It disregards the arbitrary, artificial boundaries of the academic disciplines."

In "Democracy and Education: Empowering Students to Make Sense of Their World," *Phi Delta Kappan* (January 2008), William H. Garrison contends that the best learning happens under a truly democratic system in which students assume the freedom and responsibility to make choices and direct their learning experiences. His ideas certainly reflect the basic philosophy of John Dewey and the sentiments of John Holt.

In the articles presented here Lina Bell Soares aligns herself with those in the field who feel that preoccupation with rising test scores is hurting authentic learning experiences. Gary Clabaugh argues that public schools generally lag behind society. Therefore, "Democratic Classrooms" are likely unattainable.

Lina Bell Soares

The Education Students Deserve: Building a Democratic Classroom in Teacher Education

Introduction

In 1916, Dewey postulated that democratic schools provide the foundation for students to actively participate in a democratic way of life, and to do so, the educational curriculum must be structured to engage students in authentic real-life experiences that will empower them to maintain such a way of life beyond schools' walls. Yet, scholars who have studied through varied theoretical lens (Apple & Beane, 2007; Giroux, 1988, 1989; Goodlad, 1984; Greene, 2000; Meier, 2004; Nichols & Berliner, 2007; Ravitch, 2010) assert that US public schools today are more concerned about the production of proficient test scores on state-mandated standardized tests than putting democracy into practice. Further, the consensus among these scholars is that the culture of high-stakes testing in which public schools now function under the guise of educational reform has led the US school system into troubled times and far removed from democratic ideals. In the name of reform, one wonders if this is what Dewey envisioned for democratic schools; equality achieved through a single test score.

Kahne and Middaugh (2006) maintain that participation in democracy "does not occur instinctively nor does it develop organically. Educators have a role to play—helping students in thinking carefully. . . " (p. 607). Correspondingly, teacher educators have a role to play—a role that permits preservice teachers to explore pedagogies that lead to a more social justice-oriented curriculum and develop dispositions to teach with tolerance. Further, teacher educators must empower their preservice teachers to become caring participants in their society. From this author's perspective, a good place to begin is through the implementation of democratic practices in their teaching.

In an era of high-stakes testing in US schools, it becomes necessary to engage preservice teachers in critical conversations that will sharpen their sensibilities toward societal problems in their world and ultimately remove social inequities in their classrooms. A plethora of research has found that young adult literature is a good source of critical engagement because of the many prominent themes that are integral parts of content areas, such as conflict, ethical dilemmas, gender and race issues, environmental, and even violence (Harper & Bean, 2007). Moreover, researchers have found that young adult literature provides a vehicle to support critical literacy in the classroom (Bean & Harper, 2006; Bean & Moni, 2003; Behrman, 2006; Wolk, 2009). For certification seeking teachers in middle grade education, the adoption of strategic practices in critical literacy to enable discussions that center on relevant themes in the lives of young adolescents is essential to their development for future democratic classrooms. In conjunction, the adoption of a more social justice-oriented curriculum is crucial for teacher candidates in today's diverse society.

Drawing on Dewey (1916, 1938) and on literature related to social justice and critical multicultural education (Banks, 2004; Giroux, 1989; May & Sleeter, 2010; Sleeter, 2005), in this article, I present a framework of instructional practices I use to prepare my preservice middle grade teachers to challenge the status quo (Aronowitz & Giroux, 1993) and teach for social change through an integration of young adult literature and critical literacy. I begin by offering reasons to examine controversial issues found in young adult literature, followed by a brief account of critical literacy, both the concept and pedagogy. Subsequently, I introduce a framework of critical literacy practices to establish a social justice-oriented curriculum. My purpose is twofold: 1) to teach middle grade preservice teachers how to establish a participatory democracy in their future classrooms; and 2) to prepare middle grade preservice teachers to foster fairness and justice with the lives they will one day influence.

Reasons to Teach Young Adult Literature

For diverse US classrooms, teacher educators who work with content area preservice teachers in middle grade edu-

Soares, Lina Bell. "The Education Students Deserve: Build a Democratic Classroom in Teacher Education," Critical Literacy: Theories and Practices, 7 (2), 2013, p. 69–78.

cation must do more than teach content knowledge and instructional methods. In addition, we must introduce our students to the types of experiences that lead to critical conversations about current social and controversial issues that are relevant to content studies. One method that holds promise is to expose preservice teachers in middle grade education to challenging and contentious themes in young adult literature (Walker & Bean, 2005). By integrating young adult literature into preservice teachers' development, they are given the opportunity to become part of a larger discussion that lays the foundation for caring, respectful, tolerant, and empathetic classrooms (Bean & Harper, 2004; Harper & Bean, 2007). In fact, Busching and Slesinger (2002) explicate that literature is the vehicle by which students can explore their world by focusing on issues and concerns, such as identity, discrimination, sexuality, environmental issues, and war and violence. Furthermore, McDaniel (2004) posits that when preservice teachers read and experience the controversial topics explored in diverse texts, they become aware of the injustices in the textual world, the real world, and work toward changing their world to benefit mankind. Yet for preservice teachers to be sufficiently prepared to create a democratic classroom, they must adopt a questioning stance that can be achieved through the pedagogy of critical literacy.

Critical Literacy: The Concept and Pedagogical Practices

Experts in the field of reading agree that one salient aspect of reader response is to connect students' life experiences to texts (Heron-Hruby, Hagood, & Alvermann, 2008; Rosenblatt, 1994; Sandman & Gruhler, 2007). However, response to literature requires connections beyond personal experiences. Critical literacy builds a foundation for students to engage in reader response activities that require them to read, analyze, question, and challenge all forms of text (McLaughlin & DeVoogd, 2004). It is an active approach to reading that focuses on issues of power and social inequality. Teachers who practice critical literacy engage their students in various activities designed to give them opportunities to interrogate texts (Luke & Freebody, 1997), view multiple perspectives, create alternative versions of reality (Lewison, Leland, & Harste, 2000), and then take action to put the new versions of reality into effect (Behrman, 2006). Accordingly, readers are taught to question authors' assumptions and beliefs, to question the voices heard and the voices that are silenced, and to find alternatives ways to improve their world (Au, 2009; Banks, 2004; Luke & Freebody, 1997; Sleeter, 2005). In doing so, preservice teachers come to

know the fundamentals that promote a true democratic, participatory experience.

A Framework to Promote Democracy in the Classroom

As a professor of teacher education in the US, I want my preservice teachers to do more than demonstrate the knowledge, skills, and dispositions for effective teaching. I want my students to restructure their curriculum and adopt pedagogy to foster fairness and create a democratic classroom culture of acceptance. From this perspective, I present a framework of four themes I have adapted from Ciardiello (2004): examining multiple perspectives, finding an authentic voice, recognizing social barriers, and finding one's identity to promote a participatory democratic classroom. It is important to note that Ciardiello's original framework includes a fifth theme—the call to service that provides an excellent foundation for service learning/ civic engagement projects. For purposes of this paper, I present each of the four themes in the context of young adult literature and critical literacy practices that I use with my preservice teachers.

Examining Multiple Perspectives

The theme of multiple perspectives is an important aspect of critical literacy because it teaches students that texts can have multiple meanings based on various viewpoints, beliefs, and values. The goal for classroom teachers is to help their students see that no single version tells the story (Au, 2009). There are always gaps and silences (Fairclough, 1989), as well as contradictions in telling the story. To introduce this important aspect of critical literacy, I engage my students in discussions that center on personal events, such as family disagreements or conflicts that may have occurred with professors and grades. I then have my students examine the power differential in each of the scenarios and to reflect on whose voices seemed to dominate the discussions, or whose voices were discounted or ignored. More importantly, I ask them to reflect on how they felt if perhaps the voice that had been marginalized or silenced had belonged to one of them, and I ask them if they had ever thought to question why. My goal is to raise their critical awareness by teaching them to question why their perspective was silenced, what role did power play, what affect did power have on their perspective, and what action could they have taken to change the outcome (Bean & Moni, 2003). By using questions such as these, Lewison, Leland, and Harste (2008) would posit that I am purposely teaching my students to "question the everyday world, to interrogate the relationship between language and power, to analyze popular culture and media, to understand how power relationships are socially constructed, and to consider actions that can be taken to promote social justice..." (p. 3). On a broader scale, I am providing the foundation for my students to begin to view the classroom as a society from which dialogue creates a space for constructing critical conversations about issues of social injustice.

Because critical literacy is about interrogating text and engaging in multiple perspectives, we examine many silenced voices—the silenced voices of fear, prejudice, gender bias, and discrimination that work to create the social injustices that are part of their world, and the world for many of today's students. To achieve this objective, I encourage my students to explore the viewpoints that are not heard through young adult literature in order for my students to understand that power and perspective can marginalize or even silence voices that represent a different perspective in every story. For example, I have found that *Day of Tears* by Julius Lester (2005) is an excellent reading source to engage my developing teachers in critical conversations regarding different viewpoints and perspectives. The book is based on the largest slave auction in Savannah, Georgia in 1859 and is a moving story told through many dialogues and monologues from the perspective of the slaves, the slave owners, and the auctioneer.

Despite the pervasive racism throughout the story, the book is an excellent representation of the many voices needed to tell one of the darkest chapters in American history. The social inequities found in *Day of Tears* (Lester, 2005) provide the opportunity for preservice teachers to experience deeper thinking, such as power domination and silenced voices, while building social awareness and tolerance. By examining the feelings and identities of characters who have been ignored and whose lives have been marginalized, oppressed, or perceived to be inferior from the mainstream norm, they learn to appreciate the lives of others in their world who might otherwise be ignored (Gay, 2002). Furthermore, preservice teachers learn the value in creating a classroom culture that represents a multiplicity of perspectives so that every student is acknowledged as a vital member of the learning community (Sergiovanni, 2005).

Finding Authentic Voice

Ciardiello (2004) tells readers that the theme of finding one's authentic voice in critical literacy is closely connected to the theme of multiple perspectives. In other words, as students learn that texts often silence alternative perspectives, then students begin to understand there are voices missing behind those silenced perspectives. Critical literacy is a pedagogical tool that can encourage students to question issues of power and to challenge the forces that shape inequality and oppression in their world (Beck, 2005). Shor and Pari (1999) offer:

> Critical literacy thus challenges the status quo in an effort to discover alternative paths for social and self-development. This kind of literacy—words rethinking worlds, self dissenting in society—connects the political and the personal, the public and the private, the global and the local, the economic and the pedagogical, for reinventing our lives and for promoting justice in place of inequity. (p. 1)

For young adolescents to use their "words to rethink their worlds," it is important that preservice middle grade teachers understand the power of dialogue and the need to create experiences whereby their future students can interrogate societal issues and attempt to solve social injustices in their world. To assist my developing teachers, I engage my students in reading texts that address issues of democracy, freedom, equity, and social justice, whereby critical conversations about silenced voices and marginalized groups can grow into sharper focus. I further develop lessons based on dialogue in order for my preservice teachers to participate in critical conversations that examine the injustices of privileging one group over another because of social status, race, ethnicity, and religion, and how membership in one cultural group often defines opportunities or a lack thereof. While reading, I ask them to question whose voices are heard, whose voices are missing, why the author chose to favor or reject some characters, and how could they change the social conditions to give voice to the voiceless (Bean & Moni, 2003; McLauglin & DeVoogd, 2004). These crucial conversations provide opportunities for my developing teachers to assume a critical stance, discover their voices, and more importantly, to foster a critical pedagogy that will help give voice to their future students' lives.

One piece of young adult literature that I use is *Night* by Elie Wiesel (2006). The memoir is an intensely terrifying account of the brutality, the loss of family members, and the inhumane treatment of Jews the author witnessed during his time in Hitler's death camps. The book is an incredible story because Wiesel vowed he would never revisit the personal horror. However, with encouragement from a French humanitarian, he finally broke his silence and wrote the story to speak for the six million Jews who will never speak again. A second good source of young adult literature I use to teach the concept of voice is *Speak* (Anderson, 1999). The story revolves around the life of Melinda Sordino who is an outcast in her high school for calling the police on a summer party that turned ugly. She lives with a horrible secret that she was raped during the party and cannot bring herself to speak about the trauma with her family or friends. Through her love for art, she eventually regains her voice and confronts her attacker. Melinda's silence is a significant reminder of the shame and emotional paralysis that many students experience at the hands of other students and who withdraw from life because of oppressive forces surrounding them.

After reading, my students have rewritten parts of both texts through their own voices to record their feelings of desperation, isolation, and the belief that no one would listen. Additionally, they have been given the option to share their lived experiences aloud about times of personal pain. At times, I have invited my students to write song lyrics on important issues and themes in each novel to highlight their own unique voices. At times, I have my students develop interviews with a partner, one as the main character and one as the interviewer, to give the main character a voice to discuss lived experiences with someone who would listen.

Giroux (1989) explicated that "language is inseparable from lived experience and from how people create a distinctive voice" (p. 116). With each selection of young adult literature I use with my preservice students, the goal is to teach my students that the concept of voice is closely linked to everyday lived experiences. Therefore, if lived experiences are not free to be spoken, then student voices can be silenced. By reading young adult literature, preservice middle grade teachers begin to understand the forces in society that often work to marginalize and silence some members of society. The aim is for my preservice teachers to become more sensitive to what marginalized members of society have experienced and to understand the need to create a language of possibility (Giroux, 1997) for their future students.

Recognizing Social Barriers

Kornfled and Prothro (2005) state that a classroom should be a "realm of possibility—a place in which teachers and students together examine their lived experiences and envision ways to enhance their lives and sense of efficacy in the world around them" (pp. 218-219). To be open to possibility, a classroom should be a positive learning community where all students are valued, supported, and feel a sense of belonging (Levine, 2003). Similarly, a positive learning community promotes a culture where

students are free from discrimination, ridicule, or exclusion. Ciardiello's (2004) third theme recognizes that harmful assumptions, negative stereotypes, and hurtful labels build social barriers that are divisive and counterintuitive to building a positive classroom culture. The theme of recognizing social barriers calls on teachers to bring young adolescents together by knocking down walls that separate, creating learning spaces where students can present different beliefs, values, and perspectives, and nurturing respect as caring participants in democracy.

To expand on the importance of this theme, I introduce my students to young adult literature that intentionally demonstrates how acceptance is often determined by cultural, ethnic, or class privilege. Our focus is to examine how prejudice is enacted by the dominant group. One piece of young adult literature that I frequently use is *The Outsiders* (Hinton, 1967). The story is told through the character of Ponyboy Curtis who lives with his older brothers due to the death of his parents. Throughout the novel, Ponyboy is confronted by class warfare and caught up in the bitter rivalry between the Greasers and the Socs, the nickname for Social. As a member of the Greasers, he continually faces walls of separation because of his lower social status until he is befriended by Cherry, a Soc. Through their friendship, the two teenagers realize they share many of the same dreams and fears that life can bring. Moreover, Pony Boy and Cherry portray two adolescents who let go of their misconceptions and unjust social assumptions by allowing their friendship to knock down the class barriers that segregated their lives.

For additional sources of reading, my students and I have read *The House on Mango Street* (Cisneros, 1991) which is a story of Esperanza Cordero's life in the Latino quarter of Chicago. The book is an excellent example of how one family is relegated to a life of exclusion and lower class status because they do not speak English. To examine a similar theme of exclusion, we read *Esperanza Rising* (Ryan, 2000) which is a story of a young Mexican girl whose life is shattered when her father is killed. Esperanza and her mother flee to a migrant work camp in California during the Great Depression and begin a life of poverty, fear, and living with the stigma of an undocumented worker.

Both reading selections provide my students with a glimpse of what it is like to be viewed as an outsider from the dominant perspective where power and social status determine sociological categories of sub-dominant and marginal groups. Moreover, both books illustrate the barriers of separation from life's opportunities due to language and cultural differences that many outsiders face. Through meaningful interactions with young adult literature, my preservice teachers can begin to understand the need to promote social action and knock down the walls that form barriers to learning in a democratic classroom.

Regaining One's Identity

Gee (2002) offered that identity is shaped in a situated context whereby individuals manifest certain beliefs, values, and behaviors in order to be a member of a social group. Unfortunately for many of today's young adolescents in middle grade classrooms, they struggle to form their true identities. Separated by differences in language, ethnicity, culture, and social status from the mainstream norm, many students are often marginalized in a classroom society (Gay, 2002). Nevertheless, Bishop's (1992) seminal study offered that literature can do more; "literature can act as a mechanism for the discussion and social transaction that will affect how children think about the world and children's response to literature can either validate or challenge their own ideology and world view" (p. 43). From this stance, I view young adult literature to be an agent of socialization; it is a mechanism whereby my preservice teachers can examine their implicit beliefs, attitudes, and identities while developing the knowledge of what a more just society would look like. The goal is for my preservice teachers to understand that a learning context is a society. Moreover, it must be an environment of trust that encourages adolescent identity development by signifying that each student is a significant and valued member of the classroom society.

To introduce the theme of identity, I often read aloud to my students the *Falcon and Frog: A Story of Flight from Identity and Return to Self* by Shahidi (2009). It is a delightful children's book that tells the story of how two friends help each other have the courage to be themselves and regain their identities. The message conveyed in this book is the importance of being true to oneself. The two characters in the story typify how acceptance or a lack thereof is often determined by social privilege and how prejudice is enacted by the dominant group because the two characters are judged not for whom they were on the inside, but by their outward appearance.

Before moving onto our text for this theme, I allow time for my students to share their stories when they have been the subject of others' ridicule or to recount times when they have observed others who were bullied because they were different and judged to be inferior by the dominant group. Through our discussions, we address the many sides of prejudice and the harmful effects to people's sense of selves. We then turn to our literature to read about an identity in conflict and how the conflict shapes the perception of self. *Monster* (Myers, 1999) is an excellent source to introduce my preservice teachers to the concept of identity and the struggle to regain one's true self. The main character, Steve Harmon, has been arrested and is on trial for the murder of a Harlem store owner. In this story, Steve is found guilty by association and is accused of aiding and abetting the real murderer. As the story unfolds, Steve develops a screenplay based on his time in prison and the courtroom in an attempt to come to grips with his portrayal as a monster. He is eventually set free and lives by a new code of conduct.

From reading *Monster* (Myer, 1999), my preservice teachers gain a better understanding of how characters in conflict, struggle with their identities when their world is turned upside down (Harper & Bean, 2007). Young adult literature allows my students the opportunity to analyze their sense of selves within their world and examine the concept of identity by interpreting others' actions and practices (Hagood, 2002). In essence, they learn the importance of identity to a democratic classroom society they will one day create.

Returning to Dewey

More than seventy-five years ago, Dewey (1938) wrote, "[it is] the total social set-up of the situations in which a person is engaged that is most important in interpreting his or her experiences" (p. 45). Today, those experiences have been narrowed by a classroom culture of high-stakes standardized testing in the US and have unfortunate implications in public middle school classrooms. Middle grade classroom teachers and students alike are trapped in a curriculum of anti-democratic practices. The preoccupation of raising test scores is the norm for the classroom day and meaningful curriculum that embodies authentic learning experiences to enhance a democratic way of life has given way to only content that is tested. Yet, transformation of the classroom world does not occur overnight. It requires an active commitment to challenge and disrupt the commonplace activities and curricular structures that are firmly entrenched in today's schools that deny students from educational opportunities and social equality. From this perspective, those of us in teacher education in the US are on the frontline to enact real change and we can begin by asking ourselves: Is this the education students deserve?

References

Anderson, L. H. (1999). *Speak*. New York: Penguin Group.

Apple, M., & Beane, J. (2007). *Democratic schools: Lessons in powerful education* (2nd ed.). Portsmouth, NH: Heinemann.

Aronowitz, S., & Giroux, H. A. (1993). *Postmodern education: Politics, culture, and social criticism.* Minneapolis, MN: University of Minnesota Press.

Au, W. (2009). The "building tasks" of critical history: Structuring social studies for social justice. *Social Studies Research and Practice, 4*(2). 25–35.

Banks, J. (2004). Teaching for social justice, diversity, and citizenship in a global world *The Educational Forum, 68*(4), 296–305.

Bean, T. W., & Harper, H. J. (2004). Teacher education and adolescent literacy. In T. Jetton, & J. Dole (Eds.), *Adolescent literacy research and practice* (pp. 392–411). New York: Guildford Publications.

Bean, T. W., & Harper, H. J. (2006). Exploring notions of freedom in and through young adult literature. *Journal of Adolescent & Adult Literacy, 50*(2), 96–104.

Bean, T. W., & Moni, K. (2003). Developing students' critical literacy: Exploring identity construction in young adult fiction. *Journal of Adolescent & Adult Literacy, 6*(8), 638–648.

Beck, A. S. (2005). A place for critical literacy. *Journal of Adolescent & Adult Literacy, 48*(5), 392–400.

Behrman, E. H. (2006). Teaching about language, power, and text: A review of classroom practices that support critical literacy. *Journal of Adolescent & Adult Literacy, 49*(6), 490–498.

Bishop, R. S. (1992). Multicultural literature for children: Making informed choices. In V. Harris (Ed.), *Teaching multicultural literature in grades K-8* (pp. 37–53). Norwood, MA: Christopher Gordon.

Busching, B., & Slesinger, N. A. (2002). *It's our world too: Socially responsive learners in middle school language arts.* Urbana, IL: National Council of Teachers of English.

Ciardiello, A. V. (2004). Democracy's young heroes: An instructional model of critical literacy practices. *The Reading Teacher, 58*(2), 138–147.

Cisneros, S. (1991). *The house on Mango Street.* New York: Vintage.

Dewey, J. (1916). *Democracy and education.* New York: MacMillan.

Dewey, J. (1938). *Experience and education.* New York: Touchstone.

Fairclough, N. (1989). *Language and power.* Longman: London.

Gay, G. (2002), Preparing for culturally responsive teaching. *Journal of Teacher Education, 53*(2), 106–116.

Gee, J. P. (2002). Identity as an analytic lens for research in education. In W. G. Secada (Ed.), *Review of research in education,* Vol. 25 (pp. 99–125). Washington, DC: American Educational Research Association.

Giroux, H. (1988). *Schooling and the struggle for public life: Critical pedagogy in the modern age.* Minneapolis: University of Minnesota Press.

Giroux, H. A. (1989). *Schooling for democracy: Critical pedagogy in the modern age.* London: Routledge

Giroux, H. A. (1997). *Pedagogy and the politics of hope: Theory, culture, and schooling; a critical reader.* Boulder, CO: Westview Press.

Goodlad, J. (1984). *A place called school: Prospects for the future.* New York: McGraw-Hill.

Greene, M. (2000). *Releasing the imagination: Essays on education, the arts, and social change.* San Francisco: Jossey-Bass.

Hagood, M. (2002). Critical literacy for whom? *Reading Research and Instruction, 41*(3), 247–264.

Harper, H., & Bean, T. W. (2007). Literacy education in democratic life: The promise of adolescent literacy. In J. Lewis & G. Moorman (Eds.), *Adolescent literacy instruction: Policies and promising practices* (pp. 319–335). Newark, DE: International Reading Association.

Heron-Hruby, A., Hagood, M. C., & Alvermann, D. E. (2008). Switching places and looking to adolescents for the practices that shape school literacies. *Reading and Writing Quarterly, 24*(3), 311–334.

Hinton, S. E. (1967). *The outsiders.* New York: Puffin.

Kahne, J., & Middaugh, E. (2006). Is patriotism good for democracy? A study of high school seniors' patriotic commitments. *Phi Delta Kappan, 87*(8), 600–607.

Kornfled, J., & Prothro, L. (2005). Envisioning possibility: Schooling and student agency in children's and young adult literature. *Children's Literature in Education, 36*(3), 217–239.

Lester, J. (2005). *Days of tears.* New York: Jump at the Sun/Hyperion Books.

Levine, D. (2003). *Building classroom communities: Strategies for developing a culture of caring.* Bloomington, IN: National Education Service.

Lewison, M., Leland, C., & Harste, J. (2000). Not in my classroom! The case for using multi-view social issues books with children. *The Australian Journal of Language and Literacy*, 23(1), 8–20.

Lewison, M., Leland, C., & Harste, J. (2008). *Creating critical classrooms*: *K-8 reading and writing with an edge*. New York: Lawrence Erlbaum Associates.

Luke, A. & Freebody, P. (1997). The social practices of reading. In S. Muspratt, A. Luke, & P. Freebody (Eds.), *Constructing critical literacies: Teaching and learning textual practices* (pp. 185–225). Creskill, NJ: Hampton Press.

May, S., & Sleeter, C. E., (Eds.). (2010). *Critical multiculturalism: Theory and praxis*. New York: Routledge.

McDaniel, C. (2004). Critical literacy: A questioning stance and the possibility for change. *The Reading Teacher*, 57(5), 474–481.

McLaughlin, M., & DeVoogd, G. (2004). Critical literacy as comprehension: Expanding reader response. *Journal of Adolescent & Adult Literacy*, 48(1), 52–62.

Meir, D. (2004). NCLB and democracy. In D. Meier & G. Wood (Eds.). *Many children left behind: How the No Child Left Behind Act is damaging our children* (pp. 66–78). Boston: Beacon Press.

Myers, W. D. (1999). *Monster*. New York: HarperCollins

Nichols, S. N. & Berliner, D. C. (2007). *Collateral damage: The effects of high-stakes testing on America's schools*. Cambridge, MA: Harvard Education Press.

No Child Left Behind (NCLB) Act of 2001 (2002). Pub. L. No. 107–110, § 115, Stat.1425.

Ravitch, D. (2010). *The life and death of the great American school system: How testing and choice are undermining education*. New York, NY: Basic Books.

Rosenblatt, L. (1994). The transactional theory of reading and writing. In R. B. Ruddell, M. R. Ruddell & H. Singer (Eds.), *Theoretical models and processes of reading* (4th ed., pp. 1057–1092). Newark, DE: International Reading Association.

Ryan, P. M. (2000). *Esparanza rising*. New York: Scholastic.

Sandman, A., & Gruhler, D. (2007). Reading is thinking: Connecting readers to text through literature circles. *International Journal of Learning*, 13(10), 105–114.

Sergiovanni, T. J. (2005). *Strengthening the heartbeat: Leading and learning together in schools*. San Francisco, CA: Jossey-Bass.

Shahidi, A. R. (2009). *Falcon and frog: A story of flight from identity and return to self*. New York: CreateSpace.

Shor, I., & Pari, C. (1999). *Critical literacy in action*. Portsmouth, NH: Boyonton/Cook Publishers.

Sleeter, C. (2005). *Un-standardizing curriculum: Multicultural teaching in the standards-based classroom*. New York: Teachers College Press.

Walker, N., & Bean, T. W. (2005). Sociocultural influences in content teachers selection and use of multiple texts. *Reading Research and Instruction*, 44, 61–77.

Wiesel, E. (2006). *Night*. New York: Hill and Wang.

Wolk, S. (2009). Reading for a better world: Teaching for social responsibility with young adult literature. *Journal of Adolescent & Adult Literacy, 52*(8), 664–673.

Lina Bell Soares is an Associate Professor of education at Georgia Southern University in Statesboro, Georgia.

Gary K. Clabaugh

Second Thoughts about Democratic Classrooms

... **K**ristan A. Morrison's "Democratic Classrooms: Promises and Challenges of Student Voice and Choice" argues that students must experience autonomy, freedom, and choice if schools will ever be appealing and truly embody democracy. Those who found or find school tedious, oppressive, and uninteresting may be quick to agree, but how realistic is this proposal?

Cutting Costs with Mass Production

It has been well over one hundred years since America embarked on the ambitious venture of universal public schooling. The costs of this endeavor quickly became burdensome, and it was decided to model schools on factories and emphasize mass production and cost-effectiveness, rather than democracy or individuality.

For the most part, today's public schools still are factories. Management is top-down all the way. The federal government sets basic rules. State authorities implement the rules while adding many more. School boards make decisions based on federal and state rules plus fiscal and political realities. The superintendent executes the will of the board through his or her principals. They, in turn, tell teachers what to do and when to do it, and the teachers direct the youngsters in similar manner. Knowledge is fragmented and atomized. Children are compared to one another. Social and emotional development is neglected for more measurable outcomes. Economies of scale are sought at the expense of individuality. Teachers and students are managed.

Sometimes this industrial approach produces not only undemocratic, but peculiarly inefficient, results. One superintendent of the School District of Philadelphia, for example, boasted to the press that she could tell them what was happening in any classroom in the city at any given moment. What was actually happening was administratively induced chaos, because her standardized, teacher-proof curriculum was incapable of accommodating individual differences. Second-grade teachers were forbidden to use anything other than second-grade readers and the canned lesson of the day, even if some of the kids still couldn't read. Similarly, seventh-grade math teachers were forced to "teach" algebra to kids who couldn't even do fractions or long division.

In this kind of school system, autonomy, freedom, and choice are anathema. The focus is on standardization, teacher proofing, measured outcomes, and the prison shuffle.

Compulsory Freedom?

We should also consider that democratic, freedom-based schooling would be introduced into an institution in which attendance is compulsory. True, if one can afford an alternative, there is no requirement that kids attend public school. But in every state in the union school attendance of some kind, even if it is only home schooling, is required.

"Democratic Classrooms" indicates that democratic and freedom-based education is *grounded in the premise that people are naturally curious and have an innate desire to learn and grow. If left un-fettered, un-coerced and un-manipulated . . . people will pursue their interests vigorously and with gusto. . . .* Trouble is, when people are compelled to go to school they already are fettered, coerced, and manipulated. That's what we mean by compulsion. Wouldn't compulsory education have to be abolished before freedom-based education could be meaningfully initiated?

And why imagine that youngsters' natural curiosity will be directed at constructive things? One can imagine six-year-olds happily burning insects to death with sunlight and a magnifying glass, or sixteen-year-old inner-city gang members fulfilling their urgent desire to learn small-unit military tactics. Besides which, why assume that everyone is naturally curious? I've taught seventh-graders whose curiosity seemed decidedly undersized.

Of course kids of that age are terribly concerned about peer acceptance, and that places a profound limit on their freedom. Do advocates of freedom-based education adequately consider the tyranny of peers?

The Feds Weigh In

Remember too that there is a powerful new restriction on autonomy, freedom, choice, and democracy in schooling. Emphasizing measurable results, quality control, instrumental and extrinsic motivations, and atomization and fragmentation of knowledge, No Child Left Behind represents the near-total triumph of factory-model schooling in contemporary America. The whole weight of the federal government welds the public school as factory in place as never before.

"Democratic Classrooms" offers the happy prospect of dismantling factory schools and refocusing on student voice and choice. But it's not as if the article advocates moving from A to B. Given the present environment, it advocates moving from A to Z. What are the chances?

"The Business of America Is Business"[1]

Another factor militating against the success of the "Democratic Classrooms" prescription is that most Americans spend far more time in the business world than they do where they have a voice and a choice.

What are the work world's characteristics? It's competitive; instrumental and extrinsic motivations dominate, tasks are atomized and fragmented, obedience is required, believing what one is told is valued over criticality, and a person's worth is defined by comparison to others. In short, work-world values are virtually identical to the present school values decried in "Democratic Classsrooms." Surely that is not an accident.

What would happen if business leaders suddenly found themselves confronted with employees who expected a voice and a choice? Would the CEO of General Electric or Macy's, for example, be grateful? And could our lawmakers sleep if the nation's corporate moguls were dissatisfied?

The claim here isn't that the business of America *should* be business. It is that the business of America *is* business, and this reality has to be taken into account in any prescription written for the public schools.

Freedom: A Modern Luxury?

The article comments: *In democratic and freedom-based education, students are free to decide what they study, and how, and when they study it.* The article links that to *the form of learning found in most pre-industrial societies* [in which] *the children are actively engaged in the lives of a given society; they learn skills and knowledge by means of imitation, apprenticeship, modeling and conversation rather than in any formal school setting.*

Pre-industrial education, though, was not all that free and spontaneous. In my youth, for example, I learned barbering by means of an apprenticeship that closely resembled the apprentice system of the pre-industrial guilds; I was most emphatically *not* free to decide what to learn, or how and when to learn it. The master barber decided.

Remember too that in the pre-industrial era most children grew up on farms. And while those youngsters did learn to farm by imitation, modeling, and conversation, they did *not* have the luxury of freely choosing what they wanted to do and how and when they were going to do it. That's not farm life. If you are haying and it looks like rain, you have to work like hell to get the hay in the barn before it gets wet and spoils; otherwise the livestock starves that winter. Similarly, a kid might prefer not to spend hour after hour in the broiling sun picking potato bugs, but he or she still has to do it for the family to eat potatoes.

Perhaps freedom-based education is a luxury reserved for well-fixed modern kids whom harsh reality doesn't require to do tasks of immediate and urgent importance.

The True Secret of Education

John Locke, a philosopher who inspired the nation's founders, observes in *On Education*: "[I]f the mind be curb'd, and humbled too much in children; if their spirits be abas'd and broken much, by too strict an hand over them, they lose all their vigour and industry."

But Locke also cautions that

He that has not a mastery over his inclinations, he that knows not how to resist the importunity of present pleasure or pain, for the sake of what reason tells him is fit to be done, wants the true principle of virtue and industry, and is in danger never to be good for anything.

Locke, however, does not stop there. He immediately adds:

To avoid the danger that is on either hand, is the great art; and he that has found a way how to *keep up a child's spirit easy, active, and free, and yet at the same time to restrain him from many things he has a mind to, and to draw him to things that are uneasy to him* [emphasis added]; he, I say, that knows how to reconcile these seeming contradictions, has, in my opinion, got the true secret of education.[2]

The advocates of freedom-based education, then, may have avoided the first error Locke cautions against, only to stumble into the second. They seem to be overlooking the fact that some measure of mastery over one's inclinations is necessary to ever be good at anything. How can anyone learn to accomplish a truly skilled enterprise such as ballet, glass blowing, or engineering in a reasonable time if the initiate, not the expert, decides what to learn and when to learn it?

To be sure, present-day schooling hasn't got the balance right either. Here, in Locke's words, the mind is "curb'd and humbled too much" and the youngsters too frequently "lose all their vigour and industry." That is what "Democratic Classrooms" quite rightly condemns.

The Principle of Correspondence

Historically there has always been a close correspondence between any society's social structure, values, and norms and its schooling practices. In fact, a case can be made that such correspondence is a universal feature of schooling. And "Democratic Classrooms" gets it wrong when it says, "Schools and society are reflections of one another." No, the history of education demonstrates that schooling practices reflect the values and structures of the host society.

That is not to say that alternative schools of a freer, more-democratic nature can't exist in less-free societies. Various forms of them can be found in nations as different as Israel, Japan, New Zealand, Thailand, and the United States; A. S. Neill's Summerhill, perhaps the best-known, is located in Suffolk, England.[3] But these schools owe their uniqueness to the fact that they do not serve the broad masses at public expense. They have a self-selecting clientele and do not depend on public consensus or public funding.

Still, it's instructive to know that in 1999 Summerhill ran into difficulties with the U.K.'s educational bureaucracy. Despite the school's higher-than-national-average exam pass rates and extraordinary parental and pupil satisfaction, the U.K.'s education bureaucracy inspected the school and found it wanting. It called Summerhill's pupils "foul-mouthed" and accused them of "mistaking idleness for personal liberty." In effect, the report called for Summerhill's closure if the school failed to abandon the key freedoms it afforded its pupils.

Summerhill took the government to court and won the right to continue its practices. The school survived, and in 2007 another government inspection produced entirely different results. *The Guardian* quotes the new report as saying, "Pupils' personal development, including their spiritual, moral, social and cultural development, is outstanding." Students are "courteous, polite and considerate," make "good progress," and are "well-rounded, confident, and mature" when they leave.

Zoe Readhead, the head teacher and daughter of founder A. S. Neill, said: "The government has persistently refused to acknowledge the individual philosophy of the school, such as that children can learn just as well out of the classroom. We feel vindicated." She also added, "It is not the school that changed."[4] Her point, of course, was that it was the U.K. that had changed.[5]

Undemocratic Americans

"Democratic Classrooms" seems at least as out of step with American values in 2008 as Summerhill was to the U.K.'s in 1999. Certainly the values that "Democratic Classrooms" hopes to promote are anything but widespread. Only some Americans "truly value diversity" and are "truly autonomous yet cognizant of others' needs and rights." And only some Americans "are open-minded yet equipped with critical thinking skills to analyze contradictory ideas." Other Americans angrily deny marriage to gay couples; salivate whenever Rush Limbaugh and his ilk ring a bell; and don't have the vaguest understanding of either freedom or democracy. (They eagerly deny the former to anyone who's different and think of American democracy merely as majority rule.)

Individuals of this persuasion pack a political punch. And they will undoubtedly regard as un-American the values "Democratic Classrooms" prescribes for U.S. public schools. Its new freedoms for students would be understood as self-indulgence and an attack on traditional values such as hard work, discipline, and self-denial—none of which are they particularly keen on practicing themselves.

Remember too that day-to-day U.S. public school policy is set locally by some fifteen thousand elected school boards and, except for large urban districts, broadly representative of village values. So America's public schools have achieved their undemocratic condition in a decidedly democratic manner.

Conclusion

History suggests that public schools rarely, if ever, get out ahead of society. Indeed, they generally lag behind. That is why student voice and choice and all that goes with it will have to await a freer, more-democratic America. If and when that societal change happens, the public schools will follow. Until then, support will be lacking. That's not to say that what "Democratic Classrooms" champions is undesirable. But it may be unattainable, and it is certainly unlikely in the near or intermediate future.

Happily, reform need not be all or nothing. One can, with a little luck, quietly introduce more student voice and choice into one's own classroom. And we should all congratulate any teacher who can elevate the importance of intrinsic motivation; emphasize social and emotional development as well as academics; de-emphasize mere obedience; and get kids to define their own worth rather than let others do it for them. But it had better be done without fanfare and well out of sight of the philistines.

Notes

1. A statement made by Calvin Coolidge in the 1920s.
2. John Locke, "Some Thoughts Concerning Education" (sections 41–50), in *The Harvard Classics*, available at http://www.bartleby.com/37/1/5.html.
3. See Summerhill School's Web site: http://www.summerhillschool.co.uk/pages/index.html.
4. Jessica Shepherd, *Guardian* (Manchester), December 1, 2007, available at http://www.guardian.co.uk/uk/2007/dec/01/ofsted.schools.
5. Summerhill School, available at http://www.summerhillschool.co.uk/bbc-drama.html.

. . . .

Gary K. Clabaugh is Professor of Education at La Salle University in Philadelphia and co-founder (with Edward G. Rozycki) of newfoundations.com, which explores reflective educational practice.

EXPLORING THE ISSUE

Are Truly Democratic Classrooms Possible?

Critical Thinking and Reflection

What values are sought or lost in designing democratic classrooms?

Does the federal government play a role in democratic classrooms?

How do societal values compare and contrast with school values?

How is diversity valued in a democratic classroom?

What are elements in our society that transfer to designing classrooms that are described as democratic?

Is There Common Ground?

E. D. Hirsch, Jr., the well-known core knowledge advocate, in his latest book *The Making of Americans: Democracy and Our Schools* (2009), is clearly at odds with the "truly democratic classrooms produce engaged citizens" ideology. As he has in his past works, Hirsch has no kind words for the followers of John Dewey whose progressive ideas, he claims, led to an abandonment of definite academic studies resulting in the diminishment of Americans' intellectual standing in the world. He sees hope in recent trends toward higher standards and the rise of Advanced Placement and International Baccalaureate programs in high schools. In a review of The Making of Americans, titled "I Pledge Allegiance to Core Knowledge" in *The Washington Post* (August 30, 2009), Jay Mathews states that Hirsch will settle for nothing less than "a coherent, content-based, multi-year curriculum right now to save our democracy from factionalism, inequality, and incompetence."

Another group of theorists settle in a middle-ground position between subject matter centeredness and an emphasis on student voice and choice. See, for example, "Disciplining the Mind" by Veronica Boix Mansilla and Howard Gardner in *Educational Leadership* (February 2008). They recommend the teaching of disciplinary thinking so as to prepare students to understand the real world in which they live and equip them for the future.

The following writers are supportive of Kristan A. Morrison's point of view: Dana L. Mitra, "Amplifying Student Voice," *Educational Leadership* (November 2008), who

reviews research into student voice initiatives, including student involvement in reform and the professional development of teachers, and Eric B. Freedman, "Is Teaching for Social Justice Undemocratic?" *Harvard Educational Review* (Winter 2007), who examines the "critical consciousness" approaches of Ira Shor and Paulo Freire, addressing the question "When is education democratic?"

Additional interesting sources are Thomas R. Guskey and Eric M. Anderman, "Students at Bat," *Educational Leadership* (November 2008); Deborah Meier, "Democracy at Risk," *Educational Leadership* (May 2009); Chris W. Gallagher, "Democratic Policy Making and the Arts of Engagement," *Phi Delta Kappan* (January 2008); and Stephen Macedo, "Crafting Good Citizens," *Education Next* (Spring 2004). Exploration of some of these articles will open doors to a number of important related issues.

Additional Resources

James A. Banks, "Human Rights, Diversity, and Citizenship Education," *The Educational Forum* (April 2009)w

Peter Levine, "The Civic Opportunity Gap," *Educational Leadership* (May 2009)

Richard Neumann, "American Democracy at Risk," *Phi Delta Kappan* (January 2008)

Joetta Sack-Min, "A Valued Democracy," *American School Board Journal* (January 2009)

Internet References . . .

A Hidden Downside of Democratic Classrooms

www.educationrethink.com/2013/02/a-hidden
-downside-of-democratic.html

Are Truly Democratic Classrooms Possible? Aa Prezi Ppresentation

http://prezi.com/0stlwjcb6k9y/are-truly-democratic
-classrooms-possible-character-education-and-
social
-responsibility/

Democracy in Schools: Preached but not Practiced

http://voices.washingtonpost.com/answer-sheet
/george-wood/democracy-in-schools-preached.html

Evidence of Democratic Principles in Our Schools

http://edweb.sdsu.edu/people/cmathison/truths/
truths
.html

Meaningful Practice: Democratic Classrooms

http://gordonbwest.com/critical-toolbox/democratic
-classrooms/

Selected, Edited, and with Issue Framing Material by:
Glenn L. Koonce, *Regent University*

ISSUE

Do Public Schools Have Grounds to Punish Students for Their Off-Campus Online Speech?

YES: Theodore A. McKee, from *J.S. v. Blue Mountain School District*, United States Third Circuit Court of Appeals (2011)

NO: Theodore A. McKee, from *Layshock v. Hermitage School District*, United States Third Circuit Court of Appeals (2011)

Learning Outcomes

After reading this issue, you will be able to:

- Evaluate student First Amendment Rights and their impact on the *J.S. v. Blue Mountain School District*.

- Evaluate student First Amendment Rights and their impact on the *Layshock v. Hermitage School District* case.

- Appraise social media concerns of the public schools.

- Compare and contrast the 1975 *Tinker v. Des Moines* court case as it applies to today's student rights cases involving social media.

- Assess the impact of U.S. Supreme Court decision on school officials.

ISSUE SUMMARY

YES: On February 11, 2010, a panel of judges from the Third Circuit Court of Appeals heard the *J.S. v. Blue Mountain District* case ruling against a suspended junior high school student who ridiculed her principal online using MySpace with a computer that was accessed off-campus. The student had been suspended by her school district.

NO: On the previous day, February 10, 2010, another panel of three judges from the same Third Circuit Court of Appeals heard *Layshock v. Hermitage School District* and ruled on June 3, 2010 that the school district had violated high school senior Justin Layshock's First Amendments free speech rights. A local Pennsylvania school official suspended Layshock for10 days. He was also placed in an alternative education setting and banned from extracurricular activities and graduation ceremonies for mocking his principal with a fake MySpace profile that he accessed off-campus. Both the *J.S.* and *Layshock* cases were later heard on June 3, 2011 by the Full Third Circuit Court of Appeals, with a twist and changes to the earlier ruling in J.S. due to application of a 1969 U.S. Supreme Court ruling. Chief Judge Theodore McKee wrote the court's opinion for both the Layshock & J.S. cases. In 2012, the U.S. Supreme Court declined to hear either of these social media cases.

Initial conflicting decisions in lower courts regarding student First Amendment Rights in social media disciplinary cases occurred one day apart, February 10 & 11, 2010, with two different panels of judges from the same federal appeals court. Both were Pennsylvania cases involving fake MySpace profiles that students created to mock their principal. Although neither student created their profiles on school time, used school computers, or other school resources, they were punished by school authorities. Both students and their parents sued their respective school districts. When initially heard in a district court, a Pennsylvania school officials' suspension of Layshock was upheld (*Layshock v. Hermitage School District*). The same was true for the *J.S. v. Blue Mountain School District* following a school official's suspension against a junior high school female student who ridiculed her principal online using MySpace with a computer that was accessed off-campus (*J.S. v. Blue Mountain School District*). On June 10, 2010, the full Third Circuit Court of Appeals vacated the panel rulings for both Layshock and J.S. and decided to rehear the cases.

The official court briefs for each case, as heard by the *full* Third Circuit Court of Appeals on their final rulings on June 13, 2011, are included in this issue for review of the facts and rulings by the two different panels of judges and then the *en banc* review of both cases by the full Third Circuit Court of Appeals. The uniqueness of these cases include: the similarities in the student's actions, action taken by school officials, and finally, *seemingly* oppositional rendering by the same court (Cain, 2012). Initial rulings in *J.S.* and *Layshock* outcomes were initially opposite, but as the court further reviewed the two cases, the outcomes are ruled the same, that students cannot be punished for their off campus speech baring a *substantial disruption* or the *likelihood of a substantial disruption* to the school's safe and orderly learning environment. The value in looking at this issue, grounds for punishment of students for their off campus speech, is to understand what actually occurred in these two cases, the initial incident, initial court decisions, appeals, the final rulings, decision by the U.S. Supreme Court not to hear either case, and court actions since the final rulings. This is important in school social media cases because the U.S Supreme Court has yet to hear a school social media case, resting its position on the ruling it made almost fifty years ago in *Tinker v. Des Moines Independent Community School District* (1969), commonly referred to as *Tinker v. DesMoines* or *Tinker*. This entire issues speaks to the use of critical thinking strategies in setting social media

policy in schools and acting on those policies should an incident occur.

What is the current status of free speech regarding student off campus speech and what is the key determinate for a school principal to be aware of before taking final action should an incident occur in their school? Without answering this question and understanding of the legal complexity involved, the debate becomes an emotional issue because in both cases, the students posted material that is considered offensive, even very offensive. The courts have acted on their part to weigh the constitutional protections afforded all citizens of the United States. The key factor rests on the ruling from the 1969 U.S. Supreme Court case, *Tinker v. Des Moines*, handed down over thirty years *prior* to the *Layshock* (2006) and *J.S.* (2007) cases. The debate should continue, because the incidents regarding social media will escalate in the future, as it is well known that school age children and teens primary communication through this medium. Schools are a microorganism of society and what occurs in society will likely occur in the nation's schools. In short, the problem is constant and should be discussed by all educators at all levels, students, parents, policy makers, and in particular school leaders, school board members, and school board attorneys.

Prior to the 1970s, public schools were largely immune to Constitutional law handed down by the courts. The courts were viewed as being "school friendly" and they upheld almost all school officials' decisions if the court felt those actions were *reasonable. In loco parentis* (corresponding to parental prerogatives) accompanied this status in many court cases making it unclear whether constitutional rights extended to non-adult students (Palistini & Palistini, 2012).

Clarity soon came and changed the way courts viewed student rights, especially freedom of speech and expression, with the 1969 landmark *Tinker v. Des Moines (1969)* case. In this case, the U.S. Supreme Court ruled that students do not "shed their constitutional rights" at the school house door (p. 1). Six years later another landmark U.S. Supreme Court case *Goss v. Lopez* (1975), held that students in public schools possess liberty and property interests in their education, thus are afforded due process before disciplinary action may be taken by school officials including speech and expression issues (Palistini & Palistini, 2012). Even with these transforming U.S. Supreme Court decisions, further decisions sided more with schools when a student's actions were a significant disruption to the education process or a threat to safety (weapons, serious injury, or drugs). One example is the 1986 U.S. Supreme Court case, *Bethel School District v. Fraser* where the court noted that a public high school student, Fraser, could not use sexually explicit language at a student assembly to make his nomination speech for a friend running for the office of student body vice-president. Another example is *Morse v. Fredrick* (2006), where the U.S. Supreme Court ruled against a high school student limiting student free speech rights. Joseph Frederick was an 18 year old senior in 2002 in Juneau, Alaska, who did not attend school on this particular day but did attend an off-campus school activity where he raised a banner with the words "Bong Hits 4 Jesus" (p.1). Confiscated by the principal and suspended from school, the student sued. The principal cited her actions as being appropriate since the student's sign clearly made reference to drugs. Although the student was not physically on-campus, he certainly was in the midst of the off-campus activities even having some students help him unfurl and display the banner. "It was reasonable for (the principal) to conclude that the banner promoted illegal drug use, and that failing to act would send a powerful message to the students in her charge," Chief Justice John Roberts wrote for the court's 6-3 majority (Alexander & Alexander, 2009, p. 232).

The tide has turned with the advent of social media and its disruptive or non-disruptive impact on the sacred education learning process. These are different times for schools and, for society, as growing technology has challenged school authority in matters regarding student freedom of expression. Even the U.S. Supreme Court has refused to act denying cert in the *J.S. v. Blue Mountain School District* and *Layshock v. Hermitage School District* cases. It is apparent why school officials in the Third Circuit (including Pennsylvania) may have been confused in the early 2000's and were attempting to design school board policy and actions to deal with the new social media threats to their perception of a peaceful learning environment for all. This statement still rings true today, as it parallels what school safety means for teachers, principals, and other staff, as well as, student to student threats including the growing issue of cyberbullying.

Although the *J.S.* and *Layshock* cases both involve students using social media to mock their principal, cyberbullying, particularly off-campus, by students on fellow students continues to be the primary social media issues schools are facing. Cyberbullying includes hurtful or embarrassing text or images from electronic devices that are intended to intimidate or cause emotional distress to another student. In some cases, such as with Megan Mieier, the messages have been so intensely upsetting that the student committed suicide and this unfortunate outcome led to passage of the Megan Mieier Cyberbullying Prevention Act (US Congress, 2009-2010).

Other districts have acted differently in social media cases. For example in the Fourth Circuit Court of Appeals, a West Virginia High School student was punished by the school when she invited classmates to a questionable MySpace group (*Kowalsky v. Berkeley County Schools*, 2011). Kara Kowalsky sued the school district requesting a reversal of her five-day suspension from the principal for creating a web page suggesting another student had a sexually transmitted disease and invited classmates to comment. Her major defense was that she created the site on a home computer and at a time when she was not in school. The appeals court sided with the school and indicated the learning environment had been disrupted because *Kowolsky* created the site primarily for her classmates. Different federal court jurisdictions may rule differently since the U.S. Supreme Court has not heard a school social media case continuing to rest on the ruling in *Tinker*.

In debating a position on school social media issues, it would be wise to fully review the background of the *J.S.* and *Layshock* cases, as well as, *Tinker* against more recent cases on student free speech rights. Among those cases to review in supporting school districts, the 1988 *Hazelwood v. Kuhlmeier* U.S. Supreme Court case where the court said that public high school officials could censor a student newspaper if needed to maintain a safe and orderly school learning environment. Likewise, a 2013 case in the Ninth Circuit, *Wynar v. Douglas County School District*, ruled against a student involved in Instagram messages with the intention of disturbing the school's safe and orderly learning environment through bullying and/or *disparage*. Judge Donato noted that in this case schools could punish students who established websites for bullying other students. A 23-day suspension was upheld in a Pennsylvania Federal District Court for a student who posted a Facebook post about a bomb threat (*R.L. v. Central York School District*, 2016). Using the reasonable threat of a substantial disruption the full U.S. Fifth Circuit Court of Appeals upheld a school district's punishment of a student's Facebook and YouTube postings that accused students, as well as teachers, of sexual harassment (*Bell v. Itawamba*, 2016). In addition to these cases that supported the school district, *Burge v. Colton School District* (2015) should be reviewed as the ruling favored a student. The federal district court found for a student who had posted a *rant* about a teacher who had given him a C for an assignment grade that was immediately taken down under direction from his mother. The ruling was favorable to the student because the post(s) were short lived, only seen by a few students, and not actively investigated by the school.

In the selections that follow, *Layshock v. Hermitage School District* indicates the full Third Circuit Court of Appeals in their final ruling June 13, 2011, sided with the student because the district could not convince the court that a sufficient nexus existed between the student's vulgar and defamatory profile of his principal and a resulting disruption to the

school's learning environment. In *J.S. v. Blue Mountain School District*, also heard at its final ruling on June 13, 2011, that the court reviewed the facts where the student's suspension for lewd, vulgar, and offensive profile of her principal that was created off-campus, did not pass constitutional muster as a disruption to the school learning environment.

YES ↩

Theodore A. McKee

J.S. v. Blue Mountain School District

J.S., a minor, by and through her parents, Terry Snyder and Steven Snyder, individually and on behalf of their daughter, appeal the District Court's grant of summary judgment in favor of the Blue Mountain School District ("the School District") and denial of their motion for summary judgment. This case arose when the School District suspended J.S. for creating, on a weekend and on her home computer, a MySpace profile (the "profile") making fun of her middle school principal, James McGonigle. The profile contained adult language and sexually explicit content. J.S. and her parents sued the School District under 42 U.S.C. § 1983 and state law, alleging that the suspension violated J.S.'s First Amendment free speech rights, that the School District's policies were unconstitutionally overbroad and vague, that the School District violated the Snyders' Fourteenth Amendment substantive due process rights to raise their child, and that the School District acted outside of its authority in punishing J.S. for out-of-school speech.

Because J.S. was suspended from school for speech that indisputably caused no substantial disruption in school and that could not reasonably have led school officials to forecast substantial disruption in school, the School District's actions violated J.S.'s First Amendment free speech rights. We will accordingly reverse and remand that aspect of the District Court's judgment. However, we will affirm the District Court's judgment that the School District's policies were not overbroad or void-forvagueness, and that the School District did not violate the Snyders' Fourteenth Amendment substantive due process rights.

I

J.S. was an Honor Roll eighth grade student who had never been disciplined in school until December 2006 and February 2007, when she was twice disciplined for dress code violations by McGonigle. On Sunday, March 18, 2007, J.S. and her friend K.L., another eighth grade student at Blue Mountain Middle School, created a fake profile of McGonigle, which they posted on MySpace, a social networking website. The profile was created at J.S.'s home, on a computer belonging to J.S.'s parents.

The profile did not identify McGonigle by name, school, or location, though it did contain his official photograph from the School District's website. The profile was presented as a self-portrayal of a bisexual Alabama middle school principal named "M-Hoe." The profile contained crude content and vulgar language, ranging from nonsense and juvenile humor to profanity and shameful personal attacks aimed at the principal and his family. For instance, the profile lists M-Hoe's general interests as: "detention, being a tight ass, riding the fraintrain, spending time with my child (who looks like a gorilla), baseball, my golden pen, fucking in my office, hitting on students and their parents." Appendix ("App.") 38. In addition, the profile stated in the "About me" section:

> HELLO CHILDREN[.] yes. it's your oh so wonderful, hairy, expressionless, sex addict, fagass, put on this world with a small dick PRINCIPAL[.] I have come to myspace so i can pervert the minds of other principal's [sic] to be just like me. I know, I know, you're all thrilled[.] Another reason I came to myspace is because - I am keeping an eye on you students (who[m] I care for so much)[.] For those who want to be my friend, and aren't in my school[,] I love children, sex (any kind), dogs, long walks on the beach, tv, being a dick head, and last but not least my darling wife who looks like a man (who satisfies my needs) MY FRAIN-TRAIN. . . .

Id. Though disturbing, the record indicates that the profile was so outrageous that no one took its content seriously. J.S. testified that she intended the profile to be a joke between herself and her friends. At her deposition, she testified that she created the profile because she thought it was "comical" insofar as it was so "outrageous." App. 190.

Initially, the profile could be viewed in full by anyone who knew the URL (or address) or who otherwise found the profile by searching MySpace for a term it contained. The following day, however, J.S. made the profile "private" after several students approached her at school, generally to say that they thought the profile was funny. App. 194. By making the profile "private," J.S. limited

---

Hon, Chief Judge; McKee, Theodore A. "J.S. v. Blue Mountain School District," United States Court of Appeals, June 13, 2011.

access to the profile to people whom she and K.L. invited to be a MySpace "friend." J.S. and K.L. granted "friend" status to about twenty-two School District students.

The School District's computers block access to MySpace, so no Blue Mountain student was ever able to view the profile from of school. McGonigle first learned about the profile on Tuesday, March 20, 2007, from a student who was in his office to discuss an unrelated incident. McGonigle asked this student to attempt to find out who had created the profile. He also attempted—unsuccessfully—to find the profile himself, even contacting MySpace directly.

At the end of the school day on Tuesday, the student who initially told McGonigle about the profile reported to him that it had been created by J.S. McGonigle asked this student to bring him a printout of the profile to school the next day, which she did. It is undisputed that the only printout of the profile that was ever brought to school was one brought at McGonigle's specific request.

On Wednesday, March 21, 2007, McGonigle showed the profile to Superintendent Joyce Romberger and the Director of Technology, Susan Schneider-Morgan. The three met for about fifteen minutes to discuss the profile. McGonigle also showed the profile to two guidance counselors, Michelle Guers and Debra Frain (McGonigle's wife). McGonigle contacted MySpace to attempt to discover what computer had been used to create the profile, but MySpace refused to release that information without a court order. The School District points to no evidence that anyone ever suspected the information in the profile to be true.

McGonigle ultimately decided that the creation of the profile was a Level Four Infraction under the Disciplinary Code of Blue Mountain Middle School, Student-Parent Handbook, App. 65–66, as a false accusation about a staff member of the school and a "copyright" violation of the computer use policy, for using McGonigle's photograph. At his deposition, however, McGonigle admitted that he believed the students "weren't accusing me. They were pretending they were me." App. 327.[1]

J.S. was absent from school on Wednesday, the day McGonigle obtained a copy of the profile. When she returned, on Thursday, March 22, 2007, McGonigle summoned J.S. and K.L. to his office to meet with him and Guidance Counselor Guers. J.S. initially denied creating the profile, but then admitted her role. McGonigle told J.S. and K.L. that he was upset and angry, and threatened the children and their families with legal action. App. 333–34. Following this meeting, J.S. and K.L. remained in McGonigle's office while he contacted their parents and waited for them to come to school.

McGonigle met with J.S. and her mother Terry Snyder and showed Mrs. Snyder the profile. He told the children's parents that J.S. and K.L. would receive ten days out-of-school suspension, which also prohibited attendance at school dances. McGonigle also threatened legal action. J.S. and her mother both apologized to McGonigle, and J.S. subsequently wrote a letter of apology to McGonigle and his wife.

McGonigle next contacted MySpace, provided the URL for the profile and requested its removal, which was done. McGonigle also contacted Superintendent Romberger to inform her of his decision regarding J.S. and K.L.'s punishment. Although Romberger could have overruled McGonigle's decision, she agreed with the punishment. On Friday, March 23, 2007, McGonigle sent J.S.'s parents a disciplinary notice, which stated that J.S. had been suspended for ten days.[2] The following week, Romberger declined Mrs. Snyder's request to overrule the suspension.

On the same day McGonigle met with J.S. and her mother, he contacted the local police and asked about the possibility of pressing criminal charges against the students. The local police referred McGonigle to the state police, who informed him that he could press harassment charges, but that the charges would likely be dropped. McGonigle chose not to press charges. An officer did, however, complete a formal report and asked McGonigle whether he wanted the state police to call the students and their parents to the police station to let them know how serious the situation was. McGonigle asked the officer to do this, and on Friday, March 23, J.S. and K.L. and their mothers were summoned to the state police station to discuss the profile.

The School District asserted that the profile disrupted school in the following ways. There were general "rumblings" in the school regarding the profile. More specifically, on Tuesday, March 20, McGonigle was approached by two teachers who informed him that students were discussing the profile in class. App. 322. Randy Nunemacher, a Middle School math teacher, experienced a disruption in his class when six or seven students were talking and discussing the profile; Nunemacher had to tell the students to stop talking three times, and raised his voice on the third occasion. App. 368–73. The exchange lasted about five or six minutes. App. 371. Nunemacher also testified that he heard two students talking about the profile in his class on another day, but they stopped when he told them to get back to work. App. 373–74. Nunemacher admitted that the talking in class was not a unique incident and that he had to tell his students to stop talking about various topics about once a week. Another teacher, Angela

Werner, testified that she was approached by a group of eighth grade girls at the end of her Skills for Adolescents course to report the profile. App. 415–16. Werner said this did not disrupt her class because the girls spoke with her during the portion of the class when students were permitted to work independently. App. 417–18.

The School District also alleged disruption to Counselor Frain's job activities. Frain canceled a small number of student counseling appointments to supervise student testing on the morning that McGonigle met with J.S., K.L., and their parents. Counselor Guers was originally scheduled to supervise the student testing, but was asked by McGonigle to sit in on the meetings, so Frain filled in for Guers. This substitution lasted about twenty-five to thirty minutes. There is no evidence that Frain was unable to reschedule the canceled student appointments, and the students who were to meet with her remained in their regular classes. App. 352–53.

On March 28, 2007, J.S. and her parents filed this action against the School District, Superintendent Romberger, and Principal McGonigle. By way of stipulation, on January 7, 2008, all claims against Romberger and McGonigle were dismissed, and only the School District remained as a defendant. After discovery, both parties moved for summary judgment.

After analyzing the above facts, the District Court granted the School District's summary judgment motion on all claims, though specifically acknowledging that *Tinker v. Des Moines Independent Community School District,* 393 U.S. 503 (1969), does not govern this case because no "substantial and material disruption" occurred. App. 10–12 (refusing to rely on *Tinker*); App. 17 (concluding that "a substantial disruption so as to fall under *Tinker* did not occur"). Instead, the District Court drew a distinction between political speech at issue in *Tinker,* and "vulgar and offensive" speech at issue in a subsequent school speech case, *Bethel School District v. Fraser,* 478 U.S. 675 (1986). App. 11–12. The District Court also noted the Supreme Court's most recent school speech decision, *Morse v. Frederick,* 551 U.S. 393 (2007), where the Court allowed a school district to prohibit a banner promoting illegal drug use at a school-sponsored event.

Applying a variation of the *Fraser* and *Morse* standard, the District Court held that "as vulgar, lewd, and potentially illegal speech that had an effect on campus, we find that the school did not violate the plaintiff's rights in punishing her for it even though it arguably did not cause a substantial disruption of the school." App. 15–16. The Court asserted that the facts of this case established a connection between off-campus action and on-campus effect, and thus justified punishment, because: (1) the website

was about the school's principal; (2) the intended audience was the student body; (3) a paper copy was brought into the school and the website was discussed in school; (4) the picture on the profile was appropriated from the School District's website; (5) J.S. created the profile out of anger at the principal for disciplining her for dress code violations in the past; (6) J.S. lied in school to the principal about creating the profile; (7) *"although a substantial disruption so as to fall under Tinker did not occur . . . there was in fact some disruption during school hours"*; and (8) the profile was viewed at least by the principal at school. App. 17 (emphasis added).

The District Court then rejected several other district court decisions where the courts did not allow schools to punish speech that occurred off campus, including the decision in *Layshock v. Hermitage School District,* 496 F. Supp. 2d 587 (W.D. Pa. 2007), a case substantially similar to the one before us, and which is also being considered by this Court. See App. 18–20. In distinguishing these cases, the District Court made several qualitative judgments about the speech involved in each. See, e.g., App. 18 (asserting that the statements in *Flaherty v. Keystone Oaks School District,* 247 F. Supp. 2d 698 (W.D. Pa. 2003), were "rather innocuous compared to the offensive and vulgar statements made by J.S. in the present case"); App. 19 (contending that "[t]he speech in the instant case . . . is distinguishable" from the speech in *Killion v. Franklin Regional School District,* 136 F. Supp. 2d 446 (W.D. Pa. 2001), because of, *inter alia,* "the level of vulgarity that was present" in the instant case); App. 20 (claiming that, as compared to *Layshock,* "the facts of our case include a much more vulgar and offensive profile").

Ultimately, the District Court held that although J.S.'s profile did not cause a "substantial and material" disruption under *Tinker,* the School District's punishment was constitutionally permissible because the profile was "vulgar and offensive" under *Fraser* and J.S.'s off-campus conduct had an "effect" at the school. In a footnote, the District Court also noted that "the protections provided under *Tinker* do not apply to speech that invades the rights of others." App. 16 n.4 (citing *Tinker,* 393 U.S. at 513).

Next, the District Court held that the School District's policies were not vague and overbroad. The District Court first approached the issue in a somewhat backwards manner: it concluded that because the punishment was appropriate under the First Amendment, the policies were not vague and overbroad even though they can be read to apply to off-campus conduct. App. 21. Alternatively, the District Court held that the policy language was "sufficiently narrow . . . to confine the policy to school grounds and school-related activities." *Id.* (quoting the Handbook, which provides that the "[m]aintenance of order applies during those times when students are under the direct control and supervision of school district officials," and noting that the computer use policy incorporates the limitations of the Handbook).

The District Court also held that the School District did not violate the Snyders' parental rights under the Fourteenth Amendment. The Court concluded that "the school did not err in disciplining J.S., and her actions were not merely personal home activities[,]" and that therefore the Snyders' parental rights were not violated. The Court did not address directly the plaintiffs' state law argument, but did note that Pennsylvania law allows school districts to "punish students [ ] 'during such times as they are under the supervision of the board of school directors and teachers, including the time necessarily spent in coming to and returning from school.'" App. 22 (quoting 24 Pa. Cons. Stat. § 5-510). J.S. and her parents filed a timely appeal from the District Court's entry of summary judgment in favor of the School District and from its decision to deny their motion for summary judgment.

II

The District Court had jurisdiction over the federal claims pursuant to 28 U.S.C. § 1331 and 28 U.S.C. § 1343(a)(3) and (4), and exercised supplemental jurisdiction over the state law claim under 28 U.S.C. § 1367. We exercise jurisdiction under 28 U.S.C. § 1291.

We review a District Court's disposition of a summary judgment motion *de novo. Pichler v. UNITE*, 542 F.3d 380, 385 (3d Cir. 2008) (citing *Marten v. Godwin*, 499 F.3d 290, 295 (3d Cir. 2007)). In conducting this review, we use the same standard as the District Court should have applied. *Farrell v. Planters Lifesavers Co.*, 206 F.3d 271, 278 (3d Cir. 2000). "The court shall grant summary judgment if the movant shows that there is no genuine dispute as to any material fact and the movant is entitled to judgment as a matter of law." Fed. R. Civ. P. 56(a) (setting forth the legal standard formerly found in Fed. R. Civ. P. 56(c)). All inferences must be viewed in the light most favorable to the nonmoving party, *Matsushita Elec. Indus. Co. v. Zenith Radio Corp.*, 475 U.S. 574, 587 (1986); *Farrell*, 206 F.3d at 278, and where, as was the case here, the District Court considers crossmotions for summary judgment "the court construes facts and draws inferences 'in favor of the party against whom the motion under consideration is made,'" *Pichler*, 542 F.3d at 386 (quoting *Samuelson v. LaPorte Cmty. Sch. Corp.*, 526 F.3d 1046, 1051 (7th Cir. 2008)).

"A disputed fact is 'material' if it would affect the outcome of the suit as determined by the substantive law."

Gray v. York Newspapers, Inc., 957 F.2d 1070, 1078 (3d Cir. 1992). Importantly, the nonmoving party cannot satisfy its requirement of establishing a genuine dispute of fact merely by pointing to unsupported allegations found in the pleadings. *Celotex Corp. v. Catrett*, 477 U.S. 317, 322-23 (1986). Instead, the party must raise more than "some metaphysical doubt," *Matsushita*, 475 U.S. at 586, and the court must determine that "a fair-minded jury could return a verdict for the [nonmoving party] on the evidence presented." *Anderson v. Liberty Lobby, Inc.*, 477 U.S. 242, 252 (1986); *see also Bouriez v. Carnegie Mellon Univ.*, 585 F.3d 765, 770-71 (3d Cir. 2009). It is impermissible for the court to intrude upon the duties of the fact-finder by weighing the evidence or making credibility determinations. *Pichler*, 542 F.3d at 386. Finally, when the nonmoving party is the plaintiff, he must produce sufficient evidence to establish every element that he will be required to prove at trial. *Celotex*, 477 U.S. at 322.

III

Although the precise issue before this Court is one of first impression, the Supreme Court and this Court have analyzed the extent to which school officials can regulate student speech in several thorough opinions that compel the conclusion that the School District violated J.S.'s First Amendment free speech rights when it suspended her for speech that caused no substantial disruption in school and that could not reasonably have led school officials to forecast substantial disruption in school.

A

We begin our analysis by recognizing the "comprehensive authority" of teachers and other public school officials. *Tinker*, 393 U.S. at 507. *See generally Veronia Sch. Dist. 47J v. Acton*, 515 U.S. 646, 655 (1995) (describing the public schools' power over public school children as both "custodial and tutelary"). Those officials involved in the educational process perform "important, delicate, and highly discretionary functions." *W. Va. State Bd. of Educ. v. Barnette*, 319 U.S. 624, 637 (1943). As a result, federal courts generally exercise restraint when considering issues within the purview of public school officials. See *Bd. of Educ., Island Trees Union Free Sch. Dist. v. Pico*, 457 U.S. 853, 864 (1982) ("[F]ederal courts should not ordinarily 'intervene in the resolution of conflicts which arise in the daily operation of school systems.'" (quoting *Epperson v. Arkansas*, 393 U.S. 97, 104 (1968)); see also *Hazelwood Sch. Dist. v. Kuhlmeier*, 484 U.S. 260, 266 (1988) ("[T]he education of the Nation's youth is primarily the responsibility of parents, teachers, and state and local school officials, and not of federal judges.").

The authority of public school officials is not boundless, however. The First Amendment unquestionably protects the free speech rights of students in public school. *Morse*, 551 U.S. at 396 ("Our cases make clear that students do not 'shed their constitutional rights to freedom of speech or expression at the schoolhouse gate.'" (quoting *Tinker*, 393 U.S. at 506)). Indeed, "[t]he vigilant protection of constitutional freedoms is nowhere more vital than in the community of American schools." *Shelton v. Tucker*, 364 U.S. 479, 487 (1960). The exercise of First Amendment rights in school, however, has to be "applied in light of the special characteristics of the school environment," *Tinker*, 393 U.S. at 506, and thus the constitutional rights of students in public schools "are not automatically coextensive with the rights of adults in other settings," *Fraser*, 478 U.S. at 682. Since *Tinker*, courts have struggled to strike a balance between safeguarding students' First Amendment rights and protecting the authority of school administrators to maintain an appropriate learning environment.

The Supreme Court established a basic framework for assessing student free speech claims in *Tinker*, and we will assume, without deciding, that *Tinker* applies to J.S.'s speech in this case.[3] The Court in *Tinker* held that "to justify prohibition of a particular expression of opinion," school officials must demonstrate that "the forbidden conduct would *materially and substantially interfere* with the requirements of appropriate discipline in the operation of the school." *Tinker*, 393 U.S. at 509 (emphasis added) (quotation marks omitted). This burden cannot be met if school officials are driven by "a mere desire to avoid the discomfort and unpleasantness that always accompany an unpopular viewpoint." *Id*. Moreover, "*Tinker* requires a specific and significant fear of disruption, not just some remote apprehension of disturbance." *Saxe v. State Coll. Area Sch. Dist.*, 240 F.3d 200, 211 (3d Cir. 2001). Although *Tinker* dealt with political speech, the opinion has never been confined to such speech. See *id*. at 215–17 (holding that the school's anti-harassment policy was overbroad because it "appears to cover substantially more speech than could be prohibited under *Tinker's* substantial disruption test"); see also Killion, 136 F. Supp. 2d at 455–58 (holding that the school overstepped its constitutional bounds under Tinker when it suspended a student for making "lewd" comments about the school's athletic director in an e-mail the student wrote at home and circulated to the non-school e-mail accounts of several classmates).

As this Court has emphasized, with then-Judge Alito writing for the majority, *Tinker* sets the general rule for regulating school speech, and that rule is subject to several *narrow* exceptions. *Saxe*, 240 F.3d at 212 ("Since *Tinker*,

the Supreme Court has carved out a number of narrow categories of speech that a school may restrict even without the threat of substantial disruption."). The first exception is set out in *Fraser*, which we interpreted to permit school officials to regulate "'lewd,' 'vulgar,' 'indecent,' and 'plainly offensive' speech *in school*." *Id*. at 213 (quoting *Fraser*, 478 U.S. at 683, 685) (emphasis added); see also *Sypniewski v. Warren Hills Reg'l Bd. of Educ.*, 307 F.3d 243, 253 (3d Cir. 2002) (quoting *Saxe's* narrow interpretation of the *Fraser* exception). The second exception to *Tinker* is articulated in *Hazelwood School District v. Kuhlmeier*, which allows school officials to "regulate school-sponsored speech (that is, speech that a reasonable observer would view as the school's own speech) on the basis of any legitimate pedagogical concern." *Saxe*, 240 F.3d at 214.

The Supreme Court recently articulated a third exception to *Tinker's* general rule in *Morse*. Although, prior to this case, we have not had an opportunity to analyze the scope of the *Morse* exception, the Supreme Court itself emphasized the narrow reach of its decision. In *Morse*, a school punished a student for unfurling, at a school-sponsored event, a large banner containing a message that could reasonably be interpreted as promoting illegal drug use. 551 U.S. at 396. The Court emphasized that *Morse* was a school speech case, because "[t]he event occurred during normal school hours," was sanctioned by the school "as an approved social event or class trip," was supervised by teachers and administrators from the school, and involved performances by the school band and cheerleaders. *Id*. at 400–01 (quotation marks omitted). The Court then held that "[t]he 'special characteristics of the school environment,' *Tinker*, 393 U.S.[ ] at 506 [ ], and the governmental interest in stopping student drug abuse . . . allow schools to restrict student expression that they reasonably regard as promoting illegal drug use." *Id*. at 408.

Notably, Justice Alito's concurrence in *Morse* further emphasizes the narrowness of the Court's holding, stressing that *Morse* "stand[s] at the far reaches of what the First Amendment permits." 551 U.S. at 425 (Alito, J., concurring). In fact, Justice Alito only joined the Court's opinion "on the understanding that the opinion does not hold that the special characteristics of the public schools necessarily justify any other speech restrictions" than those recognized by the Court in *Tinker*, *Fraser*, *Kuhlmeier*, and *Morse*. *Id*. at 422–23. Justice Alito also noted that the *Morse* decision "does not endorse the broad argument . . . that the First Amendment permits public school officials to censor any student speech that interferes with a school's 'educational mission.' This argument can easily be manipulated in dangerous ways, and I would reject it before such abuse occurs." *Id*. at 423 (citations omitted).

Moreover, Justice Alito engaged in a detailed discussion distinguishing the role of school authorities from the role of parents, and the school context from the "[o]utside of school" context. *Id.* at 424–25.

B

There is no dispute that J.S.'s speech did not cause a substantial disruption in the school. The School District's counsel conceded this point at oral argument and the District Court explicitly found that "a substantial disruption so as to fall under Tinker did not occur." App. at 17. Nonetheless, the School District now argues that it was justified in punishing J.S. under Tinker because of "facts which might reasonably have led school authorities to forecast substantial disruption of or material interference with school activities. . . . ." Tinker, 393 U.S. at 514. Although the burden is on school authorities to meet Tinker's requirements to abridge student First Amendment rights, the School District need not prove with absolute certainty that substantial disruption will occur. Doninger v. Niehoff, 527 F.3d 41, 51 (2d Cir. 2008) (holding that Tinker does not require "actual disruption to justify a restraint on student speech"); Lowery v. Euverard, 497 F.3d 584, 591–92 (6th Cir. 2007) ("Tinker does not require school officials to wait until the horse has left the barn before closing the door. . . . [It] does not require certainty, only that the forecast of substantial disruption be reasonable."); LaVine v. Blaine Sch. Dist., 257 F.3d 981, 989 (9th Cir. 2001) ("Tinker does not require school officials to wait until disruption actually occurs before they may act.").

The facts in this case do not support the conclusion that a forecast of substantial disruption was reasonable. In Tinker, the Supreme Court held that "our independent examination of the record fails to yield evidence that the school authorities had reason to anticipate that the wearing of the armbands [to protest the Vietnam War] would substantially interfere with the work of the school or impinge upon the rights of other students." 393 U.S. at 509. Given this holding, it is important to consider the record before the Supreme Court in Tinker and compare it to the facts of this case.

The relevant events in Tinker took place in December 1965, the year that over 200,000 U.S. troops were deployed to Vietnam as part of Operation Rolling Thunder. Justice Black dissented in Tinker, noting that "members of this Court, like all other citizens, know, without being told, that the disputes over the wisdom of the Vietnam war have disrupted and divided this country as few other issues [e]ver have." Id. at 524 (Black, J., dissenting). In fact, the Tinker majority itself noted the school authorities' concern about the effect of the protest on friends of a student who was killed in Vietnam. See id. at 509 n.3. Justice Black also emphasized the following portions of the record:

> the [ ] armbands caused comments, warnings by other students, the poking of fun at them, and a warning by an older football player that other, nonprotesting students had better let them alone. There is also evidence that a teacher of mathematics had his lesson period practically 'wrecked' chiefly by disputes with [a protesting student] who wore her armband for her 'demonstration.'

Id. at 517 (Black, J., dissenting). Based on these facts, Justice Black disagreed with the *Tinker* majority's holding that the armbands did not cause a substantial disruption in school: "I think the record overwhelmingly shows that the armbands did exactly what the elected school officials and principals foresaw they would, that is, took the students' minds off their classwork and diverted them to thoughts about the highly emotional subject of the Vietnam war." *Id.* at 518; see also *id.* at 524 ("Of course students, like other people, cannot concentrate on lesser issues when black armbands are being ostentatiously displayed in their presence to call attention to the wounded and dead of the war, some of the wounded and the dead being their friends and neighbors.").

This was the record in *Tinker*, and yet the majority in that case held that "the record does not demonstrate *any facts* which might reasonably have led school authorities to forecast substantial disruption of or material interference with school activities," and thus that the school violated the students' First Amendment rights. *Id.* at 514 (emphasis added). Turning to our record, J.S. created the profile as a joke, and she took steps to make it "private" so that access was limited to her and her friends. Although the profile contained McGonigle's picture from the school's website, the profile did not identify him by name, school, or location. Moreover, the profile, though indisputably vulgar, was so juvenile and nonsensical that no reasonable person could take its content seriously, and the record clearly demonstrates that no one did.[4] Also, the School District's computers block access to MySpace, so no Blue Mountain student was ever able to view the profile from school.[5] And, the only printout of the profile that was ever brought to school was one that was brought at McGonigle's express request. Thus, beyond general rumblings, a few minutes of talking in class, and some officials rearranging their schedules to assist McGonigle in dealing with the profile, no disruptions occurred.[6]

In comparing our record to the record in *Tinker,* this Court cannot apply *Tinker's* holding to justify the School District's actions in this case. As the Supreme Court has admonished, an "undifferentiated fear or apprehension of disturbance is not enough to overcome the right to freedom of expression." *Tinker,* 393 U.S. at 508. If *Tinker's* black armbands—an ostentatious reminder of the highly emotional and controversial subject of the Vietnam war—could not "reasonably have led school authorities to forecast substantial disruption of or material interference with school activities," id. at 514, neither can J.S.'s profile, despite the unfortunate humiliation it caused for McGonigle.[7]

Courts must determine when an "undifferentiated fear or apprehension of disturbance" transforms into a reasonable forecast that a substantial disruption or material interference will occur. The School District cites several cases where courts held that a forecast of substantial and material disruption was reasonable. See, e.g., *Doninger,* 527 F.3d at 50–51 (holding that punishment was justified, under *Tinker,* where a student's derogatory blog about the school was "purposely designed by [the student] to come onto the campus," to "encourage others to contact the administration," and where the blog contained "at best misleading and at worst false information" that the school "need[ed] to correct" (quotation marks and alteration omitted)); *Lowery,* 497 F.3d at 596 (holding that punishment was justified, under *Tinker,* where students circulated a petition to fellow football players calling for the ouster of their football coach, causing the school to have to call a team meeting to ensure "team unity," and where not doing so "woul[d] have been a grave disservice to the other players on the team"); *LaVine,* 257 F.3d at 984, 989-90 (holding that the school district did not violate a student's First Amendment rights when it expelled him on an emergency basis "to prevent [ ] potential violence on campus" after he showed a poem entitled "Last Words" to his English teacher, which was "filled with imagery of violent death and suicide" and could "be interpreted as a portent of future violence, of the shooting of [ ] fellow students").

The School District likens this case to the above cases by contending that the profile was accusatory and aroused suspicions among the school community about McGonigle's character because of the profile's references to his engaging in sexual misconduct. As explained above, however, this contention is simply not supported by the record. The profile was so outrageous that no one could have taken it seriously, and no one did. Thus, it was clearly not reasonably foreseeable that J.S.'s speech would create a substantial disruption or material interference in school, and this case is therefore distinguishable from the student speech at issue in *Doninger, Lowery,* and *LaVine.*

Moreover, unlike the students in *Doninger, Lowery,* and *LaVine,* J.S. did not even intend for the speech to reach the school—in fact, she took specific steps to make the profile "private" so that only her friends could access it. The fact that her friends happen to be Blue Mountain Middle School students is not surprising, and does not mean that J.S.'s speech targeted the school. Finally, any suggestion that, absent McGonigle's actions, a substantial disruption would have occurred, is directly undermined by the record. If anything, McGonigle's response to the profile exacerbated rather than contained the disruption in the school.[8]

The facts simply do not support the conclusion that the School District could have reasonably forecasted a substantial disruption of or material interference with the school as a result of J.S.'s profile. Under *Tinker,* therefore, the School District violated J.S.'s First Amendment free speech rights when it suspended her for creating the profile.[9]

C

Because Tinker does not justify the School District's suspension of J.S., the only way for the punishment to pass constitutional muster is if we accept the School District's argument—and the District Court's holding—that J.S.'s speech can be prohibited under the Fraser exception to Tinker.[10] The School District argues that although J.S.'s speech occurred off campus, it was justified in disciplining her because it was "lewd, vulgar, and offensive [and] had an effect on the school and the educational mission of the District." School District Br. 7. The School District's argument fails at the outset because Fraser does not apply to off-campus speech. Specifically in Morse, Chief Justice Roberts, writing for the majority, emphasized that "[h]ad Fraser delivered the same speech in a public forum outside the school context, it would have been protected." 551 U.S. at 405 (citing Cohen v. Cal., 403 U.S. 15 (1971)).[11] The Court's citation to the Cohen decision is noteworthy. The Supreme Court in Cohen held, in a non-school setting, that a state may not make a "single fourletter expletive a criminal offense." 403 U.S. at 26. Accordingly, Chief Justice Roberts's reliance on the Cohen decision reaffirms that a student's free speech rights outside the school context are coextensive with the rights of an adult.

Thus, under the Supreme Court's precedent, the Fraser exception to Tinker does not apply here. In other words, Fraser's "lewdness" standard cannot be extended to justify a school's punishment of J.S. for use of profane language outside the school, during non-school hours.[12]

The School District points out that "a hard copy or printout of the profile *actually* came into the school."

School District Br. 22. However, the fact that McGonigle caused a copy of the profile to be brought to school does not transform J.S.'s off-campus speech into school speech. The flaws of a contrary rule can be illustrated by extrapolating from the facts of *Fraser* itself. As discussed above, the Supreme Court emphasized that Fraser's speech would have been protected had he delivered it outside the school. Presumably, this protection would not be lifted if a school official or Fraser's fellow classmate overheard the off-campus speech, recorded it, and played it to the school principal.[13] Similarly here, the fact that another student printed J.S.'s profile and brought it to school at the express request of McGonigle does not turn J.S.'s off-campus speech into on-campus speech.

Under these circumstances, to apply the *Fraser* standard to justify the School District's punishment of J.S.'s speech would be to adopt a rule that allows school officials to punish any speech by a student that takes place anywhere, at any time, as long as it is *about* the school or a school official, is brought to the attention of a school official, and is deemed "offensive" by the prevailing authority. Under this standard, two students can be punished for using a vulgar remark to speak about their teacher at a private party, if another student overhears the remark, reports it to the school authorities, and the school authorities find the remark "offensive." There is no principled way to distinguish this hypothetical from the facts of the instant case.

Accordingly, we conclude that the *Fraser* decision did not give the School District the authority to punish J.S. for her off-campus speech.

Neither the Supreme Court nor this Court has ever allowed schools to punish students for off-campus speech that is not schools ponsored or at a school-sponsored event and that caused no substantial disruption at school. We follow the logic and letter of these cases and reverse the District Court's grant of summary judgment in favor of the School District and denial of J.S.'s motion for summary judgment on her free speech claim. An opposite holding would significantly broaden school districts' authority over student speech and would vest school officials with dangerously overbroad censorship discretion. We will remand to the District Court to determine appropriate relief on this claim.

IV

We next turn to the argument of J.S.'s parents that the School District violated their Fourteenth Amendment due process right to raise their child in the manner that they saw fit. Specifically, they argue that, in disciplining J.S. for conduct that occurred in her parents' home during non-school hours, the School District interfered with their parental rights.

As the Supreme Court has noted, "it cannot now be doubted that the Due Process Clause of the Fourteenth Amendment protects the fundamental right of parents to make decisions concerning the care, custody, and control of their children." *Troxel v. Granville*, 530 U.S. 57, 66 (2000). This liberty interest, however, is not absolute, *Anspach v. City of Phila.*, 503 F.3d 256, 261 (3d Cir. 2007), and "there may be circumstances in which school authorities, in order to maintain order and a proper educational atmosphere in the exercise of police power, may impose standards of conduct on students that differ from those approved by some parents," *Gruenke v. Seip*, 225 F.3d 290, 304 (3d Cir. 2000). Should the school policies conflict with the parents' liberty interest, the policies may only prevail if they are "tied to a compelling interest." *Id.* at 305.

A conflict with the parents' liberty interest will not be lightly found, and, indeed, only occurs when there is some "manipulative, coercive, or restraining conduct by the State." *Anspach*, 503 F.3d at 266. In other words, the parents' liberty interest will only be implicated if the state's action "deprived them of their right to make decisions concerning their child," and not when the action merely "complicated the making and implementation of those decisions." *C.N. v. Ridgewood Bd. of Educ.*, 430 F.3d 159, 184 (3d Cir. 2005). On the other hand, however, the level of interference required to find a conflict between the school district's policy and the parents' liberty interest may vary depending on the significance of the subject at issue, and the threshold for finding a conflict will not be as high when the school district's actions "strike at the heart of parental decision making authority on matters of the greatest importance." *Id.*

In this case, J.S.'s parents allege that the School District interfered with their ability to determine what out-of-school behavior warranted discipline and what form that discipline took. This, however, is not an accurate description of the impact that the School District's actions had upon J.S.'s parents' ability to make decisions concerning their daughter's upbringing. The School District's actions in no way forced or prevented J.S.'s parents from reaching their own disciplinary decision, nor did its actions force her parents to approve or disapprove of her conduct. Further, there was no triggering of the parents' liberty interest due to the subject matter of the School District's involvement; a decision involving a child's use of social media on the internet is not a "matter[ ] of the greatest importance." Compare *C.N.*, 430 F.3d at 184-85 (determining that no due process violation occurred when a school, without first receiving permission from parents, distributed surveys to students that included questions about sexual activity and substance abuse), with *Gruenke*, 225 F.3d at 306-07 (finding a due process violation when a school coach did not inform a student's parents of their daughter's positive pregnancy test). Under these circumstances, we cannot find that J.S.'s parents' liberty interest was implicated, and will affirm the District Court's grant of summary judgment on their Fourteenth Amendment due process claim.

V

Finally, J.S. challenges the Blue Mountain Student-Parent Handbook ("Handbook") and the Acceptable Use of the Computers, Network, Internet, Electronic Communications System and Information Policy ("AUP") as unconstitutionally overbroad and vague. Relying largely on the testimony of McGonigle and Romberger, J.S. encourages this Court to strike down these School District policies.

"A regulation is unconstitutional on its face on overbreadth grounds where there is [ ]'a likelihood that the statute's very existence will inhibit free expression' by 'inhibiting the speech of third parties who are not before the Court.'" *Saxe*, 240 F.3d at 214 (quoting *Members of City Council v. Taxpayers for Vincent*, 466 U.S. 789, 799 (1984)). "[T]he overbreadth doctrine is not casually employed," *Sypniewski*, 307 F.3d at 258 (quoting *L.A. Police Dep't v. United Reporting Publ'g Corp.*, 528 U.S. 32, 39 (1999)), and before concluding that a law is unconstitutionally overbroad, the court must first determine that the regulation is not "susceptible to a reasonable limiting construction," *Saxe*, 240 F.3d at 215. Further, a law will only be struck down as overbroad if the overbreadth is "not only real but substantial in relation to the statute's plainly legitimate sweep." *Broadrick v. Oklahoma*, 413 U.S. 601, 615 (1973). In undertaking this analysis in the public school setting, however, it is important to recognize that the school district may permissibly regulate a broader range of speech than could be regulated for the general public, giving school regulations a larger plainly legitimate sweep. *Sypniewski*, 307 F.3d at 259. Due to this consideration and concerns about the responsibilities with which public schools are tasked, we have adopted a "more hesitant application," *id.* at 259, of the overbreadth doctrine within public schools. Accordingly, "a school disciplinary policy will be struck down as overbroad only after consideration of the special needs of school discipline has been brought to bear together with the law's general hesitation to apply this 'strong medicine.'" *Id.* at 260.

J.S.'s argument that the School District's policies are overbroad in that they reach out-of-school speech fails on factual grounds, as the policies are explicitly limited to in-school speech. The Handbook states that the authority of the principals and teachers within the District is limited to "those times when students are under the direct control and supervision of school district officials." App. 58. In addition, the specific policy on computer usage in the Handbook states that "[s]tudents may not create, copy, receive, or use data, language or graphics which are obscene, threatening, abusive, or otherwise inappropriate at school or on sign out equipment at home." App. 61. The AUP is similarly limited in scope, and defines "computer" as

> any school district owned, leased or licensed or employee, student and guest owned personal hardware, software or other technology used on school district premises or at school district events, or connected to the school district network, containing school district programs or school district or student data . . . attached or connected to, installed in, or otherwise used in connection with a computer.

App. 40. We need not give these regulations a limiting construction, therefore, as the School District has already limited the reach of its policies.

What J.S. challenges here is not the policies themselves, but the interpretation of these policies that allows the School District to apply its regulations beyond the times when she was within the direct control and supervision of the School District, or beyond times when she was using a school computer. The misinterpretation of these policies by specific individuals, however, does not make the policies overbroad. Although the Handbook and AUP can be applied in a way that violates a student's constitutional rights, as happened in this case, the regulations themselves are not constitutionally infirm on the basis of being overbroad. For this reason, we will affirm the District Court's grant of summary judgment on this issue.

Our vagueness inquiry is grounded in the notice requirement of the Fourteenth Amendment's due process clause. *City of Chicago v. Morales*, 527 U.S. 41, 56 (1999). A statute will be considered void for vagueness if it does not allow a person of ordinary intelligence to determine what conduct it prohibits, or if it authorizes arbitrary enforcement. *Hill v. Colorado*, 530 U.S. 703, 732 (2000). This standard, however, is more relaxed in the school environment: "Given the school's need to be able to impose disciplinary sanctions for a wide range of unanticipated conduct disruptive of the educational process, the school disciplinary rules need not be as detailed as a criminal code which imposes criminal sanctions." *Fraser*, 478 U.S. at 686. This Court has declared that school disciplinary rules should be struck down "only when the vagueness is especially problematic," *Sypniewski*, 307 F.3d at 266, and has upheld a school disciplinary policy that required students to conform to "'an imprecise but comprehensible normative standard,'" id. (quoting *Coates v. City of Cincinnati*, 402 U.S. 61, 614 (1971)). Again, we will affirm the District Court's determination that the School District's policies were not facially unconstitutional. The policies clearly define when and where they apply. Further, the content of the regulations is not impermissibly vague. Although the AUP prohibits a broad range of uses of the School District's computers (including accessing or transmitting "material likely to be offensive or objectionable to recipients," App. 47), the addition of specific examples of impermissible usages draws this policy within the purview of Sypniewski, and articulates a comprehensible normative standard. For example, under the general prohibition against offensive material, the AUP specifically prohibits defamatory, sexually explicit, discriminatory, and violent material. App. 47–48. There can be no doubt that J.S. would have expected to have been punished under the Handbook and the AUP had she taken the same actions from a school computer or while on school grounds. In this sense, they establish a comprehensible normative standard that is appropriate for use in disciplining student misconduct. As with the discussion of over breadth above, J.S.'s argument seems to rely on specific individuals' misinterpretations of the policies, and not the invalidity of the policies themselves. It was the extension and application of these policies to speech undertaken from her personal computer at her parents' home to which she objects here. This punishment, however, was not allowed by the vagueness of the policies. Instead, it was implemented despite the fact that these policies quite clearly did not extend to the conduct at issue. As the policies are not unconstitutionally vague, much less vague in a manner that is "especially problematic," we will affirm the District Court's grant of summary judgment on this issue.

VI

For the foregoing reasons, the District Court's judgment will be affirmed in part, reversed in part and remanded.

Notes

1. In addition, Romberger testified as to her knowledge that it was actually K.L. and not J.S. who appropriated McGonigle's photograph from the School District's website. App. 305–06. Further, it was not until March 29, 2007 that the School District placed a warning on its website prohibiting the duplication of photographs or other content from the website. See App. 79, 180.

2. McGonigle testified that the other times he imposed a tenday suspension were when students brought to school a knife, razor, alcohol, and marijuana. App. 317.

3. The appellants argue that the First Amendment "limits school official[s'] ability to sanction student speech to the schoolhouse itself." Appellants' Br. 25. While this argument has some appeal, we need not address it to hold that the School District violated J.S.'s First Amendment free speech rights.

4. Indeed, although Superintendent Romberger had a duty to report allegations of inappropriate sexual contact or other misconduct by officials in the School District, she did not report McGonigle, because she believed the content of the profile was not true. App. 295–307. In fact, Romberger did not even question McGonigle as to whether any of the content was true. App. 307.

5. We agree with the appellants' argument that 24 Pa. Cons. Stat. § 5-510 also barred the School District from punishing J.S. for her off-campus speech. Section 5-510 limited the authority of the School District to:

> adopt[ing] and enforc[ing] such reasonable rules and regulations . . . regarding the conduct and deportment of all pupils attending the public schools in the district, *during such time as they are under the supervision of the board of school directors and teachers, including the time necessarily spent in coming to and returning from school.*

24 Pa. Cons. Stat. § 5-510 (emphasis added). The dissent notes that § 5-510 permits a school district to exercise "such control as is necessary to prevent infractions of discipline and interference with the educational process." *D.O.F. v. Lewisburg Area Sch. Dist. Bd. of Sch. Dirs.*, 868 A.2d 28, 36 (Pa. Commw. Ct. 2004). While that may be true, the Pennsylvania Commonwealth Court has interpreted this provision to prohibit a school district from punishing students for conduct occurring outside of school hours—even if such conduct occurs on school property. See *id.* at 35–36.

All of the integral events in this case occurred outside the school, during non-school hours.

Accordingly, § 5-510 also barred the School District from punishing J.S.

6. McGonigle testified that after this lawsuit was filed, there was a general decline in student discipline and that he believed this litigation itself encouraged other students to misbehave because they thought they could simply file a lawsuit to alleviate any trouble. App. 350-51. McGonigle's testimony in this regard is irrelevant to the issues before this Court because these disruptions did not arise out of the creation of the profile itself, but rather, were the direct result of the School District's response to the profile and the ensuing litigation. This testimony, therefore, is not relevant to determining the level of disruption that *the profile* caused in the school.

7. We recognize that vulgar and offensive speech such as that employed in this case—even made in jest—could damage the careers of teachers and administrators and we conclude only that the punitive action taken by the School District violated the First Amendment free speech rights of J.S.

   To the extent the dissent supports its arguments regarding material and substantial disruption by speculating about the possibility of discomfort by the recipients of the speech in this case, we cite then-Judge Alito's admonition in *Saxe* that "[t]he Supreme Court has held time and time again, both within and outside of the school context, that the mere fact that someone might take offense at the content of the speech is not sufficient justification for prohibiting it." 240 F.3d at 215; see also *Tinker*, 393 U.S. at 509 (holding school officials cannot prohibit student speech based upon the desire to avoid "discomfort and unpleasantness").

8. The dissent concludes that our decision creates a circuit split with the Court of Appeals for the Second Circuit, positing that that court has determined "that off-campus hostile and offensive student internet speech that is directed at school officials results in a substantial disruption of the classroom environment." Dissenting Op. 22. We disagree, largely because the dissent has overstated our sister circuit's law. Each case applying *Tinker* is decided on its own facts, see *Doninger*, 527 F.3d at 53 ("We decide only that based on the existing record, [the student's] post created a foreseeable risk of substantial disruption to the work and discipline of the school. . . ."), *Wisniewski v. Bd. of Educ. of Weedsport Cent. Sch. Dist.*, 494 F.3d 34, 40 (2d Cir. 2007) (deciding case "on this record"), so all "off-campus hostile and offensive student internet speech" will

not necessarily create a material and substantial disruption at school nor will it reasonably lead school officials to forecast substantial disruption in school. Further, the facts of the cases cited by the dissent in support of its proposition that we have created a circuit split differ considerably from the facts presented in this case. See, e.g., *Doninger*, 527 F.3d at 50-51; *Wisniewski*, 494 F.3d at 35 (involving a student "sharing with friends via the Internet a small drawing crudely, but clearly, suggesting that a named teacher should be shot and killed"). Accordingly, we do not perceive any circuit split and will continue to decide each case on its individual facts.

9. The School District seizes upon language in *Tinker* that is arguably dicta, claiming that it was justified in abridging J.S.'s First Amendment rights because the profile defamed McGonigle. School District Br. 28-33. In *Tinker*, the Court discussed its concern with "the rights of other students to be let alone." 393 U.S. at 508. As a result, the Court appeared to indicate that school officials could stop conduct that would "impinge upon the rights of other students." *Id.* at 509. Later in the opinion, the Court reiterated the point, but referred simply to "invasion of the rights of others." *Id.* at 513. Although McGonigle is not a student, the School District claims J.S's speech is not immunized by the First Amendment because McGonigle's right to be free from defamation fits within this language in *Tinker*. We are not aware of any decisions analyzing whether this language applies to anyone other than "students," but we do note that our cases have employed both of these clauses. See, e.g., *Walker-Serrano*, 325 F.3d at 416-17; *Sypniewski*, 307 F.3d at 264, 265; *Saxe*, 240 F.3d at 214, 217. We further note there is a danger in accepting the School District's argument: if that portion of *Tinker* is broadly construed, an assertion of virtually any "rights" could transcend and eviscerate the protections of the First Amendment. See generally *Snyder v. Phelps*, 131 S. Ct. 1207 (2011) (noting that the First Amendment imposes limitations on the ability to recover in tort). In any event, we agree with J.S. that, as a matter of law, McGonigle could not succeed in his claim that the profile violated his right to be free from defamation. *See Hustler Magazine, Inc. v. Falwell*, 485 U.S. 46, 57 (1988) (holding that a libel claim cannot survive where no reasonable observer can understand the statements to be describing actual facts or events); *Wecht v. PG Publ'g Co.*, 510 A.2d 769, 774 (Pa. Super Ct. 1986) ("Even the most inattentive reader would not accept this article as a factual

narrative. Considering the totality of the printed material . . . we find this publication incapable of defamatory meaning."); see also *Davis v. Monroe County Bd. of Educ.*, 526 U.S. 629, 652 (1999) (holding "simple acts of teasing and name-calling" are not actionable).

10. Indisputably, neither *Kuhlmeier* nor *Morse* governs this case.

11. Notably, in *Morse*, Chief Justice Roberts also cited Justice Brennan's concurrence in *Fraser*, which noted, "[i]f respondent had given the same speech outside of the school environment, he could not have been penalized simply because government officials considered his language to be inappropriate." *Fraser*, 478 U.S. at 688 (Brennan, J., concurring) (citing *Cohen*, 403 U.S. 15).

12. The School District notes that the courts in Doninger and Bethlehem Area School District suggested that Fraser applies to vulgar off-campus speech. See Doninger, 527 F.3d at 49 ("It is not clear . . . [whether] Fraser applies to off-campus speech."); Bethlehem Area Sch. Dist., 807 A.2d at 867 ("[W]e are not convinced that reliance solely on Tinker is appropriate."). Not only are these cases not binding on this Court, but also both Doninger and Bethlehem Area School District ultimately relied on Tinker, not Fraser, in upholding school censorship. Thus, the courts' suggestion that the Fraser standard may apply to off-campus speech is dicta. Most importantly, that dicta is undermined directly by Chief Justice Roberts's statement in Morse: "Had Fraser delivered the same speech in a public forum outside the school context, it would have been protected." 551 U.S. at 405 (citing Cohen, 403 U.S. 15). The most logical reading of Chief Justice Roberts's statement prevents the application of Fraser to speech that takes place off-campus, during non-school hours, and that is in no way sponsored by the school.

13. Note that the question of whether a school has the authority to punish a student who brings vulgar speech into school is separate from whether the school can punish the source of that speech.

THE UNITED STATES COURT OF APPEALS FOR THE THIRD CIRCUIT serves the areas of Pennsylvania, New Jersey, Delaware, and the Virgin Islands.

Theodore A. McKee

Layshock v. Hermitage School District

Mckee, *Chief Judge.*

We are asked to determine if a school district can punish a student for expressive conduct that originated outside of the schoolhouse, did not disturb the school environment and was not related to any school sponsored event. We hold that, under these circumstances, the First Amendment prohibits the school from reaching beyond the schoolyard to impose what might otherwise be appropriate discipline.

It all began when Justin Layshock used his grandmother's computer to access a popular social networking internet web site where he created a fake internet "profile" of his Hickory High School Principal, Eric Trosch. His parents filed this action under 42 U.S.C. § 1983, after the School District punished Justin for that conduct. The suit alleges, *inter alia,* that the School District's punishment transcended Justin's First Amendment right of expression. The district court granted summary judgment in favor of Justin on his First Amendment claim. We originally affirmed the district court. *See Layshock v. Hermitage School Dist.,* 593 F.3d 249 (3d Cir. 2010). Thereafter, we entered an order vacating that opinion and granting rehearing en banc. For the reasons that follow, we once again affirm the district court's holding that the school district's response to Justin's conduct transcended the protection of free expression guaranteed by the First Amendment.

Factual Background

In December of 2005, Justin Layshock was a seventeen-year-old senior at Hickory High School, which is part of the Hermitage School District in Hermitage, Pennsylvania. Sometime between December 10th and 14th, 2005, while Justin was at his grandmother's house during non-school hours, he used her computer to create what he would later refer to as a "parody profile" of his Principal, Eric Trosch. The only school resource that was even arguably involved in creating the profile was a photograph of Trosch that Justin copied from the School District's website. Justin copied that picture with a simple "cut and paste" operation

using the computer's internet browser and mouse. Justin created the profile on "MySpace."[1] MySpace is a popular social-networking website that "allows its members to create online 'profiles,' which are individual web pages on which members post photographs, videos, and information about their lives and interests." *Doe v. MySpace, Inc.,* 474 F.Supp. 2d 843, 845 (W.D. Tex. 2007).[2]

Justin created the profile by giving bogus answers to survey questions taken from various templates that were designed to assist in creating a profile. The survey included questions about favorite shoes, weaknesses, fears, one's idea of a "perfect pizza," bedtime, etc. All of Justin's answers were based on a theme of "big," because Trosch is apparently a large man. For example, Justin answered "tell me about yourself" questions as follows:

> Birthday: too drunk to remember
> Are you a health freak: big steroid freak
> In the past month have you smoked: big blunt[3]
> In the past month have you been on pills: big pills
> In the past month have you gone Skinny
>   Dipping: big lake, not big dick
> In the past month have you Stolen Anything: big keg
> Ever been drunk: big number of times
> Ever been called a Tease: big whore
> Ever been Beaten up: big fag
> Ever Shoplifted: big bag of kmart
> Number of Drugs I have taken: big

Under "Interests," Justin listed: "Transgender, Appreciators of Alcoholic Beverages." Justin also listed "Steroids International" as a club Trosch belonged to.

Justin afforded access to the profile to other students in the School District by listing them as "friends" on the MySpace website, thus allowing them to view the profile. Not surprisingly, word of the profile "spread like wildfire" and soon reached most, if not all, of Hickory High's student body.[4]

During mid-December 2005, three other students also posted unflattering profiles of Trosch on MySpace. Each of those profiles was more vulgar and more offensive than Justin's. Trosch first learned about one of the other

Hon, Chief Judge; McKee, Theodore A. "Layshock v. Hermitage School District," *United States Court of Appeals*, June 13, 2011.

profiles from his daughter, who was in eleventh grade. On Monday, December 12, 2005, Trosch told his Co-Principal, Chris Gill, and the District Superintendent, Karen Ionta, about this other profile and asked the Technology Director, Frank Gingras, to disable it. However, despite the administration's best efforts, students found ways to access the profiles. Trosch discovered Justin's profile on Thursday evening, December 15th, and a fourth profile on Sunday, December 18th.

Trosch believed all of the profiles were "degrading," "demeaning," "demoralizing," and "shocking." He was also concerned about his reputation and complained to the local police. Although he was not concerned for his safety, he was interested in pressing charges against those responsible for the bogus profiles, and he discussed whether the first profile he discovered might constitute harassment, defamation, or slander. However, no criminal charges were ever filed against Justin or any of the other student authors of profiles.

On December 15th, Justin used a computer in his Spanish classroom to access his MySpace profile of Trosch. He also showed it to other classmates, although he did not acknowledge his authorship. After viewing the profile, the students logged off of MySpace. Justin again attempted to access the profile from school on December 16th, purportedly to delete it. School district administrators were unaware of Justin's in-school attempts to access MySpace until their investigation the following week. Teacher Craig Antush glimpsed the profile in his computer lab class and told the students who were congregating around a computer and giggling to shut it down.

The School District administrators were not able to totally block students from visiting the MySpace web page at school because Gingras, the Technology Coordinator, was on vacation on December 16th. However, the school was able to control students' computer access by limiting the students' use of computers to computer labs or the library where internet access could be supervised. School officials continued to limit computer use from December 16th until December 21st, which was the last day of school before Christmas recess. Computer programming classes were also cancelled.

According to the district court, the School District's investigation revealed how many students had accessed MySpace before access to the site at school was disabled, but the school could not determine how many students actually accessed any of the Trosch profiles, or which Trosch profiles had been viewed while a student was on the MySpace website.

School District officials first learned that Justin might have created one of the Trosch profiles on December 21.

On that day, Justin and his mother were summoned to a meeting with Superintendent Ionta and Co-Principal Gill. During that meeting, Justin admitted creating a profile, but no disciplinary action was then taken against him. After the meeting, without prompting from anyone, Justin went to Trosch's office and apologized for creating the profile.[5]

Justin's parents were understandably upset over Justin's behavior. They discussed the matter with him, expressed their extreme disappointment, "grounded" him, and prohibited him from using their home computer.

On January 3, 2006, the school district sent a letter to Justin and his parents giving them notice of an informal hearing that was to be held. The letter read, in pertinent part, as follows:

> Justin admitted prior to the informal hearing that he created a profile about Mr. Trosch.
>
> This infraction is a violation of the Hermitage School District Discipline Code: Disruption of the normal school process; Disrespect; Harassment of a school administrator via computer/internet with remarks that have demeaning implications; Gross misbehavior; Obscene, vulgar and profane language; Computer Policy violations (use of school pictures without authorization).

The School District subsequently found Justin guilty of all of those charges.

In addition to a ten-day, out-of-school suspension, Justin's punishment consisted of (1) being placed in the Alternative Education Program (the "ACE" program) at the high school for the remainder of the 2005–2006 school year;[6] (2) being banned from all extracurricular activities, including Academic Games and foreign-language tutoring;[7] and (3) not being allowed to participate in his graduation ceremony.[8] The Layshocks were also informed that the School District was considering expelling Justin. Ironically, Justin, who created the least vulgar and offensive profile, and who was the only student to apologize for his behavior, was also the only student punished for the MySpace profiles.

District Court Proceedings

The Layshocks initiated this action on January 27, 2006, by filing a three count complaint pursuant to 42 U.S.C. § 1983 individually, and on Justin's behalf, against the Hermitage School District, Karen Ionta, Eric Trosch, and Chris Gill, in their official and individual capacities (hereinafter collectively referred to as the "School District" or "District"). The Layshocks also filed a motion for a temporary restraining order and/or preliminary injunction. Count I of the complaint alleged that the District's punishment of Justin violated his rights under the First Amendment. Count II alleged that the District's policies and rules were unconstitutionally vague and/or overbroad, both on their face and as applied to Justin. Count III alleged that the District's punishment of Justin interfered with, and continued to interfere with, their right as parents to determine how to best raise, nurture, discipline and educate their child in violation of their rights under the Due Process Clause of the Fourteenth Amendment.

The district court denied the request for a temporary restraining order, *Layshock v. Hermitage Sch. Dist.,* 412 F. Supp.2d 502, 508 (W.D. Pa. 2006), and the Layshocks withdrew their motion for a preliminary injunction pursuant to the district court's efforts at mediation.[9] On March 31, 2006, the district court denied the District's motion to dismiss the Layshocks' claims. The court ruled that the parents may assert a claim for a violation of their own due process right to "raise, nurture, discipline and educate their children" based on a school district's punishment of their child for speech the child uttered in the family home.

After discovery, both sides moved for summary judgment, and the court thereafter entered summary judgment in favor of Justin and against the School District only on the First Amendment claim.[10] The court concluded that a jury trial was necessary to determine compensatory damages and attorneys' fees. *See id.* at 607.

Thereafter, the district court denied the District's motion for entry of judgment pursuant to Fed.R.Civ.P. 54(b) or, in the alternative, for the issuance of a certificate of appealability pursuant to 28 U.S.C. § 1292(b).

The parties subsequently filed a joint motion in which they stipulated to damages and requested entry of final judgment while preserving all appellate issues pertaining to liability. The district court then entered a consent judgment, and the School District appealed the district court's grant of summary judgment in favor of Justin on his First Amendment claim.[11]

Summary Judgment

"Summary judgment is proper when the pleadings, depositions, answers to interrogatories, and admissions on file, together with the affidavits, if any, show that there is no genuine issue as to any material fact and that the moving party is entitled to judgment as a matter of law." *Bjorgung v. Whitetail Resort, LP,* 550 F.3d 263, 268 (3d Cir. 2008) (citation and internal quotation marks omitted). In ruling on a motion for summary judgment, the district court must view the facts in the light most favorable to the non-moving party. *Merkle v. Upper Dublin Sch. Dist.,* 211 F.3d 782, 788 (3d Cir. 2000). However, "the mere existence of *some* alleged factual dispute between the parties will not defeat an otherwise properly supported motion for summary judgment." *Anderson v. Liberty Lobby, Inc.,* 477 U.S. 242, 247-48 (1986). "As our review of a grant of summary judgment is plenary, we operate under the same legal standards as the District Court." *Bjorgung,* 550 F.3d at 268.

Discussion

The First Amendment's Application in Public Schools

In the landmark case of *Tinker v. Des Moines Indep. Cmty. Sch. Dist.,* 393 U.S. 503 (1969), a group of high school students decided to wear black arm bands to school to protest the war in Vietnam. When school officials learned of the planned protest, they preemptively prohibited students from wearing armbands. Several students who ignored the ban and wore armbands to school anyway were suspended. *Id.* at 504. Those students brought an action against the school through their parents under 42 U.S.C. § 1983, alleging that their First Amendment rights had been violated. The district court rejected that claim and upheld the constitutionality of the school officials' action, finding that it had been reasonable to preserve discipline. *Id.* 504–505. The district court's decision was affirmed without opinion by an equally divided court of appeals sitting *en banc. Id.* at 505.

The case was appealed to the Supreme Court, which held that student expression may not be suppressed unless school officials reasonably conclude that it will "materially and substantially disrupt the work and discipline of the school." *Id.* at 513. The Court concluded that the students were doing nothing more than engaging in political speech, and wearing armbands to express "their disapproval of the Vietnam hostilities and their advocacy of a truce, to make their views known, and, by their example, to influence others to adopt them." *Id.* at 514. The school district's only interest in banning the speech had been the "mere desire to avoid the discomfort and unpleasantness that always accompany an unpopular viewpoint" or "an urgent wish to avoid the controversy which might result from the expression." *Id.* at 509-10. The Court held that this interest was not enough to justify banning "a silent, passive expression of opinion, unaccompanied by any disorder or disturbance." *Id.* at 508. In one of its most famous passages, the Court explained:

First Amendment rights, applied in light of the special characteristics of the school environment, are available to teachers and students. It can hardly be argued that either students or teachers shed their constitutional rights to freedom of speech or expression at the schoolhouse gate.

Id. at 506.

Thus, although the Court concluded that the First Amendment did reach inside the "schoolhouse gate," it also recognized that the unique nature of the school environment had to be part of any First Amendment inquiry. The Court explained that it "ha[d] repeatedly emphasized the need for affirming the comprehensive authority of the States and of school officials, consistent with fundamental constitutional safeguards, to prescribe and control conduct in the schools." *Id.* at 507.

The Court next addressed the scope of the First Amendment in the context of student speech in *Bethel School District No. 403 v. Fraser*, 478 U.S. 675 (1986). There, the Court upheld the school's suspension of a high school student for delivering a nominating speech at a school assembly using "an elaborate, graphic, and explicit sexual metaphor." *Id.* at 678. The Court explained:

> The schools, as instruments of the state, may determine that the essential lessons of civil, mature conduct cannot be conveyed in a school that tolerates lewd, indecent, or offensive speech and conduct such as that indulged in by [Fraser].[12]

Id. at 683. In reaching this conclusion, the Court distinguished its prior holding in *Cohen v. California*, 403 U.S. 15 (1971). There, the Court had struck down an adult's conviction for disorderly conduct that was based on his wearing a jacket, inside a court house, that had an obscenity about the draft printed on it. The *Fraser* Court explained:

> It does not follow . . . that simply because the use of an offensive form of expression may not be prohibited to adults making what the speaker considers a political point, the same latitude must be permitted to children in public school. . . . [T]he First Amendment gives a high school student the classroom right to wear Tinker's armband, but not Cohen's jacket.

Id. at 682 (citation and internal quotation marks omitted). The Court concluded that the school could punish Fraser for his offensive nominating speech during a school assembly because the First Amendment does not prevent schools from encouraging the "fundamental values of 'habits and manners of civility,'" *id.* at 681, by "insisting

that certain modes of expression are inappropriate and subject to sanctions." *Id.* at 683. Thus, "[t]he determination of what manner of speech in the classroom or in school assembly is inappropriate properly rests with the school board." *Id.*

Similarly, in *Hazelwood School District. v. Kuhlmeier*, 484 U.S. 260 (1988), the Court held that a principal's deletion of student articles on teen pregnancy from a school-sponsored newspaper did not violate the First Amendment. The Court distinguished *Tinker* by noting that because the school had not opened the newspaper up as a public forum, the school could "exercis[e] editorial control over the style and content of student speech in school-sponsored expressive activities so long as [its] actions are reasonably related to legitimate pedagogical concerns." *Id.* at 273. The Court explained:

> The question whether the First Amendment requires a school to tolerate particular student speech—the question that we addressed in *Tinker*—is different from the question whether the First Amendment requires a school affirmatively to promote particular student speech. The former question addresses educators' ability to silence a student's personal expression that happens to occur on the school premises. The latter question concerns educators' authority over school-sponsored . . . expressive activities that students, parents, and members of the public might reasonably perceive to bear the imprimatur of the school. . . . Educators are entitled to exercise greater control over this second form of student expression.

Id. at 270–71.

The extent to which First Amendment protections apply in the public school context was most recently addressed in *Morse v. Frederick*, 551 U.S. 393 (2007). There, "[a]t a school-sanctioned and school-supervised event, a high school principal [Morse] saw some of her students unfurl a large banner conveying a message she reasonably regarded as promoting illegal drug use." *Id.* at 396. The banner read: "BONG HiTS 4 JESUS." *Id.* at 397. "Consistent with established school policy prohibiting such messages at school events, [Morse] directed the students to take down the banner." *Id.* at 396. Frederick, one of the students who brought the banner to the event, refused to remove it, and Morse "confiscated the banner and later suspended [Frederick]." *Id.* Frederick sued Morse and the school district pursuant to 42 U.S.C. § 1983, alleging a violation of his First Amendment right of expression. The district court granted summary judgment to the school district and Morse, holding that they were entitled to qualified immunity and that they had not infringed Frederick's First Amendment rights. *Id.* at 399. The Court of Appeals for the Ninth Circuit reversed.

The Supreme Court granted certiorari to determine "whether Frederick had a First Amendment right to wield his banner, and, if so, whether that right was so clearly established that the principal may be held liable for damages." *Id.* at 400.[13] The Court "resolve[d] the first question against Frederick," and, therefore, did not have to reach the second. *Id.* The Court explained that its Fourth Amendment jurisprudence recognized that "deterring drug use by school children is an important—indeed, perhaps compelling interest." *Id.* at 407 (citation omitted). The "special characteristics of the school environment, and the governmental interest in stopping student drug abuse allow schools to restrict student expression that they reasonably regard as promoting such abuse." *Id.* at 408. Thus, "a principal may, consistent with the First Amendment, restrict student speech at a school event, when that speech is reasonably viewed as promoting illegal drug use." *Id.* at 402. The Court rejected Frederick's claim that since he was across the street from the school and not on school property, he was not inside *Tinker's* "schoolhouse gate," and school officials therefore had lost authority over him. The Court reasoned that the event where the banner was unfurled occurred during school hours, and it had been approved by the school's principal as a school event. *Id.* at 400. School events and field trips off school grounds were subject to the school's rules for student conduct. *Id.* at 400-01.

It is against this legal backdrop that we must determine whether the District's actions here violated Justin's First Amendment rights.

At the outset, it is important to note that the district court found that the District could not "establish[ ] a sufficient nexus between Justin's speech and a substantial disruption of the school environment[,]" *Layshock*, 496 F. Supp. 2d at 600, and the School District does not challenge that finding on appeal. Therefore, the School District is not arguing that it could properly punish Justin under the *Tinker* exception for student speech that causes a material and substantial disruption of the school environment. *See Tinker*, 393 U.S. at 513. Rather, the District's argument is twofold:

> [A] sufficient nexus exists between Justin's creation and distribution of the vulgar and defamatory profile of Principal Trosch and the School District to permit the School District to regulate this conduct. The "speech" initially began on-campus: Justin entered school property, the

School District web site, and misappropriated a picture of the Principal. The "speech" was aimed at the School District community and the Principal and was accessed on campus by Justin. It was reasonably foreseeable that the profile would come to the attention of the School District and the Principal.

District's Br. at 9.

Justin's "Entry" onto the District's Website

The School District's attempt to forge a nexus between the School and Justin's profile by relying upon his "entering" the District's website to "take" the District's photo of Trosch is unpersuasive at best. The argument equates Justin's act of signing onto a web site with the kind of trespass he would have committed had he broken into the principal's office or a teacher's desk; and we reject it. *See Thomas v. Board of Educ.*, 607 F.2d 1043 (2d Cir. 1979).

We find the reasoning in *Thomas v. Board of Educ.*, 607 F.3d 1043 (2d Cir. 1979), far more persuasive.[14] *Thomas* involved a group of students who were suspended for producing "a satirical publication addressed to the school community." *Id.* at 1045. The articles included such topics as masturbation and prostitution, as well as more standard fare such as "school lunches, cheerleaders, classmates, and teachers." *Id.* "Some of the initial preparation for publication occurred after school hours in the classroom" of a teacher whom the students consulted "for advice on isolated questions of grammar and content." *Id.* In addition, "an occasional article was composed or typed within the school building, always after classes," and the finished magazine was stored in a "classroom closet" with the classroom teacher's permission. *Id.*

However, the students were very careful to distribute the periodical only after school and off campus, and the vast majority of their work on the publication was done "in their homes, off campus and after school hours." *Id.* The school principal learned of the magazine when a teacher confiscated a copy from another student on campus, and "following consultation with the Board of Education," the principal imposed penalties that included a five-day suspension of the students involved.[15] *Id.* at 1046. The punishment was based on the students' publication of "an allegedly 'morally offensive, indecent, and obscene,' tabloid." *Id.* at 1050 n.12.

The students sued the school board and other school officials under 42 U.S.C. § 1983. They sought "injunctive and declaratory relief from alleged deprivations of their First and Fourteenth Amendment rights." *Id.* at 1046.

The district court denied the students' request for injunctive relief based upon its conclusion that the publication "was potentially destructive of discipline in [the school], and therefore not protected by the First Amendment." *Id.* at 1047.

The Court of Appeals for the Second Circuit concluded that the students' conduct was not sufficiently related to the school to justify the school's exercise of authority. The court explained:

> [A]ll but an insignificant amount of relevant activity in this case was deliberately designed to take place beyond the schoolhouse gate. Indeed, the [students] diligently labored to ensure that [the magazine] was printed outside the school, and that no copies were sold on school grounds. That a few articles were transcribed on school typewriters, and that the finished product was secretly and unobtrusively stored in a teacher's closet do not alter the fact that [the magazine] was conceived, executed, and distributed outside the school. At best, therefore, any activity within the school itself was De minimis.

Id. at 1050.

The court reached that conclusion even though the students actually stored the offending publication inside a classroom and did some minimal amount of work on the periodical in school using school resources. Here, the relationship between Justin's conduct and the school is far more attenuated than in *Thomas*. We agree with the analysis in *Thomas*. Accordingly, because the School District concedes that Justin's profile did not cause disruption in the school, we do not think that the First Amendment can tolerate the School District stretching its authority into Justin's grandmother's home and reaching Justin while he is sitting at her computer after school in order to punish him for the expressive conduct that he engaged in there.

We realize, of course, that it is now well established that *Tinker*'s "schoolhouse gate" is not constructed solely of the bricks and mortar surrounding the school yard. Nevertheless, the concept of the "school yard" is not without boundaries and the reach of school authorities is not without limits. In *Morse*, the Court held that the First Amendment does not prevent a principal from "restrict[ing] student speech *at a* school *event,* when that speech is reasonably viewed as promoting illegal drug use." 551 U.S. at 403 (emphasis added). Nevertheless, with regard to expressive conduct that occurs outside of the school context, the Court, referring to its earlier decision in *Fraser*, was careful to note that "[h]ad Fraser delivered the same speech in a public forum outside the school context, it would have been protected." 551 U.S. at 404 (citations omitted).

It would be an unseemly and dangerous precedent to allow the state, in the guise of school authorities, to reach into a child's home and control his/her actions there to the same extent that it can control that child when he/she participates in school sponsored activities. Allowing the District to punish Justin for conduct he engaged in while at his grandmother's house using his grandmother's computer would create just such a precedent, and we therefore conclude that the district court correctly ruled that the District's response to Justin's expressive conduct violated the First Amendment guarantee of free expression.

The District Cannot Punish Justin Merely Because His Speech Reached Inside the School

As noted above, the School District also claims that Justin's speech can be treated as "on-campus" speech because it "was aimed at the School District community and the Principal and was accessed on campus by Justin [and] [i]t was reasonably foreseeable that the profile would come to the attention of the School District and the Principal."

The district court held that the School District's punishment of Justin was not appropriate under *Fraser* because "[t]here is no evidence that Justin engaged in any lewd or profane speech while in school." *Layshock,* 496 F. Supp.2d at 599–600. It also held that Justin's punishment was not appropriate under *Tinker* because the School District did "not establish[ ] a sufficient nexus between Justin's speech and a substantial disruption of the school environment." *Id.* at 600.

The School District does not dispute the district court's finding that its punishment of Justin was not appropriate under *Tinker;* it rests its argument on the Supreme Court's analysis in *Fraser*. In the School District's view, Justin's speech—his MySpace profile of Trosch—was unquestionably vulgar, lewd and offensive, and therefore not shielded by the First Amendment because it ended up inside the school community.[16] Similarly, the School District argues that under our decision in *Saxe, see* n.12, *supra,* there is no First Amendment protection for lewd, vulgar, indecent or plainly offensive speech in schools.[17]

The District rests this argument primarily on three cases which it claims allow it to respond to a student's vulgar speech when that speech is posted on the internet. The District cites *J.S. v. Bethlehem Area Sch. Dist.,* 807 A.2d 847 (Pa. 2002); *Wisniewski v. Bd. of Educ. of Weedsport Cent. Sch. Dist.,* 494 F.3d 34 (2d Cir. 2007); and *Doninger v. Niehoff,* 527 F.3d 41 (2d Cir. 2008). However, as we will explain, each of those cases involved off campus expressive conduct that resulted in a substantial disruption of the school, and the courts allowed the schools to respond to the substantial disruption that the student's out of school conduct caused.

In *J.S.*, an eighth grade student created a threatening website aimed at his algebra teacher that went so far as to explain "[w]hy Should She Die," and requested money "to help pay for the hitman." 807 A.2d at 851. The site frightened several students and parents and the algebra teacher was so badly frightened that she ended up having to take medical leave from her teaching responsibilities. As a result of her inability to return to teaching, "three substitute teachers were required to be utilized which disrupted the educational process of the students." *Id.* at 852. "In sum, the web site created disorder and significantly and adversely impacted the delivery of instruction." *Id.* at 869. The Supreme Court of Pennsylvania concluded that the resulting disruption of instruction and the educational environment allowed the school to punish the student for his expressive conduct even though the student created the website from his home.[18]

Similarly, the school suspended the student in *Wisniewski*, for creating an image on the internet from his home computer that depicted a pistol firing a bullet at a teacher's head with dots representing splattered blood above the head. 494 F.3d at 36. The words: "Kill Mr. VanderMolen" were printed beneath the drawing. VanderMolen was the student's English teacher. The student created the image a couple of weeks after his class was instructed that threats would not be tolerated at the school, and would be treated as acts of violence. The court of appeals affirmed the district court's grant of summary judgment in favor of the school district in a suit alleging a violation of the First Amendment based on the school's suspension of the student for the out-of-school conduct. The court reasoned that "[t]he fact that [the student's] creation and transmission of the icon occurred away from school property [did] not necessarily insulate him from school discipline." 494 F.3d at 39. The court reasoned that "even if [the student's] transmission of an [image] depicting and calling for the killing of his teacher could be viewed as an expression of opinion within the meaning of *Tinker*," it was not protected by the First Amendment because "it cross[ed] the boundary of protected speech and pose[d] a reasonably foreseeable risk [of] materially and substantially disrupting the work and discipline of the school." *Id.* at 38-9 (internal quotation marks omitted).

Finally, in *Doninger*, a student, who was a class officer, posted a message on her publicly accessible web log or "blog" that resulted in school authorities not allowing her to participate in an election for class office.[19] *Id.* at 43. In her message, she complained about a school activity that

was cancelled "due to douchebags in central office," and encouraged others to contact the central office to "piss [the district superintendent] off more." *Id.* at 45. When the principal learned of the student's posting, she prohibited her from running for senior class secretary "because [the student's] conduct had failed to display the civility and good citizenship expected of class officers." *Id.* at 46. The student and her parents then sought injunctive relief in the form of a court order allowing her to run for class office. The court of appeals affirmed the district court's denial of relief because the student's out of school expressive conduct "created a foreseeable risk of substantial disruption to the work and discipline of the school." *Id.* at 53.[20] "[The student] herself testified that . . . students were 'all riled up' and that a sit-in was threatened." *Id.* at 51. Accordingly, the court of appeals held that the student's mother "failed to show clearly that [the student's] First Amendment rights were violated when she was disqualified from running" for class office. *Id.* at 53.

However, for our purposes, it is particularly important to note that the court in *Doninger* was careful to explain that it "[had] no occasion to consider whether a different, more serious consequence than disqualification from student office would raise constitutional concerns." *Id.* at 53. Of course, Justin's consequences were more serious; he was suspended. Moreover, in citing *Doninger*, we do not suggest that we agree with that court's conclusion that the student's out of school expressive conduct was not protected by the First Amendment there. Rather, we cite *Doninger* only to respond to the School District's contention that that case supports its actions against Justin.

As noted earlier, the District's January 3, 2006, letter to the Layshocks advising them of Justin's suspension reads, in relevant part, that it was punishing Justin because "Justin admitted prior to the informal hearing that he created a profile about Mr. Trosch." Although the letter also mentions disruption, we have taken care to stress that the District does not now challenge the district court's finding that Justin's conduct did not result in any substantial disruption. Moreover, when pressed at oral argument, counsel for the School District conceded that the District was relying solely on the fact that Justin created the profile of Trosch, and not arguing that it created any substantial disruption in the school. However, as noted above, *Fraser* does not allow the School District to punish Justin for expressive conduct which occurred outside of the school context. *See Morse*, 551 U.S. at 404 ("Had Fraser delivered the same speech in a public forum outside the school context, it would have been protected.") (citations omitted). Moreover, we have found no authority that would support punishment for creating such a profile unless it results in foreseeable and substantial disruption of school.

We believe the cases relied upon by the School District stand for nothing more than the rather unremarkable proposition that schools may punish expressive conduct that occurs outside of school, as if it occurred inside the "schoolhouse gate," under certain very limited circumstances, none of which are present here.

As the court of appeals explained in *Thomas*: "[O]ur willingness to defer to the schoolmaster's expertise in administering school discipline rests, in large measure, upon the supposition that the arm of authority does not reach beyond the schoolhouse gate." 607 F.2d at 1045. We need not now define the precise parameters of when the arm of authority can reach beyond the schoolhouse gate because, as we noted earlier, the district court found that Justin's conduct did not disrupt the school, and the District does not appeal that finding. Thus, we need only hold that Justin's use of the District's web site does not constitute entering the school, and that the District is not empowered to punish his out of school expressive conduct under the circumstances here.

Based on those two conclusions, we will affirm the district court's grant of summary judgment to Justin Layshock on his First Amendment claim.[21]

Notes

1. MySpace is found at: http://www.myspace.com.
2. Social online networking sites allow members to use "their online profiles to become part of an online community of people with common interests. Once a member has created a profile, she can extend 'friend invitations' to other members and communicate with her friends over the MySpace.com platform via e-mail, instant messaging, or blogs." *Doe*, 474 F. Supp.2d at 846.
3. Justin explained that a "blunt" was a marijuana cigarette.
4. Justin later explained that he made the profile to be funny, and did not intend to hurt anyone. However, there was obviously nothing "funny" about the profile in the eyes of the school administration.
5. Trosch later testified that he found Justin's apology respectful and sincere. Justin followed up with a written letter of apology on January 4, 2006.
6. Students assigned to ACE meet in a segregated area of the high school for three hours each day. The program is typically reserved for students with behavior and attendance problems who are unable to function in a regular classroom.

Prior to creating the Myspace profile, Justin was classified as a gifted student, was enrolled in advanced placement classes, and had won awards at interscholastic academic competitions. The record does not reveal how the School District determined that it was appropriate to place such a student in a program designed for students who could not function in a classroom.

7. Justin had been a French tutor to middle school students.
8. Justin did graduate in 2006 and went on to attend a university in New York City.
9. The Layshocks agreed to withdraw their motion for a preliminary injunction in exchange for the District's agreement to remove Justin from the ACE program, reinstate him to his regular classes, allow him to participate in Academic Games, and attend his graduation.
10. The district court ruled that Trosch was entitled to summary judgment on all counts because he was not involved in disciplining Justin. It also held that Ionta and Gill were entitled to summary judgment on Justin's First Amendment claim based on qualified immunity, and that all of the defendants were entitled to summary judgment on the vagueness/overbreadth challenge and the parents' substantive due process claim.
11. The Layshocks filed a cross-appeal (No. 07-4555) from the district court's grant of summary judgment in favor of the School District on their Fourteenth Amendment Due Process claim. In our opinion filed on February 4, 2010, we affirmed the district court's grant of summary judgment to the School District on that claim, and the Layshocks did not seek rehearing en banc on that claim. Therefore, although we vacated the February 4, 2010, opinion and judgment as to the School District's appeal at No. 07-4464, and granted the School District's petition for rehearing en banc, we also, on April 9, 2010, ordered that "the opinion and judgment entered by this Court on February 4, 2010 stands with respect to the affirmance of the district court's grant of summary judgment to the [School District] on [the Layshocks'] Fourteenth Amendment Due Process claim."
12. In *Saxe v. State College Area School District,* 240 F.3d 200, 213 (3d Cir. 2001), we interpreted *Fraser* as establishing that "there is no First Amendment protection for 'lewd,' 'vulgar,' 'indecent,' and 'plainly offensive' speech in school."
13. The court of appeals had ruled that the principal was not entitled to qualified immunity.
14. *Thomas* was decided after *Tinker* but before *Fraser*.

15. The Principal and Superintendent of Schools had initially decided to take no action pending assessment of the publication's impact. However, they ultimately decided to act after being contacted by the President of the Board of Education. *Thomas,* 607 F.2d at 1045-46.

16. The District's argument in this regard is not crystal clear as its brief suggests that it can react to Justin's profile merely because it was lewd and vulgar. For example, the District summarizes one of its arguments as follows:

> The School District did not violate the First Amendment by punishing Justin for engaging in conduct which interfered with the School District's "highly appropriate function . . . to prohibit the use of vulgar and offensive terms in public discourse."

District's Br. at 10 (ellipsis in original).

> However, we reject out of hand any suggestion that schools can police students' out-of-school speech by patrolling "the public discourse." Accordingly, we will assume that the District is arguing that it can control lewd and vulgar speech as authorized under *Fraser.*

17. In *Saxe,* we did state: "Under *Fraser,* a school may categorically prohibit lewd, vulgar or profane language." 240 F.3d at 214. However, when read in context, it is clear that we were there referring only to speech inside *Tinker's* schoolhouse gate. Thus, we summarized the holding in *Fraser* as follows: "According to *Fraser,* . . . there is no First Amendment protection for 'lewd,' 'vulgar,' 'indecent,' and 'plainly offensive' speech *in school.*" *Id.* at 213 (emphasis added).

18. The district court believed that *J.S.* was "on point" but "respectfully reache[d] a slightly different balance between student expression and school authority." *Layshock,* 496 F. Supp. 2d at 602. However, we do not think *J.S.* is "on point" or the least bit helpful because there is no comparison between the impact of the conduct there and the impact of the conduct here.

19. "A blog (a contraction of the term 'web log') is a type of website, usually maintained by an individual with regular entries or commentary, descriptions of events, or other material such as graphics or video. . . . 'Blog' can also be used as a verb, *meaning to maintain or add content to a blog.*" (http://en.wikipedia.org/wiki/Blog) (last visited September 23, 2010).

20. The blog had resulted in numerous calls and emails to the principal, and the court of appeals noted that the blog also used inaccurate and misleading information to rally those who read it to contact the school principal.

21. The District argues in the alternative that it did not violate the First Amendment by punishing Justin because his speech was defamatory and not protected by the First Amendment. The Layshocks respond by arguing that Justin's profile is a parody that cannot constitute defamation. However, whether or not we accept the characterization of a "parody," the issue before us is limited to whether the District had the authority to punish Justin for expressive conduct outside of school that the District considered lewd and offensive.

The United States Court of Appeals for the Third Circuit serves the areas of Pennsylvania, New Jersey, Delaware, and the Virgin Islands.

EXPLORING THE ISSUE

Do Public Schools Have Grounds to Punish Students for Their Off-Campus Online Speech?

Critical Thinking and Reflection

1. How do the rulings in the *J.S. v. Blue Mountain School District and Layshock v. Hermitage court* cases apply only to the Third Circuit?
2. What types of activities should officials be focused on regarding social media issues in their schools?
3. What other U.S. Supreme Court cases impact the issues and outcomes in these two court cases?
4. Will there be more concerns in the future regarding schools and students' First Amendment rights?
5. What are the steps in a case being heard at the U.S. Supreme Court and why wasn't Layshock or J.S. heard by the highest court in the land?

Is There Common Ground?

J.S. v. Blue Mountain School District and *Layshock v. Hermitage School District* have many similarities regarding student free speech. As well, there are differences. First, it is alarming to many that the language and graphics created by both students in these cases actually occur with youth attending our schools today, and second, that in some cases school officials are strapped from being able to effectively respond to inappropriateness of the behavior. It is also difficult to understand how some students in some localities are allowed First Amendment protection yet denied in others courts across the nation. The problem is magnified considering how different circuits in the country deal with social media behavior and the legal precedents these courts follow in reaching their rulings. How are the courts viewing *nexus* to the school in these cases, defining disruption to the education learning environment, and how is the *Tinker v. DesMoines* and more recent cases factored into the decisions? For a *nexus* to occur, there must be a connection between the off-campus activity of students and the disruption, or threat of disruption, to the school. Under *Tinker,* this would be termed a disruption to the learning environment. Why hasn't the U.S. Supreme Court decided to hear a school social media case?

The common ground in social media court cases can be murky. One tactic for assuring the common ground can be identified, is to complete a meta-analysis of all the social media cases occurring in schools in all Circuit Courts. Doing so could provide data for a very relevant study and provide a clearer picture across the nation of how our judicial system views the cases under the guise of students First Amendment Rights protection. Will the common ground be brought together if the U.S. Supreme Court takes on a school social media case and makes a ruling for the entire nation?

To conclude, off campus incidents of students using social media is problematic in that no U.S. Supreme Court case specifically guides schools in their discipline of students. Schools are left to the varying decisions found in the fourteen federal circuit courts of appeal across the country. The gold standard, *Tinker*, is still the key for guidance. As noted, a bigger social media issue found in our schools is student to staff or student to student inappropriate texting and imaging. This comes as a larger part of a problem with the complexities of dealing with a technological society. Teachers and other staff have been caught using district-owned digital technology for similar behaviors as students. "Sexting" among staff and from staff to students exhibiting predatory behaviors to minors seem to occur on a regular basis around the country. Publically owned devices can be monitored by the district information technology departments. Teachers have been fired and some criminally charged with incidents like the New York special education teacher discovered using a district-owned email account to arrange sexual encounters via the website Craigslist. Another incident, some time ago, is that of a Pennsylvania superintendent texting racial slurs about students and staff between exchanges with the school's athletic director (Harold, 2013). Professional development about appropriate use of public or private devises, network, and email is vitally important, but what is the major focus on addressing appropriate use of student social media? The debate continues.

Additional References

Alexander, A. & Alexander, M. (2009). *American public school law*. Boston, MA. Wadsworth Cengage Learning.

Bethel School District v. Fraser. (1986). Retrieved from https://www.americanbar.org/groups/public_education/initiatives_awards/students_in_action/bethel.html

Cain, R. (2012). Supreme Court Denies Cert in Student's Free Speech Rights Case. *Findlaw*. Retrieved from: http://blogs.findlaw.com/supreme_court/2012/01/supreme-court-denies-cert-in-student-free-speech-rights-cases.html

Harold, B. (2013). PA Texting Scandal highlights Complexities for IT Leaders. *Education Week*, October 15. Retrieved from: www2.edweek.org/ew/articles/2013/10/16/08whistleblower.h33.html?print=1

Hazelwood School District v. Kuhlemier, 484 U.S. 260. (1988). Retrieved from https://supreme.justia.com/cases/federal/us/484/260/

Kowalsky v. Berkley County Schools. (2011). United States Court of Appeals for the Fourth Circuit. Retrieved from: www.ca4.uscourts.gov/Opinions/Published/101098.P.pdf

Morse v. Frederick, 551 U.S. 393. (2007). Retrieved from https://supreme.justia.com/cases/federal/us/551/393/

Palistini, R. & Palistini, K. (2012). *The law and American education: A case brief approach Lanham, MD*. Rowman & Littlefield.

Tinker v. DesMoines, 393 U.S.503.(1969).Retrieved from https://supreme.justia.com/cases/federal/us/393/503/

Wynar v. Douglas County School District,No. 11-17127, 9th Cir. (2013). Retrieved from https://law.justia.com/cases/federal/appellate-courts/ca9/11-17127/11-17127-2013-08-29.html

US Congress. (2009-2010). H.R.1966-Megan Meier Cyberbullying Prevention Act. Retrieved from https://www.congress.gov/bill/111th-congress/house-bill/1966

Internet References . . .

Layshock v. Hermitage School District Overview

Legal Clips: Federal court issues en banc decision in *Layshock v. Hermitage School district* violated First Amendment by disciplining student for off-campus online speech. The Source for Recent Developments in School Law.

http://legalclips.nsba.org/2011/06/15/
federal-appellate-court-issues-en-banc-
decision-holding-pennsylvania-school-
districts-discipline-of-student-for-off-campus-online-
speech-violated-the-first-amendment/

J.S. v. Blue Mountain School District Overview

Legal Clips: Federal court issues en bancdecision in J.S. v. Blue Mountain Sch. Dist..: school district violated First Amendment by disciplining student for off-campus online speech. The Source for Recent Developments in School Law.

http://legalclips.nsba.org/2011/06/15/federal-
appellate-court-issued-en-banc-decision-that-
students-off-campus-online-speech-is-not-properly-
subject-to-regulation-by-pennsylvania-school-
district/:

Third Circuit Sides with Students in Online Speech Fight Landmark Rulings Leave Some Questions Unanswered

www.splc.org/news/newsflash.asp?id=2238

Facts and Case Summary: Morse v. Frederick

www.uscourts.gov/educational-resources/get-
involved/constitution-activities/first-amendment/free-
speech-school-conduct/facts-case-summary.aspx

Supreme Court Will Not Hear Off-Campus Speech Cases

www.splc.org/news/newsflash.asp?id=2315

Selected, Edited, and with Issue Framing Material by:
Glenn L. Koonce, *Regent University*

ISSUE

Can the Common Core State Standards Be Successful?

YES: William H. Schmidt and Nathan A. Burroughs, from "How the Common Core Boosts Quality and Equality," *Educational Leadership* (2012/2013)

NO: Tom Loveless, from "The Common Core Initiative: What Are the Chances of Success?" *Educational Leadership* (2012/2013)

Learning Outcomes

After reading this issue, you will be able to:

- Identify two insistent problems in U.S. education and how the Common Core State Standards (CCSS) may be related to the problem.
- Distinguish between what the new CCSS standards can and cannot do to improve our overall national education system.
- Critique the downfalls of moving forward in support of the CCSS.
- Differentiate between standards and curriculum.
- Outline the CCSS movement in the United States.

ISSUE SUMMARY

YES: With a focus on the new math standards, Michigan State University researchers William Schmidt and Nathan Burroughs indicate the Common Core State Standards will address two tenacious problems in U.S. education: the mediocrity quality of mathematics learning and unequal opportunity in U.S. schools.

NO: Tom Loveless, a senior fellow at the Brookings Institute, takes the position that chances for the Common Core Standards to be successful are "slim at best" when compared to the claims on how well similar policies have worked in the past.

Expectations for all students to perform at a high level and be prepared for college and career readiness was reset this past fall with the arrival of the new Common Core State Standards (CCSS) to the 2013–2014 academic school year. Some feel it is the biggest challenge that teachers will face during the year. The CCSS is a voluntary state led effort to raise standards in which the U.S. Department of Education has provided some support. Five states have not yet adopted the CCSS: Alaska, Nebraska, Minnesota (English standards only), Texas, and Virginia. For

the remaining 45 states, District of Columbia, four territories, and the Department of Defense Education Activity, students Kindergarten through 12th grade in English, language arts and mathematics, are being taught the skills and knowledge necessary to collaborate and compete with their peers around the world. Social studies and science standards are currently being considered as part of the Common Core.

Educators and researchers worked together framing the Common Core standards, linking them with what colleges and employers want young people to know. With a better understanding from fewer, clearer, and higher standards, students and their families can track progress better. Parents could identify earlier, with their children, when and where problems may exist, such as in elementary school rather than in middle or even high school. This would allow for more timely intervention allowing the child to perform better. The same logic applies to the child's teacher as each child/student matriculate from grade to grade and school to school.

Prior to the CCSS each state had its own standards. Now CCSS enable collaboration between states on a range of tools and policies. According to corestandards.org (2013) these tools and policies include:

the development of textbooks, digital media, and other teaching materials aligned to the standards;

the development and implementation of common comprehensive assessment systems to measure student performance annually that will replace existing state testing systems; and

changes needed to help support educators and schools in teaching to the new standards.

Although the CCSS have many proponents, there are certainly those who disagree, even some naysayers. The naysayers say standards haven't worked in the past; they won't work in the future. They also indicate that having lofty standards is much easier than making them actually work. Two of the greatest needs for the CCSS to be successful are resources that are the least available: high quality training and teacher time to receive training (Ripley, 2013). Even within the ranks of those states that have already adopted the CCSS, there are potential push backs. Politics have been part of the controversy ensuring some resistance. A few states (Kentucky and Hawaii) adopted the standards before they were finalized causing issues. There was heated debate in Massachusetts considered by many as having the highest standards in the country. States that have refused to adopt the CCSS are relying on their own standards resulting in political debates in some of these states.

According to two national polls (Maxwell, 2013) designed to capture the view of K-12 education by the American public, the Common Core is a puzzle and the majority of those surveyed are clueless concerning the CCSS. An even murkier issue in the polls was standardized testing. There is opinion, depending on how the question was posed, that trounces testing and indicates people are fed up with it because testing has not led to better schools. Other opinions show testing is essential for knowing how well students are progressing. The poll's final tally reveals that there are issues that need attention. The Common Core is certainly one of them.

As previously indicated, the other side of standards is assessment (testing). The administration of tests, based on CCSS, will begin implementation in the 2014–2015 academic school year. The debate escalates again where there is discussion in some states regarding the use of student assessment outcomes that are linked to teacher evaluation and in some cases salary (Merit pay). If parents are clueless to the CCSS, how would they be able to reflect on this issue? The same would be true of untrained school leaders and for the teachers themselves.

The Association for Supervision and Curriculum Development (ASCD) (Association for Curriculum and Development, 2013) explored myths and fact about the CCSS. One big myth is that the CCSS were developed by the federal government when in fact they were spearheaded by the nation's governors and state education commissioners collaborating with educators, subject matter experts, and researchers. Neither did the federal government require states to adopt the CCSS because adoption is voluntary. The federal government does become involved by requiring states to adopt college- and career-ready standards in order to receive waivers from No Child Left Behind requirements. Additionally, the federal government's Race to the Top grant competition allows applicants (states) additional points for adopting college- and career-ready standards.

The fact that the CCSS is not a curriculum that dictates what and how every educator must teach eliminates another myth. The standards are to be used as a basis for districts and schools to develop their own curricula including course content, instructional strategies, and learning activities.

A final myth explored by ASCD was that the student test scores will sharply decrease on the CCSS test as opposed to current state assessments. The fact is that students will be taking newly designed tests based on the new standards. These assessments are currently designed and will require a new benchmark for student success.

State standards are not new, having been driven by textbook publishers used in series dispersed throughout all of the states for decades. We look to the new CCSS to transform education but at what financial price for design and assessment and at what price for implementation? These standards have polarized policy makers, educators, and scholars alike. Will we embrace them one year and dump them the next?

In the selections that follow Schmidt and Burroughs focus mainly on math standards, but their larger picture addresses how the CCSS will tackle the mediocrity quality and unequal opportunity in our schools. Tom Loveless takes the position that chances for the CCSS to be successful are "slim at best."

References

Association for Curriculum and Development, ASCD Policy Points: Common Core State Standards (2013). Retrieved from www.ascd.org/common-core/core-connection/10-10-13-debunking-common-core-myths.aspx

Common Core Standards Initiative. (2013) Retrieved from www.corestandards.org/

L. Maxwell, "Common Core: A Puzzle to Public." *Education Week* (vol. 33, no. 2, 2013).

A. Ripley, "The Smart Set: What happens when millions of kids are asked to master fewer things more deeply?" *Time* (vol. 182, no.14, 2013).

YES

William H. Schmidt and Nathan A. Burroughs

How the Common Core Boosts Quality and Equality

The Common Core State Standards Address Two Tenacious Problems in U.S. Education.

The adoption of the Common Core State Standards by 46 states and the District of Columbia represents a dramatic departure in U.S. education. In the past, national efforts to improve education have been directed by the federal government and have emphasized resources or organizational structure. In contrast, the Common Core State Standards in math and language arts were developed under the leadership of state governments to improve the *content* of instruction.

A tremendous commitment of time, money, and human resources has gone into creating the new standards—and even more will go into implementing them. If the ambitions of the Common Core initiative are realized, for the first time almost every public school student in the United States will be exposed to roughly the same content, especially in grades 1–8.

All of which raises the question, Is all this effort worth it? In the case of mathematics, we think the answer is *yes* because the new math standards will address two long-standing problems in U.S. education: the mediocre quality of mathematics learning and unequal opportunity in U.S. schools. In short, the Common Core State Standards have the potential to improve both quality and equality in mathematics education.

The Quality Issue

Extensive evidence points to the inadequacy of mathematics education in the United States. Only 26 percent of U.S. 12th graders reach the threshold of proficiency in math on the National Assessment of Educational Progress (National Center for Education Statistics, 2010). Moreover, U.S. 8th graders posted a mediocre performance on the 2007 Trends in International Mathematics and Science

Study (Gonzales et al., 2008) and scored below average on the 2009 Programme for International Assessment (Fleischman, Hopstock, Pelczar, & Shelley, 2010). The need to improve mathematics learning in the United States has been a primary driver of education reform efforts, including the Common Core initiative.

What New Research Shows

Although one can't say for certain what the effects of any policy will be, empirical research suggests reasons for optimism regarding the Common Core standards. A recent study examined the likelihood that the new mathematics standards would improve student achievement (Schmidt & Houang, 2012). This study involved (1) comparing the Common Core State Standards in mathematics with the mathematics standards of the countries with the highest mathematics achievement on international assessments, (2) estimating how close each state's previous math standards were to the Common Core standards, and (3) exploring whether states with standards more like the Common Core standards did better on the 2009 National Assessment of Educational Progress (NAEP) in 8th grade mathematics.

The Trends in International Mathematics and Science Study (TIMSS) demonstrated that the mathematics standards of the world's highest-achieving nations have three key characteristics: rigor, focus, and coherence. A *rigorous* curriculum covers topics at the appropriate grade level; a *focused* curriculum concentrates on a few key topics at a time; and a *coherent* curriculum adheres to the underlying logic of mathematics, moving from simple to more complex topics.

After identifying the common characteristics of the standards of those countries that did best on the TIMSS, the study compared the duration and sequence of topic coverage across grades in these "A+" standards with the Common Core State Standards for mathematics. This comparison revealed an overlap of about 90 percent. If the standards of the world's top-achieving nations are any guide, the new math standards are of high quality.

As we might expect, comparing preexisting state mathematics standards with the Common Core standards revealed wide variation in the quality of state standards. Many states will have to undertake major changes in how they're implementing their curriculums if they're to faithfully execute the vision of the Common Core standards. More important, statistical analysis of the relationship between the proximity of a state's standards to the Common Core standards and that state's average performance on the NAEP uncovered a positive relationship between the quality of a state's curriculum standards and that state's 8th grade mathematics performance.

However, some states with high standards that look very similar on paper to the Common Core standards register middling or even low NAEP scores; in contrast, other states with only average standards post higher mathematics scores on NAEP. At first glance, this might suggest that the Common Core State Standards will have little effect on student achievement—that high standards don't ensure high achievement. But such a simplistic comparison of standards to test scores neglects the crucial role of implementation (Schmidt & Houang, in press).

For example, each state has its own standards—but also its own assessments and cut scores. States with low cut scores devalue the worth of what could otherwise be strong standards, implicitly telling schools not to take the standards seriously. Once proficiency cut scores are accounted for, there's a statistically significant and positive relationship between the similarity of state standards to the Common Core State Standards and average student achievement.[1] One of the aims of the common assessments currently under development is to establish a common proficiency cut point across states, which should reduce the likelihood that states will devalue the new standards as many did their previous standards.

The Equality Issue

Much of the debate about the Common Core State Standards has focused on their potential to improve the overall quality of U.S. education. However, we have not paid enough attention to their capacity to ensure greater *equality* in content coverage among students.

We most often equate education inequality with inequality in the resources available to poorer school districts, unequal education outcomes on student assessments, the fact that underprivileged students are most likely to have inexperienced or underqualified teachers, and the fact that children from impoverished or otherwise difficult home lives are much less likely to have the same kind of supports or enrichment opportunities that their luckier peers do. All these facets of inequality are crucial for policymakers to address.

A Focus on Instructional Equality

However, what's lacking in all these discussions is any concern for inequality in *instructional content*. The U.S. education system is rife with curricular inequalities, by which we mean inequalities in the opportunity to learn challenging content (Schmidt & McKnight, 2012). If a student is never exposed to a topic, he or she can hardly be expected to learn it—a problem that's especially acute in mathematics. The mathematical content that students have an opportunity to learn varies wildly across schools, districts, and states.

The continuing variation within states effectively rebuts a common criticism that asserts that because existing state standards have had no discernible effect on student achievement, we shouldn't expect the Common Core standards to have an effect either. This claim seems to assume that the content taught at a particular grade in any given year is essentially the same in any classroom in the state.

But that's not what we find. Rather, what students have a chance to learn will be based in large measure on what community they happen to live in and what school they happen to attend. In fact, the mathematics content offered in low-income districts is more similar to that of low-income districts in other states than to middle- and high-income districts in the same state. Whether the Common Core standards will mitigate these within-state inequalities remains an open question. The seriousness of purpose accompanying the advent of the Common Core movement—with its new assessments, new textbooks, and the sheer national scope of the enterprise—is a hopeful sign. However, success will depend on effective implementation.

A Widespread Problem

When education inequality becomes a subject for public discussion, there's a strong inclination to suppose that inequality is restricted to minority and low-income children. However, data from the Promoting Rigorous Outcomes in Math and Science Education (PROM/SE) project (Schmidt & McKnight, 2012) revealed that the greatest variation in opportunity to learn mathematics content was among *middle-income districts*. There was greater variability in what topics were covered at what grade level among districts that had neither high nor low socioeconomic status (SES) than among the much more homogenous high- and low-SES districts. Inequality of opportunity to learn is a problem for every student, and for the United States as a whole.

The problem of curricular inequality goes much deeper than differences among schools or districts. The greatest source of variation in opportunity to learn mathematics is actually between classrooms (Schmidt & McKnight, 2012). Students living in the same district, attending the same school, and enrolled in the same grade can have very different classroom experiences.

This problem manifests itself in several ways. Often, classes with identical course titles and textbooks have different instructional content. The level of teacher preparation as well as teacher expectations for the student will vary (Cogan, Schmidt, & Wiley, 2001).

There's also the widespread use of tracking, a process by which students are assigned to classrooms on the basis of perceived ability. Once students are assigned to lower tracks, they almost never move up to higher ones (Schiller, Schmidt, Muller, & Houang, 2010).

Despite the fact that tracking has been roundly criticized by many scholars, policymakers, and activists, the practice remains quite common. Surveys of school administrators and teachers conducted as part of the 2011 NAEP (National Center for Education Statistics, 2011) suggest that three-quarters of 8th graders are assigned to mathematics classrooms on the basis of ability. Even more shocking, nearly a third of 4th graders are assigned in this way. Thus, many students have their long-term academic futures determined for them when they are only 9 or 10 years old.

What the New Standards Can Do

The Common Core State Standards for mathematics represent an opportunity to broaden access to rigorous educational content. Having a common set of standards certainly promotes higher-quality textbooks and assessments and makes it easier for students moving between states to fit into their new schools. However, the greater effect of the standards may be that they alter our approach to teaching mathematics.

The new math standards offer the possibility of a common curriculum within states, districts, and schools. The vision of the Common Core initiative is that teachers will cooperate across classrooms and grades in determining how they'll teach math so that there's a clear, logical progression as a student moves through school. If effectively implemented, the new standards could reduce within-state inequalities in content instruction.

The new math standards enable teachers to deepen their teaching. The new focus should shift the teaching of mathematics from a "spiraled curriculum" approach, in which too many topics are shallowly covered year after year, to one in which a few important topics are mastered at each grade level. For example, the Common Core standards call for focused instruction on fractions in grades 3–5 and on linear equations in grade 8. Because teachers will have more time to teach each topic, they should be more able to ensure that their students understand the material instead of having to cling to the vain hope that struggling students will figure things out in later years.

The new math standards discourage tracking. By insisting on common content for all students at each grade level and in every community, the Common Core mathematics standards are also in direct conflict with the concept of tracking. If the new standards were to do no more than sharply reduce this practice, the policy would be well worth the effort.

What the New Standards Don't Do

Support for the new standards cuts across ideological lines, but so does opposition. In evaluating potential benefits, it's useful to clarify what the standards don't do.

The new math standards don't hold teachers responsible for students' poor math performance. The fact that the greatest source of variation in opportunity to learn is in the classroom doesn't mean that teachers are to blame for curricular inequality. Currently, teachers are deluged with competing signals about what content to teach. State standards, state assessments, and textbooks provide conflicting guidance; and teachers receive neither the preparation nor the support they require to make effective curricular decisions. Easing this situation is one of the key objectives of the Common Core movement.

The new math standards don't end the autonomy of local schools or teachers. Curriculum is only one component of schooling, defining *what* schools should teach, not *how*. Under the present system, teachers and school districts are expected to decide both the content of instruction and the best means for helping students learn that content (along with many administrative and community responsibilities). Instead of teachers having to spend time inventing which content to teach and in what sequence, the new standards help schools and teachers focus their efforts on their core competencies and devise the best means for helping students achieve the standards.

The new math standards are not part of "market-based" education reform. Some advocates of the Common Core standards also support a range of other education reform policies, such as No Child Left Behind, merit pay, and the use of value-added models to assess teacher performance. Although there's no real inconsistency between such reforms and the Common Core State Standards, it would be a mistake to lump them together. The aim of the Common Core initiative is not to introduce market mechanisms in education but to institute high-quality standards that promote equality of opportunity to learn for all students.

The Road Ahead

A recent survey conducted on behalf of the Center for the Study of Curriculum at Michigan State University reveals both positive signs and potential pitfalls in efforts to realize the new standards.

Positive Signs

In our representative sample of more than 12,000 mathematics teachers in the 40 states that had adopted the new math standards as of January 2011, more than 90 percent said they liked the idea of having Common Core State Standards for mathematics because they provide "a consistent, clear understanding of what students are expected to learn" and "a high-quality education to our children." After reading a sample of the standards for the grades they teach, virtually 100 percent of the teachers said they would teach the new math standards. The challenges teachers identified differed little from those that educators so often express with any curriculum—lack of supporting curriculum materials and lack of parental support.

Luckily, parental support may not be an obstacle to implementing the Common Core standards. In our representative sample of more than 6,000 parents of K–8 students, most viewed math as the most important subject for their children, and nearly 70 percent thought that the Common Core State Standards for mathematics were a good idea. More than 90 percent endorsed the idea that math is important for their children's success and that their children should take math every school year, including all four years in high school.

Potential Pitfalls

The survey also suggested areas of concern. Teachers may not have a clear grasp of what's in the new math standards or how the standards differ from the status quo. Most teachers (80 percent) thought that the new standards were "pretty much the same" as previous standards, a belief that research (Schmidt & Houang, in press) shows

to be grossly mistaken. Also, many teachers believe that the new standards may require them to add new topics to their current math curriculum. Rather, the Common Core standards call for greater focus on fewer topics at each grade level.

To effectively implement the Common Core State Standards for Mathematics, teachers are going to have to be much better prepared. Fewer than half of elementary teachers we surveyed felt well prepared to teach Common Core math topics at their grade level, compared with 60 percent of middle school teachers and 70 percent of high school mathematics teachers. As for parents, those we asked still knew very little about the Common Core standards (even whether their state has adopted the standards). Moreover, a distressingly large percentage of parents (36–38 percent) believed that some children just can't "get" mathematics.

Cautious Optimism

Inadequate teacher preparation, lack of parent involvement, and insufficient resources and planning could all derail implementation efforts. Realizing the vision of the standards represents a tremendous challenge, but the potential benefits—higher mathematics achievement and greater equality of education opportunity—make it well worth the effort.

References

Cogan, L. S., Schmidt, W. H., & Wiley, D. E. (2001). Who takes what mathematics and in which track? Using TIMSS to characterize U.S. students' eighth grade mathematics learning opportunities. *Educational Evaluation and Policy Analysis, 23*(4), 323–341.

Fleischman, H. L., Hopstock, P. J., Pelczar, M. P., & Shelley, B. E. (2010). *Highlights from PISA 2009: Performance of U.S. 15-year-old students in reading, mathematics, and science literacy in an international context* (NCES 2011–004). Washington, DC: U.S. Department of Education.

Gonzales, P., Williams, T., Jocelyn, L., Roey, S., Kastberg, D., & Brenwald, S. (2008). *Highlights from TIMSS 2007: Mathematics and science achievement of U.S. fourth- and eighth-grade students in an international context* (NCES 2009–001Revised). Washington, DC: U.S. Department of Education.

National Center for Education Statistics. (2010). *The nation's report card: Grade 12 reading and mathematics 2009 national and pilot state results* (NCES 2011–455). Washington, DC: Institute of Education Sciences, U.S. Department of Education.

National Center for Education Statistics. (2011). *Percentages for mathematics, grade 8, by 8th grade assigned to math by ability [C0728011], year and jurisdiction: 2011; Percentages for mathematics, grade 4, by 4th grade assigned to math by ability [C052001], year and jurisdiction: 2011.* Data retrieved from the NAEP Data Explorer at http://nces.ed.gov/nationsreportcard/naepdata/dataset.aspx

Schiller, K. S., Schmidt, W. H., Muller, C., & Houang, R. T. (2010). Hidden disparities: How courses and curricula shape opportunities in mathematics during high school. *Equity and Excellence in Education, 43*(4), 414–433.

Schmidt, W. H., & Houang, R. T. (in press). Curricular coherence and the Common Core State Standards for Mathematics. *Educational Researcher.*

Schmidt, W. H., & McKnight, C. (2012). *Inequality for all: The challenge of unequal opportunity in American schools.* New York: Teachers College Press.

WILLIAM H. SCHMIDT is a distinguished professor at Michigan State University.

NATHAN A. BURROUGHS is research associate at the Center for the Study of Curriculum at Michigan State University.

Tom Loveless

The Common Core Initiative: What Are the Chances of Success?

The Chances are Slim at Best—and Here's Why.

Advocates of the Common Core State Standards are hopeful. They believe the standards offer a historic opportunity to boost the overall quality of U.S. education.

Hope is important in policy debates, but there's also a role for skepticism. The Common Core State Standards are not the first national education initiative to be launched with the anticipation of success. Nor is it the first time policymakers have called on education standards to guide us toward better schools.

Looking into the Claims

In a recent study (Loveless, 2012), I tried to estimate the probability that the Common Core standards will produce more learning. The study started with the assumption that a good way to predict the future effects of any policy is to examine how well similar policies have worked in the past—in this case, by examining the past effects of state education standards. The study conducted three statistical investigations using state data from the reading and math portions of the National Assessment of Educational Progress (NAEP) at both 4th and 8th grades.

The first investigation looked at whether the quality of state standards is related to past gains in student achievement. It turns out it isn't. States with poor standards have made NAEP gains comparable to states with excellent standards.

A second investigation looked at whether the levels at which states set past proficiency standards made a difference in achievement. They don't. States with low bars for student proficiency posted similar NAEP scores as those with high bars.[1]

Finally, the third analysis looked at variation in achievement. A key objective of the new standards is to reduce glaring inequalities. This doesn't mean to perfectly equalize all learning, of course. However, striving to ensure that all students possess the knowledge and skills necessary for college or careers means, statistically speaking, that a reduction in achievement variation should occur.

So how much reduction can we expect? The Common Core standards will surely not affect variation inside each individual state. Schools and districts in every state have been operating under common standards for years. The real opportunity that the initiative presents is harmonizing differences in standards among states.

How much variation on NAEP achievement is there among states? Not much. In fact, within-state variation on NAEP is four to five times greater than variation among states. Put another way, the NAEP score gap between Massachusetts and Mississippi, one of the widest between any two states, exists among different schools and districts in *every* state. Unless the Common Core standards possess some unknown power that previous standards didn't possess, that variation will go untouched.

On the basis of these findings, the most reasonable prediction is that the Common Core initiative will have little to no effect on student achievement.

How might it defy this prediction and prove successful? Advocates of the initiative are counting on two mechanisms—high-quality professional development and improvements in curriculum—to overcome the many obstacles that lie ahead.

The Problem with Professional Development

So what does high-quality professional development look like? The research on the topic is limited, producing suggestive characteristics rather than definitive prescriptions.

Limited Potential for Strong Effects

A white paper on teacher quality from the National Academy of Education (Wilson, 2009) notes that several studies have identified promising features of effective professional development. These features include a focus on subject-matter knowledge; ample time (more than 40 hours per program) with a year or more of follow-up; clear linkages to teachers' existing knowledge and skills; training that actively engages teachers; and training teams of teachers from the same school. A meta-analysis by the Council of Chief State School Officers (Blank & de las Alas, 2009) endorses a similar set of characteristics, although the best programs in this study were longer, delivering 100 hours or more of training.

Both reports note the limitations of professional development research. None of the studies that meet commonly recognized criteria for good evaluations involve middle or high school teachers, only elementary teachers. Also, the list of promising features comes from studies of disparate programs. Their effectiveness when combined into a large-scale, comprehensive program is unknown.

The only randomized field trial—the gold standard of program evaluation—of a professional development program embodying many of the recommended features produced disappointing results (Garet et al., 2008). Participants received training on early reading instruction in content-focused summer institutes, with extensive follow-up during the school year. Teachers' knowledge increased and their pedagogy changed, but there was no improvement in student achievement. The National Academy of Education report (Wilson, 2009) observes that professional development programs with strong effects have been associated with small projects, concluding that "the average teacher has a minimal chance of experiencing high-quality professional development targeted to the subjects, grades, and students he or she teaches" (p. 6).

A Word About External Assessments

To evaluate whether professional development programs had an effect on student achievement, the Council of Chief State School Officers' meta-analysis includes some studies that look at assessments specifically designed by the programs themselves as well as studies that use national, state, and local assessments to judge program effectiveness. The latter group is more relevant to the Common Core standards because the success or failure of the programs depended on how much students learned on external assessments, the type of assessments the Common Core initiative will use.

These evaluations detected educationally insignificant, even trivial, effect sizes: .17 for national norm-referenced tests, .01 for statewide assessments, and .05 for studies that used local achievement tests (Blank & de las Alas, 2009). If professional development typically yields such small effects, then expectations that it will have a significant impact in the context of the new standards are probably unwarranted.

There's an important lesson here for educators who, in coming years, will be bombarded with tales of wonderful professional development tied to the Common Core standards. Be on guard. In an extensive Institute for Education Sciences review of 1,300 studies of professional development (Yoon, Duncan, Lee, Scarloss, & Shapley, 2007), the reviewers cautioned.

The limited number of studies and the variability in their professional development approaches preclude any conclusions about the effectiveness of specific professional development programs or about the effectiveness of professional development by form, content, and intensity (p. 14).

A "Better" Curriculum—But Which One?

The Common Core website makes a point of differentiating between standards and curriculum. The page "Myths vs. Facts" declares, The Standards are not a curriculum. They are a clear set of shared goals and expectations for what knowledge and skills will help our students succeed. Local teachers, principals, superintendents, and others will decide *how* the standards are to be met. Teachers will continue to devise lesson plans and tailor instruction to the individual needs of the students in their classrooms. (National Governors Association Center for Best Practices & Council of Chief State School Officers, 2012)

The curriculum that fleshes out the new standards will, in the end, determine how teachers, parents, and students actually experience the standards. What will that curriculum contain? Given that curricular content is subject to local discretion, how broad are the boundaries for those choices?

Core Knowledge Vs. Partnership for 21st Century Skills

Consider two dramatically different views of curriculum, one supported by the Core Knowledge Foundation and the other by the Partnership for 21st Century Skills. Their philosophies are diametrically opposed, yet both organizations are convinced that the Common Core State Standards embrace their point of view.

Core Knowledge, the brainchild of E. D. Hirsch, holds that content knowledge is king. The author of the Core Knowledge blog, Robert Pondiscio (2012), lauds the Common Core initiative for reminding us "to engage children not just with rote literacy skills work and process writing, but also, and especially, with real content—rich, deep, broad knowledge about the world in which they live." For example, on the Core Knowledge website, model lessons for 8th grade language arts include the study of Greek and Latin root words; William Shakespeare's *Twelfth Night*; Pearl S. Buck's *The Good Earth* (supplemented by a research paper on Chinese culture); and Maya Angelou's *I Know Why the Caged Bird Sings*. The key to becoming a good reader is content knowledge, Pondiscio argues, and he asks, "Yet how many times have we heard it said that we need to deemphasize teaching 'mere facts' and focus on skills like critical thinking, creativity, and problem solving?"

The Partnership for 21st Century Skills promotes exactly what Pondiscio deplores. The partnership has developed a framework of skills it believes are essential to good schooling, including life and career skills; information, media, and technology skills; and what it calls the 4Cs (critical thinking, communication, collaboration, and creativity). The partnership has also published a P21 Common Core Toolkit (Magner, Soulé, & Wesolowski, 2011), which shows how the Common Core initiative and the partnership's framework are aligned. The toolkit also offers vignettes ("lesson starters") to illustrate how the Common Core standards integrate with the partnership's framework.

For example, in contrast with Core Knowledge's 8th grade lesson, an 8th grade English language arts lesson aligned to the partnership's framework proceeds as follows:

After completing a literature circle unit of teen problem novels, students brainstorm a list of significant social, emotional, or health issues that teens face today. Working in groups, students research one issue and create a public service announcement on a closed YouTube channel (viewable only by students in the class) to persuade their peers about one action they should take regarding the issue. Students will select and use references from literary readings (e.g., citing how a particular novel presents the issue) as well as research from nonfiction sources to illustrate major points (Partnership for 21st Century Skills, 2008, p. 8).

This lesson would never occur in a Core Knowledge classroom. The point here is not to settle the argument between Core Knowledge and the Partnership for 21st Century Skills. Rather, it's to illustrate the elasticity of the educational philosophy underpinning the Common Core State Standards. Philosophical ambiguity may be smart politically because it allows for a wide range of supporters—a "big tent" strategy. But if two organizations with such starkly contrasting points of view both see the standards as compatible with their definition of an ideal curriculum, then any guidance about what to teach in local schools is broad indeed.

The Curriculum Conundrum

How will educators make curricular decisions? Hopefully, the effectiveness of curricular materials and programs will factor prominently.

Unfortunately, the research on effective curriculum is as thin as the research on effective professional development. As my Brookings colleagues document in a recent report, educators are "choosing blindly" when making curriculum decisions. Instructional programs can differ dramatically in their effectiveness (Chingos & Whitehurst, 2012).

Mathematica Policy Research conducted a randomized field trial of four primary-grade math textbooks and found huge differences between the most and least effective (Agodini, Harris, Thomas, Murphy, & Gallagher, 2010). Such high-quality studies are rare, and more important, even the most robust studies cannot do the impossible—provide advice on how to choose effective materials from a sea of candidates that have never been rigorously evaluated in the first place.

So what kind of information will inform the selection of local curriculum? Note that the publishers of the four math textbooks just mentioned—both effective and ineffective alike—all advertise that their texts are now aligned with the Common Core standards. As Chingos and Whitehurst (2012) observe,

Publishers of instructional materials are lining up to declare the alignment of their materials with the Common Core standards using the most superficial of definitions. The Common Core standards will only have a chance of raising student achievement if they are implemented with high-quality materials, but there is currently no basis to measure the quality of materials. (p. 1)

Back to Where We Started?

The Common Core State Standards have been adopted by 46 states and the District of Columbia. They enjoy a huge following of well-wishers and supporters who are optimistic that the standards will boost achievement in U.S. schools. Setting aside the cheerleading and fond hopes, what are the real chances of success?

The most reasonable prediction is that the Common Core initiative will have little to no effect on student achievement. Moreover, on the basis of current research, high-quality professional development and "excellent" curricular materials are also unlikely to boost the Common Core standards' slim chances of success.

References

Agodini, R., Harris, B., Thomas, M., Murphy, R., & Gallagher, L. (2010). *Achievement effects of four early elementary school math curricula: Findings for first and second graders*. Princeton, NJ: Mathematica Policy Research.

Blank, R. K., & de las Alas, N. (2009). *Effects of teacher professional development on gains in student achievement*. Washington, DC: Council of Chief State School Officers.

Chingos, M. M., & Whitehurst, G. J. (2012). *Choosing blindly: Instructional materials, teacher effectiveness, and the Common Core*. Washington, DC: Brookings Institution. Retrieved from www.brookings.edu/research/reports/2012/04/10-curriculum-chingos-whitehurst

Garet, M. S., Cronen, S., Eaton, M., Kurki, A., Ledwig, M., Jones, W., et al. (2008). *The impact of two professional development interventions on early reading instruction and achievement*. Washington, DC: Institute of Education Sciences.

Loveless, T. (2012). *The 2012 Brown Center report on American education: How well are American students learning?* Washington, DC: Brookings Institution. Retrieved from www.brookings.edu/~/media/research/files/reports/2012/2/brown%20center/0216_brown_education_loveless.pdf

Magner, T., Soulé, H., & Wesolowski, K. (2011). *P21 Common Core toolkit: A guide to aligning the Common Core State Standards with the Framework for 21st Century Skills*. Washington, DC: Partnership for 21st Century Skills. Retrieved from www.p21.org/storage/documents/P21CommonCoreToolkit.pdf.

National Governors Association Center for Best Practices & Council of Chief State School Officers. (2012). *Myths vs. Facts*. Washington, DC: Authors. Retrieved from www.corestandards.org/about-the-standards/myths-vs-facts

Partnership for 21st Century Skills. (2008). *21st century skills map*. Tucson, AZ: Author. Retrieved from www.p21.org/storage/documents/21st_century_skills_english_map.pdf

Pondiscio, R. (2012, June 14). Nobody loves standards (and that's OK) [blog post]. Retrieved from *Common Core Watch* at www.edexcellence.net/commentary/education-gadfly-daily/common-core-watch/2012/nobody-loves-standards-and-thats-ok.html

Wilson, S. (Ed., 2009). *Teacher quality* (Education policy white paper). Washington, DC: National Academy of Education. Retrieved from http://naeducation.org/Teacher_Quality_White_Paper.pdf

Yoon, K., Duncan, T., Lee, S., Scarloss, B., & Shapley, K. (2007). *Reviewing the evidence on how teacher professional development affects student achievement* (Issues & Answers Report, REL 2007–No. 033). Washington, DC: Regional Educational Laboratory Southwest. Retrieved from http://ies.ed.gov/ncee/edlabs/regions/southwest/pdf/REL_2007033.pdf

Note

1. States that raised the bar from 2005 to 2009 did show an increase in 4th grade NAEP scores, but the correlation is weak, it does not appear in 8th grade, and the direction of causality is unclear. Rather than loftier expectations driving achievement gains, states may have raised the bar for proficiency because of rising achievement.

TOM LOVELESS is a senior fellow in governance studies at the Brookings Institution, Washington, D.C.

EXPLORING THE ISSUE

Can the Common Core State Standards Be Successful?

Critical Thinking and Reflection

1. Because the Common Sore State Standards (CCSS) are the same for each state participating, should each state also have common proficiency cut scores and common assessments (common assessments are projected in the 2014–2015 school term)?
2. Will states decide that where a student lives along with their socioeconomic factors make a difference in what is being taught?
3. Is there enough quantitative and qualitative research to support the common core initiative?
4. Will the CCSS be the answer to improving the overall quality of U.S. Education.?
5. What is your state's current policy and regulations regarding the CCSS?

Is There Common Ground?

It is a turbulent time for education and both proponents and skeptics are flexing their muscles in the Common Core State Standards (CCSS) debate. The push for these standards is not new. Policy makers, educators, parents, and the public have discussed their existence since President Eisenhower's vision of creating national goals where American students would be more competitive against other nations. The 1983 report, *A Nation at Risk*, raised a red flag noting how far American students had fallen behind other nations and the need to raise standards.

Collaboration on the assessments that allow for state by state comparison of student achievement, the National Assessment of Educational Progress (NAEP) was undertaken by President Reagan and Senator Edward Kennedy in 1988. In 1989, President H.W. Bush was involved in organizations representing the core subjects beginning to develop their own voluntary standards (i.e., The National Council of Teachers of Mathematics). The NAEP was expanded under the Clinton Administration to voluntary national testing in grades four and eight in reading and math. With mixed support and mixed results the No Child Left Behind Act (NCLB) was signed into law by President G. W. Bush in 2001 making assessment mandatory (Sloan, 2012).

Policymakers, educators, and researchers working together have shown there has been much common ground in the past regarding the development of standards in the United States. The "unevenness" of NCLB standards and failure to reauthorize them has provided impetus for the Common Core movement. The fact that the nation had 50 different standards in 50 different states

had lowered the bar in student achievement in their view of many individuals. Many asked themselves the question, "What Now?" The "What Now?" has moved the focus to the Common Core National Standards.

Reference

Sloan, W. "Coming to Terms with Common Core Standards." *ASCD Info Brief* (2012). Retrieved from www.ascd.org/publications/newsletters/policy-priorities/vol16/issue4/toc.aspx

Additional Resources

L. Calkins, M. Ehrenworth & C. Lehman, *Pathways to the Common Core: Accelerating Achievement* (Heinemann, 2012).

J. Kendall, *Understanding Common Core State Standards* (Mid-Continental Research Laboratory, 2011).

R. Marzano, D. Yanoski, J. Hoegh & J. Simms, *Using Common Core Standards to Enhance Classroom Instruction & Assessment* (Mazano Research Laboratory, 2013).

D. Reeves, *Navigating Implementation of the Common Core State Standards* (National Book Network, 2012).

H. Silver, R. Dewing & M. Perini, *The Core Six: Essential Strategies for Achieving Excellence with the Common Core* (Association for Curriculum and Development, 2013).

Internet References . . .

Florida School Board Ditches Common Core Reading Suggestions

http://blogs.edweek.org/edweek/state_
edwatch/2013/10/florida_school_board_ditches_
common-core_reading_suggestions.html

Resources for Understanding the Common Core State Standards

www.edutopia.org/common-core-state-standards-
resources

Achieve the Core

www.achievethecore.org/

Experts Speaks Against the Common Core at Wisconsin hearing

http://watchdog.org/111254/wr-common-core-expert-
speaks-out/

Implementing the Common Core State Standards: The Role of the School Counselor

www.achieve.org/publications/implementing-
common-core-state-standards-role-school-
counselor-action-brief

Selected, Edited, and with Issue Framing Material by:
Glenn L. Koonce, *Regent University*

ISSUE

Can Failing Schools Be Turned Around?

YES: Roxanne Garza and Melissa Tooley, from "Freeing Up School Turnaround Leaders," *National Association of State Boards of Education* (2018)

NO: Laura Hoxworth, from "5 Myths That Inhibit School Turnaround," *UVA Today* (2017)

Learning Outcomes

After reading this issue, you will be able to:

- Compare and contrast failing schools that struggle with failing schools that "turn around."
- Connect the No Child Left Behind (NCLB) mandates with failing schools.
- Analyze the rationale for success in schools that have been "turned around."
- Explore the Every Student Succeeds Act (ESSA) and turnaround requirements/regulations.
- Understand why the "fixation" with "fix it" efforts for struggling schools has been misguided.

ISSUE SUMMARY

YES: Policy Analyst and Director of pre-K–12 Educator Quality with the Education Policy Program at New America, Roxanne Garza and Melissa Tooley, author of *From Frenzied to Focused: How School Staffing Models Can Support Principals in Instructional Leadership*, discuss how three districts divvy up principals' duties so they can devote time to instructional leadership.

NO: Media contact, Laura Hoxworth interviews Coby Meyer, research associate professor at the University of Virginia and co-editor Marlene Darwin of the American Institutes for Research advocate addressing in their book, *Enduring Myths That Inhibit School Turnaround*, the myths that inhibit school turnaround, so that policy makers and school leaders can address them head-on.

The United States has thousands of chronically underperforming schools that are looked upon as potential sites for using a turnaround strategy to foster improvement. "Turnaround is a dramatic and comprehensive intervention in a low-performing school that (a) produces significant gains in achievement within two years and (b) readies the school for the longer process of transformation into a high performance organization" (Kutash, Nico, Gorin, Rahmatulla, & Tallant, 2010, p. 1). The concept of turning a school around from low performing to high performing got its start in the early 2000s as the No Child Left Behind

(NCLB) policies demanded accountability for improving student standardized test scores. The turnaround field has grown rapidly since then and reformers have raised awareness and provided new strategies to intervene effectively to raise test scores in troubled schools. The major focus has been on continuous improvement noted as improvement in average yearly progress the measure by which schools, districts, and states are held accountable for student performance under NCLB. The most effective turnaround efforts have involved multiple actors who collaborate in spreading effective practices, designing successful policy, building capacity, and working to ensure sustainability.

Prevalent for some time now are the four turnaround models required by the federal government for school districts to follow:

- "Turnarounds: replace the principal, rehire no more than 50 percent of the staff, and grant the principal sufficient operational flexibility (including in staffing, calendars, schedules, and budgeting) to implement fully a comprehensive approach that substantially improves student outcomes.
- Restarts. transfer control of, or close and reopen a school under a school operator that has been selected through a rigorous review process.
- School Closures: close the school and enrol students in higher achieving schools within the district.
- Transformations: replace the principal, take steps to increase teacher and school leader effectiveness, institute comprehensive instructional reforms, increase learning time, create community-oriented schools, and provide operational flexibility and sustained support. Significant debate surrounds the models" (Kutash et al., 2010, p. 5).

Many educators and turnaround specialist do not want poverty to be an excuse for student failure in school, but poverty imposes a tremendous challenge to countless students who appear at the schoolhouse every day. The question of how to best serve children of poverty has been wrestled with for decades and has become even more crucial during the long running policies associated with the NCLB. The NCLB with its focus on test-performance improvement has met with a good deal of negative reaction from frontline educators and academic theorists alike. Richard A. Gibboney, in his article "Why an Undemocratic Capitalism Has Brought Public Education to Its Knees: A Manifesto," Phi Delta Kappan (2008), put it this way: "Rather than support policies designed to reduce poverty and its toxic effects on the ability of children to succeed in school, our lawmakers are pursuing the misbegotten path of penalizing schools in poverty-stricken cities and rural areas for their failure to work educational miracles." Richard Rothstein poses the question "Whose Problem Is Poverty?" in Educational Leadership (2008), offering an inventory of deficits experienced by the poor, including a lack of health care, more lead poisoning, iron-deficiency anemia, family instability, more exposure to crime and drugs, fewer positive role models, and less exposure to culturally uplifting experiences.

Katherine Bradley, president of the CityBridge Foundation in Washington, DC, has stated that turning around chronically low-performing, high-poverty schools is the grittiest task that educators face. While the search is on to find a successful turnaround formula, Bradley, in a Washington Post (August 7, 2011) piece, expresses concern over a growing sentiment in favor of the "highly disruptive strategy of school closure and restart." Under NCLB policies, failing schools face the possibilities of "restructuring" whereby half or more of the teachers may be fired or a complete school shutdown after which the state may assume management or a replacement charter school may be authorized. In a June 29, 2010 opinion expressed on AOL News.com, Diane Ravitch pleaded "Don't Close Schools, Fix Them." She suggested that "every state should enlist a team of evaluators to visit every struggling school, document its problems, make recommendations, and stay involved to make sure that the school gets the resources it needs to improve." Ravitch has concluded that "it may take courage to close schools, but it takes, experience, wisdom, and persistence—as well as courage—to improve them and to strengthen families and communities." An elaboration of these views can be found in her Summer 2010 American Educator article entitled "In Need of a Renaissance: Real Reform Will Renew, Not Abandon, Our Neighbourhood Schools."

Andy Smarick, former COO of the National Alliance for Public Charter Schools, has been among the leaders of the movement to develop a new type of system for urban public education, a system of charter schools. In "Wave of the Future" (Education Next, 2008), he admits that charter supporters, a "motley crew of civil rights activists, free market economists, career public school educators, and voucher proponents," have yet to fashion a consistent vision. Some states have imposed caps on charter expansion and in some districts funding has been unequal. Often school boards, teachers unions, and school administrators have been antagonistic, but in some quarters, collaborative relationships have emerged.

Advocates of internally turning around troubled schools, Deborah Meier, Laura Pappano, Karin Chenoweth, Katherine Bradley, Ruby Payne, and Pamela Cantor, among others, seem to agree on many of the guidelines for resuscitating failing schools, namely staff self-assessment, teacher collaboration replacing isolation, community building, and serious in-service training. Karin Chenoweth's books, It's Being Done: Academic Success in Unexpected Schools (2007) and How It's Being Done (2009), provided a wealth of examples of regular neighborhood schools that did whatever it took to dramatically elevate student morale and achievement levels without resorting to magnet programs, charters, or outside management. Chenoweth's profiles revealed a pattern of high expectations for both teachers and students, wise use of time (with extra time devoted to low-performing students), and continual reexamination of practices, all occurring in an atmosphere of respect.

The YES and NO selections for this issue pit researchers Roxanne Garza and Melissa Tooley against Laura Hoxworth in the search for the best way to deal with failing schools and the turnaround strategy.

YES

Roxanne Garza and Melissa Tooley

Freeing Up School Turnaround Leaders

Three districts allow for divvying up duties so principals can focus on instructional leadership.

School leadership is a key factor in school turnarounds.[1] The general prescription for what school leaders should do tends to be this: set high expectations for staff and students and give strong instructional supports.[2] Most school systems recognize how tall an order this is, given everything else the principal job entails. Even principals who are ready to engage more deeply in curriculum and instruction are still expected to directly manage schedules, finances, facilities, student safety, and discipline, all while creating an engaging school culture and climate.

This bind is acute for all principals, but even more so for those working to change cultures and raise achievement in low-performing and high-need schools. Time management and distribution of tasks are of the essence. Yet many school systems are not set up to help principals use their time effectively. How can school systems make principals' roles more manageable while ensuring that teachers receive the support they need to improve instruction?

Three public school districts have been test-driving promising school leadership models that bolster principals' ability to focus on instructional leadership: Council Bluffs Community School District in Iowa; Fitchburg, Massachusetts; and District of Columbia Public Schools. The new school leadership models benefited these districts, even though they were not a panacea. For a variety of reasons, these districts still struggle to build sufficient staff capacity to address the myriad functions necessary to make schools successful.

The three districts are stressed on many levels, and each chose a model that fit its greatest perceived needs. But all sought to support high-quality teaching and learning better. Elements of the three models are compared in Table 1.

School Administration Manager

At the end of the 2006–2007 school year, Council Bluffs Community School District, a high-poverty district just across the Missouri River from Omaha, NE, learned that it had the lowest graduation rate in the state of Iowa. District leadership decided to adopt the School Administration Manager project, or SAM®, which had originally been developed for Jefferson County Schools in Kentucky.[3]

As the name suggests, the addition of a school administration manager is key. Participating principals are expected to establish goals for increasing time spent on supporting instruction and to meet with the SAM daily to review how they are spending their time during the school day. Principals also delegate specific duties to the SAM or other members of the school staff so that they are not pulled away every time an issue arises within the building.

Superintendent Martha Bruckner hoped that the SAM model would ease principals' transition from management to instructional leadership.[4] With financial support from the Iowa West Foundation, the district piloted the SAM model with seven schools beginning in the 2007–2008 school year. With additional funding from the district's general fund, by 2009–2010, every school in the district had a SAM.[5]

Council Bluffs' principals choose their SAM's tasks based on their preferences and school needs, as long as the SAM is helping free up time for the principal to focus on instruction. SAMs in the district generally take on non-instructional tasks such as maintaining the principal's calendar and school schedules, helping handle student discipline, supervising and evaluating paraprofessionals, and serving as liaison to parents. Many of the principals of the pilot SAM schools doubled the percentage of time they spent on instructional leadership activities, according to district administrators.[6] These activities included

Table 1

School Leader Models

Model Element	Council Bluff's Community School District	Fitchburg Public Schools	District of Columbia Public Schools
NSL role/initiative name	School administration manager	Student program support administrator	Director or manager of strategy and logistics
Initiative goal(s)	Increase principal focus on instruction	• Increase principal focus on instruction • Improve special education service delivery	• Increase principal focus on instruction and people management • Allow teachers to focus more time on instruction • Provide support/career paths to operations staff • Increase staff morale and retention
Key responsibilities	• Maintaining principal calendar and school schedules • Tracking principal time • Ordering supplies in response to teacher need • Overseeing building maintenance • Helping to handle student discipline • Organizing assemblies and staff meetings • Serving as liaison to parents	• Overseeing special-education-specific work • Conducting special education teacher and paraprofessional observations, evaluations • Attending grade-level and data team meetings • Facilitating teacher PD • Handling student discipline, as assigned	• Supervising school-based operations staff • Managing student information systems • Emergency planning and response • Handling building maintenance • Ordering and delivering supplies • Organizing assemblies, field trips • Budgeting • Finding coverage when teachers are absent • Maintaining school calendar
Official member of school admin team?	No	Yes	Yes
New role in schools?	Yes	Yes	Yes
NSL funding source	District general funds	District general funds	School funds
License required?	Originally not, now SAM license (unique to Iowa)	Originally teacher, now school administrator	No
Salary	Slightly less than first-year teacher (~$43,000)	Same as assistant principal (~$80,000)	Varies based on role and experience, generally similar to teacher with a bachelor's degree and 10–20 years' experience (~$68,000–$98,000)
Supervised by	Principal	Principal (and dotted line to district director of pupil services)	Principal
Supervisor of	Front office and facilities staff, paraprofessionals	Special education teachers and paraprofessionals	Front office and custodial staff

observation of classroom practice; preparation for feedback, evaluations, or instructional meetings; and working with students in the classroom.

During our focus groups, Council Bluffs' principals reported a direct, positive impact on not only the quantity but the quality of time they devoted to instructional leadership. Teachers reported that the nature of conversations with their principals changed and that they received more frequent feedback. One teacher, who spends ¾ of the day as an instructional coach indicated that the SAM allows principals' time to review and analyze assessment data, thereby allowing school decisions to be more data driven.

The district is further supporting principals' roles as instructional leaders by blending state and district resources in order to contract with the School Administrators of Iowa for SAM-related tools, such as time-tracking software, data housing, and training for SAMs.

While it is difficult with existing analysis to prove that the SAM initiative was responsible for improved student outcomes, several principals thought this was a fair "dotted line" to draw.

One noted that graduation rates have continued to rise over the past 10 years in which SAMs have been in place (Figure 1). Another offered, "I think the school is being managed better than when I was trying to do both [instructional leadership and building management] by myself because [my SAM] is so much more able to be responsive to teachers. And when people's needs are getting met, there's a direct correlation to morale."

Principals in Council Bluffs still face many demands. They say it continues to be a challenge to balance the instructional support needs of teachers with student academic needs and other student and family needs, especially when many live in poverty, deal with mental health or substance abuse issues, and face a host of other difficulties. Council Bluffs also struggles to fund its SAM positions even at low salary levels, but it has expressed a commitment to finding resources to continue doing so.

Student Program Support Administrator

Located in a former mill town 50 miles from Boston, Fitchburg Public Schools was one of the first districts in Massachusetts to pilot new educator evaluation and support systems under the state's federal Race to the Top grant in 2012–2013. As part of negotiations with its teachers' union, the district agreed that administrators would assess teacher practice through announced classroom observations, which make up the evaluative component and other nonevaluative approaches.[7] But significant time was needed to plan and complete this work. And while all schools had at least one assistant principal, that role traditionally handled discipline.

At the same time, schools and parents were pinging the central office for a more transparent, integrated approach to special education. The district had more students in special education relative to other districts in the state, with several group homes in its boundaries. It had struggled to stay in compliance on special education services and documentation.[8] Historically, evaluation team leaders (ETLs)—who were on a teacher contract but based out of the district's central office—had led the mandatory Individualized Education Program (IEP) meetings for students who required special education services. While there were some efficiencies to the ETL role (e.g., one ETL could serve several schools), parents felt that ETLs did not know their child's situation, and school staff felt ETLs did not appreciate how each school worked.[9]

The district decided in 2012–2013 to use funds that had been designated for the ETLs to create a new role,

the student program support administrator (SPSA). Like the former ETLs, the administrators facilitate, coordinate, and supervise delivery of special education services. But the new, school-level role also supports other school management responsibilities. They vary by school but typically include a mix of instructional and noninstructional duties—for example, conducting special education and paraprofessional observations and evaluations and handling student discipline.

Central office administrators in Fitchburg perceive shifts in how principals approach their work compared with five years ago. Assistant Superintendent Paula Giaquinto says principal walkthroughs of teacher classrooms used to be "an event" but is now integral, expected practice. The other big change noted was a clearer, more intentional focus on principals' data and assessment literacy and on using data to determine what to focus on next.

The other big change noted was a clearer, more intentional focus on principals' data and assessment literacy.

Fitchburg principals' report that the SPSAs enable schools to better manage and integrate special education as well as pitch in elsewhere. They perceive special education staff as more effective because of the support received from SPSAs, and they also indicate that SPSAs are slowing down the rate of referrals to special education by offering general education teachers strategies to help kids before they refer them.

Teachers perceive less of a difference in principal practice from this change. Principals surmised that teachers may not notice "behind-the-scenes" changes in administrative work (e.g., reviewing data with coaches). But many teachers do find the SPSA valuable to their own practice. Some cited using their school's SPSA as an advisor for working with struggling students, and others found their SPSAs to be proactive in offering information that would help them better serve their students with IEPs. Most of all, special education teachers say having an SPSA in the building improved their ability to strategize and receive constructive feedback about instruction, whether they were lead teachers in pullout settings or co-teachers in inclusion classrooms.

Principals expressed concern about potential turnover among SPSAs, as they have administrative licenses and can use this experience to move into leadership roles in more affluent, less demanding districts. And because the best source of new SPSAs is the special education staff, SPSA turnover often means replacing a special education teacher and an SPSA. Fitchburg Public Schools sought to equalize SPSA compensation with that of assistant principals starting in 2016–2017.

The solution was to offer schools a senior-level, operations-focused staff member who had the authority to supervise and evaluate certain staff.

Director of Strategy and Logistics

In spring 2013, an Education Resource Strategies report documented the extent to which teachers in District of Columbia Public Schools spent time on noninstructional, nonprofessional development activities.[10] In follow-up exit surveys, the district found that teachers' frustrations were rooted in not having supplies and operational support, which meant they were spending their own time (and sometimes their own money) to get them.

"We saw clear evidence that having to deal with things like fixing broken copiers, not receiving supplies on time, and so on, had a direct effect on teacher retention," said Scott Thompson, deputy chief for innovation and design in the district's Office of Instructional Practice. As a result, the Office of Human Capital started reviewing staff roles to see how they could be more effective and efficient.[11]

The district was also increasingly focused on distributed school leadership. To streamline the principal's job, the district started to help principals distribute instructional duties. But after finding that most principal time was spent on building management, the district decided to help distribute operational duties as well.

After reviewing examples from the charter sector, the district's human capital team decided the solution was to offer schools a senior-level, operations-focused staff member who had the authority to supervise and evaluate certain staff. They created a director of strategy and logistics role for supervising building management and a manager of strategy and logistics role for smaller schools, with similar qualifications and responsibilities (three years of experience and a bachelor's degree).

These administrators supervise operational functions and operational staff within the building, leaving school leaders and teachers free to focus on instruction and student learning. They handle budgeting, supervising, and evaluating front office and custodial staff, school calendars, and building maintenance issues. They do not handle student-facing work, such as school discipline.

The district piloted the new roles in 2014–2015 at nine schools. Prior to the pilot, principals reported spending about half their time on building management and operations; after the pilot, they reported spending just a fifth of their time in this area.[12] The district made the position available to all interested schools in 2015–2016, and as of 2016–2017, 60 schools had the new staff in place.

Principals in the district acknowledge they are likely to use the extra time they gained to meet with assistant principals, department chairs, and coaches rather than directly with teachers. Correspondingly, some teachers did not view their lead principal as being more focused on instruction under the new model, but most teachers report that the instructional leadership team was more visible and more likely to offer "hands-on" support: principals are seen in the halls more and assistant principals enter classrooms more frequently.

In addition, teachers in a focus group we conducted reported that the red tape that used to characterize virtually any operational or logistics request had largely been eliminated, which they attribute to the new position. Along the same lines, having a staff member designated for all things noninstructional means that building maintenance problems and supply requests have been addressed more quickly.

Figure 1

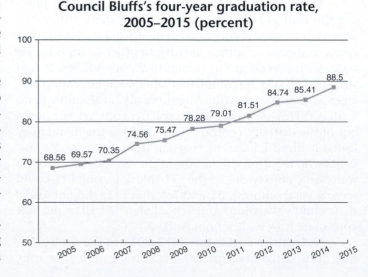

Council Bluffs's four-year graduation rate, 2005–2015 (percent)

Yet plugging one hole often means opening another. Because no additional financial resources are offered to schools to fund this position, principals may have to leave other positions unfilled in order to fund it.

For State Boards' Consideration

The experiences of these three school districts can inform other high-need districts that are considering modifying school leader roles and staffing structures to better support high-quality teaching and learning. It is difficult to draw a clear line from distributed leadership models to improved student achievement. These models cannot, for example, point to immediate higher test scores as a result of new staffing arrangements. But these models do show evidence of improvement in school culture, teacher morale, and various ways of attending to the needs of specific populations of students. As districts consider making such modifications, states should encourage districts to perform needs and resource assessments to ensure that the proposed solution matches their primary goal.

Figuring out how to meet staffing and instructional goals within budgetary constraints can also be challenging, but fortunately, the Every Student Succeeds Act (ESSA) offers states and districts a chance to support school leadership by modifying school leader roles and staffing structures as a lever for school improvement. In addition to Title I funds for school improvement, ESSA offers new flexibilities around using Title II dollars for evidence-based activities, which could include efforts like the ones we have described.13 While Title I and Title II can support school leadership efforts separately, states can also braid funding sources together for school improvement.

With or without ESSA funds, states and districts that are developing new school leadership roles should also consider the following steps:

Most teachers report that the instructional leadership team was more visible and more likely to offer "handson" support.

- Develop sample school staffing models for meeting varied assessed school needs and goals. States could support districts by providing sample staffing models such as the national SAM model, or they could point to other examples like the SPSA model in Fitchburg or the DSL/MSL model in DCPS.

- Assess whether and how principal job descriptions, expectations, and evaluation systems should change when new school leader roles are added to better reflect expectations for that role. In particular, roles and responsibilities should be clarified through standards and evaluation/development systems for school leaders and district leaders (especially principal supervisors so that they are able to support principals' changing roles).

- Develop tools, guidance, and meaningful professional development for principals and their supervisors to support this work. If districts' primary goal is to improve principal's instructional leadership, principals will also need support in developing their knowledge and skills, including time management, even with additional staff capacity.

priority areas across the four domains. Through collaborative efforts with stakeholders, state boards could set up an ongoing schedule of briefings with districts that are implementing turnaround efforts. These briefings may help scale school improvement efforts across a state as well as scaling up leading state policymakers' understanding of these efforts.

Notes

1. Kenneth Leithwood et al., *How Leadership Influences Student Learning* (Minneapolis: University of Minnesota, 2004).

2. Ibid.

3. Kenneth Leithwood et al., *Leading School Turnaround: How Successful Leaders Transform Low-Performing Schools* (Hoboken, NJ: Wiley, 2010), p. 172; Karin Chenoweth and Christina Theokas, *Getting It Done: Leading Academic Success in Unexpected Schools* (Cambridge, MA: Harvard Press, 2011); Reform Support Network, "Turnaround Leadership: How to Identify Successful School Leaders," December 2012, https://www2.ed.gov/about/inits/ed/implementation-support-unit/tech-assist/turnaroundleadership.pdf.

Mark Shellinger, then coordinator of the Wallace Foundation–funded Leading Education Achievement in Districts team in Kentucky's Jefferson County School District, based the SAM role on a position in the Victor Elementary District in Victorville, California, although that position was not part of a larger effort to track principal time use. See National SAM Innovation Project (NSIP), "SAMS

Connect," 2015, http://www.samsconnect.com/wordpress/wp-content/uploads/2015/08/SAM-Info.pdf; and Christina A. Samuels, "Managers Help Principals Balance Time," Education Week (February 11, 2008).

4. Martha Bruckner, superintendent of Council Bluffs Community School District, email exchange with authors, April 2017.

5. The exceptions are three alternative schools in the district, which do not have a SAM.

6. While principals are not required to share time-tracking data with the central office, many reported voluntarily to the Iowa West Foundation as evidence of the investment's impact.

7. Staff perceptions about this model were gathered in conversation with authors by Paula Giaquinto, assistant superintendent of Fitchburg Public Schools; Rowan Demanche, director of pupil services; Alicia Berrospe, director of special education (March 9, 2017); conversation with Andre Ravenelle, superintendent (May 2, 2017); e-mail correspondence with Rick Zeena, administrator of human resources (June 6, 2017).

8. Fitchburg teacher focus group discussion with authors, March 8, 2017; Commonwealth of Massachusetts Department of Education, "Re: Onsite Follow-up Monitoring Report: Coordinated Program Review Corrective Action Plan Verification and Special Education Mid-cycle Review," 2005.

9. Conversations with Giaquinto, Demanche, and Berrospe.

10. Education Resource Strategies, "A New Vision for Teacher Professional Growth and Support: Six Steps to a More Powerful School System Strategy" (Watertown, MA: ERS, May 2013), 27.

11. Scott Thompson, deputy chief, innovation and design, Office of Instructional Practice, DCPS, conversation with authors, December 15, 2016.

12. Ibid.

13. Rebecca Herman et al., "School Leadership Interventions under the Every Student Succeeds Act: Evidence Review," research report (Santa Monica, CA: RAND, 2017).

References

1. See Mary Klute et al., "Summary of Research on the Association between State Interventions in Chronically Low-Performing Schools and Student Achievement (REL 2016-138)," report (Washington, DC: U.S. Department of Education, 2016); Charles Thompson et al., "School Turnaround through Scaffolded Craftsmanship," *Teacher College Record* 118, no. 13 (2016): 1–26; Kenneth Leithwood et al., "Leading Data Use in Schools: Organizational Conditions and Practices at the School and District Levels," *Leadership and Policy in Schools* 9, no. 3 (2010): 292–327.

2. Kenneth Leithwood et al., "Seven Strong Claims about Successful School Leadership," *School Leadership & Management* 28, no. 1 (2008): 27–42.

3. Thompson et al., "School Turnaround through Scaffolded Craftsmanship."

4. Center on School Turnaround, "Four Domains for Rapid School Improvement: A Systems Framework" (San Francisco, CA: WestEd, 2017).

5. Barnett Berry, "Recruiting and Retaining 'Highly Qualified Teachers' for Hard-toStaff Schools," *NASSP Bulletin* 88, no. 638 (2004): 5–27; Francis Crowther et al., *Developing Teacher Leaders: How Teacher Leadership Enhances School Success* (Thousand Oaks, CA: Corwin Press, 2009); Linda Darling-Hammond et al., "Preparing School Leaders for a Changing World: Lessons from Exemplary Leadership Development Programs," report (Stanford, CA: Stanford University, Stanford Educational Leadership Institute, 2007).

6. Lucy Steiner and Sharon Barrett, "Turnaround Principal Competencies," *School Administrator* 69, no. 7 (2012): 26–29; Lucy Steiner and Emily Hassel, "Using competencies to improve school turnaround principal success," report (Chapel Hill, NC: Public Impact, 2011).

7. Center on School Turnaround, "Four Domains for Rapid School Improvement."

8. Clifford Adelman, "The Toolbox Revisited: Paths to Degree Completion from High School through College," report (Washington, DC: U.S. Department of Education, 2006); Marcia Masumoto and Sharon Brown-Welty, "Case Study of Leadership Practices and School-Community Interrelationships in High-Performing, High-Poverty, Rural California High Schools," *Journal of Research in Rural*

Education 24, no. 1 (2009): 1–18; Kristin Moore and Carol Emig, "Integrated Student Supports: A Summary of the Evidence Base for Policymakers," report (Bethesda, MD: Child Trends, 2014).

9. Linda Lambert, "A Framework for Shared Leadership," *Educational Leadership* 59 no. 8 (2002): 37–50; Karen Seashore Louis et al., "Learning from Leadership: Investigating the Links to Improved Student Learning," report (St. Paul, MN: University of Minnesota, 2010); William Saunders et al., "Increasing Achievement by Focusing Grade-Level Teams on Improving Classroom Learning: A Prospective, Quasi-Experimental Study of Title I Schools," *American Educational Research Journal* 46, no. 4 (2009): 1006–1033.

10. Rebecca Herman et al., "Turning Around Chronically Low-Performing Schools: IES Practice Guide," report (Washington, DC: National Center for Education Evaluation and Regional Assistance, 2008); Marcia Masumoto and Sharon Brown-Welty, "Case Study of Leadership Practices."

11. Joyce Epstein, *School, Family, and Community Partnerships: Preparing Educators and Improving Schools* (Boulder, CO: Westview Press, 2001); Karen Mapp and Paul Kuttner, "Partners in Education: A Dual Capacity-Building Framework for Family-School Partnerships," report (Austin, TX: SEDL, 2013); Sara McAlister, "Why Community Engagement Matters in School Turnaround," *Voices in Urban Education* 36 (2013): 35–42.

12. Rebecca Herman et al., "Turning Around Chronically Low-Performing Schools"; Marcia Masumoto and Sharon Brown-Welty, "Case Study of Leadership Practices."

13. Oregon provides such data in its district dashboard, http://www.ode.state.or.us/data/reportcard/reports.aspx.

Roxanne Garza is a senior policy analyst with the Education Policy program at New America. She is a member of the pre-K–12 team, where she provides research and analysis on policies and practices that impact teaching quality and school leadership.

Melissa Tooley is the director of Pre-K–12 Educator Quality with the Education Policy program at New America. She is a member of the pre-K–12 team, where she provides research and analysis on policies and practices that impact teaching quality and school leadership.

Laura Hoxworth

Five Myths That Inhibit School Turnaround

A new book from a University of Virginia education professor critiques the past 15 years of school turnaround efforts, examining where they have fallen short and potentially illustrating a way forward.

"Enduring Myths That Inhibit School Turnaround" is the product of Coby Meyers, a research associate professor in the Curry School of Education, and coeditor Marlene Darwin of the American Institutes for Research.

What exactly is school turnaround? Meyers defines it as "taking the lowest performing schools, identifying their most critical needs, and providing support in a structured way that instigates drastic change in a short amount of time." In other words, it's improving failing schools—fast—because traditional improvement models don't work quickly enough to give currently enrolled students a chance to succeed.

The phrase "school turnaround" entered the lexicon in the mid-2000s in the wake of the controversial No Child Left Behind (NCLB) Act. Fifteen years later, the phrase has become synonymous with that law's turnaround models, which were largely tied to standardized test scores, and the pressure those policies placed on struggling schools and their principals, teachers, and students.

Meyers has been researching school systems issues for years, since becoming fascinated with the topic while working as a teacher in Chicago. But amid recent changes in policy, funding, political climate, and general perceptions about public education in America, Meyers said now is the time to reexamine the concept of turnaround.

Here, he shares five of the most common myths inhibiting effective successful school turnaround.

MYTH No. 1: There's One Simple Solution

Addressed in the book as "the myth of single-lever turnaround," one large problem is that some practitioners and policymakers have a tendency to blame school failure—and focus school turnaround—on one single factor. Whether that's a charismatic leader, more funding or better teacher training is irrelevant. The truth is that school turnaround is complex.

"A couple of the common answers are, 'Just give them more money,' or 'Simply replace school leadership,'" Meyers said. "In actuality, turnaround requires lots of changes. If you get seduced by this 'one change' idea, you're not going to make any improvement whatsoever."

At the same time, Meyers cautions against going too far in the opposite direction—the "everything but the kitchen sink" approach. Instead, he says, "You have to focus on the biggest issues, and be laser-focused on those before you move on to the next set."

Real, systematic change—the kind of change required to transform a drastically underperforming school—requires a complex plan. A successful turnaround plan considers all of the challenges facing a certain school and then tackles them in an aggressive but structured way.

MYTH No. 2: Fundamental, Lasting Change Can Happen Fast

Studies have shown significant gains in student achievement can happen quickly—even within a single school year. But when it comes to lasting change, that's where Meyers says people often run into trouble.

"We see a lot of schools that have really significant achievement gains. But over time, those gains either plateau or they regress to the mean and fall back down," he said.

Often, you can trace these fleeting results to one impactful but nonsustainable change, such as replacing a disengaged leader with a charismatic one. Then, "When that super leader is taken to a different school or moved into district administration, the systems aren't in place to maintain the gains," Meyers said.

In general, the intense nature of turnaround isn't sustainable in the long term—and the transition from the initial turnaround phase into a traditional improvement model is often where the process breaks down. Successful turnaround requires both short- and long-term planning, including a purposeful transition period.

Meyers is also the chief of research for UVA's Darden/Curry Partnership for Leaders in Education. An intensive program that draws on innovative thinking in both business and education, which addresses the challenges of education leaders in eliciting system- and school-level improvement.

Meyers said the partnership has recently expanded its program to offer a sustainability year, which addresses the difficult transition period for struggling schools. "PLE's one-year sustainability program transitions district and school leaders from focusing on change initiatives, including foundational conditions and change leadership, to scaling solutions, which can include models of continuous improvement," he said. This deliberate focus on transition helps schools sustain positive gains long into the future.

MYTH No. 3: There's Nothing to Learn from Failing Schools

One of the biggest barriers to effective school turnaround boils down to a simple fact of human nature: addressing failure head-on is uncomfortable. When a school is struggling, Meyers said, "People feel very judged. They don't want to show you what's going poorly."

In part, the federal model of school turnaround has magnified the feeling of failure more than the understanding of and response to failure. This hesitation to examine the root causes of school failure leads to turnaround plans that don't address those causes.

In his book, Meyers and his colleagues use examples from fields outside of education—such as engineering and medicine—to argue that in order to address failure, we first have to understand it.

Meyers uses the example of engineers building a bridge: "They understand that after so much usage and so much time, that bridge is going to fail. So they are continuously studying decline and failure in order to keep that from happening.

"In education, we don't do a good job of identifying school decline and trying to get in before that happens. The presumption of failure can be really useful," he said.

MYTH No. 4: Turnaround Is the Problem of Individual Schools, Not Districts and States

Of all the myths addressed in the book, Meyers said perhaps the most important is a historic lack of accountability at the district and state levels. In the past, turnaround has been framed as a school initiative, with little to no emphasis on the district's role in the process. Meyers said that in order to move forward, we have to reframe turnaround as a systems issue—not a school issue.

"Schools alone cannot do this work," he said. "We have to be much more thoughtful about what we need from the systems at both the district and state levels, because they are the ones creating the policies and providing the resources."

The new book highlights several examples of recent policy and practitioner-oriented work that underscores the importance of examining school improvement frameworks from the district and state levels.

"If schools could turn themselves around, they would," Meyers said. "But taking responsibility for such schools is still a relatively new idea for districts and states."

MYTH No. 5: Turnaround Is Impossible

You hear it from scholars, researchers, practitioners, and all other types of people engaged with the difficult work of turning around failing schools: turnaround just doesn't work.

Some scholars call it "the failure fallacy." Despite the difficult nature of school turnaround, the fact is that turnaround is more than possible—it's proven.

"It's a fallacy because there are examples where it has worked, so clearly turnaround is possible," Meyers said.

More importantly, turnaround is necessary. Too often, he said, the failure fallacy is used as an excuse to promote a different approach entirely, such as charter schools. A critic will simply dismiss turnaround in order to advocate for a different piece of the education puzzle that doesn't address what to do with underperforming schools at all.

"It's a bait and switch," Meyers said.

The educator knows success is possible, because he sees it firsthand. "The [Partnership for Leaders in Education] works with low-performing schools daily," he said. "We see elements of the systems changing for the better. We even have examples of change occurring at the district level, where multiple schools are improving organizationally and student achievement is increasing. The work is very difficult. But success is attainable."

What's Next for School Turnaround?

Meyers said the bottom line is simple: as long as children are falling behind in underperforming schools, we can't afford to abandon turnaround efforts.

"The concept or the notion of school turnaround is not going away, regardless of whether or not the language changes," he said. "It's very clear that the idea of improving student achievement in low-performing schools at a rapid pace is here for the long haul."

For now, the language of "turnaround" is still widely used, and it gives a common shorthand to the idea of rapid school improvement. To adequately address these myths, Meyers anticipates a need to distance the process from the word "turnaround."

"For a lot of practitioners, the word has become associated with failure and punishment," he said. "A lot of the myths are driven by the language and its connection to the crushing nature of the federally funded School Improvement Grant."

In other words, "turnaround" has a branding problem. In order to move forward and make the necessary changes, we have to divorce the terminology (and its baggage) from the practice—those research-supported, systems-based methods of rapid school improvement.

Under new Every School Succeeds Act regulations, states will now have more flexibility to define and enforce school accountability on their own terms. Most states, including Virginia, will submit their plans to the federal government for feedback this September—and at least five states are adopting a new turnaround framework largely developed from the research outlined in the book.

Meyers said he hopes by addressing these myths head-on, policymakers and school leaders will be able to seize the opportunity to give school turnaround a turnaround of its own.

LAURA HOXWORTH is a writer, a marketer, and (above all) a storyteller. She has a degree in journalism and experience in magazine and book publishing (both editorial and project management), as well as marketing and communications.

EXPLORING THE ISSUE

Can Failing Schools Be Turned Around?

Critical Thinking and Reflection

1. What is the true definition of a school that has been "turned around"?
2. What are turnaround specialists, what do they do, and how successful are they?
3. How does research connect with turnaround schools?
4. What is done differently in schools that are successful in "turning around"?
5. What impact will new NCLB legislation have on turnaround schools?

Is There Common Ground?

Public schools in high-poverty areas, especially those in large urban centers, have historically suffered from neglect and underfunding. Recent budget shortfalls and declining enrollments have accelerated school closures in Chicago, Detroit, New Orleans, New York, Cleveland, Milwaukee, St. Louis, Kansas City, and Denver, creating what Monica Martinez characterizes as "Learning Deserts" in her February 2011 *Phi Delta Kappan* article. Those who champion the turnaround strategy believe that closing schools only contributes to the abandonment of urban communities, Martinez states. Others, who embrace charter alternatives, see hope in organizations attracting outside funding "to build portfolios of schools that encompass a variety of educational approaches offered by different vendors in an attempt to address intractable problems in public schools."

An analysis that goes beyond the turnarounds versus charters issue is presented in Jung-ah Choi's "Reading Educational Philosophies in Freedom Writers," *The Clearing House* (May/June 2009). The author extracts four basic philosophical elements that steered the inner-city teacher's success in the film *Freedom Writers*. They were the following: rewriting the curriculum, treating students as creators of knowledge, classroom community-building, and seeing teaching as self-realization. This entails a refusal to mechanically follow the prescribed curriculum, no longer treating students as mere recipients of knowledge, moving toward a more egalitarian relationship between teachers and students and elevating the "job" of teaching to a teaching "career."

Another slant on the issue concentrates on the wider social factors impinging upon school quality. This is treated in a Winter 2010 *Education Next* forum titled "Poor Schools or Poor Kids?" The forum features interviews with Joe Williams of the Education Equality Project and Pedro Noguera of "A Broader, Bolder Approach to Education." Among other provocative viewpoints worth considering are the following: "Tackling the Toughest Turnaround—Low-Performing High Schools." *Phi Delta Kappan* (February 2011) by Daniel L. Duke and Martha Jacobson; "Is Education the Cure for Poverty?" *The American Prospect* (May 2007) by Jared Bernstein; "Are Teachers Responsible for Low Achievement by Poor Students?" *Kappa Delta Pi Record* (Fall 2009) by David C. Berliner; and "Hidden Assumptions, Attitudes, and Procedures in Failing Schools," *Educational Horizons* (Winter 2008) by Betsy Gunzelmann.

Additional Resources

Chenoweth, K. (2007). *It's being done: Academic success in unexpected schools*. Cambridge, MA: Harvard Education Press.

Choi, J. (2009). Reading educational philosophies in freedom writers. *The Clearing House. 82:5*, 244-248. *doi:*10.3200/TCHS.82.5.244-248

Gibboney, R. (2008). Why an undemocratic capitalism has brought public education to its knees: A manifesto. *Phi Delta Kappan*. Retrieved from http://journals.sagepub.com/doi/abs/10.1177/003172170809000107

Kutash, J., Nico, E., Gorin, E., Rahmatulla, S., & Tallant, K. (2010). The school turnaround field guide. *FSG Social Impact Advisors*. Retrieved from https://www.wallacefoundation.org/knowledge-center/Documents/The-School-Turnaround-Field-Guide.pdf

Martinez, M. (2011). Learning deserts. *Phi Delta Kappan*. Retrieved from https://www.edweek.org/ew/articles/2011/01/28/kappan_martinez.html

Rothstein, R. (2008). Whose problem is poverty? *Educational Leadership*, 65/7. Retrieved from http://www.ascd.org/publications/educational-leadership/apr08/vol65/num07/Whose-Problem-Is-Poverty%C2%A2.aspx

Ravitch, D. (2010). Don't close schools, fix them. *AOL News.Com*. Retrieved from https://www.nytimes.com/2010/04/21/education/21teachers.html

Smarick, A. (2008). Wave of the future. *Education Next*. Retrieved from https://www.educationnext.org/wave-of-the-future/

Internet References . . .

Leaving no schools behind: Can bad schools be turned around?

https://whttps://epaa.asu.edu/ojs/article/view/2604ww.usatoday.com/story/news/nation/2013/04/28/failing-schools-turnaround-education/2116171/

Research on Effective Practices for School Turnaround

http://www.doe.mass.edu/turnaround/howitworks/turnaround-practices-508.pdf

Total turnaround: How LAUSD's troubled rollout became a model for tech success

https://www.iste.org/explore/articleDetail?articleid=2160

Turnaround Schools

https://www.edweek.org/ew/collections/turnaround-schools/index.html

What should America do about its worst public schools? States still don't seem to know.

https://www.washingtonpost.com/local/education/what-should-america-do-about-its-worst-public-schools-states-still-dont-seem-to-know/2017/08/06/db2d6dcc-76c6-11e7-8839-ec48ec4cae25_story.html?utm_term=.31122e2df8cc

Unit 3

UNIT

Current Specific Issues

*T*his unit probes specific questions currently being discussed by educators, policy makers, and parents, many being very "hot" issues. In most cases, these issues are grounded in the more basic questions explored in the first two Units of this edition. Views are expressed by a wide variety of writers, including Arvin Campbell, the National School Safety and Security Services, Sara Vecchiotti, Eric Christakis, James Cibulka, David Chard, Ashley LiBetti Mitchel, Chad Anderson, Paul von Hippel, Laura Bellows, Bianca Bell, Michael Zwaagstra, Michael Fitzpatrick, Margaret Hilton, Stacey M. P. Schmidt, David L. Ralph, Project Tomorrow Speak Up, William Mathis, Christopher Jepsen, Jesse Rothstein, Julien Lafortune, Diane Schanzenbach, Caitlin Emma, Derrell Bradford, Robin Lake, Trey Cobb, Roohi Sharma, Alice Opalka, Joanne Jacobs, Benjamin Herold, Kristina Riza, Jonah Elderman, Lee Walk, Marshall Lassak, Cory Bennette, Jane Robbins, Benjamin Herold, Ty Pierce, The Paper and Packaging Board, and the Accrediting Commission for Schools Western Commission of Schools and Colleges.

Selected, Edited, and with Issue Framing Material by:
Glenn L. Koonce, *Regent University*

ISSUE

Is There Support for Arming Teachers in Schools?

YES: Arvin Campbell, from "A Case for Arming Teachers and Administrators in Public Schools with Firearms," *The Bill Blackwood Law Enforcement Management Institute of Texas; Benbrook Police Department* (2016)

NO: National School Safety and Security Services, from "Arming Teachers and School Staff with Guns: Implementation Issues Present School Boards and Administrators with Significant Responsibility and Potential Liability" (2013)

Learning Outcomes

After reading this issue, you will be able to:

- Compare and contrast the pros and cons of arming trained school resource officers as opposed to arming teachers and principals in schools.
- Decide on what the criteria will be and how to determine who would be trained and allowed to be armed in a school.
- Assess if ample training and practice will be offered prior to school districts deciding on arming teachers and administrators in schools.
- Distinguish between the challenges of educational professionals teaching and serving children or having them diverted and focused on a mind-set to kill an intruder that may enter the classroom.
- Critique the Second Amendment rights to bear arms and how it relates to the school setting and safety concerns?

ISSUE SUMMARY

YES: Arvin Campbell, in a White Paper in partial fulfillment required for graduation from the Leadership Command College, Benbrook Police Department, supports arming teachers and administrators to serve as a deterrent because time is a big factor in confronting a shooter.

NO: Led by President Kenneth Trump, the National School Safety and Security Services asserts that teachers want to be armed with "textbooks and computers, not guns."

Armed police resource officers in schools are not new but the notion of arming teachers and principals in schools is new to most. Although few but growing numbers, there are school systems in the nation where teachers and administrators already are packing firearms in the schools during normal school hours. As National Rifle Association CEO Wayne LaPierre put it following the Sandy Hook massacre in 2012, "The only way to stop a bad guy with a gun is with a good guy with a gun?" (Lopez, 2018, p. 1). Many individuals agree; many do not!

The nation was horrified on February 14, 2018, when a former student opened fire at Marjory Stoneman Douglas High School in Parkland, FL, killing 17 students and staff members and injuring 17 others. In the Sandy Hook, CT, school shooting, December 14, 2012, 20 elementary school pupils, 5 teachers, and the principal were killed. "Within the span of approximately six horrific minutes, a lone shooter, armed with semiautomatic pistols and an assault rifle, entered the school and turned an entire nation upside-down" (Weatherby, 2015, p. 1). Thoughts go back to other mass school shootings among them: Columbine High School (12 students and a teacher dead), Red Lake High School (five students and two staff members dead), Amish school house shooting (five dead and five wounded), and Chardon, OH (three students dead). These mass killings have left no easy solutions for a fix. Mass shootings are not exclusive to schools; Americans live in a violent culture. In 2007, 32 persons (students and faculty) were shot and killed on the Virginia TECH campus. The Aurora, CO, movie theatre shooting ended with 12 person's dead and 70 injured in July 2012. On December 16, 2013, in the Washington, DC, Navy Yard shooting, 12 persons were killed. Fifty people were killed in the June 12, 2016, Orlando Florida night club shooting. On October 2017, 58 concertgoers at the Route 91 Harvest festival on the strip in Las Vegas were gunned down by a lone gunman from a hotel window. When the most innocent, elementary school children, are the victims it feels even more tragic. The most recent figures for school shootings were reported in the February 15, 2018, edition of *The New York Times* (Patel, 2018) from data gathered at the Gun Violence Archive, a nonprofit organization. Nationwide there have been 239 school shootings since Sandy Hook including 438 people shot, 138 of whom were killed. "Sixteen of the 239 shootings were classified as mass shootings, events in which four or more people were shot" (p. 1).

Guns in schools are not new as students have on occasion brought a gun to school that was confiscated and the student expelled. In the crackdown on school violence in the 1990s not only were students expelled but also charged by police with possession of a gun in school; zero tolerance practices regarding possession of a gun on a school campus took effect. The Gun Free-Schools Act of 1994 imposed a federal requirement for mandatory one-year expulsion from school for gun possession.

Since guns have been more common in schools, specially trained armed police officers, called School Resource Officers, are assigned to schools across the country. Most are stationed in high schools and middle schools. Some school resource officer programs have been in place for decades, like one in Chesapeake Public Schools in Chesapeake, VA, which began assigning armed and trained police officers in schools during the 1960s. This was part of a partnering police-community effort to have safe schools. Today, there is a National Association of School Resource Officers with advanced training courses. Unfortunately, there are not enough School Resource Officers for each school in the nation or even enough for each high school with funding being the major obstacle.

Not being able to solve the guns in the schools problem is part of a larger societal issue including guns in the wrong hands, frustrations of identifying and treating those suffering with mental health concerns, and protecting Second Amendment rights. Strong individual and organizational support of the right to bear arms has been around since the U.S. Constitution was signed. Most teachers do not want to be armed and, when asked, look upon their experiences in school settings across the country as almost all extremely positive. "Proponents of arming teachers seem to want to believe that the next time a shooter shows up to mow down our children, a teacher will whip out his or her rifle and shoot everyone to safety" (Cascio, 2018, p. 1). Cascio (2018) implores that arming teachers will make schools more dangerous.

As noted, there are already armed teachers and administrators in some schools in the nation but more important is the stronger call recommending training for school personnel who may or may not want to be armed. Some individuals and groups are expounding that teachers and principals are the real first responders in their schools with the obvious choice to shoot at predators if armed. It makes sense that if an intruder is the only one shooting, devastation does occur and a gun in the possession of school personnel is very powerful. Dave Parker (2013, p. 1) states, "would we rather trust our children's protection to someone with a gun that is to be used for defense, or would we simply rather hope that the unthinkable doesn't happen to them?" The question that begs answering here is: Is there support for arming the nation's teachers and principals? Shah (2013, p. 2), a reporter for *Education Week* whose beats included school safety and discipline, examined arming teachers in schools shortly after the Sandy Hook Elementary tragedy, and emphasized a comment from a Texas district superintendent who concluded that, "school personnel are the first responders."

Principals and teachers from the Harrold Independent School District in Texas, 150 miles Northwest of Fort Worth and near the Oklahoma border, are carrying concealed guns and have been doing so since unanimously approved by the school board in 2007 (Huff Post Education, 2012). Personnel allowed must have an approved state concealed-weapon permit, undergo training in crisis intervention and hostage situations, carry non-ricocheting bullets, and be individually approved by the school board. After Sandy Hook, a number of other state lawmakers in South Dakota, Oklahoma, Missouri, Oregon, and Minnesota began considering laws similar to Harrold, TX.

After Marjory Stoneman Douglas, almost all states were faced with the rising tide of support for arming teachers and administrators. As a new 2018 academic school year begins, states are arming teachers in South Dakota, Tennessee, Alabama, Texas, Kansas, Oklahoma, Wyoming, Colorado, Ohio, Utah, and Indiana (Minshew, 2018, p. 1).

The report of the National School Shield Task Force (Hutchinson, 2013) found that a properly trained armed school officer, such as a School Resource Officer, is crucial to school security and prevention of an active threat on a school campus. The report also found that due to lack of funding, armed security personnel is too expensive, and have resorted to allowing staff to carry firearms to prevent a violent incident on school property. The report goes on to recommend that a model law for all states be adopted for armed school personnel who are designated and trained for the job. A model state law is provided in the report's appendix.

There appears to be substantial majorities that firmly do not want school teachers and principals to be armed. Tom Rebotham (2013) notes that it might be a little absurd to have armed teachers simply because they have a permit to carry a concealed weapon in a school. He notes training for a concealed-weapon consisted of a three-hour class in which the individual goes to the range for 30 minutes to fire a gun at a paper target 15-feet away. The rest of the time is devoted to reviewing laws and gun safety. Certification comes with hitting the paper target with "reasonable accuracy" from the predesignated 15 feet. Robotham explains that it is a tad different pulling a gun on an intruder and determining in a split second whether or not to shoot and then hitting the gunman from the 15-foot paper target range. This is all in retrospect if, indeed, the threat is first read correctly by the teacher with a gun, in a school. It can quickly be concluded that carrying a gun to ensure the safety of school children takes intensive training over a period of months and even years. Even so, questions remain, "Should teachers and school administrators actively participate in schools' efforts to guard and protect the children in their custody by carrying weapons on their persons during the school day? Are teachers the appropriate individuals to assume the role of security guards, and are they adequately trained to use a weapon effectively during a fast-paced, traumatic, live-shooter event?" (Weatherby, 2015, p. 5).

There are no known nationwide studies or even local research on arming public school staff (Lopez, 2018). Most want armed school security in the hands of professional and trained security personnel. The figures from a Teach Plus survey look more like 80 percent opposed to arming teachers and 20 percent in favor. Teach Plus is a national advocacy group for teacher leadership (Will, 2018). Weatherby (2015, p. 1) concludes, "With education reform and teacher effectiveness at the crux of a national debate, schools should be wary of muddying the role of our educators. Instead, schools should allow teachers to focus on educating and leave the patrol-work to the properly trained experts."

In the selections that follow, Justin Moody supports arming teachers and begins his article with a scenario where 26 rural Mississippi students are victim to a gunman's random act of violence. He continues, "Picture a related set of facts—the same time, the same day. Only this time, the teacher is an enhanced, concealed-carry permit holder instead of 26 victims, there are none; the only person dead is the gunman. Unfortunately, there just is not enough armed presence in Mississippi schools." In the NO article in this issue, Kenneth Trump, president of the National School Safety and Security Services, opposes this view and makes a strong case that teachers do not want to be armed; they want to be safe.

YES

Arvin Campbell

A Case for Arming Teachers and Administrators in Public Schools with Firearms

Benbrook Police Department Benbrook, Texas February 2016

Introduction

A major issue that has taken center stage across America today is whether school teachers and administrators should be armed with firearms in public schools from Kindergarten through 12th grade. Over the last several years, there have been numerous shootings at public schools. The following is a partial list of mass murders in American schools: 12 students and 1 teacher killed at Columbine High School, a teacher, a security guard, and 5 students were killed in Red Lake Minnesota, and 20 children and 6 others were killed at Sandy Hook Elementary ("Timeline," n.d.). Many school districts have added school resource officers, but due to economic reasons, some school districts have had to either eliminate or not hire additionally needed officers. According to the US Justice Department, the number of city police officers working at schools increased almost 40 percent between 1997 and 2007 (as cited in Ferriss, 2013). Many rural school districts do not have armed police officers in any of their schools. Most elementary schools across the country do not have school resource officers. Some teachers and school administrators could be trained to carry firearms in their schools. Arming teachers would be more cost-effective for those districts that cannot afford to hire a police officer. An active shooter has many entrances to choose from to enter a school. Having teachers and administrators armed throughout the school would help mitigate this issue. School districts should have the option to arm qualified teachers and administrators with firearms in their schools.

Position

Time is a factor when dealing with a suspect armed with a gun in a school. School districts should arm teachers and administrators because they can provide an immediate armed response to confront armed suspects. When police responded in the past, they used to set up a perimeter and wait for the SWAT team to arrive to take over the incident. Police learned that their response was costing innocent lives.

Historian Jennifer Rosenberg (2003) detailed a timeline of the Columbine Massacre. In part, Eric Harris and Dylan Klebold entered Columbine High School at 11:14 A.M. and planted two 20-pound propane bombs in the crowded lunch room. They went back to their vehicles to wait for the explosions that never came. It was thought that if the bombs had detonated, up to 488 students would have been killed. Klebold and Harris started shooting students outside of the cafeteria. At 11:25 A.M., Harris exchanged gunfire with an arriving police officer, but neither were injured. Harris and Klebold entered the school and continued to shoot victims and throw bombs until at about 12:05 P.M., when they committed suicide (Rosenberg, 2003).

Now, current active shooter training instructs that a lone police officer can enter the school and confront the shooter. This has reduced the time it takes police officers to engage a suspect once they are on the scene, but it does not address the response time of officers responding from a patrol district. Arming teachers and administrators would help with this issue.

Many rural school districts in small towns rely on the state police or the sheriff's department to respond (Buerger & Buerger, 2010). Response times for these departments can be 20 minutes or more due to staffing and varied patrol responsibilities (Buerger & Buerger, 2010). Their lengthy response time can also be a result of the large areas they have to patrol. Rural schools are often much smaller and compress both distance and time which negatively affects the variables of refuge and escape (Buerger & Buerger,

2010). An active shooter could find all of the doors in a school locked in a short period of time, exit the school, and either shoot through several classroom windows and gain entry in to a classroom through a window (Buerger & Buerger, 2010). Greg Lund, a former school principal in Minnesota who works with the National Association of Certified Firearms Instructors to train gun owners, carried a gun for years on his hip at his school (Bindley, 2012). Lund said that, in a rural area, police arrival was unpredictable since the local law enforcement agency only had one officer on duty at any given time (Bindley, 2012). Nebraskan State Senator Mark Christensen said, when speaking about arming teachers, that if someone enters a school to shoot someone, it is best to have someone there to handle the situation (Khadaroo, 2011). In Texas, the Harrold Independent School District, since 2007, has allowed staff members to carry concealed handguns. The Harrold Independent School Superintendent, David Thweatt, oversees the policy and says there are people other than law enforcement who can act responsibly in regard to carrying firearms (Khadaroo, 2011).

Employing enough police officers or school resource officers at every school would be ideal, but it is not economically realistic. With shrinking budgets and hard economic times, there is a lot of competition for dwindling funds. Arming teachers and administrators is a more cost-effective way to provide security at schools that have no armed officers and can supplement schools that have some armed officers. According to the National Center for Education Statistics (as cited in Walshe, 2013), America has 132,183 schools. The National Association of School Resource Officers revealed that almost ⅓ of public schools in America have School Resource Officers (as cited in Person, 2013).

According to the Bureau of Justice Statistics, there are about 760,000 state and local law enforcement officers in America (as cited in IACP, 2012). The White House is proposing a request for $150 million to help schools hire 1,000 new police officers for schools (Ferriss, 2013). Using the figures cited by Walshe (2013), IACP (2012), and Person (2013), over 85,000 schools have no police officers assigned to them. Roughly 11 percent of all of the nation's current police officers would have to be reassigned to have an officer at every school.

Arming teachers and administrators could be a deterrent to anyone thinking about initiating an armed attack in a school. An analysis of multiple-victim public shootings from 1977 through 1999 revealed that states that enact right-to-carry laws have about a 60 percent decrease in occurrences of attacks and a 78 percent decrease in the rates that people are killed or maimed in attacks (Lott, 2005). Research also indicated that since 1997, about ⅓ of the public school shootings were stopped by the help of armed citizens before police arrived on the scene (Lott, 2005). Most active shooter school protocols involve notification of the police, lockdown procedures, minimize the target profile, and wait for the police to arrive to handle the incident (Buerger & Buerger, 2010). Although these protocols are important because they can save lives, it is not enough to actively protect children and staff. In the tragedies at Columbine and Newtown, numerous victims were killed in lockdown waiting for police response (Cafarello, 2013). The justice department found, in annual surveys of crime victims, that if confronted by a criminal, citizens are safest if they possess a gun (Lott, 2005). Lieutenant Colonel Dave Grossman, an expert on human aggression and violence, believes that a killer is more apt to attack unarmed citizens than citizens who are likely armed (Wylie, 2010). PoliceOne conducted a survey of 15,000 law enforcement officers and found that 86 percent of officers surveyed felt that casualties would have been lessened or averted if a legally armed citizen had been on the scene at the recent shootings at Aurora and Newtown (Avery, 2013). The survey also found that 81 percent of the officers believe that teachers and administrators should be armed (Avery, 2013).

Counter Position

The main opposition against arming teachers and administrators are in the areas of teacher and administrator mindset, training, mental health services, technology, and gun free zones. Critics often believe that teachers and administrators do not have the right mindset to carry a gun and possibly use lethal force. Those in the teaching field picked the profession because they wanted to teach children and be supportive, not some day have to shoot one of them in a lethal force encounter. Arming teachers seems to go against the very core beliefs of a teacher wanting to help and nurture children. Dennis Roekel, president of the National Education Association, said that most teachers do not want to be armed (Margasak, 2012). Roekel added that every school situation is different and the union has supported some schools that wanted to add trained officers (Margasak, 2012). When over 10,000 educators were surveyed by a company in Utah, they found that nearly 75 percent would not bring a firearm to school if it was permitted (Toppo, 2013). The survey also found that of those teachers and administrators who own guns, only about 33 percent would probably bring the gun to school (Toppo, 2013). Van Brocklin (2013), who has experience as a teacher and state and federal prosecutor, said she does not think that teachers should be armed.

Van Brocklin (2013) carries a gun and has completed several tactical pistol training courses alongside law enforcement officers. Van Brocklin (2013) was humbled when she failed a firearms training simulator by shooting several innocent people and getting herself killed several times without saving anyone. Van Brocklin (2013) noted that an elevated heart rate, tunnel vision, and hearing problems made simple tasks difficult.

The argument for not arming teachers is the all or nothing mentality of the opposition. This is not surprising. In 2002, news broadcasts on three major networks often described gun crime, but did not have one segment on a citizen using a firearm to stop a crime (Lott, 2005). Many allude to the fact it would be dangerous to arm all teachers and administrators. For example, Brian Siebel, an attorney at the Brady Center to Prevent Gun Violence, says not to give all teachers guns and hope nothing bad happens ("Up in Arms," 2008). Certainly, not all teachers and administrators need to be permitted or forced to be armed at school. It would be as dangerous to arm all teachers and administrators as it would be to arm everyone in society. Some people, especially in a country of over 300 million people, are just not qualified to possess firearms due to factors like age, criminal backgrounds, mental illness, poor shooting skills, inability to train, and mind-set. There would have to be standards set up by the state to govern the eligibility and requirements of teachers who could carry a firearm at school. The training would have to be more than just a concealed handgun licensing class. It would have to include training in things like firearms and crisis intervention. Texas Lieutenant Governor David Dewhurst wants the state to fund specialized training for teachers and administrators (Venturo, 2013). Dewhurst went on to say that school districts could nominate who they wanted to be armed in their schools (Venturo, 2013).

The arrival of someone with a gun on the scene of a multiple-victim shooting is the biggest factor determining the amount of injury inflicted (Lott, 2005). The focus should never be on arming teachers for the sake of arming them but to arm some qualified teachers to make the school safer. Some schools may not have anyone who can qualify to carry a firearm at school.

Other opponents to arming teachers cite technology and lockdown procedures as the root to combating school massacres. Safety experts looking back on the Sandy Hook Elementary massacre say that security measures were not lacking at the school (Shah, Maxwell, Sparks, Ujifusa, & Zubrzycki, 2013). They cited that Lanza was delayed for a few seconds from just being able to walk easily in to the school. Teachers and others herded students in to locked rooms while the principal and the school psychologist confronted Lanza (Shah et al., 2013). The executive director of the National School Safety Center said many things were done very well at Sandy Hook, but, sometimes, on the their best days, schools have limits (Shah et al., 2013). School safety expert Ken Trump told ABC News that teachers did what they could do to protect the children at Sandy Hook Elementary.

There were many acts of heroism at Sandy Hook Elementary to protect and save the children. Teachers lost their lives protecting their students. Lockdown procedures undoubtedly saved lives, but it must be supplemented with more to protect children. Merely sitting and waiting for the police to arrive may work in some instances but not all. Good intentions do not always equal good laws (Lott, 2005). Too many laws disarm law-abiding citizens, not criminals (Lott, 2005).

Other experts say that metal detectors and cameras will not prevent school massacres. On the same day of the Columbine Massacre was a one million dollar security system was installed in the school (Fratt, 2006). All of that technology did almost nothing to protect the students from being victimized. Lieutenant Colonel Grossman cited in one seminar how two unarmed security guards were the first to be shot manning a metal detector (Naese, 2013). Although the security guards were not teachers, it still demonstrates the vulnerability exposed in gun free zones. The only people who obey the gun free zone signs are the law-abiding citizens. Criminals are not going to halt their behavior just because of a gun free zone sign. That is why they are called criminals. If the guards or a teacher would have been armed, they would have at least stood a chance.

Others cite the importance of mental health screening in combating school shootings. Garret Virchick, a Boston area teacher for 25 years, said focusing on arming teachers goes against the reasons teachers went in to the field because they are caregivers (Bindley, 2012). Virchick supports mental health screening and counseling (Bindley, 2012). In reference to violent school deaths covering 2004–2005 and the first three months of the 2005–2006 school years, Dale Yeager, who is the president of Seraph Inc., a school safety training firm, said, "Every school shooting was preventable" (Fratt, 2006, p. 32). He believes that schools need to have a system to identify violent students and proactively intervene in their lives (Fratt, 2006).

Klebold and Harris were put in to a juvenile diversion program in 1998 after breaking in to a van (Rosenberg, 2003). Part of the plea agreement was that they had to meet with counselors. They convinced everyone they were sorry for what they did while they continued to plan an attack on their high school. In a report released by Connecticut Police, a nurse at the Yale Child Studies Center said Lanza's mother refused to give him prescribed antidepressants and antianxiety drugs, and she did not reschedule a follow-up appointment that he missed ("Police Release Documents," 2013). The report also said that although Lanza showed an interest in mass shootings and firearms, he did not display any aggressive or threatening tendencies ("Police Release Documents," 2013).

Opponents of arming school teachers say that school shootings are rare. They say that arming teachers makes students less safe, not safer ("Up in Arms," 2008). Randal Stephens, the executive director of the National School Safety Center, said major school violence remains rare, saying that during the 2009–2010 only 25 deaths were considered homicide (Shah et al., 2013). He went on to say there is a sense of one-upmanship in that when some of the violent plots were prevented, the would-be assailants said they planned on making Columbine look like kindergarten stuff (Shah et al., 2013). Lieutenant Colonel Grossman said there is no survival value in denial.

Grossman said that arming good guys in schools prevents massacres (Naese, 2013). Having concealed carriers on campus is a deterrent as long as it is advertised that someone on campus is armed, and an attack will be dealt with immediately (Naese, 2013).

Recommendation

Teachers and administrators should have the option of being armed at school. It should be left up to the states as to whether schools should have the option of arming their teachers. And then individual school districts should have the option of arming their teachers. Arming some teachers would help mitigate the response time of the police. It would also be more economical especially for smaller school districts that cannot afford hiring a full-time police officer. Lieutenant Colonel Grossman said concealed carriers on campus is a good thing. Grossman cited that in 2006, Utah passed a law allowing concealed carry on campus and by 2012, nearly every school had some staff carrying concealed weapons (Naese, 2013). In that time period, there were no school homicides in Utah schools (Naese, 2013).

The opposition to arming school teachers has some good points. The all or nothing mentality of the argument that all teachers cannot be trained to effectively carry firearms in schools is a dishonest argument. Anything to an extreme is bad. It is not being suggested that all teachers be armed, but only those who want to be armed and can

qualify to carry. Technology and improved mental health services are important, but they are not a cure all. When confronted with school safety measures, shooters find a way in to a school. Klebold, Harris, and Lanza had all been in counseling before they went on their rampages. As far as gun free zones, they are good as long some qualified teachers are allowed to carry concealed firearms.

It is not suggested that arming some school teachers is the only answer to making schools safer. It supplements the counterpoints when all else fails. America is a diverse country with different views on how to make schools safer. Individual states should have the right to provide security in their schools the way they see fit. Of the states that permit concealed carry on school campuses, it should be left up to the individual school districts as to arm or not arm some teachers.

References

Avery, R. (2013, April 8). Police gun control survey: Are legally-armed citizens the best solution to violence? Retrieved from http://www.policeone.com/pc_print.asp?vid=6186552

Bindley, K. (2012, December 12). Teachers carrying guns: Debate follows Sandy Hook shooting. Retrieved from http://www.huffingtonpost.com/2012/12/21/teachers-guns-sandy-hookshooting_n_2339924.html

Buerger, M., & Buerger, G. (2010, September). Those terrible first few minutes. Retrieved from http://leb.fbi.gov/2010/september/those-terrible-first-few-minutes evisiting-active-shooter-protocols-for-schools

Cafarello, N. (2013, March 16). Leave the building, don't hide in it when faced with school shooter, expert advises. Retrieved from http://www.ourtownsylvania.com/Our-Town-News/2013/03/14/Leave-the building-don-t-hide-in-it-when-faced-with-school-shooter-expert-advises.html

Ferriss, S. (2013, March 5). Analysis: Should schools have more police-or fewer? States disagree. Retrieved from http://www.nhregister.com/general-news/20130305/analysis-should-schools-have-more-police-or-fewer-states disagree-3

Fratt, L. (2006, March). Getting tough on school shootings. Retrieved from www.districtadministration.com/article/security-trends

IACP. (2012, December 21). Statement of IACP President Craig Steckler on proposal to place armed police officers in all schools [Press release]. Retrieved from http://www.theiacp.org/ViewResult?SearchID=1799

Khadaroo, S. T. (2011, January 19). School shootings: In Nebraska, a proposal to arm teachers. *Christian Science Monitor*. Retrieved from http://www.csmonitor.com/USA/Education/2011/0119/School-shootings-In-Nebraska-aproposal-to-arm-teachers

Lott, J. (2005). Teachers should be armed to prevent school violence. In A. C. Nakaya (Ed.), *Juvenile crime*. San Diego, CA: Greenhaven Press.

Margasak, L. (2012, December 28). Experts: Trained police needed for school security, not teachers. Retrieved from http://www.policeone.com/mass casualty/articles/6075711-Experts-Trained-police-needed-f...

Naese, J. (2013, March 28). Lt. Col. Dave Grossman: Keeping our schools SAFE. Retrieved from http://www.gunssavelife.com/?p=5584

Person, D. (2013, February 17). Instead of arming teachers, hire police. *USA Today*. Retrieved from http://www.usatoday.com/story/opinion/2013/02/17/armed-teachers-guns-schools/1926373/

Police Release Documents on Newtown School Massacre. (2013, December 27). Retrieved from http://www.foxnews.com/us/2013/12/27/police-release documentson-newtown-school-massacre/

Rosenberg, J. Columbine massacre. Retrieved from http://www.history1900s.about.com/od/famous crimesscandals/a/columbine.htm

Shah, N., Maxwell, L., Sparks, S., Ujifusa, A., & Zubrzycki, J. (2013, January 9). Shootings revive debates on security. *Education Week, 32*(15), 1–18.

Timeline of Worldwide School and Mass Shootings. (n.d.). Retrieved from http://www.infoplease.com/ipa/A0777958.html

Toppo, G. (2013, February 26). Teachers not gung-ho on guns at school. *USA Today*. Retrieved from www.usatoday.com/story/news/nation/2013/02/26/teachers-notgung-ho-onguns-at-school-nation wide-survey-finds/1947841

Up in Arms. (2008, October). *Current events Magazine, 108*(5), 7.

Van Brocklin, V. (2013, February). Arming teachers in schools: An argument against. Retrieved from http://www.policeone.com/pc_print.asp?vid=6126130

Venturo, J. (2013, January 12). Dewhurst proposes training, arming Texas teachers. *Star-Telegram*. Retrieved from http://article.wn.com/view/2013/01/12/Dewhurst_proposes_training_arming_Texas_teachers/

Walshe, S. (2013, May 1). Loaded: How gun manufacturers and the NRA capitalise on tragedy. Retrieved from http://www.theguardian.com/commentisfree/2013/may/01/loaded-gun-manufacturers-nra-capitalise-tragedy

Wylie, D. (2010, May 5). Active shooters in schools: The enemy is denial. Retrieved from http://www.policeone.com/school-violence/articles/2058168-Active shooters-inschools-Theenemy-is-denial/

ARVIN CAMPBELL is a lieutenant in the Benbrook Texas Police Department.

National School Safety and Security Services   **NO**

Arming Teachers and School Staff with Guns: Implementation Issues Present School Boards and Administrators with Significant Responsibility and Potential Liability

Arming persons at schools should be left to professional school public safety officials: School Resource Officers (SROs) and school police department officers.

"The vast majority of teachers want to be armed with textbooks and computers, not guns," said Kenneth S. Trump, President of National School Safety and Security Services, in response to the national discussion on arming teachers and school staff, and armed volunteers in schools.

Trump advises school districts against allowing teachers and school staff to be armed.

Trump says that while gun control and gun rights advocates typically seize on school proposals to arm teachers to further political agendas, his opposition to arming teachers and school staff focuses solely on implementation issues, not political statements and beliefs about rights to bear arms.

"School districts considering arming teachers and school staff with guns would take on significant responsibility and potential liabilities that I firmly believe are beyond the expertise, knowledge-base, experience, and professional capabilities of most school boards and administrators," Trump said. He added that school board members, superintendents, principals, teachers, school safety experts, and public safety officials he has talked with around the nation consistently do not believe that educators and school support staff should be armed.

Trump said he personally supports the Second Amendment and concealed carry laws, but believes that proposals to arm teachers and other school employees crosses the line of self-protection and protection of one's family into a different level of tasking educators and school support staff to provide public safety, law enforcement functions for hundreds or thousands of individuals in a school.

"Suggesting that by providing teachers, principals, custodians, or other school staff with 8, 16, 40, or even 60 hours of firearms training on firing, handling, and holstering a gun somehow makes a non-law enforcement officer suddenly qualified to provide public safety services is an insult to our highly trained police professionals and a high-risk to the safety of students, teachers, and other school staff," Trump said.

He said it is short-sighted for those supporting the idea to believe that educators who enter a profession to teach and serve a supportive, nurturing role with children could abruptly kick into the mindset to kill someone in a second's notice. Police officers train their entire career and enter each traffic stop and individual encounter with a preparedness and life-safety mindset that is different from the professional training and mindset of educators.

Trump, a 25-year veteran school safety expert who has trained and consulted with school and public safety officials from all 50 states and Canada, noted that school districts setting policy to allow teachers and school staff to be armed with guns would take on an enormous amount of responsibility and potential liability.

He says allowing teachers and school staff to be armed begs a number of questions:

- Does the school board have appropriate and adequate policies and procedures governing the carrying and use of firearms by teachers and school staff?
- What type of "use of force continuum" has the school district created for staff to use firearms? How does that stand up in comparison to such standards held for police officers and others who are armed and deployed in a public safety capacity?

- What types of firearms (types of guns, caliber of weapons, etc.) are staff allowed to carry and not allowed to carry? Will staff carry their own personal firearms or school district-issued firearms? If the school allows staff to carry their personal weapons for the purpose of protecting staff and students, what responsibilities do school boards and administrators thereby assume for making sure the firearms carried are functional? Does the school district have regular "inspections" of staff firearms to make sure they are functional and appropriate to policy, and if so, who on school staff is responsible for that function and what is their level of expertise and training to make such decisions?

- What type of firearms training does the school district provide on a regular, ongoing basis to those staff it authorizes to be armed with guns? Will the school district build and operate its own firearms range? Who on school staff is qualified to provide such training, operate a firearms range, etc.? Will firearms certification and recertification be added to the school district's professional development training program each year?

- What type of weapons retention training has been provided to staff who are armed and what steps have been taken to reduce risks of a teacher or staff member being intentionally disarmed by a student or other person, or for having a firearm dislodged from a staff member's control when the teacher breaks up a fight in a cafeteria or hallway?

- How is the district prepared to prevent and manage situations where teachers and/or staff members lose, misplace, or have stolen their firearms while on campus?

- How will the school district manage an accidental shooting that could occur?

- What is the impact of this type of board policy and practice on the school district's insurance and potential legal liability posture? If self-insured, is the district able to handle potential lawsuit judgments against them for cases resulting from this practice? If insured by a private carrier, what is the insurance provider's position and concerns, or will they even insure the district for such a practice?

- Most importantly, what other options have we considered as school leaders? For example, if the school district is concerned about first responder response time from the community to the school, has the school district considered employing a school resource officer (SRO) or its own trained,

commissioned and certified school police officer who is a school district employee, such as what is allowed in Texas, Florida and other states?

and many other considerations.

Trump recommends that superintendents and school boards get written opinions from their insurance carriers and school district attorneys on the risks and liability of arming non-law enforcement, school employees.

Trump has long supported school districts having school resource officers (SROs) who are city or county law enforcement officers assigned to work in schools. He also supports properly organized and operated school police departments, which are in-house school district police officers that are trained, commissioned, and certified professional peace officers in school districts where state law allows districts to have such departments.

Trump says that the arming of teachers and school staff goes is a significantly different issue that goes beyond simply the issue of an individual's right in a number of states to be licensed to carry a concealed weapon. Unlike an individual being trained and licensed under a state law to carry a firearm for personal protection at their home or on the streets, school districts that permit teachers and school staff to carry firearms on campus are in essence deploying those school employees in a public safety capacity to protect the masses with the expectation and assumption that they can and will provide a firearms-related level of public safety protection services to students and other staff. By tasking those employees with those responsibilities, Trump notes, the school district is also accepting responsibility and potential liability for implementation of such policies.

"There is a huge difference between having trained, certified and commissioned law enforcement officers who are full-time, career public safety professionals that are armed and assigned the duty of protecting students and staff versus having teachers, custodians, cafeteria workers and other non-public safety professionals packing a gun in school with hundreds of children," said Trump.

National School Safety and Security Services (www.schoolsecurity.org) is an organization dedicated to making schools safer for children, using leading edge strategies that are proven and cost effective. Kenneth S. Trump, MPA, is the President.

EXPLORING THE ISSUE

Is There Support for Arming Teachers in Schools?

Critical Thinking and Reflection

1. What impact will teachers and principals armed in schools have on what the real educational focus should be?
2. What are the liability concerns to consider in arming teachers and principals in school as opposed to trained school resource officers?
3. Will the dialogue continue to be discussed about arming school employees or will another disaster have to occur to keep it in the forefront of people's minds that are making the policy decisions?
4. What should teachers really be focused on each day in their classrooms; educational excellence or being armed for protection and safety of their students?
5. What type of firearm training should a school system provide to the faculty and staff and who will cover the economic cost of training and providing guns and ammunition?

Is There Common Ground?

Mass shootings are now a part of the fabric of America, a redefined normal for many who fear the unthinkable could happen in their school. Most people would agree that policies to reduce any violent act in our schools would be welcome. It is also apparent that any policy would be stopped at the point where teachers and administrators would be armed. It should be noted that schools are micro-organizations of society and are not immune from the violent acts committed outside the school. With automatic assault rifles becoming more common place in mass shootings and recognizing that mental health care is lacking for many deranged individuals who are capable of committing an unthinkable act, schools and society are vulnerable. In this reflection, it makes sense that if society needs armed police officers, schools also need them. The question does not appear to be, arm or not to arm, but who will be armed?

School security has come a long way in the manner in which schools are aware of the potential for extreme violence. On the other hand, schools are designed as learning facilities where teaching takes place and not every thought is for one's safety. School teachers and especially principals are not security experts. They are learning leaders whose expertise is organizing a school for maximum learning, no matter how difficult the instructional task. Security experts are generally defined as peace officers with the mandatory training and certification to be commissioned with arrest powers and the authority to carry a gun. There is a big difference between certification to be a security officer and certification to be a teacher or principal.

The debate on school violence escalates significantly after an incident of mass shooting. The rhetoric grows, followed by a period where some changes may be made. Then things appear normal and the natural thought of, "it won't happen here," pervades in schools and communities across the country once again. Of the 261 school safety bills (estimated), state legislatures have considered since the Parkland shooting, 29 bills and 6 resolutions have been enacted. Most of this legislation addressed stronger law enforcement measures, school police, guns on school property, and additional funding for school safety (Blad, 2018, pp. 1–2). By the end of the year 2018, the Federal School Safety Commission set up by President Trump after the Marjory Stoneman Douglas High School shooting will present recommendations on how to improve school safety and prevent incidents of mass violence. On August 23, 2018, *Education Week* (Cavanaugh, 2018), news broke that U.S. Secretary of Education, Betsy DeVos, is considering whether to let school districts use federal a $1.1 billion pool Title IV funding to buy guns to arm teachers. The debate is not that schools need armed protection; the question is, armed protection from whom and how soon will it happen? To conclude, although the research on guns in schools for protection is terse, there is a body of research that is very clear: "more guns, more gun deaths" (Lopez, 2018, p. 2).

Additional Resources

Blad, E. (2018). "You better make these schools safe": As school starts, violence is top of mind. *Education Week*. Retrieved from https://www.edweek.org/ew/articles/2018/08/30/you-better-make-these-schools-safe-as.html

Cascio, C. (2018). Arming teachers will make schools more dangerous. *Education Week Teacher*. Retrieved from https://www.edweek.org/tm/articles/2018/08/28/arming-teachers-will-make-schools-more-dangerous.html

Cavanaugh, S. (2018). Title IV funds for arming teachers, not ed tech? Notion draws ire of ed groups. *Education Week*. Retrieved from https://marketbrief.edweek.org/author/scavanagh/

Huff Post Education. (2012). Harrold Texas School gun policy defended after Newtown shooting. *Huffington Post*. Retrieved from http://www.huffingtonpost.com/2012/12/17/harrold-texas-school-guns_n_2316729.html.

Hutchinson, A. (2013). *Report of the national school shield task force*. Fairfax, VA: National Rifle Association of America. Retrieved from http://www.nraschoolshield.com/NSS_Final_FULL.pdf

Minshew, L. (2018). From the editorial board: On arming k-12 teachers. *The High School Journal*. The University of North Carolina Press *101*/3. Retrieved from https://muse.jhu.edu/issue/38621

Patel, J. (2018). After Sandy Hook, more than 400 People have been shot in over 200 schools. *The New York Times*. Retrieved from https://www.nytimes.com/interactive/2018/02/15/us/school-shootings-sandy-hook-parkland.html

Shah, N. (2013, February). Teachers already armed in some districts. *Education Week*, 32(21):1.

Weatherby, D. (2015, November). Opening the "Snake Pit": Arming teachers in the war against school violence and the government-created risk doctrine. *Connecticut Law Review*, 48:1.

Will, M. (2018). Nearly 20 percent of teachers would choose to carry a gun at school. *Gallop. Education Week blogs: Teacher Beat*. Retrieved from http://blogs.edweek.org/edweek/teacherbeat/2018/03/teachers_armed_surveys.html

Internet References . . .

Across the Country Measures to Arm Teachers Stall

https://www.washingtonpost.com/local/education/across-the-country-measures-to-arm-teachers-in-schools-stall/2018/05/03/7ef6193a-4193-11e8-8569-26fda6b404c7_story.html?utm_term=.f49251a36079

Arming Teachers to Give Schools Safety Essay

https://www.bartleby.com/essay/Arming-Teachers-to-Give-Schools-Safety-F3ZLCUSTC

Most U.S. Teachers Oppose Carrying Guns in Schools

https://news.gallup.com/poll/229808/teachers-op-pose-carrying-guns-schools.aspx

The Case against Arming Teachers

https://www.vox.com/policy-and-politics/2018/2/23/17041662/armed-teachers-gun-violence-mass-shootings

What Research Says about Arming Teachers

https://www.citylab.com/life/2018/03/what-the-research-says-about-arming-teachers/555545/

Selected, Edited, and with Issue Framing Material by:
Glenn L. Koonce, *Regent University*

ISSUE

Has the Time Arrived for Universal Preschool?

YES: Sara Vecchiotti, from "Transforming the Early Care and Education Workforce," National Association of State Boards of Education (2018)

NO: Erika Christakis, from "How the New Preschool Is Crushing Kids," *The Atlantic* (2016)

Learning Outcomes

After reading this issue, you will be able to:

- Evaluate solutions to successful early childhood education.
- Explain why preschool classrooms have become increasingly *fraught* spaces.
- Outline steps determining how effective the new investment in high-quality preschools will be.
- Survey the literature on how little preschool does to solve the problem of the achievement gap that puts low-income, mostly minority children, so far behind more fortunate children.
- Assess government's role in early childhood education.

ISSUE SUMMARY

YES: Dr. Sara Vecchiotti, Esq., Chief Program Officer at the Foundation for Child Development, in her support for early learning environments notes that children can receive benefits from early care and education if early childhood education professionals are adequately prepared, competent, supported, and well-compensated.

NO: Erika Christakis from *The Atlantic* posits that the same educational policies that are pushing academic goals down to ever earlier levels seem to be contributing to—while at the same time obscuring—the fact that young children are gaining fewer skills, not more.

Early childhood education can prime young minds for academic and social success. And yet in much of the country, many parents struggle to find any day care at all. Fetterman (2018), from the PEW Charitable Trust, supports early childhood education noting from her research that it supports both future academic and social successes. She bases her comments on the results of data collected from high-quality programs across many states. Fetterman collected her data from programs where the states have imposed more rigorous standards and rules on their childcare providers. Additionally, more public funds (up 47 percent) have been allocated to early education which

has led to many preschools accomplishing higher outcomes on their measures of accountability. The close scrutiny in these states have come with a cost, as many parents struggle to find day care or pay for the enhanced day care that must adhere to new rules on high-quality learning activities. But more adamant, for preschool providers, are the new regulations on sprinkler systems, radon detection, and fire escape plans. In what Fetterman calls "Child Care Deserts" (p. 10) made up of communities, many low income, with no childcare options, the situation can be dire. This scene could change rapidly with the new budget from President Trump that calls for an additional $5.8 billion for the Child Care Development Block

Grant, which will help low-income families pay for child-care. The grants would be administered by the states under federal regulations and guidelines.

The growth of preschool in the United States has been a lengthy process. Preschool education received a powerful boost when the federal Head Start program was launched in 1964, but major barriers in affordability and accessibility for those not eligible for Head Start slowed the movement. In an article titled "Preschool Education: A Concept Whose Time Has Come," Barnett (2005), director of the National Institute for Early Education Research at Rutgers University, states that "no area in education has grown like preschool in recent decades."

The most recent data by the National Center for Educational Statistics (2018, p. 50) shows:

> Among 3- to 5-year-olds who were enrolled in preschool programs in 2016, some 54 percent attended full-day programs, which was higher than the percentage who attended full-day programs in 2000 (47 percent). Among 3- to 5-year-olds attending kindergarten, the percentage attending full-day programs increased from 60 percent in 2000 to 81 percent in 2016. In every year from 2000 to 2016, the percentage of 3- to 5-year-old kindergarten students enrolled in full-day programs was higher than the percentage of 3- to 5-year-old preschool students enrolled in full-day programs.

Alarmingly, the data also showed that the United States ranked 30th in the world in the percent of 3- and 4-year-old children who enrolled in school. The 29 countries, out of 31 total, were listed ahead of the United States in preschool enrollment. All countries in the list were members of the Organization for Economic and Cooperation Development. The enrollment figures ranged from number 31, Turkey with 20 percent, to number 1, France with 100 percent.

The long-term trend for preschool growth shows that from 2000 to 2017, enrollment has risen 47 percent along with incremental improvement in early learning program standards (National Institute for Early Education Research, 2018). Adding to the support for preschool, the Council of Chief State School Officers (CCSSO) released their report, *Equity Starts Early: How Chiefs Will Build High-Quality Education*, in the spring of 2016. This report outlines five steps that, coupled with high-quality K–12 education, will contribute to strengthening student outcomes through college and career readiness (Stark & Stark, 2016). CCSSO is an organization made up of heads of K–12 state public school departments, usually state superintendents for public instruction. They are an important leadership advocates for strengthening preschool initiatives, as a key element in equal educational opportunity and as a means to eliminate achievement gaps. They are committed to working with early childhood and public education communities to implement the five action steps. These steps leverage the value of early childhood education for their state's public education systems. The five CCSSO steps are listed below:

1. Engage families and communities in early learning.
2. Connect early childhood programs and elementary schools.
3. Accelerate improvement and innovation in early childhood programs.
4. Build a high-performing early childhood workforce.
5. Increase investment to provide quality, voluntary early childhood education for all children (Stark & Stark, 2016, p. 5).

Individual states have provided more preschool programs in recent years. Oklahoma and Georgia have led the country in offering voluntary programs for 4-year olds. Florida, New York, North Carolina, and Massachusetts have moved toward universally available programs. However, neither Georgia nor Oklahoma has experienced significant improvement in students' academic performance. Christakis (2016, p. 1) agrees, in the NO article for this issue, finding that preschool classrooms today are increasingly "fraught" places, where children are less inquisitive and "less engaged than kids of earlier generations." (Preschools have been justified as a means to close the achievement gap between poor and well-off children, but they are far from reaching those lofty goals (Christakis, 2016). Lindsey Burke (2015), the Will Skillman Fellow in Education at the Heritage Foundation, a conservative think tank in Washington, DC, argues that preschool primarily benefits disadvantaged children. But the benefits dissipate over time, leaving children who attend preschool no better off academically than those who did not. For most children, "70 to 80 percent of the cognitive gains associated with attending prekindergarten have faded out by the spring of the first grade" (p. 5). *Education Next* reported in their July 16, 2018, article, "More Evidence that Benefits of Government-Funded Pre-K are Overblown," that "at best, increasing pre-K enrollment by 10 percent would raise a state's NAEP scores by a little less than 1 point five years later" (Whitehurst, 2018, p. 1). The results are not statistically significant and with the meagre, less than 1 point gain in NAEP scores 5 years later, preschool appears to have no influence on unadjusted NAEP scores. Whitehurst states, "Leaving aside the positions taken by politicians and pre-K advocates, is there good reason to believe that state pre-K is effective? Or is it another one of the periodic crazes that grip education reform in America, in the absence of or despite available evidence" (p. 2). In the YES article for this issue, Vecchiotti's position is that to have improved outcomes for children in high-quality early care and education (ECE), the ECE workforce must be adequately prepared, competent, supported, and well-compensated. Vecchiotti's article is considered a YES response to the question, has the time come for universal preschool, because it recognizes a strong link between specialized training for early care educators in the workforce and preschool classroom quality and level of child outcomes. The article also explains what the field is doing to transform the profession, for example, the Power to Profession initiative, workforce investment and strategies, Teacher Education and Compensation Helps that is focused on teacher preparation and articulation agreements in several states, the Center for Enhanced Early Learning Outcomes, and others.

Early childhood advocates support government funded pre-K as the surest way for all children to succeed in school and life. The buy-in by politicians is impressive. President Obama articulated this viewpoint in his 2013 state of the union address where he pushed for major increases in federal subsidies, with some commentators saying that the effort was second only to universal health care on the liberal policy agenda. Burke and Sheffield (2013, p. 1) describe Obama's policies on childhood education and care was part of his drive for a "cradle-to-career" government-controlled education system." In agreement with this position, Burke (2015, p. 5) of the Heritage Foundation states, "Proponents of universal government-subsidized preschool have to grapple with the fact that previous universal programs have failed and had negative social impacts on children. Evaluations of large-scale programs, such as those in Quebec and Tennessee, are a better indicator of the potential costs and benefits of universal child care than small, targeted programs are." Whitehurst (2018) notes the push for expansion of state pre-K is bipartisan indicating that about ⅓ of U.S. governors who delivered state of the state addresses in 2018 highlighted early learning initiatives.

Among the advocates of universal preschool is the Pew Center calling for a new strategy of collaboration with community-based partners back in 2009 (e.g., childcare centers, Head Start programs, and faith-based organizations) to enhance access and choice. But, there has also been disillusion with the pre-K growth movement. In an article in *The Washington Post*, "Slow the Preschool Bandwagon," Chester Finn, as quoted in Snell (2009) warned that everybody should pause before embracing universal preschool since "it dumps 5-year-olds, ready or not, into public school classrooms that today are unable even to make and sustain their own achievement gains, much less to capitalize on any advances these youngsters bring from preschool. He concludes that "done right, preschool programs can help America address its urgent education challenges, but todays push for universalism gets it almost entirely wrong" (p. 1). Sara Vecchiotti (2018), from the YES article in this issue, makes a case for continued investment in high-quality preschool by states to help kids succeed. Christakis (2016), from the NO article, sounds cautionary warnings that there is no evidence whatsoever that preschools are closing the achievement gap between poor and well-off children.

YES

Sara Vecchiotti

Transforming the Early Care and Education Workforce

Three ways state boards can elevate the profession and improve outcomes for kids.

The field of early care and education (ECE) and state boards of education alike have focused much attention on the quality and effectiveness of ECE programs.[1] Yet state boards ought also to consider the professionals that directly serve or oversee services to young children. Strong programs and strong outcomes depend on well-prepared, competent, appropriately compensated, and supported ECE professionals.

Now is the time to professionalize the ECE workforce, improve preparation and professional learning, and enhance practice. Several state boards have begun this work, exercising policy-making authority when they have it and working collaboratively with state partners and stakeholders, which all boards can do.

Why Focus on the Workforce?

Lead teachers, teacher assistants, home-based providers, coaches, master teachers, principals, and administrators comprise the ECE workforce, and all are integral to creating enriching, nurturing learning environments for young children, and ensuring high-quality teacher–child interactions.[2] Yet quality varies markedly across programs. The quality of program content, components, supports, and implementation differ, and programs are delivered inconsistently, with practices that fail to reflect recent developmental science.[3] Likewise, early educators have varied competencies, qualifications, compensation, and professional supports, all of which affect program and classroom quality and help achieve positive child outcomes.[4]

The status of the ECE profession reflects the complex, fragmented, disparate ECE system itself. In all 50 states, early educators' educational backgrounds and qualifications differ depending on whether they teach in state prekindergarten, Head Start, or childcare, as well as

compared with family childcare settings.[5] Further, 35 of 59 state pre-K initiatives require the lead teacher to have a bachelor's degree, 51 require specialized training in pre-K, and 19 require teacher assistants to have a child development associate credential or equivalent.[6]

National Survey of Early Care and Education data reveal overall that education levels were higher for those serving children aged 3–5 (45 percent with at least a four-year degree) than for those serving younger children (19 percent with at least a four-year degree).[7] These variances are important: research suggests a link between specialized training in ECE to acquire key competencies and classroom quality and child outcomes.[8]

However, obtaining a degree does not guarantee teacher competence. Teacher preparation programs within institutions of higher education also vary widely in terms of coursework, clinical/field-based preservice practice, and induction supports, as well as whether developmental science informed program design.[9] Therefore, there is room to align definitions of what ECE professionals should know and be able to do in instructing and supporting children's learning with determining standards for what curricula, field experiences, and induction supports adequately prepare student teachers.

A focus on training and knowledge is not enough. Improving compensation and supporting well-being is also essential. ECE professionals are routinely compensated at low-income levels, even for those with high levels of educational attainment. In fact, large percentages of the workforce need public assistance to support their own children and families—34 percent of prekindergarten and kindergarten teachers and 46 percent of childcare workers. Compare this with the 13 percent of elementary and middle school teachers and 53 percent of fast-food workers receiving assistance.[10] Economic worry leads to stress and depression, potentially affecting teacher well-being, which in turn can hamper teachers' ability to be supportive of and responsive to children in the classroom.[11]

Large percentages of the workforce need public assistance to support their own children and families.

Well-being also stems from whether professionals feel supported within their work environment, which includes their ability to access supports for professional learning. Professional development that is of high quality, intentional in purpose and design, and focused on effective instructional strategies can improve teacher practice and thereby improve child outcomes.[12] However, not all ECE professionals have such opportunities for ongoing learning.[13]

Moving toward more unified ECE professional systems—from preparation to competencies to compensation and professional supports—can help reduce the wide variability in program and classroom quality and better support children.

What Is the Field Doing?

Much is happening in the field of ECE to transform the profession. For example, the Power to the Profession initiative convenes 15 ECE professional and member organizations in a national taskforce to define a shared framework of knowledge and competencies, qualifications, and compensation for all professionals working with children birth through age 8.[14] Currently, five states within the Power to the Profession initiative are engaged in intensive state-based communications and advocacy building work.[15] As a follow-up to the groundbreaking workforce report from the Institute of Medicine/National Research Council (IOM/NRC) in 2015, the National Academies of Sciences, Engineering, and Medicine has organized implementation teams in several states that are focused on realizing specific recommendations from the report.[16]

In addition, the National Governors Association supported six states in development of a policy agenda to strengthen the ECE profession through workforce investments and strategies; another cohort of states is scheduled for 2018.[17] Teacher Education and Compensation Helps focused efforts on teacher preparation articulation agreements and compensation in several states.[18] The Center for Enhanced Early Learning Outcomes and the BUILD Initiative sponsored roundtables that convened states

on instruction tools, credentialing, and implementing IOM/NRC recommendations.[19] The Foundation for Child Development has supported the National Association of State Boards of Education (NASBE), the National League of Cities, and the National Association for the Education of Young Children (NAEYC) to help several states and cities focus on ECE workforce issues.[20]

What Can State Boards Do?

There are several ways state boards can exercise their policy-making authority and their roles as advocates and consensus builders to strengthen the ECE workforce. Boards have varied roles in this domain: setting requirements for core early learning standards, advancing workforce credentialing and preparation, and improving professional development opportunities. Across the country, 16 state boards have authority over standards, 32 have authority over pre-K–12 teacher licensure, and 28 have sole authority over teacher preparation programs.[21]

All boards have the power to transform the workforce. Table 1 shows how board authorities align with the recommendations of the IOM/NRC report and three key goals: professionalize the field, improve preparation and professional learning, and enhance practice.

Goal 1: Professionalize the Field. The 32 state boards with authority over pre-K–12 teacher licensure can set core competencies for early learning educators as the basis for certification and licensing, thereby strengthening competency-based qualifications.[22] Rather than starting from scratch, states can benefit from the ongoing efforts of the Power to the Professions taskforce, which is working toward defining these competencies.[23]

In rethinking competencies, state boards should ask these questions: Do current qualification and certification requirements align with what teachers and principals should know and be able to do to support children's learning? Are the required competencies informed by child developmental science? Are they informed by what the field and ECE profession see as needed competencies? Are the ECE administrator and principal leaders who are included in planning representative of mixed-delivery systems? Boards can work to answer such questions and, in conjunction with other state agencies, can examine

Boards can examine qualifications and adopt competencies for professionals across the birth to age 8 continuum.

qualifications and adopt competencies for professionals across the birth to age 8 continuum.

The IOM/NRC report provides a starting point for establishing core knowledge and competencies.[24] For example, it suggests that all ECE professionals should know how children develop and learn across the developmental domains (cognitive, socioemotional, etc.), and they should know how the areas of development interact to promote children's learning and further development. Armed with such knowledge, early educators can create goal and objective-based learning opportunities and use a portfolio of instructional strategies to support individual learning trajectories.

Goal 2: Improve Preparation and Professional Learning. Another relevant area of board authority relates to establishing standards for accreditation of preparation programs for teachers and administrators, and such standards should align with the competencies required for teacher certification and licensure. Through such accreditation, state boards can influence how early educators are prepared and align preparation standards with core competencies.

Questions to consider in rethinking standards for teacher preparation: Are teacher education programs adequately preparing students to meet the demands of ECE settings? Are programs preparing administrators and principal leaders who are well versed in ECE? Is content, curriculum, and pedagogy aligned with the required competencies? Are efforts focused on recruiting and retaining a diverse ECE student population? Are programs effectively providing preservice clinical, field-based practical experiences and supporting graduates in their first years of teaching? Do institutions of higher education have articulation agreements supportive of a career ladder?[25]

Goal 3: Enhance the Quality of Professional Practice. State boards have a significant role, alongside their education agencies, in planning and implementing the Every Student Succeeds Act (ESSA) and administering federal assistance programs, as well as developing rules and regulations for the administration of state programs, including state pre-K.

Questions to consider: Does the state have an overall vision and plan for ECE? How can a state use ESSA to strengthen the ECE workforce and coordinate it with other state plans and efforts? How can opportunities for professional learning and collaboration within ESSA be used to improve the quality of ECE practice? Are early educators and kindergarten and elementary school teachers themselves compensated at a level equivalent to that of secondary educators? Boards can help direct ESSA implementation toward a focus on the ECE workforce and provide opportunities for gaining the following:

- sustained, embedded, and data-driven professional development for ECE teachers and leaders (Titles I and II);
- specialized knowledge in professional development for curricula, literacy, assessment, family engagement, school readiness, and dual language learners (Titles I and II);

Figure 1

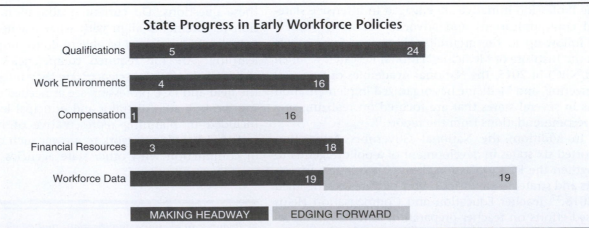

State Progress in Early Workforce Policies

	MAKING HEADWAY	EDGING FORWARD
Qualifications	5	24
Work Environments	4	16
Compensation	1	16
Financial Resources	3	18
Workforce Data	19	19

Source: Marcy Whitebook et al., *"Early Childhood Workforce Index 2016"* (Berkeley, CA: Center for the Study of Child Care Employment Institute for Research on Labor and Employment, University of California, 2016).

Table 1

ECE Workforce Recommendations, Goals, and Board Authorities.

Recommendation	Goal	Authority
1. Strengthen competency-based qualification requirements for all care and education professionals working with children from birth through age 8.	Professionalize the field	Certification and licensure
2. Develop and implement comprehensive pathways and multiyear timelines for transitioning to a minimum bachelor's degree qualification requirement, with specialized knowledge and competencies, for all lead educators working with children from birth through age 8.	Professionalize the field	Certification and licensure
3. Strengthen practice-based qualification requirements for all lead educators working with children from birth through age 8.	Professionalize the field	Certification and licensure
4. Build an interdisciplinary foundation in higher education for child development.	Improve preparation and professional learning	Accreditation of preparation programs
5. Develop and enhance programs in higher education for care and education professionals working with children from birth through age 8.	Improve preparation and professional learning	Accreditation of preparation programs
6. Support the consistent quality and coherence of professional learning supports during ongoing practice for professionals working with children from birth through age 8.	Enhance the quality of professional practice	Professional development systems and ESSA implementation
7. Develop a new paradigm for evaluation and assessment of professional practice for those who work with children from birth through age 8.	Enhance the quality of professional practice	Professional development systems and ESSA implementation
8. Ensure that policies and standards for care and education leaders encompass the foundational knowledge and competencies needed to support high-quality practices for child development and early learning.	Professionalize the field	Certification and Licensure
9. Strengthen collaboration and communication among professionals and systems within the care and education sector and with closely related sectors, especially health and social services.	All three goals	All authorities
10. Support workforce development with coherent funding, oversight, and policies.	All three goals	All authorities
11. Collaboratively develop and periodically update coherent guidance that is foundational across roles and settings for care and education professionals working with children from birth through age 8.	All three goals	All authorities
12. Support comprehensive state- and local-level efforts to transform the professional workforce for children from birth through age 8.	All three goals	All authorities
13. Build a better knowledge base to inform workforce development and professional learning services and systems.	All three goals	All authorities

Source: Institute of Medicine/National Research Council, "*Transforming the Workforce for Children Birth Through Age 8: A Unifying Foundation,*" 2015.

- staff coaching by experienced teachers, principals, and faculty through higher education partnerships (Title II);
- induction programs and ongoing evaluation for administrators and teachers in pre-K-3 (Titles I and II);
- residency programs for teachers, principals, and other school leaders (Title II).

ESSA implementation also gives boards opportunities to support recruitment, hiring, and selection of promising, diverse, effective ECE educators (Title II). Boards can also work through ESSA implementation and in their advocacy role to ensure appropriate compensation. Establishing parity for teachers in community-based organizations with public school counterparts for Title I preschool programs and state pre-K is an important first step.

Four State Boards Make a Start

Much work remains to develop supportive ECE workforce policies at the state level (Figure 1). To support state efforts, the Foundation for Child Development provided funding to NASBE to work with four state boards that committed to focus on the ECE workforce by rethinking early educator competencies and certification, preparation programs, career pathways and professional development, and evaluation. Below is a brief description of the work occurring in each state:

- The Iowa State Board of Education is working with its department of education to define early learning standards for every K–3 classroom and strengthen policies to support Iowa's ECE workforce. Part of the work includes developing knowledge and skill-based competencies and providing professional learning for K–3 educators that aligns with early learning standards.
- Michigan's state board is developing a strategic framework for an infrastructure to support a qualified ECE workforce serving children birth through age 8. The work involves integrating personnel development systems across the ECE workforce; aligning career pathways to core knowledge and competencies; examining licensure programs, standards, tests, and grade bands; determining professional learning opportunities; and proposing policy recommendations to support the ECE workforce.
- Nebraska's state board is reviewing requirements for ECE leaders and expanding professional development opportunities (e.g., online training) for teachers, principals, and other administrators with responsibilities for educating children from birth through third grade.
- The New York State Board of Regents established a Blue Ribbon Committee on Early Learning to help launch a unified, competency-based early educator preparation program that addresses the diverse needs of children in their early years and a professional development system for the ECE workforce.

While the state boards are working individually, they will also collaborate in other ECE workforce efforts that the National League of Cities and NAEYC are leading.

Such joint work and peer-to-peer learning is expected to link and leverage varying levels of government systems (state boards of education and municipal leaders) and professional associations (state/local NAEYC affiliates) to create a more effective, inclusive policy-making approach.

Conclusion

There is ample opportunity for state boards to improve outcomes for children by strengthening the early care and education workforce and thereby improving the quality of early care and education. Ensuring that ECE professionals have the knowledge, supports, and resources they need to support children's learning is one avenue to improving the quality of teacher–child interactions and of children's learning environments.

Children will not receive benefits from early care and education unless ECE professionals are adequately prepared, competent, supported, and well-compensated. By enhancing the ECE workforce, state boards can ensure that all children have a chance to receive a high-quality early education. Unless states focus on the ECE workforce, the extant context of fragmented, inconsistent ECE systems and varying ECE program quality will continue. Moreover, children will continue to miss opportunities for equitable, high-quality ECE experiences that can help them reach their full potential.

Children will not receive benefits from early care and education unless ECE professionals are adequately prepared, competent, supported, and well-compensated.

Notes

1. E. S. Peisner-Feinberg et al., "The Children of the Cost, Quality, and Outcomes Study Go to School: Technical Report" (Chapel Hill, NC: University of North Carolina at Chapel Hill, Frank Porter Graham Child Development Center, 2000); W. T. Gormley et al., "The Effects of Universal Pre-K on Cognitive Development," *Developmental Psychology* 41, no. 6 (2005), 72–84; U.S. Department of Health and Human Services, Administration for Children and Families, Head Start Impact Study, Final Report (Washington, DC, January 2010); Yoshikawa et al., "Investing in Our Future: The

Evidence Base on Preschool Education" (New York and Washington: Foundation for Child Development and Society for Research in Child Development, October 2013); Deborah A. Phillips et al., "The Current State of Scientific Knowledge on Pre-Kindergarten Effects" (Washington, DC: Brookings Institution and the Duke Center for Child and Family Policy, April 20, 2017).

2. In 2015, the Institute of Medicine/National Research Council (IOM/NRC) released "Transforming the Workforce for Children Birth Through Age 8: A Unifying Foundation." The consensus report stemmed from multidisciplinary, independent, objective, and nonpartisan expert committees that provided thorough issue reviews and evidence-based recommendations. The IOM/NRC report highlighted the importance of the ECE workforce for program quality and positive outcomes for young children. See also Institute of Medicine, *From Neurons to Neighborhoods: The Science of Early Childhood Development* (Washington, DC: The National Academies Press, 2000); B. K. Hamre, "Teachers' Daily Interactions with Children: An Essential Ingredient in Effective Early Childhood Programs," *Child Development Perspectives* 8, no. 4 (2014): 223–30; Diane Early et al., "Teachers' Education, Classroom Quality, and Young Children's Academic Skills: Results from Seven Studies of Preschool Programs," *Child Development* 78, no. 2 (2007): 558–80.

3. Center on the Developing Child, Harvard University, "From Best Practices to Breakthrough Impacts: A Science-Based Approach to Building a More Promising Future for Young Children and Families" (Boston, MA, 2016); Phillips et al., "Current State of Scientific Knowledge."

4. Center of Developing Child, "From Best Practices to Breakthrough Impacts"; Ajay Chaudry, "The Promise of Preschool Education: Challenges for Policy and Governance" in Phillips et al., "Current State of Scientific Knowledge," 75–84.

5. Marcy Whitebook et al., "Early Childhood Workforce Index—2016" (Berkeley, CA: Center for the Study of Child Care Employment, University of California, Berkeley, 2016).

6. National Institute for Early Education Research, "The State of Preschool 2016: State Preschool Yearbook" (New Jersey: Rutgers University, 2017).

7. National Survey of Early Care and Education Project Team, "Number and Characteristics of Early Care and Education Teachers and Caregivers: Initial Findings, National Survey of Early Care and Education," *OPRE Report* #2013-38 (Washington, DC: Office of Planning, Research and Evaluation, Administration for Children and Families, U.S. Department of Health and Human Services, 2013).

8. IOM/NRC, "Transforming the Workforce"; M. Bueno, et al. "A Matter of Degrees: Preparing Teachers for the Pre-K Classroom" (Washington, DC: Pew Center on the States, 2010).

9. IOM/NRC, "Transforming the Workforce"; Marcy Whitebook, "By Default or by Design? Variations in Higher Education Programs for Early Care and Teachers and Their Implications for Research Methodology, Policy, and Practice" (Berkeley, CA: Center for the Study of Child Care Employment, University of California, Berkeley, 2012); Marcy Whitebook and Lea J. E. Austin, "Early Childhood Higher Education: Taking Stock across the States" (Berkeley, CA: Center for the Study of Child Care Employment, University of California, Berkeley, 2015).

10. Whitebook et al., "Early Childhood Workforce Index."

11. E. J. De Schipper et al., "Cortisol Levels of Caregivers in Child Care Centers as Related to the Quality of Their Caregiving," *Early Childhood Research Quarterly* 24, no. 1 (2009): 55–63; Lieny Jeon, et al., "Pathways from Teacher Depression and Child Care Quality to Child Behavioral Problems," *Journal of Consulting and Clinical Psychology* 82 (2014): 225–35; R. C. Whitaker et al., "Workplace Stress and the Quality of Teacher–Children Relationships in Head Start," *Early Childhood Research Quarterly* 30 (2015): 57–69.

12. Ruben Fukkink and Anna Lont, "Does Training Matter? A Meta-Analysis and Review of Caregiver Training Studies," *Early Childhood Research Quarterly* 22, no. 3 (2007): 294–311; U.S. Department of Education, Office of Planning, Evaluation and Policy Development, Policy and Program Studies Service, "Toward the Identification of Features of Effective Professional Development for Early Childhood Educators, Literature Review" (Washington, DC, 2010).

13. IOM/NRC, "Transforming the Workforce"; McCormick Center for Early Childhood Leadership, "Quality Standards Drive Professional Development Opportunities" (Wheeling, IL: National Louis University, 2016).

14. The program is described here: http://www.naeyc.org/ profession/overview.

15. The states participating are Indiana, Iowa, New Mexico, New York, and Wisconsin.

16. IOM/NRC, "Transforming the Workforce." The project is described at http://www.nas.edu/i2I. The states participating are California, Colorado, Illinois, Indiana, Minnesota, Nebraska, New York, Virginia, and Washington, and the region of Washington, DC, Maryland, and Northern Virginia is also participating.

17. Governors in the following states participated: Iowa, Minnesota, New Jersey, New York, Utah, and Washington.

18. States participating in these efforts are Alabama, Arizona, Florida, Indiana, Iowa, Michigan, Nebraska, North Carolina, Ohio, Texas, West Virginia, and Wisconsin. In addition, TEACH is also active in Colorado, Delaware, Kansas, Minnesota, Missouri, Nevada, New Mexico, Pennsylvania, Rhode Island, South Carolina, Utah, Vermont, and Washington, DC.

19. The states that participated are California, Florida, Georgia, Illinois, Indiana, Louisiana, Massachusetts, Mississippi, Nebraska, New Jersey, North Carolina, Pennsylvania, Rhode Island, South Carolina, Tennessee, and Washington.

20. The states participating include Iowa, Michigan, Nebraska, and New York. The cities participating include Hartford, Connecticut; Jacksonville, Florida; Kansas City, Missouri; and Richmond, Virginia. Rochester, New York, San Francisco, and Seattle serve as advisor cities.

21. Winona Hao, "Advancing the Early Learning Workforce through State Policies," *Policy Update* 23, no. 25 (Alexandria, VA: NASBE, 2016); e-mail communication from Winona Hao, September 22, 2017.

22. See IOM/NRC recommendations 1, 2, 3, and 8.

23. The four states in NASBE's early learning group will be considering these competencies as part of their efforts.

24. IOM/NRC, "Transforming the Workforce," pp. 496–501.

25. Table 1 shows state boards could be instrumental in implementing IOM/NRC recommendations 4 and 5 regarding preparation and high-quality practice.

SARA VECCHIOTTI is the vice president, Research and Program Innovation at the Foundation for Child Development, and is responsible for Research, Program and Grant development and monitoring, as well as Communications strategies.

Erika Christakis

How the New Preschool Is Crushing Kids

Today's young children are working more, but they're learning less.

STEP INTO an American preschool classroom today and you are likely to be bom-barded with what we educators call a print-rich environment, every surface festooned with alphabet charts, bar graphs, word walls, instructional posters, classroom rules, calendars, schedules, and motivational platitudes—few of which a 4-year-old can "decode," the contemporary word for what used to be known as reading.

Because so few adults can remember the pertinent details of their own **preschool** or kindergarten years, it can be hard to appreciate just how much the early-education landscape has been transformed over the past two decades. The changes are not restricted to the confusing pastiche on classroom walls. Pedagogy and curricula have changed too, most recently in response to the Common Core State Standards Initiative's kindergarten guidelines. Much greater portions of the day are now spent on what's called "seat work" (a term that probably doesn't need any exposition) and a form of tightly scripted teaching known as direct instruction, formerly used mainly in the older grades, in which a teacher carefully controls the content and pacing of what a child is supposed to learn.

One study, titled "Is Kindergarten the New First Grade?," compared kindergarten teachers' attitudes nation-wide in 1998 and 2010 and found that the percentage of teachers expecting children to know how to read by the end of the year had risen from 30 to 80 percent. The researchers also reported more time spent with workbooks and worksheets, and less time devoted to music and art. Kindergarten is indeed the new first grade, the authors concluded glumly. In turn, children who would once have used the kindergarten year as a gentle transition into school are in some cases being held back before they've had a chance to start. A study out of Mississippi found that in some counties, more than 10 percent of kindergartners weren't allowed to advance to first grade.

Until recently, school-readiness skills weren't high on anyone's agenda, nor was the idea that the youngest learners might be disqualified from moving on to a subsequent stage. But now that kindergarten serves as a gatekeeper, not a welcome mat, to elementary school, concerns about school preparedness kick in earlier and earlier. A child who's supposed to read by the end of kindergarten had better be getting ready in **preschool**. As a result, expectations that may arguably have been reasonable for 5- and 6-year-olds, such as being able to sit at a desk and complete a task using pencil and paper, are now directed at even younger children, who lack the motor skills and attention span to be successful.

Preschool classrooms have become increasingly fraught spaces, with teachers cajoling their charges to finish their "work" before they can go play. And yet, even as preschoolers are learning more pre-academic skills at earlier ages, I've heard many teachers say that they seem somehow—is it possible?—less inquisitive and less engaged than the kids of earlier generations. More children today seem to lack the language skills needed to retell a simple story or to use basic connecting words and prepositions. They can't make a conceptual analogy between, say, the veins on a leaf and the veins in their own hands.

New research sounds a particularly disquieting note. A major evaluation of Tennessee's publicly funded **preschool** system, published in September, found that although children who had attended **preschool** initially exhibited more "school readiness" skills when they entered kindergarten than did their non-**preschool**-attending peers, by the time they were in first grade their attitudes toward school were deteriorating. And by second grade they performed worse on tests measuring literacy, language, and math skills. The researchers told New York magazine that overreliance on direct instruction and repetitive, poorly structured pedagogy were likely culprits; children who'd been subjected to the same insipid tasks year after year after year were understandably losing their enthusiasm for learning.

That's right. The same educational policies that are pushing academic goals down to ever earlier levels seem to be contributing to—while at the same time obscuring—the fact that young children are gaining fewer skills, not more.

PENDULUM SHIFTS in education are as old as our republic. Steven Mintz, a historian who has written about the evolution of American childhood, describes an oscillation in the national zeitgeist between the notion of a "protected" childhood and that of a "prepared" one. Starting in the early 2000s, though, a confluence of forces began pushing preferences ever further in the direction of preparation: the increasing numbers of dual-career families scrambling to arrange child care; a new scientific focus on the cognitive potential of the early years; and concerns about growing ability gaps between well-off and disadvantaged children, which in turn fueled the trend of standards-based testing in public schools.

Preschool is a relatively recent addition to the American educational system. With a few notable exceptions, the government had a limited role in early education until the 1960s, when the federal Head Start program was founded. Before mothers entered the full-time workforce in large numbers, private **preschools** were likewise uncommon, and mainly served as a safe social space for children to learn to get along with others.

In the past few decades, however, we have seen a major transfer of child care and early learning from home to institution: Nearly three-quarters of American 4-year-olds are now in some kind of nonfamily care. That category spans a dizzying mix of privately and publicly funded **preschool** environments, including family-run day cares, private **preschools** in church basements, and Head Start programs in public elementary schools, to name a few. Across all of them, the distinction between early education and "official" school seems to be eroding.

When I survey parents of preschoolers, they tend to be on board with many of these changes, either because they fear that the old-fashioned pleasures of unhurried learning have no place in today's hypercompetitive world or because they simply can't find, or afford, a better option. The stress is palpable: Pick the "wrong" **preschool** or ease up on the phonics drills at home, and your child might not go to college. She might not be employable. She might not even be allowed to start first grade!

Media attention to the cognitive potential of early childhood has a way of exacerbating such worries, but the actual academic consensus on the components of high-quality early education tells another story. According to experts such as the Yale professor Edward Zigler, a leader in child-development and early-education policy for half a century, the best **preschool** programs share several features: They provide ample opportunities for young children to use and hear complex, interactive language; their curriculum supports a wide range of school-readiness goals that include social and emotional skills and active learning;

they encourage meaningful family involvement; and they have knowledgeable and well-qualified teachers.

As an early-childhood educator, I've clocked many hours in many **preschool** classrooms, and I have found that I can pretty quickly take the temperature from the looks on kids' faces, the ratio of table space to open areas, and the amount of conversation going on in either. In a high-quality program, adults are building relationships with the children and paying close attention to their thought processes and, by extension, their communication. They're finding ways to make the children think out loud.

The real focus in the **preschool** years should be not just on vocabulary and reading, but on talking and listening. We forget how vital spontaneous, unstructured conversation is to young children's understanding. By talking with adults, and one another, they pick up information. They learn how things work. They solve puzzles that trouble them. Sometimes, to be fair, what children take away from a conversation is wrong. They might conclude, as my young son did, that pigs produce ham, just as chickens produce eggs and cows produce milk. But these understandings are worked over, refined, and adapted—as when a brutal older sibling explains a ham sandwich's grisly origins.

Teachers play a crucial role in supporting this type of learning. A 2011 study in the journal Child Development found that **preschool** teachers' use of sophisticated vocabulary in informal classroom settings predicted their students' reading comprehension and word knowledge in fourth grade. Unfortunately, much of the conversation in today's **preschool** classrooms is one-directional and simplistic, as teachers steer students through a highly structured schedule, herding them from one activity to another and signaling approval with a quick "good job!"

Consider the difference between a teacher's use of a closed statement versus an open-ended question. Imagine that a teacher approaches a child drawing a picture and exclaims, "Oh, what a pretty house!" If the child is not actually drawing a house, she might feel exposed, and even if she is drawing a house, the teacher's remark shuts down further discussion: She has labeled the thing and said she likes it. What more is there to add? A much more helpful approach would be to say, "Tell me about your drawing," inviting the child to be reflective. It's never possible to anticipate everything a small person needs to learn, so open-ended inquiry can reveal what is known and unknown. Such a small pedagogic difference can be an important catalyst for a basic, but unbounded, cognitive habit—the act of thinking out loud.

Conversation is gold. It's the most efficient early-learning system we have. And it's far more valuable than most of the reading-skills curricula we have been implementing: One meta-analysis of 13 early-childhood literacy programs "failed to find any evidence of effects on language or print-based outcomes." Take a moment to digest that devastating conclusion.

I WAS RECENTLY ASKED to review a popular **preschool** curriculum that comes with a big box of thematic units, including lists of words and "key concepts" that children are supposed to master. One objective of the curriculum's ocean unit, for example, is to help preschoolers understand "the importance of the ocean to the environment." Children are given a list of specific terms to learn, including exoskeleton, scallop shell, blubber, and tube feet. At first glance, this stuff seems fun and educational, but doesn't this extremely narrow articulation of "key concepts" feel a little off? What's so special about blubber, anyway? Might a young child not want to ponder bigger questions: What is water? Where do the blue and green come from? Could anything be more beautiful and more terrifying than an ocean?

The shift from an active and exploratory early-childhood pedagogy to a more scripted and instruction-based model does not involve a simple trade-off between play and work, or between joy and achievement. On the contrary, the preoccupation with accountability has led to a set of measures that favor shallow mimicry and recall behaviors, such as learning vocabulary lists and recognizing shapes and colors (some-thing that a dog can do, by the way, but that is in fact an extraordinarily low bar for most curious 4-year-olds), while devaluing complex, integrative, and syncretic learning.

Last year, I observed some preschoolers conversing about whether snakes have bones. They argued at length among themselves, comparing the flexible serpentine body with dinosaur fossils and fish, both of which they had previously explored. There was no clear consensus on how these various creatures could contain the same hard skeletons, but I watched, transfixed, as each child added to the groundwork another had laid. The teacher gently guided the group as a captain might steer a large ship, with the tiniest nudge of the wheel. Finally, a little boy who had seen a snake skeleton in a museum became animated as he pantomimed the structure of a snake's spine in a series of karate chops: "One bone, one bone, one bone," he informed his friends. "I think we're all going to have to do a lot more research," the teacher replied, impressed. This loosely Socratic method is a perfect fit for young minds; the problem is that it doesn't conform easily to a school-readiness checklist.

The academic takeover of American early learning can be understood as a shift from what I would call an "ideas-based curriculum" to a "naming-and-labeling-based curriculum." Not coincidentally, the latter can be delivered without substantially improving our teaching force. Inexperienced or poorly supported teachers are directed to rely heavily on scripted lesson plans for a reason: We can

point to a defined objective, and tell ourselves that at least kids are getting something this way.

But that something—while relatively cheap to provide—is awfully thin gruel. One major study of 700 **preschool** classrooms in 11 states found that only 15 percent showed evidence of effective interactions between teacher and child. Fifteen percent.

We neglect vital teacher-child interactions at our peril. Although the infusion of academics into **preschool** has been justified as a way to close the achievement gap between poor and well-off children, Robert Pianta, one of the country's leading child-policy experts, cautions that there is "no evidence whatsoever" that our early-learning system is suited to that task. He estimates that the average preschool program "narrows the achievement gap by perhaps only 5 percent," compared with the 30 to 50 percent that studies suggest would be possible with higher-quality programs. Contrasting the dismal results of Tennessee's preschool system with the more promising results in places such as Boston, which promotes active, child-centered learning (and, spends more than twice the national average on **preschool**), lends further credence to the idea that preschool quality really does matter.

It's become almost a cliché to look to Finland's educational system for inspiration. As has been widely reported, the country began to radically professionalize its workforce in the 1970s and abandoned most of the performance standards endemic to American schooling. Today, Finland's schools are consistently ranked among the world's very best. This "Finnish miracle" sounds almost too good to be true. Surely the country must have a few dud teachers and slacker kids!

And yet, when I've visited Finland, I've found it impossible to remain unmoved by the example of **preschools** where the learning environment is assessed, rather than the children in it. Having rejected many of the pseudo-academic benchmarks that can, and do, fit on a scorecard, **preschool** teachers in Finland are free to focus on what's really essential: their relationship with the growing child.

Here's what the Finns, who don't begin formal reading instruction until around age 7, have to say about preparing preschoolers to read: "The basis for the beginnings of literacy is that children have heard and listened . . . They have spoken and been spoken to, people have discussed [things] with them . . . They have asked questions and received answers."

For our littlest learners, what could be more important than that?

ERIKA CHRISTAKIS is an American early childhood educator and author of The Importance of Being Little.

EXPLORING THE ISSUE

Has the Time Arrived for Universal Preschool?

Critical Thinking and Reflection

1. What has been the government's role in early education?
2. Why do some feel that preschool is a strategy to close the achievement gap?
3. What does a high-quality preschool look like?
4. Is preschool just another year of school? Explain.
5. What are key concepts that children are supposed to master in a preschool curriculum?

Is There Common Ground?

There is a prominent ongoing debate focused on the expansion of publicly funded preschool education. It is not a new debate as studies and surveys have been a part of the preschool landscape through the years. A combined report from the Society for Research in Child Development and Foundation for Child Development in 2013, *Investing in Our Future: The Evidence Base on Preschool Education*, asserts, "While there is clear evidence that preschool education boosts early learning for children from a range of backgrounds, we also see a convergence of test scores during the elementary school grades so that are diminishing differences over time on tests of academic achievement between children who did and did not attend preschool" (Yoshikawa et al., 2013, p. 14). Snell (2008), reported 10 years ago on her web posting, "Preschool's Failures: Where Are the Long-term Benefits?" evidence that the high-quality preschool program in Tennessee produced no statistical achievement difference between those who attended preschool and those who did not. In Oklahoma, where preschool had been in place for two decades, math and reading scores were still below the national average. Around the same time, in his book, *Re-route the Pre-school Juggernaut*, Chester E. Finn, Jr. (2009) attempted to stifle the momentum of the universal preschool campaign spearheaded by then secretary of education Arne Duncan, David L. Kirp, Libby Doggett of Pre-K Now, W. Steven Barnett, and others. Precisely as these strategists intend, he claims, "Many Americans are coming to believe that pre-kindergarten is a good and necessary thing for government to provide; indeed that not providing it will cruelly deprive our youngest residents of their birthrights, blight

their educational futures, and dim their life prospects." The result, he contends, has been strong public support for the movement with little consideration of how it will be paid for. Also at the time, Federal funding supported the work of the State Advisory Councils on Early Childhood Education and Care as a strategic investment by the Obama Administration for Children and Families in early childhood infrastructure. This foundational work was accomplished not only as a result of federal investment but also as a state investment. See the U.S. Department of Health and Human Services and U.S. Department of Education websites for specific and current information on the Federal role in preschool education.

Douglas Besharov and Douglas Call (2008) raised concerns about the preschool movement in their works "The New Kindergarten" and "Preschool Puzzle: As State After State Expands PreK Schooling, Questions Remain." In these documents Besharov addresses the problem of whether a preschool program can reduce the racial/ethnic achievement gap and the issue of who should receive expanded funding for early care and education. The May 2010 issue of *Phi Delta Kappan* offers nine articles on universal preschool. The 2016 CCSSO report, *Equity Starts Early: How Chiefs Will Build High Quality Early Education*, mentioned earlier in this issue is more recent, relevant, and ready as a strategy to improve outcomes, narrow achievement gaps, and convey long-term benefits for children in school and life (Stark & Stark, 2016). Christakis (2016, p. 2) in the NO article for this issue, states that:

> even as preschoolers are learning more pre-academic skills at earlier ages, I've heard many

teachers say that they seem somehow—Is it possible?—less inquisitive and less engaged than the kids of earlier generations. More children today seem to lack the language skills

needed to retell a simple story or to use basic connecting words and prepositions. They can't make a conceptual analogy between, say, the veins on a leaf and the veins in their own hands.

With all the naysayers who doubt the benefits of preschool for students across the nation, there are many who feel just the opposite. Recently, a group of top researchers in early childhood education, including Deborah Phillips of Georgetown University, Mark W. Lipsey of Vanderbilt, Kenneth Dodge of Duke, and Ron Haskins of the Brookings Institution, gathered in Washington, DC, to end the debates over the benefits of preschool. "They came away with one clear, strong message: Kids who attend public preschool programs are better prepared for kindergarten than kids who don't" (Sancez, 2017, p. 1).

Additional Resources

Barnette, S. & Frede, E. (2010). The promise of preschool: Why we need early education for all. *American Educator*. 34:1.

Burke, L. (2015). *Research review: Universal preschool may do more harm than good*. Heritage Foundation. Retrieved from https://www.heritage.org/education/report/research-review-universal-preschool-may-do-more-harm-good

Burke, L. & Shefield, R. (2013). *Universal preschools' empty promise*. Heritage Foundation. Retrieved from http://www.heritage.org/research/reports/2013/03/universal-preschools-empty-promises

Fetterman, M. (2018). *More money—and stricter scrutiny—for child care*. The PEW Charitable Trust. Retrieved from http://www.pewtrusts.org/en/research-and-analysis/blogs/stateline/2018/07/06/more-money-and-stricter-scrutiny-for-child-care

Finn, C. (2009). *Re-route the pre-school juggernaut*. Stanford, CA: Hoover Institution Press Publication.

National Center for Educational Statistics. (2018). *The condition of education 2017*. Preschool and kindergarten enrolment. Retrieved from https://nces.ed.gov/pubs2017/2017144.pdf

National Institute for Early Education Research. (2018) *State of preschool 2017*. Retrieved from http://nieer.org/wp-content/uploads/2018/07/2018-07-03-change_over_time.jpg

Stark, D. & Stark, F. (2016). *Equity starts early: How chiefs will build high-quality education*. Council of Chief State School Officers. Washington, DC. Retrieved from file:///C:/Users/Glenn/Downloads/EquityStartsEarly3242016.pdf

Whitehurst, G. (2018). More evidence that benefits of government-funded pre-k are overblown. *EdNext.org*. Retrieved from https://www.educationnext.org/evidence-benefits-government-funded-pre-k-overblown/

Sancez, C. (2017). Preschool: Decades worth of studies, one strong message. *nprEd*. Retrieved from https://www.npr.org/sections/ed/2017/05/03/524907739/pre-k-decades-worth-of-studies-one-strong-message

Yoshikawa, H., Weiland, C., Brooks-Gunn, J., Burchinal, J., Espinosa, L., Gormley, W., Ludwig, J., Magnuson, K., Phillips, D., & Zaslow, M. (2013). *Investing in our future: The evidence base on preschool education*. Society for Research in Child Development and Foundation for Child Development. Retrieved from http://fcd-us.org/sites/default/files/Evidence%20Base%20on%20Preschool%20Education%20FINAL.pdf

Internet References . . .

Do We Already Have Universal Preschool?

https://www.brookings.edu/research/do-we-already-
have-universal-preschool/

Public Preferences for Targeted and Universal Preschool

http://journals.sagepub.com/doi/
full/10.1177/2332858417753125

The Push for Pre-kindergarten: Has the Time Come for Universal Early Education?

https://www.syracuse.com/news/index.ssf/2013/04/
the_push_for_pre-kindergarten.html

Three Reasons Universal Preschool Is Valuable

https://www.parents.com/toddlers-preschoolers/
starting-preschool/preparing/3-reasons-universal-
preschool-is-valuable/

Universal Pre-K is Hard to Find and Harder to Fund

http://www.governing.com/topics/education/gov-
universal-pre-kindergarten.html

Selected, Edited, and with Issue Framing Material by:
Glenn L. Koonce, *Regent University*

ISSUE

Should Teacher Preparation and Licensing Be Regulated by the Government?

YES: James Cibulka, from "Strengthen State Oversight of Teacher Preparation," *Education Next* (2013)

NO: David Chard, from "Training Must Focus on Content and Pedagogy," *Education Next* (2013)

Learning Outcomes

After reading this issue, you will be able to:

- Assess the need to include courses on the science of reading instruction or on mathematics content in all elementary-educator preparation programs as well as various culture studies due to dramatic shifts in the demographics of our country.

- Evaluate the need to bring public, private, and not-for-profit sectors together to forge a concrete plan for studying and strengthening teacher preparation programs.

- Research the need for a reformed teacher-licensure system in our knowledge-based, globally competitive economy.

- Critique options for ways to improve practices and incentives to help attract high-quality teachers to the educational field of teaching.

- Analyze the difference between increased government licensure regulations and focusing on training in content and pedagogy.

ISSUE SUMMARY

YES: Council for the Accreditation of Educator Preparation President Jim Cibulka states that tightening government licensure regulation is needed to assure candidate and program quality that can result in a more favorable learning environment for Pre-K–12 students.

NO: David Chard indicates that current state control of teacher preparation and licensing does not ensure that teachers will be of high quality.

Licensing of teachers in most states is a function of state boards or state department of education. The common pathways to licensing are through state approved college or university teacher preparation programs. The goal of these preparation programs is to produce teachers who will be successful in attaining higher student academic achievement.

The lack of consistently high student achievement in the United States has been blamed on a variety of groups in almost a sequential order. First, students were blamed for poor work and study habits. Parents followed, being blamed for anything from not helping their children with school work to broken homes and living in poverty. The focus then shifted to blaming schools themselves and the teachers who taught in them. Principals and other school leaders followed. Over the past decade much has been said and written concerning how college and university schools of education are sending ill-prepared teachers into the field. This fact is not the only reason given for poor student achievement but the movement is continuing to grow especially regarding who is accountable for preparation programs success. The government acts with policy and regulation, and colleges and universities respond with their, now, sole accreditor, the Council for the Accreditation of Education Preparation (CAEP). CAEP is actually the blending of the only two accreditors for teacher preparation, the National Council for Accreditation of Teacher Education (NCATE), founded in 1954, and the Teacher Education Accreditation Council (TEAC), founded in 1997. CAEP is viewed in many higher education circles as an opportunity for assisting teacher preparation programs ultimate outcomes which is improved student academic achievement as graduates go into the field.

The downside of teacher preparation is reflected in report after report issuing scathing indictments of schools across the United States who graduates new teachers. The most recent "scathing" report of teacher training programs was issued by the National Council on Teacher Quality (NTCQ) with results published in U.S. News and World Report (June 18, 2013). Though the report's methodologies have been criticized by some educators, it describes teacher preparation as "an industry of mediocrity," accepting students who are generally not high achievers. Upon graduation and assigned to their first students, those students experience a significant loss in learning. Although many schools in the report received higher rankings, Kate Walsh, president of the NTCQ indicated that part of the motivation for the study was to "pressure teacher preparation programs to deliver better teachers" (Adams & Baron, 2013).

Among the most pressing issues in American education is helping teachers get better earlier (Schorr, 2013) and be closer to the real classroom earlier in their studies, especially in places where schools are struggling. Research has shown that a strong teacher makes a huge difference in educational outcomes from students. Much of the current approach to preparing teachers amounts to "weak tea" and supports Art Levine's 2006 study that indicated "more than three in five teachers said their training left them unprepared for the classroom—and principals agreed." (Schorr, 2013).

With half of all new teachers abandoning the profession within five years, how is the crisis in preparation being confronted? Many preparation programs are feeling the pressure. CAEP accreditation is vigorously upgrading and improving their standards, principals, and policies for both teacher and principal preparation programs. CAEP's (caep.org) "mission is to advance excellent educator preparation through evidence-based accreditation that assures quality and supports continuous improvement to strengthen P-12 student learning." People are not ignoring CAEP's critiques.

With the founding of CAEP, tougher standards that emphasize performance were approved in the summer of 2013. For the first time minimum admissions criteria and an emphasis on selecting reliable and valid evidence were addressed. Some programs may close down because they either won't be able to meet the standards, do not have the resources for the cost-intensive and labor intensive requirements, or they simply lack high quality candidates (Sawchuk, 2013).

Accreditation alone is not enough as acknowledged by the organization itself. Standards for teachers such as the Interstate New Teacher Assessment and Support Consortium (INTASC) have been seen as good building preparation programs but have not shown a correlation to a teacher's ability to promote student achievement. To do so, preparation programs for teachers need the following (Education Commission of the States, 2013):

- need for quality students to enter the programs and not drop out
- less focus on "soft" pedagogical knowledge and more on subject matter depth
- not being prepared to teach to student performance standards
- providing more intensive real world practical experience
- be more responsive to the need of nontraditional teacher candidates, especially minorities and mid-career adults
- more rigorous accreditation standards
- greater involvement with the arts and sciences faculty
- emphasize outcomes such as pass rate on state teacher licensure exams
- building solid partnerships between universities and school districts or individual schools
- alternative teacher preparation programs

The basic issue is that not all teacher programs are equal. Not all offer the ten items listed and are ill-equipped to provide a strong faculty, collaboration with other schools and partners, careful oversight of quality student teaching experiences, or the big picture that high achieving applicants be admitted who understand the mission and calling to be a moral and ethical teacher.

In the selections that follow, Jim Cibulka believes that state oversight of teacher preparation can be strengthened and CAEP accreditation is part of the solution. David Chard believes there has been and continues to be a steady decline in the quality of candidates attracted to teaching and that state control does not ensure that teachers will be of high quality.

References

J. Adams & K. Baron, Critical report on teacher preparation programs spark debate. EdSource Today (June 18, 2013). Retrieved from: www.edsource.org/today/2013/critical-report-on-teacher-preparation-programs-sparks-debate/33721#.UnFjAzXD9y0

Education Commission of the States, Teaching Quality Preparation (2013). Retrieved from: www.usnews.com/education/articles/2013/06/18/us-news-releases-nctq-teacher-prep-ratings

S. Sawchuk, S. (2013). "Tougher Requirements Ahead for Teacher Prep." *Education Week* (vol. 32, no. 36), p. 20.

Schorr, J. (2013). A Revolution Begins in Teacher Prep. *Stanford Social Innovation Review* (Winter 2013). Retrieved from: www.ssireview.org/articles/entry/a_revolution_begins_in_teacher_prep

YES

James Cibulka

Strengthen State Oversight of Teacher Preparation

As the president of the sole specialized accreditor for educator preparation, I certainly agree with Dr. Chard's assertion that "[i]mproving educational attainment for all students in today's schools can only happen if we improve the quality of teaching." As Dr. Chard mentions in his essay, the Council for the Accreditation of Educator Preparation (CAEP) is already working toward some of the solutions proposed through development of the next generation of accreditation standards for educator preparation as well as convening a data task force to provide guidance and help determine some of the very research questions for studying and strengthening educator preparation, as Dr. Chard suggests.

While one of the hallmarks of CAEP as a new kind of accreditor is its focus on research and evidence that will further advance the field of educator preparation, this does not negate the need for a reformed teacher-licensure system.

Like many other features of our Pre-K–12 school system, the current design of teacher licensing, or certification as it's often called, has outlived its usefulness. It was suited to a bygone era when the nation's principal concern was to produce teachers that "do no harm" to their students. This concept of *primum non nocere*, originally applied to medical ethics, set a low bar for entrants to teaching. It seems strangely out of place today, when expectations for teachers emphasize their competence to help all learners become successful in a knowledge-based, globally competitive economy. Yet eliminating teacher licensure altogether likely would be to *worsen* the current dysfunctions. I will offer strategies for reforming teacher licensure that I believe have greater potential for success.

The Impact of Teacher Licensing

Some economists argue that the social and economic costs of licensure outweigh its benefits by reducing economic growth and/or the distribution of economic benefits. They argue that by invoking licensure, government improperly values the special interests of the practitioner over other interests. These criticisms date back to Adam Smith, but were given currency by Milton Friedman, who argued that government and professional associations were using licensure to reassert the monopoly of cartels by creating market entry restrictions.

Other economists, however, reject this critique of licensure in favor of a theory of "market failure." According to this perspective, governmental intervention in the market, via such activities as professional licensing, can be justified when the market fails to operate efficiently. Market failure occurs when it is difficult for the consumer to judge the qualifications of a provider or the quality of a provider's work.

The empirical evidence is mixed. With the pathways into teaching growing in number, including training programs offered outside of higher education, it is hard to argue that current licensure policies substantially restrict entry, for example. And even critics acknowledge that licensing may lead to benefits such as higher-quality outcomes for those who obtain services from licensed professionals.

For many critics of teacher licensure, the gold standard is whether it promotes or impedes student learning. Yet research on the impact of licensure on student outcomes is inconclusive, with some studies finding little, if any, difference among traditionally certified and uncertified teachers and others finding substantially higher student test scores among traditionally certified teachers.

The comparisons in a number of such studies are complicated by the fact that teachers self-select into teaching with different skills sets and training, and they are not, of course, randomly assigned to schools, making inferences about their productivity imperfect at best. Moreover, labels can be confusing. Alternative approaches to licensure often are equated with the term "uncertified," yet individuals taking an alternative route are typically intending to become fully licensed while they teach. Alternative paths to certification may produce different outcomes in the field than traditional paths. An analysis by Paul Peterson and Daniel Nadler found that states that encourage alternative licensure have greater diversity in their teacher pools, for example (see "What Happens When States Have Genuine Alternative Certification?" *check the facts*, Winter 2009). Given these complications, the most that can be said is that the research has not shown licensure by itself to have a negative or positive effect on student learning.

Teacher Licensure in the States

Current licensure requirements vary significantly among states, as reported by the testing company Educational Testing Service (ETS):

Praxis: Thirty-six states accept the Praxis exam to establish basic skills proficiency (Praxis I), content knowledge (Praxis II), or both. Thirty-four of these require either the Praxis I or II specifically for at least one level of licensure, generally for the initial level. However, the score required to pass varies considerably: on a 100-point scale, the most demanding states tend to set a cut score 20 to 30 points above those of the least-demanding states, whose cut scores are below what is recommended by ETS.

Bachelor's degrees: All states require some form of bachelor's degree, yet requirements for content-specific degrees are variously defined and inconsistently applied. The standard requirement is a major in the subject, although most states allow substitution of a major with course credits. Due to the inconsistent approaches within higher education, the Praxis examination has, by default, become the threshold for entering the profession.

Master's degrees: Twenty-five states require a master's degree in order to obtain one or more kinds of certification. However, states are moving away from this type of requirement toward outcome-based induction programs.

Alternative routes to licensure outside of higher education: According to a 2010 U.S. Department of Education report, 8 percent of teacher preparation programs were designated as "alternative, not based in institutions of higher education," provided instead by for-profit or non-profit organizations. Combined, the states of Alabama, Florida, Oklahoma, New Jersey, and Texas produce 74 percent of teacher candidates trained outside of institutions

of higher education. There is wide variation in the quality of teachers produced both within higher education and via alternative pathways, a signal that the systems of quality control need to be overhauled through regulation and market mechanisms.

Licensing Can Be Improved

Teacher licensure has little impact on teaching quality because it sets too low a bar for entry into teaching. Also, licensure policies have often been relaxed to assure that an adult is in each classroom, but not necessarily a *qualified* adult. In short, educator licensure suffers from weak controls:

- Licensure regulations in some states focus only on courses and degrees for some pathways into teaching. As soon as they enter the classroom, graduates of preparation programs should show evidence of their ability to teach diverse learners according to rigorous college- and career-ready standards.
- Many licensure tests lack rigor. Worse still, most states use low cut scores that further weaken their rigor. Licensure tests must be redesigned to focus on the more rigorous content required for Pre-K–12 students, general pedagogy, and pedagogy within a discipline (pedagogical content knowledge).
- Current licensure policies make little use of performance-based assessments that capture a candidate's actual preparedness to teach on entering a classroom. Some states are moving away from licensure based on paper-and-pencil tests in favor of assessments that demonstrate competence to teach and to raise Pre-K–12 student learning.

Addressing basic licensure issues could have a considerable impact on teacher quality. More focus on performance assessments such as those noted above would, among other things, lessen unduly burdensome course requirements for nontraditional applicants entering college and university preparation programs. A shift to a focus on measuring outcomes will open the licensure process to high-quality alternative pathways into teaching and encourage innovation among higher education providers who wish to compete on cost and quality rather than on traditional curriculum and seat-time requirements.

Relicensure requirements for practicing teachers should be aligned with improved initial licensure requirements. They should specify a more advanced level of practice with accompanying evidence, including instructional practices, student learning, and other measures. Similarly, advanced master's programs should be redesigned to serve this purpose as well.

More rigorous licensure requirements should focus on meeting the needs of today's diverse learners, whatever the school setting. Also, licensure requirements should complement new, more rigorous teacher-evaluation systems that capture the context within which teachers work, using teacher observation protocols, student learning measures, and student surveys that measure student engagement and related evidence of a teacher's effectiveness. Neither a licensure system nor evaluation alone can accomplish what these quality-control mechanisms can do if they are complementary and rigorous.

Leverage State Authority

If the teacher licensing bar is to be raised, more rigorous state program-approval authority for teacher preparation programs is also needed. The recent report of the Council of Chief State School Officers found that state program-approval policies for preparation programs, both those for "traditional higher education programs and for new pathways, suffer from weak and inconsistent regulation." Weak controls at the front end lead to highly inconsistent quality among entrants to teacher preparation programs and ultimately new hires. This pattern contributes to high retraining costs for school districts and to destabilizing and costly turnover rates. States could use their authority over teacher preparation programs to strengthen the qualifications of beginning teachers and lower costs to districts by focusing on the recruitment and admission

of a qualified pool, rigorous clinical preparation, and collecting evidence of program impact (hiring rates, graduate and employer satisfaction, Pre-K–12 student learning, and related measures). States should work closely with CAEP, as the new accrediting body for educator preparation, in aligning program approval and licensure policies with accreditation standards.

Tightening regulation to assure candidate and program quality is likely to lead to a more qualified pool of graduates competing to teach, better hiring decisions, less attrition, and a more favorable learning environment for Pre-K–12 students. Markets have their place as mechanisms for introducing quality. However, the market will work much better if government regulates the providers more effectively and if preparation programs produce graduates whose readiness to teach can be clearly identified by the school districts that hire them.

As Dr. Chard indicated, the efforts of individual groups like CAEP are not enough: we must approach education reform holistically and at a systemic level. In coming years, a record number of new teachers will be hired to replace those retiring. As a nation, we cannot afford to fail. We will have a once-in-a-generation chance to get it right.

JAMES CIBULKA, prior to his appointment as President of the Council for the Accreditation of Educator Preparation (CAEP), was president of the National Council for Accreditation of Teacher Education (NCATE), and before that served as dean of the College of Education at the University of Kentucky.

David Chard

Training Must Focus on Content and Pedagogy

What happens inside the classroom is the most critical ingredient in ensuring that all students are able to achieve their career goals. Improving educational attainment for all students in today's schools can only happen if we improve the quality of teaching.

Just over 30 years ago, I decided to become a classroom teacher, specifically a teacher of mathematics and chemistry. I was prepared at a midsize university in the Midwest. Despite the university's great reputation for teacher preparation, faculties in mathematics and chemistry discouraged me from the profession, noting that I was not going to be adequately compensated, would work in difficult conditions, and would be much happier in industry. This should have been a message to me that as a society we had moved down a path that dissuades the best and brightest from seeing teaching as a viable career option.

Nevertheless, I was hired to teach mathematics in California in 1985. At the time, like today, far fewer individuals were being prepared to be mathematics teachers in California than the state needed. Many of us were hired from the Midwest and from eastern states, and given emergency certification in California conditioned on passing a course on California history and the National Teacher Exam in mathematics. I didn't realize then that my experience in California was the beginning of 30 years of slow but steady decline in the quality of candidates we were attracting and preparing to teach in our schools.

Over that period, it has become clear that current state control of teacher preparation and licensing does not ensure that teachers will be of high quality. State regulations that promote a one-size-fits-all approach to teacher preparation have limited our ability to innovate, customize, and study features of preparation programs that may positively affect student achievement. Bold new approaches to teacher preparation that are thoroughly evaluated for effectiveness in the classroom are long overdue.

What's Wrong with the System

Each state sets standards for teacher certification largely through its regulation of the teacher preparation programs that are operated by the institutions of higher education located within its boundaries. With few exceptions, this approach is unsatisfactory. In most states, in order for a program to recommend teachers for certification, it must meet a series of requirements that read like a laundry list. In my home state of Texas, for example, the State Board for Educator Certification (SBEC) requires that in addition to the content standards specified for each grade band, the curriculum for teacher preparation programs must include 17 specific subjects of study. On the surface, there is nothing wrong with any of them. However, given as a list, none appear to have any particular emphasis (i.e., learning theories (#5) seems as important as parent communication (#13) and motivation (#4)); they are not tailored to fit the needs of teachers in any specific context (i.e., urban or rural, turnaround or successful); and they do not consider the developmental stage of the student as it relates to each topic. Perhaps most importantly, this approach assumes a state-held knowledge base on optimal teacher preparation, which simply doesn't exist. The insistence that all preparation programs cover these topics discourages innovation or research on more effective approaches to teacher preparation.

What Makes Teachers Effective?

By all accounts, it is difficult to define precisely what sets good teachers apart from ineffective teachers or even average teachers. We do know that effectiveness in today's classroom is multidimensional.

It is difficult to conceive of an effective teacher who doesn't have a deep understanding of content knowledge. Deep understanding starts with the content itself (e.g., proportional reasoning, Shakespeare, the Krebs cycle), learned through disciplinary study. Content knowledge has to be backed up with experience in designing instruction that conveys content most effectively, enabling students to achieve mastery. In other words, knowing how to solve mathematical problems using proportions falls short of the content knowledge needed for teaching proportional reasoning. An effective teacher must be able to determine where students' understanding has broken down and how to support their cognition.

Unfortunately, it is difficult and time-consuming to master content knowledge and even more so to become an expert teacher. Mastery comes only with adequate experience and professional support. Certainly, in the process of preparation, we can instruct new teachers in how to recognize when students don't understand and how to identify their needs, but the numerous possible variations that underlie students' difficulties reduce the likelihood that new teachers will be experts from the start.

Pedagogical knowledge and skills require an understanding of a child's development involving biology, developmental psychology, cognitive psychology, linguistics, behavioral psychology, and cultural anthropology. That's just to work with one child. When we place students together in groups, we have to consider sociocultural factors, systems dynamics, learning histories, and relationship histories. Then we get down to the engineering of instruction: how to plan and deliver content to groups of students who enter the classroom each day or each period. Teachers must estimate students' level of understanding and take an approach to teaching that will stimulate curiosity and engagement with the content.

I highlight these two components of teaching because they seem to be the most central to the work of teacher preparation programs. In short, they represent the development of a teacher's knowledge of the "what" and "how" of teaching. Recent advancements in education research have brought a new lens to these two areas and suggest that in many cases, teacher preparation programs are not currently designed to provide adequate content knowledge or to teach pedagogical practices that are supported by research evidence. The National Council on Teacher Quality (NCTQ) (see "21st-Century Teacher Education," *features*, Summer 2013) has launched an initiative that will identify those teacher-preparation programs that set high standards with regard to content and pedagogy. As NCTQ found in its analysis, far too few teacher-preparation programs currently provide what is necessary for a new teacher to be successful.

Ideally, our system of teacher preparation would also determine who has the personality and disposition to be a teacher before preparation begins, and ensure that they develop the skills and professionalism needed to be effective within a school. These areas lie on the margin of what is currently in the purview of teacher preparation programs. In addition, there is compelling evidence that the quality of the individuals who are attracted to the field may be more powerful than differences in teacher preparation programs. Recent efforts by the newly formed Council for the Accreditation of Educator Preparation (CAEP) to establish stronger criteria for selecting top-notch candidates are a step in the right direction.

Setting the bar higher is only the first step, however. Over the past several decades, fewer and fewer well-qualified candidates have seen teaching as an acceptable career choice. On average, U.S. teachers earn only about two-thirds of the salaries of other professions with comparable preparation, there is little room for advancement within the profession, and the working conditions in many public schools are challenging at best. Teacher preparation programs alone can't adequately attract a pool of strong new teachers to the field. One of the most promising outcomes of initiatives such as Teach For America (TFA) is that it helps bring to schools well-educated college graduates who might otherwise not have considered education as a career option. But even TFA falls short of filling the need for new teachers in the next decade. Without powerful new incentives, it seems fewer high-quality teachers will be drawn to the field.

What's the Solution?

In an effort to create immediate and enduring improvements in student outcomes, most states have adopted Common Core State Standards or other content standards that reflect higher expectations for student learning than previous iterations. Efforts to establish similarly comprehensive standards for teacher preparation, such as those being developed by CAEP, should be applauded. We should not simply adopt new teacher competencies, however, without a thoughtful and strategic plan for evaluation and evidence-based revision of our teacher-preparation programs.

I envision the first steps in this process to be a broad and inclusive conversation that brings the public, private, and not-for-profit sectors together to forge a concrete plan for studying and strengthening teacher preparation. While the conversation would be broad, the agenda should be narrow and focus on three immediate needs: 1) radically improving the quality of candidates coming to the field; 2) identifying the specific content of coursework necessary to improve teacher knowledge; and 3) and detailing the practical experiences that new teachers need in order to ensure they are effective in the types of classroom contexts in which they plan to teach. This conversation will require a thoughtful analysis of why our system of teacher preparation has not changed appreciably for decades and what we need to do to make needed changes happen.

In terms of the optimal content of teacher preparation programs, we have only begun to understand what specific amounts of knowledge and skills one needs to possess to be an effective classroom teacher. We also know very little about how those needs change depending on students' developmental stages (e.g., pre-K, middle school) and the teaching context (e.g., urban, suburban, rural). It's easy to see where content is absent, however. Even without empirical evidence, we can make logical decisions about how to improve the quality and quantity of the most important knowledge and skills. For example, it is common in many elementary-educator preparation programs to see few courses on the science of reading instruction or on mathematics content. These limitations should be immediately addressed. Another example involves how little teachers understand about the home language and culture of their students. This is particularly important given the dramatic demographic shifts we are witnessing in most of our country. Efforts to understand the knowledge, skills, and dispositions that are critical to sustained success in the classroom are under way, but further state and federal investment in research is needed to guide the reform of preparation programs.

Finally, we need to encourage experimentation with the practical requirements of teacher preparation. At my institution, we assume that more experience in the classroom than is required by state regulation provides teacher candidates with valuable practice and important information regarding their choices of where to teach. However, the "more is better" approach has not been adequately evaluated. As an example, teacher residency programs have captured interest nationally, but we have only limited evidence of their effectiveness compared to more traditional teacher-preparation programs. Again, logical analyses remain our only short-term tool for making informed decisions, but more evidence is needed to improve our practice.

At a recent dinner for incoming merit scholars to our university, I asked several of them whether they had considered teaching as an option. There was collective nervous laughter. One young lady said that they would never teach because they knew it paid poorly, the working conditions were not good, there was little respect for teachers, and there were no opportunities to advance and lead. Here was a high school senior unwittingly communicating key changes that need to be made to attract high-quality teachers to our field. We will need to set a significantly higher bar for admission to the teaching field and, at the same time, muster financial and professional incentives (e.g., salary, retirement, and career opportunities) to boost interest among our very best candidates for teaching. In addition, attracting top-notch teachers will require more investment in our knowledge of the impact of pay-for-performance models.

Shortly after the turn of the last century, physician preparation in the United States was examined critically for its quality. The results were significant improvements in medical school quality, higher standards for admission, and higher medical costs overall. Similar improvements to teacher preparation could result in better teaching and improved learning outcomes for students. Likewise, these changes will likely require a significant investment in research and development to fuel improved practices and to inform teacher preparation. If we want better teaching, we will have to pay for it.

DAVID CHARD is dean of the Annette Caldwell Simmons School of Education and Human Development at Southern Methodist University and holds a PhD in special education.

EXPLORING THE ISSUE

Should Teacher Preparation and Licensing Be Regulated by the Government?

Critical Thinking and Reflection

1. Will including a design to provide adequate content knowledge and teach pedagogical practices provide what is necessary for a new teacher to be successful?
2. Should the newly formed Council for the Accreditation of Education Preparation (CAEP) be the sole accreditor for teacher preparation and licensing programs?
3. What can be done in the future to convince well educated college graduates to be drawn to the field of teaching?
4. Should the government regulate the Pre-K–12 program providers and tighten regulations to assure candidates and program quality?
5. What is wrong with the current teacher certification standards and what direction should be taken to assure positive change in the future leading to top quality teachers in all classrooms?

Is There Common Ground?

The quality of teaching must improve whether one believes government should play a particular role or not in teacher preparation programs. Teachers must master content knowledge as well as pedagogical knowledge and skills. One solution for common ground is having comprehensive standards for teacher preparation programs, such as those being developed by the Council for the Accreditation of Educator Preparation (CAEP) that are evidence based and offer a strategic plan. The new standards include establishing minimum admissions criteria and the use of "value added" measures. Preparation programs would be assessed on the evidence they produce to meet each standard.

The ultimate outcome for teacher and principal preparation programs is that student's achieve. Using standardized test scores of the students of a university's program are a key measure that is supported by the U.S. Education Department. This is also a measure that CAEP would like to find in their evidence while accrediting preparation programs (The Answer Sheet, 2013). The week of August 16, 2013 the New York City Department of Education released this headline: "New York City becomes the First Major School System in the Country to Comprehensively Collect and Analyze Data on New Teacher Hires from Post-Secondary Schools of Education." The intent is to use the data in the report to support improvement at many levels and as a "first step" to "opening a dialogue" with teacher preparation programs

concerning how to improve what they do (The Answer Sheet, 2013). Not many college programs, of any type have indicated they are tracking their graduates into the field to see how they perform.

Since the evidence for significant program improvement is not readily available, there are those who believe innovations and ongoing evaluations need to occur. Perhaps the effort of the New York City Department of Education is the starting point for forming common ground.

Reference

V. Strauss, The big problem with new evaluations of teacher prep programs. *The Answer Sheet* (August 16, 2013). Retrieved from: www.washingtonpost.com/blogs/answer-sheet/wp/2013/08/16/the-big-problem-with-new-evaluations-of-teacher-prep-programs/

Additional Resources

M. Cockran-Smith & K. Zeichner, *Studying Teacher Education: The Report of the AERA Panel on Research and Teacher Education* (Taylor & Francis e-Library, 2009).

L. Hammond, *Powerful Teacher Education: Lessons from Exemplary Programs* (2013).

L. Hammond & J. Bransford, eds., *Preparing Teachers for a Changing World* (John Wiley & Sons, 2005).

T. Lasley, Why Do Teacher-Education Programs Fear a New Rating System? The Chronicle of High Education (2011). Retrieved from: http://chronicle.com/article/Why-Do-Teacher-Education/129654/

S. Sherman, *Teacher Preparation as an Inspirational Practice: Building Capacities for Responsiveness* (Routledge Taylor & Francis Group, 2013).

Internet References . . .

National Council of Teacher Quality

www.nctq.org/siteHome.do

Council for the Accreditation of Educator Preparation

http://caepnet.org/

Educating School Teachers by Art Levine

www.edschools.org/pdf/Educating_Teachers_Report.pdf

Group Urges Feds to Yank Aid from Poor-Performing Teacher-Prep Programs

http://blogs.edweek.org/edweek/teacherbeat/2013/09/report_urges.html

Teacher Education Accreditation Council and the National Council for the Accreditation of Teacher Education

www.teac.org/ and http://www.ncate.org/

Selected, Edited, and with Issue Framing Material by:
Glenn L. Koonce, *Regent University*

ISSUE

Though the Law Has Been Rescinded, Should Teacher Preparation Programs Be Rated under the Higher Education Act?

YES: Ashley LiBetti Mitchel and Chad Aldeman, from "Plotting a New Course on Teacher Preparation Reform," *National Association of State Boards of Education* (2017)

NO: Paul T. von Hippel and Laura Bellows, from "Rating Teacher-Preparation Programs," *Education Next* (2018)

Learning Outcomes

After reading this issue, you will be able to:

- List the three potential paths forward to encourage teacher preparation program accountability.
- Describe the evaluation measuring "value-added" to student scores on standardized tests.
- Summarize the various ways of measuring teacher and program quality.
- Consider how the Every Student Succeeds Act (ESSA), as well as the Higher Education Acts, might encourage teacher preparation programs to improve.
- What does the literature reveal about teacher preparation program accountability?

ISSUE SUMMARY

YES: Ashley LiBetti Mitchel, a senior analyst, and Chad Aldeman, a principal at Bellwether Education Partners, state that the regulation to rate teacher preparation programs deserved more attention as a way to hold them accountable.

NO: Paul von Hippel, an associate professor in the LBJ School of Public Affairs, University of Texas in Austin, and Laura Bellows, doctoral student at the Sanford School of Public Policy at Duke University, noting attention to the body of research comparing teacher preparation programs has produced inconsistent results, and they question why officials at U.S. Department of Education dismissed this research when originally setting the policy.

"**O**ne of the only things Republicans and Democrats in Washington, DC, can agree on is that they don't like the accreditation system in higher education" (Horn, 2018, p. 1). University teacher preparation programs are accredited in order to merit awarding degrees, along with accompanying licensure by the state, to graduates who successfully complete the program of studies. The nation's teacher preparation programs have long been criticized for a lack of rigor and too little classroom practice. In addition, according to Dubin (2017), our schools face a national teacher shortage, including the challenge of recruiting and retaining teachers of color.

In the October 31, 2016, *Federal Register*, Office of Postsecondary Education, U.S. Department of Education (DOE), a new regulation, *34 CFR, part 612*, was posted under "Teacher Preparation Issues" to update, clarify, and improve the regulations, at the time, on teacher preparation program accountability and align them with Title II reporting system data ("Teacher Preparation Issues," 2016, p. 75494). One area of focus was the annual report, or assessment, of program performance and improvements to the program(s). The overall intent was on having accurate information on the quality of teacher preparation programs within a state to ensure members of the public, prospective teachers and employers (districts and schools), the states, the Institutes of Higher Education (IHE), and the programs themselves could evaluate program effectiveness. Specifically addressed in the regulations was the fact that "thousands of novice teachers enter the profession every year and their students deserve to have well-prepared teachers" (p. 1). The impetus for the new regulation came from a U.S. Government Accountability Office report that some states were not following the law assuring that teacher preparation programs in their state were being assessed for low performance. Having this accountability could help prospective teachers make the best decision for selecting a program that would fully prepare them to educate children in the public schools of the nation. Identified low-performing programs could receive the technical assistance they would need to improve. Under the Title II reporting system, it was determined that the data being reported by teacher preparation programs was not very useful by those needing the accountability information. In addition, over ½ of the teacher preparation programs themselves and none of the staff surveyed in the school districts were using the data. It was hoped by the U.S. DOE that a rating system to improve teacher preparation programs would have a strong impact on the teacher preparation field that would yield higher student achievement outcomes in K–12 schools. One other impact the new regulation would have was on the eligibility for teacher preparation programs to be identified as high quality for Teacher Education Assistance for College and Higher Education (TEACH) Grant eligibility purposes ("Teacher Preparation Issues," 2016). TEACH is a "federal grant that provides up to $4,000 per year to students who agree to teach for four years at an elementary school, secondary school, or educational service agency that serves students from low-income families. If the service obligation is not met, the grant is converted to a Direct Unsubsidized Loan" (U.S. Department of Education, 2018, Letter "T").

In a press release from the U.S. Department of Education (2016, p. 1), the new regulation was being touted as a means "to help ensure that new teachers are ready to succeed in the classroom and that every student is taught by a great educator, to bring transparency to the effectiveness of teacher preparation programs, to provide programs with ongoing feedback to help them improve

continuously, and to respond to educators across the country who do not feel ready to enter the classroom after graduation." Teacher preparation programs across the country began seriously looking at how they were following their state program accountability requirements and how they align these requirements in data they were reporting for the Title II reporting system. Most of these programs were already immersed in their state program approval processes and/or national accreditation from the Council for the Accreditation of Educator Preparation (CAEP), a combination of two organizations, National Council for the Accreditation of Teacher Education and the Teacher Education Accreditation Association (TEAC), that had begun to merge in 2010. CAEP Standards became the sole accreditation criteria for teacher preparation in fall 2016 and is a recognized accreditor by the Council for Higher Education Accreditation. CAEP defines accreditation as "quality assurance through external peer review in reviewing departments, schools, and colleges which prepare teachers and other educators" (Council for the Accreditation of Educator Preparation, 2018, p. 1). Will (2018) reports that 147 providers of educator preparation programs (teacher and school leader) have been accredited under CAEP standards, 13 are on probation, 3 accreditations have been revoked, and 1 denied accreditation.

The U.S. DOE ("Teacher Preparation Issues," 2016) noted that the new regulation did not infringe on a state's authority to establish, use, and report other criteria for valid and reliable assessment of their teacher preparation program's performance, to include accreditation from CAEP. A number of states use CAEP as their vehicle to both accredit and approve teacher preparation programs in their state.

There was concern from states that the U.S. DOE's proposal to "establish four performance levels including 21 indicators by which teacher preparation programs were to be rated, what a state must consider in identifying low-performing or at risk teacher preparation programs, and the actions a state would take with respect to low-performing programs" was federal overreach of state's authority to approve their own teacher education programs (p. 17). In addition, it was felt this federal overreach "represents a profound and improper shift in the historic relationship among institutions, States, school districts, accrediting agencies, and the federal government in the area of teacher preparation and certification" (p. 35). The U.S. DOE noted that these requirements simply clarified the requirements already in place by Congress in Title II reporting and that the federal government had a direct interest in the subject because of Federal student loan assistance. Using 2013–2014 data, the U.S. Department of Education (2016) stated that there were approximately 460,000 individuals enrolled in teacher preparation programs who needed to have basic information about whether their programs had been successful in preparing completers for the rigors of an entry level classroom well prepared for teaching. The need for a strong and diverse preparation programs is needed to generate pipelines of new teachers to meet the needs of the nation's diverse learners including hard to staff schools in high-need areas.

The Every Student Succeeds Act (ESSA) is a shift in the one-size-fits all approach to education that has been growing more difficult to manage since the passage of the No Child Left Behind Act in 2001. ESSA is an attempt to reduce the federal role in education which in turn can empower parents as well as local and state leaders. The same focus by the Trump administration was directed to the Higher Education Act. In an effort to reduce the federal imprint in higher education, the Trump administration nixed the regulation to rate teacher preparation programs before it got off the ground. In the "YES" article for this issue, a case and a recommendation is made to "execute the regulation to serve as the foundation for a new, more flexible program approval strategy that ensures high program quality standards while encouraging innovation" (Mitchel & Aldeman, 2017, p. 34). In the "NO" article, von Hippel and Bellows (2018) indicate that there does not appear to be more than negligible differences in the evaluation of teacher preparation programs, noting that in review of the U.S. DOE's decision to require the rating system, it acknowledged—then dismissed—inconsistencies in the research. Additional analysis indicated that program rankings were error prone, gave false positives to high-ranking programs, and that the findings were consistent across six different locations (states)—Texas, Florida, Louisiana, Missouri, Washington State, and New York City. von Hippel and Bellows also raise concerns about this oversight and state that there may be better ways to hold programs accountable for their quality.

YES ←

Ashley LiBetti Mitchel and Chad Aldeman

Plotting a New Course on Teacher Preparation Reform

State boards have at least three means for changing how they hold prep programs accountable. www.nasbe.org

State boards could push their state education agencies (SEAs) to design a public website that houses programs' completer data and allows potential teacher candidates and their employers to compare data by program.

In early 2017, Congress used an obscure law called the Congressional Review Act to rescind two education regulations passed late in the Obama administration. One of those, which attempted to define and implement the Every Student Succeeds Act (ESSA), received the bulk of the media attention at the time. It was the first crack at defining some of ESSA's vaguer passages, and it also was more urgent, with states busy planning how to implement the new law in the 2017–2018 school year.

But the second regulation that was rescinded, which would have redefined the way states held teacher preparation programs accountable, deserved more attention than it got. It would have defined legislative language originally inserted into the 1998 reauthorization of the Higher Education Act by asking states to design rating systems for their preparation programs based on the outcomes of their graduates, including whether they found jobs, remained as teachers, and demonstrated effectiveness in classrooms.

The policy would have provided crucial information about the effectiveness of preparation program completers, and thus it could have nudged teacher preparation programs to improve and changed the way teachers get hired in schools. But it had no natural political constituency, and therefore few people fought to retain it when the Trump administration cut it. States (rightfully) pointed out that the regulation came with no new money, congressional Republicans called it a federal overreach, and national teachers' unions disagreed with the premise that

preparation programs were responsible for the student learning gains of their graduates.

With the regulation gone, and with states well under way in implementing their ESSA plans, what steps can state boards of education take to encourage teacher preparation programs to improve? We see at least three potential paths forward:

1. Execute the Proposed Regulation Anyway

Our first recommendation to state boards is to act as if the proposed teacher preparation regulation had not been rescinded. Despite being politically unpopular at the federal level, the proposed regulation was based on facts that are still true:

- Most states hold preparation programs accountable via inputs—things like admission criteria and certain coursework. Historically, states relied on these inputs because they were thought to be predictive of teacher effectiveness and because the data were readily available and easily measured.
- There is very little evidence that these input measures actually affect student learning.

Taken together, these facts suggest that states need to change the way they hold preparation programs accountable. The proposed regulation offers an alternative—one that mirrors work already happening in more than a dozen states. **Louisiana** and **Tennessee** were some of the first: as early as 2000, Louisiana started assessing teacher preparation programs based on the outcomes of their graduates. In recent years, other states shifted to outcomes-focused accountability frameworks to capitalize on their access to a multitude of data on program completers.

State boards, especially those with explicit authority over teacher preparation programs, could push to adopt rules that look similar to the proposed regulation and work done in other states. Specifically, state boards should collect and publicly report program completer data and use those data to foster continuous improvement at the program level.

State boards could also work to amend educator preparation program standards to require that the state collects and publicly reports data on program completer placement rates, retention rates, and classroom effectiveness. Rhode Island, for example, rewrote their state standards in 2013 to explicitly assess programs on their evaluation and employment outcomes, including placement, retention, and measures of professional practice.[1]

Florida takes this work one step further: its state board annually analyzes statewide data to identify critical teacher shortage areas, habitually high-need content areas, and high-priority locations.[2] The state then assesses programs on their production of teachers in those critical areas.

Further, state boards could push their SEAs to design a public website that houses programs' completer data and allows "consumers"—potential teacher candidates and their employers—to compare data by program. Of the states currently doing this work, almost all of them make these data publicly available but not necessarily in a way that lets the end user glean the information they need. For example, a state may publish provider-level reports in PDF format. If a teacher candidate wanted to determine which program produces graduates with consistently high evaluation scores, they would have to manually toggle to compare a single data point across multiple PDFs for multiple programs and years. It would not be impossible, but it would be tedious.

There are real barriers to finding the right teacher preparation program, but data formatting should not be one of them. Massachusetts provides a good example of how one could design a format to compare data across potential providers.[3]

Collecting and publishing outcome data will likely have only some effect on preparation programs' practices, however. To foster significant and continuous improvement, state boards should urge their SEAs to ask strategic questions about program quality and practice and to analyze program data. How effective are specific program practices? Under what circumstances? For whom? By looking at program data across the state, the SEA could identify programs that consistently perform well on state metrics

and then work to determine which elements of the program's practice produced those effects.

If the SEA cannot conduct those analyses at the state level, state boards should encourage programs to do this work as a smaller networked learning community. Where programs are in the driver seat and intentionally using data to inform continuous improvement rather than solely providing data for use as an accountability tool, sustainable improvement becomes possible.

2. Help Districts Make Better Decisions

Even if states decide not to collect new information on their teacher preparation programs, they could still benefit from shifting their thinking away from a primary focus on licensing initial teachers. Instead, they should turn to helping their school districts make smarter decisions about whom to hire in the first place. Under this strategy, states should consider how to expand district access to actionable data that already exists.

This recommendation bucks against recent trends, where states have tried to "raise the bar" on the teaching profession. Counterintuitive though it may seem, states would be better off acknowledging the limits of setting hard barriers to entry and instead turn toward softer strategies to influence teacher recruitment efforts.

Why not just raise the bar? State leaders must recognize that it is almost impossible to know in advance, based on paper credentials, who will be a good teacher. In this context, all metrics that states use to set barriers to entry suffer from similar flaws. Today, 46 states and the District of Columbia require teacher candidates to pass some form of ETS's Praxis assessments, which focus on math and reading content knowledge.[4] A 1999 analysis found that its questions were roughly as difficult as what we ask of most high schoolers.[5] Still, lots of would-be teachers cannot pass it. But that does not necessarily mean they will be bad teachers.

www.nasbe.org.

A recent report from the Arkansas Center for Research in Economics was able to approximate the effect of raising the passing score on Praxis by comparing results in Arkansas and Louisiana, two states with different cut scores in 2010.[6] The study found that, from a statistical perspective, teachers who performed better on the Praxis math test on average were better math teachers. But the differences were tiny, and there was wide variation at nearly every score. Some great teachers scored poorly on the Praxis, and some poor teachers scored well.

If Arkansas were to raise its Praxis cut score to match Louisiana's minimum, it would effectively block some lower-performing teachers from ever becoming teachers, but it would also lose many teachers who could have performed at similar levels—or even better than average. Rather than weeding out bad teachers, the policy change would mostly just limit the supply of new teachers.

The Arkansas study mirrored findings from an earlier one looking at Praxis test-takers in North Carolina,[7] as well as another one looking at principal candidates taking a common licensure exam in Tennessee. The Tennessee[8] study had another troubling finding: although white test-takers tended to score higher than nonwhite candidates, they performed no better on measures of job performance like evaluation ratings or surveys of teachers' perceptions of school leadership. In effect, the state's licensure exam was screening out minority candidates, even though the exam had no ability to distinguish between good and bad prospective principals.

More recently, a number of states have moved beyond the multiple-choice, fill-in-the-blank Praxis test for teachers, requiring assessments tied to specific subject areas. There are now multiple Praxis II tests, all pitched to a particular content area or pedagogical skill set. These should produce more discerning results, but the same Arkansas study found that they do not. Even the edTPA—a portfolio-based assessment based on videos of teacher candidates delivering actual lessons, teacher lesson plans, student work, and candidate reflections—had similar results. A study of teacher candidates in Washington State found that the edTPA was not much better than the Praxis as a policy tool.[9] There was no clear-cut point at which a state would want to set its passing score, and every point higher they raised the bar meant they would lose teachers, some of whom would have been good and some not so good.

Instead of continuing down this policy path, states should shift their gaze to helping school districts make better hiring decisions. They could start by opening up existing information to school districts. States have a unique role in providing access to teacher data, or at least allowing districts to request it, and a district choosing between two otherwise identical teachers should want to give the edge to the teacher with the better credentials, assuming they have access to that information. This is true of traditional licensure test scores and whether candidates are able to meet a state's expectation on their first try as well as newer requirements like edTPA.

edTPA in particular has a host of information that would aid districts' hiring efforts. Any edTPA state could explicitly allow districts to request the same teacher videos that were scored as part of the edTPA. While not all districts can require teacher candidates to do an in person practice lesson, opening up the edTPA videos to future employers would allow districts to evaluate potential teachers based on performance. States could also build websites to help match teacher candidates with prospective employers and include dedicated space for candidates to upload their performance videos.

There is evidence that these types of activities can boost the quality of incoming teachers. In Spokane, Washington, for example, the district uses a screening mechanism that helps identify future teaching ability.[10] And as part of sweeping reforms to its recruiting process, the **District of Columbia Public Schools** (DCPS) now requires all candidates to either conduct in person lessons or submit a video of actual teaching. Those mock teaching lessons strongly predict future classroom effectiveness and have enabled DCPS to significantly improve the caliber of its incoming teachers. Districts may not necessarily pursue these reforms on their own, but states can help create the conditions for more districts to do so. Helping districts improve their hiring practices could have other positive benefits. It could help districts recruit more candidates per opening, hire candidates earlier in the year, and land a higher percentage of their preferred candidates, leaving fewer unfilled openings at the start of the school year. All this would, in turn, lead to more effectively run school systems and to better teachers coming into schools.

3. Spur Innovation among High-performing Programs

Finally, state boards should explore how they can encourage innovation among high-performing preparation programs. Boards involved in the state's program approval process can offer high-performing programs the option to forgo some of the more arduous program approval requirements in exchange for developing and piloting innovative, evidence-based practices.

Opening up the edTPA videos to future employers would allow districts to evaluate potential teachers based on performance.

State boards, with the support of state legislatures, can create a bucket of money to expand high-quality programs—based on completer performance data, specifically in shortage areas.

Only programs with a history of complying with program approval requirements and evidence of producing effective program completers should be given this opportunity, but doing so will create the space for high-performing programs to innovate and incentivize other programs to focus on their completers' performance data. The types of flexibility that states can offer programs depend on a state's approval process, but two options are shorter, lighter touch program approval visits and longer approval timelines. State boards, with the support of state legislatures, can also offer programs' financial incentives to innovate. They can create a bucket of money to expand high-quality programs—based on completer performance data, specifically in shortage areas. Additionally, states can encourage high performers to adopt innovative program models through use of the 5 percent of Title II funding set aside for this purpose.

Boards involved with their states' program approval processes can also encourage innovation by approving certain alternative pathways to teacher licensure. Most, though not all, states allow alternative certification programs, but the requirements for program approval—and the degree to which they allow innovation—varies by state. State boards must carefully balance program approval requirements for alternative certification pathways; requirements that are too stringent and prescriptive stifle innovation, while lax requirements encourage low program quality. (Our first recommendation—to execute the proposed Higher Education Act regulation—can also serve as the foundation for a new, flexible program approval strategy that ensures high program quality standards while encouraging innovation.)

State boards have a number of options for encouraging teacher preparation programs to improve, even in the absence of federal requirements. These recommendations, in their most basic forms, propose that state boards pursue a simple strategy: figure out how preparation programs are performing, help program "consumers"—specifically districts—make better "purchasing" decisions, and give high-performing programs flexibility to innovate.

We are going to start conversations immediately about technical changes that need to be made to the plan and how we can think bigger.

What Are Your Expectations for ESSA Plan Implementation?

State Superintendent Smith: At the beginning, there were people who did not really believe that their input would show up in the plan. But we kept showing up, and the drafts changed based on stakeholder input. We were trying to change the relationship between the field and the state agency to build trust and relationships so that we could do the real work of implementing. Conversations are ongoing on how the plan works, and it is going to take feedback from the field to implement this plan. How we are going to eliminate performance gaps and pay attention to equity are going to take dialogue. We believe we have built some relationships to be a part of that dialogue. It is the relationship that makes it possible to transform outcomes so we can create more opportunities for kids.

Board Member Jacobson: Next steps are really important to District of Columbia. We know our plan is not perfect and plans should evolve over time. At our immediate meeting after the approval of the state plan, we considered a resolution to set up a task force that is broader than the board's previous committee. We started our work on ESSA with just board members around the table. Although we did go out into our communities, we did not involve some communities as robustly as we could in the crafting of the plan and in our daily engagement. Our board set up a working group that will include members of the public charter sector and traditional schools, parents, students, business groups, teachers, and others. We are going to start conversations immediately about technical changes that need to be made to the plan and how we can think bigger. We wanted to start small and grow over time. There are big ideas out there, and we want to try those out. This working group will be our mechanism to conduct our work in a really targeted and thoughtful manner over the next year.

Notes

1. Rhode Island Department of Education, "Rhode Island Standards for Educator Preparation," http://www.ride.ri.gov/Portals/0/Uploads/Documents/TeachersandAdministrators-Excellent-Educators/Educator-Certification/Becoming-an-Educator/RIPA_Standards_2013.pdf.

2. Florida Department of State, "Educator Standards, Preparation and Performance," Florida Administrative Code Rule 6A-5.066, https://www.flrules.org/gateway/ruleNo.asp?ID=6A-5.066.

3. Massachusetts Department of Elementary and Secondary Education, "Educator Preparation Employment by Program," School and District Profiles database, http://profiles.doe.mass.edu/state_report/epppempratebyprogram.aspx.4. ETS, "State Requirements," https://www.ets.org/praxis/states.

Though the Law Has Been Rescinded, Should Teacher Preparation Programs Be Rated Under the Higher Education Act? by Koonce

175

5. "Not Good Enough: A Content Analysis of Teacher Licensing Examinations," *Thinking K-16* 3, no. 1 (Washington, DC: Education Trust).

6. James Shuls, "Can We Simply Raise the Bar on Teacher Quality?" (Arkansas Center for Research in Economics, 2016, http://uca.edu/acre/files/2014/11/Shuls_RaisingtheBar_05312016.pdf).

7. Dan Goldhaber, "Everyone's Doing It, but What Does *Journal of Human Resources* 42, no. 4 (fall 2007): 765–94.

8. Jason A. Grissom et al., "Principal Licensure Exams and Future Job Performance: Evidence from the School Leaders Licensure Assessment," *Educational Evaluation and Policy Analysis* 39, no. 2 (2017): 248–80, https://doi.org/10.3102/0162373716680293.

9. Dan Goldhaber et al., "Evaluating Prospective Teachers: Testing the Predictive Validity of the edTPA," Working Paper 157 (Washington, DC: National Center for Analysis of Longitudinal Data in Education Research, American Institutes for Research, November 2016).

10. Dan Goldhaber et al., "Screen Twice, Cut Once: Assessing the Predictive Validity of Teacher Selection Tools," Working Paper 120 (Washington, DC: National Center for Analysis of Longitudinal Data in Education Research, American Institutes for Research, December 2014).

Ashley LiBetti Mitchel, MPP, conducts research and policy analysis, specializing in early childhood education, teacher preparation, and charter schools, for Bellwether Education Partners in Washington, DC.

Chad Anderson is a principal at Bellwether Education Partners.

Paul T. von Hippel and Laura Bellows

Rating Teacher-Preparation Programs

Can Value-Added Make Useful Distinctions?

Recent policies intended to improve teacher quality have focused on the preparation that teachers receive before entering the classroom. A short-lived federal rule would have required every state to assess and rank teacher-preparation programs by their graduates' impact on student learning. Though the federal rule was repealed, last year some 21 states and the District of Columbia opted to rank teacher-preparation programs by measures of their graduates' effectiveness in the classroom, such as their value-added scores.

But what does the research say? Do teachers from different preparation programs differ substantially in their impacts? Can outcomes like student test performance reliably identify more or less effective teacher-preparation programs?

To address these questions, we reanalyzed prior evaluations of teacher-preparation programs from six locations: Florida, Louisiana, Missouri, Texas, Washington State, and New York City. We found negligible differences in teacher quality between programs, amounting to no more than 3 percent of the average test-score gap between students from low-income families and their more affluent peers. Differences between programs were negligible even in Louisiana and New York City, where earlier evaluations had reported substantial differences and fueled the push for program accountability.

Most differences between programs would be too small to matter, even if we could measure them accurately. And we can rarely measure them accurately. The errors we make in estimating program differences are often larger than the differences we are trying to estimate. With rare exceptions, we cannot use student test scores to say whether a given program's teachers are significantly better or worse than average. If policy makers want to hold preparation programs accountable for the quality of their graduates, there may be better ways to do it.

A Push for Accountability

Four days before the 2016 election, the U.S. Department of Education (DOE) issued a regulation requiring every state to publish an annual "report card" on the quality of its teacher-preparation programs. Report cards would rate programs by their outcomes, such as graduates' impacts on student performance on standardized tests, rather than program characteristics like curriculum and faculty credentials. Programs would be assigned one of four performance categories: low-performing, at-risk of being low-performing, effective, or exemplary. The report cards would be published on the web. Like college ratings, they would provide feedback to preparation programs, help prospective teachers choose among programs, and help schools and districts evaluate job applicants from different programs. Programs persistently rated as low-performing would lose eligibility for federal TEACH grants, which provide $4,000 per year to students who train and then teach in a high-need subject or a high-poverty school.

The regulation was part of a larger plan to improve teacher recruitment and preparation nationwide, inspired by widespread concerns about the quality of teacher-training programs (see "21st-Century Teacher Education," *features,* Summer 2013). Released in 2011, the plan won early support from some program providers, unions, and advocates. But when the specifics of the regulations were published in draft form in October 2016, they were criticized by congressional Republicans and union leaders as an example of burdensome federal overreach. President Randi Weingarten of the American Federation of Teachers said the regulation was fundamentally misguided. "It is, quite simply, ludicrous," she said, "to propose evaluating teacher preparation programs based on the performance [test scores] of the students taught by a program's graduates."

DESPITE A FEDERAL REPEAL, report cards on teacher-preparation programs remain a live policy at the state level.

The regulation was never implemented. In early 2017, after Republicans regained the White House, the rule was repealed by Congress. At a public signing ceremony, President Trump declared the repeal had removed "an additional layer of bureaucracy to encourage freedom in our schools."

However, report cards on teacher-preparation programs remain a live policy at the state level. In Louisiana, the practice dates back more than a decade; evaluators began to collect data in 2003–2004 and first published a report card that named individual programs in 2008. In 2010, 11 states and the District of Columbia received funding to develop program report cards as part of their federal Race to the Top grants. By 2017, according to the National Council on Teacher Quality, 21 states and the District of Columbia were "collect[ing] and publicly report[ing] data that connect teachers' student growth data to their preparation programs."

Looking for a Research Base

On what did states and DOE base their decision to require report cards? Research comparing teacher-preparation programs has produced inconsistent results. Some research, from Louisiana and New York, claimed that differences between teacher-preparation programs were substantial. Other research, from Missouri and Texas, claimed that the differences between teacher-preparation programs were minuscule, and that it was rarely possible to tell which programs were better or worse.

In its 129-page regulation, DOE spent less than a sentence acknowledging—and dismissing—inconsistencies in the research. "While we acknowledge that some studies of teacher preparation programs find very small differences at the program level . . . we believe that the examples we have cited above provide a reasonable basis for States' use of student learning outcomes" to evaluate teacher-preparation programs. It is unclear why officials at DOE dismissed research that didn't support the idea of program rankings. It is also unclear why officials felt a need to issue a national regulation requiring all 50 states to rate teacher-preparation programs when research had not reached a consensus that rankings would be practical or useful.

In fact, in the public debate over the federal regulation, research carried no weight at all. Research had been published in academic journals and summarized in more popular outlets like *Kappan* and the *Washington Post*. Yet teachers' unions did not cite research, and neither did members of Congress. Research went unmentioned in a 2015 Government Accountability Office report on teacher-training programs. When the DOE regulation listed 11 stakeholder groups that state governments must consult when specifying the data and analysis that would go into program report cards, neither researchers nor evaluators made the list.

Ranking Programs by Value-Added

Programs evaluated in a state report card may be "traditional" programs, in which a college student majors in education and completes student teaching to earn a degree and a teaching certificate. Or they may be "alternative" certification programs, which provide coursework and training to certify adults who already hold a bachelor's degree in other subjects. Alternative programs are often run by school districts or nonprofits like Teach For America or The New Teacher Project, but the fastest growing programs are run by for-profit corporations like Kaplan University or Teachers of Tomorrow.

A program that produces exceptional teachers may do so for different reasons. The program might provide excellent training that gives teachers the knowledge and skills they need to succeed in the classroom. Or the program could be very selective about the applicants that it accepts. State report cards don't measure whether the teachers coming out of a program are good because of training or selectivity. As long as the program is putting effective teachers in the classroom, the report card will give it a positive review.

At least, that is what is supposed to happen. In principle, comparing the effectiveness of teachers from different programs sounds pretty simple. But in practice, there is a lot that can go wrong.

Let's start with the simple part. Teachers are commonly evaluated by measuring their "value-added" to student scores on standardized tests. Value-added models begin by asking what students would be expected to score given their previous scores, poverty levels, and other characteristics. If students score above expectations, their teacher gets credit for the excess and her value-added is positive. If students score below expectations, the teacher gets credit for the shortfall and her value-added is negative.

To rank teacher-preparation programs, report cards average the value-added of teachers who have graduated from each program in the past few years. This approach to evaluating programs isn't perfect, but it stands up to some common knocks. In criticizing the federal regulation, for example, Weingarten claimed that "the flawed framework . . . will punish teacher-prep programs whose graduates go on to teach in our highest-needs schools, most often those with high concentrations of students who live in poverty and English language learners." But value-added models commonly adjust for poverty and English proficiency. And the federal regulation gave extra credit to programs that placed teachers in high-need schools.

The problem with ranking programs on value-added is not that the rankings are biased; the problem is that the rankings are almost random. Once random noise is sifted out of the rankings, the true differences between programs are usually too small to matter.

The Role of Randomness

We first looked at these issues in a 2016 study of 95 teacher-preparation programs in Texas. We ranked each program by estimating its teachers' average value-added to math scores. The graph of rankings is seductive (see Figure 1). Once you see the graph, it's hard not to think that the "best" programs—the ones that turn out the best teachers—are on the right, and the "worst" programs are

on the left. You could even slice the graph into groups of programs that look as if they have similar quality, such as "effective" programs, "low-performing" programs, and "at risk" programs. That's what the federal regulation would have required.

In fact, though, these programs are less different than they look. The differences that look so compelling in the graph are mostly random. There's random error in student test scores, there's random variation in the particular group of teachers who complete a program in a given year, there's random variation in where those teachers end up working, and there's random variation in how responsive their students are. These random factors vary from year to year, for reasons beyond a program's control. So where a program falls in a given year's rankings, and whether it moves up or down from one year to the next, is typically more a matter of luck than of quality.

THE PROBLEM WITH RANKING PROGRAMS ON VALUE-ADDED is not that the rankings are biased; the problem is that the rankings are mostly random.

It's hard for almost everyone, even trained researchers, to appreciate how much the apparent differences between programs are due to random estimation error. We are often "fooled by randomness"—when we see a random pattern, we think it means more than it does.

To highlight the role of random error, we calculated the "null distribution," or what the distribution of

Figure 1

Comparing a State's Teacher Prep Programs

When the 95 teacher preparation programs in Texas are ranked based on their graduates' average value-added to student test scores, it appears as though there are clear distinctions to be made between the "worst" programs, clustered on the left of the figure, and the "best" programs, clustered on the right.

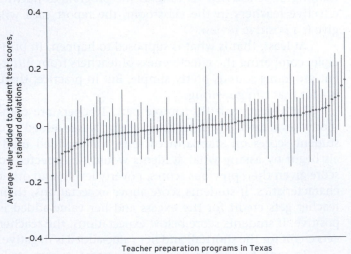

Source: Authors' calculations

Note: Each point represents an estimate of the average value-added to student test scores of recent graduates of one of the 95 teacher preparation programs in Texas. The line extending vertically from each point represents the estimate's 95 percent confidence interval.

Figure 2

The Role of Random Estimation Error

If all of the programs were identical and ranked based on estimation error alone, the distribution of the program estimates would be flat in the middle and flare at the ends.

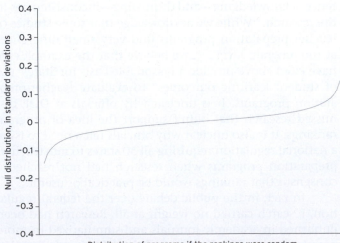

Source: Authors' calculations

program rankings would look like if all the programs were actually identical and nothing but random estimation error were present. The null distribution looks an awful lot like our actual results: it is almost flat in the middle and flares at the ends (see Figure 2).

In fact, when we lay the null distribution over the Texas results, the fit is almost perfect (see Figure 3). Remember, the null distribution shows what program rankings would look like *if they were entirely random*. So the tight fit of the null distribution suggests that the rankings are, if not entirely random, then darn close. Even the programs that appear to stand out may stand out because of error. In fact, ¾ of the variation in Texas rankings—¾ of the reason that one program ranks above another—is random chance. Only ¼ of the variation has anything to do with program quality.

When true differences are small and estimates are noisy, it is hard to single out specific programs as different from average. Here, too, it is easy to fool ourselves. According to the conventions of statistics, about 5 percent of the time we are permitted to make a "type 1 error" that singles out a program as "significantly different" when it is truly average. That risk might be acceptable in a state with just a couple of programs, but in Texas, where there are almost 100 programs, a 5 percent error rate ensures that we'll erroneously label about five ordinary programs as exceptional. In fact, when we conducted our Texas evaluation, we found seven programs that were "significantly different" from average. Quite possibly five of these differences, or even all seven, were type 1 errors. Quite possibly just two of the programs, or none, were truly different.

A Six-State Review

After finishing our report card on Texas, we were a little confused. Our Texas results suggested there was little difference in effectiveness between teachers from various programs. Research from Missouri agreed. Yet there were reports from Louisiana and New York City suggesting larger differences. And there were reports from Florida and Washington State that we wanted to look at more closely.

Adding to the confusion, in each state, researchers had compared programs using different statistical methods. So when researchers reached different conclusions, we couldn't be sure if it was because of their programs or because of the methods used to compare them.

To clear things up, we reanalyzed the results from different states using a uniform set of statistical best practices. When we did that, we found that results from different states were actually very similar. In every state, the differences between most programs were minuscule. Having a

Figure 3

Fooled by Randomness

The distribution of programs ranked by estimation error looks very similar to the actual results for the teacher preparation programs in Texas; when the two are overlaid, the fit is almost perfect.

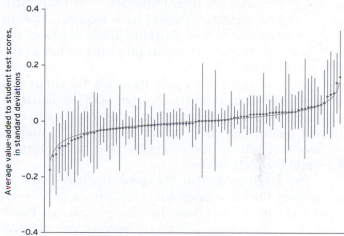

Teacher preparation programs in Texas, with null distribution overlaid

Source: Authors' calculations

Note: Each point represents an estimate of the average value-added to student test scores of recent graduates of one of the 95 teacher preparation programs in Texas. The blue line extending vertically from each point represents the estimate's 95 percent confidence interval. The pink line represents the null distribution, or what the distribution of program estimates would look like if the programs were identical and ranked based on estimation error alone.

teacher from one program or another typically changed student test scores by just .01 to .03 standard deviations, or 1 to 3 percent of the average score gap between poor and nonpoor children.

Remarkably, these patterns held in every state we looked at—not just in Missouri and Texas, where program differences were already thought to be negligible, but also in Louisiana and New York City, where larger differences had been reported previously. For example, when we reanalyzed estimates for the 15 largest teacher-preparation programs in New York City, we found no significant differences between programs (see Figure 4). The estimates hewed very close to the null distribution, suggesting that little but estimation error was present. Similar patterns also held in Florida and Washington.

Why Ranking Programs on Value-Added Won't Work

The differences between programs are typically too small to matter. And they're practically impossible to estimate with any reliability. The errors that we make in estimation will often be larger than the differences we are trying to estimate. Program rankings will consist largely of noise, and program rankings will bounce up and down randomly from one year to another.

This means that we cannot rank programs in a meaningful order. And we cannot justify classifying programs by performance level ("effective," "at risk," etc.), as the federal regulation would have required. Statistically, at most one or two programs stand out from the pack in any given state. The other programs are practically indistinguishable.

None of this means that there are no differences between *individual* teachers. A large body of literature shows that some teachers are better than others, and that teacher quality can have meaningful effects on student success—not just on test scores but also on graduation rates and even job success.

The problem is that the good teachers don't all come from the same programs. The differences between good and bad teachers from the same program are much larger than the average differences between one program and another. So even if we could do a better job ranking

programs, knowing what program prepared a teacher would give employers little guidance about how effective the teacher was likely to be.

We also don't believe that *all* teacher-preparation programs are the same. Although the vast majority of programs are practically indistinguishable, there are exceptions—at most one or two per state, our results suggest—that really do produce teachers whose average impacts on test scores are significantly better than average.

For example, we know that Teach For America and UTeach both produce above-average teachers, although their effects are moderate in size and limited to math and science. But we don't know that from state report cards. We know it from evaluations that focused specifically on UTeach and Teach For America.

Our results suggest there may also be an occasional program whose teachers are significantly worse than average. It could be valuable to look more closely at these rare outliers. But trying to rank other programs on value-added will just create confusion.

Should We Rank Programs in Other Ways?

It's not helpful to rank a state's programs by teachers' value-added. With rare exceptions, the true differences between programs are so small that rankings would consist mostly of noise. But can we look at other measures of program quality? Student test scores are not the only way to evaluate programs. In fact, although the federal regulation required that no program be classified as "effective" unless its graduates had an exceptional impact on test scores, it did require that programs be evaluated using other indicators of quality as well.

One of those indicators was the ratings of a program's graduates by principals or supervisors conducting teacher observations. However, we believe it is premature to require principal ratings in a formal ranking system. While principal ratings do vary across programs, there is research evidence that principal ratings are biased. They are biased in favor of teachers with advantaged students, and they are biased toward teachers whom the principal likes, or at least has evaluated positively in the past. Ratings by impartial outsiders are less biased, but teacher-rating forms still have a lot of room for improvement. While teacher observations remain a good topic for research, until observation forms get better they are not something that regulations should require or that states should use to rank programs.

THE DIFFERENCES BETWEEN GOOD AND BAD TEACHERS FROM THE SAME PROGRAM are much

Figure 4

Replicating the Pattern in New York City

When the 15 largest teacher-preparation programs in New York City are compared on the basis of their graduates' average value-added to student test scores, the distribution is also almost identical to what it would be if all of the rankings were entirely random.

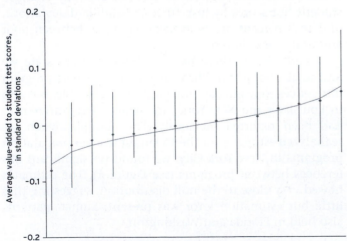

Source: Authors' calculations

Note: Each point represents an estimate of the average value-added to student test scores of recent graduates of one of New York City's 15 largest teacher-preparation programs. The blue line extending vertically from each point represents the estimate's 95 percent confidence interval. The pink line represents the null distribution, or what the distribution of program estimates would look like if the programs were identical and ranked based on estimation error alone.

Though the Law Has Been Rescinded, Should Teacher Preparation Programs Be Rated Under the Higher Education Act? by Koonce

181

larger than the average differences between one program and another.

The federal regulation also suggested reporting teachers' ratings of their own preparation programs. Whether these ratings should be required is debatable. There is little research on teachers' ratings of preparation programs, and there is a danger that some ratings may be noisy or biased. Still, prospective teachers may want to know what their predecessors thought of the training offered by a given program.

Finally, the federal regulation suggested tracking programs' record of placing and retaining graduates in the teaching profession, especially at high-need schools. We think this is an excellent idea. If a large percentage of a program's graduates are not becoming teachers, or not persisting as teachers, that is clearly a concern. Likewise, if a large percentage of graduates are persisting, especially at high-need schools, that is a sign of success. And placement and retention are straightforward to measure by linking

program rosters to employment records. We favor reporting the percentage of program graduates who enter and persist in the field for which they were trained—not just for teacher-preparation programs but for other college majors and training programs as well.

PAUL VON HIPPEL, PhD, is an associate professor of Public Affairs at the LBJ School of Public Affairs. He is an expert on research design and missing data and studies evidence-based policy, educational inequality and the relationship between schooling, health, and obesity.

LAURA BELLOWS, PhD, MPH, RD, is an associate professor at Colorado State University whose research interests revolve around the impact of community-based interventions on public health outcomes.

EXPLORING THE ISSUE

Though the Law Has Been Rescinded, Should Teacher Preparation Programs Be Rated under the Higher Education Act?

Critical Thinking and Reflection

1. Do you see edTPA as a hiring trend for teachers in the future?
2. If there is an accreditation system in place, is there really a need for a rating system? Why or why not?
3. What is the best way for a student to currently search for the best teacher preparation program?
4. Was the annual "report card" a good idea? Explain.
5. If there is no accreditation process for teacher preparation programs, how can these programs be held accountable?

Is There Common Ground?

An old tale in education circles explains that part of the reason for students not achieving success in high school is because the middle school did not prepare them properly for high school. The middle school pushes the blame to the elementary school's lack of preparing students for middle school. The elementary school complains that the preschool just didn't do their job, and the preschools focus the main reason on the parent did not preparing their child for success in school when they had nurtured and watched them grow for five years. Should we now say that teachers preparing at the university were not adequately prepared by the high school to be successful in their teacher preparation programs? Blaming is not very fertile territory for common ground in the issue of preparing teachers in universities across the country to teach in the nation's schools. Most everyone would agree that teacher preparation programs should be held accountable for the outcomes of their students, to include, being successful teachers in the K–12 schools across the country.

The common ground can be found in the changing tide for the nation's schools being redefined under regulations found in the Every Student Succeeds Act (ESSA). A major driver in this legislation has been to lessen the federal mandates that have been the hallmark of the No Child Left Behind (NCLB), testing and test preparation. With punitive measures for schools and school districts not making Adequate Yearly Progress troublesome and pervasive, the NCLB policies had reached and surpassed their effectiveness. As the years under NCLB progressed,

many states put in place accountability systems that did just the opposite of what they were charged to do for student achievement and success. ESSA plans and their implementation offers state leaders an opportunity to change outdate NCLB practices and help students who have been underserved for so long. As ESSA plans are formalized in the U.S. Department of Education review process, implementation can proceed and hopefully common ground by all stakeholders can be found that can also impact how teachers are prepared and teacher preparation programs held accountable.

For the nation's teacher preparation programs, the rating system that was put into place in 2016 has been reversed, noting the same overreach and elimination of the large footprint that the federal government has on K–12 schools across the nation. In a bipartisan response that has spurned the passage of the ESSA, new opportunities lie ahead for finding common ground, but its passage doesn't totally answer the question, where do those desiring to be teachers find the best programs? In a survey by Teach Plus (Will, 2018, p. 10) that asked "755 teachers from 26 states views on teacher-prep program accountability, almost half (46%) want more transparency on how well these programs are preparing teachers to teach." Perhaps, with the elimination of the rating system, CAEP could gain ground as the national accreditor for teacher preparation programs, providing some measure of a program's success for an individual interested in finding a successful program. Even though the law has been rescinded, should legislatures revisit the teacher preparation program rating system under the ESSA?

Additional Resources

Council for the Accreditation of Educator Preparation. (2018). *CAEP scope of accreditation.* Retrieved from http://caepnet.org/accreditation/about-accreditation/what-is-accreditation

Dubin, J. (2017). Investing wisely in teacher preparation. *American Educator.* Retrieved from https://www.aft.org/sites/default/files/periodicals/ae_fall2017_dubin.pdf

Hill, M. (2018). After five years, a bold set of teacher-preparation standards still faces challenge. *Education Week.* Retrieved from https://www.edweek.org/ew/articles/2018/08/29/after-five-years-a-bold-set-of.html

Mitchel, A. and Anderson, C. (2017). *Plotting a new course on teacher preparation reform.* National Association of State Boards of Education. Retrieved from http://www.nasbe.org/wp-content/uploads/2017/09/Mitchel-Aldeman_Sept-2017-Standard.pdf

Office of Federal Student Aid. (2018). *Teacher Education Assistance for College and Higher Education (TEACH) Grant.* Washington, DC: U.S. Department of Education.

"Teacher Preparation Issues," 34 CFR part 612 *Code of Federal Regulations*, 81 FR 75494-75622. 2016 ed. Retrieved from https://www.federalregister.gov/documents/2016/10/31/2016-24856/teacher-preparation-issues

U.S. Department of Education. (2016). *Education department releases final teacher preparation regulations.* Retrieved from https://www.ed.gov/news/press-releases/education-department-releases-final-teacher-preparation-regulations

von Hippel, P. and Bellows, L. (2018). Rating teacher-preparation programs," *Education Next.* 18/3.

Will, M. (2018). Make teacher-prep programs accountable for graduate's performance, teachers say. *Education Week.* Retrieved from http://blogs.edweek.org/edweek/teacherbeat/2018/07/teacher_preparation_programs_accountability_survey.html

Internet References . . .

America's Teacher—Training Programs Aren't Good Enough

https://www.theatlantic.com/national/archive/2013/06/americas-teacher-training-programs-arent-good-enough/276993/

Improving Teacher Preparation: Building on Innovation

https://www.ed.gov/teacherprep

Ohio Teacher Preparation Programs Shine in New Ranking

https://edexcellence.net/articles/ohio-teacher-preparation-programs-shine-in-new-ranking

Raising the Bar on Teacher Prep

https://www.nctq.org/review

Ranking Teacher-prep Programs on Value-added Is Usually Futile

https://www.educationnext.org/ranking-teacher-prep-programs-value-added-usually-futile/

Selected, Edited, and with Issue Framing Material by:
Glenn L. Koonce, *Regent University*

ISSUE

Should There Be No-Zero Grading Policies in Schools?

YES: Bianca Bell, from "From Zero to Hero: A Teacher's Academic Freedom and Professional Judgment Upheld," *Education Law Journal* (2016)

NO: Michael Zwaagstra, from "Zero Support for No-Zero Policies," *Frontier Centre for Public Policy* (2012)

Learning Outcomes

After reading this issue, you will be able to:

- Understand general purposes and overall function of grades in schools.
- List alternatives to assigning grades of zero for missed work.
- Substantiate reasons for having a no-zero policy.
- Identify specific rationale in defense of a no-zero grading policy.
- Describe the research findings that support a minimum grading policy.

ISSUE SUMMARY

YES: Articulating student at Ursel Phillips Fellows Hopkinson LLP, Bianca Bell reports the outcome from a court case where a teacher's use of zeros, in deference to the principal's policy, was upheld in court.

NO: Teacher, education researcher, and author Michael Zwaagstra posits no-zero policies are logically flawed, unsupported by research, and mathematically unfair.

"**W**ith a no-zero grading policy, the glass is always half full," because even if a student turns in no work at all, they cannot be assigned a grade of less than 50 (Minero, 2018, p. 1). New grading systems that ban student grades of zero continue to grow across the country. Identified as a no-zero policy or minimum grading policy, the system works like this: "if a student has completed an assignment— no matter how late or poorly done—he has shown a *good faith* effort, and therefore deserves somewhere between a zero and 49" (Walker, 2016, p. 1). The no-zero grade movement is focused on adopting grading practices that make it more difficult for students to fail a class because of work habits, effort, punctuality, or homework. Examples of this movement can be found in Fairfax County Public Schools in Virginia, one of the largest districts in the country, nearby Prince George's County Public Schools in

Maryland, and Philadelphia School District, in Pennsylvania. Philadelphia recently approved policies where no student who made a "reasonable attempt" or a "good faith effort" would receive a grade lower that 50, on 100-point scale (Balight, 2016, p. 1; Minero, 2018, p. 1). Even more concerning for many is the extended national movement to do away with grades all together and lowering the value of school assessment staples like the Scholastic Aptitude Test and Advanced Placement exams.

Supporters of the no-zero policy argue that no-zero grades help struggling students with opportunities to retake exams or turn in late work. It allows for practices that are more conducive for student learning, are fairer, allow an opportunity for students to catch up when they are behind, and keeps many students from dropping out (Balight, 2016). There are legitimate concerns from those that oppose no-zero policies. They assert that the message being sent to students is that hard work and homework are not important. When students do not take pride in their work they do not aspire to more challenging tasks. Teachers also lose an important tool to enforce diligence in a no-zero grading policy, their professional judgment. Furthermore, any *artificial boost* to student grades can mask student failure. Because of this perspective, it is logical for opponents of no-zero policies to feel that students are not being held accountable for the material they need to know to be successful. No-zero policies lead to students being unprepared for the world of work and the expectations for succeeding in college. This hits home for most because if an individual goes to their employer and says, "Here's my work, its two weeks late," they are likely to get fired. The controversy continues to grow as more school districts implement no-zero policies (Walker, 2016, p. 2).

Like many changes made in the education system for K–12 students, there is an absence of empirical data and clear comparative analysis of the conflicting points of view regarding no-zero policies. In the case of evaluating grading practices, research studies are almost nonexistent. In a 2014 literature review exploring the grading practices for the last 200 years, Minero (2018, p. 2) concluded, "grades increase anxiety and decrease the interest in learning for students who struggle." There is cynicism in the failure of research to provide direction on such a controversial, but important issue. One of the longest established and almost sacred traditions in American education is the *A–F* or *100–0* grading system. It is not surprising that supporters of the traditional grading system do not see a need to change. The most common arguments against the no-zero grading policy are the following statements. Zero-grading policies are:

- Unfair toward students that work to complete assignments on time;
- Not preparing students for real-world situations in which incomplete or late work is not acceptable and often results in loss of employment or failure in college;
- Rewarding laziness and encouraging students to avoid work;
- Inappropriately inflating student grades;
- Damaging the academic reputation of the school and its teachers;
- Interfering with teachers' ability to use their own discretion in grading (Hanover Research, 2013, p. 10);
- Softening competency requirements and contributing to grade inflation;
- Offering unfair and unearned assistance to low-performing students—making it too easy for

them; Giving students a falsely optimistic view of their abilities (Cariflo & Carey, 2009, p. 27);
- Undermines instruction allowing students to subvert the system; who learn to do nothing the first two ¼ and collect their 50s, do well on the next two ¼ and the final, and pass for the year (Minero, 2018, p. 2).

Asserting that the arguments against no-zero policies are compelling, Zwaagstra (2012, p. 4), in the NO article for this issue, states that no-zero policies "prohibit teachers from giving marks of zero for incomplete work." Some recently implemented no-zero policies across the country make it harder to fail students. Many of these policies do not allow a zero even when students have cheated on work turned in for a grade. Many feel that cheating is a very serious issue that needs teacher intervention strategies to assure the behavior does not reoccur, not a no-zero policy.

The phrase *No work–No credit* rings as a strong emotional attachment for teachers assigning a zero to students who submit nothing for an assignment. Should the thought not be, the student failed to turn in an assignment and as a consequence, that student received a failing grade of a zero? The logic for this mind-set is timeless. Teachers understand it, parents understand it, and certainly students understand it. Teachers have been assigning zeros, seemingly, forever. Why would assigning a zero be toxic to so many people today? A decade ago, Reeves (2008) provided some insights to answering this question, stating that the most effective thing to reduce the student failure rate is to challenge prevailing grading practices. Schools do not need a new curriculum, a new principal, new teachers, or even new technology to reduce the failure rate; they need a better grading system. Failure for students can result from just two or three zeros in the course of an entire semester. A few course failures can devastate a student's grade point average to the point that they drop out of high school. Most of these students who fail to graduate incur a lifetime of personal and social consequences. The logic for assigning a zero appears steep under these conditions.

The YES article for this issue is the result of a recent court case supporting a teacher's academic freedom and professional judgment for refusing to follow a school-wide grading policy that directed teachers to give letter grades instead of a zero for students who failed to turn in an assignment (Bell, 2016). Norrell's (2015) opposing opinion is that the use of zeros can cause a student to withdraw from learning and is toxic as a grading policy. Norrell noted that it is "nearly impossible to recover academically from one or multiple zeros" (p. 2), the impact of no-zero grading affects high-achieving students as well as students who struggle.

Likewise, no-zero policies greatly impact teachers, who may be less than even-tempered by the presumption that if they give a student a zero, it is motivated only by the desire to punish. Most teachers assign grades after material has been taught; therefore, students are engaged in learning activities and then evaluated on assessments designed to measure that learning. Teachers dedicate much time in their review of student work to evaluate and assign grades. The issue of grades and grading policies are very important and ethically based for teachers. In deference to this position, many teachers use zeros as instruments of control. Professor at the University of Kentucky and researcher in grading policies Thomas Guskey (2004, p. 2) states that the zero is the "ultimate grading weapon used to punish students for not putting forth adequate effort or for failing to demonstrate appropriate responsibility." (To these teachers, the zero is justified and deserved when established deadlines are not met, students misbehave, and/or students fail to heed the teacher's warnings. Guskey notes that "few teachers even recognize that many of their grading practices serve precisely this purpose" (p. 2). Students respond in a serious way once they realize the teacher is serious about their grading practices. Teachers assigning a zero hits home with many students. Even if a zero is retracted after the inappropriate behavior improves, it is a powerful force in the hands of some teachers. Most would be wise to the gaming possibilities of students playing the system to produce little work and still pass. And really, what parent would want their child to receive a passing grade for work they never even submitted? In this sense, teachers feel reinforced when their actions help students to remediate their learning or behavior issues before they become major problems.

Hanover Research (2013) profiled no-zero grading policies at eight different districts and secondary schools, finding that there is much controversy when no-zero grading policies are introduced. Another key finding was that proponents in favor of no-zero grading argued "the use of zero in traditional 100-point grading systems excessively punishes students for missed assignments, distorts the ability of grades to reflect student mastery of academic subjects, and is ineffective at altering student behavior" (p. 3). This report also asserted that grades "first and foremost should reflect students' learning and mastery of academic material" (p. 3).

The value of grading is diminished when a zero is assigned to students as a measure of mastering established learning standards or achieving specific learning goals. When the zero is assigned for inadequate effort or poor performance, it is argued the grade become punitive. Guskey, as quoted in Hanover Research (2013, p. 7), agrees, claiming that there are "no studies to support the use of low grades or marks as punishment." When punishment occurs and results in low grades, students may become discouraged and continue in a cycle of failure. Using grades to motivate, punish, or sort students' results in "diluting" a grade's efficiency and usefulness. When this occurs, "we are using grades to manipulate students" (p. 7). Proponents of eliminating zeros stress that there should be consequences for inappropriate behavior, but grading should not be that consequence.

The clash of views continues in the zero-grade policy debate. Even though zero-grading policies are gaining in popularity, there are districts that have implemented such a policy and then abandoned it, citing that zero grade is a major step backward in the progress for greater student accountability. Minimum grading policies are no magic bullet for improving student achievement. According to the experts, "neither no-zero nor zero policies are silver bullets" and grading should be more focused on how the teacher conceptualizes the grade by providing expectations and clear and specific feedback" (Minero, p. 3). Since the issue of permitting (or not) zeros in student grades has not been resolved, it is likely the debate will continue and unfortunately usurp resources that could be directed toward other strategies to improve student success.

YES

Bianca Bell

From Zero to Hero: A Teacher's Academic Freedom and Professional Judgment Upheld

Edmonton School District No. 7 v. Dorval[1]

Labor law—Teacher dismissal—Just cause—Board of Reference—Remedies—Reinstatement—Damages—School Act (Alta.), ss. 105(1) (2), 135, 138(2), 143(1)

Introduction

In *Edmonton School District No. 7 v. Dorval*, the Alberta Court of Appeal upheld a decision of a Board of Reference (Board) that found a School Board had unjustly terminated a high-school teacher for refusing to follow his principal's grading policy because of a difference of opinion about teaching philosophy. The Court of Appeal's decision enhances support for teachers who exercise their professional judgment when choosing methods of assessment and teaching, even when their opinions and beliefs on educational strategies conflict with those of their superiors.

Background

Mr. Dorval, the teacher in this case, was terminated for refusing to follow a school-wide grading policy that was unilaterally imposed by the principal. The policy directed teachers to give letter codes instead of a zero to students who failed to hand in an assignment. Each letter code was meant to reflect the behavioral reason behind a student's failure to submit his or her homework.

Based on his 35 years of experience as a teacher, Mr. Dorval disagreed with the new policy. He believed that zeros, which could be replaced upon completion of an assignment, encouraged accountability, encouraged students to complete assignments, and resulted in "work-based evaluation." Mr. Dorval, together with several other teachers, contended that the letter coding policy inflated grades and provided little incentive to students to submit

their outstanding work. Mr. Dorval believed that, as a professional, *he* had the primary responsibility for fashioning student assessment. The principal believed otherwise.

After Mr. Dorval advised the principal that he would not replace zeros on his assignments with the letter codes, the principal issued him a letter of reprimand for refusing to use the codes and failing to attend various staff meetings. Mr. Dorval responded that the Collective Agreement provided that teachers could carry out their duties in accordance with School Board policies, and that no board-wide policy existed that necessitated the use of the letter codes.[2] Mr. Dorval also detailed his attendance at staff meetings, demonstrating a near-perfect attendance record. Subsequently, Mr. Dorval received another letter of reprimand for insubordinate and disrespectful behavior toward the principal and a further failure to attend departmental meetings.

Following the second letter of reprimand, the principal submitted a recommendation to the Superintendent that Mr. Dorval be suspended for his refusal to use the letter grading system. Following a hearing held by the Superintendent, Mr. Dorval was suspended from his duties. According to the Superintendent, although it would be acceptable for Mr. Dorval to disagree with pedagogical and philosophical guidelines, the implementation of the Policy had been made mandatory. Mr. Dorval was ordered to turn in all school property, leave the campus immediately, and not enter the school during his suspension.

During the suspension, the principal continued to contact Mr. Dorval to demand exams and assignments that the teacher had mistakenly taken home in the chaos of packing up quickly. This request resulted in Mr. Dorval's attending the school to drop off the exams. The principal chastised Mr. Dorval's presence at the school as well as his failure to mark all of the exams before he was suspended. The principal subsequently recommended that Mr. Dorval be terminated, relying on the same grounds he had used to justify the suspension, as well as Mr. Dorval's purported "neglect of duty as a professional teacher" and continued "insubordination" during the suspension.

A termination hearing was held by the Superintendent who had previously suspended Mr. Dorval. That Superintendent ultimately decided that Mr. Dorval had a cavalier attitude and contempt for the principal which, compounded with the suspension, justified termination. Mr. Dorval appealed his termination to the Board of Reference.

Board of Reference Decision

After a hearing, the Board of Reference found that Mr. Dorval's actions with respect to the new assessment policy were not a deliberate refusal to obey lawful instructions as alleged by the principal, but rather the "'lawful and professional exercise of his teaching responsibilities."[3] It further suggested that insubordination does not necessarily flow from a refusal to follow policy if there is a reasonable explanation for the difference of opinion. The Board remarked that

> [t]he Teacher had professional obligations to the students and the responsibility to use his judgment in the selection of teaching and assessment methods, to achieve completion of the curriculum. The Principal had a professional obligation to supervise the fulfillment of those professional responsibilities, while respecting the professional judgment of the Teacher.[4]

With respect to the initial suspension, the Board held that assessment was only a portion of Mr. Dorval's responsibilities, he was not incompetent in other areas, and his attendance at staff meetings was above average. It ultimately held that the suspension was not reasonable or fair. After considering the evidence concerning the events leading to the termination, the Board held that Mr. Dorval's failure to return school property, unauthorized entry of the school, and attitude toward the employer were reasonable, adequately explained, and did not involve any deliberate misconduct.

Ultimately, the Board found no just cause for discipline and awarded Mr. Dorval lost wages back to his termination

date. Although the Board held the opinion that the principal should have the final say in school-related matters, it ultimately stressed the importance of respecting the professional judgment of Mr. Dorval and mining the experience of senior teachers when attempting to accomplish educational goals. The School Board appealed the Board of Reference's decision to the Court of Appeal of Alberta.

Court of Appeal Decision

On appeal, the court found the Board's decision should be reviewed on the standard of reasonableness: whether it was justifiable, transparent, and intelligible. The court reviewed five issues.

(a) Was the Board Entitled to Consider the Events Leading up to the Suspension?

The appellant School Board argued that because Mr. Dorval had not appealed the suspension, the events leading up to the suspension could not be taken into account in determining whether the termination was justified. The court dismissed this argument pointing out that the events leading up to the suspension were the subject of extensive focus at the termination hearing and were directly connected to the events underlying the termination.

(b) Did the Board Err in Its Identification and Application of the Law?

Next, the appellant submitted that the Board did not apply the proper legal test for workplace discipline. The court found this argument was without merit because there is a difference between employees who are required to obey lawful orders from persons in authority and professional employees who may be expected to exercise a degree of independent judgment in their performance of duties.[5] It confirmed that, as a professional employee, Mr. Dorval had a legal obligation to his students and was entitled to exercise his professional judgment regarding what was in the best interest of his students' learning.

With respect to the claim that the Board had erred in applying the legal test for insubordination, the court concluded that disagreement does not necessarily constitute insubordination.[6] The court affirmed that, on these facts, Mr. Dorval had explained his concerns about the grading system and asked for information to substantiate it, which the principal refused to supply. The court also found it relevant that several other teachers who had also challenged the principal over this issue had not been disciplined.

Ultimately, the court found that Board had not erred in applying the legal test for insubordination.

(c) Did the Board Err by Failing to Consider All Grounds for Termination and Ignoring Relevant Evidence?

The court quickly dismissed this argument, suggesting decisions must be reviewed as a whole and not parsed into specific errors or decisions. It held that all complaints made by the School Board were included as evidence in the hearings and that this evidence led to a reasonable determination that Mr. Dorval was unfairly terminated.

(d) Did the Board Err by Making Irrelevant Findings?

The appellant also argued that the Board had made irrelevant comments about the personality conflict between Mr. Dorval and the principal. The court dismissed this ground of appeal given the Board's extensive analysis of the important legal principles that applied to the case.

(e) Did the Board Err in Concluding There Was No Just Cause for Termination?

Finally, the court had to determine whether the Board had been reasonable in finding that the Superintendent did not have just cause to terminate Mr. Dorval. The Board had applied the test for reasonableness set out under the *School Act*,[7] which requires elements of both substantive and procedural unreasonableness to overturn a termination.[8] The Board had found that there were unreasonable substantive elements to the termination, including the imposition of the grading policy without consultation, the overriding of Mr. Dorval's professional judgment and his professional rights and duties regarding assessment, the principal's having ignored concerns about the policy, the lack of adequate communication to the community about the new policy, and the discriminatory singling out of Mr. Dorval for discipline. The Board had also found that certain procedural elements of termination were unreasonable, including the conduct surrounding the discipline after Mr. Dorval had been suspended, as well as the biased nature of the termination hearing. Based on these considerations, the court concluded that the Board had properly considered both the substantive and procedural elements of the test set out in the Act.

Mr. Dorval's cross-appeal of the Board's refusal to grant reinstatement rather than damages was denied by the court, despite arbitral jurisprudence recognizing reinstatement as the presumptive remedy. The court noted that, according to the Supreme Court of Canada,[9] this presumption may not apply in certain circumstances. The deterioration of the relationship between Mr. Dorval and the principal embodied such circumstances and thus the Board's decision on the remedy issue had been reasonable.

Commentary

This decision clearly exemplifies the tensions between professional autonomy in the classroom and the push to standardize education policy across a province. Although the Court of Appeal did not go as far as recognizing anything like academic freedom for public school educators, it did affirm that considerable weight must be given to a teacher's exercise of professional judgment in fashioning effective and appropriate assessment methods. Sometimes a teacher's duty to his/her students will trump his/her duty to obey directives from management. Although principals remain a source of authority on educational assessment methods, this decision makes clear that it does not necessarily constitute insubordination to resist policies that are developed at the local level around issues in which a legitimate difference in pedagogical opinion exists.

It is important, however, to appreciate the decision's affirmation of a teacher's professional judgment in its greater context. In this case, the policy at issue was developed without consultation with the Union or individual teachers, and was unilaterally imposed at only one school. The court may have come to a different conclusion if the grading policy had an unshakable pedagogical basis and had been implemented at the School Board level following an appropriate consultation process.

References

1. *Edmonton School District No. 7 v. Dorval*, 2016 ABCA 8, 2016 CarswellAlta 32 (Alta, CA).

2. *Ibid.* at para. 10.

3. *Ibid.* at para. 30.

4. *Ibid.* at para. 7.

5. *Ibid.* at para. 49 (emphasis added).

6. *Ibid.* at para 53.

7. R.S.A. 2000, c. S-3 s. 107(2).

8. The Board had used the test from *Gazdarica v. Calgary Roman Catholic Separate School District No. 1*, 1988 CarswellAlta 120, 91 A.R. 194 (Alta. Bd. of Ref. under the School Act) at paras. 5–6.

9. *A.U.P.E. v. Lethbridge Community College*, 2004 SCC
28, 2004 CarswellAlta 533, 2004 CarswellAlta 534,
(sub nom. *Alberta Union of Provincial Employees v.
Lethbridge Community College*) [2004] 1 S.C.R. 727
(S.C.C.) at para. 56.

BIANCA BELL received her JD from Osgoode Hall Law
School in 2015 and practices at UPFH in the areas of labor
law on behalf of trade unions and associations, employment law, and human rights, criminal law in the context
of criminal allegations in the workplace.

Michael Zwaagstra

Zero Support for No-Zero Policies

Executive Summary

- Many school boards and individual schools across the country have implemented no-zero policies as part of their formal guidelines for teachers. These policies prohibit teachers from giving marks of zero for incomplete work or for academic misconduct such as plagiarism. Since no-zero policies obviously have a major impact on assessment practices, it is important to carefully evaluate the arguments made in favour of this approach.

- It is difficult to quantify how widespread no-zero policies are across Canada, since school boards tend not to advertise their existence. Nevertheless, the media report enough examples of no-zero policies to demonstrate that this practice is widespread.

- The research on no-zero policies is surprisingly weak. In fact, the assessment consultants regularly cite each other as their only sources when defending no-zero policies, and they rarely refer to actual research evidence to support their position.

- There are many reasons why school administrators should avoid no-zero policies. First, they inevitably bring controversy with them, something that is acknowledged by even their strongest proponents.

- Second, no-zero policies unreasonably interfere with the professional discretion of teachers to determine grades. Teachers know their students and realize it is unrealistic to expect the same technique to work with every student. They use a variety of methods to hold students accountable.

- Third, no-zero policies fail to prepare students for life after school. Employees are not paid for doing nothing, and universities do not grant credit to students who choose not to hand in their assignments.

- The arguments against no-zero policies are compelling. No-zero policies always encounter fierce resistance from parents and teachers, unreasonably interfere with the professional discretion of teachers, penalize students who complete all their assignments on time and fail to prepare students for life after school. These are all excellent reasons for school administrators to avoid stepping into the quagmire of no-zero policies.

Introduction

Many school boards and individual schools across the country have no-zero policies as part of their formal assessment guidelines for teachers. No-zero policies prohibit teachers from giving their students marks of zero for incomplete work or for academic misconduct such as plagiarism. Rather, teachers are expected to use a variety of interventions (such as scheduled homework time during lunchtime or after school) to make sure students complete the assigned work.

Unsurprisingly, no-zero policies are highly controversial among teachers and parents. Many parents think that schools are not preparing students for the real world when they impose policies that make it impossible for students to receive zeros. Many teachers oppose no-zero policies because they undermine their professional autonomy to determine appropriate grades.

Nevertheless, no-zero policies receive strong endorsements from most assessment consultants in the field of education. Ken O'Connor, Damian Cooper, Douglas Reeves and Thomas Guskey are some of the best-known authors who claim that no-zero policies make sense because there is substantial research evidence supporting them.

Some people are skeptical of this approach. The recent suspension of Edmonton high school teacher Lynden Dorval for defying a no-zero directive at Ross Sheppard High School garnered attention across the country. Largely because of the public outcry, trustees with the Edmonton Public School Board agreed to review their assessment policies and practices. The outcry also prompted other jurisdictions to reconsider their assessment policies and practices.

Since no-zero policies obviously have a major impact on assessment practices in schools, it is important to carefully evaluate the arguments made in favour of this approach. This includes the theoretical arguments and the evidentiary research base. If evidence for this approach is lacking, school administrators should question the wisdom of no-zero policies.

The Current Approach to Assessment

Grading practices have changed significantly over the years. Teachers used to determine students' grades without input from school boards. Understandably, this led to a wide variety of practices, some more valid than others. However, starting approximately 20 years ago, researchers began paying closer attention to how teachers graded their students.[1]

While assessments are primarily associated with unit tests, project marks and final grades, assessment consultants emphasize that this type of evaluation is only one component of a proper assessment protocol. Formative assessment, also known as assessment for learning, now receives a great deal of emphasis.[2] Such assessment provides specific feedback to students about their progress and is generally not included in their final grades. It supports the learning process and gives students the opportunity to practice their skills in a non-judgmental environment. In contrast, assignments and tests given for the purpose of evaluation are summative assessment or assessment of learning.

Research strongly supports the importance of feedback as part of the learning process. In his examination of more than 900 meta-analyses consisting of approximately 60,000 research studies, John Hattie, the director of the Melbourne Education Research Institute in Australia, found that feedback has "twice the average effect of all other schooling effects" and it "places in the top ten influences on [students'] achievement."[3] Thus, there is good reason for the attention given to formative assessment.

Assessment consultants also emphasize the importance of ensuring that grades are valid and reliable. "Validity" means that grades convey appropriate information about the specific achievement in question, and "reliability" means that grades are accurate on a consistent basis.[4] Some argue that combining all of the scores in one subject into a single grade may increase the risk of a measurement error, since some teachers fail to ensure validity and reliability when determining grades.[5]

One way to address this concern is to implement a clear separation between data about achievement and data about behaviour and attitudes.[6] Assessment consultants tend to be highly critical of incorporating behavioural

factors such as attendance, attitude, effort, participation and punctuality into final grades. They argue that behavioural factors should be reported separately on the report card and that they should not affect a student's final academic grade.[7]

Because the time an assignment is turned in is considered a behavioural factor, many assessment consultants say that students should not receive academic penalties for lateness or incomplete work. Similarly, given that plagiarism is also a behavioural choice, consultants argue that it is inappropriate for guilty students to receive a mark of zero. In these cases, students should redo the work properly, and their marks should accurately reflect their achievement rather than their behaviour.[8]

As a result, assessment consultants who support an absolute separation of behaviour from academic achievement insist that a no-zero policy is the only reasonable policy for school boards. As such, a significant number of Canadian school boards have enacted such policies.

No-Zero Policies Across Canada

It is difficult to quantify how widespread no-zero policies are since school boards tend not to report these policies to the public. Generally, the public becomes aware of a no-zero policy when the media reports on controversial cases. Nevertheless, there are enough examples to demonstrate that this practice is quite widespread.

The most famous case in Canada is at Ross Sheppard High School in Edmonton. Teachers there cannot give students a zero for any incomplete work. Instead, they are required to enter a three-digit behaviour code. This code does not affect the students' final mark.[9] In May 2012, the Edmonton Public School Board suspended physics teacher Lynden Dorval for failing to comply with his school's no-zero policy. While the Edmonton Public School Board does not have a division-wide no-zero policy, some schools under its jurisdiction, such as Ross Sheppard, have implemented one.[10]

Public response to this issue has been overwhelmingly on Dorval's side. Students rallied to his defence, teachers spoke out in support of his position and newspaper pages were filled with letters attacking the no-zero policy. Even an online poll conducted by the *Edmonton Journal* reported that more than 97 percent of the 12,486 respondents opposed the no-zero policy.[11] Largely in response to this public pressure, the school trustees voted at their June meeting to review their assessment practices.[12]

Edmonton is not the only place in Alberta with a no-zero policy. Greater St. Albert Catholic Schools has had one for the last five years.[13] In addition, at least one school in the Calgary Board of Education, Dr. E. P. Scarlett High School, has a no-zero policy.[14]

In Saskatchewan, at least two school divisions have no-zero policies. Saskatoon Public Schools prohibits teachers from deducting marks for lateness or plagiarism. Not surprisingly, the board faced substantial public criticism when the policy became known.[15] Prairie Spirit School Division, located north of Saskatoon, also has a similar policy.[16]

For a number of years, Manitoba had a province-wide policy that prohibited teachers from deducting marks for late or missing assignments. Nevertheless, in November 2010, Education Minister Nancy Allan announced a reversal of that policy and made it clear that teachers may decide how to handle late or missing work.[17] The official policy document released by the Manitoba government now permits teachers to deduct marks for late or missing work and for academic dishonesty.[18]

A similar about-face on assessment took place in Ontario. Guidelines from the provincial department of education originally stipulated that teachers could give marks of zero only as a last resort. Because of this guideline, a number of schools implemented formal no-zero policies. However, the Minister of Education released a new set of guidelines in 2010 that explicitly gave teachers the option of giving a mark of zero for incomplete work.[19] This reversal received the enthusiastic endorsement of Ken Coran, president of the Ontario Secondary School Teachers' Federation.[20]

No-zero policies have even made their way to Canada's East Coast. The Eastern School District in St. John's, Newfoundland, explicitly prohibits teachers from deducting marks for late or missing work or for plagiarism.[21] Despite opposition from the Newfoundland and Labrador Teachers' Association, this district has kept its no-zero policy.[22]

Regardless of where a no-zero policy is implemented, it usually generates controversy when the public becomes aware of its existence. However, the strong pushback from many parents and teachers makes it difficult to implement these policies. Public opposition to no-zero policies shows no sign of subsiding.

Arguments in Support of No-Zero Policies

Advocates of no-zero policies think that there are good reasons for them. Among other things, they point to documents produced by provincial education departments. For example, the Alberta Education Learner Assessment Branch recently produced a 150-page report that provides a number of formal recommendations to schools. Among other things, it says, "No-zero policies support student-learning outcomes" and consequently the report recommended that teachers should accept late assignments without penalty.[23]

Several recurring themes appear regularly in defense of no-zero policies. Let us look at them.

1) Empirical research strongly supports no-zero policies.

This is potentially the strongest argument offered in support of no-zero policies. If empirical research studies clearly point to the superiority of the no-zero approach, then we would need to give it serious consideration, even when there is public opposition.

However, the research on no-zero policies is surprisingly weak. In fact, the various assessment consultants regularly cite each other as sources when defending no-zero policies, but they rarely refer to research data in support of their position. For example, Mark Weichel, the director of curriculum for the Papillion-La Vista School District in Nebraska, wrote, "Not one study has shown that assigning a zero is effective in improving student achievement,"[24] and he cites an article written by Guskey that appeared in *Principal Leadership* in November 2004 to support that view.[25]

However, this argument cuts both ways, since no-zero advocates cannot avoid the fact that the burden of proof rests with them. They are the ones proposing that schools completely revamp their assessment practices, and for this reason, they should be able to produce research evidence that supports their position. It is revealing that neither Weichel nor Guskey cite even one research study showing that no-zero policies effectively improve student achievement. Since all jurisdictions in Canada and the United States have at least some standardized testing, it should be possible to produce research that shows how no-zero policies improve scores on standardized tests. However, none has been produced.

On its website, the Edmonton Public School Board links to two articles in support of no-zero policies.[26] One of these is an article by Guskey that appeared in the October 2004 edition of *Principal Leadership* called "Zero Alternatives."[27] In it, he boldly claims that zeros rarely provide an accurate picture of what students have learned, and he cites only one source for that claim. His source is English teacher Barry Raebeck's paper presented to the National Middle School Association at its 1993 conference in Portland, Oregon.[28] While Raebeck's paper describes the use of zeros as a questionable grading practice, nowhere does he cite any research evidence to support this position. Thus, Guskey's key argument against zeros is based on one English teacher's opinion-based presentation at a conference almost 20 years ago.

Interestingly, Guskey repeats the same claim about zeros in several of his books and cites the same presentation by Raebeck.[29] Even if we assume Guskey meant to refer to Raebeck's more recent book *The Teacher's Gradebook*, it still does not help Guskey's argument. While Raebeck strongly opposes the use of zeros, his book cites no research evidence in support of no-zero policies.[30]

In his book *How to Grade for Learning*, O'Connor states that zeros are a problem because low grades cause students to withdraw from learning.[31] To support this statement, he cites an article by Guskey that appeared in the *NASSP Bulletin* in 2000.[32] In this article, Guskey cites only one source for this particular claim—a 1992 article in the *British Columbia Journal of Special Education* by Deborah Selby and Sharon Murphy.[33] There, Selby and Murphy describe the experiences of six learning-disabled students in mainstream classrooms. These students had negative experiences with letter grades and blamed themselves for their poor marks.

It should be obvious that it is absurd to generalize from the experiences of six learning-disabled students to the rest of the student population. Yet, Guskey regularly cites this article when he makes the claim that grades of zero have a negative impact on students. Even a more recent article by Guskey that appeared in the November 2011 edition of *Educational Leadership* contains the same claim with the same Selby and Murphy article again providing the only research support.[34]

The Edmonton Public Schools' website lists an article in *Phi Delta Kappan* written by Douglas Reeves that also supports no-zero policies.[35] He asserts that grading as punishment is an ineffective strategy but cites only one source—Thomas Guskey and Jane Bailey's book *Developing Grading and Reporting Systems for Student Learning*.[36] As noted earlier, Guskey's claims about zeros are based upon articles that do not support his position.

Even the 150-page assessment study commissioned by Alberta Education yields little empirical evidence for recommending no-zero policies.[37] Although the report endorses no-zero policies, the main references are articles and books by O'Connor, Reeves and Guskey—all of which we have examined here—and none of which provides any empirical evidence in support of the policies.

In short, the claim that no-zero policies are supported by empirical evidence is false. Any defense of no-zero policies must rely solely on other arguments.

2) Behaviour and attitude must remain separate from achievement.

This argument rests on the premise that teachers must "separate student work habits from their academic achievement."[38] The goal of separating achievement from behaviour is laudable but not always practical in classroom settings. Once students know there is no academic consequence for late or missing work, some of them will take advantage of this opportunity. While marks should be based primarily on achievement, it is reasonable for teachers to use their professional discretion when dealing with late or missing work.

That there ought to be some discretion explains why the assessment consultants themselves often make exceptions to their rule about separating behaviour from achievement.[39] Even Raebeck, the English teacher frequently cited by Guskey, openly states that he enforces deadlines in his classroom by deducting marks for late assignments.[40] He goes on to say: "... [N]o matter what we would like to believe about ourselves, we cannot separate a student's attitude from his or her performance. Nor should we."[41]

On this point, Raebeck is correct. Teachers work with real students who do not always conform to the latest educational theory promoted by idealistic consultants. Implementing an absolute separation between behaviour and performance on report cards may sound good in theory, but it often does not translate well in a regular classroom setting.

3) Zeros unfairly skew a student's average mark downward.

Reeves argues that the use of zeros on a 100-point scale with letter grades is unfair to students, because there is a much bigger interval between a D and an F than between the other letters. Since an A is typically 90 to 100, a B is 80 to 89, etc., the interval between D (60) and F (0) skews a student's mark downward farther than is reasonable.[42]

However, this argument is only applicable to schools that convert percentages to letter grades. In Canadian schools, grades often remain in percentages, especially at the high school level. This means there are many different achievement levels possible within a failing mark. For example, a student could receive a mark of 0, 12, 37, or 48 on an assignment. Most teachers can easily point out the difference between someone earning a mark of 48 and someone getting 12, even though these are both failing marks. If an assignment never comes in, a mark of zero is fully appropriate, since the student has produced zero evidence of learning.

As for schools that use letter grades, Reeves' argument still only holds weight if the conversion to a letter grade takes place on the assignment itself. In many cases, teachers use percentages for assignments and tests and only convert a student's mark to a letter grade when calculating final report card marks.[43] Thus, students have the same range of performance below 50 percent as they do above 50 percent.

Even if Reeves is correct about the disproportionate effect of a zero, one has to ask why this is such a serious problem. After all, any student who does not like the negative effect a zero has on his or her average can avoid it by simply doing the assignment. Dorval, the Edmonton teacher suspended for disobeying his school's no-zero policy, said that showing students the impact zeros have on their marks motivated them to complete their assignments.[44]

4) Zeros make it easy for students to avoid taking responsibility for their learning.

It is ironic that no-zero advocates will, on the one hand, argue that zeros have a disproportionate impact on a student's final grade but then say that letting students "take a zero" is the easy option.[45] In addition, this argument relies on the premise that teachers who hand out zeros do not use any other forms of intervention to get students to complete their assignments and hand them in on time.

However, there is no evidence that most teachers simply hand out a zero to students at the first sign of trouble. Rather, they often work with students, adjust deadlines when necessary and provide extra support outside of regular classroom hours. Despite all these interventions, there are times when the work is just not handed in. At this point, teachers have to decide on an appropriate consequence, and many think that a zero is reasonable. They know what the zero means, and so do the students.

5) There are more-effective ways of dealing with late or missing assignments.

O'Connor argues that the appropriate way of dealing with missing assignments is to record an "I" for incomplete. In his view, this mark should not have a direct impact on a student's average. Instead, the teacher makes a judgment call as to whether the student has provided enough evidence of learning from other assignments. If there is enough evidence for the teacher to assess the student, then the incomplete assignment should not count against his or her mark.[46]

Ross Sheppard High School in Edmonton took this recommendation to heart and devised a long list of letter codes to replace zeros. Some of the "marks" students can receive include MPA (missed performance assessment),

AMP (academic malpractice), NHI (not handed in) and CNA (chose not to attempt).[47] However, instead of simplifying the grading process, this new alphabet soup grading system makes the teachers' work much more complex. Many teachers at Ross Sheppard were finding it more difficult to get students to complete their work, and they supported Dorval's opposition to the new system.[48]

In addition, a system of letter codes is ultimately worthless if it does not have an impact on the final grades. Students who want to do less work will quickly figure out that they can choose which assignments they hand in. As for the pyramid of interventions recommended by O'Connor and other assessment consultants, there is no reason why they cannot be implemented with the zeros in place. Teachers do not stop providing support and encouragement to students just because they have the option of giving a zero for work the students do not hand in.

Why No-Zero policies Are a Bad Idea

There are many reasons school administrators should avoid no-zero policies. One is that the no-zero policies inevitably bring controversy with them, something acknowledged by even their strongest proponents.[49] Many parents and teachers strongly oppose no-zero policies, and this makes it difficult to implement them. If a school chooses to use a no-zero policy, it can expect that controversy will likely overshadow other more important initiatives. For this reason, school administrators need to ask themselves whether a no-zero policy is worth the opposition they are certain to face.

No-zero policies also unreasonably interfere with the professional discretion of teachers to determine grades. Teachers know their students, and they realize it is unrealistic to expect the same strategies to work with every student. Most teachers use a variety of methods to hold their students accountable. All a no-zero policy does is take away one of the significant consequences that teachers can use for students who fail to submit their work.

Since no-zero policies prohibit teachers from giving a zero for incomplete work, a student who hands in an assignment and receives a grade of only 30 percent or 40 percent would actually be better off not submitting it. In fact, students will figure out that it is in their best interest to choose the assignments they submit. Conscientious students who do all their work could be at a significant disadvantage in the grades they receive.

Finally, no-zero policies fail to prepare students for their working lives after school. Employers do not pay employees to do nothing, and universities do not give credit to students who choose not to hand in their assignments. A pilot who never flies a plane, an electrician who never wires a house and a journalist who never hands in a story can all expect not to be paid. Employers are not going to accommodate employees who do not submit their work. Teachers need to prepare students for this reality.

Conclusion

No-zero policy advocates claim there is overwhelming evidence for their position. However, as we have seen, this claim is demonstrably false. The number of articles and books cited in defense of no-zero policies is limited, and they do not justify the grand claims made by the no-zero supporters.

Other arguments for no-zero policies also fall flat. They do not improve the accuracy of final grades; they do not encourage students to take responsibility for their work; and they make it difficult for teachers to hold students accountable. The arguments made by no-zero advocates are little more than a house of cards that easily collapses.

In contrast, the arguments against no-zero policies are compelling. No-zero policies always encounter fierce resistance from parents and teachers, unreasonably interfere with the professional discretion of teachers, make teachers work longer on their grading, penalize students who complete their assignments on time and fail to prepare students for life after school. These are all very good reasons for school administrators to avoid no-zero policies.

Thus, no-zero policies are logically flawed, unsupported by research, mathematically questionable and an administrative nightmare. Consequently, no-zero policies deserve zero support.

Endnotes

1. Susan Brookhart, *Grading*, Upper Saddle River, NJ: Pearson Education, Inc., 2004, pp. 15–23.

2. Rick Stiggins, "Assessment for Learning," *Ahead of the Curve: The Power of Assessment to Transform Teaching and Learning*, Douglas Reeves, Ed., Bloomington: Solution Tree Press, 2007, pp. 59–76.

3. John Hattie, *Visible Learning for Teachers: Maximizing Impact on Learning,* New York: Routledge, 2012, p. 116.

4. Brookhart, op. cit., pp. 9–10.

5. Robert J. Marzano, *Transforming Classroom Grading,* Alexandria: Association for Supervision and Curriculum Development, 2000, pp. 6–8.

6. Damian Cooper and Ken O'Connor with Nanci Wakeman, "Redefining 'Fair': Assessment and Grading for the 21st Century," *Changing Perspectives,* February 2009, pp. 27–31.

7. Ken O'Connor, *How to Grade for Learning K-12, Third Edition,* Thousand Oaks: Corwin, 2009, pp. 90–109.

8. Ibid.

9. Ross Sheppard School Assessment, Grading and Reporting Practice 2011–12. Available at: http://shep.epsb.ca/images/stories/Assessment_Policy_2011–12.pdf.

10. Andrea Sands, "Ross Sheppard Teacher Kicked Out of Class for Giving Students Zeros," *Edmonton Journal,* June 1, 2012. Available at: http://www.edmonAtonjournal.com/news/Ross+Sheppard+teacher+kicked+class+giving+students+zeros/6709514/story.html.

11. David Staples, "Good Reason for Popular Uprising against No Zeros Policy," *Edmonton Journal,* June 6, 2012. Available at: http://www.edmontonjournal.com/opinion/Good+reason+popular+uprising+against+Zeros+policy/6735090/story.html.

12. CBC News, "Edmonton School Board to Review Grading Policy," June 26, 2012. Available at: http://www.cbc.ca/news/canada/edmonton/story/2012/06/26/edmonton-school-board-meeting-no-zero.html.

13. Megan Sarrazin, "Local Boards Differ on 'No Zero' Policy," *St. Albert Gazette,* June 30, 2012. Available at: http://www.stalbertgazette.com/article/20120630/SAG0801/306309985/local-boards-differ-on-no-zero-policy.

14. "Building High School Teachers' Comfort with Assessment For Learning." Available at: http://projects.cbe.ab.ca/area5/deps/building-teacher-comfort-assessment/.

15. Robert J. LeBlanc, "The Limits to Reform: A Critical Assessment of the Saskatoon Public School Board's Assessment Controversy," *In Education,* Summer 2011. Available at: http://ineducation.ca/article/limits-reform-critical-discussion-saskatoon-public-school-boards-assessment-controversy.

16. Prairie Spirit School Board, "Quality Assessment in Prairie Spirit School Division," *Board of Education*

Focus, October 3, 2011. Available at: http://www.spiritsd.ca/schoolboard/Board%20Focus%20-%20October%203%202011.pdf.

17. Nick Martin, "Minister Refutes Idea of 'No-Fail' Policy," *Winnipeg Free Press,* November 18, 2010. Available at: http://www.winnipegfreepress.com/local/minister-refutes-idea-of-no-fail-policy-108891049.html.

18. Manitoba Education, *Provincial Assessment Policy Kindergarten to Grade 12: Academic Responsibility, Honesty, and Promotion/Retention,* 2010. Available at: http://www.edu.gov.mb.ca/k12/assess/docs/policy_k12/full_doc.pdf.

19. CBC News Ottawa, "Ontario Schools Will Get Tougher on Late Assignments," August 25, 2010. Available at: http://www.cbc.ca/news/canada/ottawa/story/2010/08/25/ontario-education.html.

20. Siri Agrell, "Do-Over Generation Set to Meet Deadline Shock," *The Globe and Mail,* August 27, 2010. Available at: http://www.theglobeandmail.com/news/national/do-over-generation-set-to-meet-deadline-shock/article1378509/.

21. Eastern School District, "Administration Regulations Policy IL—Assessment and Evaluation," October 5, 2011. Available at: http://www.cbc.ca/news/pdf/nl-evaluation-regulations-20111005.pdf.

22. CBC News Newfoundland & Labrador, "N.L. School Board's Cheating Policy Irks Teachers," October 24, 2011. Available at: http://www.cbc.ca/news/canada/newfoundland-labrador/story/2011/10/24/nl-cheating-students-school-board-1024.html.

23. Charles F. Webber et al., The Alberta Student Assessment Study: Final Report (Edmonton: Alberta Education), June 2009, p. 135. Available at: http://education.alberta.ca/media/1165612/albertaassessmentstudyfinalreport.pdf.

24. Mark Weichel, "Lowering High School Failure Rates," *The Principal as Assessment Leader,* Thomas Guskey, Ed., Bloomington: Solution Tree Press, 2009, p. 207.

25. Thomas Guskey, "Are Zeros Your Ultimate Weapon?" *Principal Leadership,* November 2004, pp. 49–53. Available at: http://www.haslett.k12.mi.us/education/page/download.php?fileinfo=R-3Vza2V5Xy1fQXJlX1plcm9zX1lvdXJfVWx0aW1hdGVfV2VhcG9uLnBkZjo6Oi93d3cvc2Nob29scy8scy89uLnBkZg==

26. Edmonton Public Schools' Assessment Practices, June 6, 2012. Available at: http://news.epsb.ca/2012/06/edmonton-public-schools-assessment-practices/.

27. Thomas Guskey, "Zero Alternatives," Principal Leadership, October 2004, pp. 49–53. Available at: http://www.hsd.k12.or.us/Portals/0/district/Grading%20Reporting/Grading/zero%20alternatives%20-%20guskey.pdf.

28. Barry Raebeck, *Exploding Myths, Exploring Truths: Humane, Productive Grading and Grouping in the Quality Middle School,* a paper presented at the annual conference and exhibit of the National Middle School Association, 1993. Available at: http://www.eric.ed.gov/ERICWebPortal/search/detailmini.jsp?_nfpb=true&_&ERICExtSearch_SearchValue_0=ED366462&ERICExtSearch_SearchType_0=no&accno=ED366462.

29. Thomas R. Guskey and Jane M. Bailey, *Developing Grading and Reporting Systems for Student Learning,* Thousand Oaks,CA: Corwin Press, 2001, p. 143; and Thomas R. Guskey, Ed., *Practical Solutions for Serious Problems in Standards-Based Grading,* Thousand Oaks: Corwin Press, 2009, p. 16.

30. Barry Raebeck, *The Teacher's Gradebook: Strategies for Student Success,* Lanham: The Scarecrow Press, 2002.

31. O'Connor, op. cit., p. 164.

32. Thomas Guskey, "Grading Policies that Work against Standards…and How to Fix Them," *NASSP Bulletin,* 84(620), 2000, pp. 20–29. Available at: http://www.minnetonka.k12.mn.us/academics/gradingandreporting/Documents/Gradingarticle-GUSKEY.pdf.

33. Deborah Selby and Sharon Murphy, "Graded or Degraded: Perceptions of Letter-Grading for Mainstreamed Learning-Disabled Students," *British Columbia Journal of Special Education,* 16(1), 1992, pp. 92–104.

34. Thomas R. Guskey, "Five Obstacles to Grading Reform," *Educational Leadership,* 69(3), November 2011, pp. 16–21. Available at: http://www.ascd.org/publications/educational-leadership/nov11/vol69/num03/Five-Obstacles-to-Grading-Reform.aspx.

35. Douglas B. Reeves, "The Case against the Zero," *Phi Delta Kappan,* 86(4), December 2004, pp. 324–325. Available at: http://www.leadandlearn.com/sites/default/files/articles/caseagainstzero.pdf.

36. Guskey and Bailey, op. cit.

37. Webber, op. cit.

38. Tammy Heflebower, "Proficiency: More Than a Grade," *The Teacher as Assessment Leader,* Thomas R. Guskey, Ed., Bloomington: Solution Tree Press, 2009, p. 127.

39. Marzano, op. cit., pp. 37–39.

40. Raebeck, op. cit., p. 17.

41. Ibid., p. 52.

42. Reeves, op. cit. pp. 324–325.

43. Brookhart, op. cit., p. 25.

44. Joe O'Connor, "Edmonton Teacher May Lose Job for Refusing to Let Kids Skip Assignments," *National Post,* June 2, 2012. Available at: http://news.nationalpost.com/2012/06/02/edmonton-teacher-may-lose-job-for-refusing-to-let-kids-skip-assignments/.

45. Ken O'Connor, op. cit., pp. 163-167.

46. Ibid.

47. Ross Sheppard School Assessment, *Grading and Reporting Practice,* 2011–12. Available at: http://shep.epsb.ca/images/stories/Assessment_Policy_2011–12.pdf.

48. Dean Bennett, "Alberta Teacher Suspended for Giving Out Zeros Fears Colleague Will Be Punished," *The Canadian Press,* June 13, 2012. Available at: http://www.winnipegfreepress.com/canada/alberta-teacher-suspended-for-giving-out-zeros-fears-colleague-will-be-punished-158927075.html.

49. Reeves, op. cit.

MICHAEL ZWAAGSTRA is a public school teacher and a research fellow at the Frontier Centre for Public Policy who specializes in education policy.

EXPLORING THE ISSUE

Should There Be No-Zero Grading Policies in Schools?

Critical Thinking and Reflection

1. Are zeros ever an acceptable measure of discipline in any educational setting? Support the position taken.
2. As an educator, reflect on a past situation where a student received a zero; what were the circumstances and what was the outcome?
3. How important is teacher input in the decision-making process when changes affecting a district's grading policies are made?
4. Should students' learning be about knowledge, behavior, or a combination of the two?
5. Design a real-life scenario regarding a zero for a student grade on an assignment not submitted to the teacher. Take a stand on the no-zero position taken providing clear and specific rationale for the action taken.

Is There Common Ground?

The arguments in favor of zero-grading appear to be equal to those against it. Since a number of school districts have recently moved (or are considering moving) to minimum grading, it is worthy of much debate as a sound educational grading practice. On one side, there are those who say "No" to the no-zero policy of grading. Leading the way for this opposition are those who believe that lowering academic expectations will only hurt students in the long run. They note that teaching students to be lazy is a terrible lesson for them to learn. In relation to when schools lower their expectations for academics, Careva (2013, p. 2) calls this a "monopoly-like, get out of jail free card," Careva continues, "We are not being honest with our students when we say, 'you don't have to work hard to pass, you can miss half of your assignments in all of your classes and you can still graduate from our school'" (p. 2). Most colleges would not apply this principle for what they expect from their students. Likewise, there are not many training opportunities or business practices that would embrace this minimum evaluation standard. Failing to give students the real consequences for their homework does not prepare them for their future careers. For the most part, parents can ally with teachers on this issue. No parent wants their child to be set up for failure in the future. Would their grown-up child get paid at a job for work they didn't do? Should a teacher's grading policy be any different?

The argument against no-zero policies appears overwhelming. One can certainly support the merits of this position. Others say "Not the case" because those in favor of zero-grading policies continue to justify and expand their presence. This is evidenced by the number of school districts that have moved to minimum grading and the numerous districts planning the move in the near future. Some estimate that over half of the school districts in the nation have or are considering no-zero grading policies. Most of the positive engagement and growth with no-zero policies has resulted from the stance taken that not assigning zeros helps struggling students to stay motivated. Supporters contend that these policies can improve the dropout rate across the country. Those in favor of a no-zero policy want the focus of grades to be on effective assessment of student learning rather than student behavior. Students feel that handing out a zero for a missed assignment is a punitive disciplinary measure and not a representation of their learning. Those who disagree with this mind-set are in favor of assigning zeros as best practice for success, now and in the future. The two positions create the continuing seesaw debate on minimum grading policies, as well as challenges directed at any magic bullet for improving student success.

Perhaps the common ground comes from the way a no-zero policy is navigated. Making it a part of a wider assessment practice can address the system of rewards and punishment that support student learning. Guskey (2004) writes about alternatives to assigning zeros, stating there are far better ways to motivate and encourage students. The first alternative is to assign an "*I*" or "*Incomplete*" grade instead of a zero (p. 51). Another alternative is to report academic progress and behavioral aspects of students' progress separately. The third alternative is to change the grading scale entirely from the A = 90–100 percent, B = 80–89 percent, C = 70–79 percent, and so on, to whole number scales where A = 4, B = 3, C = 2, and so on (Guskey, 2004, p. 52). These options may be direct, immediate, and academically sound, but would likely face much analysis and lead to further debate. Reasons for discernment include additional funding to support the mechanisms required for implementation of the no-zero grading policy, the possible creation of additional work for teachers, and the conflict that naturally arise from the change process.

Lacking the resources to effectively change the system of grading, no matter what the alternative, requires candid discussions about the purpose of grading and reporting of the grades. The questions to ask include: What do teachers want to communicate through grading? Who is the primary audience for the message? And, what is the intended goal? These are recommendations from Guskey (2004) as a means to address and resolve the use of zeros. The first step in seeking common ground for the no-zero issue is to have grades become a part of learning and not the conclusion of learning. Minero (2018, p. 1) asserts, "Teaching is hard work. Let's have grades that reflect actual learning."

Additional Resources

Balight, M. & St. George, D. (2016, July 5). It is becoming too hard to fail. *The Washington Post*. p. 12.

Cariflo, J. & Carey, T. (2009, November–December). A critical examination of current minimum grading policy recommendations. *The High School Journal* 93:23–37.

Careva, G. (2013). *For students' sake, say no to no-zero policy on grading. Catalyst Chicago*. Retrieved from http://catalyst-chicago.org/2013/10/students-sake-say-no-no-zero-policy-grading/

Guskey, T. (2004). *O alternatives. PL*. Retrieved from http://www.hsd.k12.or.us/Portals/0/district/Grading%20Reporting/Grading/zero%20alternatives%20-%20guskey.pdf.

Hanover Research. (2013). *Replacing zero grading at the secondary level*. Washington, DC. Retrieved from http://www.grading4impact.com/wp-content/uploads/2015/05/Hanover_ReplacingZero-Grading.pdf.

Minero, E. (2016). Do no-zero policies help or hurt students? *Edutopia*. Retrieved from https://www.edutopia.org/article/do-no-zero-policies-help-or-hurt-students

Norrell, T. (2015). *Less than zero*. National School Boards Association. Retrieved from https://www.nsba.org/newsroom/american-school-board-journal/latest-edition/less-zero

Reeves. D. (2008). Leading to change: Effective grading policies. *Educational Leadership*. 65:5.

Walker, T. 2016. *Teachers divided over controversial "no-zero" grading policy*. National Education Association. Retrieved from http://neatoday.org/2016/08/04/no-zero-policy-pro-con/.

Internet References . . .

A New Kind of Classroom: No Grades, No Failing, No Hurry

https://www.nytimes.com/2017/08/11/nyregion/mastery-based-learning-no-grades.html

Is Our Grading System Fair?

https://www.edutopia.org/discussion/our-grading-system-fair

No-zero Policy: A Failure of One-Size-Fits-All Education Reform

https://www.fraserinstitute.org/blogs/no-zero-policy-a-failure-of-one-size-fits-all-education-reform

Teacher Divided Over "No-Zero" Policy

http://neatoday.org/2016/08/04/no-zero-policy-pro-con/

The Case against the Zero

https://www.ccresa.org/Files/Uploads/252/The_Case_Against_Zero.pdf

Selected, Edited, and with Issue Framing Material by:
Glenn L. Koonce, *Regent University*

ISSUE

Is the "21st Century Skills" Movement Practical?

YES: **Michael F. Fitzpatrick,** from "Presenting a Practitioner's Response to the 21st Century Skills Debate," Mass.gov (2015)

NO: **Margaret Hilton,** from "Preparing Students for Life and Work," *Issues in Science and Technology* (2015)

Learning Outcomes

After reading this issue, you will be able to:

- Distinguish between academic concepts and life skills in the 21st Century Skills model.
- Identify and explain the three broad concepts that cluster around 21st Century Skills.
- Assess the statement, "Important challenges remain for 21st century competencies."
- Analyze how school districts effectively blend 21st century skill development into the school curriculum.
- Evaluate the 21st Century Skills model as it applies to school improvement.

ISSUE SUMMARY

YES: Michael Fitzpatrick, a member of the American Association of School Administrators, presents a research-based view that concludes school leaders can and should promote challenging and meaningful structure for 21st century skill development.

NO: Margaret Hilton, a senior program officer of the Board on Science Education and the Board on Testing and Assessment at the National Research Council, argues that the "Achilles" heel of the growing movement for 21st century skills is the absence of agreement on what these skills are and that important challenges to this concept remain.

Calls for adoption of national standards, national tests, and even a national curriculum have certainly been on the increase. As Walter Isaacson of the Aspen Institute stated in a *Time*, April 15, 2009 article, "How to Raise the Standard in America's Schools, without national standards for what our students should learn, it will be hard for the United States to succeed in the 21st century economy." But the prospect of such a development has been politically explosive. Isaacson characterizes it this way: "The right chokes on the word national, with its implication that the feds will trample on the states' traditional authority over public schools, and the left chokes on the word standards, with the intimations of assessments and testing that accompany it." The present-day reality, according to a 2014

Harvard University Think Tank—Education for the 21st Century, Executive Summary, is that

> "student achievement results are mediocre in international comparisons, too many students drop out of school before completing high school, many students begin community college or college poorly prepared to meet the academic requirements, college completion is low, and many of those who do graduate are not seen by employers as ready for the workforce" (p. 2).

A number of movements were afoot, some time ago, to define what is most needed in the realm of school improvement. States led the development of the Common Core State Standards. In 2009, state leaders, including governors and state commissioners of education from 48 states, two territories and the District of Columbia, came together and decided to develop common, college-and career-ready standards in mathematics and English language arts. The National Governors Association Center for Best Practices (NGA Center) and the Council of Chief State School Officers (CCSSO) collaborated with the states to complete the work needed to put the common core in place. With financial support from private foundations and federal support from the "Race to the Top" fund, the Common Core State Standards Initiative (CCSSI) moved to cover tests, curriculum, and teacher training. The federal government was not involved in the development of the standards. The final standards were published in June 2010 and available for each state to review, consider, and voluntarily adopt. To date, as of 2017, 42 states and the District of Columbia have joined the effort. English language arts and math were the subjects chosen for the Common Core State Standards, but other subject areas are being considered, such as science, world languages, and the arts.

Starting out as a push by states to improve learning standards, the Common Core has made education an even more contentious issue. The 2016 ACT National Curriculum Survey® looked at educational practices and college and career expectations, with results taken from surveys completed by thousands of K-12 teachers and college instructors in English and writing, math, reading, and science. The results show a disconnect between what is emphasized in the Common Core and what some college instructors perceive as important to college readiness.

The Thomas B. Fordham Institute produced a document in 2010 compiled by Chester E. Finn, Jr. and Michael J. Petrilli titled *Now What? Imperatives & Options for "Common Core" Implementation & Governance*. The report called for a Common Core Coordinating Council as a starting point, with the purpose of preserving independence from Washington. It appears that the "Now What?" movement is still a charge for the Common Core Coordinating Council.

The Center for Public Education in Alexandria, Virginia issued a report in July, 2009, titled *Defining a 21st Century Education* by Craig D. Jerald. The report analyzed the major forces reshaping skill demands (automation, globalization, corporate changes, demographics, and personal risk and responsibility).

The Partnership for 21st Century Skills in Tucson, Arizona, which has broad support from the business and technology communities and the Association for Career and Technical Education has kept in its Framework for 21st Century Learning, critical thinking, problem solving, communication, and collaboration. The Framework delineates core subjects and 21st-century themes (such as global awareness) and life and career skills (such as adaptability, self-direction, productivity, and cross-cultural understanding). Paige Johnson, in "The 21st Century Skills Movement," *Educational Leadership* (September 2009), states that "to successfully face rigorous higher-education courses and a globally competitive work environment, schools must align classroom environments and core subjects with 21st century skills." Or, as Richard H. Hersh, in "A Well-Rounded Education for a Flat World," *Educational Leadership* (September 2009) puts it, we need "a pervasive school culture that refuses to define education as the passive reception of knowledge and instead celebrates demanding, profoundly engaging, and authentic educational experiences." More specifically, Bernie Trilling, global director of the Oracle Education Foundation, in "Leading Learning in Our Time," *Principal* (January/February 2010), espouses "inquiry- and design-based projects rooted in driving questions and real-world problems" that would engage students in a deeper understanding and effective use of knowledge.

Those who have reservations about the 21st Century Skills model are concerned that it may just become another pedagogical fad, that it demands too much change too fast, that it is too oriented to economic forces, that the skills emphasis downplays subject matter content, and that the recommended skills are in need of more specific definition. The Harvard University Think Tank notes, "Alongside current problems, employers, civil and social leaders increasingly see that the educational system needs to develop a new set of 21st century skills for students. Without new efforts to help students gain the competencies that prepare them to meet the demands of democracy, competitiveness and life, schools are increasingly irrelevant. These competencies include critical thinking, collaboration, communication skills, and creativity. Other important skills include life skills, capacity for life-long learning, technological and financial literacy, global awareness, and skills for effective civic engagement" (p. 2).

Remembering the debate from the 2009 Forum for Youth Investment conference in Washington, D.C., "21st Century Skills: Doomed Pedagogical Fad or Key to the Future," it is certain that the debate continues today. Supporters believe that their main goal is in fact to integrate 21st century skills into core subjects along with increasing and "better" standards, improved professional and learning environments, increased assessment options, and making core subjects more relevant to students. Critics of the movement argue that 21st century skills and content knowledge are not independent of one another, noting that a base of knowledge must be present to gain deeper knowledge and build skills. Critics further believe the 21st century skills movement erodes opportunities for a well-rounded education and further forces schools to reduce subject matter options in order to increase 21st century skills. It doesn't appear that either side of the issue has evaluated the impact that No Child Left Behind (NCLB) has had on the 21st century skills movement, nor what the impact will be as we move into the era of Every Student Succeeds Act (ESSA). No matter which stance taken in the debate over 21st century skills, school reform, economic competitiveness, and career and college readiness are not issues that will be going away.

In the first of the following selections, Michael Fitzpatrick captures divergent views on the present debate regarding 21st century skills. In the second selection, Margaret Hilton addresses the lack of shared vision and meaning for 21st century skills.

YES ↵

Michael F. Fitzpatrick

Presenting a Practitioner's Response to the 21st Century Skills Debate: Encouraging and Promoting THINKING Beyond TASK

The viewpoint put forth in this position paper is intended, among other challenges, to effectively capture divergent views on the present debate regarding 21st century skills. The opinion which follows is anchored in recent research findings by respected policy analysts and incorporates views both from the private sector and from a wide variety of educational professionals from across the Commonwealth of Massachusetts. It also has the benefit of direct feedback from individuals aligned closely with both sides of the national debate, including the president of the Partnership for 21st Century Skills and the executive directors of Massachusetts-based Pioneer Institute for Public Policy Research and the Massachusetts Business Alliance for Education, among others. Given the Commonwealth's proven success with the Massachusetts Comprehensive Assessment System (MCAS) and assessment driven growth, this reference point serves as a viable lens for colleagues to revisit, refine, and invigorate a new educational direction.

From my perspective, the present political debate is unnecessarily polarized. One viewpoint has been characterized as suggesting the dire need to move from theoretical academic concepts into concrete workplace/life skills. The other side argues that the identified 21st century skills are immeasurable and would result in a departure from empirically-driven basic framework competencies. Regardless of the view to which one subscribes, the obvious question remains: Why must we give up one thing to secure or protect the other? The argument should not be controlled by reactors or contributors who focus on teaching either academic concepts or life skills. As school superintendents are charged with ensuring that students are prepared for success in an ever more challenging global society, the position of school executive officers in Massachusetts and across the nation must be that it is possible, and in fact vital to the success of education reform efforts, to effectively blend the two.

In the mid-1990s, the official response to the Massachusetts Education Reform Act of 1993 first dictated that MCAS—which set out to measure student achievement on purely academic subjects—should be applied equally to students in the Commowealth's vocational technical and its non-vocational public school systems. The initial reaction from many vocational technical practitioners was that it would be unfair to measure career-oriented students by the same academic standards as students who spend their entire school day focused on academic pursuits. Yet the reality that, in order to succeed, career and technical students must have the same foundation of learning as their non-vocational counterparts could not be denied and the argument that any measurement system must include all students prevailed. Faced with the prospect of a poor showing on a statewide academic assessment, the state's career and technical delivery system responded to the call for greater academic rigor and made sweeping changes within its curricula to promote increased student achievement in academic subject areas. Without losing their focus on imparting technical skills for a specific trade or career goal, vocational technical systems found ways to link academic learning to practical lessons and discovered that the resulting applied learning models created more motivated learners. The results have surpassed most expectations and garnered an enhanced image and unprecedented demand for enrollment in career and technical schools across Massachusetts.

Today, all schools are faced with a growing awareness that success in the 21st century requires more than just core academic knowledge. As economic, technological, informational, and demographic changes transform the way people live and work, and as these changes continue to accelerate, it is increasingly apparent that future success will depend upon one's ability to adapt to inevitable changes and to constantly learn and relearn. In much the same way that career and technical systems found new ways to incorporate academic learning within their workforce preparation curricula, all Massachusetts schools now must develop new approaches which protect MCAS and other assessment-driven growth, while diversifying instructional methodology and pedagogy to include promoting workplace/life talents.

In order to develop new strategies, one must first identify, compare, and contrast several 21st century skill delineations. When thinking about the skills needed to succeed in today's society, the traits most frequently identified are clarity and simplicity of communication (both verbal and written), reasoning and problem-solving, financial and business literacy, and global awareness. Confidence, innovation, tactical and strategic vision, and the ability to shape a clear mission are other attributes that employers value, along with enthusiasm, persuasiveness, an ability to accept criticism and make refinements, and a willingness to move outside of one's comfort zone.

Many of the think tanks and policy analysts who have developed positions on the need to promote 21st century skills have created their own delineation of those skills. For example, the Partnership for 21st Century Skills, in its 2002 publication Learning for the 21st Century, identified three broad categories of learning skills: information and communication skills, thinking and problem-solving skills, and interpersonal and self-directional skills. Those categories are further delineated in the chart identified as Appendix A.

Significantly, the Partnership for 21st Century Skills credited its delineation of 21st century learning skills as having been adapted not only from employer needs, but also from the work of the American Library Association, the Association of College and Research Libraries, The Big 6 model for solving informational problems, the Center for Media Literacy, Educational Testing Service, the National Skills Standards Board, North Central Regional Educational Laboratory's enGauge, and the Secretary's Commission on Achieving Necessary Skills (SCANS).[1]

In similar fashion, the Massachusetts Business Alliance for Education, in its October 2006 report Preparing for the Future: Employer Perspectives on Work Readiness Skills, and again in its October 2008 publication Educating a 21st Century Workforce: A Call for Action on High School Reform, examined the need for students to master a set of college and career readiness skills that spans disciplinary boundaries. In the latter report, the MBAE Commission on Educating a 21st Century Workforce drew upon focus group studies and anecdotal discussions with employers to identify four categories of skills, including: 21st century themes such as global awareness and financial literacy; broader skills of learning and innovation; information, media, and technology skills; and life and career skills. More specific skills identified within these categories include economic, business, and entrepreneurial literacy; civic and health literacy; creativity and innovation; critical thinking and problem-solving; communication and collaboration; flexibility and adaptability; productivity and accountability; and leadership and responsibility.[2] See Appendix B.

The Pioneer Institute, long a champion of greater academic rigor in Massachusetts' schools and more recently a key player in opposing the Massachusetts movement to add measurements of workplace and life skills to the state's academic assessment system, nonetheless identified so-called 21st century skills in its policy brief Strengthening Standards-Based Education: Recommendations to Policy Makers on 21st Century Skills. It listed oral communication, information processing, critical thinking, problem-solving, teamwork and collaboration, self-directed learning and leadership, and other less easily defined or measurable attributes such as creativity and innovation, media literacy, global awareness, and cultural competency.[3]

A subsequent publication by the Pioneer Institute Center for School Reform, A Step Backwards: An Analysis of the 21st Century Skills Task Force Report, took issue with many aspects of a task force recommendation to the Massachusetts Board of Elementary and Secondary Education, yet acknowledged that students need a variety of social, technical, and communication skills to compete successfully in a global economy, including critical thinking, problem-solving, and financial, economic, and business literacy. Pioneer Institute Executive Director Jim Stergios has pointed out that many aspects of these specific skills are already embedded in the state's academic curriculum frameworks, but that they will continue to need further emphasis.[4]

Schematics or inventories of skill sets such as these create a reference point for teachers or curriculum developers to brainstorm how to foster and measure those characteristics within subsequent lessons without loss of integrity of the lesson. While the 2008 Pioneer Institute policy brief called for pilot testing the teaching of 21st century skills to prospective teachers in four or five schools of education over the next five years to determine how teachable and measurable they are, one need not wait for the results of such a pilot to begin integrating diversified instructional methodology into the curriculum.

For example, a social studies lesson might be delivered via student simulation, role playing, team assignments, and student presentations. Classroom activities of this nature would necessitate many of the decision making, prioritization, and communication skills expected in a successful worker or college student, yet not be taught at the expense of the framework. A math lesson might be taken off-campus to integrate math skills and concepts into hands-on, inquiry-based projects, as Monson's Granite Valley Middle School math teacher, Jeffrey Sitnik, did when he took students to a local farm to learn about farming from seed to market.5 That and other joint school and business activities funded by DESE's "Collaborative Partnerships for Student Success" grants show students real-life applications for math and other academic subjects and provide opportunities to reinforce workplace/life skills. The benefits of inquiry-style lessons versus the passive lecture format have been clearly documented. By encouraging inquiry-based learning and lesson plans at new levels of frequency, we are promoting the development of the workplace and life skills that will allow students to succeed in the global skills race.

Given the wide variety of disparate careers from which today's students choose, any proposal for incorporating skill development within academic learning cannot stifle individuality. The inclinations of the on-line entrepreneur need to be given as much opportunity to thrive as the caring, attentive attributes of a nurse. For that reason, 21st century lesson planning must strive to introduce a whole range of critical thinking, media literacy, and teamwork aspects to classroom activities. It will not be sufficient for classroom teachers to focus on only one or two of the many life skills in the wide spectrum of 21st century skills and hope that other essential skills will be promoted in other subject areas or in subsequent grades. Each teacher must accept responsibility for student outcomes that demonstrate proficiency in critical thinking and problem-solving, communication and collaboration. At the local level, instructors should adopt assessment practices that at once measure proficiency in core subjects and reward students for initiative and self-direction, productivity, accountability, and responsibility. At the same time, strategies must be devised to encourage adaptability and ingenuity within the context of some students' inherent individual personality traits such as shyness or resistance to change.

The Massachusetts Business Alliance for Education listed including 21st century skills across the curriculum as one if its key tactics for aligning the high school curriculum with the demands of college and career. It suggested that essential life and learning skills should be incorporated across the curriculum in such a way that students learn and apply these skills in the course of core subject learning, thus reinforcing the connection between what students learn in the classroom and the real-world skills they will need once they graduate.6

The Partnership for 21st Century Skills has advocated for federal funding to assist states in revising standards to reflect 21st century skills, developing and implementing approaches to assess those skills, creating professional development programs to enhance teacher understanding of the skills, and conducting research and evaluation to identify best practices for teaching, attaining, and measuring the skills. Massachusetts is one of thirteen leadership states that have joined the Partnership and committed to infusing 21st century skills into their education and workforce development systems. As executive officers of the state's educational agencies, Massachusetts school superintendents are a vital component of that commitment and should enthusiastically endorse the opportunity to redefine rigor as mastery of both academic subjects and 21st century skills.

As MBAE Executive Director Linda Noonan and Jill Norton, Executive Director of the Rennie Center for Education Research & Policy, asserted in a guest column published late last year in several Massachusetts newspapers, "Both educators and employers agree that the skills necessary to be successful in college and careers include a combination of content mastery, as well as technological skills and the ability to innovate, communicate, and think creatively."7

Ken Kay is president of Partnership for 21st Century Skills and CEO and founder of e-Luminate Group, an education consulting firm specializing in marketing communications and 21st century skills services. When invited to comment on this white paper, he acknowledged the success of career and technical education in imparting life and career skills and suggested that effective school reform will build upon CTE expertise in those skills to ensure that all teachers become equally adept at imparting important workplace and life skills to their students as they are in teaching academic content. He noted that "critical thinking" and "problem-solving" actually present a higher threshold than mere content mastery and cited his preference to use the term "21st century rigor" to talk about the higher threshold of melding content and skills together. Kay noted that CTE and academic teachers have a great deal to learn from each other and, if they could meet in the middle, would be able to design a curriculum that brings content and skills to every child.

Hans Meeder, former Deputy Assistant Secretary of the U.S. Department of Education Office of Vocational and Adult Education, and now a consultant on promising educational practices, concurs that innovative practices which break down the traditional barriers between rigorous academic content and relevant career-related content and skills are clearly worthy of significant investment and study. In a report prepared for the Association for Career and Technical Education, he noted that "as state and local policymakers are requiring students to take more and higher levels of academic courses to improve their prospects for college and work readiness, a balance must be struck between increasing academic rigor and providing students with relevant and 'real-world' instruction."[8]

In my opinion, to effectively blend 21st century skill development into the school curriculum, school systems will need to make it a priority and promote shared leadership expectations. Teachers must be given targeted professional development opportunities which will encourage them to move outside of their individual and collective comfort zones and modify instructional methodology. At the same time, the administrators who supervise them must embrace the challenge and themselves receive the necessary professional development resources to hone evaluation and observation skills which foster improved integrated instruction. Although the realities of day-to-day school operations all too often cause school administrators to be caught up in crisis management, any successful recipe will require better time management and a major commitment by school leaders to provide meaningful classroom observation feedback.

Much of the disagreement about 21st century skill development is centered on how to measure and otherwise assess student attainment of the talents and traits needed for success. While we may be challenged to develop the right balance of external and internal assessments to effectively measure the impact of new instructional approaches that impart real life skills, the current inability to precisely quantify student attainment of those skills should not become an excuse to not even try to teach them. We must recognize the importance of this new educational direction and its relevance to our ability to remain competitive, and seize every opportunity to explicitly and purposefully integrate the development of career and college readiness skills into each school curriculum.

That being said, we cannot retreat from the consistent and high standards in academic content that the Massachusetts Curriculum Frameworks and MCAS have established. The state's impressive NAEP and TIMSS rankings and Massachusetts students' constantly improving MCAS scores provide solid evidence that a rigorous system

Appendix A: Partnership for 21st Century Skills—Learning Skills

INFORMATION AND COMMUNICATION SKILLS	INFORMATION AND MEDIA LITERACY SKILLS Analyzing, accessing, managing, integrating, evaluating, and creating information in a variety of forms and media. Understanding the role of media in society. COMMUNICATION SKILLS Understanding, managing, and creating effective oral, written, and multimedia communication in a variety of forms and contexts.
THINKING AND PROBLEM-SOLVING SKILLS	CRITICAL THINKING AND SYSTEMS THINKING Exercising sound reasoning in understanding and making complex choices, understanding the interconnections among systems. PROBLEM IDENTIFICATION, FORMULATION, AND SOLUTION Ability to frame, analyze, and solve problems. CREATIVITY AND INTELLECTUAL CURIOSITY Developing, implementing, and communicating new ideas to others; staying open and responsive to new and diverse perspectives.
INTERPERSONAL AND SELF-DIRECTIONAL SKILLS	INTERPERSONAL AND COLLABORATIVE SKILLS Demonstrating teamwork and leadership; adapting to varied roles and responsibilities; working productively with others; exercising empathy; respecting diverse perspectives. SELF-DIRECTION Monitoring one's own understanding and learning needs, locating appropriate resources, transferring learning from one domain to another. ACCOUNTABILITY AND ADAPTABILITY Exercising personal responsibility and flexibility in personal, workplace, and community contexts; setting and meeting high standards and goals for one's self and others; tolerating ambiguity. SOCIAL RESPONSIBILITY Acting responsibly with the interests of the larger community in mind; demonstrating ethical behavior in personal, workplace, and community contexts.

of standards and accountability can indeed improve student achievement. We simply cannot rely on academic proficiency alone to ensure that our students and the future workforce will remain competitive in a constantly evolving global economy. The wide open 21st century marketplace offers tremendous opportunity for those who are equipped with finely tuned interpersonal and communication skills, an understanding of cultural differences, and ever higher levels of creativity and innovation. Educators must accept responsibility for preparing students for success in an increasingly competitive environment. To do that, they must teach students not only what they need to know, but how to think and problem-solve beyond the specific task at hand so they become life-long learners.

In conclusion, it would be presumptuous to suggest there is a single solution to the complex issues of school reform, economic competitiveness, and 21st century skill development. Yet, by remaining open to new instructional approaches which recognize diverse learning styles of multiple learners, school leaders can, and should, promote challenging and meaningful instruction via a lens and a process which examines and refines individual teaching and learning.

Educational practitioners have a particularly relevant perspective to bring to the debate and should be eager to contribute to the meaningful discussion on how best to equip students for future success.

Appendix B: MBAE Description of Skills[9]

- **Core Subjects and 21st Century Themes.** Mastery of core subjects and 21st century themes is essential for students in the 21st century. Core subjects include: English, reading or language arts; world languages; arts; mathematics; economics; science; geography; history; and government and civics. In addition to these subjects, schools must move beyond a focus on basic competency in core subjects to promoting understanding of academic content at much higher levels by weaving 21st century interdisciplinary themes into core subjects. These include: global awareness; financial, economic, business and entrepreneurial literacy; civic literacy; and health and wellness awareness.
- **Learning and Innovation Skills.** Learning and innovation skills increasingly are being recognized as the skills that separate students who are prepared for increasingly complex life and work environments in the 21st century, and those who

are not. A focus on creativity, critical thinking, communication and collaboration is essential to prepare students for the future.
- **Information, Media, and Technology Skills.** People in the 21st century live in a technology and media-suffused environment, marked by access to an abundance of information, rapid changes in technology tools, and the ability to collaborate and make individual contributions on an unprecedented scale. To be effective in the 21st century, citizens and workers must be able to exhibit a range of functional and critical thinking skills related to information, media and technology.
- **Life Skills.** The ability to navigate the complex life and work environments in the globally competitive information age requires students to pay rigorous attention to developing adequate life and career skills. These skills include: flexibility and adaptability; initiative and self-direction; social and cross-cultural skills; productivity and accountability; leadership and responsibility.

References

1. Partnership for 21st Century Skills. 2002. Learning for the 21st Century, p.9. Retrieved from http://www.21stcenturyskills.org/images/stories/otherdocs/p21up_Report.pdf

2. Massachusetts Business Alliance for Education, October 2008. "Educating a 21st Century Workforce," p.14. Retrieved from http://www.mbae.org/uploads/06102008230519EducatingA21stCenturyWorkforce.pdf

3. Jim Stergios and Jamie Gass, Pioneer Institute Policy Brief Strengthening Standards-Based Education, November 2008, p. 1-2. Retrieved from http://www.pioneerinstitute.org/pdf/081111_pb_21st_century.pdf

4. Jim Stergios, Pioneer Institute Policy Brief A Step Backwards: An Analysis of the 21st Century Skills Task Force Report, February 2009, p.1. Retrieved from http://www.pioneerinstitute.org/pdf/090217_pb_a_step_backwards.pdf

5. Nancy H. Gonter, "Students learn math on the job," Springfield Republican, May 31, 2009. Retrieved from http://www.masslive.com/chicopeeholyoke/republican/index.ssf?/base/news-20/1243668588103590.xml&coll=1

6. Massachusetts Business Alliance for Education, p. 14.

7. Linda M. Noonan and Jill Norton, "Moving beyond the basics," Milford Daily News, December 21, 2008. Retrieved from http://www.milforddailynews.com/opinion/x268040592/Noonan-Norton-Moving-beyond-the-basics

8. ACTE, February 2009, Joining Forces for Student Success, p.1. Retrieved from http://www.acteonline.org/uploadedFiles/Publications_and_Online_Media/files/academic_integration_paper_WEB.pdf

9. Massachusetts Business Alliance for Education, p. 25.

Michael Fitzpatrick is superintendent-director of the Blackstone Valley Vocational, Regional School District in Upton, Massachusetts.

Margaret Hilton

Preparing Students for Life and Work

Employers, educational policymakers, and others are calling on schools and colleges to develop "21st century skills," such as teamwork, problem-solving, and self-management that are seen as valuable for success in the workplace, citizenship, and family life. For example, 19 states are working with the Partnership for 21st Century Skills, a nonprofit association of education and business leaders, to infuse 21st century skills into their curricula, assessments, and teaching practices. (see http://www.p21.org/members-states/partnerstates). On Capitol Hill, bipartisan sponsors in the House and Senate introduced the 21st Century Readiness Act, with the goal of including attention to 21st century skills in the pending reauthorization of the Elementary and Secondary Education Act. The bipartisan Congressional 21st Century Skills Caucus, formed by Rep. Thomas Petri (R-WI) and Rep. Dave Loebsack (D-IA) in the 112th Congress, provides a forum for discussions about the importance of 21st century skills in preparing all students for college, career, and life.

The Achilles heel of the growing movement for 21st century skills is the absence of agreement on what these skills are. The Partnership for 21st Century Skills framework includes four learning and innovation skills—critical thinking, communication, collaboration, and creativity—along with life and career skills, information, media, and technology skills, and core academic subjects. The Hewlett Foundation focuses on "deeper learning," including mastery of core academic content, critical thinking and problem solving, collaboration, effective communication, self-directed learning, and an academic mindset. Other individuals and groups see information technology skills as most valuable for career success. To address this lack of a shared vision, the National Research Council (NRC) conducted a study of deeper learning and 21st century skills and published the report *Education for Life and Work: Developing Transferable Knowledge and Skills in the 21st Century* (National Academies Press, 2012).

To understand the importance of 21st century skills, including their relationship to learning of school subjects, the committee reviewed research not only from the cognitive sciences, but also in social psychology, child and adolescent development, economics, and human resource development. As a first step toward improved definitions, the committee clustered various lists of 21st century skills into three broad domains of competence:

- The cognitive domain, which involves reasoning and memory;
- The intrapersonal domain, which includes the capacity to manage one's behavior and emotions to achieve one's goals (including learning goals); and
- The interpersonal domain, which involves expressing ideas and interpreting and responding to messages from others.

To prepare for an uncertain 21st century economy, where workers can expect to frequently change jobs (whether as a result of layoffs or to explore new opportunities), students need to go beyond memorizing facts and taking multiple-choice tests. They need deeper learning, which the committee defined as the process through which a person becomes capable of taking what was learned in one situation and applying it to new situations—in other words, learning for transfer. Through the process of deeper learning, students develop 21st century competencies—transferable knowledge and skills. In contrast to a view of 21st century skills as general skills that can be applied across various civic, workplace, or family contexts, the committee views these competencies as aspects of expertise that are specific to—and intertwined with—knowledge of a particular discipline or topic area. The committee uses the broader term "competencies" rather than "skills" to include both knowledge and skills. In mathematics, for example, these competencies include content knowledge together with critical thinking, problem solving, constructing and evaluating evidence-based arguments, systems thinking, and complex communication.

Competency Counts

The committee set out to identify the competencies that were most valuable for success at work, in education, and in other settings. It found that the research base is limited, based primarily on correlational rather than causal studies. Thus, the committee could draw only limited conclusions:

- More studies have focused on cognitive competencies than on interpersonal and intrapersonal competencies, showing consistent, positive correlations (of modest size) with desirable educational, career, and health outcomes. For example, many studies have found that higher levels of general cognitive ability are correlated with higher occupational levels and earnings.
- Among interpersonal and intrapersonal competencies, conscientiousness (a tendency to be organized, responsible, and hardworking) is most highly correlated with desirable educational, career, and health outcomes. Anti-social behavior, which has both intrapersonal and interpersonal dimensions, is negatively correlated with these outcomes.

In contrast to the limited evidence of the importance of cognitive, interpersonal, and intrapersonal competencies, the committee found much stronger evidence of a causal relationship between years of completed schooling and higher adult earnings, as well as better health and civic engagement. Moreover, individuals with higher levels of education appear to more readily learn new knowledge and skills on the job.

The strong relationship between increased years of schooling and higher adult earnings suggests that formal schooling helps develop a mixture of cognitive, interpersonal, and intrapersonal competencies that is not measured by current academic tests, but is valued by the labor market. Further research is needed to examine this hypothesis. This would entail longitudinal tracking of students with controls for differences in individuals' family backgrounds and more studies using statistical methods that are designed to approximate experiments.

Many educators are well aware of the importance of nurturing broader competencies, as reflected in their development of the Common Core State Standards in mathematics and English language arts and the Next Generation Science Standards, based on the NRC Framework for K-12 Science Education. All three standards documents highlight the importance of a cluster of cognitive competencies including critical thinking and non-routine problem solving. For example, the mathematics standards and the NRC science framework include a "practices" dimension, calling for students to actively use their knowledge to tackle new problems, while the English language arts standards call on students to synthesize and apply evidence to create and effectively communicate an argument. Although all three documents expect students to develop the cognitive and interpersonal competencies needed to construct and evaluate an evidence-based argument, the disciplines differ in their views of what counts as evidence and what the rules of argumentation are.

The Common Core standards and the NRC framework represent each discipline's desire to promote deeper learning and develop transferable knowledge and skills within that discipline. For example, the NRC framework aims to develop science knowledge that transfers beyond the classroom to everyday life, preparing high school graduates to engage in public discussions on science-related issues and to be critical consumers of scientific information. At a more basic level, deeper learning of a school subject over the course of a school year develops durable, transferable competencies within the subject that students can apply when continuing to learn about that subject in the following school year.

However, research is lacking on how to help learners transfer competencies learned in one discipline or topic area to another discipline or topic area or how to combine and integrate competencies across disciplines.

Research to date has identified a number of practices and principles that contribute to deeper learning and transfer within a discipline or topic area. Instruction for deeper learning begins with a focus on clearly delineated learning goals along with assessments to measure student progress toward and attainment of the goals. It requires the development of new curriculum and instructional programs that include research-based teaching methods, such as:

- Using multiple and varied representations of concepts and tasks, such as diagrams, numerical and mathematical representations, and simulations, combined with activities and guidance that support mapping across the varied representations.
- Encouraging elaboration, questioning, and explanation—for example, prompting students who are reading a history text to think about the author's intent and/or to explain specific information and arguments as they read—either silently to themselves, or to others.
- Engaging learners in challenging tasks, while also supporting them with guidance, feedback, and encouragement to reflect on their own learning processes and the status of their understanding.

- Teaching with examples and cases, such as modeling step-by-step how students can carry out a procedure to solve a problem and using sets of worked examples.
- Priming student motivation by connecting topics to students' personal lives and interests, engaging students in collaborative problem solving, and drawing attention to the knowledge and skills students are developing, rather than grades or scores.
- Using formative assessments to: make learning goals clear to students; continuously monitor, provide feedback, and respond to students' learning progress; and involve students in self- and peer-assessment.

But will these same methods be effective in developing interpersonal and intrapersonal competencies, such as teamwork or self-regulation? It seems likely that they would, but the reality is that we don't have the evidence to support this assumption. The research challenge is to first more clearly define and develop reliable methods for assessing students' intrapersonal and interpersonal competencies in order to study and compare various approaches for developing them. A new NRC study of assessing intrapersonal and interpersonal competencies will begin to address this challenge.

The political environment creates additional barriers to the creation of an educational system that fosters deeper learning and transferable 21st century competencies. Many states are now pushing back against the Common Core standards that were initiated by a wide coalition of education and business leaders. Even in states that have embraced the new standards, the extent to which 21st century competencies will be taught and learned will depend on developments in educational assessment. Although research indicates that formative assessment by teachers supports deeper learning and development of transferable competencies, current educational policies focus on summative assessments that measure mastery of content. State and federal accountability systems often hold schools and districts accountable for improving student scores on such assessments, and teachers and school leaders respond by emphasizing what is included on these assessments. Traditionally, education leaders have favored the use of standardized, on-demand, end-of-year assessments. Composed largely of multiple-choice items, these tests are relatively cheap to develop, administer, and score; have sound psychometric properties; and provide easily quantifiable and comparable scores for assessing individuals and institutions. Yet, such standardized tests have not been conducive to measuring and supporting deeper learning in order to

develop 21st century competencies. In the face of current fiscal constraints at the federal and state levels, policymakers may seek to minimize assessment costs by maintaining lower-cost, traditional test formats, rather than incorporating into their systems relatively more expensive, performance- and curriculum-based assessments that may better measure 21st century competencies.

Recent developments in assessment may help to address these challenges. Two large consortia of states, with support from the U.S. Department of Education, have developed new assessment frameworks and methods aligned with the Common Core State Standards in Mathematics and English Language Arts. These new assessment frameworks include some facets of 21st century competencies represented in the Common Core State Standards, providing a strong incentive for states, districts, schools, and teachers to emphasize these competencies as part of disciplinary instruction. Next Generation Science Standards have been developed based on the NRC framework, and assessments aligned with these standards are currently under development. If the new science assessments include facets of 21st century competencies, they will provide a similarly strong incentive for states, districts, schools, and teachers to emphasize those facets in classroom science instruction.

Next Steps

Because 21st century competencies support deeper learning of school subjects, their widespread acquisition could potentially reduce disparities in educational attainment, preparing a broader swath of young people for successful adult outcomes at work and in other life arenas. However, important challenges remain. For educational interventions focused on developing transferable competencies to move beyond isolated promising examples and flourish more widely in K-12 and higher education, larger systemic issues and policies involving curriculum, instruction, assessment, and professional development will need to be addressed. As noted previously, new types of assessment systems, capable of accurately measuring and supporting acquisition of these competencies will be needed and this, in turn, will require a sustained program of research and development. In addition, it will be important for researchers and publishers to collaborate in developing new curricula that incorporate the research-based design principles and instructional methods we described previously. Finally, new approaches to teacher preparation and professional development will be needed to help current and prospective teachers understand how to support students' deeper learning and development of 21st century competencies in the context of mastering core academic content. If teachers are to not only understand these ideas, but also translate them into their daily instructional practice, they will need support from school and district administrators, including time for learning, shared lesson planning and review, and reflection. States and school districts should implement these changes, while private foundations and federal agencies should invest in research on assessment and curriculum development to foster widespread deeper learning and development of 21st century competencies.

Margaret Hilton is a senior program officer of the Board on Science Education and the Board on Testing and Assessment at the National Research Council.

EXPLORING THE ISSUE

Is the "21st Century Skills" Movement Practical?

Critical Thinking and Reflection

1. Where is much of the disagreement about 21st century skill development centered?
2. Why can't educators agree on what to include in the 21st Century Skills model?
3. What new assessment frameworks and methods align with 21st Century Skills model?
4. What are next steps in the 21st century skills movement?
5. Why can't educators identify the competencies that were most valuable for success at work, in education, and in other settings?

Is There Common Ground?

The focus of this issue has been on the 21st Century Skills model for school improvement and the concerns about its appropriateness and its potential effect on traditional elements of the curriculum. The larger context is the growing desire in many quarters for a nationwide consensus on what needs to be taught and how it should be taught. The 21st century skills movement is seen as one of the logical movements for improving our schools because it is addressing what students need to be career and college ready. Margaret Hilton states that teachers are to not only understand 21st century skills, but also translate them into their daily instructional practice. To do this successfully, they will need support from school and district administrators, including time for learning, shared lesson planning and review, and reflection. Fitzpatrick does not disagree here acknowledging, "Educational practitioners have a particularly relevant perspective to bring to the debate and should be eager to contribute to the meaningful discussion on how best to equip students for future success" (p. 6). This common ground speaks to how important teachers and school leaders are to successful 21st century skills implementation.

Bob Pearlman, a 21st Century School and District Consultant and Senior Education Consultant to the Los Angeles Area Chamber of Commerce, states that "Designing 21st century schools and new learning environments starts with asking 'What knowledge and skills do students need for the 21st century?' But real design needs to go much further and address the following questions as well:

- What pedagogy, curricula, activities, and experiences foster 21st century learning?
- What assessments for learning, both school-based and national, foster student learning of the outcomes, student engagement, and self-direction?
- How can technology support the pedagogy, curricula, and assessments of a 21st century collaborative learning environment?
- And lastly, what physical learning environments (classroom, school, and real world) foster 21st century student learning (p. 1)?"

A decade ago, the National Education Association (NEA) helped establish the Partnership for 21st Century Skills (P21) and in 2002 began a 2-year journey to develop what became known as a *Framework for 21st Century Learning*, highlighting 18 different skills. NEA continues in their document *Preparing 21st Century Students for a Global Society* that over the years it became clear that the "framework was too long and complicated" (p. 1). Should this finding end the work for harnessing the 21st century skills as a strategy to improve schools?

The Harvard University Think Tank asserts, "The problems in the educational system are deep and complex." They continue, "Solutions require innovation and thinking outside the building (which goes far beyond thinking *out of the box*)" (p. 14). It may be that the solutions themselves require a 21st century skills mindset (creativity, innovation, and critical thinking), requiring bringing multiple people and organizations together to solve the important problems facing K-12 education.

Additional Resources

J. Bellanca & R. Brandt, eds., *21st Century Skills: Rethinking How Students Learn* (2012).

K. Kay & V. Greenhill, *The Leader's Guide to 21st Century Education: 7 Steps for Schools and Districts* (2012).

T. Matthewson. San Jose Public School Uses Project-Based Learning to Engage Student. P21 Partnership for 21st Century Learning. Retrieved from http://www.p21.org/ (2016, September 28).

B. Trilling & C. Faddell, *21st Century Skills: Learning for Life in Our Times* (2012).

T. Wagner, *The Global Achievement Gap: Why Even Our Best Schools Don't Teach the New Survival Skills Our Children Need—and What We Can Do About It* (2008).

Internet References . . .

Partnership for 21st Century Skills

www.p21.org/

What Are 21st Century Skills?

http://atc21s.org/index.php/about/what-are
-21st-century-skills/

Center for 21st Century Skills

www.skills21.org/

ASCD: 21st Century Skills

www.ascd.org/research-a-topic/21st-century
-skills-resources.aspx

California Department of Education: Partnership for 21st Century Schools

http://www.cde.ca.gov/eo/in/cr/p21cskls.asp

Selected, Edited, and with Issue Framing Material by:
Glenn L. Koonce, *Regent University*

ISSUE

Should Educators Be Cautious Regarding Flipped Classrooms?

YES: Stacy M.P. Schmidt and David L. Ralph, from "The Flipped Classroom: A Twist on Teaching," *The Clute Institute* (2016)

NO: Project Tomorrow Speak Up, from "Speak Up 2014 National Research Project Findings: Flipped Learning Continues to Trend for Third Year," *Flipped Learning Network* (2015)

Learning Outcomes

After reading this issue, you will be able to:

- Identify five reasons to implement the flipped classroom with caution.
- Compare and contrast the pros and cons of a flipped classroom.
- Explore the criticisms and downsides to flipped learning.
- Explain why the lack of access to technology by students makes it unattractive for teachers to use.
- Construct rationale for teachers flipping their classrooms using videos they have found online or that they are creating themselves.

ISSUE SUMMARY

YES: Professors Stacy Schmidt from California State University at Bakersfield and David Ralph from Pepperdine University advocate for more research and funding for the flipped classroom noting five reasons to use caution in implementing flipped classrooms.

NO: Speak Up's 2014 National Research Project Findings assert that school leaders, teachers, librarians, and students are increasingly interested in flipped learning to transform the learning experience and a growing number of teachers who are moving to the concept, so "why fight it?"

Note: The Flipped Learning Network (2014) indicates flipped classroom and flipped learning are not interchangeable because "Flipping a class can, but does not necessarily, lead to Flipped Learning. To engage in flipped learning, teachers must incorporate four pillars into their practice: (1) Flexible Environment;(2) Learning Culture;(3) Intentional Content; and(4) Professional Education" (pp. 1–2). In this issue, flipped classrooms are considered a major element of flipped learning.

The *New York Times* (Rosenberg, 2013) uses the phrase "Turning Education Upside Down" (p. 1) as the title for its article that describes the flipped classroom. Reported as being in its early stages and not rigorously studied, the new pedagogical concept has an impressive track record in schools. Most of these reports were identified from short anecdotal online blogs and academic-oriented newspaper articles. In addition, there are numerous websites being created that are dedicated to promoting the flipped classroom ideology. The Flipped Learning Network reports that in 2011 there were 2500 teacher members on its social media site. The number rose to 9000 teachers in 2012 (Goodwin & Miller, 2013). This is a hot topic in education technology circles and its explosive growth will continue unabated over the next five to ten years (Lancaster & Read, 2015). The popularity and *buzz* surrounding flipped classrooms also includes a number of marketing materials designed to assist teachers who want to implement the Flipped model in their classrooms. Bishop and Verlinger (2013) state that the main focus of these materials are resources for making "screencasts and Khan Academy-style instructional videos" (p. 3). One company awards a certificate for "certified" flipped classroom instructors (p. 3).

The term "flipped classroom" or "flipped learning" has just recently *popped* up in educational settings across the country. Bormann (2014) indicates that the terms are a relatively new pedagogical technique. Hayeborne & Paerret (2016) describe a flipped classroom as a teaching technique in which "what was once considered homework is now done in the classroom, and what was once done in classroom is now done during out-of-class time" (p. 1). Although a vast majority of its growth has occurred over the past few years, flipped classrooms or inverted learning can be found as early as 2000 and is connected with the online learning movement. In addition, technology growth has had a major impact on the opportunity to flip learning. In 2001, Massachusetts Institute of Technology (MIT) announced its OpenCourseWare (OCW) initiative allowing open access to information that had previously only been available to tuition-paying MIT students. The trend continued when in 2006, MIT graduate Salman Khan founded the Khan Academy which released over 3200 videos and 350 practice exercises. Khan's work and others that followed have led to the conclusion that for conveying basic information, video lectures are as effective as in-person lectures. This concept has been key to the thinking behind flipped classrooms: "pre-recorded lectures can be assigned to students as homework, leaving class time open for interactive-activities that cannot be automated or computerized" (Bishop & Verlanger, 2013, p. 4).

Often referred to as the pioneers in flipped learning, two Colorado chemistry teachers, Jonathan Bergman and Aron Sams, were instrumental in the coming of age for flipped classrooms. Being classroom teachers in a very rural area, they frequently had students who missed class, end-of-day activities, competitions, games, or other events at their home school or other school sites. Beginning in 2007 they began using live video recordings and Screencasting software among other technology tools to record lectures and activities for their students. The reported results were very favorable with student interaction rising in classrooms and much flexible time being available for individual attention (Hamden, McKnight, McKnight, & Arfstrom, 2013).

The literature does not indicate a consensus definition for flipped (or inverted) classrooms mainly due to the limited amount of scholarly research on its effectiveness (Bishop & Verlinger, 2013). Basically, as noted earlier, flipped classes work as they sound: "students work on homework in class and watch their teacher's lectures videotaped and uploaded online-at home" (Hutchins, 2013, p. 1). Bishop and Verleger state that in the flipped class "events that have traditionally taken place inside the classroom now take place outside the classroom and vice versa" (p.3). In a white paper written by Hamden et al. (2013) a more elaborate definition for flipped learning was noted:

> "In a Flipped Learning setting, teachers make lessons available to students to be accessed whenever and wherever it is convenient for the student, at home, in class, during study hall, on the bus to a game, or even from a hospital bed. Teachers can deliver this instruction by recording and narrating screencasts of work they do on their computers, creating videos of themselves teaching, or curating video lessons from trusted internet sites. Students can watch the videos or screencasts as many times as they need to, enabling them to be more productive learners in the classroom. Since direct instruction is delivered outside the group learning space, teachers can then use in-class items to actively engage students in the learning process and provide them with individualized support" (p. 4).

As noted earlier, two major players in the "Flipped" model are Aaron Sams and Jonathan Bergmann who co-authored "Flip Your Classroom," a how-to manual for flipped learning. They indicate that students become inquisitive and in charge of their own learning through a "Flipped" model. Sams and Bergmann also note that lectures are out of the classroom and more individualized instruction, labs, and/or projects takes their place. Terms found in the "Flipped" learning model include active learning, student engagement, hybrid course design, and both individual inquiry teamed with collaborative effort. Sams and Bergmann have new careers based on their success working and consulting in the field with workshops and conferences (LaFee, 2013).

On the other hand, there are skeptics who question whether significant numbers of students possess or have access to the technology in their homes to be active and successful independent learners. In addition, do students possess the necessary motivation, understanding, and training to make it work? The same is true for teachers who would have different preparation and in-class instruction modalities to master as they move to a flipped model. Preliminary research at Harvey Mudd College "suggests that the benefits of flipping a classroom are dubious" (Atteberry, 2013), noting flipped classrooms might not make any difference at all in student learning. In his article, The Flipped Classroom is a Lie, Aviles (2014) purports that flipped learning is no "silver bullet" (p. 1), it will not make a teacher great or students successful.

In May 2014, Bormann released his study *Affordances of Flipped Learning and its Effects on Student Engagement and Achievement* finding both positive support for flipped learning and areas that still remain unclear, thus creating fertile grounds for continuing debate. In other studies, Amy Roehl, Shweta Linga Reddy, and Gayla Jett Shannon (2013) provide high praise for "this blended method of learning" in their experiment comparing a flipped classroom to a traditional lecture classroom. William Heyborne, an assistant professor in the Department of Biology at Southern Utah University and Jamis Perrett, a product analysis lead at Monosato Company in St. Louis, found mixed results in their study of flipped learning as compared to traditional learning. Regarding the superiority of either pedagogical approach, Heyborne and Perrett state that "there does seem to be a trend toward performance gains using the flipped pedagogy" (p. 36). Heyborne and Perrett strongly advocate for a larger multiclass study to further clarify the importance of the growing flipped learning culture. Regardless of outcomes, flipped learning is being touted as a "powerful strategy to address some of the weaknesses of traditional teaching," while at the same time, "it is essential that flipped learning is not exploited as a means of reducing contact time" between student and teachers (Lancaster & Read, 2015, p. 1).

References

Atteberry, E. (2013, December 5). 'Flipped Classrooms' May Not Have Any Impact on Learning. *USA Today*. Retrieved from http://www.usatoday.com/story/news/nation/2013/10/22/flipped-classrooms-effectiveness/3148447/

Bormann, J. (2014). Affordances of Flipped Learning and its Effect on Student Engagement and Achievement (Master's thesis: University of Northern Iowa). Retrieved from http://www.

flippedlearning.org/cms/lib07/VA01923112/Centricity/Domain/41/bormann_lit_review.pdf.

Bishop, J. & Verleger, M. (2013, June). The Flipped Classroom: A Survey of the Research. Paper presented at the American Society for Engineering Education Annual Conference & Exposition, Atlanta, GA.

Flipped Learning Network. (2014). What is Flipped Learning? Retrieved from http://flippedlearning.org/cms/lib07/VA01923112/Centricity/Domain/46/FLIP_handout_FNL_Web.pdf.

Goodman, B. & Miller, K. (2013). Research Says/Evidence on Flipped Classrooms Is Still Coming in. *Educational Leadership*. 70:6.

Hamden, H. McKnight, P. Mcknight, K., & Arfstrom, K. (2013). A White Paper Based on the Literature Review Titled: A Review of Flipped Learning Flipped Learning Network. Retrieved from http://flippedlearning.org/wp-content/uploads/2016/07/WhitePaper_FlippedLearning.pdf

Hayeborne, W. & Paerret, J. (2016). *To Flip or Not to Flip? Analysis of a Flipped Classroom Pedagogy in a General Biology Course*. National Science Teachers Association. Retrieved from https://www.nsta.org/store/product_detail.aspx?id=10.2505/4/jcst16_045_04_31.

Hutchins, S. (2013, November 25). More Teachers Switch to Flipped Classroom Techniques. *The Virginian-Pilot*. Retrieved from http://hamptonroads.com/print/698071.

LaFee, S. (2013, March). Flipped Learning. School Administrator (3/70). American Association of School Administrators.

Lancaster, S. & Read, D. (2015). Flipping lecture and inverting classrooms. *Education in Chemistry*. Retrieved from http://www.rsc.org/Education/EiC/issues/2013september/flipped-classroom-inverting-lectures.asp.

Rosenberg, T. (2013, October 9). Turning Education Upside Down. *The New York Times*. Retrieved from http://opinionator.blogs.nytimes.com/2013/10/09/turning-education-upside-down/?_php=true&_type=blogs&_r=1&.

YES

Stacy M.P. Schmidt and David L. Ralph

The Flipped Classroom: A Twist On Teaching

Introduction

The traditional classroom has utilized the I Do, We Do, You Do as a strategy for teaching for years. The flipped classroom truly flips that strategy. The teacher uses You Do, We Do, I Do instead. Homework, inquiry, and investigation happen in the classroom. At home students participate in preparation work including watching videos, PowerPoints, and completing readings. After completing the preparation work, students arrive in class ready to start solving problems, analyzing text, or investigating solutions.

The flipped classroom is fairly new in the teaching field as a strategy for teaching. It has been used by teachers from elementary school to graduate school. As with most strategies, the flipped classroom has a variety of ways to implement in the classroom.

Why the Flipped Classroom

The term flipping comes from the idea of swapping homework for classwork (Ash, 2012). When students go home to work on homework, some of them have well educated parents that can assist them with the work while others have parents that are not knowledgeable in the content and cannot assist them with their homework. Thus according to Ash (2012), students are able to return to class with the content and then receive assistance with the homework from the expert in the field—the teacher during class time. The flipped classroom provides the students with in class support for completing work. The flipped classroom provides more time for hands on activities and content inquiry and analysis. Fulton (2012) also found that the flipped classroom causes "students to take more responsibility for their own learning". Students also have access to the content at home so if they are absent due to illness they can easily catch up and do not miss out on vital lectures.

Flipping Your Classroom: The Research

Flipping your classroom does not mean you can never lecture or that your classroom is always flipped. The teacher is still necessary in the flipped classroom. The teacher still has to plan and prepare for every class. The flipped classroom also does not require technology to use.

Ash (2012) suggested the following 5 tips for flipping your classroom:

1. Don't get hung up on creating your own videos.
2. Be thoughtful about what parts of your class you decide to "Flip" and when.
3. If possible, find a partner to create videos with.
4. Address the issue of access early.
5. Find a way to engage students in the videos.

A common practice of teachers utilizing a flipped classroom is videos of the lectures. The videos are used in various ways. Teachers found that the use of short 10–15 minute videos is the best way to incorporate the videos. Resources have surfaced on the web of content information in a wide range of subject matter. Some websites provide premade videos, tutorials, and interfaces on the subject matter. The most successful flipped classrooms report that they utilize videos of the content that they have gotten from a variety of places. By obtaining videos from other sources the students indicate they are more engaged and found the information refreshing. Videos from the same person can become mundane and boring. Taking boring lectures and recording them and making students watch them on their own time is not the purpose of the flipped classroom. Voice-over PowerPoints are also mundane and boring. Students will disengage and are likely not going to watch them with their full attention. One means of making the videos is the use of simple "one take" videos (Brunsell & Horejsi, 2013). "To create these videos, all you need is an inexpensive digital camera, tripod, white panel board, and dry erase markers. Teachers outline their presentation with visual aids on a series of small whiteboards. Then, they simply record themselves talking through the series of whiteboards. The benefit of this approach is that videos can be created quickly; and by having the teacher on camera, students connect with both the content and their teacher."

Budget constraints do not have to prevent a teacher from utilizing the flipped classroom. The first consideration that must be made when incorporating a flipped classroom is what technology is available to not only the teacher but the students as well. If a teacher requires students to use the internet or view videos for homework, the students need to have access to this technology. Some teachers are shocked to discover how many of their students still do not even have a computer at home let alone access to the internet. Some teacher's work addresses this by creating a means to provide access to these students while other teachers change their medium away from the computer. Whether it is watch videos or complete a reading, the teacher cannot just require the task to be completed. The student needs to be engaged in the process to assure its completion and the students acquiring the knowledge presented. This can be done in many ways. Teachers are even getting creative with this aspect of the flipped classroom. It can be as simple as having the students complete a worksheet or answer questions as they read or watch the video. Having the students write questions about what further information they need is helpful in moving to the in class portion of the lesson. Having the students identify and define words they were not familiar with is also helpful.

In some instances the flipped classroom provides a solution to budget issues. "A Minnesota high school with severe budget constraints enlisted YouTube in its successful effort to boost math competency scores (Fulton, 2012)." The school did not have money for new textbooks and were utilizing outdated material. The teachers used YouTube to store videos to accompany materials they created and implemented themselves. Working together the math teachers were able to create videos and then create activities, worksheets, and projects that were utilized in the class. "Unable to afford an expensive course management system, they turned to Moodle, a free online learning management system" (Fulton, 2012). Moodle is free to use and provides you with the opportunity to use a variety of online tools. This can be used to store documents, videos, and information for students if your school cannot afford an online portal of their own.

The flipped classroom should not just be a band wagon that all teachers jump on to use in their classrooms. It is vital that teachers approach the flipped classroom with care and knowledge.

Neilsen (2012) identified the following five reasons to implement the flipped classroom with caution:

1. Many of our students don't have access to technology at home
2. Flipped homework is still homework and there are a growing number of parents and educators who believe mandatory homework needlessly robs children of their after-school time.
3. Flipping instruction might end up just providing more time to do the same type of memorization and regurgitation that just doesn't work.
4. If we really want transformation in education, one thing we must do is stop grouping students by date of manufacture, which the flipped classroom is ideally suited for. True flipping should include a careful redesign of the learning environment, but this is often overlooked.
5. The flipped classroom is built on a traditional model of teaching and learning: I lecture, you intake

On the other hand, Millard (2012) found 5 reasons the flipped classroom works:

1. Increases student engagement
2. Strengthens team-based skills
3. Offers personalized student guidance
4. Focuses Classroom Discussion
5. Provides Faculty Freedom

The flipped network (2012) conducted a study of teachers incorporating the flipped classroom at the junior high and secondary school. The study indicated that 99% of the teachers that incorporated the flipped classroom will continue to use it. 67% reported improvements in student performance and 80% reported improvements in student engagement. 71% of the teachers put 50% or more of their instruction online. Science was the most flipped subject at 46%, math was 32% and ELA was only 12%. 95% of the study consisted of secondary teachers.

Flipping Your Classroom: The Study

Classroom teachers were surveyed regarding the flipped classroom. 58 teachers responded to the survey. Of the 58 teachers 21 were brand new teachers with 1–2 years experience. 13 teachers had 2–5 years of experience and 24 teachers had more than 5 years of teaching experience.

Years of Teaching

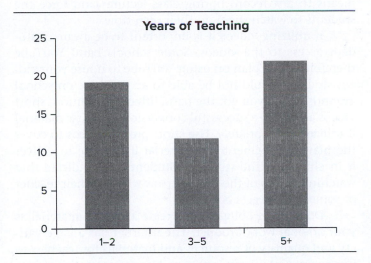

Of the 58 teachers only 3 teachers utilized a flipped classroom.

Use Flipped Classroom

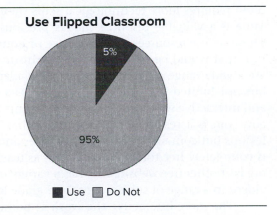

One class was high school math, one class was a high school Social Science, and one class was an elementary classroom. Of the 58 teachers, 15 were knowledgeable of the flipped classroom, 13 were somewhat knowledgeable, and 30 were not very knowledgeable.

The three flipped classrooms utilized different strategies and techniques. All of the teachers reported increased student engagement, improved student scores, and less incomplete assignments. The next paragraphs describe the different flipped classrooms utilized.

For the at home work, the high school math teacher incorporated fully online resources. The teacher utilized an online resource, the Khan Academy. Students were assigned videos to watch, interactive challenges, and quizzes. The Khan Academy website is located at

Knowledge of the Flipped Classroom

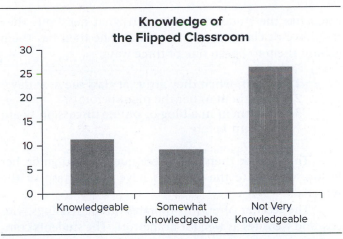

khanacademy.org. The teacher is referred to as a Coach on the site. The teacher selects which information to assign to the students. The students watch the videos, practice problems, and take quizzes. The teacher has access to the results instantly on the website. This provides the teacher with information on what the students have mastered and what information needs further instruction. Teachers then use this information for instruction in class the following day. The students arrived at class with questions from the lesson and the teacher immediately dove into working out problems with the students and answering their questions. The teacher reported that the students were more engaged in class as a result of using the flipped classroom.

The teacher also stated that the students reported that this method provided them with an opportunity to get better support working out the problems. The students often do not realize they do not understand a concept until they start actually analyzing and solving problems. Some students have parents at home that can assist them when they struggle with the math but a majority of the students do not have anyone at home that has enough knowledge in the content area of mathematics to help them. So with the flipped classroom they arrive and class and start to solve questions and the expert (the teacher) monitors their progress and is available for guidance. Thus, the result is improved scores for the mathematics students. In addition, the students are less likely to get frustrated and give up working on the math when the teacher is there to further explain the information and processes.

The High School Social Science teacher used both online and offline resources in her flipped classroom. She often has the students read the textbook for homework. Whenever textbook readings are assigned, the teacher always requires the students complete a task while reading the text. These activities can be a graphic organizer, sentence frames, or open ended questions. The teacher often has the students write down what questions they still have or clarifications they need. She then has them submit them to her in one of three ways:

1. Hand in when they arrive at class the next day
2. Email them to her the night before
3. Write them in a blog or online discussion board the night before

The teacher then uses these questions to guide her lesson and assure the students have a full grasp of the material.

The teacher often incorporates online readings, videos, and websites as well for homework. The students complete these assignments at home. While completing these assignments, the students often complete activities while doing the homework. Sometimes this works is taking notes of the reading or creating an outline of the material. Then in class, the teacher skips the lecture and begins with analysis, application, and comparisons. The result is that discussions are more engaging and deeper the teacher reports.

The elementary teacher is faced with many students that do not have access to technology at home. Some students have no computers and some that have computers have no internet access. Therefore, the elementary teacher uses an exclusively offline flipped classroom. The teacher assigns the students to complete readings including the textbooks. While completing the readings, students are sometimes required to highlight key points in one color, new vocabulary in another color, and confusing or points that need clarification in another color. Other times students are required to write notecards of specific information. It might be main characters, key dates, points for clarification, or vocabulary cards for example. This frontloads the material and exposes the children to the information prior to coming to class. Some students still do not complete the homework reports the teacher. The teacher makes it clear that the flipped classroom is not a solution to incomplete homework. On the other hand, she did report that students are more encouraged to be prepared for class as the expectation is for students to know the material and be able to actively participate in the class activities and discussions

Conclusion

The flipped classroom is a lot of work to utilize and the lack of access to technology by students make it unattractive for teachers to use. As access is more readily available and more data is available to support the improved learning and student engagement, more teachers will be willing to implement a flipped classroom. The flipped classroom can be used to enhance learning and is not meant as a means to just record boring class lectures and force the students to watch them on their own time.

If utilizing videos it is important to be aware of student access to the videos. Some schools band YouTube therefore, if you plan on using YouTube to house your videos students would not be able to access these on school grounds unless you got the band lifted. In addition, short videos are key to a successful conversion of course material if utilized appropriately. Use short precise videos to cover the material. Segment the material if possible to deliver it in chunks to the students. Students also indicate that watching videos of the same person whether their teacher or someone else gets boring.

Do not feel obligated to create all of the material as your original work product. The internet has a large variety and quantity of resources and materials for teachers to incorporate into their classroom. Not only does this reduce the workload for the teacher but provides variety for the students. Sometimes creating your own online resources often requires more technological skills then you possess. Time is a valuable resource that is precious to teachers. These online resources take the place of hours of preparation that would be required to create this material. There are a wide range of resources that are available including but not limited to: online readings, videos on YouTube, and interactive websites. The Khan Academy at khanacademy.com is a resource that not online has online video lessons but contains interactive activities and quizzes and is completely free for students as well as teachers. Sophia.org is another free website that has a variety of lessons and videos in a range of subject areas and grade levels.

The more interactive the work at home is the more successful the flipped classroom. Students will be more apt to complete the at home work when they are engaged and interested. Variety in content, activities, and videos will engage students. As the flipped classroom becomes more and more utilized, more research and resources will need to be completed.

References

Ash, K. (2012) Educators View 'Flipped' Model' With a More Critical Eye. *Education Week*, pS6–S7.

Brunsell, E. and Horejsi, M. (2013) Flipping Your Classroom in One 'Take'. *The Science Teacher*, p. 8.

Flipped Learning Network (2012) What do teachers who've flipped their classrooms have to report? *Technology and Learning*, p. 12.

Fulton, K. (2012) The Flipped Classroom: Transforming Education at Byron High School, *T.H.E. Journal*, p. 18–20.

Millard, E. (2012) 5 Reasons Flipped Classrooms Work. *University Business*, p.26–29.

Nielsen, L. (2012) Five Reasons I'm Not Flipping Over The Flipped Classroom. *Technology and Learning*, p. 46.

Stacy M.P. Schmidt is the director of teacher education, Antelope Valley Campus, California State University at Bakersfield and David L. Ralph is professor of marketing, Department Chair of Marketing, Law, Economics at Pepperdine University.

Project Tomorrow Speak Up  **NO**

Speak Up 2014 National Research Project Findings: Flipped Learning Continues to Trend for Third year

During the fall of 2014, over 521,865 K-12 students, teachers, administrators, parents, and community members participated in the 12th annual Speak Up online surveys facilitated by the national education nonprofit organization, Project Tomorrow© in conjunction with the Flipped Learning Network™.

For the third year in a row, specific questions were asked of teachers, librarians, and building and district administrators on flipped learning and the use of videos in the classroom. Educators and administrators weighed in on professional development when learning how to flip a class. Students lent their voices on flipped learning, videos as homework, and how (and how often) they use learning and social media tools.

Results were released at AASA: The School Superintendents Association's National Conference on Education on February 28, 2015.

Flipped Learning—Trending for Three Years

For the third consecutive year, 4,326 building and district administrators from 2,600 school districts are seeing a significant increase in teachers flipping their classrooms using videos they have found online or that they are creating themselves. Over the past three years, school leaders at all grade levels have seen increases from 23 to 32 percent of teachers using videos found online, with a slightly larger overall increase in the number of teachers who are creating their own videos moving from 19 to 29 percent.

When school technology leaders were asked about popular approaches to digital learning that have had positive results in their schools, they specifically selected "flipped learning" 48 percent of the time. They also selected "digital content, which includes videos, simulations and animations" 84 percent of the time and two-third selected "digital media tools for student content creation." Both of these categories are directly related to flipped learning.

Coupled with the number of teachers and administrators who have NEVER heard of flipped learning, we know the growth and sustainability of this particular teaching method will continue to grow. In 2013, the first year questions were asked about flipped learning in this survey, 18 percent of teachers and 12 percent of administrators had never heard of it; three years later only 12 percent and seven percent, respectively, had never heard of it.

Amongst school administrators, 28 percent identify flipped learning as already having a significant impact on transforming teaching and learning in their districts. The majority of middle (38 percent) and high schools (40 percent) are implementing flipped learning with "positive results," but elementary schools (17 percent) are increasingly using it in their classrooms too.

Both librarians and teachers were asked about digital content they either recommend to the educators they work with, or in the case of teachers, that they currently use in their classrooms. Librarians indicated that 55 percent have found online videos from places such as YouTube, Khan Academy or NASA (an increase from 44 percent three years ago) for teachers to use in their classroom, with 61 percent of teachers doing likewise (an increase from 47 percent). Likewise, the number of librarians who have created their own videos increased from 13 to 24 percent, and teachers from eight to 12, again over three years.

A Call for More Professional Development

The national research measured an increased number of teachers who are using video for their own professional development. In the past year, 62 percent of educators indicated they had used an online video to learn how to do something themselves and 11 percent indicated they had created their own videos of lectures or lessons for their students to watch. With teachers utilizing video for their own learning or for transferring knowledge to others, this trend continues to support the idea of flipped learning. Educators who were not yet flipping, indicated they were interested in "trying flipped learning" in their classrooms and schools; an increase from 15 percent to 17 percent from last year.

A fifth of teachers at all grade levels are asking for professional development in this area; 21 percent indicated that learning how to "implement a flipped classroom model" is on their "wish list for professional development" in the coming year. A secondary question was asked whether or not they wished to receive training on "how to create videos of lessons and lectures for students to watch," which was at 18 percent. There were fewer teachers asking for instruction on "finding high quality videos" this year (16 percent). So even if teachers were not fully aware of the term flipped learning used in the survey, they were interested in learning more about the concept.

Also increasing from last year's survey to this year was the number of administrators who indicated they were "providing specific training" on flipped learning for their teachers, which increased from five to seven percent. School librarians are providing much of the PD with 17 percent stating they helped teachers set up a flipped classroom in the past year.

School administrators are expecting new teachers to know how to flip their classrooms prior to completing their certification process. Last year, 41 percent of school leaders indicated that pre-service teachers should "know how to set up a flipped learning classroom," this year that increased to 46 percent. Of the same group, 68 percent indicated that pre-service teachers should come to their new jobs with the "ability to create and use video, podcasts and other media" in their classrooms. Even when broken down by grade levels (elementary, middle, or high schools), the averages of the responses do not differ by more than a few percentage points; administrators are expecting new hires to come with these skills no matter the grade or subject taught.

Students' Voices on Flipped Learning

Of the 431,241 students in grades kindergarten through twelfth who took the online survey in the fall of 2014 almost half indicated they regularly used videos as part of their homework—either videos they found online or videos created by their teachers. While the flipped learning model is not necessarily predicated on videos as homework, many commonly use that interpretation. For the Flipped Learning Network's definition of a flipped classroom and flipped learning, [visit http://flippedlearning.org/definition-of-flipped-learning/]. Specifically, when students in grades 6–12 were asked if they participated in a "flipped class where students watch/listen to lectures or lessons at home and then use the class time to do projects or get homework help," seven percent indicated they did.

Yet, on average, 40 percent of students stated they found videos online (e.g. YouTube and Khan Academy) to help with homework or studying. Interestingly, half of all kindergarteners, first and second graders said they had used a video for additional assistance. When asked if they had watched a video created by their teacher for class, 26 percent of all K-12 students indicated they had, with most being middle or high school students. Again, another indicator of growth for this method of teaching.

The majority of polled students in grades 3-12 agreed with these statements on why using technology was helping them to learn: I am able to learn at my own pace (59 percent); I have more control over my learning (50 percent); and I am learning in a way that better fits my learning style (49 percent). While students are not known to endorse or encourage homework, 37 percent did agree with this statement: My learning does not stop at the end of the class period or school day; I can go home and continue learning after school.

To get a sense of the acceptance rate of videos by students consider this: the number of students in middle and high school who said they "never" use Facebook is 41 percent, and 30 percent said they never access Instagram, yet only 4.5 percent never go to YouTube. Even more telling is that 44 percent of students said they use YouTube "all the time" with 35 percent selecting the same response for Instagram, yet only 14 percent marked that for Facebook. Video is the means for youth to access social media in their free time so it goes that they are very comfortable using video for their formal and informal learning.

Stumbling Blocks to Implementing Flipped Learning

Always a concern for educators and administrators is student access to teacher created or curated videos away from school, but the decrease from the first year is an indicator of ongoing acceptance of this ideology. For instance, half of all teachers (49 percent) are concerned about students not being able to access videos at home, a decrease of four percentage points from year one. Administrators have not changed their level of concern and remained steady at 47 percent from year one to three.

Another concern is ensuring that educators have enough training to properly implement flipped learning. There has been an overall decrease in the number of teachers who indicated they needed instruction "in how to make the videos," how to "find high quality videos," and "how to best utilize class time." Interestingly, teachers decreased their concerns from year one to three on how to make and find videos (by 5 to 8 percentage points), but there was only a percentage point decrease in their need for training on how to best utilize class time once they have flipped their classes. This is clearly an area for school leaders to concentrate on when offering flipped training. Ironically, administrators stated that their employees needed more training in all three areas more than teachers did by an average of 16 percentage points! This disconnect needs to be further explored.

Next Steps

Once again the message is clear—school leaders, teachers, librarians and students are increasingly interested in flipped learning to transform the learning experience.

Administrators want their teachers to utilize this method of instruction. Educators and pre-service teachers want more professional development. Librarians and other media specialists need support to assist with implementations. Students continue to use video as their go to method of formal and informal learning, so why fight it?

While the number of teachers and administrators who had never heard of flipped learning declined over the past three years, more teachers seem to be embracing this method without knowing of the research or pedagogy behind it. Research such as this annual survey and subsequent report will help to guide this ongoing conversation. Both Project Tomorrow and the Flipped Learning Network look forward to continuing to research and provide guidance to support educators and administrators who are interested in this highly innovative approach to learning.

Each year, the Speak Up Research Project on Digital Learning asks K-12 students, parents, and educators about the role of technology for learning in and out of school.

EXPLORING THE ISSUE

Should Educators Be Cautious Regarding Flipped Classrooms?

Critical Thinking and Reflection

1. Why are school leaders, teachers, librarians, and students increasingly interested in flipped learning to transform the learning experience?
2. What are some digital media tools for flipped learning?
3. Is the flipped classroom a fad that may soon go away or is it a transformational teaching method that is here to stay?
4. What resources does the Khan Academy provide for flipped learning?
5. Do budget constraints prevent a teacher from utilizing the flipped classroom?

Is There Common Ground?

Focusing more of the responsibility for learning and achievement on to the student certainly is a worthy goal and outcome for education. Much can be said for the state of current technology that supports a flipped pedagogical approach to teaching and learning. Research during the past decade consistently shows teaching as the first and most important among school-related influences on learning. Do the flipped learning and/or flipped classroom model change this fact? Whether or not a change is made in pedagogy, it appears that traditional classrooms and flipped classrooms point to the teacher for successful student outcomes.

Student responsibility for learning, instructional use of technology, and teacher pedagogy are areas educators can gravitate to, but student achievement is the accountability measure to which all teachers are held. The question for consideration is, are flipped methods effective? The common ground for responding to this question is further study. Controlled studies should be employed comparing traditional pedagogy versus flipped pedagogy. Quantitative, qualitative, and mixed methods should be designed and both theory and practice examined. From this, best practices will emerge revealing any common ground for the issue question.

Comparing the love affair growing in the use of flipped learning to the cries announcing "Don't flip," there is little data affirming one or the other is the only way to go in schools across the nation. Even so, flipping is rapidly moving into the mainstream, at the same time it is being viewed as a fad. What the flip does particularly well is to bring about a distinctive shift in priorities—from merely covering material to working toward mastery of it. As the flipped classroom becomes more and more utilized, more research and resources will need to be completed. Research can provide guidance to support educators and administrators who are interested in this highly innovative approach to learning. Results from further study will help understand where there is common ground.

Additional Resources

K. Walsh, *Flipped Classroom Workshop in a Book (Learn How to Implement Flipped Instruction in Your Classroom)*. eBook from EmergingEdTech (2016).

J. Bergman, "How to Flip Your Class for Students with Little Access to Technology," Video: http://www.jonbergmann.com/how-to-flip-your-class-if-your-students-have-limited-access-to-technology/ (2016).

J. Bergmann, *Flipped Learning; Gateway to Student Engagement* (2014).

J. Bretzmann, *Flipping 2.0: Practical Strategies for Flipping Your Class* (2013).

J. Bergmann, *Flip Your Classroom: Reach Every Student in Every Class, Every Day* (2012).

Internet References . . .

Flipped Learning Model Dramatically Improves Course Pass Rate for At-Risk Students

http://assets.pearsonschool.com/asset_mgr/current/201317/Clintondale_casestudy.pdf

Flipped Learning Simplified

http://www.jonbergmann.com/

How "Flipping" the Classroom Can Improve the Traditional Lecture

http://chronicle.com/article/How-Flipping-the

-Classroom/130857/

Things You Should Know About Flipped Classrooms

https://net.educause.edu/ir/library/pdf/eli7081.pdf

What Is Flipped Learning?

http://flippedlearning.org/wp-content/uploads/2016/07/FLIP_handout_FNL_Web.pdf

Selected, Edited, and with Issue Framing Material by:
Glenn L. Koonce, *Regent University*

ISSUE

Does Class Size Affect Student Achievement?

YES: William J. Mathis, from "The Effectiveness of Class Size Reduction," *National Education Policy Center* (2016)

NO: Christopher Jepsen, from "Class Size: Does It Matter for Student Achievement?" *IZA World of Labor* (2015)

Learning Outcomes

After reading this issue, you will be able to:

- Summarize the positive benefits of smaller class size on student achievement.
- Compare and contrast the benefits of class size on the productivity of student learning.
- Research the cost benefits of having fewer students in a classroom.
- Distinguish between the three categories of class-size reduction studies: randomized experiments, natural experiments, and sophisticated mathematical models.
- Evaluate the short-term and long-term effects of small classes in the early grades.

ISSUE SUMMARY

YES: William J. Mathis, the managing director of the National Education Policy Center at the University of Colorado Boulder, states that the literature on class-size reduction finds it as an effective strategy for improved learning.

NO: Christopher Jepsen states that smaller classes are often associated with increased achievement, but evidence is far from universal.

Educators, researchers, policy makers, parents, and politicians have debated and analyzed for decades whether class size effects student achievement. The logical view would be, "yes it does" if class size is small, has been reduced, or is in the process of being reduced. Giving teachers fewer students to teach makes sense as a strategy to raise student achievement and is very popular, seemingly, with everyone. However, the mere number of students present in a classroom is much more complex to evaluate, and there is conflicting evidence in the body of class-size research as to its effectiveness. In theory, having fewer students in a classroom allows the teacher to give more individual attention to students and allocate more time for different methods of teaching and assessment, and there are less students to motivate and maintain appropriate behavior. But other factors should be considered regarding class-size effects on student achievement. The overall school environment and teacher quality are two facets, as well as individual student backgrounds and the mix of students being taught in a particular classroom. One disconnect in the long-range impact of smaller classes is the time required to continue the types of studies needed to produce high-quality research.

When reviewing the literature on class size, it is important to distinguish the difference between *class size* and *student–teacher ratio*. Class size refers to the actual number of students in a classroom, while the student–teacher ratio divides the total number of enrolled students in a school by the number of credentialed professional educators that support the classroom (teachers, librarians, special education counselors, etc.). Whitehurst and Chingos (2011), from the Brown Center on Education Policy at the Brookings Institute, caution that not all studies found in the large body of literature on class-size effects on student achievement are of high quality. Conclusions from even the small pool of credible studies differ in terms of the setting, methods, grades, and variation in the magnitude of the number of students in the class. Whitehurst and Chingos have asserted that there are three categories of "credible" class-size policy reduction studies:

- randomized experiments, in which students and teachers are randomly assigned to smaller or larger classes;
- natural experiments in which, for example, a sudden change in class-size policy allowed a before-and-after analysis of its effects; and
- sophisticated mathematical models for estimating effects that take advantage of longitudinal data on individual students, teachers, and schools. (Krasnoff, 2014, p. 4)

Krasnoff's meta-analytic findings of existing studies on class-size reduction are mixed as to any "discernable effects on student achievement" (p. 4). He states that "there is no reason to expect consistent improved student performance under a class size reduction policy" (p. 4).

The results of the meta-analysis conducted by Krasnoff (2014) support the main finding in the NO article for this issue. In the NO article, Jepsen (2015) concludes that only modest improvement in students' achievement results when class size is reduced. He indicates that these slight improvements appear more in the early primary grades (K–3) than in higher grade levels (4–12). Even with students showing modest gains in lower elementary level grades, the evidence is not universal as to higher achievement gains. Jepsen supports Krasnoff's assertion that since the number of students in each studied classroom is not determined randomly, rigorous analysis of the causal relationship between class size and student achievement is complicated. The most significant outcome from Jepsen's work is that "several high quality studies find no relationship between class size and student achievement" (p. 1).

Opposing positions exist to the notion that there are only slight improvements in student outcomes when class size is small. McKee, Sims, and Rivkin (2015) cite 11 studies between 1990 and 2011 that found significant and lasting impact of smaller class sizes on student achievement. Overall, the findings in these studies generally support increased achievement in grades 5 and below. In the YES article for this issue, Mathis (2016, p. 3) concluded that the "literature on class size reduction is clear and positive, the 'overwhelming majority' of peer-reviewed papers find it an effective strategy." In a National Council of Professors of Education Administration Policy Brief on the Tennessee Student/Teacher Achievement Ratio (STAR) experiment and other related class-size studies by Charles Achilles (2012) showed that there are both short-term and long-term benefits for students in kindergarten through third grade. Achilles, in a "high-intensity experimental design" (p. 1), using a large sample and random assignment, found improved test outcomes and school engagement, reduced grade retention, and greater benefits for poor, minority, and male students in small size classrooms. The original results in this study applied to grades K–3 from 1985 to 1989. Achilles continued his study on the same STAR database of 11,601 students as they matriculated through grades 4–8, from 1990 to 1996 (*Lasting Benefits Study*). The *Enduring Effects Phase* took place between 1996 and 2011 where Achilles noted long-term advantages of small classes in early grades.

A Northwestern University National Policy Center brief developed by Schanzenbach (2014) reinforces Achilles' earlier writings that academic research supports the positive impact of small classes on student test scores. Describing the importance of research design, Schanzenbach explains that less sophisticated analysis, using simple correlations in comparing class size, can lead to misleading outcomes. In the case of low-achieving or special needs, students systematically being assigned to a smaller class, the estimated relationships between class size and outcomes can be negatively biased.

Schanzenbach (2014) believes the STAR study is the best evidence on the impact of reducing class size because it employed a randomized experiment, which is the gold standard of social science research. The population studied were *randomly* assigned to either a small or regular class and not assigned because of the achievement level of the students, their socioeconomic background, or involvement of their parents in the school. The STAR experiment also produced additional long-range outcomes that found smaller class size had a positive impact on students after the experiment ended. Schanzenbach noted a positive impact on the following list of later life outcomes: juvenile criminal behavior, teen pregnancy, high school graduation, college enrollment and completion, quality of college attended, savings behavior, marriage rates, residential location, and home ownership.

Urging more attention to the issue of class size, a National Council of Teachers of English (NCTE) (2014) report, *Why Class Size Matters Today*, asserts from their review of the research that students in smaller classes perform better than their peers in large classes in all subjects and on all assessments. The report indicates that students in smaller classes are as much as "one to two months ahead in content knowledge and that they score higher on standardized assessments" (p. 2). The positive effects are strongest in elementary grades and endure the longer students remain in smaller classes. In addition, these benefits continue into upper elementary and/or middle school. The NCTE report advises that these benefits are not consistent across all levels and across all student populations. Other benefits in the report included student engagement and long-term success. Students *talk more* and *participate more* in smaller classes. They interact more with their teacher, develop better relationships with peers, and display less disruptive behaviors. Finally, they spend more time on task and have greater access to technology. Long-term benefits of smaller classes include life successes, defined as increased earning potential, improved citizenship, and decreased crime and welfare dependence. Students also have a higher probability of attending college.

The argument made in Schanzenbach's recommendations regarding the long-term "human capital" (p. 10) gains is directed at another item to consider for reducing class size: costs. Substantial social and educational costs in the future could be offset by any additional funding that would be allocated in the future for smaller classes. Jepsen (2014) agrees, stating that reducing class size is a very expensive policy reform measure. Generally, the American public wants immediate results from their hard-earned tax dollars. For the *money matters* supporters, class-size reductions require cost/benefit analysis including staffing and in some cases facilities to house additional classrooms. Where to spend the money is a question for all sides, realizing that class size is only one of a number of policy options that can be pursued for improving student learning. Competing with the revenue available for school reform include tutoring, extending learning time by starting school earlier or enhanced early childhood opportunities for school readiness, digital learning and smart use of technology initiatives, pay and performance for results, improving teacher quality, and comprehensive reform programs with alternative funding streams. Policy makers who fund class-size decisions will have to look at both short- and long-range outcomes for the most cost-effective policy overall.

Class size is a major factor in student learning, and as this introduction has argued, more quality research is needed to determine its effect on student achievement and to guide policy and funding decisions. Considerations include the belief that without effective teaching, class size does not matter, and that there are cost-effectiveness as well as funding issues in reducing class size.

YES

William J. Mathis

The Effectiveness of Class Size Reduction

Ask a parent if they want their child in a class of 15 or a class of 25. The answer is predictable. Intuitively, they know that smaller classes will provide more personalized attention, a better climate, and result in more learning. Ask teachers, and they will wax eloquent on the importance of small classes in providing individual support to their students. But ask a school board or district administrator, contending with a tight budget. They ask whether the average class size can be a bit bigger.

Teacher pay and benefits are the largest single school expenditure, representing 80 percent of the nation's school budgets.[1] Thus, small class size is a costly, important, contentious, and perennial issue.

The Research on Class Size

There are many studies of the impact of smaller classes and they vary widely in quality.[2] As a result, proponents from all perspectives can cherry-pick studies that support their point of view.

But let's look closer. There is, in fact, an independent consensus on what we know:

This material is provided free of cost to NEPC's readers, who may make non-commercial use of the material as long as NEPC and its author(s) are credited as the source. For inquiries about commercial use, please contact NEPC at nepc@colorado.edu.

One of the earliest influential meta-studies was by Glass and Smith in 1979.[3] They statistically analyzed 300 reports involving almost 900,000 students. Once the class size fell below about 15, learning increased progressively as class size became smaller.

The most prominent study supporting smaller class sizes was the Tennessee Student/Teacher Achievement Ratio (STAR) experiment. The STAR experiment was a four-year statewide random-assignment experiment. Students in Kindergarten in the same schools were randomly assigned to classes of 13–15, to classes of 22–25 with a teacher's aide, or to classes of 25 without a teacher's aide. In the early studies, these students were followed through grade 3. In practice, the small classes ranged in size from 13 to 18 and the large classes from 22 to 28. It is worth noting that even the larger classes were smaller than most classes in those grades in Tennessee at the time. The smaller classes performed substantially better by the end of second grade in test scores, grades, and fewer disciplinary referrals.[4]

The gains lasted. The students that had been assigned to smaller classes were more likely to graduate in four years, more likely to go to college, and more likely to get a degree in a STEM field. The positive effect was twice as large for poor and minority students, and thus narrowed the achievement gap. The original STAR study and follow-up reports, called the *Lasting Benefits Studies*, and subsequent *Project Challenge*[5] had an impact in the political arena. President Bill Clinton proposed a $12 billion class-size reduction program in his 1998 State of the Union address that was subsequently adopted by Congress.

Molnar et al. (1996–2001), in a well-designed series of five annual evaluations of the Wisconsin Student Achievement Guarantee in Education class-size reduction program utilizing a quasi-experimental design, reproduced the STAR results.[6] With class sizes of 15, they found significant and substantial effect sizes of 0.2 standard deviations, indicating that class size was a very effective school improvement strategy. Gains were greatest for African American students, and teachers reported better classroom climates and fewer discipline problems. The continuation of small class sizes into the higher grades increased its impact. But cost considerations resulted in class-size reduction activities being concentrated in the lower grades, mostly among economically deprived and children of color.[7]

Over the years, Erik Hanushek of the Hoover Institute has taken a more skeptical look. He performed a "meta-analysis" of 277 studies in 1997, claiming that class-size reduction was not an effective school reform strategy. He argued that class sizes have dropped over the last half of the twentieth century with no corresponding increase in achievement scores.[8] In summary:

> Surely class size reductions are beneficial in specific circumstances—for specific groups of students, subject matters, and teachers. Second, class size reductions necessarily involve hiring more teachers, and teacher quality is much more important than class size in affecting student outcomes. Third, class size reduction is very expensive, and little or no consideration is given to alternative and more productive uses of those resources.[9] (p. 5)

Hanushek's analysis was criticized on methodological grounds in that he gave more weight to studies that showed no impact from lowering class size, while also treating weak studies as equivalent to those that were experimental and/or of much higher quality. He was also questioned about his claim that teacher quality was more important than class size in affecting student outcomes. Moreover, in reanalyzing the Tennessee STAR data, Alan Krueger not only concluded that class-size reduction had economic benefits that outweighed the costs, and even within the large cohort of 22–25 students, the smaller the class, the better the student outcomes.[10] Mosteller also reported sustained effects and "the effect size for minorities was about double that for majorities."[11]

Krueger noted, as have many others, that class-size reduction most benefits minority and disadvantaged students and would be expected to narrow the racial achievement gap by about ⅓. He also estimated that the economic gains of smaller classes in the early grades outweighed the costs two to one.[12] While experimental studies have not been done for the middle and upper grades, there are many controlled studies, including longitudinal studies, showing gains in student outcomes for smaller classes at these grade levels.[13] Many of these studies also show improvements in student engagement, lower dropout rates and better noncognitive skills. One longitudinal study revealed that smaller classes in eighth grade led to improvements in persistence and self-esteem, and that for urban schools, the economic benefits from investing in smaller classes would likely save nearly twice the cost. A study done for the US Department of Education analyzed the achievement levels of students in 2,561 schools, as measured by performance on the NAEP (national) exams. After controlling for student background, the only objective factor found to be positively correlated with student performance was class size. Student achievement was even more strongly linked to smaller classes in the upper grades.[14]

In recent work (2015), Jackson, Johnson, and Persico investigated the effects of school finance reform in 28 states. They followed the infusion of new money between 1970 and 2010, and found, ". . . a 10% increase in per-pupil spending each year for all 12 years of public school leads to 0.27 more completed years of education, 7.25 percent higher wages, and a 3.67 percentage-point reduction in the annual incidence of adult poverty." They concluded that the gains were achieved primarily by lower student-to-teacher ratios, increases in teacher salaries, and longer school years. Gains were strongest for economically disadvantaged children and were sufficient to eliminate from ⊠ to 100 percent of the adult outcome gaps (i.e., wages, education level, and percent in poverty) between those raised in poor and nonpoor families.[15]

Overall, the literature on class-size reduction is clear and positive. The "overwhelming majority" of peer-reviewed papers find it an effective strategy.[16]

Further Policy Considerations

Supply of Teachers

An oft-heard reservation about class-size reduction is that there are not enough well-qualified teachers to make the system work. However, in California's billion-dollar class-size reduction initiative, achievement increased for all groups, but there was little or no evidence that the need to hire more teachers led to lower quality teachers in the long run. When the Los Angeles Unified School District needed to triple its hiring of elementary teachers following the state's class-size reduction initiative, there was no reduction in mean teacher effectiveness.[17] In addition, some studies point to lower teacher attrition rates when class sizes are reduced, which would likely lead to a more experienced and effective teaching force overall.[18]

Wash-out Effects

Most of the research has been conducted in the early grades (K–3). This led some to questioning whether the effects are lasting or are cost-effective.[19] Though Harris contended the effects wash out by seventh grade,[20] Krueger and Schanzenbach found gains in college entrance exams and especially among minority students. In fact, they concluded that small classes through eighth grade cut the achievement gap by 54 percent.[21] Dynarski et al. found gains in college attendance, graduation rate, and a higher likelihood of graduating with a STEM degree.[22] Jackson, Johnson, and Persico found sustained long-term social and economic effects in their 28-state work. Chetty et al. found that students from smaller classes in kindergarten had a greater likelihood of attending college, owning a home, and holding a 401K more than 20 years later.[23]

Noncognitive Effects

In addition to the gains listed above, college attendance, graduation rate, student engagement, persistence, and self-esteem is reported as higher.[24] The gains in test scores are attributed to the greater individualization of instruction, better classroom control and, thus, better climate. Teachers have more time for individual interactions with children, consulting with parents, and giving greater attention to grading papers.[25]

As Compared to Other Reforms

There is little evidence indicating that other reforms would be more effective at a lower cost.[26] While teacher quality is undoubtedly important, those who argue that improving teacher quality would be more cost-effective present no comparative data from experimental or controlled studies.

Recommendations[27]

- Class size is an important determinant of student outcomes, and one that can be directly determined by policy. All else being equal, lowering class sizes will improve student outcomes.
- The payoff from class-size reduction is greater for low-income and minority children. Conversely, increases in class size are likely to be especially harmful to these populations—who are already more likely to be subjected to large classes.
- While lowering class size has a demonstrable cost, it may prove the more cost-effective policy overall particularly for disadvantaged students. Money saved today by increasing class sizes will likely result in additional substantial social and educational costs in the future.[28]
- Generally, class sizes between 15 and 18 are recommended, but variations are indicated. For example, band and physical education may require large classes, while special education and some laboratory classes may require less.

Notes and References

1. *Public School Expenditures* (2016, May). Washington, DC: National Center for Education Statistics. Retrieved May 26, 2016, from http://nces.ed.gov/programs/coe/indicator_cmb.asp

2. Glass, G. V., & Smith, M. L. (1979). Meta-analysis of research on class size and achievement. *Educational Evaluation and Policy Analysis*, *1*(1), 2–16.

Chingos, M., & Whitehurst, G. (2011). *Class size: What research says and what it means for state* policy. Washington, DC: Brown Center on Education Policy at the Brookings Institution. Retrieved May 28, 2016, from http://www.brookings.edu/research/papers/2011/05/11-class-size-whitehurst-chingos

3. Glass, G. V., & Smith, M. L. (1979). Meta-analysis of research on class size and achievement. *Educational Evaluation and Policy Analysis*, *1*(1), 2–16.

4. Finn, J. D., & Achilles, C. M. (1999). Tennessee's class size study: Findings, implications, and misconceptions. *Educational Evaluation and Policy Analysis*, *21*(2), 97–110.

5. Mosteller, F. (2008). The Tennessee study of class size in the early school grades. *The Future of Children*, 113–126. Retrieved June 8, 2016, from https://www.princeton.edu/futureofchildren/publications/docs/05_02_08.pdf

6. Molnar, A., Smith, P., Zahorik, J., Palmer, A., Halbach, A., & Ehrle, K. (1999). Evaluating the SAGE program: A pilot program in targeted pupil-teacher reduction in Wisconsin. *Educational Evaluation and Policy Analysis*, *21*(2), 165–177. Retrieved May 28, 2016, from http://epsl.asu.edu/sage/documents/evalsage.pdf

Maier, P., Molnar, A., Percy, S., Smith, P., & Zahorik, J. (1997, December). *First year results of the student achievement guarantee in education program.* Milwaukee, WI: Center for Education Research, Analysis, and Innovation. Retrieved June 7, 2016, from http://nepc.colorado.edu/publication/first-year-results-student-achievement-guarantee-education-program

Molnar, A., Smith, P., & Zahorik, J. (1998, December). *1997–98 Evaluation results of the Student Achievement Guarantee in Education (SAGE) program.* Milwaukee, WI: Center for Education Research, Analysis, and Innovation. Retrieved June 7, 2016, from http://nepc.colorado.edu/publication/1997-98-evaluation-results-student-achievement-guarantee-education-sage-program

Molnar, A., Smith, P., & Zahorik, J. (1999, December). *Evaluation Results of the Student Achievement Guarantee in Education (SAGE) Program, 1998–99.* Milwaukee, WI: Center for Education Research,

Analysis, and Innovation. Retrieved June 7, 2016, from http://nepc.colorado.edu/publication/1998-99-evaluationresults-of-student-achievement-guarantee-education-sage-program

Zahorik, J., Smith, P., & Molnar, A. (2000, December). *1999–2000 Evaluation results of the Student Achievement Guarantee in Education (SAGE) program.* Milwaukee, WI: Center for Education Research, Analysis, and Innovation. Retrieved June 7, 2016, from http://nepc.colorado.edu/publication/1999-2000-evaluation-results-student-achievement-guarantee-education-sage-program

Molnar, A., Smith, P., & Zahorik, J. (2001, December). *2000–2001 Evaluation results of the Student Achievement Guarantee in Education (SAGE) program.* Milwaukee, WI: Center for Education Research, Analysis, and Innovation. Retrieved June 7, 2016, from http://nepc.colorado.edu/publication/2000-2001-evaluation-results-student-achievement-guarantee-education-sage-program

7. Betts, J. R., & Shkolnik, J. L. (1999). The behavioral effects of variations in class size: The case of math teachers. *Educational Evaluation and Policy Analysis, 21*(2), 193–213.

Rice, J. K. (1999). The impact of class size on instructional strategies and the use of time in high school mathematics and science courses. *Educational Evaluation and Policy Analysis, 21*(2), 215–229.

8. Hanushek, E. (1997). Assessing the effects of school resources on student performance: An update. *Educational Evaluation and Policy Analysis, 19*(2), 141–164.

9. Hanushek, E. (February 1998). *The evidence on class size.* Occasional Paper Number 98-1. Wallis Institute of Political Economy. University of Rochester. Retrieved May 28, 2016, from http://hanushek.stanford.edu/sites/default/files/publications/Hanushek%201998%20HouseTestimony%20Class%20Size.pdf

Hanushek, E. (2002). Evidence, politics and the class size debate. In L. Mishel & R. Rothstein (Eds.), *The class size debate.* Washington, DC: Economic Policy Institute. Retrieved June 5, 2016, from http://hanushek.stanford.edu/sites/default/files/publications/Hanushek%202002%20ClassSizeDebate.pdf

10. Krueger, A. (2002). *Economic considerations and class size.* NBER Working Paper No. 8875. Retrieved June 5, 2016, from http://www.nber.org/papers/w8875

11. Mosteller, F. (2008, May). The Tennessee study of class size in the early school grades. *The Future of Children, 5*(2), 117. Retrieved June 8, 2016, from https://www.princeton.edu/futureofchildren/publications/docs/05_02_08.pdf

12. Krueger, A. (2002). A response to Eric Hanushek's "Evidence Politics, and the Class Size debate." In L. Mishel & R. Rothstein (Eds.), *The class size debate.* Washington, DC: Economic Policy Institute. Retrieved June 5, 2016, from http://hanushek.stanford.edu/sites/default/files/publications/Hanushek%202002%20ClassSizeDebate.pdf

13. Dustmann, C., et al. (2015). Class Size, Education and Wages. *Journal of Labor Economics, 33*(3), 711–750.

Fredriksson, P., Öckert, B., & Oosterbeek, H. (2011). Long-term effects of class size. IZA Discussion Paper # 5879. Retrieved June 6, 2016, from http://ftp.iza.org/dp5879.pdf

Babcock, P., & Betts, J. (2009). Reduced class distinctions: Effort, ability, and the education production Function. *Journal of Urban Economics, 65,* 314–322. Retrieved June 6, 2016, from http://econweb.ucsd.edu/~jbetts/Pub/A60%20babcock%20and%20betts%20JUE%202009.pdf

Blatchford, P., Bassett, P., & Brown, P. (2008). *Do low attaining and younger students benefit most from small classes? Results from a systematic observation study of class size effects on pupil classroom engagement and teacher pupil interaction.* Paper delivered to the American Educational Research Association Annual Meeting, New York. Retrieved June 6, 2016, from http://www.classsizematters.org/wp-content/uploads/2011/04/Blatchford_2008.pdf

14. McLaughlin, D., & Drori, G. (2000). *School-level correlates of academic achievement: Student assessment scores in SASS Public Schools.* U.S. Department of Education. National Center for Education Statistics NCES 303. Retrieved June 6, 2016, from http://nces.ed.gov/pubs2000/2000303.pdf

15. Jackson, C. K., Johnson, R. C., & Persico, C. (2015). *The effects of school spending on educational and economic outcomes: Evidence from school finance reforms* (No. w20847). Cambridge, MA: National Bureau of Economic Research. Retrieved June 1, 2016, from http://www.nber.org/papers/w20847

16. Zyngier, D. (2014). Class size and academic results, with a focus on children from culturally, linguistically and economically disenfranchised communities. *Evidence Base, 2014*(1). Retrieved June 5, 2016, from http://www.classsizematters.org/wp-content/uploads/2014/05/EvidenceBase2014Issue1.pdf

17. Jepsen, C., & Rivken, S. (2009). Class reduction and student achievement: The potential tradeoff between teacher quality and class size. *Journal of Human Resources, 44*(1), 223–250.

    Gordon, R., Kane, T., & Staiger, D. (April 2006). *Identifying effective teachers using performance on the job*. Hamilton Project, Retrieved June 6, 2016 from http://www.brookings.edu/views/papers/200604hamilton_1.pdf

18. Isenberg, E. (2010, February). *The effect of class size on teacher attrition: Evidence from class size reduction policies in New York State*, US Census Bureau Center for Economic Studies, Paper No. CESWP-10-05.

    Bohrnstedt, G., & Stecher, B. (2002, September). *What we have learned about class size reduction in California, technical appendix, APPENDIX C: Class size reduction and teacher migration*. Retrieved June 6, 2016, from http://www.classiz.org/techreport/CSRYear4_final.pdf

19. Clinton Demands $1.4 Billion to Reduce Class Size. (1999, April). *Education Reporter, 159*. Retrieved May 30, 2016, from http://www.eagleforum.org/educate/1999/apr99/class_size.html

20. Harris, D. (2007). Class size and school size: Taking the trade-offs seriously. In F. Hess & T. Loveless (Eds.), *Brookings papers on education Policy 2006-2007 (137-61)*. Washington, DC: Brookings Institution.

21. Krueger, A., & Whitmore, D. (2000, April). *The Effect of attending a small class in the early grades on college-test taking and middle school test results: Evidence from Project STAR*. Working Paper 7656. Retrieved May 30, 2016, from http://www.nber.org/papers/w7656

22. Dynarski, S., Hyman, J., & Schanzenbach, D. (2011, October 16). *Experimental evidence on the effect of childhood investments on postsecondary attainment and degree completion*. Retrieved June 5, 2016, from http://www.classsizematters.org/wp-content/uploads/2012/10/dynarski-120426.pdf

23. Chetty, R., et al. (2010, September). How does your kindergarten classroom affect your earnings? Evidence from project star. *The Quarterly Journal of Economics, 126*(4), 1593–1660. Retrieved June 6, 2016, from http://qje.oxfordjournals.org/content/126/4/1593.full

24. Dee, T., & West, M. (2011). The non-cognitive returns to class size. *Educational Evaluation and Policy Analysis, 33*(1), 23–46.

25. Maier, P., Molnar, A., Percy, S., Smith, P., & Zahorik, J. (1997). *First year results of the student achievement guarantee in education program*. Retrieved May 30, 2016, from http://nepc.colorado.edu/files/yearend97_0.pdf

26. Chingos, M., & Whitehurst, G. (2011, May 11). *Class size: What research says and what it means for state policy*. Washington, DC: Brookings Institute. Retrieved June 5, 2016, from http://www.brookings.edu/research/papers/2011/05/11-class-size-whitehurst-chingos

27. Schanzenbach, D.W. (2014). *Does class size matter?* Boulder, CO: National Education Policy Center. Retrieved May 30, 2016, from http://nepc.colorado.edu/publication/does-class-size-matter

28. Schanzenbach, D.W. (2014). Does class size matter? Boulder, CO: National Education Policy Center. Retrieved May 30, 2016, from http://nepc.colorado.edu/publication/does-class-size-matter

*This is a section of **Research-Based Options for Education Policy-making**, a multipart brief that takes up a number of important policy issues and identifies policies supported by research. Each section focuses on a different issue, and its recommendations to policy makers are based on the latest scholarship. **Research-Based Options for Education Policy-making** is published by The National Education Policy Center and is made possible in part by funding from the Great Lakes Center for Education Research and Practice.*

The National Education Policy Center (NEPC), housed at the University of Colorado Boulder School of Education, produces and disseminates high-quality, peer-reviewed research to inform education policy *discussions*. Visit us at: http://nepc.colorado.edu.

WILLIAM J. MATHIS is the managing director of the National Education Policy Center at the University of Colorado Boulder and the former superintendent of schools for the Rutland Northeast Supervisory Union in Brandon Vermont.

Christopher Jepsen

 **NO**

Class Size: Does It Matter for Student Achievement?

Smaller classes are often associated with increased achievement, but the evidence is far from universal

Elevator Pitch

Numerous economic studies have considered the relationship between class size and student achievement, the majority of which have focused on elementary schools in the US and Europe. While the general finding is that smaller classes are associated with increased student achievement, a few high-quality studies find no relationship. Further, empirical research on the costs and benefits of smaller classes concludes that other education policies,

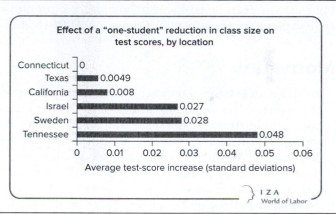

Sources: Connecticut [1]; Texas [2]; California [3]; Israel [4]; Sweden [5]; Tennessee [6] and [7].

Key Findings

Pros

- In general, smaller classes are associated with increased student achievement, usually measured by standardized tests in multiple subjects such as mathematics and reading.

- There are benefits of smaller class sizes when variation in class size (due to maximum class-size rules) and random fluctuations in population are taken into consideration.

- The positive relationship between smaller class size and student achievement holds for students in different grades as well as in different countries and across continents.

- Reducing class size is a clear education policy that is popular with students, parents, teachers, and policymakers, and hence easy to argue for.

Cons

- Several high-quality studies find no relationship between class size and student achievement.

- Reducing class size is a very expensive policy reform relative to other reforms, which may also provide better value.

- Because most studies focus on elementary schools, much less is known about the relationship between class size and student achievement in secondary schools.

- Reducing class size in many schools in developing countries is unlikely to improve achievement as these schools have more fundamental challenges, such as high teacher absenteeism.

such as tutoring, early childhood programs, or improving teacher quality would be better investments.

Author's Main Message

Reducing class size is a popular education policy measure with parents, teachers, and policymakers. However, research shows that reducing class size leads to, in most cases, only modest improvements in student achievement. Also, students in early grades appear to gain more from smaller classes than older students. Despite extensive research on class size, much about this relationship is still unknown. Policymakers should be aware that reducing class sizes can be costly, is no guarantee of improved achievement, and is only one of many possible reforms.

Motivation

Class size is an extremely popular education reform among many stakeholders, including students, parents, teachers, school administrators, and educationalists. With such broad appeal, reducing class size is also popular among policymakers. Intuitively, students in smaller classes should have better learning outcomes than students in larger classes—for example, the teacher can provide more individualized attention in smaller classes, and classroom discipline is easier with fewer students [6].

At the same time, reducing class size is an expensive education policy. For example, a class-size reduction policy instituted in California in 1996 reduced class size from an average of 30 students per class to a maximum of 20 students per class, but as a result increased the number of teachers by approximately half [3]. To illustrate this calculation, consider a grade with 60 students; the legislation would increase the number of teachers from two to three, which is an increase of 50%. Teacher salaries constitute the vast majority of schools' non-capital expenses, and in the first two years of California's class-size reduction, over 25,000 additional teachers were hired.

Research indicates that the costs of reducing class size are more likely to exceed the benefits and that other education policies, such as tutoring, early childhood programs, or improving teacher quality, would be better investments [6].

In addition, a simple comparison of achievement across classrooms of different sizes will not reflect the true relationship between class size and student achievement, for a number of reasons. For example, in the US, where the biggest source of funding is local property tax revenue, schools in wealthier areas are more likely to have smaller classes and higher achievement due to students'

more advantaged backgrounds, rather than being a casual effect of smaller classes [6]. In contrast, if a school provides smaller classes for its most "at-risk" students, the result would be higher achievement in the larger classes, again for reasons unrelated to class size.

Therefore, a rigorous analysis of the causal relationship between class size and student achievement is complicated, as the number of students in each classroom is not determined randomly. And while smaller classes are generally associated with higher student achievement, the evidence is not universal.

Discussion of Pros and Cons

Influential Research

It is quite challenging to isolate the effect of class size from other determinants of student achievement, as schools explicitly decide class sizes, and they often base class-size decisions, as well as the assignment of specific students to classes of different sizes, on prior student achievement (i.e., test scores). Consequently, researchers view the class-size experiment conducted in Tennessee in the late 1980s as the highest-quality study on the topic. Over 11,000 students and their teachers were randomly assigned between small classes of 15 students and regular classes of 23 students [6]. If it is assumed that class-size effects are linear (in order to make comparisons between studies with difference changes in class size), then the "per-pupil" effect of the Tennessee experiment was 0.048 standard deviations [6], [7]. In other words, each "one-student" reduction in class size is associated with an increase in student achievement of 0.048 standard deviations.

However, the bulk of research on the relationship between class size and student achievement is based on techniques other than random experiments. Such studies, often called "quasi-experimental" or "non-experimental," attempt to isolate the effect of class size in several ways. One compelling way, first used in an analysis of Israeli schools, is to focus on small changes in student enrollment that correspond with changes in the number of teachers, thus leading to differences in class size [4]. This approach is often called the "maximum class-size rule" (or Maimonides' Rule, after the 12th-century scholar who proposed it).

As an example of this, in Israel, the maximum number of students in a classroom is 40. This means that a school with 39 people in a grade has one teacher with a class size of 39, whereas a school with 42 people in a grade has two teachers with an average class size of 21. The underlying idea is that natural fluctuations in area population generate potentially large, and presumably random, changes in average class size. However, researchers and policymakers using this type of analysis should carefully investigate the extent to which these fluctuations in class size appear to be random. The study for Israel is very carefully investigated and shows that smaller classes are associated with sizable improvements in achievement for fifth-grade students, but with smaller effects for fourth-grade students. In terms of a "per-student" reduction, the effect is around 0.036 standard deviations for fifth grade and approximately 0.018 for fourth grade [4].

Another technique that has been frequently used is to study yearly fluctuations in class size, thereby attempting to isolate presumably random changes in class size that occur as a result of student population variation (i.e., students moving into and out of schools and classrooms). This approach typically involves using detailed data on a large number of students over multiple years, as a given grade or school may have very little fluctuation between one year and the next. This approach was first applied to data on students in late elementary grades in Texas [2]. In the fifth grade, a one-student reduction in class size is associated with an increase of 0.0055 standard deviations in mathematics and 0.0043 standard deviations in reading (in their most sophisticated analyses). In the sixth and seventh grades, the authors could not refute the proposition that class size is unrelated to student achievement. This approach has also been used to estimate the effect of class-size reduction in California, with effects of 0.006–0.01 standard deviations for third grade reading and mathematics, respectively [3].

A similar approach looked instead at variations in the population of school-age children, rather than the actual student population. Estimates from this approach are much smaller than those using more detailed student-level data. In Connecticut, for example, there is no evidence that reductions in class size are associated with gains in student achievement, using data from the 1980s and 1990s [1]. The results are similar when using the maximum class-size rule, referred to earlier.

Further Evidence in the US

A class-size reduction program was also conducted in Florida. This was undertaken across all grades (as opposed to the Californian study, which focuses on kindergarten through third grade) and had both district-level and school-level components. The results show little, if any, improvement in achievement resulting from the reductions in class size [8].

In Minnesota, researchers used changes in the school-age population (as opposed to the actual school population) to study the relationship between elementary school class size and student achievement. However, over half the schools have missing data on either the school-age population or the class size. Among the schools without missing data, a "one-student" reduction in class size is associated with smaller achievement gains than those found in the most influential studies of class size.

Several studies use state-level datasets with detailed information on class size and student achievement, as well as student demographic information and information on teachers. These data typically cover entire school districts, or even states, such as New York, North Carolina, and San Diego. The data are available for multiple years. With these data, researchers studied the determinants of student achievement in general, often with a focus on teacher characteristics. Almost all of these studies include class size, even if it is not the main focus of the analysis. The majority of these studies find a negative relationship between class size and student achievement as measured by standardized test scores, indicating that the bigger the class size the lower the test scores. In other words, the research typically concludes that smaller classes are associated with higher student achievement.

Studies in Europe

In Europe, the most influential studies use the maximum class-size rule. In Sweden, a "one-student" reduction in class size in grades four to six is associated with an increase in test scores in mathematics and Swedish, at ages 13 and 16, of 0.023–0.033 standard deviations respectively [5]. Similarly, in France, numerous researchers have applied this technique and identified a smaller, positive relationship between smaller classes and student achievement, both in elementary and secondary grades [9]. Two studies in Denmark, using different data sets and statistical techniques, also demonstrate small benefits of reduced class sizes for both test scores and year of schooling.

However, the findings from Europe are far from universal. A study of 11 countries, predominantly in Europe, shows substantial cross-country variation in the relationship between class size and student achievement, with most countries having a small or no benefit from smaller class sizes [10]. In Norway, two studies using the maximum class-size rule obtain different results. One study finds a positive effect of smaller class sizes on student achievement in the early years of secondary school, whereas another study, using similar methods (on a larger data set), essentially finds no effect. Using a variant of the maximum class size based on the government's school funding formula, researchers were not able to discern a clear relationship between class size and student achievement for fourth, sixth, and eighth grade students in the Netherlands.

Studies Outside the US and Europe

Class-size research is rare outside the US and Europe. In Japan, smaller classes are associated with higher achievement in fourth and sixth grades, but there is no evidence of a positive relationship for ninth grade. As of July 2015, there are, to the author's best knowledge, no studies on class size in Canada, Australia, or New Zealand in the main database of economics literature, EconLit (https://www.aeaweb.org/econlit/).

In developing countries, few high-quality studies of class size exist. One of these high-quality investigations is for Bolivia, which finds a positive relationship between student achievement and smaller classes [11].

In general, the problem of isolating the effect of smaller classes from other factors is more challenging in developing countries than in developed countries. Basic services, such as having a teacher (or even a substitute teacher) are often missing in schools in many locations. If the teacher is not present, then the size of the class is irrelevant.

In Kenya, for example, a reduction in class size from 82 to 44 is not associated with improved achievement, but the use of a locally hired contract teacher (i.e., a teacher who is hired on an annual, renewable contract) is associated with improved achievement. The likely explanation for this is that absenteeism is much lower among contract teachers.

Therefore, in many developing countries, more fundamental issues, such as adequate staffing and facilities, need to be addressed before focusing attention on possible class size effects on student achievement.

Do Certain Types of Students Benefit More Than Others?

The takeaway message from the existing research is that smaller classes are associated with improved student achievement more often than not, though some high-quality studies find no relationship. But what does past research tell us about whether some students benefit more than others from smaller classes?

As with the overall pattern of results, smaller classes do not clearly benefit (or harm) specific groups of students. The studies finding no relationship between class size and achievement generally report analyses for different types of student groups, and none of them finds that any particular group of students would benefit significantly more from smaller classes.

The closest thing to consensus on class-size effects is that when smaller classes are beneficial, they tend to be more beneficial for younger students than for older students. This finding is demonstrated, for example, by empirical research in Texas and Japan.

Some evidence suggests that disadvantaged students receive larger benefits, as shown in the class-size experiment in Tennessee and the maximum class-size rule in Israel [4], [5]. However, this pattern of results is not echoed elsewhere in the literature. In Europe, the effects do not appear to differ much by student demographics such as gender, parental income, race, and ethnicity. In Japan, the benefits associated with smaller class sizes appear to be larger for wealthy students and for class sizes under 20 students.

Cost–Benefit Analysis

It is important to measure the potential benefits of smaller classes against their costs. Assuming there is no change in enrollment, a reduction in class size corresponds with an increase in the number of classrooms. Thus, the two primary costs of reducing class sizes are the cost of additional teachers and the cost of creating additional classroom space. On this basis, studies from the US suggest that each "one-student" reduction in class size has a cost of $200–250 per pupil [6]. However, it is important to consider that there may also be additional costs involved, such as electricity and other costs of operation.

Another approach in estimating costs is a simple "back-of-the-envelope" calculation, with the assumption that all costs are variable. In other words, a 10% reduction in class size would produce a 10% increase in per-student costs. Under this simplistic approach, the estimated cost of a "one-student" reduction in class size is even higher, in excess of $400 per student [6].

In addition, a comprehensive cost–benefit analysis of smaller classes should include all benefits of smaller classes, including short- as well as longer-term improvements in achievement. These benefits would also include future values for students, such as increased earnings, decreased unemployment, improved health, etc.

US studies that compare costs and benefits usually find that the total benefits of smaller class sizes—not just the benefits associated with improved achievement—do not exceed the costs. Even in the study with the largest effects of smaller classes (the experiment in Tennessee), the benefits are roughly equal to the costs [6], [7]. In other programs, where the perceived benefits are noticeably smaller, the benefits are even lower relative to the costs.

The cost–benefit ratio seems even less favorable in Europe, where the predicted effects of smaller classes are less consistent than in US studies. That being said, however, the study from Sweden argues that the benefits of smaller classes do exceed the costs [5]. This study follows students from school until they are middle-aged. It can therefore directly estimate the increase in wages associated with reduced class sizes. The corresponding estimates show larger wage increases than the indirect effects used elsewhere in the literature; this includes indirect effects measured in Sweden (when the actual wage data are not used). Although other studies do not explicitly model the cost–benefit analysis, the smaller benefits of class size suggest that the benefits do not significantly outweigh the costs. However, the study from Sweden shows that predicting the effects of smaller classes on future wages will produce "estimated" wage gains that are smaller than the "actual" wage gains. It is unclear whether researchers would find a similar relationship in other countries.

The "Opportunity Cost" of Reducing Class Size

So far, the discussion of costs and benefits has been in terms of monetary costs. An *economic* cost–benefit analysis, however, would compare the benefits and costs of class size to those of an alternative use of the money [6]. The comparison with the "next-best" alternative use of money is known in economics as the "opportunity cost." With this in mind, given that the benefits of reducing class size do not exceed the costs in nearly all studies, a rational conclusion would be that smaller class sizes do not exceed the benefits of the next-best alternative: i.e., that the "opportunity cost" is not significant.

For most of the studies reviewed in this contribution, the costs of reducing class size generally exceed the benefits, with the exception of the study from Sweden [5]. Studies looking at the costs and benefits of smaller classes (i.e., the "opportunity cost" of reducing class size) have concluded that other education policies, such as tutoring, early childhood programs, or improving teacher quality, would be better investments [6]. For example, the study of class size and teacher characteristics in Texas concluded that improving teacher quality, such as replacing the most ineffective teachers, would have significantly large returns—much larger than any conceivable class-size reduction program [2]. However, in many countries, including the US, the ability to replace low-quality teachers is complicated by the tenure system, which protects teachers from dismissal; teachers with tenure are quite difficult, if not impossible, to remove from their positions. Alternatively, reassigning ineffective, tenured teachers to non-classroom duties is very expensive.

Limitations and Gaps

The Tennessee experiment is considered the "gold standard" for class-size research, in large part because it is the only sizable class-size experiment that has been conducted since the early 20th century. However, even random experiments, such as this, have their limitations. Fewer than half the students randomly assigned to small or regular classes in kindergarten or pre-school are recorded in the data four years later [6], [7]. Hence it is not possible to track students over time. In addition, only schools with at least three classrooms per grade are included in the study, which results in an overrepresentation of urban schools and of schools with sizable non-white student populations. Both are likely to bias results.

Another potential concern is that teachers assigned to smaller classes may exert extra effort to increase the likelihood of being assigned to smaller classes in the future [1], [6]. However, there is evidence that, even among the regular classes, those with slightly smaller class sizes have better student outcomes than those with larger class sizes [6], [7].

Studies using other techniques, such as the maximum class-size rule, also have their limitations. The studies in Sweden and Bolivia are limited to smaller schools, so it is not clear whether class size has similar effects in larger schools in these countries [5], [8]. One study from Japan is based on one year of data (2002) only, while another study is limited to the city of Yokohama. Again, there are concerns about whether the class-size effects are similar in other years and in other parts of Japan.

Another major limitation is the issue of "external validity." In other words, it is not clear to what extent the results from one study in one location or time period can inform the likely benefits of smaller classes in a different location or time period, or in a school of a different size or in a different country.

To illustrate the point, consider two of the highest-quality studies: the Tennessee experiment and the Israeli study using the maximum class-size rule. In Tennessee, the class-size experiment compared students in "regular" classes of 23 with students in "small" classes of 15. In Israel, the maximum class-size rule is 40 students. Therefore, one of the smallest possible class sizes in Israel—21 students (say in a grade of 42 students)—would be considered a "regular" class size in Tennessee (or elsewhere, such as Denmark). The few high-quality studies that exist only study a small set of possible changes in class size. Consequently, research provides only little insight on the effectiveness of class size across the possible, or even probable, distribution of class sizes. Researchers simply cannot identify the optimal class size (yet).

Another fundamental gap in the literature is the lack of high-quality studies in secondary schools [6]. Given the above concerns regarding external validity, the studies from primary schools are of little use when evaluating the relationship between class size and student achievement in secondary schools, particularly in the later grades of secondary school (grades 10–12). One challenge in studying class size in secondary school is that, in most locations, students in secondary schools have different teachers for different subjects. For outcomes such as subject-matter test scores, the class size in that subject is the most relevant, but the relevant class-size measure for overall outcomes, such as graduation or grade-point-average, is less clear.

An additional gap in the research is the absence of studies in many locations. Clearly, more high-quality research is needed in places where little, if any, such research is currently available, such as in Germany or Australia. However, identifying the relationship between class size and achievement can be challenging in some settings. For example, many schools in Ireland, particularly in urban areas, have very little variation in class size due to school policies. Consequently, the techniques used elsewhere, such as the maximum class-size rule, are unlikely to work in Ireland, as there may not be enough classrooms with different sizes to compare achievement.

Summary and Policy Advice

In summary, smaller classes are generally associated with higher student achievement, but the evidence is far from unanimous. The few studies that find no effect of smaller classes use data from similar (if not identical) locations to studies that find positive effects of smaller classes. The studies, by and large, use the same statistical techniques. Thus, advocates of smaller classes cannot simply dismiss the studies finding no effect as being somehow inferior or being confined to particular locations. Instead, the conclusion for policymakers and researchers is that reducing class sizes is no guarantee of improved achievement, even though the majority of past research finds such a positive relationship.

Even in situations where smaller class sizes are associated with improved student achievement, resources may be better spent on other reforms, such as teacher "quality" (as opposed to teacher "quantity").

In general, the effectiveness of education reforms is difficult—and in some cases virtually impossible—to estimate, especially as these reforms usually overlap. For example, in the late 1990s, California instituted several educational reforms, such as expanded school accountability, in addition to reducing class sizes.

Policymakers must also keep in mind that policies designed to change class size are likely to have unintended consequences. In line with this, the class-size reduction program in California led to a dramatic increase in the number of teaching positions in the state. As a consequence, many teachers in low-performing schools in poor neighborhoods left for newly created positions in higher-quality schools in more affluent areas, leaving the low-performing schools to hire new teachers with less experience (and, presumably, less ability) [3].

Also, in response to strong financial incentives to keep class sizes as small as possible, many schools in California combined students from different grades into the same classroom. These multi-grade classrooms tended to have lower achievement than otherwise similar classrooms with students from only one grade.

So, what should policymakers do regarding class size? Many stakeholders in education, including teachers and parents, strongly believe that smaller classes are better for students. However, policymakers should be aware that reducing class size is an expensive reform that will not automatically increase student achievement, although it will likely please teachers, parents, and students. They should consider class size as only one of many possible reforms. A more holistic approach would be to consider the potential costs and benefits of many possible reforms, with the understanding that these costs and benefits are imprecise at best and completely unknown at worst.

Many parts of the world have little or no information on the effectiveness, or ineffectiveness of smaller classes. For developing countries, schools often face more fundamental challenges, such as teacher absenteeism, that will reduce (if not eliminate) any benefits of smaller classes. In these places, policymakers would be better served to solve the more pressing issues before turning their attention to potential class size effects.

If policymakers wish to understand the relationship between class size and student achievement in their area, then the easiest, quickest, and least costly way to determine that is to begin by studying the data available to them. High-quality data increase, but do not ensure, the likelihood that researchers can identify the past relationship between class size and achievement. The possibility of conducting a class-size experiment, as in Tennessee, is extremely challenging and expensive, and it still may not provide conclusive evidence on the effects of smaller classes, even after years of study.

In sum, the relationship between class size and achievement is not clear. Research suggests that policymakers should be aware that reducing class sizes is no guarantee of improved achievement and is only one of many possible reforms.

References

Further Reading

Hanushek, E. A. "Evidence, politics, and the class-size debate." In: Mishel, L., and R. Rothstein (eds).

The Class Size Debate. Washington, DC: Economic Policy Institute, 2002; pp. 37–66.

Hanushek, E. A. "The economic value of higher teacher quality." Economics of Education Review 30:3 (2011): 466–479.

Krueger, A. B. "Understanding the magnitude and effect of class size on student achievement." In: Mishel, L., and R. Rothstein (eds). The Class Size Debate. Washington, DC: Economic Policy Institute, 2002; pp. 7–36.

Key References

1. Hoxby, C. M. "The effects of class size on student achievement: New evidence from population variation." Quarterly Journal of Economics 115:4 (2000): 1239–1285.

2. Angrist, J., and V. Lavy. "Using Maimonides' Rule to estimate the effect of class size on scholastic achievement. Quarterly Journal of Economics 114:2 (1999): 533–575.

3. Rivkin, S. G., E. A. Hanushek, and J. F. Kain. "Teachers, schools, and academic achievement." Econometrica 73:2 (2005): 417–458.

4. Krueger, A. B. "Experimental estimates of education production functions." Quarterly Journal of Economics 114:2 (1999): 497–532.

5. Chingos, M. "The impact of a universal class-size reduction policy: Evidence from Florida's state-wide mandate." Economics of Education Review 31:5 (2012): 543–562.

6. Chingos, M. "Class size and student outcomes: Research and policy implications." Journal of Policy Analysis and Management 32:2 (2013): 411–438.

7. Jepsen, C., and S. Rivkin. "Class size and student achievement: The potential tradeoff between teacher quality and class size." Journal of Human Resources 44:1 (2009): 223–250.

8. Fredriksson, P., B. Öckert, and H. Oosterbeek. "Long-term effects of class size." Quarterly Journal of Economics 128:1 (2013): 249–285.

9. Gary-Bobo, R. J., and M.-B. Mahjoub. "Estimation of class-size effects, using 'Maimonides' Rule' and other instruments: The case of French junior high schools." Annales d'Economie et de Statistique 111–112 (2013): 193–225

10. Wössmann, L., and M. West. "Class-size effects in school systems around the world: Evidence from between-grade variation in TIMSS." European Economic Review 50:3 (2006): 695–736.

11. Urquiola, M. "Identifying class-size effects in developing countries: Evidence from rural Bolivia." Review of Economics and Statistics 88:1 (2006): 171–177.

Online Extras

The full reference list for this article is available from: http://wol.iza.org/articles/class-size-does-it-matter-for-student-achievement

View the evidence map for this article: http://wol.iza.org/articles/class-size-does-it-matter-for-student-achievement/map

CHRISTOPHER JEPSEN is a lecturer and assistant professor at the University College, School of Economics in Dublin, Ireland.

EXPLORING THE ISSUE

Does Class-Size Affect Student Achievement?

Critical Thinking and Reflection

1. Is there current research to support smaller classes in middle school and high school?
2. Are school districts more concerned about their districts' fiscal budget and not so much concerned about student achievement?
3. Should there be a standardized student–teacher ratio per grade level?
4. Draw from your own personal experiences, either in your childhood or as an educator, and reflect on your personal beliefs about smaller class size.
5. Survey a random sampling of students about how class size makes a difference in their learning and then analyze the findings.

Is There Common Ground?

The simple idea of using class size as a strategy to raise student achievement has been tossed about in academia for decades. Although some levels of success have been cited for the very early grades, the debate continues. Researchers have had a hard time isolating and measuring the effects of class size on student achievement. Likewise, there is disagreement on whether any benefits that are found outweigh its costs. It is very expensive. The debate becomes highly politicized and tense during times of tightening budgets.

Smaller classes or reducing class size is naturally very attractive to parents who feel lower numbers translate into higher level of success for their children. Smaller classes are popular with parents, who support it as a strategy for school reform. Politicians who are strong advocates for education are often drawn into the debate in support of small classes and class-size reduction. Many educators feel small classes and class-size reduction efforts are worthy undertakings. But are these just intuitive reflections when compared to the research reviewed by Jepsen and others, which note that several high-quality studies found no relationship between class size and student achievement?

Conversely, it is safe to say that results from researchers, such as Achilles (2012), present evidence suggesting the additional resources expended on class-size reductions do result in gains to student achievement. Further, some of these studies support long-term positive outcomes for students who have been in small classes. While the large literature base on class-size reduction includes some

contradictory conclusions, it also includes those with robust findings that small classes positively impact student achievement.

Rather than looking at conflicting research and feeling obligated to choose a side, common ground for class size can be found with the teacher. A well-prepared and effective teacher in the classroom yields positive academic results, whether in a small or a large classroom.

Poor instructional practices in a small class typically lead to lower levels of competence and student progress. Should the focus of the class-size debate then move to teacher quality? Seeking out and hiring highly qualified teachers, providing effective professional development and supportive instructional resources, and incorporating strong retention practices that include teacher participation in decision-making, competitive pay, and strong supportive instructional leadership are better investments than simply reducing class size. Reducing class size is costly. Failing to account for these costs in comparing the conflicting research on class size's impact on student achievement may cause funding concerns in other important areas. Quality classroom space, opportunities for teachers to work and plan together, and the items noted on supporting high-qualified teachers in the introduction of this issue should not be compromised. The stakes are high when undertaking these initiatives. The argument that it is teacher quality, rather than the size of the class, that drives student achievement provides common sense as well as common ground.

Additional Resources

Achilles, C. (2012). Class size policy: The STAR experiment and related class size studies. *NCPEA Policy Brief*. Retrieved from http://www.ncpeapublications.org/attachments/article/524/ClassSize.pdf

Krasnoff, B. (2014). *What the research says about class size, professional development, and recruitment, induction and retention of highly qualified teachers*. Retrieved from http://www.k12.wa.us/titleiia/program/pubdocs/CompendiumofT2AStrategies.pdf

McKee, G., Sims, K., & Rivkin, S. (2015). Disruption, learning, and the heterogeneous benefits of smaller classes. *Empirical Economics*. 48/3.

National Council of Teachers of English (NCTE). (2014). *Why class size matters today*. Retrieved from http://www.ncte.org/positions/statements/why-class-size-matters

Schanzenbach, D. (2014). *Does class size matter?* Retrieved from http://www.greatlakescenter.org/docs/Policy_Briefs/Schanzenbach_ClassSize.pdf

Whitehurst, G. & Chingos, M. (2011). *Class size: what research says and what it means for state policy*. Retrieved from https://www.brookings.edu/research/class-size-what-research-says-and-what-it-means-for-state-policy/

Internet References . . .

Class Size and Student Achievement

https://www.psychologicalscience.org/journals/pspi/pdf/pspi2_1.pdf?origin=p

Class Size and Student Achievement

http://www.centerforpubliceducation.org/research/class-size-and-student-achievement

Effect of Class Size of Student Achievement in Secondary School

https://pdfs.semanticscholar.org/7a65/1cd5f2c473d26fd153ea1d96c883111dae7a.pdf

Reducing Class Size Is Popular with Parents but Not Education Experts, New Research on CA Program Might Change That

https://www.the74million.org/reducing-class-sizes-is-popular-with-parents-but-not-education-experts-new-research-on-ca-program-might-change-that/

The Class-Size Debate: What the Evidence Means for Education Policy

https://gspp.berkeley.edu/research/featured/the-class-size-debate-what-the-evidence-means-for-education-policy

Selected, Edited, and with Issue Framing Material by:
Glenn L. Koonce, *Regent University*

ISSUE

Does Funding Improve Student Achievement?

YES: Jesse Rothstein, Julien Lafortune, and Diane Whitmore Schanzenbach, from "Can School Finance Reforms Improve Student Achievement?" *Washington Center for Equitable Growth* (2016)

NO: Caitlin Emma, from "Here's Why $7 Billion Didn't Help America's Worst Schools," *Politico* (2015)

Learning Outcomes

After reading this issue, you will be able to:

- Cite the many factors that impact school funding and student achievement.
- Review and explain *the empirical evidence on school choice* and its impact on student achievement.
- Describe the differences between Cost-Function and Production-Function research studies.
- Outline the educational school funding issues since the U.S. Supreme Court *Brown v. Board of Education* case in 1954.
- Explain the socioeconomic factors related to student achievement as described in the *Coleman Report*.

ISSUE SUMMARY

YES: Jesse Rothstein, a PhD candidate at the University of California, Berkley Economics Department, Julien Lafortune, a professor of Public Policy and Economics at the University of California, and Diane Whitmore Schanzenbach, a chair of the Program on Child, Adolescent, and Family Studies at Northwestern's Institute for Policy Research and a senior fellow at the Brookings Institute, find that "money matters for student achievement" and through a new strand of research have found positive effects of additional funding on student achievement.

NO: Caitlin Emma, Politico reporter covering education, inquires as to why the government pumped $3 billion dollars of economic stimulus money into School Improvement Grants when six years later the program failed to produce only modest or no gains in student achievement.

Education is the nation's largest and most important industry, using tax dollars and other sources to develop its product. Investment in education is linked directly to the productivity of the nation. A student's success in school allows for greater opportunities to attain a better job, gains to social mobility, and higher economic status, which ultimately leads to a higher standard of living. To attain and retain these benefits to society, financing education must remain a high priority. The Gallup Poll on the biggest problems facing public education consistently ranks lack of financial support at the top. Unfortunately, there are many unsolved problems with funding mechanisms, equality in funding, funding reform, and funding cuts. The Center on Budget and Policy Priorities maintains that funding is an "urgent priority," reporting that 31 states provided less funding per student in 2014 than in 2008, and 15 have cut their general funding per student over 10 percent (Leachman, Albares, Matterson, & Wallace, 2016, p. 1). In addition, local school districts have cut 297,000 jobs since 2008, while student enrollment has increased by 804,000 during the same time period (Leachman et al., 2016). Much discussion in the public domain results from frequent criticism of America's public school systems as wasteful and inefficient, and that spending has not made schools better.

Even though the Trump administration wants to cut funding, the $67.9 (National Center for Education Statistics, 2018) to $71 (Ujifusa, 2018) billion dollars that the United States will spend in 2019 on public K–12 education (including on average of over $12,00 per student) fuels the ongoing academic debate as to whether or not funding improves student achievement. In the recently passed new education law, the Every Student Succeeds Act requires, for the first time, that states should report to the public on each school's annual per-pupil spending amount (Burnette, 2018). Districts will be reporting by individual school and not the entire school district and could result in some "thorny" (p. 1) technically and political challenges.

Research shows a dichotomy of conclusions regarding the effects of school funding on student achievement. Ample studies support the position that funding improves student achievement. For example, Bruce Baker, a professor in the Graduate School of Education at Rutgers University, wrote in a *Shanker Education Report* (2012) that based on a compilation of empirical evidence in relationships between financial resources and student outcomes, money matters. He asserts, "School resources which cost money are positively associated with student outcomes" (p. 2). "Money matters, of course," states Stanford professor and Hoover Institute Fellow E. Hanushek (as cited in Turner et al., 2016, p. 17):

> Hanushek continues, "make no mistake, money makes a difference in the classroom if money reaches students who need it the most, the increase comes steadily year after year, and the money stays in the classroom paying for training and supporting strong teachers, improving curriculum and keeping class sizes manageable" (pp. 17, 18).

Likewise, there are numerous studies that do not support the position that funding improves student achievement. A classic study on funding and student achievement dates back to the 1966 *Coleman Report* (Coleman, 1966). Coleman found that funding was not closely related to student achievement and that socioeconomic factors were a more accurate predictor. Coleman focused on questions of racial equality by examining student-standardized test scores and the socioeconomic status and education levels of their parents. The debate has continued for decades, as educators envision what additional funds could provide for student achievement. At the same time, many politicians seeking reelection on platforms of tax reduction cite limited public resources and a lack of research indicating increased funding produces higher student achievement. Further complicating this issue are the numerous restraints in compiling and comparing data about funding across 50 states and over 13,500 public school districts, with revenue sources streaming from the federal, state, and local levels (National Center for Education Statistics, 2018). Teacher salaries, funding formulas, priorities in budgets, cost-effectiveness, maintaining and expanding facilities and resources, equalization, school choice, mismanagement, professional development, and impact of legislation and litigation have been identified as some of the concerns with identifying the actual expenditures for K–12 education. Most scholars who take a position on this issue also realize that there are many factors that impact student success in school. Hiring and retaining the best teachers and school leaders, readiness, achievement gaps, class size, demographics, free and reduced lunch, and accountability measures are included as some of the areas that have an impact on student achievement.

Citing a study by Hoffman in 2013, "Districts that are able to expand more funds to pay more teachers, hire more instructional aides, provide more extensive professional development, buy more supplies, better maintain and expand buildings, purchase new equipment and technology tend to have significantly higher test scores which are usually linked to improve readiness for college and career" (p. 5). John Mackenzie (2008, p. 1) from the University of Delaware challenged the common argument that "throwing more money at schools will do little or nothing to improve them." In a study correlating school funding with College Board SAT I scores, Mackenzie found that a "1,000 increase in per-pupil funding would yield a 9.28% increase in SAT I scores" (p. 2). Noting that various participation rates may bias the results when correlating SAT I scores, Makenzie also included National Assessment of Education Progress (NAEP) results in his study. NAEP are nationwide fourth- and eighth-grade student reading and mathematics scores reported and compared state to state. When testing the relationship between scores on the NAEP and per-pupil funding, as reported by the Census Bureau's Public Elementary-Secondary Education Finance Data, there was a positive relationship between funding and student performance (Makenzie, 2008). In addition, Mackenzie (2008) found that for both the SAT I and NAEP, states with higher per-pupil spending outscored states with lower per-pupil spending.

Snell (2013) cites Hanushek's, along with finance attorney A. Lindseth's, extensive body of national and international studies, which found, "Difference in either the absolute spending level or spending increases bear little or no consistent relationship to difference in student achievement" (p. 2). Hanushek observed that decades since the Coleman Report "pouring money into schools does not necessarily fix them" (Turner et al., 2016, p. 1). A highly regarded Cato Institute study, *State Education Trends: Academic Performance and Spending the Last 40 Years,* used U.S. Department of Education data for costs, number of employees, student enrollment, test results, and other figures, and found no relationship between spending and academic outcomes (Coulson, 2014). Andrew Coulson, director for the Center of Education Freedom, lamented after his decade's long body of work that "the takeaway from this study is that what we've done over the last 40 years hasn't worked" (p. 1).

Given the conflicting views from the research on student achievement and funding, the emerging questions for this issue may address ways in which schools spend the money, not how much they spend. Where can the nation get the biggest bang for the instructional buck in advancing student achievement? How many times can

state school funding regulations be overhauled? Should educators change the way success is defined for students? Turner et al. (2016, p. 19) asks, "Is it just about test scores? Or should the focus widen to include wages, incarceration rates, and other life outcomes of kids many years after they have left the nation's schools?" Not all school funding can be expected to improve test scores or result in higher student achievement. Kirabo Jackson, a researcher from Northwestern University's School of Education and Social Policy, states that "important social-emotional skills-sharing, cooperation, persistence—may not show up in a test score, but cultivating them in schools can help a child succeed in later life" (p. 16). This opinion is seriously taken when considered that today the country pays $88,000 a year to incarnate a juvenile, compared to $12,000 a year to educate them. The fiscal costs of incarcerated juveniles to a community are high and they compete with resources needed for schools.

Will the statements "more money will not fix our schools" and "throwing more money at public schools will do little or nothing to fix them" be the continuing mantra for school funding (Mackenzie, 2008, p. 1)? Or, will these myths be debunked, suggesting that most U.S. schools are underfunded? The introduction of this school funding and student achievement issue provides opportunities for debate between spending and academic achievement.

YES

**Julien Lafortune, Jesse Rothstein, and
Diane Whitmore Schanzenbach**

Can School Finance Reforms Improve Student Achievement?

Introduction

The achievement gap between rich and poor students in the United States is large—roughly twice as large as the gap between black and white students—and growing.[1] On average, children from low-income families have lower test scores and rates of high school and college completion, and eventually lower earnings than their peers from higher income families. Addressing these disparities is key to breaking the cycle of poverty and inequality across generations.

Recent education policy discussions have started from the premise that one can't just "throw money at the problem." Instead, solutions to the achievement gap must come from accountability, school choice, or other reforms designed to obtain better outcomes using a fixed set of resources. But largely outside of the public eye, a number of states have made dramatic changes to their finance systems to redirect funding to low-income school districts. Taken together, these reforms are the largest anti-inequality education effort in this country since school desegregation. Are school finance reforms merely a waste of effort? Or does money really matter, and does funding reform have the ability to make a dent in the achievement gap?

Our recent paper, "School Finance Reform and the Distribution of Student Achievement," explores these questions.[2] We examine the impacts of so-called "adequacy"-based finance reforms, designed to ensure that low-income schools have adequate funding to achieve desired outcomes. These reforms began in 1990 in Kentucky, with the Kentucky Education Reform Act. Since then, 26 additional states have enacted their own reforms. We draw on rarely used student-level data from the National Assessment of Educational Progress (NAEP) to identify the effects of these reforms on the relative achievement of students in high- and low-income school districts.

The importance of additional school resources for student achievement has long been debated, with many researchers arguing that school resources do not matter much in explaining differences in student achievement between schools, and therefore that money does not matter.[3] But these studies have generally compared districts or states that spent more to those spending less, without the ability to control for the factors that determined the disparities in funding. As a result, the estimated effect of resources is confounded by other factors (such as student need) and may not identify the true causal effect of additional funding. By examining state-level reforms, we are able to identify the causal effects of funding through reform-induced changes in the resources available to districts. Importantly, these changes in funding are driven by shifts in state policy rather than unobserved local determinants that might confound the effect of funding. We are therefore able to identify the policy-relevant effect of funding: What is the impact of changes in state policies that send funding to low-income districts, often with few or no strings attached?

We show that school resources play a major role in student achievement, and that finance reforms can effect major reductions in inequality between high- and low-income school districts. Accordingly, while states that did not implement reforms have seen growing test score gaps between high- and low-income school districts over the last two decades, states that implemented reforms saw steady declines over the same period. The effect is large: finance reforms raise achievement in the lowest-income school districts by about ⅒ of a standard deviation, closing about ⅕ of the gap between high- and low-income districts. There is no sign that the additional funds are wasted. On the contrary, our estimates indicate that additional funds distributed via finance reforms are more productive than funds targeted to class-size reduction.

School Finance Reforms Increase School Spending in Low-income Districts

Traditionally, U.S. public schools have been funded through local property taxes. Because wealthy families tend to live in communities with larger tax bases and fewer needs, their children's schools have typically spent much more per student than have schools in poor districts.

Beginning in the 1970s, many states reformed their school finance systems to address this inequality. Often reacting to mandates from courts that found local finance systems unconstitutional, states have moved away from funding based primarily on property taxes and have implemented state aid formulas that direct more money to low-income and low-tax-base school districts.

These reforms can be divided into two waves:

In the 1970s and the 1980s, state school finance reforms were focused on equity, or on reducing funding gaps between districts. These reforms often involved redistribution from high-income or high-tax-base districts to low-income or low-tax-base districts. They have been much studied,[4] and some scholars have argued that they induced political dynamics that led to reduced funding across the board.[5]

In 1989, the Kentucky Supreme Court ruled in *Rose v. Council for Better Education* that "each child, every child . . . must be provided with an equal opportunity to have an adequate education." This set off a second wave of reforms, beginning in Kentucky and followed by 26 other states, focused on "adequacy" rather than on "equity." The goal was to ensure an adequate level of funding in low-income school districts, regardless of whether that was more than, the same as, or less than funding levels in high-income districts.[6] As a consequence, states facing adequacy standards were much less prone to achieve equality by reducing overall funding; instead, they were forced to raise absolute and relative funding in the poor districts. However, there has been little evidence available about their actual impacts. Our new paper helps to close that gap.

Average revenue per pupil in elementary and secondary schools in the United States amounts to roughly $13,000 a year. In 2011, low-income districts spent an average of 8 percent more per pupil than did high-income districts in states that have implemented reforms. This is a dramatic reversal from historical experience—as recently as 1990, low-income districts in these states averaged 9 percent less than high-income districts.[7]

In order to estimate how much adequacy-based school finance reforms have contributed to this reduction, we use an "event study" design, which essentially looks at the result of three successive differences for each school finance reform. We compare outcomes in high-income and low-income districts (difference #1), in states where school finance reforms have been implemented and where reforms haven't been implemented (difference #2), and before and after the reform (difference #3). This identification strategy allows us to disentangle the impact of school finance reforms from other contemporaneous changes in school funding and from other differences between states that did and did not implement finance reforms.

Figure 1 shows the evolution of funding gaps between high- and low-income districts. We divide states into two groups: those that have reformed their finance systems since 1990 and those that have not. In 1990, rich districts in both groups of states were spending an average of $750 more per year per pupil than poor districts. (Average spending between 1990 and 2011 was about $10,000 per pupil.) Over the next two decades, not much changed in the states that did not reform their finance systems: the gap remained $800 in 2008, narrowing only during the 2009–2011 state fiscal crisis and never doing better than parity. By contrast, the states that implemented reforms saw dramatic reversals, so that by 2011 they spent an average of $1,150 more per pupil in low-income than in high-income districts.

Our more formal event study analysis confirms this basic pattern, while zeroing in on the timing of school finance reforms to ensure that we distinguish the effects of these reforms from other factors. It shows that state-level school finance reforms markedly increased the progressivity of school spending, and that this increase was not accomplished by redistributing money from rich to poor districts, but rather by increasing state funding across the board, with larger increases in low-income districts.

Figure 1

Evolution of the funding gap between low-income and high-income school districts.

Funding per pupil for students in low-income districts minus funding per pupil in high-income districts

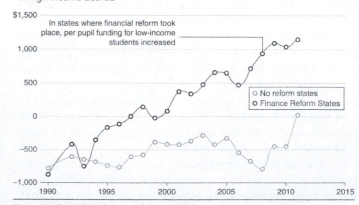

Source: Author's Calculations using our database of school finance reforms, district-level finance data from the National Center for Education Statistics' (NCES) Common Core of Data (CCD) school district finance files and the Census of Governments, and district household distributions form the 1990 Census School District Data Book.

©2016 Washington Center for Equitable Growth.

Increasing School Spending Helps Students Achieve Better Outcomes

Did this sharp and immediate increase in funding for low-income school districts lead to better student outcomes? This is the most important question about school finance reform, but has been the hardest to answer due in large part to a shortage of nationally comparable student achievement data. We take advantage of rarely used student-level data from the NAEP, which are ideally suited for this purpose.

We find that finance reforms did indeed produce higher achievement for students in low-income school districts, helping to reduce the achievement gap between high- and low-income districts (see Figure 2). In states that did not implement reforms, test scores in low-income districts deteriorated relative to high-income districts between 1990 and 2011, a reflection of rising inequality over this period. But in states that implemented reforms, the gap closed slightly.

Again, the event study strategy confirms this basic story. Ten years after a reform, test scores in low-income school districts had risen by about 0.08 standard deviations relative to those in higher-income districts. Reforms raised relative funding in the low-income districts by about $500 per pupil, which implies that increasing funding by $1,000 per pupil—about 10 percent of average funding over the period—raises test scores by 0.16 standard deviations.

One way to get a sense of the size of this impact is to compare it with the effect of other investments of similar size. The effect that we estimate of school finance reforms is twice as large as the effect implied by a $1,000 investment in class-size reduction, as measured by Project STAR—a much-studied four-year experiment in the state of Tennessee in the mid-1980s. The school finance reform impact is also large when we compare the costs of the extra funds to the additional earnings that students benefitting from those funds can be expected to earn later in life.

One important result of our study, therefore, is that granting additional funds to school districts, largely without strings, does not lead to the money being wasted—the funds are used productively. This does not necessarily mean that districts spend the money as efficiently as possible—it is possible that some alternative use would have been even more productive. But their usage compares favorably to other activities that might have been thought to contribute importantly to student achievement (and that, indeed, the cost of the additional funds is outweighed by the benefits on student learning). The extra funding has important impacts that, while not enough to close the

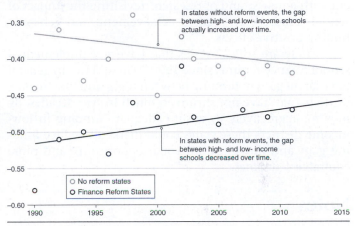

Figure 2

Evolution of the achievement gap between low-income and high-income school districts

Mean test scores in high-income districts minus mean test scores in low-income districts

In states without reform events, the gap between high- and low- income schools actually increased over time.

In states with reform events, the gap between high- and low- income schools decreased over time.

○ No reform states
○ Finance Reform States

Source: Author's calculations using our database of school finance reforms, student achievement data from the national assessment of Educational Progress (NAEP), and household income distributions from the 1990 Census School District Data Book. ©2016 Washington Center for Equitable Growth.

achievement gap between high- and low-income districts, can contribute toward narrowing it. Indeed, we find that a reform closes about ⅕ of the pre-reform gap. There are no other policies that have been implemented at a large scale that have had impacts of this size.

A final result of our study is less encouraging. While school finance reforms did successfully reduce achievement gaps between high- and low-income districts, they did not have measurable impacts on gaps between high- and low-income students. This is because low-income students (and, for that matter, minority students) are not overwhelmingly concentrated in low-income school districts, so an improvement in the relative performance of those districts does relatively little for the relative performance of low-income students. To make substantial progress on closing overall achievement gaps, policies to address disparities in outcomes within school districts are still needed.

Conclusion

School finance reforms are perhaps the largest national effort we have made to increase equality of educational opportunity since the school desegregation movement. Although national attention has been focused elsewhere, there have been dramatic improvements in equality of school funding over the last two decades, many spurred by a series of state court rulings demanding more adequate school funding. We show that these reforms translated into sharp and immediate increases in funding in low-income districts.

We also find that reforms lead to improvements in student achievement in low-income districts—that money matters for student achievement. Our findings are consistent with a new strand of research[8] revisiting the impact of school resources on student achievement, and generally finding positive effects.

There are still 22 states that have not implemented school finance reforms since 1990.[9] These states in general have larger gaps in funding between high- and low-income districts that have not shrunken much in two decades. By moving aggressively to ensure adequate funding in low-income districts these states could markedly reduce funding gaps and move toward equal opportunity and more equitable outcomes.

Notes

1. Here, "rich" and "poor" families are those at the 90th and 10th percentiles of the income distribution, respectively. See Sean F. Reardon, "The Widening Academic Achievement Gap Between the Rich and the Poor: New Evidence and Possible Explanations," in Greg J. Duncan and Richard Murnane, eds., *Whither Opportunity? Rising Inequality, Schools, and Children's Life Chances* (New York: Russell Sage Foundation, 2011).

2. Julien Lafortune, Jesse Rothstein, and Diane Whitmore Schanzenbach, "School Finance Reform and the Distribution of Student Achievement," *Working Paper No. 22011*, National Bureau of Economic Research (2016).

3. See, for example, Eric A. Hanushek, "School resources," in Eric A. Hanushek and Finis Welch, eds., *Handbook of the Economics of Education*, vol. 2 (The Netherlands: North Holland, 2006).

4. Eric A. Hanushek and Alfred A. Lindseth, *Schoolhouses, Courthouses and Statehouses: Solving the Funding-Achievement Puzzle in America's Public Schools* (Princeton: Princeton University Press, 2009); Sean Corcoran and William N. Evans, "Equity, Adequacy, and the evolving State Role in Education Finance," in Helen F. Ladd and Margaret E. Goertz, eds., *Handbook of Research in Education Finance and Policy*, 2nd edition (New York: Routledge, 2015); David Card and A. Abigail Payne, "School finance reform, the distribution of school spending, and the distribution of test scores," *Journal of Public Economics* 83 (1) (2002): 49–82; Sheila E. Murray, William N. Evans, and Robert M. Schwab, "Education-finance reform and the distribution of education resources," *American Economic Review* 88 (4) (1998): 789–812.

5. See, for example, William A. Fischel, "Did Serrano cause Proposition 13?" *National Tax Journal* 42 (4) (1989): 465–473; Caroline M. Hoxby, "All school finance equalizations are not created equal," *Quarterly Journal of Economics* 116 (4) (2001): 1189–1231.

6. We record that the following states implemented school finance reforms between 1990 and 2011: Alaska, Arizona, Arkansas, California, Colorado, Connecticut, Idaho, Indiana, Kansas, Kentucky, Maryland, Massachusetts, Missouri, Montana, New Hampshire, New Jersey, New Mexico, New York, North Carolina, North Dakota, Ohio, Tennessee, Texas, Vermont, Washington, West Virginia, and Wyoming.

7. High- and low-income districts are defined here as districts with average household incomes in the top and bottom quintiles, respectively, of the state's distribution.

8. See, for example, David P. Sims, "Suing for your supper? Resource allocation, teacher compensation, and finance lawsuits," *Economics of Education Review* 30 (5) (2011): 1034–1044; Raj Chetty and others, "How does your Kindergarten classroom affect your earnings? Evidence from Project STAR," *Quarterly Journal of Economics* 126 (4) (2011): 1593–1660; C. Kirabo Jackson, Rucker C. Johnson, and Claudia Persico, "The Effects of School Spending on Educational and Economic Outcomes: Evidence from School Finance Reforms," *Quarterly Journal of Economics* 131 (1) (2016): 157–218.

9. We do not count Hawaii or the District of Columbia, each of which has only a single school district.

JESSE ROTHSTEIN is a PhD candidate at the University of California, Berkley Economics Department.

JULIEN LAFORTUNE is a professor of Public Policy and Economics at the University of California.

DIANE WHITMORE SCHANZENBACH is a chair of the Program on Child, Adolescent, and Family Studies at Northwestern's Institute for Policy Research and a senior fellow at the Brookings Institute.

Caitlin Emma

Here's Why $7 Billion Didn't Help America's Worst Schools

What two troubled high schools tell us about why the government got so little for so much money?

In 2009, the Obama administration saw a chance to tackle a problem that had bedeviled educators for decades.

"Our goal is to turn around the 5,000 lowest-performing schools over the next five years, as part of our overall strategy for dramatically reducing the dropout rate, improving high school graduation rates and increasing the number of students who graduate prepared for success in college and the workplace," said Arne Duncan, the administration's new secretary of education in August of that year.

The administration pumped $3 billion of economic stimulus money into the School Improvement Grants program. Six years later, the program has failed to produce the dramatic results the administration had hoped to achieve. About ⅔ of SIG schools nationwide made modest or no gains—not much different from similarly bad schools that got no money at all. About ⅓ of the schools actually got worse.

Even Duncan acknowledges the progress has been "incremental."

School turnaround is "hard, but it's not rocket science," said Sarah Yatsko, a senior research analyst at the Center on Reinventing Public Education. "We know a lot about what an effective turnaround strategy looks like."

But then why has the SIG program, created in 2007 under President George W. Bush, produced such uneven results at a total cost of about $7 billion?

A comparison by POLITICO of two troubled high schools—one in Miami and one in Chicago—both of which received millions in SIG funds, both of which followed a similar turnaround strategy, reveals that education officials at the federal, state, and local levels paid too little attention to a key variable for success. One school made impressive gains, rebounding in three years from an "F" rating to a "B." At the other, less than 10 percent of

juniors are proficient at reading, math, and science—the same level as before the grant.

The difference between the schools was in their readiness to make use of the sudden infusion of money. In Miami, school district officials had prepared for the grants. They had the support of teachers, unions, and parents. In Chicago, where teachers fought the program and officials changed almost yearly, schools churned through millions of dollars but didn't budge the needle.

Now, the Department of Education is preparing for another multi-million grant competition. But interviews by POLITICO with nearly two dozen analysts, teachers, administrators, and policymakers, who have studied the performance of SIG schools, raise questions about whether any of the changes ordered by the Department of Education or Congress will actually yield better results for the money spent.

"Reviewers need to spend more time focusing on who's ready and who isn't," Yatsko said. "One thing that people have glommed on to is that the program offered a tremendous amount of money and a lot of it was wasted."

Ready in Miami

When Duncan made his pronouncement, Alberto Carvalho had been the superintendent of the Miami-Dade public schools for about a year. It was "a dark time for Miami schools," Carvalho told POLITICO. The state of Florida was threatening to shut down a number of them. Huge achievement gaps divided poor, black, and Hispanic children and their more affluent, white peers.

But Carvalho, 51, had an advantage going in. He knew what didn't work.

As a deputy to former Miami Superintendent Rudy Crew, Carvalho had his hand on federal funding for the district's failing schools and he had seen up close the implementation of Crew's School Improvement Zone plan. That initiative had mixed results, which critics attributed to its lack of focus on developing effective teachers and administrators.

In his new job, Carvalho went looking for expertise and he hired Nikolai Vitti, Florida's deputy chancellor of school improvement, to head Miami's Education Transformation Office. Vitti drew on lessons he learned at the state level, while Carvalho, who had to weather a mini-scandal over a romantic affair with a local reporter, deftly cleared political barriers, securing buy-in from the school board and the community.

When the $43 million in SIG money arrived in 2010, Carvalho and Vitti knew that improving personnel in the failing schools would be the key to their success. That meant moving weak teachers out and replacing them with stronger teachers from high-performing schools.

In order to do that, the district and the United Teachers of Dade signed a memorandum of understanding to help ease teachers through the changes. The union took pains to ensure that transferred teachers were happy with their new placements. For example, some were moved to better schools closer to home, cutting down commutes.

Miami Edison Senior High School was one of the 19 schools in the Miami-Dade district that got SIG money in the first round of grants. Located in Miami's impoverished Little Haiti neighborhood, it was known as a dropout factory—less than half of students graduated during the 2007–2008 school year. A year later, just 12 percent of students were reading at or above grade level.

After years of failure, the state ordered Edison to hire a new principal, who started in 2009. Then, with the help of nearly $1.5 million over three years in federal grant money, officials changed out more than ½ of the school staff. The district brought in Teach For America recruits and held teacher recruitment fairs. Top teachers who volunteered to work at Edison were given financial incentives, like signing bonuses and extra pay for boosting student test scores.

The strategy worked.

Over the three-year period, test scores went up and students made significant learning gains. Nearly, ¾ earned a diploma the first year after the grant ran out.

"When you feel empowered to do your job, who wouldn't get results?" said Dannielle Boyer, a former teacher at Miami Edison. Boyer volunteered to transfer to another SIG school, North Miami Senior High School, so she could work with the school's Haitian students. She also received a stipend.

The results were similar across the district. In 2013, at the end of the first round of grants, the number of Miami schools receiving a "D" or "F" grade was cut in half—from 19 schools to 9. Test scores went up. And the district cut the number of days spent on out-of-school and in-school suspensions by a ¼. Carvalho tried to ensure the gains would last through a strong succession of leaders.

Vitti left during the 2012–2013 school year, the last year of Edison's SIG grant, to be superintendent of schools in Jacksonville, FL. Miami Edison Principal Pablo Ortiz, who saw results at his school under SIG, took Vitti's place in the district office. And the district, which had

Gains Follow Grants

The Majority of students at Miami Edison Senior High School are black and living in poverty. Many of the students are of Haitian descent and about a ¼ are English language learners. Under the three-year school Improvement Grant, test scores went up and students made significant learning gains.

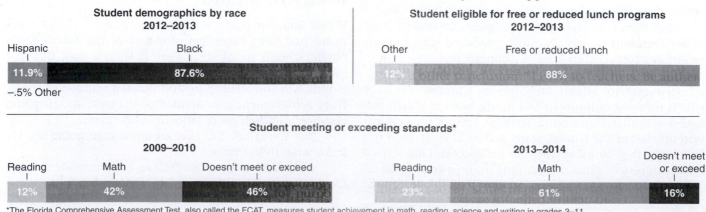

Student demographics by race 2012–2013

Hispanic	Black
11.9%	87.6%

−.5% Other

Student eligible for free or reduced lunch programs 2012–2013

Other	Free or reduced lunch
12%	88%

Student meeting or exceeding standards*

2009–2010

Reading	Math	Doesn't meet or exceed
12%	42%	46%

2013–2014

Reading	Math	Doesn't meet or exceed
23%	61%	16%

*The Florida Comprehensive Assessment Test, also called the FCAT, measures student achievement in math, reading, science and writing in grades 3–11.

Source: The National Center for Education statistics and the Florida Department of Education.

been grooming education leaders for tough jobs, picked Trynegwa K. Diggs as Edison's new principal.

Diggs, 42, had worked in struggling schools. She shadowed a model principal at another SIG-grant school. A common thread runs through all struggling schools, she said, but each one is "extremely unique."

Despite its gains, Edison still struggles with proficiency rates, particularly in reading. Before the grant, just 12 percent of students were reading at grade level or better. The year after the grant, the percentage of students nearly doubled to 23 percent, but that's still very low.

"Some students have no knowledge of the English language," Diggs said, referring to the ¼ of the school's 800 students who are Haitian. "Some had no formal education in Haiti, but you're still responsible for making sure that they graduate."

The teachers are used to visiting students' homes, particularly when Haitian parents aren't involved in their child's education. Even physical education teacher Nehemy Cher-frere makes home visits.

"I tell the parents, 'You're not in Haiti now, you need to come to the school and talk to the teachers,'" he said. "You have to be a teacher, a father figure and a friend."

Resistant in Chicago

If leadership was key to Miami's readiness, the revolving door at Chicago Public Schools has been that district's undoing. Six different interim and permanent leaders have occupied the top office since Arne Duncan left in 2009 when Obama asked him to come to Washington. One of them, Barbara Byrd-Bennett, pleaded guilty in October to wire fraud for steering multimillion-dollar no-bid contracts to a former employer.

"Before I was here, there was CEO Paul Vallas for about seven years. I did about 7½, so you had two CEOs over 15 years. You had some stability," Duncan said in April. "And that kind of lack of continuity, that lack of stability . . . this is what makes me sad."

A powerful and combative teachers' union in Chicago added to the challenge.

Timothy Meegan, a high school civics teacher and union delegate who ran for alderman, said teachers at his school circulated petitions to keep the grant money out because they heard "horror stories" from other schools. Principals and administrators were "secretive" about the grant process, Meegan said. Unlike teachers in Miami, teachers in Chicago didn't feel involved and felt that they were losing control over their classrooms as the emphasis shifted to testing.

"Sometimes these interventions only reach in, break everything up and leave it again," said Mary Ann Pitcher codirector of the Network for College Success, which has partnered with SIG schools in Chicago. "All of that trauma and transition hinders and prevents progress."

All of these factors were on display at Christian Fenger Academy, located in one of the poorest and most violent neighborhoods on Chicago's South Side. The high school had been on probation for more than a dozen years for poor student performance. Teacher turnover was high

Money for Nothing

The vast majority of students attending Christian Fenger Academy High School in Chicago are black and living in poverty. Despite a three-year School Improvement Grant, test scores remain exceedingly low. During the 2014–2015 school year, only about ½ of the students graduated within five years and less than ½ enrolled in college.

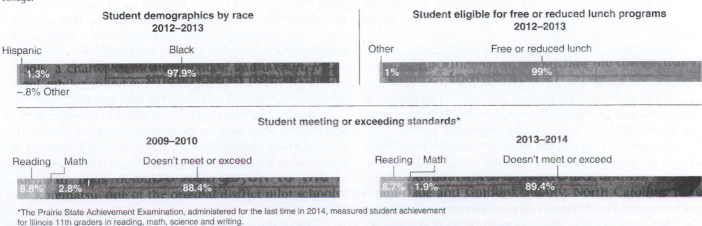

*The Prairie State Achievement Examination, administered for the last time in 2014, measured student achievement for Illinois 11th graders in reading, math, science and writing.

Source: The National Center for Education Statistics, Chicago Public Schools and the Illinois state Board of Education.

and instruction was suffering. In 2009, the beating death of a 16-year-old student captured on a two-minute video rocked the school and the community.

Like Edison in Miami, Fenger replaced the principal and overhauled the staff. But the similar strategy produced very different results. Last year, just 5 percent of Fenger's juniors met or exceeded state standards in reading, math, and English—compared with the district average of 33 percent. Only about ½ of the students graduated within five years. Less than ½ enrolled in college.

Liz Dozier, 37, arrived at Fenger to take the principal's job in 2009. The school had about 1,200 students at the time. But new charter schools opened and families sought suburban or out-of-state schools. During the last school year, Fenger's enrollment had plummeted to about 270 students, nearly all black and from low-income families.

Dozier, along with Mayor Rahm Emanuel, starred in CNN's "Chicagoland," a 2014 documentary that demonstrated problems at Fenger continued unabated after the SIG money ran out. "Test scores have always been a struggle," Dozier told POLITICO, but the school is better off because of the grant. More freshmen are now on track to graduate high school and more students are graduating on time, she said.

The story was more or less the same at all four of the Chicago schools that received the funds in 2010: test scores in reading on the state's Prairie State Achievement Examination declined over the course of the three-year grant. After the grant ran out, the percentage of students reading at or above grade level still hovered around 10 percent.

What really hampered the turnaround effort, Dozier said, was not the turmoil in the district office or pushback from the union, it was the short life of the grant. As students left, so did staff, draining away institutional knowledge about the school's improvement efforts, she said. Dozier left Fenger in July, for reasons she won't divulge.

In addition, violence, unemployment, the economic well-being of the community "all ripple into how and whether kids are able to learn," Dozier added. "The school faces some really unique issues," she said. "The challenge hasn't changed because unfortunately, the kids who enter our school still have needs, social-emotional needs."

Progress in Chicago has been minimal because "these schools are constantly being tinkered with," said Meegan, the civics teacher and alderman candidate. "There's no stability, there are no resources . . . those schools have always had trouble and they always will until poverty is addressed."

But some say leaning on poverty and other social ills is not an acceptable excuse.

Andy Smarick, a partner at Bellwether Education Partners, said, "The excuse that poverty is going to stop us from providing a good education to kids is the kind of excuse that makes adults feel good."

"If they think that poor kids are never going to learn, then why did we just spend $7 billion?"

Learning from Mistakes

The Obama administration was flying blind at the onset of the stimulus funding, said Michael Casserly, executive director of the Council of the Great City Schools.

"They didn't have a whole lot of SIG evaluation data to go on," Casserly said, a program supporter. "But at this point, I would hope that they've learned a lot about what produces results and what doesn't."

But the results are in, and it's not clear that schools are being held to the standard set by Miami.

"We've seen some schools and districts that have been very committed to implementation and they've made double digit gains," said Ann Whalen, a senior adviser to Duncan who oversees School Improvement Grants. "And we've seen others take this opportunity and continue doing what they've done before."

Duncan told reporters in October that the SIG program hasn't been perfect. But it's more about "challenging folks to think about—is the right idea to start a new school? Is the right idea longer instructional time? Is the right idea more social workers and counselors? Is the right idea more parental engagement?

"It was appropriate for us not just to talk about it, but to put huge resources, very significant resources behind this," Duncan said. "And I can tell you, just anecdotally, that I've been to I would say potentially dozens of schools that have been transformed. And to see in two or three years the difference there—none of them are perfect, none are where they want to be—but it's unbelievably motivating. Same buildings, same neighborhoods, same socioeconomic challenges, same everything, just different expectations and different results."

That said, the agency should continue to make sure schools are prepared, Whalen, his deputy, said.

But it has always been up to states to consider school and district readiness, among other factors, she said. The goal of the program was to give states and districts an incentive to help local leaders implement rigorous reform.

"We're trying to make sure that we don't overreach," Whalen said. "We're not going to tell [states] how to run their process."

But that hasn't stopped Congress from tinkering with the rules for the SIG program. Congressionally ordered changes to the program took effect this year, with the goal of giving schools more flexibility to divert from the four approved turnaround models—becoming a charter, closing the school and sending students elsewhere, changing the principal and ½ the staff, or only changing the principal and overhauling teacher evaluations. (Three-quarters of schools chose the fourth option, considered by far the least disruptive.) Many consider the models too restrictive and say they aren't grounded in good research. The new changes expand the number of intervention models to seven.

The changes also allow schools and districts to spend a full year on planning and preparation, which will help with readiness, Whalen said. They lengthen the grant period from three years to five years to help schools avoid backsliding when the money runs out.

Many worry that additional flexibility is the last thing states need.

"It's remarkable to me that people bought into the view that the problem with the program is that it was too constraining," Smarick said. "Why do failing districts and failing schools need more leeway to make these decisions?"

Whalen said flexibility is a

"double-edged sword," providing "opportunities for people to be less rigorous or more innovative."

"We're constantly trying to help build the capacity for people on the ground making these decisions to make better decisions to support kids," she said. "But nothing is going to be fixed solely from D.C."

Several studies have shown that states often lack the resources and expertise to adequately turn around low-performing schools. More than ¾ of states surveyed said they lacked expertise for supporting school turnaround in 2012, according to a report released by the National Center for Education Evaluation and Regional Assistance earlier this year. Eighty percent of states said the same in 2013.

"Study after study has shown that our state departments of education are under-resourced and do not have the capacity to do what we ask of them," said Maria Ferguson of the Center on Education Policy.

But if the grant application process focused less on compliance and more on readiness at every level of government—ensuring that schools and districts have the right leaders, expertise, vision and buy-in from teachers and the community—then experts and turnaround leaders say the program might have generated better results.

"I wonder if the government could set higher bars around the aligning of the stars that need to happen," said Yatsko of the Center on Reinventing Public Education. "It wouldn't be too hard to look at an application and determine readiness, making sure that all the elements are in place."

Nathan Gibbs-Bowling, recently named one of America's top teachers, has watched the SIG grants play out in his Tacoma, Washington, school district. He said if the states and feds focus on one readiness factor, it should be leadership.

"If I was designing the program, I'd be investigating what's on the ground in schools and districts to make sure that's in place," he said. "If the feds are going to keep giving out grants this large, it makes sense to create leadership teams that have to go in and take a look at this."

"But I don't think states or feds are willing to do that kind of granular investigation," he added.

Whether the changes to the program lead to better results—and whether the Obama administration has learned its lessons—remains to be seen.

And the School Improvement Grants program may soon disappear. Congress is close to reauthorizing No Child Left Behind, and both the House and Senate version of the bill would do away with the SIG program. There would still be money to fix the lowest-performing schools—the federal government just wouldn't have a say in how to do it.

Regardless, the "federal government needs to be held accountable for spending billions of dollars on a program that all the experience told us wouldn't produce the changes that they said it would," Smarick said. "That's something they're going to have to explain."

CAITLIN EMMA is a reporter covering state and federal education policy news for POLITICO.

EXPLORING THE ISSUE

Does Funding Improve Student Achievement?

Critical Thinking and Reflection

1. Should student achievement be caught up in the political tug-of-war over funding? Why or why not?
2. How is the impact of school funding on student achievement measured?
3. What controls the funds budgeted to each school?
4. What kind of statistical test data is needed to monitor whether funding has an impact on student achievement?
5. Does the difference in the socioeconomic background of the student directly impact funding and student achievement?

Is There Common Ground?

The common economic theory "you get what you pay for" may not accurately reflect the view that if more is spent on education, student performance will improve. There are mixed results from the existing evidence on student academic achievement when correlated with school funding. Snell (2013) states that there is a non-relationship between spending and student achievement to levels of funding. Hoffman et al. (2013) link student achievement to levels of funding. They assert that significantly higher student scores result from spending more money to pay more teachers, hire more instructional aides, provide more extensive professional development, buy more supplies, better maintain and expand buildings, and purchase new equipment and technology (Hoffman et al., 2013). This statement makes sense, as school budgets increase and student outcomes (as measured by the National Assessment of Educational Progress, American College Testing, Scholastic Aptitude Test and numerous other assessments) rise too. Snell (2013, p. 1) counters with, "a beautiful building is no guarantee of student learning and neither are large increases in funding." This is quite a stark contrast in the search for common ground.

A 2014 study published by the Kansas Association of School Boards (Carter, 2014), using linear regression and correlation analysis, concluded that increased funding significantly predicts student performance. In opposition to this finding, the reports on school spending from the *Coleman Report* and the Cato Institute support that there is little to no link between spending and academic achievement. To further support the Coleman and Cato stance is a part of the long-running school funding lawsuit in the state of New Jersey that began in 1990. *Abbott v. Burke* resulted in increased spending in 31 of New Jersey's then-poorest school districts. The new money for schools soon eclipsed spending in some of the wealthiest districts in the states. In 2016, all these years later, many of these districts are still "spending 2.5 times the national average, and there's no real evidence that they're closing the achievement gap or that they are doing significantly better" (Turner et al., 2016, p. 8).

For the contrasting positions on school finding and student achievement, the common ground may be better reflected not on how much is spent on schools, but on how the money is spent. Simply throwing more dollars at education does not appear to be the wise course of action. The important points of agreement between all education stakeholders, who span both the political as well as ideological viewpoints, may recognize that school funding and student achievement depend upon each other. Maybe it's not a debate at all, even though lawmakers, educators, and communities continue to battle over equitable school funding. For those who take the position that school funding does not play a large role in determining student achievement, it is necessary to look at what does. Teacher quality would likely be near or at the top of that list. Poverty has a large impact on student achievement and paying for the things (and people) that are most likely to help vulnerable students would be important. To make this happen, many schools need more money. Efforts to improve students' performance should focus on how to allocate available, as well as new, educational resources more effectively. Getting the money into the correct programs to address the specific needs of underserved students should be monitored and evaluated. Assessment and analysis provide opportunities for further research that would give greater understanding to spending and its direct effects on achievement.

Additional Resources

Burnette, D. (2018). What is ESSA's new school-spending transparency requirement, and how will it work? *Education Week*. Retrieved from https://www.edweek.org/ew/articles/2018/08/09/what-is-essas-new-school-spending-transparency-requirement.html

Carter, T. (2014). *Educational funding and student outcomes: The relationship as evidenced by state level data*. Research Reports. The Kansas Association of School Boards. Retrieved from http://files.eric.ed.gov/fulltext/ED560044.pdf

Coleman, J. (1966). *The Coleman report*. National Center for Educational Statistics. Retrieved from http://files.eric.ed.gov/fulltext/ED012275.pdf

Coulson, A. (2014). No link between school spending and student achievement. *CBS DC*. Retrieved from http://washington.cbslocal.com/2014/04/07/study-no-link-between-school-spending-student-achievement/

Hoffman, M., Wiggall, R., Dereshiwsky, M. & Emanuel, G. (2013). State school finance system variance impacts on student achievement inadequacies in school funding. *eJournal of Education Policy*. Retrieved from https://files.eric.ed.gov/fulltext/EJ1158691.pdf

Leachman, M., Albares, N., Matterson, K., & Wallace, M. (2016). Most stales have cut school funding and some continue cutting. *Center on Budget and Policy Priorities*. Retrieved from http://www.cbpp.org/research/state-budget-and-tax/most-states-have-cut-school-funding-and-some-continue-cutting

Mackenzie, J. (2006). *Public school funding and performance*. Whitepaper. Department of Applied Economic & Statistics. Retrieved from http://www1.udel.edu/johnmack/research/schoolfunding.pelf (2008).

National Center for Education Statistics. (2018). *Fiscal year 2019 budget summary and background information*. Retrieved from https://www2.ed.gov/about/overview/budget/budget19/summary/19summary.pdf

Shanker Education Report. (2012). Money matters, affects student performance, outcomes. *Huffington Post*. Retrieved from http://www.huffingtonpost.com/2012/01/09/shanker-education-report-_n_1195064.html

Turner, K. McCory, L. Worf, S. Gonzalez, K. Carapezza, & C. McInerny, (2016). Can money fix America's schools? *nprEd How Learning Happens*. Retrieved from http://www.npr.org/sections/ed/2016/04/25/468157856/can-more-money-fix-americas-schools

Ujifusa, A. (2018). Education funding bill progresses in house after school safety money restored. *Education Week*. Retrieved from http://blogs.edweek.org/edweek/campaign-k-12/2018/07/education_spending_bill_house_advances_school_safety_money_restored.html

Internet References . . .

Can More Money Fix America's Schools?

https://www.npr.org/sections/ed/2016/04/25/468157856/can-more-money-fix-americas-schools

Can Student Finance Reforms Improve Student Achievement?

https://equitablegrowth.org/can-school-finance-reforms-improve-student-achievement/

Does Money Matter?

http://edpolicy.education.jhu.edu/wp-content/uploads/2017/05/Does-Money-Matter-Commentary.pdf

Does Spending More on Education Improve Academic Achievement?

https://www.heartland.org/publications-resources/publications/does-spending-more-on-education-improve-academic-achievement?source=policybot

The Effect of School Spending on Student Achievement: Addressing Biases in Value-added Models

https://rss.onlinelibrary.wiley.com/doi/full/10.1111/rssa.12304

Selected, Edited, and with Issue Framing Material by:
Glenn L. Koonce, *Regent University*

ISSUE

Should Charter Schools Be Expanded?

YES: Derrell Bradford, from "Strengthening the Roots of the Charter-School Movement," *Education Next* (2018)

NO: Robin Lake, et al., from "Why Is Charter Growth Slowing?" *Education Next* (2018)

Learning Outcomes

After reading this issue, you will be able to:

- Compare and contrast charter schools with traditional public schools.
- Evaluate the pros and cons between all-district charter schools, a mix of charter schools and traditional schools.
- Briefly summarize why charter schools are a "Bad Deal" for students, teachers, and taxpayers in the Metro Nashville Public Schools, as well as numerous other districts.
- Explain why charter schools are more prevalent in urban areas.
- Analyze the reasons that educators may choose public schools over charter schools.

ISSUE SUMMARY

YES: Derrell Bradford, executive vice president of 50CAN, a national nonprofit that advocates for equal opportunity in K–12 education and senior visiting fellow at the Thomas B. Fordham Institute, notes that we would be better advised to provide leaders of charter schools with more support because they allow the autonomy and flexibility to do what some districts can't or won't.

NO: Robin Lake, director of the Center on Reinventing Public Education at the University of Washington Bothell, where Roohi Sharma is research coordinator and Alice Opalka is special assistant to the director, Trey Cobb, a graduate student at the University of Notre Dame and a middle school math teacher, share their study of charter school growth and decline in the San Francisco Bay area of charter schools over the last five years and they note that districts have become skilled at limiting charter growth.

As a wide-reaching K–12 school reform initiative, the charter school movement originated in New England during the 1970s. This initiative gained a foothold in Minnesota which passed the first charter school law in 1991, followed by California in 1992. By 1995, 19 states had followed suit. In 2018, 44 states, Puerto Rico, and the District of Columbia had charter school laws on the books serving 3.2 million students in 7,000 charter schools across the nation (National Alliance for Public Charter Schools, 2018, p. 1). The National Alliance for Public Charter Schools is the leading national nonprofit organization

committed to advancing the public charter school movement. The Alliance measures and ranks charter schools in the United States and provides an annual report on their website.

There has been consistent broad-based support from governors, state legislators, and secretaries of education for charter schools. Presidential backing began with the Clinton administration and has been maintained during the Bush and Obama education agendas. In an opinion piece by Conor Williams (2018), senior researcher at the New American's Policy program and noted expert on school choice and education equity, regarding the Trump administration's position on charter schools, the following questions were posed:

> How should a charter network run by progressives committed to embattling racism navigate the Trump administration's vocal support of charters? How should it respond to criticism from progressives who accuse it of undermining public education? Charter schools are homeless (p. 1).

In the current political climate, charter school advocacy is in a constant battle for legitimacy. Most charter schools serve struggling/needy students in mostly urban settings. The logic emanating from the Trump administration on charters is that authorizing and accountability must be made at the state level. Although the rapid expansion of charter schools is likely to continue, conflicting views remain as to this growth and to their success, leading one to question, should charter school be expanded? Some view charter schools as controversial and instead focus on the question, do they work? Both supporters and opponents dig into their positions and the debate continues.

Charter Schools face many political challenges. They have deliberately been concentrated in communities of color where high rates of poverty define the neighborhoods. In Philadelphia, Oakland, Chicago, Houston, Los Angeles, Washington, DC, and other urban centers with high poverty rates, charter schools are part of an effort to overcome the inequities in race and class that afflict American public education. In addition, some of the antagonistic views on charter schools are grounded in the deeply cynical term *public funding*. Corporate, financial elite and sponsoring elected officials compose the boards that govern many charter schools, leaving community representatives, educators, and families of students out of the decision-making process or prohibited at all from sitting on charter school boards (Casey, 2015, p. 3).

A question often asked about charter schools is directed to the federal government's role in charter school expansion. How will this federal role be articulated and how will it align with the recently enacted Every Student Succeeds Act (ESSA) in the future? Advocates of charter schools have praised and supported ESSA for advocating for high-achieving charters. These successful charters can receive federal grants under ESSA, but what does this say about the many charter schools that struggle to achieve student success, who close their doors due to a mired of concerns and problems?

Opposing research (both current and previous) regarding charter school expansion forms the premise for this issue. Most of this research is directed at student outcomes. Writing in a fall issue of *Education Week*, Prothero (2016, p. 1) noted contradictory findings from two "high quality" studies on who earns more money in adulthood: public school students or charter school students. A study conducted by Georgia State University, Vanderbilt University, and Mathematica Policy Research found charter school students in Florida earn significantly more in adulthood than their public school peers. A Harvard University and Princeton University study found just the opposite, public school students in Texas earn more in adulthood than their charter school peer (*Education Week*, 2016).

The often cited *National Charter School Study 2013*, by the Center for Research on Education Outcomes (CREDO, 2013) at Stanford University, examined results from charter schools in 27 states and New York City to identify differences in student performance at charter schools versus traditional schools. The 2013 study was a follow-up to its earlier 2009 report, *Multiple Choices: Charter School Performance in 16 States*, and emphasized any trends in charter school performance over the four-year time span. The first finding indicated that there was an 80 percent increase in student enrollment over the four years. A second finding noted that in the four years both reading and math aggregate scores showed improvement, as compared to the earlier report. When all 27 states' results were pooled in the 2013 report, learning gains in reading were higher for students in charter schools over their peers in traditional public schools. However, the report found that "across the states and across schools, charter school quality is uneven" (CREDO, 2013, p. 3).

Soon after the release of the findings from the 2013 report, the National Educational Policy Center in Boulder, Colorado, which provides academically sound reviews of selected publications, challenged these findings asserting that "even setting aside its analytical flaws, the CREDO study merely confirms that charter schools perform on par with traditional schools" (Mathis and Maul, 2013, p. 1). The Brookings Institute's response to the CREDO study is "much ado about tiny differences" (Loveless, 2013, p. 1). In this Brookings' response, the focus was on whether the differences in the CREDO study were statistically significant. Citing an "enormous" sample size (1.5 million charter students matched with a group of traditional public school students) and the size or "magnitude" of the effect (p. 1) makes small differences appear much larger than they really are (p. 5).

CREDO (2015) released a different report two years later, *Urban Charter School Study Report on 41 Regions 2015*, comparing charter school performance in urban areas to traditional public schools in the community. The study included data from 41 urban areas in 22 states. This report indicated significantly higher levels of annual growth in both math and reading scores from students in the charter schools. Additionally, significantly larger gains were found for charter school African American, Hispanic, low-income, and special education students. It was noted in the report that even though many of these charter schools "demonstrate the ability to educate all students to high levels, some continue to struggle" (p. vi).

Similar to the CREDO 2013 report, there are critics of the more recent CREDO 2015 findings. The National Center for Policy Analysis cites critics Gabor and Fung who indicate they are skeptical of the finding that charters outperform city public schools in reading and math (Haynes, 2015). The major problems identified included a "number of anti-public school biases" and violating their own methodology in data collected.

Referring to these type of reports (i.e., CREDO, 2015) as "horse race charter school studies," DiCarlo (2015, p. 1) writing for the Albert Shanker Institute states that charter versus regular school studies are important for evaluating performance and trends. However, DiCarlo adds these studies are not particularly useful to judge charter schools "en-masse" (p. 1), particularly when test scores are the measures being evaluated. The merits of the charter school's primary premise is to try things differently, to vary policies and practices within districts, and to experiment. DiCarlo concludes that math and reading coefficients that are estimated with many different policy environments found in charter schools are not the sole summation of their success. The huge variety of different models and the impact of these *treatments* is what should be equally, if not, more focused on evaluating.

Despite the mixed reviews, Yousuf (2016) comments on both the 2013 and the 2015 CREDO reports, along with other empirical evidence, that charter schools be expanded in the United States. Yousuf states, "The charter schools produce 40% better results in both math and reading scores per dollar spent" (pp. 4–5). Yousuf surmised these and other results from numerous studies conducted between 2002 and 2010, a meta-analysis of 30 empirical studies that investigated the value-added effects of charter schools, data from the CREDO reports, and two additional studies conducted in 2014. He notes that charter schools will continue to grow. To demonstrate the expansion of

charter schools, Denver Colorado, who in June of 2018 won the 2018 Broad award for Public Charter Schools, will open its first preschool through 12th-grade charter outside the city to a suburb just north in Adams 14 school district (Robles, 2018). Meanwhile, on August 20, 2018, a Florida judge threw off the November ballot a proposed constitutional amendment that would have made it easier to establish a charter school in the state.

The CREDO website includes more recent evaluations of state outcomes regarding their charter schools. The most recent work of CREDO (2018) was the evaluation of the Charter Restart Model in New Orleans. Charter schools that performed low in New Orleans were partnered with high achieving Charter Management Organizations (CMOs) that exhibited a proven model to improve student learning. Results were dismal after tabulating results of the program over a five-year period. Of the 21 schools evaluated, none met the original targets in both reading and math, nor did they out perform their peer charter schools in the city. CREDO's work is often criticized as it is with any organization that conducts research studies experience. Specifically, CREDO has been criticized for a lack of a thorough literature review, methodology, trivial effect sizes, and others. CREDO has addressed each concern on their website noting that their work is only a piece of the larger landscape of study regarding charter schools and that other studies should not be ignored.

Are charter schools better? Are they revolutionizing public schools as we know them? How many charter schools are just right for a school district? Will traditional public schools or charter schools lead the charge for virtual schools? What is the federal government's role and the policy implications from the newly enacted ESSA on charter school expansion? Are charter schools doing a better job of educating students than traditional public schools? Can the question of quality charter schools be answered—what explains success in high-quality education? What do the continuing rise in charter schools say about the system of public schools in the United States? What are parents and educators to do with such contradiction in so many of the studies being conducted on student outcomes between charter schools and public schools? This debate is likely to escalate as questions like these continue to be asked and debated by both charter school naysayers and charter school supporters.

YES

Derrell Bradford

Strengthening the Roots of the Charter-School Movement

How the Mom-and-Pops Can Help the Sector Diversify and Grow

Over the past quarter century, charter schools have taken firm root in the American education landscape. What started with a few Minnesota schools in the early 1990s has burgeoned into a nationwide phenomenon, with nearly 7,000 charter schools serving more than three million students in 43 states and the nation's capital.

Twenty-five years isn't a long time relative to the history of public and private schooling in the United States, but it is long enough to merit a close look at the charter-school movement today and how it compares to the one initially envisaged by many of its pioneers: an enterprise that aspired toward diversity in the populations of children served, the kinds of schools offered, the size and scale of those schools, and the background, culture, and race of the folks who ran them.

Without question, the movement has given many of the country's children schools that are now among the nation's best of any type. This is an achievement in which all charter supporters can take pride.

It would be wrong, however, to assume that the developments that have given the movement its current shape have come without costs. Every road taken leaves a fork unexplored, and the road taken to date seems incomplete, littered with unanswered and important questions.

While the charter sector is still growing, the rate of its expansion has slowed dramatically over the years. In 2001, the number of charter schools in the country rose by 26 percent and, the following year, by 19 percent. But that rate steadily fell and now languishes at an estimated 2 percent annually (see Figure 1). Student enrollment in charter schools continues to climb, but the rate of growth has slowed from more than 30 percent in 2001 to just 7 percent in 2017.

And that brings us to those unanswered questions: Can the charter-school movement grow to sufficient scale for long-term political sustainability if we continue to use "quality"—as measured by such factors as test scores—as the sole indicator of a successful school? What is the future role of single-site schools in that growth, given that charter management organizations (CMOs) and for-profit education management organizations (EMOs) are increasingly crowding the field? And finally, can we commit ourselves to a more inclusive and flexible approach to charter authorizing in order to diversify the schools we create and the pool of prospective leaders who run them?

In this final query, especially, we may discover whether the movement's roots will ever be deep enough to survive the political and social headwinds that have threatened the chartering tree since its first sprouting.

One School, One Dream

Howard Fuller, the lifelong civil rights activist, former Black Panther, and now staunch champion of school choice, once offered in a speech: "CMOs, EMOs . . . I'm for all them O's. But there still needs to be a space for the person who just wants to start a single school in their community."

In Fuller's view, one that is shared by many charter supporters, the standalone or single-site school, and an environment that supports its creation and maintenance, are essential if we are to achieve a successful and responsive mix of school options for families.

The standalone or single-site school and an environment that supports its creation and maintenance are essential if we are to achieve a successful and responsive mix of school options for families.

But increasingly, single-site schools appear to suffer a higher burden of proof, as it were, to justify their existence relative to the CMOs that largely set the political and expansion strategies for the broader movement. Independent schools, when taken as a whole, still represent the majority of the country's charter schools—55 percent of them, according to the National Alliance for Public Charter Schools. But as CMOs continue to grow, that percentage is shrinking.

Examining the role that single-site schools play and how we can maintain them in the overall charter mix is not simple, but it uncovers a number of factors that contribute to the paucity—at least on the coasts—of standalone schools that are also led by people of color.

Access to Support

If there is a recurring theme that surfaces when exploring the health and growth of the "mom-and-pops"—as many charter advocates call them—it's this: starting a school, any school, is hard work, but doing it alone comes with particularly thorny challenges.

"Starting HoLa was way harder than any of us expected," said Barbara Martinez, a founder of the Hoboken Dual Language Charter School, or HoLa, an independent charter school in Hoboken, NJ. "We ran into problems very early on and had to learn a lot very, very quickly." Martinez, who chairs HoLa's board and also works for the Northeast's largest charter network, Uncommon Schools, added: "When a CMO launches a new school, they bring along all of their lessons learned and they open with an already well-trained leader. At HoLa, there was no playbook."

Michele Mason, executive director of the Newark Charter School Fund, which supports charter schools in the city and works extensively with its single-site charters, made a similar point, noting that many mom-and-pops lack the human capital used by CMOs to manage the problems that confront any education startup. "[Prior to my arrival we were] sending in consultants to help school leaders with finance, culture, personnel, boards," Mason said. "We did a lot of early work on board development and board support. The CMOs don't have to worry about that so much."

Mason added that the depth of the talent pool for hiring staff is another advantage that CMOs enjoy over the standalones. "Every personnel problem—turnover, and so on—is easier when you have a pipeline."

Access to Experts

Many large charter-school networks can also count on regular technical support and expertise from various powerhouse consultants and consulting firms that serve the education-reform sector. So, if knowledge and professional support are money, some observers believe that access to such wired-in "help" means the rich are indeed getting richer in the charter-school world.

Leslie Talbot of Talbot Consulting, an education management consulting practice in New York City, said, "About 90 percent of our charter work is with single-site schools or leaders of color at single sites looking to grow to multiple campuses. We purposely decided to focus on this universe of schools and leaders because they need unique help, and because they don't have a large CMO behind them." Talbot is also a member of the National Charter Collaborative, an organization that "supports single-site charter-school leaders of color who invest in the hopes and dreams of students through the cultural fabric of their communities."

What are the kinds of support that might bolster a mom-and-pop's chances of success? "There are lots of growth-related strategic-planning and thought-partnering service providers in [our area of consulting]," offered Talbot. "Single-site charter leaders, especially those of color, often are isolated from these professional development opportunities, in need of help typically provided by consulting practices, and unable to access funding sources that can provide opportunities" to tap into either of those resources.

Connections and Capital

The old bromide "It's who you know" certainly holds true in the entrepreneurial environment of charter startups. As with any risky and costly enterprise, the power of personal and professional relationships can open doors for school leaders. Yet these are precisely the relationships many mom-and-pop, community-focused charter founders lack. And that creates significant obstacles for prospective single-site operators.

A 2017 Thomas B. Fordham Institute report analyzed 639 charter applications that were submitted to 30 authorizers across four states, providing a glimpse of the tea leaves that charter authorizers read to determine whether or not a school should open. Authorizing is most certainly a process of risk mitigation, as no one wants to open a "bad" school. But some of the study's findings point to distinct disadvantages for operators who aren't on the funder circuit or don't have the high-level connections commanded by the country's largest CMOs.

For instance, among applicants who identified an external funding source from which they had secured or requested a grant to support their proposed school,

Figure 1

Slowing Growth in the Charter Sector

1a) After a decade of climbing by rates as high as 6-9 percent per year, the number of charter schools in recent years has increased by only about 2 percent annually.

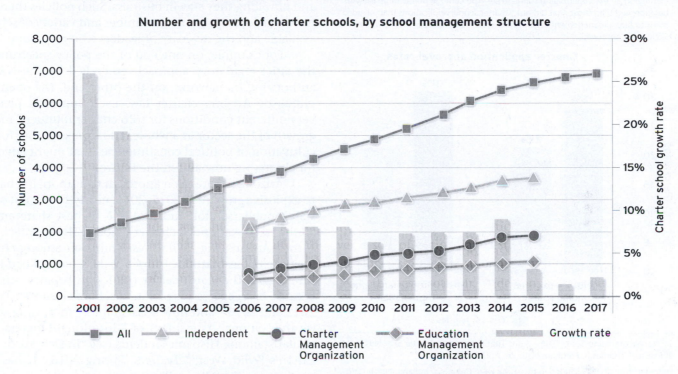

Number and growth of charter schools, by school management structure

1b) The growth rate in student enrollment at charter schools has also declined steadily since 2001.

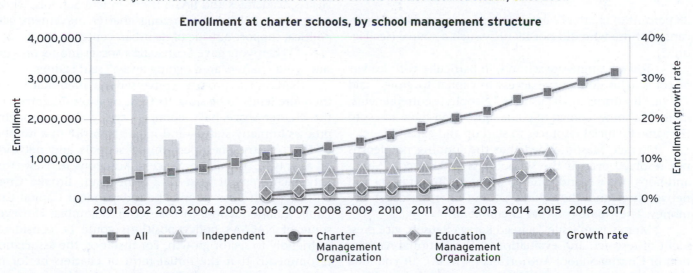

Enrollment at charter schools, by school management structure

Source: National Alliance for Public Charter Schools, Data Dashboard (2000–2015); National Alliance for Public Charter Schools, A Closer Look at the Charter School Movement (2016); National Alliance for Public Charter Schools, Estimated Charter Public School Enrollment 2016–2017 (2017).

Note: Data are presented by calendar year in which the school year ends. Data are estimates for 2016 and 2017. In Figure 1b, approximately 20 percent of the enrollment in each year on average cannot be categorized by management structure, owing to data limitations.

Figure 2

Likelihood of Charter Application Approval

A study of 639 charter school applications in four states found that applications identifying an external funding source were 7 percentage points more likely to be approved than those that did not. Charter school applications that included plans to hire a management organization were 10 percentage points more likely to be approved.

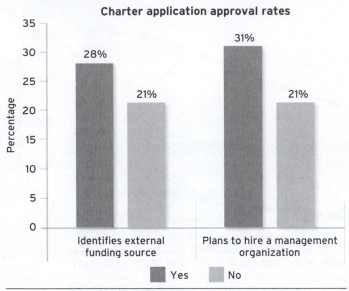

Charter application approval rates

Source: Nicotera and Stuit, "Three Signs That a Proposed Charter School Is at Risk of Failing," Thomas B. Fordham Institute, April 2017.

Note: The four states included in the study were Colorado, Indiana, North Carolina, and Texas.

28 percent of charters were approved, compared to 21 percent of those who did not identify such a source (see Figure 2).

"You see single-site schools, in particular with leaders of color, who don't have access to capital to grow," said Talbot. "It mirrors small business." Neophyte entrepreneurs, including some women of color, "just don't have access to the same financial resources to start up and expand."

Michele Mason added that the funding problem is not resolved even if the school gets authorized. "Mom-and-pops don't spend time focusing on [fundraising and networking] and they don't go out there and get the money. They're not on that circuit at all."

"Money is an issue," agreed Karega Rausch, vice president of research and evaluation at the National Association of Charter School Authorizers (NACSA). "If you look at folks who have received funding from the federal Charter Schools Program, for instance . . . those are the people getting schools off the ground. And this whole process is easier for a charter network that does not require the same level of investment as new startups."

Authorizing and the Politics of Scale

Charter-school authorizing policies differ from state to state and are perhaps the greatest determinant of when, where, and what kind of new charter schools can open—and how long they stay in business. Such policies therefore have a major impact on the number and variety of schools available and the diversity of leaders who run them.

For example, on one end of the policy spectrum lies the strict regulatory approach embodied by the NACSA authorizing frameworks; on the other end, the open and pluralistic Arizona charter law. Each approach presents very different conditions for solo charter founders, for the growth of the sector as a whole, and, by extension, for the cultivation of political constituencies that might advocate for chartering now and in the future.

Arizona's more open approach to authorizing has led to explosive growth: in 2015–2016, nearly 16 percent of the state's public school students—the highest share among all the states—attended charter schools. The approach also earned Arizona the "Wild West" moniker among charter insiders. But as Matthew Ladner of the Charles Koch Institute argues, the state's sector has found balance—in part because of an aggressive period of school closures between 2012 and 2016—and now boasts rapidly increasing scores on the National Assessment of Educational Progress, particularly among Hispanic students (see "In Defense of Education's 'Wild West,'" *Features,* Spring 2018). It has also produced such stellar college-preparatory schools as Great Hearts Academies and BASIS Independent Schools, whose success has helped the Arizona charter movement gain political support outside of its urban centers.

"When you have Scottsdale's soccer moms on your side, your charters aren't going away," said Ladner.

NACSA's approach, conversely, is methodical and therefore tends to be slow. Its tight controls on entry into the charter space have come to typify the authorizing process in many states—and have given rise to a number of the country's best-performing schools and networks of any type, including Success Academy in New York City, Achievement First in Connecticut, Brooke Charter Schools in Boston, and the independent Capital City Public Charter School in District of Columbia. However, some of NACSA's policy positions could be considered unfriendly to sector growth. For instance, the association recommends that the initial term of charters be for no more than five years, and that every state develop a provision requiring automatic closure of schools whose test scores fall below a minimum level. Such provisions may have the most impact on single-site, community-focused charters, which might be concentrating on priorities other than standardized test scores and whose test results might therefore lag, at least in the first few years of operation.

Certainly, responsible oversight of charter schools is essential and that includes the ability to close bad schools. "Despite a welcome, increasing trend of closing failing schools [over] the last five years, closing a school is still very hard," Rausch said. "Authorizers should open lots of innovative and new kinds of schools, but they also have to be able to close them if they fail kids. We can't just open, open, open. We need to make sure that when a family chooses a school there's some expectation that the school is OK."

"You have this conundrum where [there are] leaders of color, with one to two schools, serving the highest-needs population, who also have the least monetary and human capital support to deal with that challenge."

The issue of quality is anchored in the pact between charter schools and their authorizers (and by extension, the public). Charter schools are exempt from certain rules and regulations, and in exchange for this freedom and flexibility, they are expected to meet accountability guidelines and get results. Over time, authorizers have increasingly defined those results by state test scores.

By this measure, the large CMOs have come out ahead. Overall, schools run by them have produced greater gains in student learning on state assessments, in both math and reading, than their district school counterparts, while the mom-and-pops have fared less well, achieving just a small edge over district schools in reading and virtually none in math (see Figure 3).

But some charter advocates are calling for a more nuanced definition of quality, particularly in light of the population that most standalone charters—especially those with leaders of color—plan to serve. This is a fault-line issue in the movement.

"Diverse leadership is a key element if we want to catalyze both authentic community and political engagement to support the movement's future."

"In my experience, leaders of color who are opening single sites are delivering a model that is born out of the local community," said Talbot. "We've witnessed

Figure 3

Larger Academic Gains at Charters Operated by Charter Management Organizations

Compared to their local peers in district schools, students attending charter schools operated by charter management organizations gain the equivalent of 17 days of learning in both math and reading. Independent charter schools produce smaller though still significant gains in reading, but have no clear effect in math.

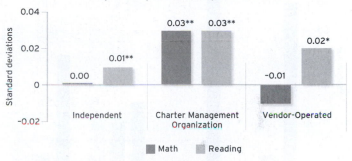

Impact of charter sector attendance on student academic growth, by school management structure

* Statistically significant at the 95% confidence level
** Statistically significant at the 99% confidence level

Source: Center for Research on Education Outcomes, "Charter Management Organizations 2017."
Note: Vendor-operated schools are operated by education service providers that support multiple schools on a contracted basis but do not hold the charters for the schools they serve. The majority of vendor-operated schools are for-profit. Many vendors can be classified as for-profit education management organizations (EMOs).

single-site charters headed by leaders of color serve large numbers of students who have high needs. Not at-risk . . . but seriously high needs—those ongoing emergent life and family conditions that come with extreme poverty," such as homelessness. "When you compound this with [a school's] lack of access to capital and support . . . you have this conundrum where you have leaders of color, with one to two schools, serving the highest-needs population, who also have the least monetary and human-capital support to deal with that challenge. And as a result, their data doesn't look very good. An authorizer is going to say to a school like that, 'You're not ready to expand. You might not even be able to stay open.'"

When it comes to attempting a turnaround, standalone schools are again at a disadvantage relative to the CMOs. "What happens with the mom-and-pops is that if they don't do well early—if their data doesn't look good—there's no one there to bail them out," said Mason. "They don't have anyone to come and help with the programming. The academic supports. And if they don't have results early, then they're immediately on probation and they're climbing uphill trying to build a team, get culture

Figure 4

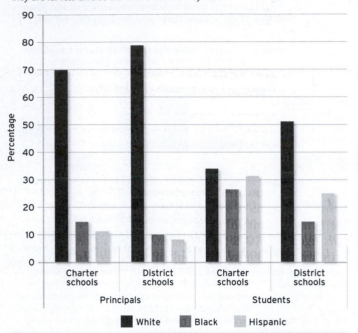

School Leaders Less Diverse Than Students across Sectors

Charter school principals are more diverse than principals of district schools, but they are far less diverse than the students they serve.

Legend: White (black) / Black (dark gray) / Hispanic (light gray)

Source: Data for principals from U.S. Department of Education, "Characteristics of Public Elementary and Secondary School Principals in the United States," August 2017; data for students from the National Center on Education Statistics, Digest of Education Statistics.

better advised to provide these leaders with more support in several areas: building better networks of consultants who can straddle the worlds of philanthropy and community; recruiting from nontraditional sources to diversify the pool of potential leaders, in terms of both race and worldview; and allowing more time to produce tangible results. Such supports might help more mom-and-pops succeed and, in the process, help expand and diversify (in terms of charter type and leader) the movement as a whole while advancing its political credibility.

The numbers tell the story on the subject of leadership. Charter schools serve a higher percentage of black and Hispanic students than district schools do, and while charter schools boast greater percentages of black and Hispanic principals than district schools, these charter-school leaders overall are far less diverse than the students they serve (see Figure 4). Though many may view charter schools primarily through the lens of performance, it seems that many of the families who choose them value community—the ability to see themselves in their schools and leaders—substantially more than we originally believed. Diverse leadership, therefore, is a key element if we want to catalyze both authentic community and political engagement to support the movement's future.

More Is Better

A schooling sector that does not grow to a critical mass will always struggle for political survival. So what issues are at play when we consider the future growth of charter schools, and what role will single sites and a greater variety of school offerings play in that strategy? There's no consensus on the answer.

A more pluralistic approach to charter creation—one that embraces more-diverse types of schools, academic offerings, and leadership and helps more independent schools get off the ground—might entail risks in terms of quality control, but it could also help the movement expand more quickly. And steady growth could in turn help the movement mount a robust defense in the face of deepening opposition from teachers unions and other anti-charter actors such as the NAACP. (Last year the NAACP released a task force report on charter schools, calling for an outright moratorium on new schools for the present and significant rule changes that would effectively end future charter growth.)

Another viewpoint within the movement, though, points out that the sector is still growing, though at a slower pace and even if there is a coincident reduction in the diversity of school types.

and academics in place. CMOs have all the resources to come in and intervene if they see things going awry."

Then, too, a charter school, especially an independent one, can often fill a specialized niche, focusing on the performing arts, or science, or world languages. "As an independent charter school, you have to be offering families something different, . . . and in our case it's the opportunity for kids to become fully bilingual and bi-literate," offered Barbara Martinez of HoLa. "It's not about being better or beating the district. It's about ensuring that you are not only offering a unique type of educational program, but that you also happen to be preparing kids for college and beyond. For us, [charter] autonomy and flexibility allow us to do that in a way that some districts can't or won't."

In short, the superior performance of CMO schools vis-à-vis test scores does not imply that we should only focus on growing CMO-run schools. Given the resource disadvantages that independent operators face, and the challenging populations that many serve, we would be

"We know the movement is still growing because the number of kids enrolled in charter schools is still growing," said NACSA's Rausch. "It's just not growing at the same clip it used to, despite the fact that authorizers are approving the same percentage of applications." He also noted that certain types of growth might go untallied: the addition of seats at an existing school, for instance, or the opening of a new campus to serve more students.

Rausch notes that one factor hampering sector-wide growth is a shrinking supply of prospective operators, single site or otherwise. "We've seen a decline overall in the number of applications that authorizers receive," he said. "What we need are more applications and more people that are interested in starting new single sites, or more single sites that want to grow into networks. But I'm also not sure there is the same level of intentional cultivation to get people to do this work [anymore]. I wonder if there is the same kind of intensity around [starting charters] as there used to be."

Many charter supporters, however, don't believe that an anemic startup supply is the only barrier to sector expansion in general, or to the growth of independent schools. Indeed, many believe there are "preferences" baked into the authorizing process that actually hinder both of these goals, inhibiting the movement's progress and its creativity. That is, chartering is a movement that began with the aspiration of starting many kinds of schools, but it may have morphed into one that is only adept at starting one type of school: a highly structured school that is run by a CMO or an EMO and whose goal is to close achievement gaps for low-income kids of color while producing exceptional test scores. This "type" of charter is becoming synonymous with the term "charter school" across most of America. Among many charter leaders and supporters, these are schools that "we know work."

In many regions of the country, these charters dominate the landscape and have had considerable success. However, given the pluralistic spirit of chartering overall, the issue of why they dominate is a salient one. Is it chance or is it engineered? Fordham's report revealed that only 21 percent of applicants who did not plan to hire a CMO or an EMO to run their school had their charters approved, compared to 31 percent for applicants who did have such plans, which *could* indicate a bias toward CMO or EMO applicants over those who wish to start stand-alone schools. As Fordham's Michael Petrilli and Amber Northern put it in the report's foreword: "The factors that led charter applicants to be rejected may very well predict low performance, had the schools been allowed to open. But since the applications with the factors were less likely to be approved, we have no way of knowing."

> *"It's important to remember** that every network started as a single school. We need to continue to support that. I don't think it's either CMO or single site. It's a 'both/and.'"*

The institutional strength implied by a "brand name" such as Uncommon Schools or IDEA might give CMO schools more traction with authorizers and the public. "The truth is that telling a community that a school with a track record is going to open is significantly easier than a new idea," offered Rausch. "But it's important to remember that every network started as a single school. We need to continue to support that. I don't think it's either CMO or single site. It's a 'both/and.'"

If there is a bias toward CMO charters as the "school of choice" among authorizers, why might that be, and what would it mean for single sites? Some believe the problem is one where the goal of these schools is simply lost in the listening—or lack of it—and that the mom-and-pops could benefit from the assistance of professionals who know how to communicate a good idea to authorizers and philanthropists.

The language of "education people in general, and people of color in education specifically . . . doesn't match up with the corporate language [that pervades the field and] that underpins authorizing and charter growth decisions," said Talbot. "I think more [charter growth] funds, philanthropists, foundations, need . . . let's call it translation . . . so there is common ground between leaders of color, single-site startups, foundations, and other participants in the space. I think this is imperative for growth, for recognition, and for competitiveness."

What Now?

The future of chartering poses many questions. Admittedly, state authorizing laws frame the way the "what" and "who" of charters is addressed. Yet it is difficult to ignore some of the issues that have grown out of the "deliberate" approach to authorizing that has typified much of recent charter creation.

Some places, such as Colorado, have significant populations of single-site schools, but overall, the movement doesn't seem to be trending that way. Rausch noted that certain localities, such as Indianapolis, have had many charter-school leaders of color, but the movement, particularly on the coasts, is mainly the province of white school leaders and organizational heads who tend to hold homogeneous views on test scores, school structure, and "what works." And while some Mountain States boast charter populations that are diverse in ethnicity, income, and location, in the states with the greatest number of charters, the schools are densely concentrated in urban areas and largely serve low-income students of color. Neither of these scenarios is "right," but perhaps a clever mix of both represents a more open, diverse, inclusive, and sustainable future for the charter movement. In the end, the answers we seek may not lie in the leaves that have grown on the chartering tree, but in the chaotic and diverse roots that started the whole movement in the first place.

Derrell Bradford is an executive vice president of 50CAN, a national nonprofit that advocates for equal opportunity in K–12 education and a senior visiting fellow at the Thomas B. Fordham Institute.

Robin Lake et al.

Why Is Charter Growth Slowing?

Lessons from the Bay Area

Since the nation's first charter-school law was passed in 1991, charter schools throughout the United States have enjoyed steady and relatively rapid growth. Today, they serve more than three million students nationwide—nearly three times as many students as a decade ago. In cities like New Orleans and Detroit, which have especially robust charter sectors, more students attend charters than district schools.

But the rate of growth is slowing. Until 2013, the total number of U.S. charter schools was increasing by 6–8 percent each year. Since then, that number has fallen steadily, to less than 2 percent in 2016 (see Figure 1). At the same time, waiting lists remain long for many charter schools, and their overall academic performance is strong. So why is growth slowing, and what can charter leaders, policy makers, and communities do to regain momentum and keep pace with demand?

To explore this question, we study charter growth in a single region as a case study: the Bay Area, which includes San Francisco and the cities, suburbs, and rural areas that surround it. California is one of the nation's leading charter-school states, and charters have boomed in the Bay Area in particular. The area also is in the midst of a five-year decline in the rate of charter growth, mirroring the national trend. We survey charter operators and analyze the policy environment, market forces, and other dynamics contributing to an overall slowdown in expansion.

Our study finds that charter schools are encountering a set of interlocking barriers to growth that essentially reflect the price of success. As charters have become a more significant presence, especially in their target cities, they are encountering scarce facilities, increased competition with one another, and heightened political opposition. These intense new dynamics exacerbate the already challenging realities of a maturing sector: after a period of rapid expansion, many charter networks are also choosing to pause growth to attend to internal needs, including improving instruction and talent development. These conditions call for a range of interventions to restore strong charter growth, such as new measures to expand access to school facilities, increased coordination among charter operators, and stronger partnerships between charters, local districts, and state officials.

Figure 1

National Charter School Growth Rate Drops

Until 2014, the charter sector enjoyed a steady growth rate, with the total number of charter schools increasing by 6–9 percent each year. That growth rate has fallen sharply since, dipping below 2 percent in 2015 and 2016.

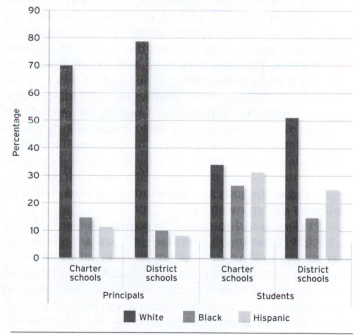

Source: National Alliance for Public Charter Schools.
Note: Data presented by calendar year in which the school year ends.

While the specific factors constraining growth in the Bay Area may not be strictly relevant elsewhere, they do shed light on factors potentially at play in multiple settings nationwide. And with an estimated half million students on waiting lists across the United States, breaking through barriers to more quickly expand high-quality charters is an urgent need.

After a Charter Boom

Charter schools have a relatively long history in California, where the state legislature first authorized them in 1992. Several aspects of that law made it one of the fastest-growing charter states. Unlike many other states, charter growth is not tightly capped, with an additional 100 schools allowed to open each year. Local school districts are the primary authorizer for most charters, but charter schools can also be approved by their county or the state board of education if rejected by their district. This diverse pool of authorizers, loose cap, and strong appeals process work together to ensure applications are not arbitrarily denied. Today, California has the largest charter-school enrollment and greatest number of charter schools in the country, with 630,000 students at 1,275 schools statewide.

Charters have flourished in particular in the Bay Area, the five-county region we focus on in our study: Alameda, Contra Costa, San Francisco, San Mateo, and Santa Clara. The region includes 108 school districts in all, which enrolled 834,000 students in 2016–2017. While demographics differ from county to county, each one serves a majority of nonwhite students and significant populations of students who are economically disadvantaged and enrolled in English Language Learner programs. There are currently 178 charter schools, serving about 10 percent of all students. Some 110 charter schools were part of a network or management organization, while 68 schools were freestanding.

While individual school performance varies, charter schools generally outperform district schools in the Bay Area. In a 2015 report, Stanford University's Center for Research on Education Outcomes (CREDO) found that the average charter-school student in the Bay Area attained significantly more growth in reading and math than similar students in nearby district schools—and that this difference increased the longer he or she stayed in a charter school. In addition, a 2016 analysis by Innovate Public Schools found the majority of Bay Area public schools achieving above-average results for low-income Latino and African American students were charter schools. Demand for charters has remained strong, based on data from schools' self-reported waiting lists. A 2015 study

by Bellwether Education Partners found 91,000 students on charter school waiting lists in California as a whole, including 2,261 in Oakland.

However, the pace of new charter school openings and enrollment growth in the Bay Area has slowed in recent years (see Figure 2). New schools continue to open each year, but the rate slowed considerably from its peak in 2012–2013, when more than 18 percent additional students enrolled compared to the previous year. Since then, the sector has added fewer students every year, enrolling about 4 percent additional students in 2017–2018. Non-charter enrollment in the Bay Area has been almost flat during the same period.

We set out to learn what factors are inhibiting charter growth in the Bay Area, and to identify how they can be addressed. Our goal was to confirm or deny the many hypotheses that could explain the slowdown, and determine what strategies would support faster growth.

We conducted telephone interviews with representatives from organizations that operate 74 different Bay Area charter schools, taking care to seek evidence and to corroborate with other interviews as a check on individual views. We examined data on school authorizations, openings, closings, and enrollment, and reviewed information on Bay Area charter authorizers from the National Association of Charter School Authorizers (NACSA). Our research also included reviewing media coverage, public polling data, demographic data, and facilities leasing and purchasing information.

The available data were limited, and further analysis is needed to quantify more precisely some of the challenges we identify here. Still, we find clear, consistent barriers to charter school growth: a lack of access to affordable school buildings, increased competition among charter schools for students and resources, and a political backlash to the growing presence of charter schools. We also identify areas that are *not* directly contributing to the recent slowdown, such as parent demand and the availability of trained teachers. Below, we detail the three major speed bumps along with interventions that our research suggests could help overcome them—both in the Bay Area and in communities facing similar challenges.

Barrier #1: Too Few School Facilities

The most immediate and overwhelming single-factor constraining charter school growth in the Bay Area is a lack of access to affordable school buildings. This phenomenon is common across the United States, with charters fighting for space in high-cost cities without the legislative and

> *The average charter-school student in the Bay Area attained significantly more growth in reading and math than similar students in nearby district schools.*

financial supports that district schools enjoy (see "Whose School Buildings Are They, Anyway?" *features*, Fall 2012).

Facilities were named the primary reason that charters are not growing more quickly by the operators we interviewed and surveyed. The scarcity of school buildings acts as a hard cap on growth, because no matter what other assets a charter school has, no building means no school. As one charter leader said, "Our growth plan for the next year will be either 100 percent successful or 100 percent catastrophic if I don't find a property in the next three months."

Several factors contribute to the facilities squeeze, including the high cost of real estate and a policy environment in which district leaders can more easily access commercial real estate than charter leaders. Buildings in the Bay Area that are suitable for school facilities are both limited and expensive, making it very difficult to find affordable long-term leases on the private market. The logical buildings to look to, then, are those owned by local school districts.

A 2000 state initiative was supposed to help. California Proposition 39 compels districts to provide facilities for students within their boundaries who attend charter schools. But too often, the buildings made available to them are insufficient for charters' needs. And because the rule mandates that districts provide facilities only for students who live within the district, charter schools that serve students from multiple districts often are offered facilities that cannot house all of the students in their school.

Alternatively, districts are required to give local charters first refusal to rent or purchase "surplus" space or buildings. But that option is only helpful when districts identify "surplus" space, and charter operators report that many have been unwilling to share their facilities or consolidate under-enrolled schools in order to do so.

Further complicating matters, Proposition 39 only requires districts to issue one-year leases, which are often inconvenient, inefficient, and expensive. For example, a charter school that serves 200 students might be offered two spaces capable of housing 100 students each in different buildings, sometimes not even near each other. Having disparate locations hampers school functions like student recruitment, school culture, and potentially,

Figure 2

Charter School and Enrollment Growth Stall in the Bay Area

Until 2014, the charter sector enjoyed a steady growth rate, with the total number of charter schools increasing by 6–9 percent each year. That growth rate has fallen sharply since, dipping below 2 percent in 2015 and 2016.

2a) Growth in the number of charter schools in the Bay Area has mirrored the national trend, with a sharp slowdown in recent years.

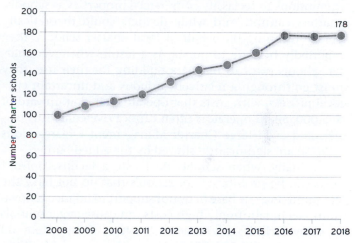

2b) The enrollment growth rate in Bay Area charter schools peaked in 2013, with over 18 percent more students attending than in the previous year. Growth has slowed steadily since and fell to 3.8 percent in 2018. District enrollment in the Bay Area has been almost flat since 2009.

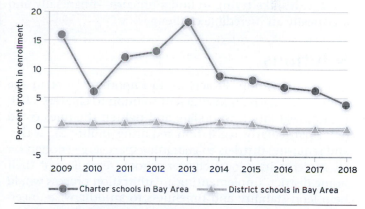

Source: California Charter Schools Association.
Note: Data presented by calendar year in which the school year ends. In Figure 2b, data for 2018 are estimates.

student learning and enrichment opportunities. And without long-term commitments, charters often have to move. One operator explained the burden this creates: "It's hard to build continuity for staff and families if you don't know by May where the school will be in August."

Districts also have reportedly become more sophisticated about fighting Proposition 39 requests, and those bureaucratic delays can make it too time-consuming and expensive for a charter school to fight a resistant district for space. When district rental agreements are not available or renewed, and charter schools cannot secure another location, they must close.

Another facilities option is to rezone commercial buildings for school use, but again, the regulations in place make this far more difficult for charters than for school districts. While districts can exercise zoning exemptions to reclassify commercial properties as schools, charters cannot. And while districts could theoretically pursue rezoning on behalf of local charter schools, they reportedly hesitate to do so. As a result, whenever charter schools want to rezone a building for their use, they must go through a relatively arduous and uncertain city-level process, with costs that operators cited at upward of $65,000. Small operators often cannot overcome this barrier, and even large Charter Management Organizations (CMOs) are significantly slowed by the added burden.

Finally, when schools do locate a facility, upfront costs can be prohibitive for schools that do not have the per-pupil revenue base or donor support to finance renovations. Such dauntingly high costs can cause larger schools to delay facilities investments by years. While state aid under Senate Bill 740 (SB740) does support some facilities expense, that program is not currently sufficient to offset the true cost. One operator described the situation neatly: "District Prop 39 policies are prohibitive, and the market is crazy. It's like trying to find a unicorn—financially and logistically an incredible challenge."

Solutions

While Proposition 39 acts as an important "foot in the door," it remains an insufficient solution to charters' challenges. Legislation to update and tighten the rules could help, particularly legislation requiring multi-year leases, and requiring districts to guarantee space large enough for all students in a local charter school, regardless of their home district. Implementing an arbitration process would help lend stability and timeliness to an otherwise uncertain dispute process.

We see other potential legislative or regulatory fixes as well. Mandating that districts house charter students before the district seeks bond funding could help relieve facility shortages. Allowing charter schools to access the zoning exemptions that districts use to turn commercial facilities into schools would also open up more options. Zoning flexibility for schools with nontraditional approaches (like small-group instruction or one-to-one blended learning models) would make it easier for

innovative schools to find space that fits their needs, such as using office occupancy standards instead of the usual school standards for rezoning. And retooling SB740 to keep better pace with charters' facilities costs could also help.

Ultimately, the growth of charters will be fundamentally constrained as long as districts fail to consolidate or close under-enrolled district schools. Serious attention needs to go into developing a strategy that mandates or creates incentives for these actions and provides political backing to district and board officials. The state could offer "consolidation grants" to districts willing to use their space to maximum efficiency; levy a "tax" on districts with unutilized space, for failing to use public buildings to public benefit; or take building ownership rights away from districts that fail to manage them efficiently. Or the state could simply require that districts that fail to reduce costs responsibly get out of the property-ownership business, either by having the state assume ownership, by placing the buildings into a third-party trust, or by establishing a cooperative to which charter schools have equal rights.

Barrier #2: Internal Challenges

New charters in the Bay Area—particularly in Oakland—are spending a lot of time and energy competing with other charter schools for facilities and resources. In interviews, leaders point to fierce competition for the few available and affordable buildings, as well as missed opportunities to coordinate on common issues like staff recruitment. And because there are so many high-quality management organizations interested in expansion, little attention has been paid to providing support and incubation for new school operators. For example, we spoke to one community member whose group had managed to navigate the politics of the application process and get approved at the state level after being denied at the district and county levels, only to find they couldn't secure a facility.

Charter advocates in the Bay Area seem to subscribe to a "survival of the fittest" ethic, which holds that because running a successful charter school requires so much capacity, if potential operators are scared off from pursuing an application without a lot of handholding, it's probably for the best. This was a reasonable strategy in

---

Charters are fighting for space in high-cost cities without the legislative and financial supports that district schools enjoy.

---

the early days when the supply of savvy entrepreneurs was plentiful and charters were booming, but it may be time to look deeper for quality operators and provide more support.

Larger management organizations, which have traditionally fueled a major portion of Bay Area charter expansion, are increasingly rethinking their growth plans in order to refine and improve their models. For some, recent results from new Common Core–aligned tests were a wake-up call that their students were not learning concepts deeply enough. Other organizations are dealing with labor issues, such as stepped-up efforts by the California Teachers Association to organize charter school teachers. And many organizations are shifting toward sharing knowledge with district-run schools rather than simply growing as many schools as quickly as possible. At least two well-recognized Bay Area management organizations have recently decided against further expansion for the time being and are instead starting consulting efforts or creating structured professional-development workshops and materials for district-run schools.

Overall, most charter leaders we spoke to felt that start-up funding is reasonably easy to secure, especially for school networks with a strong track record of success. However, because of the political and facilities impediments described above, the rising cost of doing business has made substantial growth untenable for most charter schools. Smaller management organizations and standalone schools in particular lack the resources and connections to fight the various battles required to grow.

Meanwhile, the funding community is not sufficiently supporting these smaller players to make it worth their while. In interviews, many leaders told us they believe that the Bay Area's supply of effective schools is limited today by the philanthropic funding strategies used in the past. In particular, there is a consistent perception that single-site schools and school leaders of color who are not tied into local funder networks have historically not been connected to dominant funding channels.

Further hampering growth, the charter leaders we interviewed said that start-up dollars are the hardest to come by in the communities they consider most viable for charter school expansion. Operators are finding it easy to access philanthropic funding in urban Oakland and San Francisco, but see those places as "over-saturated" and gentrifying. By contrast, in the less urban area of western Contra Costa County, there are more available facilities and a growing population of students that match most charter schools' target populations—but fewer opportunities to access philanthropic dollars to start up new schools.

As one charter-school operator said, "People are moving farther and farther away from cities [because they can't afford to live there] and into poor-performing school districts. An organization like KIPP—if they want to double in the next five years—they'll need to go in these areas. But charters are not going there because there is no funding there."

Solutions

Charters share common challenges and can coordinate to support common solutions. A legal action fund to promote sector-wide interests in the Bay Area and to engage in lawsuits around Proposition 39 and other barriers to growth could benefit all charter schools, especially the small schools that don't have the resources to engage in protracted legal battles.

Funders should consider supporting growth where charter operators believe the need is greatest and barriers to entry are low. No data exist on the prevalence of charter leaders of color, so we have no way to assess the impact of past or present funding efforts. It may be time to start collecting these data and to create even more avenues for identifying and supporting promising school and management organization founders who are not on funders' radars.

A centralized process or organization to help single-site schools and small networks outsource facilities searches, such as through the state charter-school association, could also help ease a shared burden. In addition, small operators would benefit if start-up costs were supported with more subsidies or loan programs, or with more philanthropic support. Many facilities funding programs are lease or reimbursement programs that rely on schools raising funds or collateral, but upfront funds remain elusive.

Barrier #3: Political Backlash

Political opposition has always been a reality for charters, but leaders we interviewed report that it is growing, in part because of national politics and in part because of local resistance to the charters' expanding presence and the perceived fiscal impact on districts.

Districts facing financial strains often see charters as responsible for their challenges (whether this perception is accurate or not). As a result, charter growth becomes an enemy of district financial security in the minds of some school boards. In response, districts have become skilled at limiting charter growth, not only by blocking access to facilities but also by bringing lawsuits against growing schools and making charters' compliance with state regulations more difficult. In addition, charters are being asked to jump through bureaucratic hoops and comply with complex public-records requests and onerous administrative requirements, which one leader described as "death by a thousand cuts."

Teachers unions also have reportedly stepped up their resistance strategies and are increasingly coordinating opposition campaigns with local school districts and attorneys. Statewide advertising campaigns and targeted local resistance efforts are increasingly common nationwide. An annual poll by *Education Next* in 2017 showed that public support for charter schools has recently fallen, particularly among Democrats, and opposition has grown (see "The 2017 *EdNext* Poll on School Reform," *features*, Winter 2018).

On the other hand, charter advocacy also is on the rise, often resulting in successful campaigns for school board races. By one accounting, the California Charter Schools Association spent more than $12 million on candidates for school board and other races in 2016 and 2017. Also in 2017, charter advocates celebrated the successful election of two charter-friendly board members to the Los Angeles Unified School District, leading to a reform-friendly board majority. The Oakland and San Francisco boards have seen similar electoral shifts.

Solutions

Diffusing political fights isn't a matter of just winning elections. Truly stabilizing charters' role and ensuring their expansion can keep pace with demand calls for a new way of thinking about the charter–district school relationship. One interviewee suggested that the Bay Area would do well to help district leaders think of their jobs as overseeing a broad portfolio of educational options with various governance models, to potentially include having all schools operate with charter-like autonomies. As one charter authorizer said: "If there's one thing I could change, it would be portfolio management. If a district [leader] can go to bed each day and think, 'what we can do for our kids?' If the kid goes to a district or charter shouldn't matter."

This sort of thinking could be especially helpful in addressing the facilities challenge. One possibility would be to found an independent commission of civic leaders empowered to advise district authorizers on where to place new charters. This commission would help site new charters in underserved neighborhoods and minimize competition for scarce facilities, for example. It is crucial that such a commission is impartial to the self-interest of

---

Districts have become skilled at limiting charter growth, not only by blocking access to facilities but also by bringing lawsuits and making charters' compliance with regulations more difficult.

---

particular networks and district self-interests, and base facilities decisions on school quality, student need, and efficient usage.

The Cleveland Transformation Alliance (CTA) provides something of an example of what's possible. The independent CTA is governed by a board of representatives from Cleveland's mayor's office, the school district, multiple charter operators, and local community organizations. The board monitors school quality, provides information to families, and tracks the overall portfolio of options. Less formally, more than 20 cities, through the Gates Foundation–funded District-Charter Collaboration Compacts, have established cooperative working groups focused on a range of topics, such as solving shared problems, addressing gaps in service across sectors for students and families, and sharing innovative practices.

Fueling Faster Charter Growth

It may be that, to help charters grow, we must first help districts cope with their particular challenges, including legacy costs. This issue is causing significant pain in places like San Jose and Oakland, which might otherwise be open to more charter schools.

We have recently suggested potential "grand bargains" between districts, state education agencies, and charter operators that might work to pool their strengths to address one another's challenges, in a 2017 paper titled "Better Together." In such arrangements, the state might grant funding or loosen rules for districts and charters that want to become more nimble and work in partnership with one another. For example, charters might gain access to facilities or special education supports, and would help contribute to a fund to buy down pension obligations in exchange.

Already, some cities are finding political advantage in creating "hybrid" or "partnership" schools that have the

---

Truly stabilizing charters' role and ensuring their expansion can keep pace with demand calls for a new way of thinking about the charter–district school relationship.

---

full autonomy of a charter school but operate on contract with districts within district-provided buildings, generally created by state legislation. Examples include schools in Indianapolis; Tulsa; Atlanta; and Camden, NJ. Besides gaining access to district buildings, these schools also tend to attract principals and teachers who like the idea of working more closely with districts and being part of systemic reform. These new models also help address the problems of saturation and economies of scale by operating in collaboration with the district. There are potential downsides, such as the risk of diluted autonomy and accountability, but given the intensity of the challenge in the Bay Area and cities across the United States, this could be a good option to explore.

Even beyond so-called "grand bargains," many of these paths forward will be challenging, requiring a greater deal of coordination and collaboration from districts, charter operators, funders, and other stakeholders than is the current custom. But through innovation and cooperation, charter schools in the Bay Area and beyond can nurture a second generation of impact, both in the students they serve and the broader systemic improvements they inspire.

What Comes Next After Easy Growth Ends

Our study has revealed a Bay Area charter sector that, now well into its second decade, must adjust to its own maturity. At the most basic level, Bay Area charters have simply been priced out of a very expensive facilities market. That is a critical issue, but the story is complicated by a set of interlocking factors that are, in part, the natural outgrowth of what has been a very successful school-improvement movement and, in part, a normal maturation process. Facilities scarcity, driven by political discord between charters and districts, puts a hard cap on charter growth. Funder preferences for certain locales, combined with the failure of districts to adjust to enrollment loss, create a pressure cooker for political backlash. The supply of operators is constrained by authorizers and funding decisions, as well as by reliance on highly motivated and savvy management organizations to single-handedly provide most of the needed schools. Meanwhile, those organizations are experiencing growing pains of their own.

The easy days of Bay Area, and possibly national, charter growth may be over. Anyone serious about finding a way to meet the still-desperate need for better education in the region can't afford to sit back and hope the old strategies will eventually work. While there are many potential paths forward to reinvigorate the growth of quality charter schools in the Bay Area, doing so will require new ideas and new strategic investments.

ROBIN LAKE is a director of the Center on Reinventing Public Education at the University of Washington Bothell.

ROOHI SHARMA is a research coordinator.

ALICE OPALKA is a special assistant to the director.

TREY COBB is a graduate student at the University of Notre Dame and a middle school math teacher.

EXPLORING THE ISSUE

Should Charter Schools Be Expanded?

Critical Thinking and Reflection

1. Is charter-school expansion the beginning of a phasing out of public school education as we know it today?
2. Should charter schools be open options for all students or continue to be isolated to a select group?
3. Why choose charter schools over a public school education?
4. What does the argument "confusing structure with rules" mean for both the charter schools in the District of Columbia and New Orleans?
5. Cite reasons for the growth of charter schools since first legislated in the 1990s.
6. How many charter schools is "just right"?

Is There Common Ground?

The enduring debate on charter-school expansion is focused on whether charter schools do a better job of educating students than traditional public schools. Even with mixed results in the literature, charter schools continue to expand, particularly in large urban districts where up to 30 percent of children attend a charter school. Not specifically addressed in this issue is the "searing criticism that charter schools are accelerating the resegregation of American public education and whether there is harmful lack of diversity in the publicly funded, but independently run schools of choice" (*Education Week*, 2016, p. 4). Nathan (2016) states that despite the powerful opposition to charter schools, the movement is helping to solve some of the nation's toughest educational problems. A strong positive impact is being made on students who live in poverty and youngsters from troubled backgrounds. Because successful charter schools are identified with high student achievement, many are having their contracts renewed.

Of the 50 million K–12 public school students in the country, only 5 percent are enrolled in charter schools. Even 5 percent is significant when the only game in town for education has been a traditional public school. Charter schools are posing the only credible competition to the traditional system of educating the nation's youth. Serving almost exclusively high-poverty minority students, charter schools make significant gains, as noted in the CREDO 2015 report. Gabelman (2016) takes the opposite viewpoint, in that the extensive expansion of charter schools in the Nashville metropolitan area is bad for students, teachers, and taxpayers. Gabelman wants zero growth for charter schools.

Gabelman concludes that the picture is not all rosy. There is much frustration with unsuccessful charter schools that produce lackluster student performance. The number of failed charter schools is likely to increase in the coming years. This disrupts the education process and leaves students and their families "adrift" (Bowman, 2016, p. 25). In a review of 50 charter schools across Minnesota, most families are "beset with financial and managerial problems" (p. 26). Typically, confidence in the charter-school movement erode when this occurs, and the call for a clearer accountability system is made. Where will the line be drawn between autonomy, which is central to the charter idea, and accountability?

Where is the common ground? The *public* wants better schools, particularly for those students who struggle the most and have the least amount of resources. Maybe the best route for providing better education is opportunity, choice, and responsibility. These are the things charter schools tout for attaining higher student achievement outcomes. Creating new public schools in ways that aren't currently possible in most states is seen as a very natural evolution in addressing school reform. Many envision innovation in education as moving away from the direct district run concept with a school board, superintendent, and a large central office that oversees a system of schools. The concept of schools run by faculty, parents, and/or other community leaders may address the redefining of U.S. public education in the future. The incentive to improve student progress without crippling our current systems of public schools appears to be the common ground, but "when it comes to education politics today, it seems to be the last thing anyone wants to talk about" (Williams, 2018, p. 1).

Additional Resources

Bowman, D. (2016). Charter closings come under scrutiny. *Education Week*. Retrieved from http://www.edweek.org/media/ebooks/charter-school-movement-ebook.pdf

Education Week. (2016). *The charter school movement: 25 years in the making*. Bethesda, MD. Retrieved from http://www.edweek.org/media/ebooks/charter-school-movement-ebook.pdf

Casey, L. (2015). The charter school challenge. *New Labor Forum*. Retrieved from http://newlaborforum.cuny.edu/2015/01/17/the-charter-school-challenge/

Center for Research on Education Outcomes (CREDO). (2013). *National charter school study 2013*. Stanford University. Retrieved from http://credo.stanford.edu/documents/NCSS%202013%20Final%20Draft.pdf

Center for Research on Education Outcomes (CREDO). (2015). *Urban Charter School Study Report on 41 Regions 2015*. Stanford University. Retrieved from https://urbancharters.stanford.edu/download/Urban%20Charter%20School%20Study%20Report%20on%2041%20Regions.pdf

Center for Research on Education Outcomes (CREDO). (2018). *An evaluation of the 13 validation grant: Scaling the New Orleans charter restart model*. Stanford University. Retrieved from http://nolai3eval.stanford.edu/

DiCarlo, M. (2015). *Lessons and directions from the credo urban charter school study*. Albert Shanker Institute. Retrieved from http://www.shankerinstitute.org/blog/lessons-and-directions-credo-urban-charter-school-study

Haynes, C. (2015). *New CREDO study is seriously flawed, says critics*. National Center for Policy Analysis. Retrieved from http://educationblog.ncpa.org

Loveless, T. (2013). *Much ado about tiny differences*. The Brookings Institute. Retrieved from https://www.brookings.edu/research/charter-school-study-much-ado-about-tiny-differences/

Mathis, W. & Maul, A. (2013). *CREDO's significantly insignificant findings*. National Education Policy Center. Retrieved from http://nepc.colorado.edu/newsletter/2013/07/review-credo-2013

Nathan, J. (2016). The charter school movement is growing because it's working. *Education Week*. Retrieved from http://www.edweek.org/media/ebooks/charter-school-movement-ebook.pdf

National Alliance for Public Charter Schools. (2018). *Charter law database*. Retrieved from https://www.publiccharters.org/our-work/charter-law-database

National Charter School Resource Center. (2016). *What's a charter school?* Retrieved from https://www.charterschoolcenter.org/

Prothero, A. (2016). Does graduating from a charter school help or hinder future earnings? *Education Week*. Retrieved from http://www.edweek.org/ew/articles/2016/09/14/does-graduating-from-a-charter-help-or.html?cmp=eml-enl-eu-news2

Robles, Y. (2018). *Denver area charter prepares to expand into the suburbs, bringing a new option to Adams 14*. Retrieved from https://www.chalkbeat.org/posts/co/2018/06/21/denver-area-charter-school-kipp-prepares-to-expand-into-suburbs-new-option-adams-14/

Williams, C. (2018, June 2). Betsy Devos loves charter schools: That's bad for charter schools. *The New York Times*. Retrieved from https://www.nytimes.com/2018/06/02/opinion/sunday/betsy-devos-charter-schools-trump.html

Yousuf, S. (2016). The impact of charter schools on student achievement in the United States. *International Journal on New Trends in Education and their Implications 7*(1). Retrieved from http://www.ijonte.org/FileUpload/ks63207/File/08._sajid_ali_yousuf_zai_.pdf

Internet References . . .

Celebrate Charter-School Success

https://www.usnews.com/opinion/knowledge-bank/
articles/2017-10-05/expanding-the-best-charter-
schools-brings-more-education-success

Charter Schools and the Achievement Gap

https://futureofchildren.princeton.edu/sites/futureof-
children/files/resource-links/charter_schools_com-
piled.pdf

**Charter Schools Are Reshaping America's
Education System for the Worse**

https://www.thenation.com/article/charter-schools-
are-reshaping-americas-education-system-for-the-
worse/

**Exploring the Consequences of Charter-
school Expansion in U.S. Cities**

https://www.epi.org/publication/exploring-the-conse-
quences-of-charter-school-expansion-in-u-s-cities/

**Six Reasons Why Charter School
Expansion Is a Problem**

http://www.buildingbetterschools.com/2017/06/19/
six-reasons-why-charter-school-expansion-is-a-
problem-2/

Selected, Edited, and with Issue Framing Material by:
Glenn L. Koonce, *Regent University*

ISSUE

Is the Use of Technology Changing How Teachers Teach and Students Learn?

YES: Joanne Jacobs, from "Beyond the Factory Model: Oakland Teachers Learn How to Blend," *Education Next* (2014)

NO: Benjamin Herold, from "Why Ed Tech Is Not Transforming How Teachers Teach: Student-Centered, Technology-Driven Instruction Remains Elusive for Most," *Education Week* (2015)

Learning Outcomes

After reading this issue, you will be able to:

- Identify the positive effects that technology has on student learning according to Jacobs.
- xplain some reasons for the slow movement to use technology to enhance student learning.
- Examine a variety of ways that technology is changing how teachers teach.
- List reasons why some teachers aren't as proactive in using technology in their classrooms.
- Describe a student centered classroom and how effective digital teaching can change teaching and learning.

ISSUE SUMMARY

YES: Former San Jose Mercury News editorial writer and columnist for K-12 education, Joanne Jacobs, provides evidence from the field that technology use through Blended Learning strategies has a positive effect on student learning outcomes even though she acknowledges it is not "transformational" right now.

NO: Benjamin Herold posits that a mountain of evidence indicates that teachers have been painfully slow to transform the way they teach despite the massive influx of new technology into their classrooms.

Schools across the nation have made an enormous investment in technology in order to keep up with the demands of twenty-first century learners. According to an Ed NET Insight report, the cost is considerable—$10 billion a year and rising (Schaffhauser, 2016). These costs include hardware, software, teacher training, and tech support, but is this technology truly changing how teachers teach and students learn? Whether it is teacher pedagogy or student knowledge, skills and abilities, creating meaningful technological change in America's classrooms is complex. Conflicting views about the impact of technology on teaching and learning abound in the literature. One side provides evidence that educational technology is changing the face of traditional classrooms, while the contrary side finds that technology use for student learning, especially achievement gains, is elusive. Recently published articles provide evidence of the conflicting views. For example, "Technology Is Changing the Way Educators Teach" by Angie Mason in a December 5, 2013, How to Learn blog post reinforces the view that technology is indeed changing the way teachers teach. On the other hand, Benjamin Herold's June 10, 2015 Education Week blog post titled "Why Ed Tech Is Not Transforming How Teachers Teach" (the NO article in this issue) takes the opposite viewpoint.

An AdvancED study involving 140,000 direct classroom observations in K-12 schools in 39 states and 11 countries showed that in just over half (52.7 percent) of the observations, students were not using technology to gather, evaluate, or use information for learning (Broekhuizen, 2016). Almost two-thirds (66 percent) of the observations showed students were not using technology for problem solving, conducting research, or working collaboratively (Broekhuizen, 2016). Further, at a recent Arizona State University and Global Silicon Valley summit in San Diego, philanthropist Bill Gates told thousands in attendance that education technology is still at its earliest stages and has yet to live up to its promise, stating, "We really haven't changed student academic outcomes with technology" (Molnar, 2016, p. 2). Once a national and international leader in Learning Technology, Maine's 1-to-1 Computing initiative is under scrutiny for lack of demonstrating its impact on student achievement (Herold & Katz, 2016).

Many teachers spend more time using technology for the administrative requirements of their classroom than for student outcome activities. When they do, students are typically engaged in routine practices like drills, practice exercises, and reading assignments. Teachers use technology primarily for supplemental support, and not for collaboration among students for critical thinking, problem solving, or to imbed technology in their instruction as a pivotal teaching strategy. Teaching strategies remain print-based, while many students come to class fully engaged and fully proficient technology users in mobile devices and other tools. Some teachers are also very skeptical of any claims that technology will have a dramatic impact on student learning. For many teachers, using technology is challenging; to get some to reach farther out of their comfort zone when using technology is very difficult. Time, energy, and teaching using technology every day are a huge commitment. Others feel that their school leaders must support the desired new learning found in technology with time to do it, adequate training, resources, and a reward for taking on the extra work.

In contrast to AdvancED and Bill Gates, a 2010 Motorola report asserts that the "burgeoning revolution" in learning technology, specifically the Internet and online learning, is "transforming" the K-12 learning experience (p. 2). This report cites Christenson, Horn, and Johnson from their book Disrupting Class, that 50 percent of high school courses will be online by 2019 (p. 3). The report also notes that teachers will not become obsolete, but their roles will change to more of a guide and facilitator for student learning. In 2014, 4 years after the Motorola report, there had been an 80 percent increase in students taking part in online/blended learning, 50 percent increase in districts offering online/blended learning, and a 58 percent increase in online public schools (Connections Academy, 2014). As per EdNET Insight report, spending

for educational technology was up again in 2015, noting that 46 percent of school districts spent more on expansion and hardware and 38 percent spent more on teacher training (Schaffhauser, 2016). Included in the hardware were desktop computers, laptops, interactive projectors, interactive whiteboards, flat panels, and as a high priority, Chromebooks (Schaffhauser, 2016). A steady pace for growth continues. For example, today, publically funded full-time online charter schools enroll 200,000 students across 26 states (Herold, 2016). The indication would be that with the billions being spent on technology, teaching and learning would continue to change, and student outcomes would be enhanced. In addition, teachers would be fully engaged and excited about new strategies for teaching while using technology.

Costley (2014) presents evidence that "Technology has a positive effect on student learning and outcomes: 1) increased student motivation; 2) increased student engagement; 3) increased student collaboration; 4) increased hands-on learning opportunities; 5) allows for learning at all levels; 6) increased confidence in students; and 7) increased technology skill (p. 9).

A note of caution should prevail while reading that technology is revolutionizing the way teachers teach and students learn. The massive inundation of computers, iPads, Web 2.0, whiteboards, touchscreens, social media/social learning, YouTube, Prezi's, digital textbooks, online learning, Cloud computing, and a host of other technology tools into schools have not improved student achievement. According to the NO article, author (Herold, 2015) in this issue, there are "numerous culprits" for the lack of student outcomes including, "teachers' beliefs about what constitutes effective instruction, their lack of technology expertise, erratic training and support from administrators, and federal, state, and local policies that offer teachers neither the time nor the incentive to explore and experiment" (p. 1).

Managing the changing technology landscape of education requires school leaders and policymakers to support a strong framework for harnessing and evaluating the value of different technologies for student engagement and achievement. What is needed from technology to transform schools for the twenty-first century are leaders who seize the momentum of the digital world movement, build capacity in schools and school districts, and provide resources that will motivate teachers and students and ensure success. School and district technology plans must be built collaboratively with teachers and the entire school community.

Transparent to either the YES or NO view of technology for teaching and learning is the fact that technology is not going away. It involves much more than purchasing and installation into classrooms. The rapid developments in educational technologies and failure of leader training to keep up have left many educators completely unprepared for teaching in the digital classroom. A commonly shared view is that technology cannot replace traditional teaching and learning. Other teachers have embraced the dynamic evolvement of digital learning, choosing to be fully engaged in the techniques, skills, methods, and processes of a tech-savvy classroom. There is no doubt that in today's K-12 school, students come highly engaged in using technology. Generation Z (GenZ) or iGeneration (iGen) grew up using the Internet and are proficient users of social media. Communication, as well as education, is "different" for them (as compared to baby-boomers and millennials). The influence of technology on the toys they grew up with and the entertainment choices they have today can all be combined into a device they hold in their hand; they are just an app away from their next learning experience. They live in a digital world, expect digital engagement, and often come to school expecting a digital learning experience. Educators wish they could spend the same quality time on their school's learning achievement as they do on their daily cell phone interactions.

The YES and NO selections in this issue present differing views on how technology is, or is not, changing how teachers teach and students learn. Although the YES article reveals positive outcomes with technology use, it is not a full endorsement of technology in the classroom. What the YES article posits is that there are strong reasons to go "beyond the factory model" phasing out the tradition of direct instruction approach to student learning (Jacobs, 2014, p. 40). There will continue to be challenges and opportunities when it comes to the use of technology in education. Successes will likely be accompanied by a proactive stance, active engagement in effective technology use in the classroom, and willingness to change core teacher practices. It's not likely that there will ever be a perfect environment for teaching and learning, but technology plays a significant role in today's society and needs to play a similar role in America's schools.

References

L. Broekhuizen, The Paradox of Classroom Technology: Despite Proliferation and Access, Students Not Using Technology for Learning AdvancED, Alpharetta, GA. Retrieved from http://www.advanc-ed.org/sites/default/files/AdvancED_eleot_Classroom_Tech_Report.pdf (2016).

Connections Academy, Retrieved from http://www.connectionsacademy.com/news/growth-of-k-12-online-education-infographic (2014).

K. CostleyThe Positive Effects of Technology on Teaching and Student Learning. International Electronic Journal of Elementary Education. Retrieved from http://files.eric.ed.gov/fulltext/ED554557.pdf (2014).

B. Herold, Technology in Education: An Overview. Education Week, February 5, 2016. Retrieved from http://www.edweek.org/ew/issues/technology-in-education/ (2016).

B. Herold & J. Katz, Maine 1 -to-1 Computing Initiative Under Microscope. Education Week, August 30, 2016. Retrieved from http://www.edweek.org/ew/articles/2016/08/3 (2016).

M. Molnar, Bill Gates: Ed Tech Has Underachieved, But Better Days are Ahead. EdWeek Market Brief. Retrieved from https://marketbrief.edweek.org/marketplace-k-12/bill-gates/ (2016).

Motorola. How Technology Is Changing the Ways Students Learn and Teachers Teach. White Paper Report, Schaumburg, IL. Retrieved from http://www.motorolasolutions.com/content/dam/msi/docs/business/solutions/industry_solutions/education/document/_staticfile/wp_edu_ro-22-105.pdf (2016).

D. Schaffhauser, Report: Education Tech Spending on the Rise. The Journal. Retrieved from https://thejournal.com/articles/2016/01/19/report-education-tech-spending-on-the-rise.aspx (2016).

YES ↵

Joanne Jacobs

Beyond the Factory Model

Like many high-poverty middle schools, Oakland's Elmhurst Community Prep is trying to reach students who are academically all over the map. One-third of the students are working at grade level in reading and math, says Principal Kilian Betlach. Another third are one to two years behind. The remaining third are three or four years behind—or more. "You can't teach them by aiming for the middle and providing these little supports," says Betlach.

Differentiation—teaching students at very different levels of achievement in the same class—is "the greatest challenge facing America's schools today," writes Michael Petrilli (see "All Together Now?" features, Winter 2011).

"Teachers are told to sprinkle your differentiation fairy dust," says Betlach. With 32 students in a class, and no aides, "it's not possible."

What is possible?

A foundation-funded experiment is testing whether "blended learning" can personalize instruction in eight Oakland schools. Blended learning combines brick-and-mortar schooling with online education "with some element of student control over time, place, path, and/or pace" of learning, according to the Clayton Christensen Institute definition of the term.

The Rogers Family Foundation, created in 2003 by T. Gary and Kathleen Rogers, launched a blended-learning pilot in four Oakland Unified schools, including Elmhurst, in fall 2012. Two more district schools and two charters were added in 2013. The foundation focuses on improving Oakland's troubled schools and is funding the pilot with help from the Quest Foundation, the Bill and Melinda Gates Foundation, and others.

Urban schooling doesn't get much tougher than in Oakland. More than two-thirds of Oakland Unified School District students are Latino or African American; 80 percent qualify for free or reduced-price lunch. One-third are English language learners (ELLs). Only half of disadvantaged 9th graders earn a high school diploma in four years.

Pressured by community groups, the district created small, autonomous, quasi-charter schools like Elmhurst starting in 2001. Scores began rising but remain low.

Despite this bleak picture, Oakland schools do have one advantage as they attempt to transform through blended learning: nobody thinks the status quo is good enough.

Blend and Rotate

"Student control" over the pace of learning is on display in Will Short's Math 8 class at Elmhurst. Laptop users are working on Khan Academy quizzes geared to each student's skill level. At the front of the class, a display charts their "energy points," a measure that includes "on taskness" and the percentage of correct answers. Students receive instant feedback.

Freed from whole-class instruction by the technology, Short has time to reteach concepts to individual students or small groups. Advanced students can move ahead.

At Bret Harte Middle School, which joined the pilot in the second year, Chantel Parnell divides her 6th-grade math students into three groups. On a day in late October, some are using Khan Academy or Google Drive on Chromebooks, while another group is constructing box plots at their desks. The rest are sitting in a circle with the teacher. "Do you understand why you got this answer?" Parnell asks a student.

At that moment, a girl in the Chromebook group raises her hand. A student walks over to help. Oakland schools can't afford aides in mainstream classrooms, so Parnell has asked students to volunteer to coach their classmates.

Like Parnell, most pilot teachers use the "station rotation model." Students move between computers, teacher-led discussions, and, sometimes, group projects or independent desk work.

A few teachers use the PC lab. Some of Patricia Wong's students are working on adding and subtracting negative numbers. Wong explains $4 + (-5)$ to a boy. "Plus a minus is subtraction," she says. "What do you do? . . . Why?"

Jacobs, Joanne. "Beyond the Factory Model: Oakland Teachers Learn How to Blend," Education Next, 14 (4), 2014, p. 35–41. Copyright ©2014 by Education Next Institute, Inc. All rights reserved. Used with permission.

Meanwhile, one girl is drawing a number line on the screen. Another has moved on to multiplying and dividing with negative numbers. Advanced students are doing word problems. One boy is taking the "mastery challenge," which pops up randomly. The challenge asks him to add 2.83 + 3.5.

Blended learning isn't just for math classes at Bret Harte. Teacher Amy Colt uses the online learning program Achieve3000 to teach English and social studies. The program provides Associated Press news stories rewritten to match each user's reading level, plus a reading quiz to check comprehension and a writing test. Colt circulates, talking to students individually.

First-Year Evaluation

SRI Education researchers conducted an evaluation of the program's first year for the Rogers Foundation. Below are some highlights from that report:

Most teachers used digital content for remediation. They had little faith that students would learn new concepts or develop higher-order skills online. Using instructional videos to introduce new concepts was too difficult for most students, teachers said.

Although all digital-content providers claim their content is aligned with Common Core standards, most teachers were dubious about the software's rigor. "The technology piece is mediocre," reported a middle-school math teacher.

Despite that, teachers gave online programs high ratings. That may reflect their decision to use digital content to teach basic skills.

Teachers struggled to teach students to work independently and rotate quickly, while also troubleshooting the computers and leading small-group discussions. Over time, students learned to focus, persevere, and cope with problems, teachers said. They helped each other.

Those students who started way behind could see their progress, even if they remained below grade level. Students said they tracked their progress closely and felt "rewarded and empowered" when they improved. "The data helped them make the link between their hard work and learning."

Using the data wasn't easy, however. "It's hard for a kid to sift through it all and pinpoint exactly what specific activity is holding them back or what specific skill they are missing," a teacher said.

Using data was hard for teachers, too. Only a few teachers became comfortable analyzing data to "inform instructional decisions," despite tools provided by the digital content providers.

Many teachers mistrusted data from tests they hadn't written themselves. One teacher told her principal that students were "getting little medals and trophies saying that they know their math facts [but] when it comes to paper-and-pencil timed tests they don't know their math facts."

(She was using a pencil-and-paper test that was the "best of the factory model," Klein explained. She switched to an online program that matched her assessments.)

The ability to monitor student progress easily helped teachers use their time more efficiently. One pilot teacher said, "I'm spending a lot less time grading and more time actually looking at the data and planning for reteaching lessons."

Students were eager to retake math quizzes, said a middle-school teacher. Once they achieved proficiency, the teacher let students explore Khan Academy videos on other topics. "She joked that she would often find her middle schoolers watching videos about art history and theology when they had time to explore."

A few teachers had help from a student teacher or special education aide. Madison Park had AmeriCorps volunteers who served as blended-learning coaches. Rogers's blended-learning specialists rotated among classrooms. But most teachers had to go it alone most of the time.

In some classrooms, blended learning built "a sense of community and collaboration." At one middle school, Rogers's blended-learning specialist trained a group of girls to refurbish older PC desktops. "Not only did the students learn a valuable skill that they felt good about, it also allowed the school to scale up its technical capacity quickly and cheaply. Now, if a computer goes down, one of the students can bring it back to life," the report said.

Several teachers used IT-skilled students to set up computers and troubleshoot problems. Even in elementary school, some students served as tech support for their teachers.

"I loved having the ability to teach to a smaller group of kids; every kid was more engaged, participated more," one teacher said. "I did different things with different kids depending on their needs."

Source: Woodworth, K., Greenwald, E., Tyler, N., Comstock, M. (2013). *Evaluation of the First Year of the Oakland Blended Learning Pilot.* Menlo Park, CA: SRI International.

The Launch

The idea for the pilot came from Oakland principals who had received earlier Rogers grants. They "weren't having the impact they wanted with technology" and wanted to do "something larger and deeper," says Greg Klein, director of blended learning for the Rogers Foundation. Klein is coauthor of "Blended Learning in Practice: Four District School Journeys," a case study of the Oakland project written with Carrie McPherson Douglass, who's now with the Cities for Education Entrepreneurship Trust, an umbrella organization for urban reform groups nationwide.

Teachers said, "I don't have enough time to meet the needs of my highest-skilled students or my ELLs. It would be great to personalize instruction." Those proved to be "gateway drug conversations," says Klein.

Tracey Logan, who manages technical services for Oakland Unified, was enthusiastic. "We saw an opportunity that was aligned to where we want to go," she says.

Schools competed for the chance to participate. Working with Education Elements, a company that designs "personalized learning solutions," the foundation initially chose EnCompass Academy (K–5), Korematsu Discovery Academy (K–5), Madison Park Academy (grades 6–9), and Elmhurst Community Prep (6–8). All are district-run schools in high-poverty, high-crime areas.

"We looked for principals who were strong leaders able to implement change," says Jane Bryson, who directs the education team at Education Elements. Like their principals, all the teachers within the schools that implemented blended learning were "early adopters" who wanted to try something new. They committed to spending one hour a week after school on collaboration and training, which Rogers funded. That time proved to be critical, says Bryson.

But the pilot's first year was difficult.

Education Elements trained and supported Madison Park and Korematsu teachers. The company's software platform lets students sign in to a home page that shows all the learning programs available. Teachers can access a data dashboard to see all the data on each student and create assessment tools.

All of Madison Park's math teachers and two other teachers volunteered to be in the pilot. At Korematsu, two 4th-grade teachers volunteered to use blended learning to teach both reading and math.

Hoping to test a different approach as well, Rogers brought in Junyo, a small company, to work with Elmhurst and EnCompass Academy. Junyo tried to develop its own platform with a portal for students and a data dashboard for teachers but gave up in mid-September, returned the money, and quit the pilot. Klein and the foundation's two blended-learning specialists took over tech support and training for the two schools. But lingering effects of the Junyo experiment added to what were already significant challenges.

At the former Junyo schools, the lack of a single portal meant that a student might need to log in separately to five different programs. Klein made sure they could use the same username and password at least.

Rogers had planned to try blending in just 4th and 5th grade at EnCompass, but Junyo signed up all the teachers. Many didn't realize how much work it would take, says Klein. Implementation was "shallow."

Elmhurst had a "failure to launch" in what Betlach calls "Year 0." Junyo's "advice on devices was divisive and faulty." Teachers never had reliable Internet access.

Elmhurst's building, shared with another small middle school, was erected in 1906 and partially rebuilt in the 1920s after a fire.

To make room for desktop computers, the foundation paid to have built-in cabinets removed, something teachers had wanted for a long time. But there weren't enough wireless access points.

On the software front, Rogers learned a lot from the first year about what not to do, says Klein. "We asked teachers to learn multiple education tech tools at the same time." It was too much.

Across the four schools, pilot middle-school teachers used a number of different learning programs, including Achieve3000, i-Ready, Khan Academy, ST Math, iLearn, and iPass, according to an SRI International report on the pilot's first year (see sidebar). At the elementary level, Google Drive, Achieve3000, Mangahigh, Khan Academy, Digital Passport, and i-Ready were popular.

"Online content providers can look like bright, shiny objects," says Bryson. And Rogers was paying.

"It was overwhelming," says Keara Duggan, an Education Elements staffer who worked with teachers.

"Now we say, start with Khan, and then add more as you see the need," says Klein. The pilot's new motto: "Go slow to go fast."

His other conclusion: "Listen to teachers. Be authentically humble."

"We did way too much too fast," says Logan.

"This is really, really hard," teachers told her. "It's like being a first-year teacher all over again."

A Leap of Faith

Once teachers gain experience with blended learning, they don't want to go back, says Logan. "They say, 'I wouldn't do it any other way.'"

Technology will "change what teaching looks like"—eventually, she predicts. Right now, however, "it's a bit of a leap of faith."

Technology can "make the best use of teacher time, adapt to meet students where they are, and encourage collaboration and creativity," Logan says. It can "expand the classroom. Students don't just have access to what a teacher knows or what's in the science book." Most of all, she wants students to "take ownership of their learning."

Jessica Tucker wants that for her students, too. Every Friday, Tucker would give a math quiz to her 6th graders at Madison Park. Half would fail. She'd try to reteach the lesson the following week, while introducing the next concept. On Friday, once again, half would fail.

After making the transition to blended learning, Tucker asked students to signal if they were ready for a quiz. Thumbs-up meant ready, thumbs-down meant no way, and a sideways thumb meant "not sure."

On one Friday, 15 students put their thumbs up. Those students all passed the quiz. Tucker taught an extra lesson for those who needed it before they took the quiz. "It was effective because they felt they had a choice," she said in a video on differentiation in a blended classroom. "I did an extension lesson at a higher level" for the ones who took the quiz first.

"I've done that every Friday since," says Tucker. "It has improved mastery scores a lot."

She uses a program called MasteryConnect to design her own tests. If a student does poorly, "I can say, 'before you retake the test, I want you to go to these four Khan videos.' The kids who didn't get it after two lessons with me, they're obviously not going to get it with another lesson with me."

Tucker wants to instill the belief that "you can't not master a concept. I don't care how many times you have to take it. You can't leave until you learn."

Year 2 and Beyond

In Year 2 of the pilot, Rogers added two district middle schools, a charter elementary school, and a charter K–8 school, while serving more grade levels at the original four schools.

ASCEND, a district school turned K–8 charter, has a Chromebook for every student and every teacher. Aspire's Millsmont Elementary, a charter, has gone in a different direction, by designing a mobile computer lab that groups students in "pods" of four.

Korematsu, one of the original district pilot schools, is blending in nearly every classroom now. EnCompass simplified its program, and the principal hired teachers who are eager to use digital learning.

This year, Elmhurst's Internet works consistently at a high speed thanks to newly installed access points. Blended learning is starting to work, says Betlach.

"It allows you to gather data on student performance much more quickly," says the principal. The "exit ticket"—a mini-quiz at the end of each lesson—gives students instant feedback. "Kids say, 'I really like to know how I did right away.'"

Teachers can track trends and patterns: Which question was problematic? What needs reteaching? "Better data let you target instruction to where kids are," says Betlach. With students at widely different skill levels, teachers can have "different groups working on different things."

All the 8th-grade teachers are participating in the blended pilot this year. So are two special-education classes and one 6th-grade math/science class. Teachers who've tried it are spreading the word, says Betlach. Nonpilot teachers ask him, "When do I get my Chromebooks?"

Blending More, Spending Less

Rogers is learning how to blend without overspending. The foundation "overpaid" for hardware in Year 1, spending $670 per student, says Klein. Schools bought MacBook Airs, Lenovo PCs, and Windows desktops. This year, the four new schools and the new teachers at Year 1 schools bought Chromebooks for $249 apiece. The price already has fallen to $199, says Klein.

Chromebooks hold up, require less tech support, and have a battery that lasts all day, says Klein. "Google has a cloud-based interface to manage the devices. You can buy 20 Chromebooks and 30 seconds later they're set up and away you go."

Teachers are using more free software this year. "You can get a lot of value out of Khan Academy at zero cost," says Klein. "Then, when you go shopping for premium content, you have a better idea of what you need."

Because of savings on computers and software, the Year 2 cost is $10,000 per school, half the cost of Year 1, says Klein.

With hardware and software spending going down, Rogers is focusing on helping teachers use technology to improve learning. That's what really counts, says Klein.

His don't-go-there example is Los Angeles Unified, which spent $500 million to buy iPads for every student. Implementation was a disaster. Other districts, such as Miami-Dade and Guilford County, North Carolina, have put laptops-for-all programs on hold.

The Rogers pilot is having a ripple effect in Oakland and beyond. Schools that didn't make the Rogers pilot, both district and charter, are "trying to blend with very little money," says Klein.

Learning Without Limits (LWL), a district-run elementary that recently converted to a charter, applied for the blended-learning pilot but didn't make the cut. The school went ahead anyhow. With few computers in the early grades, LWL blends in 4th and 5th grades.

School PTAs and local donors are helping. Some use very low-cost computers refurbished by Oakland Technology Exchange West. Others can afford Chromebooks.

Before the pilot started, only one or two "bleeding edge" charters in Oakland were trying to use blended learning, says Rogers's Year 2 report. "Just two years later, our eight pilot schools are joined by at least five more district schools, and practically every charter in the city is actively leveraging adaptive online content to personalize instruction." A majority of Oakland schools have asked the foundation how they could try blended learning.

Oakland Unified is investing $3.5 million—half of its one-time Common Core implementation dollars from the state—to upgrade networks at every school. The district won a $100,000 Gates Foundation planning grant to design a personalized blended learning system at all its schools and is seeking funding for implementation.

Nearby districts have adopted blended learning on their own. Thirty-five miles to the south, next to San Jose, Milpitas Unified is blending instruction in two-thirds of elementary-school classrooms; the district's teachers designed the plan. At Milpitas High School, the district has provided Chromebooks for students and teachers to use across the curriculum.

Phasing Out the Factory Model

It will take some time to determine how well blended learning works in the Oakland schools. Even though most teachers reported that students were highly engaged when working

Figure 1

Engagement Boost

Pilot teachers reported that students were highly engaged with digital learning content; they were less optimistic about the impact of blended learning on student test scores.

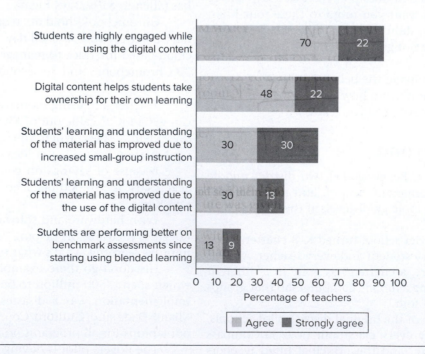

Source: Woodworth, K., Greenwald, E., Tyler, N., Comstock, M. (2013). Evaluation of the First Year of the Oakland Blended Learning Pilot. Menlo Park, CA: SRI International, Exhibit 10.

with digital content and were better able to learn the material, only one-fifth of Rogers pilot teachers said their students did better on benchmark tests the first year (see Figure 1).

Results on the 2013 California Standards Tests were "mixed," says Klein. Madison Park's 6th graders outperformed the district average in math and algebra students also showed progress. Korematsu, which blended only in 4th grade, showed gains in reading, where blended learning was concentrated, and smaller gains in math.

Rogers predicts "dramatic changes to student outcomes in years two, three, and beyond" as personalized learning takes hold.

Because there's no control group, it will be difficult to tell whether higher scores are due to the pilot or other factors. And California's state testing system will not report scores next year because of the transition to Common Core standards, which will make it even harder to track progress. The district gives the Scholastic Reading Inventory exam three times a year, however, which will enable

the pilot schools focusing on English language arts to see what's working (see Figure 2). In addition, some online content programs have built-in assessments that can be used to evaluate students' progress.

The foundation is surveying teachers and students to see how attitudes are changing.

In the pilot's first year, "blended learning . . . encourage[d] experimentation," wrote Klein and Douglass in a January 2013 update to the case study. "We see teachers dramatically changing their schedules, grouping structures and habits more frequently and with more excitement and openness than ever before."

In the second year, "we have a handful (and growing number) of teachers who are truly innovating at each site and are pushing their peers to both play and learn alongside their students," they wrote in an earlier update.

The foundation's focus now is on training teachers on programs and tools, connecting them to coaches, and helping teachers collaborate with each other.

Figure 2

Reading Gains

During the second year of the program, the proportion of students reading at grade level increased by between 10 and 25 percentage points at three of the four pilot schools, matching or outpacing average gains in the district as a whole.

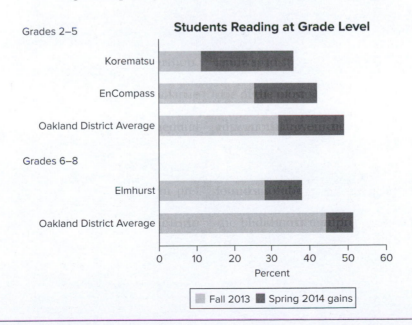

Notes: Reading at grade level is measured using the Scholastic Reading Inventory. Achievement data are not yet available for Madison Park Academy.

Source: Rogers Family Foundation

Education technology often is used to do the same old thing—only with less paper, says Klein. Technology must change teaching in order to make a difference. That's the foundation's goal in Oakland. Yet Klein recognizes that much has stayed the same at the pilot schools. "Our pilots highly disrupt the status quo at schools, but it's the same teaching staff ratio, grade levels, and bell schedule."

"We're not necessarily funding next-generation models," says Klein. "We're less funding the future and more funding the breakdown of the past. It's the beginning of the end of the factory model."

"Next-generation learning" will go much deeper, Klein predicts. But, first, he wants to show that the blended pilot is helping students learn more.

"In education, we took down the chalkboards and put up the whiteboard, but it probably didn't make a lick of difference in academics," says Klein. "Now we're moving to student-facing devices. We're hopeful we can help Oakland do it well. How can we transfer teaching and learning in a daily way in core classes?"

Blended learning is "not transformational right now," he says. He thinks it will be.

JOANNE JACOBS is a former San Jose Mercury News editorial writer and columnist for K-12 education and community colleges.

Benjamin Herold

 **NO**

Why Ed Tech Is Not Transforming How Teachers Teach

Student-Centered, Technology-Driven Instruction Remains Elusive for Most

Public schools now provide at least one computer for every five students. They spend more than $3 billion per year on digital content. And nearly three-fourths of high school students now say they regularly use a smartphone or tablet in the classroom.

But a mountain of evidence indicates that teachers have been painfully slow to transform the ways they teach, despite that massive influx of new technology into their classrooms. The student-centered, hands-on, personalized instruction envisioned by ed-tech proponents remains the exception to the rule.

"The introduction of computers into schools was supposed to improve academic achievement and alter how teachers taught," said Stanford University education professor Larry Cuban. "Neither has occurred."

Indeed, a host of national and regional surveys suggest that teachers are far more likely to use technology to make their own jobs easier and to supplement traditional instructional strategies than to put students in control of their own learning. Case study after case study describe a common pattern inside schools: A handful of "early adopters" embrace innovative uses of new technology, while their colleagues make incremental or no changes to what they already do.

Researchers have identified numerous culprits, including teachers' beliefs about what constitutes effective instruction, their lack of technology expertise, erratic training and support from administrators, and federal, state, and local policies that offer teachers neither the time nor the incentive to explore and experiment.

The net effect, said Leslie A. Wilson, the chief executive officer of the One-to-One Institute, a nonprofit based in Mason, Mich., that has consulted with hundreds of schools and districts across the country and world, is

that schools rarely realize the full promise of educational technology.

"There's nothing transformative about every kid having an iPad unless you're able to reach higher-order teaching and learning," Ms. Wilson said. "If schools take all this technology, and use it like a textbook, or just have teachers show PowerPoint [presentations] or use drill-and-kill software, they might as well not even have it."

Modeling Good Digital Teaching

A clear description of what student-centered, technology-driven classroom instruction entails is laid out in standards developed by the Washington-based International Society for Technology in Education.

"You can do student-centered teaching without technology. There have been teachers doing that for a long time," said Wendy Drexler, ISTE's chief innovation officer. "But tech is not going away, and we want to have teachers using it effectively."

In the digital age, the ISTE standards say, teachers should be expected, among other strategies, to "engage students in exploring real-world issues and solving authentic problems using digital tools and resources." They should also "develop technology-enriched learning environments that enable all students to become active participants in setting their own educational goals, managing their own learning, and assessing their own progress."

That pretty much describes Robyn L. Howton's Advanced Placement English class at the 1,100-student Mount Pleasant High School, a neighborhood comprehensive high school with just-above-average state test scores, located on the outskirts of Wilmington.

On a warm May morning, 26 Mount Pleasant 11th graders were scattered around Ms. Howton's room, sitting in groups of three or four. They were midway through a project-based unit on social-justice movements. Their goal: Produce independent research papers on topics of their choice, then collaboratively develop a multimedia presentation of their findings with classmates researching the same issue.

After a brief welcome and introduction, the teens were on their own. The 15 iPads on a cart in the back of the room were quickly gobbled up.

Nicole Collins, Courtney Norris, and Quincy Vaughn, all 17, went to work at a small table. Using iPads and a cloud-based tool called Google Slides, they collaborated in real time on their group presentation about injustices in the U.S. criminal-justice system.

Ms. Collins said she had chosen the topic because "my own family has problems with the law, so I understand part of it."

Mr. Vaughn expressed a different motivation: "With everything that's going on with Ferguson and Baltimore, it's a little overwhelming," he said, referring to the police killings of black men and the resulting protests in each city. "Sometimes, you need to speak out."

The trio worked enthusiastically for 25 minutes without any interaction with their teacher. Ms. Howton slid to the back of the room. On her laptop, she logged into the Google platform to check students' work. Occasionally, she circulated around the room, asking probing questions or issuing challenges to individual groups.

"I've probably stood in front of that class for three hours the entire school year," said the 24-year teaching veteran, who has received intensive training in technology integration from a local foundation and a consortium of Delaware school districts that promote personalized learning. "I decided my personal goal was to turn my classroom into a model so other teachers who want to start down this pathway have someone to come and [observe]."

But Mount Pleasant Principal Heather Austin said that only about 5 percent of her school's teachers are even in the same ballpark as Ms. Howton when it comes to making effective use of classroom technology. Another 5 percent are extremely resistant to use just about any ed tech.

"The 90 percent in the middle, they all have overhead projectors, there's a teacher computer, they use some sort of PowerPoint," Ms. Austin said. "They're using [technology] to enhance what they're doing, but they haven't really given students control over it."

Research suggests that's more or less the standard distribution of technology use in most schools nationwide.

The most authoritative national study on teacher technology use was conducted by the National Center for Education Statistics in 2009. A survey of 3,159 teachers found that when teachers did allow students to use technology, it was most often to prepare written text (61 percent of respondents reported that their students did so "sometimes" or "often") conduct Internet research (66 percent), or learn/practice basic skills (69 percent).

Far more rare were teachers who reported that their students sometimes or often used technology to conduct experiments (25 percent), create art or music (25 percent), design and produce a product (13 percent), or contribute to a blog or wiki (9 percent).

Student-centered use of classroom technology "isn't going to happen overnight," said Ms. Drexler of ISTE. "This is about the diffusion of innovation."

A Pessimistic View

Mr. Cuban of Stanford has a more pessimistic take.

"Most teachers have 'domesticated' innovative technologies by incorporating them into their existing repertoire of teacher-directed practices," he wrote in his 2013 book, Inside the Black Box of Classroom Practice: Change Without Reform in American Education.

In his research for that book, Mr. Cuban revisited the technology-rich Silicon Valley high school featured in his seminal 2001 book, Overused and Oversold: Computers in the Classroom.

At the turn of the 21st century, he had found that "most teachers [at the school] had adapted an innovation to fit their customary practices."

More than a decade later, some things had changed. More teachers regularly used digital devices for classroom instruction. And many of those teachers had incrementally changed their approach, using technology to plan lessons more efficiently, communicate with their colleagues more frequently, and access information via the Internet more regularly.

Still, Mr. Cuban wrote, "all but a few of the teachers at [the school] used a familiar repertoire of instructional approaches: lecturing, conducting a discussion, and occasional use of technologies such as overhead projectors, videos, and computers." For the most part, he concluded, "even in computer-based classes, teacher-centered instruction with a mix of student-centered practices was the norm."

Similar findings resulted from a 2010 study of 21 Texas middle schools by private researcher Kelly S. Shapley and her colleagues. The schools had been provided with abundant technology, including laptops for every student and teacher, wireless upgrades for schools, digital curricula and assessments, and professional development, paid for with $20 million in federal funds.

The End Result?

"In general, teachers at many schools seemed to view technology as a more valuable tool for themselves than for their students," Ms. Shapley wrote.

While spotty Internet connections and Wi-Fi networks continue to cause problems in some places, access to technology is no longer the main barrier to transforming instruction, most researchers point out.

Instead, their focus is now on so-called "second order" obstacles.

In 2010, for example, researchers Peggy A. Ertmer of Purdue University, in West Lafayette, Ind., and Anne T. Ottenbreit-Leftwich of Indiana University, in Bloomington, took a comprehensive look at how teachers' knowledge, confidence, and belief systems interact with school culture to shape the ways in which teachers integrate technology into their classrooms.

One big issue: Many teachers lack an understanding of how educational technology works.

But the greater challenge, the researchers wrote, is in expanding teachers' knowledge of new instructional practices that will allow them to select and use the right technology, in the right way, with the right students, for the right purpose.

A 2014 paper by researchers at Michigan State University, in East Lansing, provides a tangible example: Teachers and students in the small-scale study were found to be making extensive use of the online word-processing tool Google Docs. The application's power to support collaborative writing and in-depth feedback, however, was not being realized. Teachers were not encouraging group-writing assignments and their feedback focused overwhelmingly on issues such as spelling and grammar, rather than content and organization.

Even more important than knowledge of how to use classroom technology, Ms. Ertmer and Ms. Ottenbreit–Leftwich wrote, may be teachers' level of confidence in trying it out in their classrooms. If they do not believe that they can use technology to accomplish their classroom goals, they appear unlikely to seriously attempt it.

On top of that, teachers' "pedagogical beliefs" are increasingly believed to play a central role in their willingness to use ed tech.

In a forthcoming study by researcher Emily Rodgers of The Ohio State University, in Columbus, and her colleagues, 1st graders in low-performing elementary schools showed statistically significant gains in their ability to identify letters after using an iPad app called LetterWorks. Their teachers, however, expressed reluctance about continuing to use the app, in large part because they held a philosophical belief that tactile learning is important for young children.

Classroom Realities

Those barriers to good technology use are made worse by school-based factors and problematic policies.

Researchers have found, for example, that even innovative teachers can be heavily affected by pressure to conform to more traditional instructional styles, with a teacher as the focal point for the classroom. Newer teachers inclined to use technology in their classrooms can also be deterred by experienced teachers who feel differently.

And the current test-based accountability system isn't exactly supporting the transition to student-centered, technology-driven instruction, said Ms. Drexler of ISTE. "We're telling teachers that the key thing that is important is that students in your classroom achieve, and we're defining achievement by how they do on [standardized] tests," she said. "That's not going to change behavior."

Perhaps the most obvious—and overlooked—barrier to effective ed-tech use is that totally changing the way you do your job takes a ton of time and work.

That's the challenge facing Scott Bacon, a 13-year-veteran educator who now teaches 9th grade economics at Mount Pleasant High.

As his students returned from lunch on that recent May day, they settled into paired desks, all facing the front of the room.

Mr. Bacon launched into a combination PowerPoint presentation-lecture about various types of unemployment.

Periodically, he stopped to ask a question of the whole class. A few students' hands shot up. After hearing from one or two of the students, Mr. Bacon continued, clicking a button to bring up his own answers to his questions on the PowerPoint.

When the lecture turned to "technological unemployment," Mr. Bacon joked to the class: "Eventually, everyone is going to be replaced by a robot, right? I'm being replaced by computers as we speak. You can just watch Khan Academy now, right?"

Later, he described his own experience trying to implement the technology-integration training he has received through the same multidistrict consortium on personalized learning in which Ms. Howton takes part.

While he's very motivated to make his instruction more student–centered, Mr. Bacon said, "What I'm finding is I'm having a hard time doing it that right way, a wholesale change. "His attempts to move in that direction have been frustrating and draining.

He described, for example, an earlier lesson in which he conducted an experiment involving a National Public Radio segment on recent federal unemployment statistics. The whole class listened together. Mr. Bacon asked half his students to write a summary and reaction using a pencil and notecards and half to do so using the online discussion forum on the school's new learning management system.

Describing his own experience during the experiment, Mr. Bacon said, "I'm up there juggling different remotes, a mouse up here versus a mouse [attached to a computer in the back of the class]. It felt crazy. Doing that was a lot more work than if I had just given them all notecards."

Ingredients for Success

So how can schools and districts better support teachers in transforming the way they teach?

Most often, that discussion begins with professional development. There are a lot of ideas and theories on what can make such training more effective, but rigorous, independent research remains frustratingly rare.

One strategy that most researchers and experts seem to agree on: so-called "job–embedded" professional development that takes place consistently during the workday and is tied to specific classroom challenges that teachers actually face, rather than in the isolated sessions often preferred by district central offices and written into districts' contracts with their teachers.

"When learning experiences are focused solely on the technology itself, with no specific connection to grade or content learning goals, teachers are unlikely to incorporate technology into their practices," concluded Ms. Ertmer and Ms. Ottenbreit–Leftwich, the researchers who wrote the 2010 paper on the factors influencing teachers' use of educational technology.

Another oft-cited strategy is putting to work those "early adopters" inside a school who are making innovative, student-centered use of technology in their classrooms. "The smarter districts use those teachers to teach other teachers how to integrate tech into their lessons," Mr. Cuban said. "The dumb ones use vendors to provide professional development and force teachers to attend those sessions."

That smarter strategy is what Ms. Austin, the Mount Pleasant principal, is attempting. But even as she described her approach to scaling up student-centered, technology-driven instruction during an interview in her office, a whiteboard loomed over her shoulder. On it was a circle, representing a Mount Pleasant student. Surrounding that circle were 19 other shapes, each representing a major initiative or issue the school is currently trying to balance, from new online exams linked to the Common Core State Standards to Delaware's intensive new teacher-evaluation program.

BENJAMIN HEROLD is an education reporter at WHYY in Philadelphia, Pennsylvania.

EXPLORING THE ISSUE

Is The Use of Technology Changing How Teachers Teach and Students Learn?

Critical Thinking and Reflection

1. What will technology look like in a classroom the next 10 to 20 years?
2. Will Bill Gates statement about technology "still being in the early stages" hold true to the future educational classroom setting?
3. How will educators be trained to teach our future Generation Z or iGeneration students?
4. What will the financial picture look like for teacher training and school upgrades to turn our current schools in to twenty-first century schools?
5. Are educational teacher preparation programs incorporating sufficient technology in their curriculum to train teachers?
6. What is your vision for the future in using technology in the classroom to impact student achievement?

Is There Common Ground?

Technology is everywhere and creates a different possibility for teaching and learning. Something happens when the huge door of technology is opened in the classroom. Teachers are faced with learning new tools and overcoming challenges of technology integration, many feeling out of their comfort zone while doing so. They may not have the appropriate skill set to be successful or the mindset to be comfortable when using technology, but many are challenged to integrate it into their classroom to transform learning. Students who have grown up in a technological world are leaving their backpacks at home and going digital. They welcome learning using their "devices." New technologies allow teachers to reach students in ways that are appealing to them. In many ways technology can help teachers and students find common ground as they use their devices to interact, allowing new ways to communicate. Technology, when used correctly, can positively impact their achievement, as noted by Costley (2014).

In another camp, there are those who argue that technology in the classroom can be a detriment to learning and a distraction to students. Certainly, this is not a boost to student engagement and can be a reason why students do not perform well. Too many students and their parents cannot afford the digital devices for engagement in their learning. Unfortunately, there are those who continue to promote expensive technologies without evidence of their effectiveness for student learning. It wasn't too long ago that there were those who believed technology could,

or would, replace teachers. This concept is foreign to the research that finds, a teacher is the most important factor in student learning. This fact is not likely to go away or even fade in the discussion on teaching and learning.

Teachers are active agents for change in implementing and designing technological innovations. Technology, in the hands of professionals, trained teachers and their students, can make these innovations the most effective and productive. When this happens, student outcomes are positively impacted. Teachers should be the ones at the center of policy development that can make technology tools the most effective. A proactive stance on a teacher's value to what kinds of technology work best for teaching, learning, and improved student achievement is the answer to the question, "Is the use of technology changing how teacher's teach and student's learn?"

Still, there are those who feel that teaching and learning involve more than clicking a button or socially networking on a digital device. There is research that supports the notion that the frills, bells, and whistles of student hands-on devices and other technologies have not improved student learning, nor do they appear likely to do so in the future.

Common ground is bringing the two opposing camps together for opportunities to engage directly with others: teachers with teachers, teachers with administrators, teachers with students, and teachers with technology entrepreneurs, researchers (who study student learning outcomes), techies, inventors, designers, and dreamers. Common ground is a bigger window for the number one factor in student success—the teacher—to interact, collaborate, and be part of how best to use technology for student success. Involvement of teachers in all facets of technology use for teaching and learning is a very powerful educational strategy, as well as a trend for higher levels of student success.

Additional Resources

Eady, M. & Lockyer, L., Tools for Learning: Technology and Teaching Strategies. Queensland University of Technology (2013).

Efaw, J., No Teacher Left Behind: How to Teach with Technology. EDUCAUSE QUARTERLY (2005).

Grinager, H., How Education Technology Leads to Improved Student Achievement. Education Issues (2006).

Halverson, R. & Smith, A., How New Technologies Have (and Have Not) Changed Teaching and Learning in Schools. Journal of Computing in Teaching Education (2009–10).

McManis, L. & Gunnewig, S., Finding the Education in Education Technology with Early Learners. Technology and Young Learners (2012).

Internet References . . .

Five Positive Effects Technology Has on Teaching and Learning

https://blog.kurzweiledu.com/2015/02/12/5-positive
-effects-technology-has-on-teaching-learning/

How Has Technology Transformed the Role of a Teacher?

https://www.theguardian.com/teacher-network/
teacher
-blog/2013/jun/18/technology-transform-teaching
-students-schools

Technology Changing How Students Learn, Teachers Say

http://www.nytimes.com/2012/11/01/education
/technology-is-changing-how-students-learn
-teachers-say.html?_r=0

Use of Technology in Teaching and Learning

http://www.ed.gov/oii-news/use-technology-teaching
-and-learning

What's Tomorrow Student Look Like?

http://askatechteacher.com/2014/08/28/whats
-tomorrows-digital-student-look-like/

Selected, Edited, and with Issue Framing Material by:
Glenn L. Koonce, *Regent University*

ISSUE

Should Students Be Allowed to Opt Out?

YES: Kristina Rizga, from "Sorry, I'm Not Taking This Test," *Mother Jones* (2015)

NO: Jonah Edelman, from "This Issue Is Bigger Than Just Testing," *Education Next* (2016)

Learning Outcomes
After reading this issue, you will be able to: • Describe the key points that parents choose to allow their child to opt out of testing. • Examine some of the types of students that are opting out of state tests. • Research to best understand the purpose for standardized testing in the educational arena. • Analyze how students that opt out can affect the overall school testing data results. • Describe how quality standardized tests help the teacher assess each students' overall success and academic achievement in school.

ISSUE SUMMARY

YES: Kristina Rizga, a former education correspondent at *Mother Jones* and author of *Mission High,* argues that with so much controversy revolving around the effects of testing on struggling students and schools, it's hard to remember that the movement's original goal was to level the educational playing field.

NO: Jonah Edelman, an American advocate for public education and the cofounder and Chief Executive Officer of Stand for Children deeply values teachers' perspective on how students are progressing academically, but he also wants a more objective gauge of whether students are on grade level in math, reading, and writing.

"**O**pt Out poses a challenge to a cornerstone of federal and state education policy in the United States: standardized testing" (Pizmony-Levy & Cosman, 2017, p. 5). The two articles being presented in this issue certainly offer diverse sides of the issues and are appropriately titled: "*Sorry, I'm Not Taking This Test*" (Rizga, 2015) and "*The Issue Is Bigger than Just Testing*" (Edelman, 2016). Although standardized tests have been around since before the Civil War, growth after the Civil War was limited to college entrance exams until the turn of the century. In 1905, Alfred Binet designed initial work that would eventually be developed into the modern IQ test, known as the Stanford Binet Intelligence test. A short time later, tests of mental capacities were needed to help place soldiers in jobs that supported the troops fighting in World War

I. About the same time, Columbia University developed standardized achievement tests in arithmetic, handwriting, spelling, drawing, reading, and language ability. Soon a large number of high school tests, vocational tests, and athletic ability test began appearing between the two World Wars that were being administered as part of statewide testing programs. Over a hundred standardized tests in all elementary and secondary subjects were increasingly being used to classify students. The Scholastic Aptitude Test was designed and began with 315 questions with a time period of 90 minutes for completion. In the 1930s, high-speed computing and test scanners were being developed and used to produce test reports for analysis. IOWA tests begin spreading across the country. The next big growth period for testing came with the passage of the Elementary & Secondary Act of 1965 where norm-referenced test was being used to evaluate curriculum and instruction programs. Testing continued to grow to the point where almost every child in the country was being tested on a regular basis. The No Child Left Behind Act (NCLB) of 2001 mandated standardized testing as means of assessing school performance through Adequate Yearly Progress (AYP). Perhaps in a demonstration of testing going full circle, the new federal Every Student Succeeds Act (ESSA) deemphasizes test scores in favor of multiple measures of student outcomes for accountability.

At the same time, the ESSA was being delivered for President Obama's signature in 2015, the New York State Opt Out movement was in full swing. Twenty percent of public school students in New York had opted out from taking state standardized tests in mathematics and English language arts. An examination of public opinion on this Opt Out movement was written by Pizmony-Levy and Cosman (2017) at Teachers College, Columbia University. The elephant in the room regarding this report was that students across the country were opting out of taking standardized tests, not just the students from New York. The Opt Out movement was also very strong at the time in California, Colorado, and Florida, as well as other pockets across the country. Even so, the study conducted by Pizmony-Levy and Cosman was a somewhat new phenomenon—polling public opinion on the Opt Out movement. According to the authors of the study, "public opinion can offer support for, and endorsement of, the challenges posed by social movements and can affect public policy by signaling to elected officials where the public stands on various issues" (p. 9). In seeking public opinion on the Opt Out movement, the authors noted two limitations found in their study: (1) the survey responses could not assess the extent to which the general public engaged with the Opt Out movement and support of parents who participated in it and (2) most surveys used the term "standardized tests," rather than specify the target of the Opt Out movement: mathematics and English arts state standardized tests for third through eighth graders, skewing data in favor of standardized tests (p 10).

In reporting the findings, the national sample consisted of 2,107 adults aged 18 and older on their responses to a combination of responses on two surveys conducted in February and May, 2015. Examples of survey questions include:

> As you may know, in recent years a growing number of parents across the nation are opting their children out of state standardized tests in math and reading. These parents say that they have a

right to decide whether or not their children take the tests.

1. How much, if anything, have you heard about this group of parents?
   a. Nothing at all
   b. A little
   c. A fair amount
   d. A lot
2. If you have heard about this group of parents, where have you heard about it?
   a. National Media (newspapers, television, online)
   b. Local Media (newspapers, television, online)
   c. Social Media
   d. Parents
   e. School Officials
   f. Other
   g. I haven't heard about these parents
3. How well, if at all, do you feel you understand the goals of this group of parents?
   a. Not at all well
   b. Not too well
   c. Fairly well
   d. Very well
4. To what extent do you support or oppose parents opting their children out of state standardized tests in math and reading?
   a. Strongly oppose
   b. Somewhat oppose
   c. Neither oppose or support
   d. Somewhat support
   e. Strongly support (p. 34).

Survey findings include;

1. Close to ⅔ of Americans had heard of the Opt Out movement;
2. Slightly more than ½ of Americans who had heard about the movement said they understood the goals of the movement;
3. About ⅓ of Americans said they supported parents who take part in the movement;
4. Respondents were more likely to report supporting parental action described in ethical/political terms than in a neutral term;
5. Notably, framing the Opt Out movement in the context of "parental rights" had no statistically significant effect on public engagement;
6. The general public relies more heavily on traditional media, whereas Opt Out activists relies more heavily on social media; and
7. The general public believes Opt Out activists oppose the Common Core and are critical of standardized testing's impact on teachers (teach to

the test), whereas, Opt Out activist report a more expansive set of motivators, including opposing using student's performance on standardized tests to evaluate teachers and believing standardized tests takes away too much instructional time (pp. 31, 32).

Recommendations include:

1. Districts should reduce unnecessary testing;
2. Educators and policy makers should improve communication with parents about the value gained from having all students take the assessments;
3. Policy makers should discourage opting out; and
4. Policy makers should support appropriate uses of test scores (Pizmony-Levy & Cosman, 2017, p. 37).

Education Next conducted a poll that was cited in an ACT Research & Policy issue brief from 2015 (Croft), and found that "a majority of the general public, 59 percent, and 52 percent of parents, did not support letting parents decide whether to have their children take state and math reading tests" (p. 1). In the same year, a combined Phi Delta Kappa and Gallop poll found that "59% of public school parents would not excuse their own child from taking standardized tests" (p. 1). However, in the three states noted earlier (New York, Colorado, and Florida) a large number of parents opted their students out of testing. Croft (2015) also identified additional states where significant numbers of parents opted their children out of testing: Washington State, Oregon, Maine, Michigan, New Jersey, and New Mexico. Reasons given ranged from concerns about testing, curriculum, and state departments of education, to types of tests, length and number of tests, and how the tests are administered. At the time, 2015, legislation bodies were introducing bills regarding opt out.

In a follow-up policy issue brief, Croft (2016) noted that 30 states and the District of Columbia had statues that required all students to participate in standardized testing. Yet, additional states were being added to the list of states with significant opt outs including Connecticut,

Delaware, Idaho, Rhode Island, Utah, and Wisconsin. Some of these states received notices from the U.S. Department of Education that they needed to develop plans to reduce the number of opt outs. At the time, legislation in state government ranged from *no* consequences for opt outs (Oklahoma) to two states (Oregon and Utah) that allow opt outs and notice to parents of their right to opt out. Of the 87 Opt Out bills introduced in state legislature in 2015 and 2016 only 5 bills passed (Oregon, Utah, Colorado, Wisconsin, and a new state to the list, Georgia).

With the passage of the ESSA, the policy regarding testing remained rigid, thus creating a challenge to policy-making in states that have contested testing policies found in the policies of the NCLB. "The Every Student Succeeds Act (ESSA) requires that states assess 95% of all students, and 95% of each 'subgroup' in every school with federally mandated annual state tests in English and math. It says that in calculating average school test scores, a school must include in the denominator the greater of either all test takers, or 95% of eligible test takers. If more than 5% of students are not tested, the lowest possible score will be assigned to non-test takers beyond 5%" (FairTest, 2018, p. 1). Are some states ignoring their own law that very clearly states, parents can opt their children out of standardized testing? This contradiction is one that all educators must stay tuned to, particularly as states move forward with approved ESSA plans and their implementation.

The YES article for this issue shares a very personal student's view of testing and of opting out of testing. The student notes that she is missing out on a chance to learn in her daily classroom activities due to the fact that standardized tests set the pace for all learning. The impact on teacher's lost opportunities for student learning is also addressed in the article (Riga, 2015). Edelman (2016), in the NO article, supports testing. He makes his case on how standardized testing provides invaluable information that can be used to improve public education for everyone. Will the Opt Out movement be a political battle, a psychological one, or somewhere in between? For sure, the debate will continue.

YES ⤶

Kristina Rizga

Sorry, I'm Not Taking This Test

The average US student takes more than 113 standardized tests before graduation. More and more are now saying: Enough.

One hot morning in May, Kiana Hernandez came to class early. She stood still outside the door, intensely scanning each face in the morning rush of shoulders, hats, and backpacks. She felt anxious. For more than eight months, she had been thinking about what she was about to do, but she didn't want it to be a big scene.

As her English teacher approached the door, she blocked him with her petite, slender frame. Then, in a soft voice, she said, "I'm sorry. I'm not going to take the test today." The multiple-choice test that morning was 1 of 15 that year alone, and she'd found out it would be used primarily as part of her teacher's job evaluation. She'd come into class, she said, but would spend the hour quietly studying.

The teacher stared at her dark-brown eyes in silence while students shuffled past. "That's a mistake," he said with a deep sigh.

By her own estimate, Kiana had spent about three months during each of her four years at University High in Orlando preparing for and taking standardized tests that determined everything from her GPA to her school's fate. "These tests were cutting out class time," she says. "We would stop whatever we were learning to prepare." The spring of her senior year, she says, there were three whole months when she couldn't get access to computers at school (she didn't have one at home) to do homework or fill out college applications. They were always being used for testing.

Kiana had a 2.99 GPA and is heading to Otterbein University in Ohio this fall. She says she did well in regular classroom assignments and quizzes, but struggled with the standardized tests the district and state demanded. "Once you throw out the word 'test,' I freeze," she tells me. "I get anxiety knowing that the tests count more than classwork or schoolwork. It's a make or break kind of thing."

Junior year had been particularly hard. She'd failed the Florida reading test every year since sixth grade and had been placed in remedial classes where she was drilled on basic skills, like reading paragraphs to find the topic sentence and then filling in the right bubbles on a practice test. She didn't get to read whole books like her peers in the regular class or practice her writing, analysis, and debating—skills she would need for the political science degree she dreamed of, or for the school board candidacy that she envisioned. (Sorting students into remedial classes, educational research shows, actually depresses achievement among African American and Latino students in many cases, yet it remains common practice.)

Kiana was living with her mother, and times were tough. Some days there was no food in the house. "The only thing that kept me going to school was my math teacher," Kiana says. "The only place that I felt that I had worth was Mr. Katz's class. That's the thing that kept me going every day."

On the news, Kiana saw pictures of students and parents carrying signs reading "Opt-Out: Boycott Standardized Testing." Her high school didn't have activists like that. In the library, Kiana made flyers that read: "Are you tired of taking time consuming and pointless tests? Boycott Benchmark Testing! When given the test, open the slip and do NOT pick up your pencil. Refuse to feed the system!" She passed them out to her classmates, but they were worried that opting out would hurt their GPAs.

Kiana talked about this with Mr. Katz, who regularly met with students who needed extra help during his lunch hour and after school. One day during their tutoring session, he mentioned Gandhi. Kiana went to the library and found some of Gandhi's essays. She determined that what it took to make change was someone taking a personal stand.

Next, she researched state education rules and discovered that the end-of-course tests that Florida required in every subject were being used primarily for job evaluations. (She says one teacher told her: "Please take [the test]. My paycheck depends on it.")

The English teacher started passing out the computer tablets used to take the test. He put one on her desk. Kiana raised her hand. "I'm sorry," she said again. "I'm not going to take this test."

The noise dropped abruptly.

"You should wait until you are done with high school before you try to change the world," the teacher said.

Kiana reached into her backpack and pulled out a notebook to prepare for her psychology final.

Critics have long warned that a flood of standardized testing is distorting American education. But in recent months, an unprecedented number of students like Kiana, along with teachers and parents across the country, have chosen to take matters into their own hands—by simply refusing to take part.

"This school year saw by far some of the largest numbers of families opting out from standardized tests in history," Bob Schaeffer, director of public education at the advocacy group FairTest.org, told me this spring. In New Jersey, 15 percent of high school students chose not to take state tests in the 2014–2015 school year. In New York state, only a few districts reported meeting 95 percent participation, the minimum required by federal rules, according to a *New York Times* investigation. There are opt-out activists in every state, and in Florida—thanks in part to the hardcore protesting policies implemented by former Gov. Jeb Bush—the backlash is especially severe.

"Half the counties in Florida have an opt-out group," Cindy Hamilton, a parent and cofounder of Opt Out Orlando, told me. She said her group is not against tests per se but against the process being taken out of the hands of teachers and schools and turned over to outside vendors. (As NPR's Anya Kamenetz has documented, the testing industry, controlled by a handful of companies such as CBT/McGraw-Hill, Harcourt, and Pearson, has grown from $263 million worth of sales in 1997 to $2 billion.) "Our movement," Hamilton said, "is civil disobedience against the gathering of all of this data by for-profit companies that doesn't help students learn."

Students in American public schools today take more standardized tests than their peers in any other industrialized country. A 2014 survey of 14 large districts by the Center for American Progress found that third to eighth graders take 10 standardized tests each year on average, and some take up to 20. By contrast, students in Europe rarely encounter multiple-choice questions in their national assessments and instead write essays that are graded by trained educators. Students in England, New Zealand, and Singapore are also evaluated through projects like presentations, science investigations, and collaborative assignments, designed to both mimic what professionals do in the real world and provide data on what students are learning.

In the past three years, I interviewed hundreds of students across the nation while reporting my book, *Mission High*. In schools, both urban and suburban, affluent and struggling, students told me that preparing for such tests cut into things that advanced their education—projects, field trips, and electives like music or computer classes.

"Testing felt like such a waste," Alexia Garcia, a 2013 graduate of Lincoln High in Portland, Oregon, told me. "It felt really irrelevant and disconnected from what we were doing in classes." As a senior, Garcia became a lead organizer with the Portland Student Union, a coalition with members in 12 area high schools that has been one of the most visible student groups in the national student opt-out movement. Garcia, who is now at Vassar College, told me that this year—thanks to the Black Lives Matter movement—students are also increasingly talking about how standardized testing contributes to inequality and ultimately the "school-to-prison pipeline."

Joshua Katz, Kiana Hernandez's math teacher, says he tests his students using a variety of challenges and quizzes, but the only ones that officially count are the fill-in-the-bubble variety. "They tell me I must have data, and they don't consider tests data unless it comes from multiple-choice," Katz told me.

Every nine weeks, Katz has to stop whatever his students are doing and make time for the district's benchmark tests measuring student progress toward the big Common Core exam in the spring. (Proponents of the Common Core standards, now in place in 43 states, promised fewer tests and less of a focus on multiple-choice. But most of the teachers told me there had been no change in the number of standardized assessments. "This year was a circus—16 weeks of testing scheduled at the high school level," Katz said.)

And University High, whose neighborhood and student population is largely middle class, didn't bear as heavy a load of tests and drills as its poorer counterparts: One recent study found that urban high school students spend 266 percent more time taking district-level exams than their suburban counterparts. That's in part because the stakes for these schools are so high: test scores determine not just how much funding a school will get, but whether it will be allowed to stay open at all. In response, some administrators have been taking desperate measures, including pushing the lowest-performing students out entirely. Suspensions have been growing across the country, especially among African American and Latino students, and many researchers correlate this with pressure to raise scores. And in the 2011–2012 school year, the Government Accountability Office reported that officials in 33 states confirmed at least one instance of school staff flat-out cheating.

With so much controversy revolving around the effect of testing on struggling students and schools, it's hard to remember that the movement's original goal was to level the educational playing field. In 1965, as part of the War on Poverty, the Johnson administration sent extra federal funding to low-income schools, and in return asked for data to make sure the money was making an impact. As more states started using standardized tests in the 1970s and 1980s, urban education researchers were able to identify which schools were helping students of color and those from poor families achieve—giving the lie to the idea that these students couldn't succeed.

By the late '80s, many educators were pushing to deploy reliable, external data to measure student progress, a movement that culminated in the bipartisan support for President George W. Bush's No Child Left Behind (NCLB) initiative. With NCLB, states were required to gather and analyze vast amounts of testing data by race, ethnicity, and class. Researchers soon started mining this information, convinced that they could reveal what really worked in education. One 2006 study found that putting students in a top-rated teacher's class raised average scores by 5 percentage points. Another connected increases in test scores to higher earning levels, lower pregnancy rates, and higher college acceptance rates.

> "They tell me I must have data, and they don't consider tests data unless it comes from multiple-choice," teacher Joshua Katz told me.

Findings like this encouraged two major beliefs in policy circles: first, that test scores were a key factor in how students would do later in life. And second, that the best way to improve teaching was to reward the top performers and fire the bottom ones, based in large part on their students' scores. High-profile charter schools like KIPP and Uncommon Schools, whose model relied in part on avoiding teacher tenure, helped cement that belief.

By 2009, President Barack Obama used his Race to the Top initiative to promote using test scores to hire, fire, and compensate teachers. Today, 35 states require teacher evaluations to include these scores as a factor—and many states have introduced new tests just for this purpose.

Until this year, Florida used end-of-course tests in virtually every subject to give bonuses to some teachers and punish others. When Kiana's math teacher, Joshua Katz, was downgraded to "effective" from "highly effective" this year, his salary was slated to drop by $1,100.

But while using student test scores to rate teachers may seem intuitive, researchers say it actually flies in the face of the evidence: decades of data indicates that better results come not from hiring innately better teachers, but from helping them improve through constant training and feedback. Perhaps that's why no other nation in the world uses annual, standardized tests to set teacher salaries. (Other countries use test scores to push teachers to improve but not to punish them.)

Nor do other developed nations have such a drastic gap in funding between rich and poor schools. Mission High School in San Francisco, for example, spends $9,780 per student, while schools in Palo Alto, just 30 miles away, spend $14,995. New York spends $19,818 per student, California just $9,220. The per student funding gap between rich and poor schools nationwide has grown 44 percent in the last decade—even as the number of needy students has grown. In 2013, for the first time in at least 50 years, a majority of US public school students came from low-income families.

In July, EdBuild released an analysis of child poverty in some 13,000 school districts nationwide. In the districts outlined in red, more than 40 percent of students came from impoverished households.

All this presents a significant risk for a country that has relied on schools as the primary avenue for social mobility. Prudence L. Carter, a professor in the school of education at Stanford University, says in fact, kids have very different opportunities: affluent students ride through the education system in what amounts to a high-speed elevator supported by well-paid teachers, intellectually challenging classes, and private tutors. Middle-class kids are on an escalator. Their parents may struggle to keep up, but still can access resources to help their children prepare for college. And then there are low-income students like Kiana, who are left running up a staircase with missing steps and no handrails.

When it comes to standardized testing, this means that schools that educate low-income students start out at a disadvantage: they are much more likely to have lower-paid and less-qualified teachers; lack college preparatory classes, books, and supplies; and offer fewer arts and sports programs. When their students don't make it to the same "proficiency" benchmarks on yearly tests as their wealthier counterparts, politicians label them and their teachers as "failing." And that begins a vicious cycle: struggling students are pushed into remedial classes that zero in on what's measured on the tests, further limiting their opportunities to learn the advanced skills they'll need in college or the workplace.

"What I observed was egregious," Ceresta Smith, a 26-year veteran teacher in Miami and a cofounder of United Opt Out National, told me about a predominantly African American, low-income school where she worked from 2008 to 2010. Some teachers tried to incorporate writing and intellectually engaging readings, she said, but most resorted to remediation of basic skills. "Students are reading random passages and practice picking the correct multiple-choice. It was very separate and unequal."

The proponents of testing-based reform like to argue that—while imperfect—the current approach has been working better than any other, leading to rising graduation rates and standardized test scores. But as Stanford researcher Linda Darling-Hammond has pointed out, there's a bit of circular logic at work here: a system singularly focused on producing better test scores leads to . . . better test scores. Meanwhile, though, American students' performance compared to other nations—on tests that measure skills and knowledge more broadly—remained flat or declined between 2000 and 2012.

Most importantly, test-based accountability is failing on its most important mandate—eliminating the achievement gap between different groups of students. While racial gaps have narrowed slightly since 2001, they remain stubbornly large. The gaps in math and reading for African American and Latino students shrank far more dramatically before NCLB—when policies focused on equalizing funding and school integration, rather than on test scores. In the 1970s and 1980s, the achievement gap between black and white 13-year-olds was cut roughly in ½ nationwide. In the mid-'70s, the rates at which white, black, and Latino graduates attended college reached parity for the first and only time.

In the decades since, the encouraging news is that the black–white achievement gap has kept slowly shrinking. But at the same time, the gap between students from poor and affluent families has widened into a chasm, growing by 40 percent between 1985 and 2001. Sean Reardon, a Stanford professor who focuses on poverty and inequality in education, says this is not surprising—affluent families can spend more than ever on enrichment activities. He argues it's up to government to level the playing field, by making sure low-income students get the opportunity to succeed. But in many places, government is instead pulling back from the civil rights era's focus on educational inequality.

Today, many students of color are once again going to segregated, high-poverty schools that struggle to offer advanced classes and attract teachers and counselors. Some 40 percent of black and Latino students now are in schools at which 90–100 percent of the student body are kids of color.

To be sure, the test-based reform movement still has powerful proponents—politicians like Jeb Bush and Secretary of Education Arne Duncan, philanthropists like Bill Gates, some teachers, and prominent civil rights organizations such as the NAACP and National Council of La Raza. "For the civil rights community, data provide the power to advocate for greater equality under the law," a coalition of 12 groups argued in a recent joint statement criticizing the opt-out movement. "We cannot fix what we cannot measure." Some teachers I spoke to echo that message: Lauren Fine, an elementary-school teacher in Denver, believes that without the standards and annual assessments, we won't be able to maintain "a high bar for every student." President Barack Obama agrees with this line of reasoning and recently said that as Congress debates rewriting the NCLB law, he won't sign any bills that don't include requirements for annual testing, accountability, and state interventions.

But a growing list of others, from the students and parents in the opt-out movement to youth and labor groups and education researchers, are arguing that the push for standardized testing has in fact exacerbated inequities. Journey for Justice is a coalition of grassroots youth and parent groups in 21 cities. "Our concern is that the people who are most directly impacted by these education policies are never consulted," director Jitu Brown told me.

Brown, who saw firsthand the impact of the recent closures of 50 low-scoring schools in his native Chicago, says politicians should look at the real world rather than listening to "education entrepreneurs who are implementing mediocre interventions in our communities." In Chicago, he notes, "you had young people being displaced as the one stable institution in our community was eliminated. You had the massive firing of black teachers, as if they were the problem—when equity never existed."

So assume for a moment that the opt-outers succeed: we'd still need ways to improve teaching, assess what students are learning, and reduce the achievement gaps. How should that happen instead?

I found some answers as I spent two years in classrooms with Pirette McKamey, a highly respected teacher at Mission High, and Ajanee Greene, a bright, resilient senior who had just finished a powerful 10-page research paper—even though, as a freshman, she got a D in English at her old school. As I watched McKamey and her colleagues design lesson plans and pore over Ajanee's writing together, I realized that a focus on accountability doesn't have to sacrifice teachers' growth or students' love of learning.

One winter morning in 2013, McKamey and seven other teachers sat in an empty classroom at Mission High. A light February rain drummed against the windows as Shideh Etaat passed around roasted almonds and talked about her weekend plans. The teachers had convened for one of their three weekly planning hours. This one was dedicated to in-depth case studies of individual students' math worksheets, essay drafts, and written notes for science lab investigations.

Etaat, a first-year English teacher, had brought in a poem written by a junior named Jay, who came to California from Thailand two years ago. "Jay is that student who will say, 'Oh, I don't write poetry. I'm not creative,'" Etaat said. "But I find that English learners are able to see outside of the box. They have an ability to play with language in this really creative way."

Etaat explained that she'd given her students photos of five different pairs of shoes. She'd asked them to pick a pair they would not wear, and to create a character to go with them. She passed out the "scaffolding" documentation for her lesson—directions for how to develop a character, some sample stanzas, a poem she had written herself based on the assignment. Educational theorists call this teaching in the "zone of proximal development": that place where we can't progress by ourselves, but we can with targeted assistance and constructive feedback.

The wind whistled through the old window frames as the teachers read Jay's poem.

My shoes look like a pair of cheap running shoes
Full of sweat and heat
In his shoes, he works hard every day
He sees himself working in the mud
And sleeping on the street with other hobos
In my shoes, I see a student running in the hallway
Trying to get his lunch as early as possible
In his shoes, he hears the heavy metal noise of his hammer
Striking at that thick jet black rock until it resolves
In my shoes, I hear the noisy noise coming out of the classroom
The sound of electronic devices and ceaseless hip hop music
In his shoes, he feels pain coming from his body,
The pain of loneliness and betrayal.

"It's very hard to scaffold creativity just right," said Dayna Soares, a second-year math teacher. "Sometimes teachers give you a blank paper and that's too much freedom. I'm always struggling with this—how can I give my students just enough structure, but in a way that doesn't make them fill in the blanks?"

They talked about the craft of grading and commenting on student work. When teachers provide feedback on writing, research shows, many default to a "what's wrong with this paper" strategy, instead of writing responses that promote growth. "Every time a student does an assignment, they are communicating something about their thinking," McKamey told the group. "And even if it's far away from what I thought they'd do, they are still communicating the ways they are putting the pieces together. There are so many opportunities to miss certain students and not see them, not hear them, shut them down. It takes a lot of skill, experience, and patience not to do that." Looking over multiple-choice questions doesn't help teachers detect these signals, McKamey told me, because they won't tell you where and why someone got stuck.

In other words: it's not just students who miss out on a chance to learn when standardized tests set the pace. Teachers, too, lose opportunities to improve their craft and professional judgment—for example, detecting where their students' thinking hits what McKamey calls a "knot" and figuring out how they can improve. That's when many fall back on the only available option: repetitive instruction, more testing, and remediation.

What's essential for teachers to grow, McKamey told me, is collaboration with fellow professionals—and that mutual accountability, she said, is more effective than test scores or even financial bonuses. "What teachers care about," she said, "is the feedback they get from students, parents, and peers they respect."

Max Anders, a first-year English teacher, told me that working with McKamey helped him learn how to teach every student individually. "My understanding before was you give work for the middle," explained Anders, who was teaching Plato's "The Allegory of the Cave" at the time. "But the best approach is to give rigorous work that challenges everyone and learn how to break it up and scaffold it just right."

McKamey's small, sunlit office is lined with binders filled with the lesson plans she has built up over the last 27 years of teaching, including one for Tim O'Brien's Vietnam War memoir, *The Things They Carried*. Every year she teaches the novel, McKamey adds material to the binder, because she learns new things from her students and colleagues each time. Underneath her heavy desk, three pairs of shoes sit neatly lined up: black loafers and Mary Janes for teaching and coaching, light-gray sneakers for dance class after school.

I talked to Ajanee Greene in that office one afternoon. Independent and astute, Ajanee wrote the strongest research papers in the English classes I'd been observing. She was about to become the first in her family to graduate from high school and had started filling out college applications.

From the moment she stepped into McKamey's classroom, Ajanee told me, she started to feel like an intelligent person. "By middle school, I could tell which teacher is looking at my grades and test scores and is just teaching me basics without opportunities to challenge myself. Just because I struggle with some grammar rules doesn't mean I can't think deeply. Ms. McKamey believed in me and then pushed me to work really, really hard."

Ajanee and McKamey had just finished their lunch meeting, an occasional check-in to talk about life and school. As McKamey left for a meeting, Ajanee told me that she'd chosen the topic for her paper—titled "Black on Black Violence: Why We Do This to Ourselves"—because she'd lost her stepfather and several close friends to gun violence.

> At school, Ajanee said, "you learn about math and reading, but you rarely learn new ways of looking and thinking about life."

For the paper, Ajanee had read and analyzed about 20 articles and studies and, with McKamey's encouragement, had interviewed her neighbors and added her own point of view. She didn't like how the local paper described her stepfather as a "flashy" man who had recently purchased a piece of new jewelry—implying, it seemed to her, that greed might have been the reason he'd been shot.

Ajanee wanted her readers to understand that her stepdad was a dedicated father of four who was home with his seven-year-old nephew when he was killed. The violence didn't just affect the victims; it scarred the survivors, Ajanee wrote. "Personal, private, solitary pain is more terrifying than what anyone can inflict. The violence stays with families and becomes a part of their lives. Nobody feels the same and family relationships get strained." She also added a section on the history of slavery and Jim Crow, writing, "The epidemic of African Americans killing each other didn't start because we just hate each other. It started when we began to believe the things other races said about us and began to hate ourselves."

"When you go to school, you learn about math and reading, but you rarely learn new ways of looking and thinking about life," Ajanee explained. "Learning the skills to research and write this paper helped me learn so much: how many people are dying, why they are dying, how to tell the stories of others and learn about the world. It gave me a better understanding."

She got an A– for the paper. "When they told me the grade, I thought it must have been a mistake," she says—she'd read her classmates' drafts and didn't think hers measured up. "Before this, the longest paper I wrote was three pages. Now, if I have to write 15 pages in college next year, I feel ready," she told me. (That was in 2013. This year, after two years in community college, Ajanee transferred to Jackson State University in Mississippi.)

But as politicians, economists, and philanthropists focus on ever more sophisticated number crunching, opportunities for teachers to nurture students' intellect the way McKamey does have grown more limited. Mission High teachers never complained to me about being overworked, but they worked more hours than anyone I met in the corporate world. For more than a decade, McKamey woke up at 5 A.M., got to school by 6:30, left for dance class at 4:30 P.M., and then worked almost every evening and every Sunday. Most teachers I met worked with students after school and colleagues on weekends, without pay.

And yet the story of Mission High holds out hope for a different kind of school reform—one that builds on resources that already exist in thousands of schools and doesn't require spending a dime on the next generation of tests, software, or teacher evaluation forms. That's because Mission has already been through exactly the kind of harsh treatment for "failing" schools that the standardized-testing movement supports—and then it found another way.

In the mid-1990s, Mission had rock-bottom test scores and was targeted by the district for "reconstitution." The principal was removed and ½ the teachers were reassigned. Yet in 2001, the school once again had some of the lowest test scores and attendance rates among all of San Francisco's high schools, and more teachers were leaving it than almost any other school in the district.

Then Mission High tried something new. Instead of bringing in consultants, it mobilized a small group of teachers—including McKamey—to lead reforms on their own. It increased paid time for them to plan lessons together, design assessments, and analyze outcomes. The teachers made videos of students talking about what kind of instruction helped them succeed. They read research about how integrated classes, personalized teaching, and culturally relevant curriculum increased achievement. They asked successful teachers to coach colleagues who needed help.

To focus their efforts and keep each other accountable, McKamey and her colleagues regularly pore over data, both qualitative and quantitative. They look at achievement gaps, attendance, referrals, graduation rates, and test scores. They also walk through classrooms, delve into student work, and interview teachers and students. "We are always looking at and trying to understand different kinds of data, including anecdotal," McKamey told me. "Then we can settle on something we need to concentrate on each year." One year, social studies teachers discovered that too many students didn't fully grasp the difference between summarizing a text versus analyzing it, so they spent the next year building more opportunities to practice those skills. The math department, meanwhile, focused on one-on-one coaching to help set up effective group work.

By contrast, back in Florida, Katz told me that the typical way he receives professional development entails an observation of a model lesson by a district consultant demonstrating how to teach Common Core standards. While University High struggles to keep teachers, Mission High has very low attrition. It is no longer considered a "hard-to-staff" school by the district. "Mission High is famous at the district because it is known as a learning community and a good, supportive place to work," Soares told me. "It's hard to get a job here."

The school does well on a bevy of other metrics, as well. The graduation rate went from among the lowest in the district, at 60 percent, to 82 percent; the graduation rate for African American students was 20 percent higher than the district average that year. Even though close to 40 percent of students are English learners and 75 percent are poor, college enrollment rose from 55 percent in 2007 to 74 percent by 2013. Suspensions plummeted, and in the annual student and parent satisfaction survey from 2013, close to 90 percent said they liked the school and would recommend it to others.

That doesn't mean there aren't challenges. Standardized test scores went up 86 points, to 641 (out of 1,000) in 2012, but that was still far from California's target for all schools of 800. The numbers of African American and Latino students in AP math and science classes don't fully mirror the student body, and their passing rates on the California high school exit exam went down in 2013 and 2014. The work continues, but so does the commitment of teachers to keep at it. "No one here does 7:45 to 3:10 and then calls it quits," science teacher Becky Fulop, who has worked at Mission High for more than a decade, told me. "That by itself doesn't necessarily make teachers effective, but the dedication here is extraordinarily high."

Nationally, there are thousands of struggling schools like Mission where teachers are engaged in similar hard, messy, and slow work. What if instead of spending more money on new rounds of tests, we focused on their ability to learn and lead on the job?

No country has ever turned around its educational achievement by increasing standardized tests, according to research conducted by Lant Pritchett at the Center for Global Development. The best systems, it turns out, invest in supporting accountability at the school level—like those teacher meetings at Mission High.

"It's always an attempt to hijack the effort by the teacher to think about education," McKamey told me one morning as we talked about the dozens of reform efforts she's seen come and go in 27 years of working in inner-city schools. The only thing none of the politicians, consultants, and philanthropists who came in to fix education ever tried, she said, was a systemic commitment to support teachers as leaders in closing the achievement gap, one classroom at a time.

"Let me remind you what analysis is," she said a few hours later, standing in the middle of her class with those black leather loafers from under her desk. "When I was little, I used a hammer and screwdriver to crack a golf ball open. As I cracked that glossy plastic open, I saw rubber bands. And I went, 'Ha! I didn't know there were rubber bands in golf balls. I wonder what's inside other balls?' It made me curious about the world. So we are doing the same thing. We'll analyze the author's words to dig in deeper."

The 25 seniors had just finished reading a chapter from *The Things They Carried* titled "The Man I Killed." When they were done, McKamey asked them to pick out a quote they found intriguing.

David, a shy, reflective teenager whose face lit up when the class read poetry, raised his hand:

> He was a slim, dead, almost dainty young man of about twenty. He lay with one leg bent beneath him, his jaw in his throat, his face neither expressive nor inexpressive. One eye was shut. The other was a star-shaped hole.

"What do you notice in this passage?" McKamey probed.

"The man the narrator killed is the same age as him," Roberto commented.

"Exactly," she replied. "Now you are one step deeper. What do I feel inside when I think of that?"

"Guilt, regret," Ajanee jumped in.

"That's right," McKamey commented. "I personally would use the word *compassion*. But what you said is 100 percent correct. And what does that do when we realize that this man is the same age as us?"

"It makes me think that he's young, likes girls, probably doesn't want to fight in a war," Roberto said.

"Exactly. Now take that even deeper."

"It's like he is killing himself?" Roberto said more hesitantly, glancing at her for affirmation.

"Perfect! Now you made a connection," McKamey said, excitement in her voice. "That's what this quote is really about. Now, why is O'Brien saying 'star-shaped hole'? Why not 'peanut-shaped' hole?"

Ajanee raised her hand. "The image in his mind is burned."

"Exactly!" McKamey replied. "O'Brien wants us to keep that same image in mind that he had as a young soldier in *his* mind. It's the kind of image you never forget."

KRISTINA RIZGA is a former education correspondent at *Mother Jones* and covers education, focusing primarily on how school reforms affect students and teachers in the classrooms, and how policies create or reduce racial disparities in schools. She is the author of *Mission High*.

Jonah Edelman

This Issue Is Bigger Than Just Testing

What do we hear from those who oppose testing? Schools burden students with excessive test preparation. Districts force students to take standardized tests throughout the school year that aren't aligned to what students are learning. Some states and districts have unfairly penalized teachers during this period of transition to common standards of learning.

What might come as a surprise to some is that I agree with all of the criticisms. There *is* too much test preparation. There *are* too many unaligned tests given throughout the year. And some states and districts haven't given enough thought to how to evaluate teachers during the transition period. All that said, I firmly believe that tests are fundamentally necessary and that the new tests aligned with the Common Core State Standards, which are better and fairer than former assessments, are a key tool for educators and parents to ensure their students are on track for college and career.

Last year, roughly 20 percent of New York State public school students refused to sit for standardized tests. In the state of Washington, 48,000 students didn't take the state assessment. A few other states, such as New Jersey and Colorado, also gained media attention when large numbers of students refused to take tests.

When we look further at these opt-outs, we find an interesting trend. Students who didn't take the assessments in New York were more likely to be white, well off, and from upscale cities and towns (see Figure 2a). They were also modestly lower achieving than those who took the tests (see Figure 2b). In Washington State, the vast majority of those opting out were from economically advantaged households, and a high percentage were 11th graders. As they prepare for college, many 11th graders take the Scholastic Aptitude Test or ACT and perhaps Advanced Placement exams as well, and they probably don't relish the idea of also having to take state standardized tests.

Despite the media hype and the overheated and often irresponsible rhetoric of test-refusal activists (which only adds to students' anxiety), this issue is about common sense and equity. Test refusers commonly try to throw all

Figure 1

Who Is Opting Out?

(2a) Students who opted out of New York's 2015 state tests were much less likely to be economically disadvantaged or English language learners.

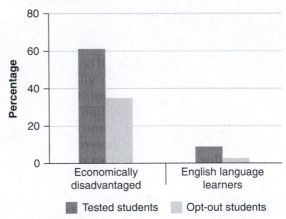

(2b) Opt-out students were also modestly lower achieving on average, despite the fact that their families tended to be more advantaged.

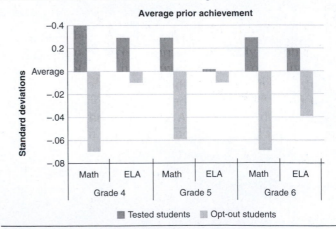

Source: American Institution for Research, "2014–15 Growth Model for Educator Evaluation. Technical Report," February 2016.

Notes: Tested students are those who participated in New York's statewide testing program in 2013–2014 and 2014–2015; opt-out students are those who participated in New York's statewide testing program in 2013–2014 but did not participated in 2014–2015. Analysis is based on all students linked to teachers for evaluation under the New York Growth Model for Educator Effectiveness. Date in Figure 2a are for Students in Grade 4; patterns are similar in graders 5–7.

of education's ills into the sink. There is no doubt that there was a rocky transition with the Common Core and the aligned tests, but instead of joining a productive debate and coming together with solutions, opt-out activists have taken unilateral action. The ones being harmed are those commonly stuck in the middle—the students. The simple question we need to keep at the center of this issue is, are we counting every child and ensuring that he or she is on a path to college and career? That needs to be our singular focus when it comes to talking about the value of testing as a tool in educators' and parents' toolboxes.

All parents, regardless of socioeconomic background, race, ethnicity, or their child's disability designation, need to know how their child is doing in reading, writing, and math. Just because a student attends an advantaged school does not mean that he or she is automatically on track for college or career. Conversely, a student attending a chronically underperforming school is not necessarily achieving below grade level. Yearly assessments provide a piece of critical information for parents who in many cases may not be getting the full picture from their children's report cards.

The fact is, no parent gets excited about his or her child taking a standardized test, just as we don't get excited about taking our kids for annual checkups at the doctor's office. My organization, Stand for Children, has championed legislation in multiple states to significantly reduce testing time. We also support the idea of districts conducting thoughtful audits of their assessment practices in order to weed out unnecessary testing.

Students should *only* take tests that (1) are aligned to what they're learning, (2) are high quality, and (3) serve a useful purpose. While you wouldn't know it based on the shallow media coverage, many educators consider the new generation of standardized tests to be far superior at assessing student learning than any previous tests. For instance, Massachusetts educators strongly prefer the PARCC exam over the Massachusetts Comprehensive Assessment System, which isn't fully aligned with the state curriculum frameworks. And a recent report by the Thomas B. Fordham Institute, comparing the new tests with older ones, indicated that the PARCC and Smarter Balanced exams had the strongest matches with the criteria that the Council of Chief State School Officers developed for evaluating high-quality assessments.

Personally, I'm glad my sons, now fifth graders, are required to take a standardized test annually from third through eighth grade. I deeply value their teachers' perspective on how they're progressing academically and in other ways, but I also want a more objective gauge of whether they're on grade level in math, reading, and writing. For the same reason, I strongly believe in taking

my sons for an annual medical checkup, even if they seem healthy to me.

Every child in our country needs to learn how to read, write, and do basic math. If children can't master these fundamental skills, they can't learn and progress in other key ways, and can't possibly get a good job when they grow up. And they may well end up incarcerated or chronically unemployed.

That's why educators, parents, advocates, and policy makers need to know how students are doing in reading, writing, and math throughout the K–12 years. For all students, but particularly for the tens of millions of American students growing up in poverty, it's a life-defining question.

High-quality standardized tests help:

- parents know whether their children are on track so they can work with teachers to resolve issues before it's too late;
- teachers know how their students compare with others across the state, and help the next grade's teachers know what kind of support incoming students need;
- educators use data to inform instructional decisions in future years based on cohort performance;
- school leaders know which teachers are doing well and which ones may need extra attention;
- school administrators know which schools are doing well and which ones need careful review;
- policy makers and the public know how marginalized students—including low-income students of color and those with disabilities—are doing and help prevent school systems and society itself from ignoring their needs.

Let's stay on that last point for a moment. There is a reason the Elementary and Secondary Education Act was signed into law in 1965 at the height of the Civil Rights movement, as there was clear disparity in states across the country in how students were educated based simply on the color of their skin, income level, or ability. Without standardized tests, how would we even know if disproportionate numbers of low-income children and children of color in a particular school or community are behind? How would parents in underserved communities with a high percentage of low-performing schools have any idea their children are attending a failing school? How else but with standardized tests?

These aren't abstract questions. Given that the majority of public school students in our nation are nonwhite and come from low-income families, they are also defining questions for the future of our nation.

At Stand for Children, we work with thousands of low-income parents and guardians in underserved communities all across the nation, from Phoenix to Indianapolis, Boston to Baton Rouge, Denver to Chicago, Tulsa to Tacoma. Like the vast majority of low-income parents, the parents and guardians (including many grandparents raising grandchildren) with whom we work are deeply committed to their children getting a good education, knowing it's their only hope for a better life. And yet, committed as they are, it's frighteningly common for parents and guardians with whom we work to believe wrongly that their children are on track because they're bringing home good grades. It's also sadly common for these parents to think their children are in good schools—when that couldn't be further from the truth.

I'm talking about the African American grandmother in Memphis who was horrified to discover after we taught her how to interpret standardized test results that her four grandchildren—*all* of whom were getting As and Bs in school—were up to *three* grades behind in reading. With the assistance of Stand for Children, she found the children extra help right away, and they've caught up.

I'm thinking of the many dozens of Latino immigrant parents we worked with in the Murphy School District in Phoenix who were dismayed to learn their district was chronically failing to educate their children. Armed with that information and empowered by the state's open-enrollment law, they moved their children to better public schools.

Then there are the African American parents we supported at School 93 in a low-income neighborhood of Indianapolis, who, after learning their school was one of the worst-performing in the state of Indiana, advocated to bring a proven local school-improvement model called Project Restore to their school. The result has been a dramatically improved instructional focus, a positive school climate, and marked progress for students.

How would that caring Memphis grandmother have known her grandchildren were behind if it weren't for standardized tests? Without standardized tests, how would the committed Murphy parents have known their district was wantonly failing? How would the School 93 parents have found out there was a problem with their children's school? What would have happened to all of those children if they didn't have this critical information point to add to the others?

I can tell you this with confidence: standardized tests aren't a nuisance to the families we work with, nor for me. For the families we serve, whose children are more apt to attend low-performing schools and have less-effective teachers than their privileged peers, the time taken for standardized tests is a reasonable cost for receiving vital information about how their children are doing academically. The same should hold true for more affluent families choosing to opt out of the annual assessment. If children who are experiencing success in schools or for whom schools generally "work" (i.e., white, middle-class, nondisabled children) don't participate in the assessment, their parents lose valuable information. And decision makers lose valuable information about where there may be bright spots to learn from and where improvement or intervention is needed.

That's why civil rights organizations such as the Leadership Conference on Civil and Human Rights, the National Urban League, the National Disability Rights Network, and National Council of La Raza campaigned so hard—and successfully—during the debate over the Every Student Succeeds Act to convince Congress and the Obama administration to continue to require annual measurements of student progress.

Opponents of standardized tests often ignore the vital role assessments play in the struggle for educational equity. They also commonly argue that the United States tests students more than most countries. That's simply untrue.

Andreas Schleicher of the Organization for Economic Cooperation and Development (OECD), which oversees the multinational Program for International Student Assessment (PISA) exam, expressed wonderment at U.S. news coverage of test refusals. "The U.S. is not a country of heavy testing," Schleicher noted. In fact, he told the *Hechinger Report* and *U.S. News & World Report* that *most* of the 70 OECD nations give their students *more* standardized tests than we do in the United States. The Netherlands, Belgium, and several Asian countries—all of which have high-performing education systems—test students much more.

Standardized tests are common the world over because they serve an essential purpose—to provide information about learning in schools. That said, standardized tests obviously don't measure the myriad other ways children need to develop to be contributing members of society, and we need to make sure that schools don't overly focus on core subjects and fail to educate the whole child. We also need to ensure that instruction is relevant and engaging so that students are motivated to come to school and learn.

Furthermore, there are ways in which we can improve standardized testing in our country.

An issue that gets little attention from the news media is that too many schools lack the technology or bandwidth to enable efficient standardized testing to take place. This situation must be remedied, so we can minimize the time needed to administer standardized tests (and enable more students to benefit from better technology throughout the school year).

In addition, test providers should deliver assessment results more quickly so parents and teachers can use the information right away. And perhaps we need to consider shifting toward shorter assessments taken at intervals throughout the year. That approach needs further exploration, but it could provide teachers and parents with more immediately useful information. There are such tests on the market, but most don't align with what students are learning, and they don't yet enable monitoring of how educators, schools, districts, and states are doing.

For now, I hope that more parents will begin to recognize that standardized tests provide invaluable information that can help us move toward equity in public education and improve the system for everyone. Let's stop this battle and instead work together for solutions that help all students get the education they deserve.

*This piece is part of a **forum on the testing opt-out movement**. For an alternate perspective, see "**Opt-Out Reflects the Genuine Concerns of Parents**" by Scott Levy.*

JONAH EDELMAN is an American advocate for public education and the cofounder and a chief executive officer of Stand for Children.

EXPLORING THE ISSUE

Should Students Be Allowed to Opt Out?

Critical Thinking and Reflection

1. What is the argument for giving students an option to opt out of standardized test in K–12 schools?
2. Has standardized testing taken away from the creativity and individualization of teachers' lessons in the classroom?
3. How is the new trend in standardized testing beginning to change the current landscape of the educational classroom?
4. Are school districts using the testing data to improve student achievement?
5. How will opt out students be prepared to enter higher education?

Is There Common Ground?

The common ground possibly rests on testing reforms and responsiveness of state officials to clearly understand and properly implement the Every Student Succeeds Act (ESSA) regulations. Those who do not support significant assessment reform may be replaced with officials, elected or appointed, who do. Will these officials state that a student can opt out but the state will penalize the school if the student does opt out? Ignoring laws already in place does not seem to be the ethical way to proceed. If a significant number of students opt out in their own state standardized tests, will it render state testing data useless (FairTest, 2018)? As indicated previously, a number of states already have significant numbers of students who have opted out. Eldeman (2016), on the NO side of this issue, states that he actually agrees that there is too much testing and test preparation, but as he continues on, firmly believes that to ensure students are on track for college and career that testing is necessary. He also wants testing to be aligned with the Common Core which presents another set of issues, as there are many parents who are opposed to the Common Core. Other key reasons identified in the literature on why parents support opting their children out of testing include:

- the growing role of corporations in schools;
- the growing role of the federal government in schools;
- opposition to privatization;
- opposition to using students' performance on standardized tests to evaluate teachers;
- children complain about standardized tests;
- children do not do well on standardized tests;

- standardized tests force teachers to teach to the test; and
- standardized tests take away too much instructional time (Pizmony-Levy & Cosman, 2017, p. 34).

The rational just noted for a reduction in the testing of students is not just complaints from parents. Educators, educational organizations, even school boards share much of the common ground for opposition to over-testing and over-preparing for standardized testing in the nation's schools. With the passage and planning for implementation of the ESSA, perhaps a common thread for test reform can be found in the discussions that will answer the question, does opt out of testing make sense? If students do opt out, will any penalty come to that student, the student's school, and/or the student's school district? Since ESSA puts states in the driver's seat for their own ESSA plans and implementation of these plans, it seems fitting that responsiveness from state officials on the issue will be key to understanding both sides of the issue as well as the common ground.

Additional Resources

FairTest. (2018). Federal law & regulations on opting out under ESSA. *National Center for Fair and Open Testing*. Retrieved from https://www.fairtest.org/federal-law-and-regulations-opting-out-under-essa

Croft, M. (2015). Opt-outs: What is lost when students do not test. *ACT Research & Policy Issue Brief*. Retrieved from https://www.act.org/content/dam/act/unsecured/documents/5087_Issue_Brief_Opt_Outs_Web_Secured.pdf

Croft, M. (2016). State legislatures opting in to opting out. *ACT Research & Policy Issue Brief.* Retrieved from https://www.act.org/content/dam/act/unsecured/documents/MS489-Issue-Brief-State-Legislatures-Opting-in-to-Opting-Out.pdf

Pizmony-Levy, O., & Cosman, B. (2017). *How Americans view the Opt Out movement.* Research Report. New York: Teachers College, Columbia University.

Internet References . . .

Just Say No to Standardized Tests: Why and How to Opt Out

http://www.fairtest.org/get-involved/opting-out

Should Kids Be Allowed to Opt Out of Standardized Test? Many Americans Say "No"

https://www.huffingtonpost.com/2015/03/17/standardized-test-opt-out-poll_n_6880688.html

Should You Opt Your Child Out of Standardized Testing?

https://www.psychologytoday.com/us/blog/singletons/201510/should-you-opt-your-child-out-standardized-testing

The Opt Out Reckoning

https://www.usnews.com/opinion/articles/2016-05-09/who-does-the-movement-to-opt-out-of-standardized-testing-help

Three Reasons Students Should Opt Out of Standardized Tests—and Three Reasons They Shouldn't

https://hechingerreport.org/three-reasons-students-opt-standardized-tests-three-reasons-shouldnt/

Selected, Edited, and with Issue Framing Material by:
Glenn L. Koonce, *Regent University*

ISSUE

Does Homework Matter?

YES: Lee Walk and Marshall Lassak, from "Making Homework Matter to Students: More Meaningful Homework Is an Easily Achievable Goal," *Mathematics Teaching in the Middle School* (2017)

NO: Cory A. Bennette, from "'Most Won't Do It!' Examining Homework as a Structure for Learning in a Diverse Middle School," *American Secondary Education* (2017)

Learning Outcomes

After reading this issue, you will be able to:

- Briefly explain the four types of homework assignments given to students in the pre-algebra middle school classroom. Choose the one that you feel would be the most beneficial to student learning and discuss why.

- Expand on the four categories of cognitive demands and how each of these relates to the questions, Does Homework Matter?

- Describe how the number of years on the teaching job affects his or her opinion on homework assignments.

- Discuss some of the differences in the qualitative findings about homework between teachers, parents, and students.

- Compare and contrast the concerns that parents have about homework.

ISSUE SUMMARY

YES: Lee Walk who teaches eighth-grade math and science at Cumberland Middle School in Toledo, IL, and Marshall Lassak who teaches at Eastern Illinois University in Charleston, SC, believe that with an appropriate level of demand and timely feedback students can learn from their homework and be confident that the work they do outside of class is meaningful.

NO: Cory Bennett, an associate professor of Education at Idaho State University, provides recommendations for homework policy and practice that requires critical examination of practices and beliefs.

For millions of school children who have attended school in the United States for decades, homework has been a staple in their homes between the times the last bell rings in the school day until the next morning when they arrive once again back in school. What parent has not said to their children, *have you finished your homework?* To these parents and their students, teachers, and school leaders the question is posed, does homework matter? "After decades spent trying to assess the value of homework, researchers still argue over the simplest findings" (Crawford, 2018, p. 1). Yet, for better or worse, homework is on the rise in the United States, the ante being upped as teachers and school administrators respond to increasing pressure for their students to perform better on state-mandated tests. The debate continues as it started, decades ago, on the importance of homework. It appears this debate is just as prevalent today as it has always been. Much of the literature on this issue point to homework being a stressor for students, even extending some of the stress element to parents and teachers who must enforce the homework regime. Crawford (2018, p. 1) states that "by taking away precious family time and putting kids under unneeded pressure, homework is an ineffective way to help children become better learners and thinkers." Crawford points to books like *The End of Homework*, *The Homework Myth*, and *The Case Against Homework*, as well as, the film *Race to Nowhere* to affirm her statement. In a Brown Center Report on Homework (Loveless, 2014), anti-homework sentiment hit a high peak from 1998 to 2003 when national publications ran cover stories on the evils of homework including *Newsweek*, *Time*, and *People*. Perhaps the most onerous came in 2003 from *People* titled: "Overbooked: Four Hours of Homework for a Third Grader? Exhausted Kids (and Parents) Fight Back." Perhaps even better, from a 2013 article found in *Atlantic* that told the story of a Manhattan writer who joined his middle school daughter in her homework assignments for a week. He titled his article, "My Daughter's Homework is Killing Me."

One stellar example of the homework issue put the question to test, legal test that is. In a serious dispute that ended up in the Supreme Court of Canada, a couple argued that there was no evidence that homework improved academic performance. The verdict was a win for the parents and an exemption from all homework for their two children—these children never have to do homework again in their current school (*The Guardian*, 2009). It would be fair to say that in this case, the parents did their homework on homework!

Although a review of the literature on homework has not shown statistically significant results that it has any benefits for elementary school students, it did correlate with students' academic achievement in middle school from results of a study conducted at Duke University (*Virginia Teacher*, 2018). Key findings included that with homework, students are better able to retain subject matter, and there is more propensity for a deeper understanding of future course material. In deference, the study found that the more time students spent on homework, beyond 90 minutes a day, the less the correlation. For high schoolers, that time factor rises to 120 minutes. As the guide for high schoolers according to the Duke University study, homework should be no more than 10 minutes per subject. Recommendations found in this study included additional benefits for students from lower-income backgrounds or English language learners who may not have the resources available or supportive parents with higher levels of education at home to encourage and guide their children. It was suggested that these students be given additional in-classroom support.

A recent qualitative research design study conducted by Bennett (2017) noted in his findings that the effectiveness of homework was mixed and that there were a very limited number of studies on the perspectives of the issue from students and educators. Bennett also found differences between students and educators on homework in a culturally and socioeconomically diverse middle school. As an example, one of the open-ended questions asked how homework made students feel. Some keyword responses from students included: "boring, frustration, hard, helpful, and irritating." On the other hand, responses from teachers to the same question included: "enrich, responsibility, reinforcement, and useful with support" (p. 28). Interviews were also conducted for further reflection on the homework issue. The major conclusion in Bennett's study was that educators must be cautious when adopting practices the research refers to as one-size-fits-all. This is particularly true when there are mixed reviews and no conclusive evidence that homework is an effective practice that results in higher academic achievement. Quoting Linda Darling-Hammond, in Bennett (2017, p. 35), "Depending on teacher's interpretation of homework and their philosophical beliefs towards learning, homework can become a senseless and ineffective tool in supporting, assessing, and measuring students' learning." This is a fairly strong statement from a nationally recognized leader who has written extensively on educational issues. Darling-Hammond's statement puts the educator squarely in front of the issue to provide evidence of the effectiveness of homework for their students. The answer certainly cannot be a simple yes or no, good or bad, effective or ineffective. The value of homework must be studied in the school arena in a valid and reliable way and evaluated using critical thinking analysis. Bennett (2017, p. 35) noted in his conclusion, that in deference to homework, "differentiated learning, group projects, whole-class discourse, and open-ended explorations are but a few of the instructional strategies that have shown to increase students' understanding."

A resourceful website to view how the homework issue plays in a debate can be found at Debate.org (2018). The debate question to search for at this site is: Should Students Have Homework? According to the tally from reviewers who responded to the online survey question, 76 percent said, "no" (p. 1). A sample of the debater's responses include: "No more homework please; It is a good use of time; I think we should have homework because it teaches us more in the long run; it causes stress; and No, it is a longer school day that stays at home; and Homework is less than beneficial for students" (pp. 1–3). More arguments can be loaded to the questions and responses, thus ensuring a lively debate on the topic.

After yielding to the numerous, seemly overwhelming, negative connotations of homework on school students, there is another side. The articles noted earlier in this introduction from *Time*, *Newsweek*, and *People* drew sharp criticism about the homework controversy when they were circulated between 1998 and 2003. A 2003 Brown Center Report on American Education included, at the time, a study on the homework issue. To the dismay of writers of the mostly demeaning articles of the impact of homework on students, the Brown report released its findings from the most reliable empirical evidence gathered at the time. The study concluded that "the dramatic claims about the evils of homework were unfounded." In addition, the following results were noted: "that an overwhelming majority of students had spent less than an hour on homework each night, parents were not upset indicating they thought homework was about right, and parents that wanted more homework outnumbered those who wanted less" (Loveless, 2014, p. 1). The Brown Center Report on American Education's homework status was replicated again, 10 years later, in 2013 using data from the National Assessment of Educational Progress. The survey looked at long-term trends in homework over the preceding three decades. The question asked the participants was "How much time did you spend on homework yesterday?" Results were very much different from the statements made by parents in 2003. Participants described themselves as being very unhappy with the amount of homework their children were bringing home. The 2013 Brown Report, emphasized that "these unhappy people are real, but they may also be atypical" (p. 17) and not representative of the common household experience with school-age children and their homework, thus, bringing even more rhetoric to the homework issue. Walk and Lassak (2017, p. 547), in the YES article for this issue, agree that homework indeed matters and that teachers "must be clear about their goals and expectations for student homework." They also must provide timely feedback and allow students to correct mistakes in order to learn from their homework. It is not likely that the issue of homework will go away anytime soon.

YES

Lee Walk and Marshall Lassak

Making Homework Matter to Students

More Meaningful Homework Is an Easily Achievable Goal

During my teaching career (author Walk), I have been frustrated with student assignments being handed in incomplete, rushed through, or not at all. It made me wonder what students saw as the purpose of homework. I tried to impart the idea that the purpose of homework was to help students improve their understanding of mathematical concepts, practice skills, and act as a formative assessment that could help me see what they currently comprehended. Unfortunately, many students seemed to think that homework was just another unpleasant task to finish as quickly as possible without thinking deeply about what they were doing.

Two studies (Trautwein, 2007; Dettmers et al., 2010) show a positive correlation between high-quality homework and mathematics achievement. Students who completed their homework assignments scored better on assessments. However, these studies also showed no relationship between time spent on homework and resulting student achievement. This helped verify that although homework can be a valuable tool for learning, more time spent on daily homework is not necessarily a good idea.

In continuing to research effective homework styles and implementation, I found in many studies that student collaboration was important in developing mathematical reasoning. Wieman and Arbaugh (2014) discuss how students could use homework as an opportunity to work together. However, they also emphasize that teachers must be clear about their goals and expectations for student homework:

> Students may think that they are supposed to be able to complete all the homework problems quickly and easily, and that referring to their notes or asking a friend for help is somehow "cheating." (p. 162)

Students must understand the difference between asking another student for help in thinking through a problem and simply asking for the answer. Homework does not need to be completed independently if the primary goal is to learn about mathematics.

Levels of Demand

Smith and Stein (1998) argue that the highest learning gains for students result from engagement in high levels of cognitive thinking and reasoning. They break down tasks in terms of four categories of cognitive demand:

1. Memorization
2. Procedures without connections to concepts or meaning
3. Procedures with connections to concepts
4. Doing mathematics

Keeping in mind the appropriate level of homework challenge, it appears that most homework tasks should be in the third category (procedures with connections to concepts). The first two categories are considered to have a lower-level demand for students because they can be solved with limited or no cognitive demand. The third and fourth categories of tasks require deeper thinking and understanding. These tasks might be more complex and often have multiple solution paths.

Although the fourth level may be appropriate for classroom learning, it is likely to be too difficult for homework on a regular basis and could negatively impact student effort.

Changing My Approach

All this research led me to wonder if my students would be more successful in completing and learning from their homework if they were given fewer problems with a higher level of cognitive demand. I already knew that some students have difficulties with procedural questions and that

Figure 1

Students were given this format and asked to find and fix the mistake.

1) $5x + 4x - x$ $9x$ **Explain mistake:** **Correct answer:**	2) $5 - (x - 2)$ $5 - x - 2$ $3 - x$ **Explain mistake:** **Correct answer:**	3) $2(x + 5)$ $2x + 5$ **Explain mistake:** **Correct answer:**

Figure 2

Jennifer produced this explanation.

3) $2(x + 5)$
$2x + 5$ $2x + 10$

Explain mistake:

The person did not distribute the 2 to the 5

Correct answer: $2x + 10$

Figure 3

Connor found these errors; he was unable to obtain the correct answer for problem 5.

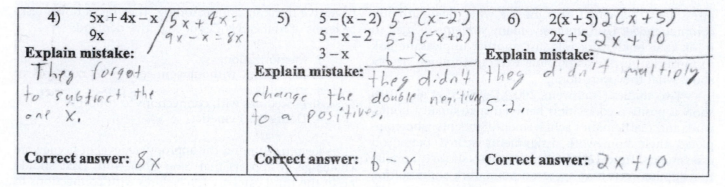

4) $5x + 4x - x$ $5x + 9x =$ $9x$ $9x - x = 8x$ **Explain mistake:** They forgot to subtract the one x. **Correct answer:** $8x$	5) $5 - (x - 2)$ $5 - (x - 2)$ $5 - x - 2$ $5 - 1(-x + 2)$ $3 - x$ $6 - x$ **Explain mistake:** they didn't change the double negitive to a positive. **Correct answer:** $6 - x$	6) $2(x + 5)$ $2(x + 5)$ $2x + 5$ $2x + 10$ **Explain mistake:** they didn't multiply $5 \cdot 2$. **Correct answer:** $2x + 10$

Figure 4

Kim produced these explanations.

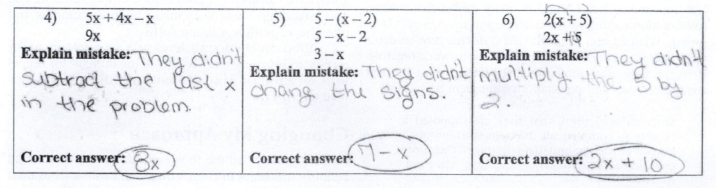

4) $5x + 4x - x$ $9x$ **Explain mistake:** They didn't subtract the last x in the problem. **Correct answer:** $8x$	5) $5 - (x - 2)$ $5 - x - 2$ $3 - x$ **Explain mistake:** They didn't change the signs. **Correct answer:** $7 - x$	6) $2(x + 5)$ $2x + 5$ **Explain mistake:** They didn't multiply the 5 by 2. **Correct answer:** $2x + 10$

even those students who are able to answer such questions often have a difficult time explaining the reasoning for their methods.

When teaching pre-algebra to my eighth-grade students, I typically assign skill-and-drill questions accompanied by one short-response problem. Skill-and-drill problems give students repeated practice of a particular procedure and are intended to help them gain fluency. The majority of my students completed the homework problems, but those who often did not explained that they did not have "enough time" or did not understand what to do. These students were typically habitual offenders in failing to complete their assignments, and the homework never seemed important to them. I tried to motivate my students and access self-motivation by putting more control of the homework into their hands through additional time and choices.

Focusing on the algebraic concept of solving linear equations, I implemented a change in my homework style for several weeks. Manipulating and solving equations is a central concept for my students, and it is a skill that many have difficulty in mastering. I thought this would be a good time to provide a better homework experience. My class received "cognitive" homework with fewer problems that had a higher level of demand. Weekly homework

assignments contained suggestions about the number of questions to be completed each day. The presentation of the material for the unit and the structure of the classroom still allowed for time spent reviewing homework questions.

In changing the type of homework, I tried not to change my method of assessment or how I integrated homework into my lessons. I continued to collect and check homework for completion and accuracy. Students were allowed and encouraged to ask questions about homework ideas as part of daily lessons. Weekly quizzes were used to help determine student progress throughout the unit.

I emphasized that the new homework had fewer problems for them to complete and that daily assignments

Figure 5

Revisiting ideas often allowed for better class discussion and participation

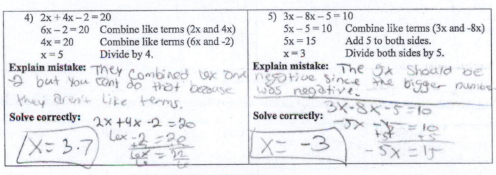

(a) Donna's work

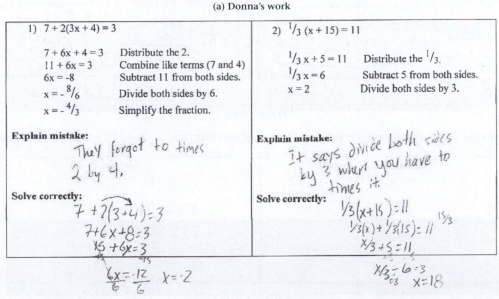

(b) Lois's work

Figure 6

These students sorted equations by using common characteristics

7) Take the six equations from the previous section and sort them into 2 groups by common characteristics

Group 1 Subtraction sign	Group 2 addition sign
$f - 15 = ^-1$	$y + 12 = ^-10$
$d - 15 = ^-19$	$n + 19 = 0$
	$c + 6 = 1$
	$g + 8 = 1)$

(a) Connor's work

7) Take the six equations from the previous section and sort them into 2 groups by common characteristics

	Group 1		Group 2
1) $y + 12 = ^-10$ $y = 22$	these are addition	2) $F - 15 = ^-1$ $F = 14$	these are subtraction
3) $n + 19 = 0$ $n = ^-19$		4) $d - 15 = -14$ $d = 1$	
5) $g + 8 = 13$ $g = 5$		6) $C + 6 = 1$ $c = ^-5$	

(b) Mary's work

7) Take the six equations from the previous section and sort them into 2 groups by common characteristics

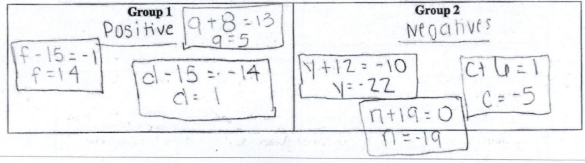

(c) Jane's work

7) Take the six equations from the previous section and sort them into 2 groups by common characteristics

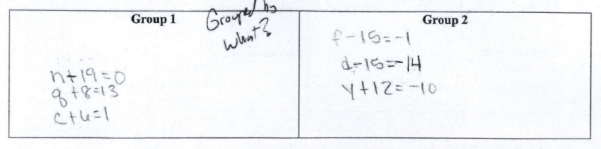

(d) Debbie's work

were only suggestions; nothing was due until the end of the week. This meant that if they were busy on a given night, they could get it done later in the week. I tried to motivate them by putting more control of the homework into their hands.

To foster student cooperation, I told students that they could ask me for help but reminded them that they could also rely on their classmates. On several occasions, I told students that they could work with a partner or in small groups to work out problems at the end of class. The class also engaged in think–pair–share activities to jump-start thinking and discussion.

The new homework problems I created and assigned were influenced by suggestions obtained from reading work done by Wieman and Arbaugh (2014), Lange, Booth, and Newton (2014), and Friedlander and Arcavi (2012), all of whom offered advice on particular homework style questions as well as questions to elicit the type of thinking and activity advocated by Smith and Stein (1998).

Find and Fix the Mistake

Find and Fix the Mistake problems (see Figure 1) were the most commonly used tasks throughout the new homework implementation. Students were instructed to identify the mistake, explain it, and simplify the expressions or solve the equations correctly. One advantage of these problems was that they required students to use correct mathematical vocabulary. Jennifer (see Figure 2) includes the term distribute in her response, which was discussed several times in class.

Connor (see Figure 3) and Kim (see Figure 4) both demonstrated their procedural knowledge; writing about the problem helped them participate in class discussion. During this time, I found that students were more confident in class discussions when they had had a chance to think before class about these ideas. Rather than just solving the equations with varying levels of procedural fluency, students were thinking more about the problems and how to explain errors.

Students like Donna and Lois (see Figure 5) were improving on their answers and explanations from previous assignments. These two students—as well as others—were also more likely to volunteer their opinions in class when they had their explanations already on paper. This led to better class discussions in that more students engaged with the ideas. From my perspective, Find and Fix the Mistake problems made it clear what students did and did not understand in terms of mathematical procedures and concepts.

Problem Sorts

Problem Sort questions asked students to sort equations they had already solved into two groups by using common characteristics, such as operations (shown by Connor and Mary's work in Figures 6a and b), properties, nature of the solution (shown by Jane in Figure 6c), and so on. The open-ended nature of choosing the sorting criteria made this type of question challenging for students. Quite often I received answers like Debbie's (see Figure 6d), which appears to show a separation by operation but no explanation. This type of problem does not seem to exceed the cognitive level of the class, yet its usefulness in helping students better understand solving linear equations remains unclear to me.

Create Your Own Word Problem

Students were asked to write a story that matched a given equation and expressions; basically, a word problem in reverse (an example is shown in Figure 7).

The level of demand for this task is much greater than those of previous assignments because students must

- understand how the expressions relate to the equation;
- determine what the equation is asking; and
- make a meaningful story to go with the problem.

Unfortunately, the level of demand was evidently too high for students in the class.

One determinant of how important or useful a problem was to students was whether they actually completed the problem. The Create Your Own Word Problem task was one of the most skipped problems in any of the homework assignments. Figure 8 shows that Kim and Connor gave answers that were nearly correct. They both solved the equation correctly but had difficulty in determining the number of cups needed for each ingredient. Kim's answers for each ingredient did not match the equation. Connor found a solution to the equation but not for each ingredient in the problem.

I did notice improvement for some students as they gained more experience with this type of problem. Figure 9 shows how Jane struggled with the first version of this problem and then a few weeks later how she improved with a different version. Improvement was evident for several students, and although the level of demand may have been high, the problem was useful in determining

Figure 7

This grid illustrated a word problem in reverse.

2) The art teacher is making salt dough for an upcoming project. The ratio of flour to salt to water used to make salt dough is shown below.

Making Sour Dough	Story
Cups of flour: 2c	
Cups of salt: c	
Cups of water: ¾ c	
2c + c + ¾ c = 60 cups	

   a. Write a story that matches the expressions and equation shown above.
   b. Solve the equation. How many cups of each ingredient is the art teacher planning to use?

Figure 8

These students had difficulty determining the number of cups needed for each ingredient.

Making Sour Dough	Story
Cups of flour: 2c	Mrs. Need is making salt dough.
Cups of salt: c	The ratio of the flour is 2c the
Cups of water: ¾ c	ratio of the salt is a amount of cups
2c + c + ¾ c = 60 cups	and the ratio of the water is ³/₄c
2c + c + ³/₄c = 60 cups	and the total ratio is 60cups.

   a. Write a story that matches the expressions and equation shown above.
   b. Solve the equation. How many cups of each ingredient is the art teacher planning to use?

$$\frac{3.7}{3.75}c = \frac{60}{3.75} \quad \boxed{C = 16 \text{cups}} \quad \boxed{\text{Flour} = 2c \quad \text{Water} = 3/4\,c \\ \text{Salt} = 16c}$$

(a) Kim's work

Making Sour Dough	Story
Cups of flour: 2c	An art teacher is making special
Cups of salt: c	dough for a project. The ingredients are
Cups of water: ¾ c	two cups of flour, one cup of salt,
2c + c + ¾ c = 60 cups	and three quarters of water. Make an
2c+c+³/₄c = 60cups	equation to find how many cups of
3c+³/₄c = 60cups	ingredients : the teacher is going to
3.75c/3.75 = 60cups/3.75	use.
C = 16cups	

(b) Connor's work

students' understanding and misconceptions of certain types of linear equations.

Justify Your Reasoning

This type of problem is designed to help students analyze why linear equations can have one, none, or infinitely many solutions. The concept of a math equation not having a solution was a new idea for many of the students

at this grade level. This question was asked after students were already solving linear equations that might not have had a solution.

Many students, including Sharon (see Figure 10a), repeated phrases that were discussed in class. Although these statements may be true, students did not offer any justification or evidence that they really understood how the inequality and the no-solution equation were related. Amy (see Figure 10b) also tried to relate the problem directly to class conversation. Like Sharon, Amy may simply be repeating what others have said in class, making it more difficult to perceive individual reasoning. Other students were able to provide some insight into how they viewed the problem. Kim attempted to describe actions she took to solve these types of problems (see Figure 10c). This does not necessarily demonstrate understanding; rather, it is an observed connection between the process and end result.

Connor's response (see Figure 10d) dug a little bit deeper. Connor was able to explain his answer by talking about how inequalities went with no solutions because the equations were "never true in the first place." He continued to describe how these equations may initially look

Figure 9

Jane struggled with the first version of this problem. Weeks later, she improved with a different version

Making Sour Dough	Story
Cups of flour: 2c	How to make
Cups of salt: c	2 cups of mashed potatoe flakes
Cups of water: ¾ c	w = how many cups of water
2c + c + ¾ c = 60 cups	3/4 a cup of milk
2c + c + ³/₄c = 60	2c + w + ³/₄c = 60 cups
	3c + ³/₄c = 60
	3⁸/₄c = 60

(a)

Fixing Your Car	Story
Time (hours): h	I got my car repaired + they charged by hour.
Cost of Mike's Mechanics: 15h + 75	Mike Mechanics cost 15 dollars a hour plus the parts which are 75 $
Cost of Bubba's Body Shop: 25h	Bubba's Body Shop cost 25 dollars a hour
15h + 75 = 25h	Either way its going to take the same amount of hours.
h = 7.5 −15 −15	
75 = 10h	The hours they will spent on
10 10	

   a. Write a story that matches the expressions and equation shown above.
   b. Solve the equation.
   c. Interpret the answer.

my car will take 7.5 hours.

(b)

like the others but do not hold up under mathematical investigation.

Students completed the Justify Your Reasoning problems relatively quickly, and most students attempted them. Allowing students to explain their responses in class helped them to make connections with other students and their ideas.

Positive Perception of Homework

I feel that these tasks had a positive impact on my students' perception of homework. A careful selection of homework tasks can help students practice, understand, and explore mathematical concepts. If students are confused about what a question is asking or how to begin, they are not as likely to persevere through the problem.

Teachers and students evaluate homework questions differently, and they cannot be labeled as simply easy or difficult. The appropriateness of the level of demand of the problem is important when considering what students should gain from completing a task. Questions such as those in Find and Fix the Problem were very popular and successful with students. They had clear expectations, and students were able to determine answers that they thought made sense and were acceptable to them.

I found the benefits of using this style of homework to include the following:

- Improved class discussions: Students were able to explain the mathematical concepts with more confidence and use better vocabulary in the classroom setting.
- Teacher insights: Explanations for and justification of the homework problems made it easier for me to determine current levels of understanding as well as notice common misconceptions shared by the class.

This small change in my homework approach helped me gain information about students' perception of homework in a different way. Although the process did not determine why some students continually fail to complete their homework, it did help me see why certain students skip the occasional problem. In working with new homework practices, I learned how important it is for homework to contain an appropriate level of demand. Skills-practice problems are beneficial to students' math knowledge, but good cognitive problems require students

Figure 10

These students sorted equations by using common characteristics

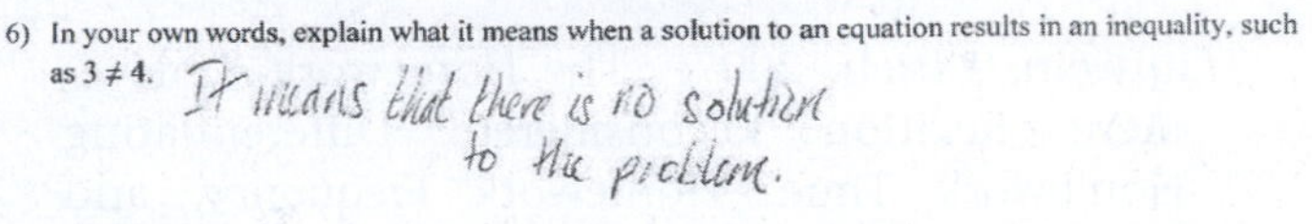

6) In your own words, explain what it means when a solution to an equation results in an inequality, such as $3 \neq 4$. *It means that there is no solution to the problem.*

(a) Sharon's work

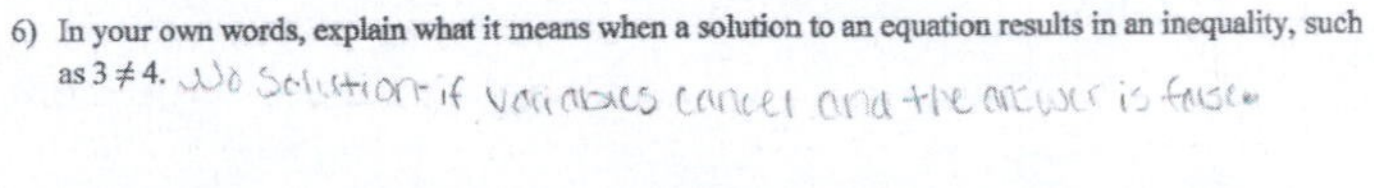

6) In your own words, explain what it means when a solution to an equation results in an inequality, such as $3 \neq 4$. *No solution if variables cancel and the answer is false*

(b) Amy's work

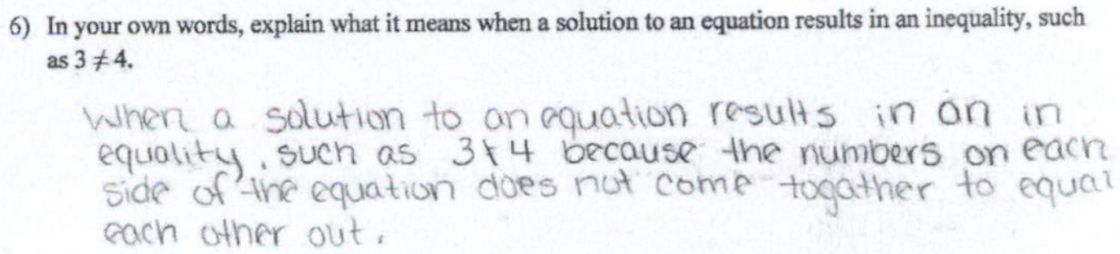

6) In your own words, explain what it means when a solution to an equation results in an inequality, such as $3 \neq 4$.

When a solution to an equation results in an inequality, such as 3 ≠ 4 because the numbers on each side of the equation does not come together to equal each other out.

(c) Kim's work

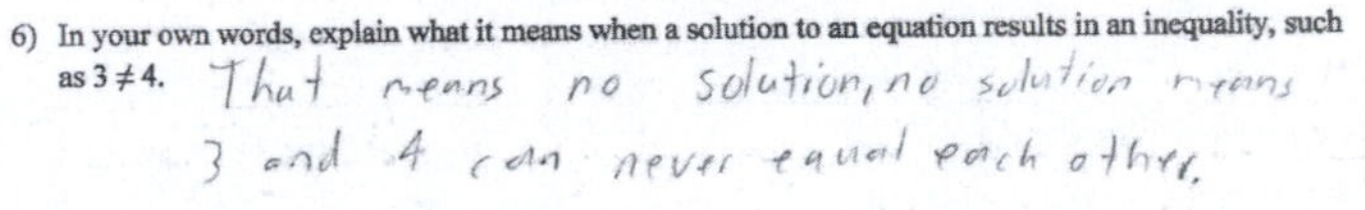

6) In your own words, explain what it means when a solution to an equation results in an inequality, such as $3 \neq 4$. *That means no solution, no solution means 3 and 4 can never equal each other.*

(b) Connor's work

to invoke deeper levels of thinking. I plan to continue to adjust my homework structure to include skills practice and cognitive thought. Problems with an appropriate level of demand and timely feedback allow students to learn from their homework and be confident that the work they do outside of class is meaningful.

References

Dettmers, S., Ulrich Trautwein, Oliver Lüdtke, Mareike Kunter, and Jurgen Baumert. 2010. "Homework Works If Homework Quality Is High: Using Multilevel Modeling to Predict the Development of Achievement in Mathematics." *Journal of Educational Psychology* 102 (May): 467–82.

Friedlander, Alex, and Abraham Arcavi. 2012. "Practicing Algebraic Skills: A Conceptual Approach." *The Mathematics Teacher* 105 (April): 608–14.

Lange, Karin E., Julie L. Booth, and Kristie J. Newton. 2014. "Learning Algebra from Worked Examples." *The Mathematics Teacher* 107 (March): 534–40.

Smith, Margaret Schwan, and Mary Kay Stein. 1998. "Selecting and Creating Mathematical Tasks: From Research to Practice." *Mathematics Teaching in the Middle School* 3 (February): 344–50.

Trautwein, Ulrich. 2007. "The Homework-Achievement Relation Reconsidered: Differentiating Homework Time, Homework Frequency, and Homework Effort." *Learning and Instruction* 17 (3): 372–88.

Wieman, Rob, and Fran Arbaugh. 2014. "Making Homework More Meaningful." *Mathematics Teaching in the Middle School* 20 (October): 160–65.

LEE WALK teaches eighth-grade math and science at Cumberland Middle School in Toledo, IL.

MARSHALL LASSAK teaches at Eastern Illinois University in Charleston.

Cory A. Bennett

"Most Won't Do It!" Examining Homework as a Structure for Learning in a Diverse Middle School

The learning outcomes desired for students today are greatly different than they were even a ¼ of a century ago. Attention has shifted toward helping students to develop as complex thinkers and creative problem solvers within communities of collaboration (Partnership for 21st Century Skills, 2015). However, many schools still reflect practices and structures from the turn of the previous century (Kliebard, 2004). In secondary schools, learning structures need to be appropriate for creating experiences that are developmentally responsive to the nature and needs of adolescents (*Association of Middle Level Education* [AMLE], 2010). Learning experiences should, therefore, not only support required learning outcomes but also be adapted to the actual circumstances of learning.

Much could be done to restructure the framework for enacting teaching and learning in middle schools in ways that would support students' academic and affective development (*AMLE*, 2010; Roney, Anfara, & Brown, 2008). Far too often, however, the structures of day-to-day educational experiences have become so engrained that their appropriateness is rarely questioned. Homework is one of these engrained structures. This is not to say that homework cannot be effective, but rather that the construct of homework needs to be examined. This study examined homework in one middle school by analyzing the extent to which students, teachers, and administrators valued it as an effective learning practice.

Questioning the Benefits of Homework

As a middle school mathematics teacher in a culturally, linguistically, and socioeconomically diverse community, I encountered many students who struggled with mathematics. During my first year of teaching, I had implemented several different homework policies with the hope of finding a policy that would help the students produce higher quality work that allowed me to assess their learning. These policies succeeded only in producing inadequate data from which no useful information could be gleaned, and when students got stuck, they would often stop working.

The majority of my students' parents confessed to not being "a math person" and did not believe they could help their student at home. Many of those parents worked multiple jobs and were not at home after school. This often meant that students were responsible for taking care of the home and looking after their younger siblings after school. Sometimes chores at home required them to work well into the night. It became clear to me that homework in my class, and as traditionally conceptualized, was not promoting the kind of student learning I had intended.

In my current work in professional development with experienced teachers, I often hear those teachers question the role and nature of homework, but due to pressures from their district, school, or colleagues, they rarely change their practice. These experiences made me wonder about how other teachers and students perceived homework as an instructional structure for supporting student learning.

Review of Literature

Many assumptions are made about the benefits of homework. Two of the most commonly cited benefits are an increase in academic achievement and the development of personal traits such as responsibility and time management that are needed throughout life. These assumptions are not, however, always supported by research. Previous studies have examined homework as a means to increase academic achievement (Chen & Stevenson, 1989; Cooper,

1989; Vatterott, 2009), but Cooper and Valentine (2001) stated that much of the research is conceptually or methodologically flawed. Studies have found that homework was linked to higher grades but not higher achievement on standardized tests (Krashen, 2013).

Although some studies have shown various gains in achievement (Marzano & Pickering, 2007), the relationship between academic achievement and homework is so unclear (Cooper & Valentine, 2001) that using research to definitively state that homework is effective in all contexts is presumptive. If the academic benefits of homework are suspect, then the question that remains is whether or not homework has nonacademic benefits.

Some research has suggested that homework negatively impacted students' affective development (Bennett & Kalish, 2006; Kralovac & Buell, 2001), and academic achievement may falter if students feel rejected or perceive themselves as inadequate in comparison to their peers (Van Hoose, Strahan, & L'Esperance, 2001).

Jackson and Davis (2000) discussed how students with more support, with deeper relationships with peers, develop greater self-efficacy. Such support is actually a predecessor to academic attainment and is directly correlated with school success and self-esteem (Telljohann, Symons, & Pateman, 2004). Gibson and Jefferson (2006) suggested that student self-esteem and self-efficacy must be addressed before efforts to increase academic achievement are undertaken (Kralovac & Buell, 2001). Thus, the time spent working on relationships is valuable to both an individual student's affective development and academic success.

Gibson and Jefferson (2006) noted that one of the most effective ways to encourage interpersonal worth is through meaningful relationships with families, peers, and other mentors. The dilemma that can arise is that students may not be able to further strengthen these relationships if they are required to spend substantial amounts of time doing homework after school. Homework may actually obstruct the efforts of the educational system by impeding students' affective developmental outside of school.

Because the findings from research on homework are so mixed, it is important for school leaders and teachers to carefully consider how specific findings relate to their student demographics and the specific courses. A "one-size-fits-all" approach to supporting students with homework would seem to disregard what is known about individual differences in learning.

Purpose of the Study

There is evidence to suggest that homework has strong learning benefits for some students (Carr, 2013; Marzano & Pickering, 2007), but individual school districts, schools, and classrooms need to carefully examine the situations of their particular students, including the resources that are available to those students outside of school, in order to determine which learning strategies are likely to be effective. The question is not whether homework *can* be effective, but rather the extent to which the intent, structure, and implementation of homework are routinely and purposefully examined.

A Hawaiian proverb states that not all knowledge is taught in the same school. For middle schools, this proverb suggests the need to keep in mind the larger goals of education and to consider how other people and positive environments that promote healthy relationships with students support academic achievement. Increasing academic achievement is not the only reason students are in school, and school is not the only place where learning occurs, so supporting student learning can become more difficult when instructional structures are left unchecked and unevaluated. The purpose of this qualitative case study was to better understand educators' and students' perceptions of homework as an instructional structure for supporting student learning within one culturally and socioeconomically diverse middle school (Bempechat et al., 2011).

Examining the assumptions about homework, or any instructional learning experience, should be a critical process in the classroom as teachers develop policies and learning experiences that best suit the needs of their students (Darling-Hammond, 2000). Routinely using practices without understanding how the intended learning outcomes are realized for students should never happen. Comparing the perceptions of teachers, students, and administrators can lead to a more accurate understanding of the benefits of homework in increasing academic achievement and the implications on adolescents' affective development.

Perceptions matter because teachers' perceptions toward pedagogical practices and the enactment of the curriculum determine the learning experiences for students (Brown, 2001). Additionally, Bempechat and colleagues (2011) indicated that students' perceptions around homework are not well understood. This research attempts to add to the current body of knowledge. The research question that guided this study was, therefore, "What are administrators, teachers' and students' perceptions towards homework as an instructional structure supporting student learning and to what extent do these perceptions align?"

Method

I used an exploratory qualitative case study design for this study (Bogdan & Biklen, 2007). Such an approach was suitable for capturing a middle school setting that was rich in cultural, linguistic, and socioeconomic diversity.

Setting

Mountain Middle School is located in a rapidly growing suburban community where many of the families still remember the community's agricultural past. At the time of this study, the two largest reported ethnicities within the school were Filipino and Part-Hawaiian with other ethnic representations including Caucasian, Samoan, Japanese, African American, and Hawaiian (see Table 1). Six other identified ethnicities were reported and comprised roughly 6 percent of the entire student population.

Enrollment at the school was 1,367 with 41 percent of these students receiving free or reduced-cost lunch, an indicator often used to determine poverty levels within a school. Additionally, 9.4 percent of the students were identified as being enrolled in Special Education programs. In contrast, there were just over 70 teaching faculty, the majority of whom were not of the predominate cultures within the community. Mountain Middle School was also identified as an academically struggling school by local and state education departments because of habitual low scores on standardized state assessment tests. All classrooms were heterogeneous and inclusion based. Students with special needs and English language learners were included in the general education setting.

Mountain Middle School was chosen for this project because of the diversity represented within the student body, specifically with respect to ethnicity, socioeconomic status, and cultures. Additionally, the size of the school meant there were more teachers within one building and thus more diversity with teachers, too. In this case, teaching diversity included the number of years teaching, cultural norms, and ontological views about learning. Although some secondary schools may be more homogeneous in the student and teacher demographics, choosing a school that encompassed a richer population of students and teachers allowed for more complex and distinct beliefs around the use of homework as a means of supporting all students learning.

Participants

All participants were purposefully chosen (Creswell & Plano-Clark, 2010) and included 45 students from two seventh-grade classrooms and 11 teachers responsible for teaching various content areas for those students. The teachers in this study were from two teams each of which consisted of five teachers from different content areas. Two administrators were selected to participate because of their involvement in supporting these instructional teams.

Data Collection and Analysis

A three-phase design was used in this study. Phase 1 began with a questionnaire for teachers to determine the value they placed on homework as an instructional structure to support all of their students. The questionnaire included six open-ended questions and six scaled questions that focused on learning preferences and perspectives toward homework. Students were chosen to complete the questionnaire based on the stratified results of the teachers' responses (Bogdan & Biklen, 2007). Once the 11 teachers had been identified, their students were given a questionnaire with both closed- and open-form questions. Responses were used to identify groups who also placed a high and low value on the use of homework to promote learning.

Phase 2 consisted of semi-structured interviews (Slavin, 2007) with teachers and administrators. There were two types of semi-structured interviews: focus groups interviews with students and one-on-one interviews with teachers and administrators. For the students, small focus groups were created based on their responses in the questionnaire.

Table 1

Percentage of major ethnicities reported by families at Mountain Middle School						
Filipino	Part-Hawaiian	Caucasian	Samoan	Japanese	African American	Hawaiian
41.1	15.9	7.1	4.7	4.3	3.9	3.6

Two teachers were selected for semi-structured interviews based on their responses to their questionnaire. One of the teachers had a strong and overwhelming belief that homework was an invaluable tool in student learning and assigned homework daily, while the other teacher believed that homework had little value for his students and felt that it did not support student learning and thus assigned little to no homework. Due to administrators' time constraints, they did not complete the questionnaire from phase 1, but questions from the teachers' open-form questionnaire were asked during the interviews to capture their beliefs on the same questions. Principals did not review and provide comments on their interview transcripts, but statements were summarized and repeated back to ensure clarity in their meaning and intent. No follow-up interviews were conducted with principals after the completion of this study. The final phase of the study merged the two previous phases to construct meaning and generate theories that answered the research question (Teddlie & Tashakkori, 2009).

Findings

The findings included data from the questionnaire's scaled items and open-ended questions. The interviews provided narrative data. The student and teacher data from the questionnaires was reported as compared together, and the interview data was reported according to their respective participants.

Questionnaires

Two open-ended questions were included in the questionnaire to further probe the perceptions of teachers and students on homework. One of the questions asked teachers and students to describe homework using one or two words. Key words were recorded, sorted into three categories: (a) those responses that suggested a more favorable opinion of homework, (b) those that had a less favorable opinion of homework, and (c) those that were neutral in their connotation. Students frequently responded with less favorable words for homework, while teachers provided more favorable responses. While a few student responses included the words "fun" or "easy" the overwhelming word of choice as reported by the students was "boring" as seen in Table 2. Other words students used included "irritating," "hard," "stressful," and "frustrating." On the other hand, the teachers overwhelmingly responded with words of a more favorable nature such as "confidence builder," "useful," "reinforces," and "enriches."

The second question examined how homework makes the students feel. Again, students frequently reported less favorable comments toward homework with "bored" being the most common response. Other common responses included "confusing," "frustrated," and "tired," though a few reported feeling "smarter" and "more organized." The teachers' responses were all of a less favorable nature with the most common words reported being

Table 2

Comparison of one to two word description of homework; listed alphabetically				
Key word responses by students on homework			**Key word responses by teachers on homework**	
Annoying	Boring	Boring	Confidence builder	Enforce
Boring	Boring	Boring	Enrich	Learning tool
Boring	Boring	Boring	Most won't do it	Reinforcement
Boring	Boring	Boring	Responsibility	Useful
Boring	Boring	Boring	Useful	Useful with support
Cool	Critical	Easy	Useless without support	
Easy	Exciting	Extra		
Frustrating	Frustrating	Hard		
Hard	Hard	hard		
Hard	Helpful	Helpful		
Irritating	Irritating	Learning		
Long	Long	Persuasive		
Review	Rigorous	Sad		
Smart	Stressful	Thinking		
Useful	Work	Work		

Table 3

Reported amounts of homework students complete			
1 (none to very little)	2	3	4 (All to nearly all)
Teachers	2	6	3	0
Students	0	2	17	24

"angry," "frustrated," and "overwhelmed." This seemed to match the general feelings that the students had toward homework.

For the first scaled question, students and teachers were asked how much homework is completed with a 1 indicating none to very little and a 4 indicating all of the homework, as evident in Table 3. Students typically reported doing all, or nearly all, of the homework that was assigned to them, while most teachers reported that students completed little of the homework they were assigned. None of the students marked a 1 (none to very little homework), only two students marked a 2, 17 marked a 3, and 24 marked a 4 (all or nearly all homework). For the teachers, two marked a 1, six teachers marked a 2, and three teachers marked a 3.

Interviews

Narrative data were collected from two administrators as well as two teachers and from six students. The questions for these interviews stemmed from the questionnaire results but were also open to emergent themes during the interviews. Perspectives on homework varied for each group. Although there were some common themes, each group tended to have a unique view on the role and purpose of homework.

Administrators. The administrators were asked about homework as it applied to the school as a whole rather than a particular classroom or content area. As with the surveys, a couple questions provided more elaborate information. One of these questions dealt with giving a two or three word definition of homework; similar to that of the survey question for the teachers and students. Both of the administrators suggested that homework needs to be "relevant" or an "extension" of learning that occurred in the classroom and not "something new," meaning it should be content that has previously been learned or explored enough to ensure successful learning on students' own time.

The first administrator interviewed, Mr. Anderson, stated that homework was "supposed to be relevant." He went on to say that he did not feel that this relevance

was prevalent in a "meaningful" way at Mountain Middle School: "I think homework gets used a lot here but I am not sure that it is meaningful to students. I am not sure it helps their learning much." Meaningful was described as activities that involved families or the community and not worksheets or a set number of problems out of a book.

As with Mr. Anderson, the second administrator, Ms. Bell, also felt frustrated about how homework was used and the amount that was expected of children to complete. Ms. Bell shared her experiences raising her own children as well as helping her grandchildren and how homework tended to be a contentious issue. Her children were often "bombarded with copious amounts of homework that filled up their backpacks leaving little time after school for much else." Ms. Bell also mentioned how overwhelmed, frustrated, and sometimes angry her children became with homework; reactions she often saw with students at Mountain Middle School. "I've been in education for a long time and I am not convinced that homework, as it is done now, is the way to go."

A second question asked what the administrators thought helped the students at Mountain Middle School learn the best. Both Mr. Anderson and Ms. Bell agreed that the students learn best if there were "hands on" explorations. Mr. Anderson stated "there are different ways to learn but [hands on] is how they learn the best. They see it. They do it. And then they teach it to others. This is how we should be supporting our students." This idea of "doing" and then "teaching" was shared by Ms. Bell, too. She believed that "when students are doing whatever it is they are learning and then applying it; then it becomes reinforcement."

Although both administrators felt that the idea of homework as a means of meaningful reinforcement of the learning that occurred in the classroom was a desired outcome, there were also concerns about the ability of parents to assist their students with the homework assigned. "I have a lot of parents that don't understand the homework. They just don't know how to help," said Ms. Bell. She went on to say that when this happens she thinks, "The parents and the students become frustrated and the homework doesn't get done."

Teachers. The first teacher interviewed, Mrs. Jensen, was a mathematics teacher who believed homework had a "great impact on student learning" and she assigned a set number of questions from a book nearly every day; usually 20–30. When I asked Mrs. Jensen how she knew homework had a "great impact" she stated that it was evident in the "look in the student's eyes" and the fact that they raised their hand during class.

You can see it. When they go home and do the work, they come back to class with this look in their eye. I mean, some don't do it, but those that do have this look in their face. And, a lot of hands go up so I know they are learning.

With that said, Mrs. Jensen also reported feeling frustrated because her daughter had a lot of homework every night and this had often put a strain on family time. When asked if the experience with her daughter, who was the same age as her students, had changed her policies or practices in the classroom, Mrs. Jensen said that she was aware that it can be a problem but that she tried not to overwhelm them with too much. I then asked Mrs. Jensen how her students would respond if they did not have homework. She said that "they would be so frustrated because they wouldn't know what is going on in class." Several times she commented that being a student was like having a job. "It is the student's job to learn and therefore they have to have homework."

The second teacher that was interviewed, Mr. Carter, was a social studies teacher, and he said that he never assigned homework because it was not useful. Mr. Carter believed that most students were not interested in doing homework and would rather be doing other things. "Most don't do it, and the couple that do get it don't really need to do the homework; they already get it!" He went on to say that he used to assign homework but found that many students did not have access to the Internet at home, a computer, or other resources, human or otherwise, available. "Homework might be helpful if I knew they were going to interact with an adult or older sibling at home but many of my kids have to watch their younger siblings so they don't even have time for it."

Another major reason Mr. Carter did not give homework was because the school did not have an updated textbook in social studies that addressed the state standards. When asked if he would assign homework if he had such a text, Mr. Carter replied that he might, but it would not be just "rote, answer the questions at the end of the chapter kind of thing. It would have to get them thinking about what we were doing in class." As with both administrators, Mr. Carter also expressed doubts about families being able to assist their student with the homework they were assigned because "most of the parents don't have researching skills; they don't know how to help." Mr. Carter felt that this caused students to "copy and paste" from Internet sources and not really learn how to synthesize information.

Students. The first focus group, which had three students, believed that homework was not useful in their learning. These students reported feeling frequently confused, frustrated, or bored, which in turn led them to not do the work. A lack of help at home was another reason homework was not completed. One student, Kelly, said

When I get stuck my mom says to go ask my dad for help but when I go ask my dad he says he didn't have this until high school and he doesn't remember it anyway. So I just don't do it.

Kelly later stated that she generally did not feel like she could get help with her homework except "maybe from friends; if I ask." The other two students also reported that they did not mind doing homework if it was fun, short, or a project of some kind. Jason, another student in this group, said, "I like projects, especially if I get to work with my friends. I don't like math because we don't do projects and I don't get to talk to my friends about it."

All three students in this subgroup, even Jason who seemed to be the most opposed to homework, suggested that homework would be acceptable if they thought it was useful. Of further note, when asked who it was that helped them the most, a little, and the least with their homework all three students placed family at the bottom of the list; two said friends and one said their teacher (see Table 4).

The second focus group, which also had three students, had a more favorable perception toward homework. These students stated that homework often helped them to better understand what was going on in class. Rachel, one student from this group, did not care for group work or projects as much because she often felt stressed out working with others who, "never do their part of the project and then I get stuck doing everything." She preferred having individual work, like homework, count for a grade. Another student, Sarah, believed that homework was helpful in her learning because it helped her learn organizational skills and because "it makes me feel smarter." While

Table 4

Comparison of students' perceptions on who provides the most help with homework

	The most help	A little help	Very little help
Student 1	Friends	Parents	Older sister
Student 2	Friends	Teacher	Parents
Student 3	Teacher	Friends	Parents
Student 4	Teacher	Parents	Brother
Student 5	Mom	Friends	Sister
Student 6	Friends	Teacher	Parents

Sarah felt homework could be helpful she also said that she felt like there was too much. Eric, the third student in this group, shared Sarah's belief and said that "homework can be stressful" and this caused him to feel "tired if there is too much to do. It is hard to stay focused." When I asked the group to classify who provided the most help when it came to completing their homework, one student indicated their teacher, one their parent, and one their friend.

Discussion

The purpose and effectiveness of homework is becoming increasingly scrutinized and questioned (Vatterott, 2009). Gaining the perspectives of the school administration, teachers, and students at Mountain Middle School highlighted the polarity in perspectives at this school and provided support for critically analyzing and reevaluating instructional practices. Analysis of the data revealed three areas of particular interest for better understanding the views of stake holders. The first area deals with the frequent use of the word "bored" in relation to homework and the learning implications when students feel bored. The second was the contrast between students' and teachers' perceptions on the amount of homework completed by students. The third deals with the inconsistent perspectives of the administrators, teachers, and students toward homework.

Boredom

The majority of students indicated that they felt homework was boring or that they became bored as a result of doing homework. Effective instruction and learning experiences do not create situations wherein students are bored. An abundance of research indicates that a lack of engagement, the investment, attention, interest, and effort students put into their learning leads to diminished learning (Black, 2005; Bryson & Hand, 2007; Jackson & Davis, 2000; Smith, Rook, & Smith, 2007).

When students become bored with their homework, they become disengaged, and their learning potential diminishes for the given task. This matches students' comments in the interviews saying that they gave up on doing homework when they no longer understood what to do or how to do it. Although both administrators, one of the teachers interviewed, and several of the students believed that homework should be a "meaningful extension" to learning, it did not seem as though homework was used in this fashion. When homework is a quality extension to the classroom instruction, meaningful learning can occur (Darling-Hammond & Ifill-Lynch, 2006; Marzano & Pickering, 2007).

How Much Homework Is Completed?

There is the discrepancy in perception of how much homework is completed (see Table 3). With the students reporting higher rates of homework completed than teachers, these students feel they are finishing the majority of their homework, while their teachers believe that students are not doing this. It should be noted that the actual amount of homework completed was unknown and the reported differences were only the perceptions of the given parties. Nonetheless, some teachers felt that students were not doing their homework, but those teachers continued using homework because they believed doing homework was the "student's job" and that it would promote desirable personal habits such as responsibility and accountability. Research does not support this assumption unless these habits are deliberately designed and taught by teachers (Brock, Lapp, & Fisher, 2011; Cooper & Valentine, 2001; Epstein & Van Voorhis, 2001). Many of the students expressed a desire to have less homework and more group projects all of which are appropriate practices for adolescents that further support student learning (*AMLE*, 2010; Powell & Van Zandt Allen, 2001).

Finally, teachers' perceptions of homework were not aligned with administrators or students. It would seem that many teachers were using homework even though the students did not see much value in it as a tool to support their learning; they were bored when doing it. The continuation of instructional practices that do not engage students do little to promote learning or increase students' academic achievement. As previously mentioned, students must become actively engaged in their academics if meaningful learning is to occur.

Limitations

Several limitations in this study are worth highlighting in further detail. First, due to the nature of this qualitative case study, it is inappropriate to generalize results to other schools across the country. Readers must determine the extent to which findings in this study might be relevant to their own contexts. Also, findings from this study might be clarified by using other sources of data such as student work samples from across content areas. Follow-up interviews with the same students over time might better capture the nuances of their perspectives. In this study, homework was loosely defined to encompass a broader collection of artifacts for multiple content areas as perceived by different stakeholders (i.e., students, teachers, and principals). Focusing future work on specific kinds of homework, especially those uniquely tailored to individual students, could provide greater insight into the perceived effectiveness of homework between students, teachers, and school leaders. It is also recommended that additional research consider such things as the impact of individualized homework on student achievement.

Recommendations for Homework Policy and Practice

Homework, in and of itself, is not an ineffective practice to support students, but understanding the role it may, or may not play, in schools requires careful consideration. While it is impossible to establish a set of recommendations for schools in general, there are some things to consider that are relevant to all schools when examining the role homework plays in students' academic experiences.

First, it is worth considering how, specifically, homework fits in with the larger assessment outcomes of the school. That is, does the school have a clear assessment plan in place that aligns with the standards and instructional materials (Wiggins & McTighe, 2007)? Recognizing the role of assessments, including a variety of formative assessments, will be helpful in understanding what role homework will have in the learning of students.

Second, educators should ask, "What policies, procedures, and practices are in place for students to get more focused assistance with the learning in the classroom?" This question relates to a well-developed and enacted multitiered student support system that is dynamic and flexible at the classroom level (Fuchs & Fuchs, 2006). It should be noted that a system may be in place from a school-wide perspective, but the implementation of that plan may have tremendous variation within classrooms. This means that administrators and other school leaders (i.e., curriculum coordinators and academic coaches) should have an active role in helping to improve the instructional practices across the school to better understand the kinds of additional academic support students need.

Lastly, it is strongly recommended that teachers and administrators openly examine and discuss the evidence they have on the effectiveness of homework within their schools. The nature and complexity of evidence should help to guide the policies about homework. However, it is equally irresponsible to do away with practices with no evidence to support the decision. Also, be careful in thinking that a lack of evidence suggests an effective practice. Just because something worked for a small group of students does not mean it is having the larger impacts on student learning across the school.

Conclusion

Cooper (1989, p. 7) defined homework as "tasks assigned to students by school teachers that are meant to be carried out during non-school hours." That is an innocuous and fair definition, but what matters is not the definition but the interpretation and enactment of homework within the classroom. The decisions that teachers make impact student learning in monumental ways (Darling-Hammond, 2000). Depending on teachers' interpretation of homework and their philosophical beliefs toward learning, homework can become a senseless and ineffective tool in supporting, assessing, and measuring students' learning (Darling-Hammond & Ifill-Lynch, 2006).

Examining the effectiveness of homework is an important question and one worth understanding. However, the implications of implementing policies without critically examining their impact on learning are perhaps just as important to consider. It is a disservice to students to narrow the discussion on homework to a dichotomy of variables such as good or bad, effective or ineffective in increasing achievement, or even a little or a lot of homework.

Classroom structures that develop more complex thinking skills and the opportunity for students to meaningfully interact with the people they feel can best support their learning should be further developed and supported across learning environments. Differentiated learning, group projects, whole-class discourse, and open-ended explorations are but a few instructional strategies that have shown to increase students' understanding (Chapin, O'Connor, & Anderson, 2003; Frey, Fisher, & Everlove, 2009; Garner, 2007). Furthermore, practices that lead to frustrations, disengagement, and decreased self-efficacy should be closely scrutinized and carefully reconsidered (Darling-Hammond & Ifill-Lynch, 2006). Although it may be easier said than done, scrutiny of this kind would also require some teachers to question or shift their philosophical beliefs about learning and the nature of knowledge; constructs that are not easily changed (Pajares, 1992).

Increasing student achievement is an ongoing process, and effective change requires critical examination of practices and beliefs. Making a deliberate effort to better understand how all stakeholders perceive given practices and applying current research on best practices within the context of each school should be an ongoing and dynamic process. To assume that one practice will be beneficial for all students is unproductive at best. No school or classroom is the same and no school or classroom should generally encourage practices that do not support all students.

Lounsbury (2009, p. 35) stated that if schools are not mindful of educating the whole-child, creating experiences that support students' academic and affective development, and helping students become "responsible, self-reliant, and clear-thinking individuals, [then] they will have failed at what is, ultimately, their most important responsibility." Schools and classrooms do not need to reinvent the wheel, but they do need to continually reevaluate beliefs and practices with respect to student learning. This means being deliberate in providing multitiered levels of support as needed for students and being extremely cautious in systematically "adopting" practices that are not clearly supported by research. "One-size-fits-all" practices that do not support students' specific learning needs or help achieve school-wide objectives, or practices that do not promote engagement for all students should be questioned. If an instructional strategy does not promote or create engaged student learning, why use it?

References

Association of Middle Level Education. (2010). *This we believe: Successful schools for young adolescents.* Westerville, OH: Association of Middle Level Education.

Bempechat, J., Li, J., Neier, S. M., Gillis, C. A., & Holloway, S. D. (2011). The homework experience: Perceptions of low-income youth. *Journal of Advanced Academics, 22(2)*, 250–278.

Bennett, S., & Kalish, N. (2006). *The case against homework: How homework is hurting our children and what we can do about it.* New York, NY: Crown.

Black, S. (2005). Listening to students. *American School Board Journal, 192*(11), 39–41.

Bogdan, R., & Biklen, S. K. (2007). *Qualitative research for education* (5th ed.). Boston, MA: Pearson.

Brock, C., Lapp, D., & Fisher, D. (2011). Homework practices: Myth and realities. *California Reader, 45*(1), 21–26.

Brown, D. F. (2001). Middle level teachers' perceptions of the impact of block scheduling on instruction and learning. *Research in Middle Level Education Annual, 24*, 121–141.

Bryson, C., & Hand, L. (2007). The role of engagement in inspiring teaching and learning. *Innovations in Education and Teaching International, 44*(4), 349–362.

Carr, N. S. (2013). Increasing the effectiveness of homework for all learners in the inclusive classroom. *School Community Journal, 23*(1), 169.

Chapin, S. H., O'Connor, C., & Anderson, M. C. (2003). *Classroom discussions: Using math talk to help students learn, grades K-6.* Sausalito, CA: Math Solutions.

Chen, C., & Stevenson, H. W. (1989). Homework: A cross-cultural examination. *Child Development, 60*(3), 551–561.

Cooper, H. (1989). *Homework.* White Plains, NY: Longman.

Cooper, H., & Valentine, J. C. (2001). Using research to answer practical questions about homework. *Educational Psychologist, 36*(3), 143–153.

Creswell, J. W., & Plano-Clark, V. (2010). *Designing and conducting mixed methods research.* Thousand Oaks, CA: Sage.

Darling-Hammond, L. (2000). Futures of teaching in American education. *Journal of Educational Change, 1*(4), 353–373.

Darling-Hammond, L., & Ifill-Lynch, O. (2006). If they'd only do their work! *Educational Leadership, 63*(5), 8–13.

Epstein, J. L., & Van Voorhis, F. (2001). More than minutes: Teachers' roles in designing homework. *Educational Psychologist, 36*(3), 181–193.

Frey, N., Fisher, D., & Everlove, S. (2009). *Productive group work: How to engage students, build teamwork, and promote understanding.* Alexandria, VA: ASCD.

Fuchs, D., & Fuchs, L. S. (2006). Introduction to response to intervention: What, why, and how valid is it? *Reading Research Quarterly, 41*(1), 93–99.

Garner, B. K. (2007). *Getting to "got it!" Helping struggling students learn how to learn.* Alexandria, VA: ASCD.

Gibson, D. M., & Jefferson, R. (2006). The effect of perceived parental involvement and the use of growth-fostering relationships on self-concept in adolescents participating in "gear up." *Adolescence, 41*(161), 111–125.

Jackson, A., & Davis, G. A. (2000). *Turning points 2000: Educating adolescents in the 21st century.* New York, NY: Teachers College Press.

Kliebard, H. M. (2004). *The struggle for the American curriculum, 1893-1958.* New York, NY: Routledge-Falmer.

Kralovac, E., & Buell, J. (2001). End homework now. *Educational Leadership, 58*(7), 39–42.

Krashen, S. (2013). The hard work hypothesis: Is doing your homework enough to overcome the effects of poverty? *Multicultural Education, 20*(3/4), 16–19.

Lounsbury, J. (2009). Deferred but not deterred: A middle school manifesto. *Middle School Journal, 40*(5), 31–36.

Marzano, R. J., & Pickering, D. J. (2007). The case for and against homework. *Educational Leadership, 64*(6), 74–79.

Pajares, M. F. (1992). Teachers' beliefs and educational research: Cleaning up a messy construct. *Review of Educational Research, 62*(3), 307–332.

Partnership for 21st Century Skills. (2015). *A framework for 21st century learning.* http://www.p21.org/our-work/p21-framework.

Powell, R. (2001). Middle school curriculum. In V. A. Anfara (Ed.), *The handbook of research in middle level education* (pp. 107–124). Greenwich, CT: Information Age Publishing.

Roney, K., Anfara, V., & Brown, K. (2008). *Creating organizationally healthy and effective middle schools: Research that supports the middle school concept and student achievement.* Westerville, OH: AMLE.

Slavin, R. E. (2007). *Educational research in an age of accountability.* Boston, MA: Pearson.

Smith, K. S., Rook, J., & Smith, T. W. (2007). Increasing student engagement using effective and metacognitive writing strategies in content areas. *Preventing School Failure: Alternative Education for Children and Youth, 51*(3), 43–48.

Teddlie, C., & Tashakkori, A. (2009). *Foundations of mixed methods research: Integrating quantitative and qualitative approaches in the social and behavioral sciences.* Thousand Oaks, CA: Sage.

Telljohann, S. K., Symons, C. W., & Pateman, B. (2004). *Health education: Elementary and middle school applications.* Boston, MA: McGraw Hill.

Van Hoose, J., Strahan, D., & L'Esperance, M. (2001). *Promoting harmony: Young adolescent development and school practices.* Westerville, OH: AMLE.

Vatterott, C. (2009). *Rethinking homework: Best practices that support diverse needs.* Alexandria, VA: ASCD.

Wiggins, G., & McTighe, J. (2007). *Schooling by design: Mission, action and achievement.* Alexandria, VA: ASCD.

CORY BENNETT is an associate professor of Education at Idaho State University.

EXPLORING THE ISSUE

Does Homework Matter?

Critical Thinking and Reflection

1. How did changing the approach to completing math homework assignments in the Walk/Lassak article change the overall motivation of the classroom?
2. Compare and contrast the opposition to homework at the different grade levels in elementary, middle, and high school.
3. Has concerns regarding homework really changed over the decades? Explain.
4. List any key studies related to the question, does homework matter.
5. What did the Supreme Court in Canada decide about their homework issue?

Is There Common Ground?

Should we believe reports from the press that students are overburdened with homework and their parents up in arms because of the amount of time their children spend on homework? Or is it the opposite, reported as the results from studies conducted on the issue indicating that this is not the case and that the students and parents in the study were atypical? Which portrait of the homework burden issue is accurate and what is actually going on? Why all the horror homework stories? Loveless (2014) sheds some light on the issue that may extend beyond homework to other areas of concern parents may harbor about schooling. The following items were indicated as potential causes of the discontent after analyzing a Met Life survey of parents conducted in 2013. The study results indicate numerous items that may be fanning the homework conflict that are, more than likely, still are today:

- Many parents have much larger ongoing complaints and concerns about their children's schooling.
- Many parents are truly alienated from their child's school.
- Many parents convince themselves that the numbers in opposition of homework is larger than it actually is.
- Even schools of choice get their share of complaints about homework.
- Horror stories about homework should be read in a proper perspective that originate from the personal discontent of a small group of parents.
- There is always a clique of parents who are happy with the amount of homework.

- Many parents prefer more homework, not less.
- If there are issues, policies should be reviewed in regard to homework with parents on a case-by-case basis.
- Complaints about homework have existed for more than a century and they show no signs of going away (Loveless, 2014, p. 24).

Homework is inseparable with students, parents, teachers, and schools. For the most part, homework is perceived as positive with robust activities outside the actual classroom for learning, practice, and/or preparation for classroom teaching and learning activities. Homework too is quite often a two-edged sword requiring debate in order to find and move on common ground to resolve the homework controversy.

Additional Resources

Bennett, C. (2017). Most won't do it: Examining homework as a structure for learning in a diverse middle school. *American Secondary Education*: 45/2. Retrieved from https://eric.ed.gov/?id=EJ1142297

Crawford, L. (2018). Does homework really work? *Great!Schools.org*. Retrieved from https://www.greatschools.org/gk/articles/what-research-says-about-homework/

Debate.org. (2018). *Should students have homework?* Retrieved from http://www.debate.org/opinions/should-students-have-homework

Loveless, T. (2014). Homework in America: Part II. *Brown Center Report on American Education*. Brooking's.

The Guardian. (2018). Canadian parents win legal battle against homework. Retrieved from https://www.theguardian.com/world/2009/nov/18/canada-homework-milley

Virginia Teacher. (2018). Homework: Necessary inconvenience. Retrieved from http://www.vateacher.com/homework-necessary-inconvenience-or-unnecessary-evil/

Internet References . . .

Does Homework Design Matter? The Role of Homework's Purpose in Student Mathematics Achievement

https://www.researchgate.net/publication/281393258_Does_homework_design_matter_The_role_of_homework's_purpose_in_student_mathematics_achievement

Does Homework Matter? An Investigation of Teacher Perceptions about Homework Practices for Children from Nondominant Backgrounds

http://journals.sagepub.com/doi/10.1177/0042085907304277

Does Homework Really Work?

https://www.greatschools.org/gk/articles/what-research-says-about-homework/

Homework: Is It Worth the Hassle?

https://www.theguardian.com/teacher-network/2017/feb/07/homework-is-it-worth-the-hassle

Making Homework Matter: Don't Ban It, Fix It

https://psmag.com/education/making-homework-matter-dont-ban-it-fix-it

Selected, Edited, and with Issue Framing Material by:
Glenn L. Koonce, *Regent University*

ISSUE

Is There Opposition to Using Technology to Track Student Social–Emotional Learning?

YES: Jane Robbins, from "Invited Testimony of Jane Robbins, American Principles Project Foundation before the U.S. House Committee on Education and the Workforce" (2018)

NO: Benjamin Herold, from "How (and Why) Ed-Tech Companies Are Tracking Student's Feelings," *Education Week* (2018)

Learning Outcomes

After reading this issue, you will be able to:

- Identify the key factors of the various ways that the government can compile personal data with Social–Emotional Learning.
- Consider some of the pros and cons of "Panorama Education" programs.
- Trace the evolutionary startup of one of the digital companies or government agencies covered in Social–Emotional Learning.
- Create a timeline, from the 1960s to the present, tracking the social emotional movement in the United States.
- Research the best practices for measuring SEL traits by Marzano and others and analyze the rubrics for each.

ISSUE SUMMARY

YES: Speaking to the U.S. House Committee on Education and the Workforce, Jane Robbins is opposed to using technology to track student social emotional behavior because she feels the government will have enormous leeway to disclose personal information on individual students without their consent.

NO: Benjamin Herold comments on both sides of the issue, but identifies school districts that have already implemented SEL assessment and comments favorable on the growing push to use educational technology to measure, monitor, and modify students' emotions, mindsets, and ways of thinking.

Maria Shea-Michiels states in her 2018 article, *Need a "silver bullet"? Try SEL*, that there is really "no silver bullet when it comes to education, but there is a research-backed approach that may come close: social-emotional learning" (p. 1). Social–emotional learning hit the education scene in the 1960s, making its way into the lexicon in the early 1990s. The movement took off and recently, interest in social–emotional learning (SEL) has exploded. Now, all 50 states have SEL standards at the preschool level and more states are instituting SEL standards for kindergarten through 12th grade. The premise is that integrating thinking, emotions, and behavior produce positive school outcomes. SEL goes by numerous titles/identifiers across the country, as well as in the literature, from character education, 21st-century skills, soft skills, skills for success, inter- and intrapersonal competencies, and noncognitive skills. Practitioners, policy makers, and parents typically use the term that best identifies with their understanding from various theoretical approaches

(Jones & Doolittle, 2017). Many educators were connected to SEL from their use of soft skills found in character education and helping students to resolve conflict. For teachers and school leaders, these soft skills have evolved into the long-standing concept of educating the whole child. With the 2015 passage of the new federal law governing K–12 education, the Every Student Succeeds Act (ESSA), signed into law by President Obama in December 2015, school districts are looking to emphasize nonacademic concepts and whole child issues and their place in student outcomes, school accreditation, as well as district success. The ESSA allows for multiple measures of student success and proponents, see SEL assessment as one of numerous multiple measures' possibilities. The additional indicator in school accountability being required by ESSA, beyond test scores, can be seen in the work of a coalition of California districts who suggest using measures of social emotional learning (Blad, 2016).

In the early-nineteen nineties, the violence in schools movement evolved to eradicate serious threats to school safety with many districts instituting zero-tolerance policies for certain disciplinary infractions (guns, drugs, and violence). The Collaborative to Advance Social Emotional Learning (CASEL) was organized in 1994 and met that same year to bring educators together with researchers and other key individuals and groups to address the rising tide of violence in schools. CASEL associates collaborated to author *Promoting Social and Emotional Learning: Guidelines for Educators* that helped define the field and has driven the SEL forward since that time (Elias et al., 1997). CASEL (2018) defines SEL as:

> the process through which children and adults acquire and effectively apply the knowledge, attributes, and skills necessary to understand and manage emotions, set and achieve positive goals, feel and show empathy for others, establish and maintain positive relationships, and make responsible decisions (par. 1).

Currently, as noted in the NO article for this issue, the SEL field is being challenged by the use of technology to track student's emotions (feelings) in order to "measure, monitor, and modify student's emotions, mindsets, and ways of thinking" (Herold, 2018). The result is a "highly dimensional psychometric profile" (p. 2) that can be improved with practice and is being tied to greater potential for academic success. Assessments are being developed, with some already available, to measure student SEL. "The interplay between digital technology and

human emotion is not science fiction nor a hypothetical dream for the future. It is a growing reality with powerful implications for today's student outcomes" (McGraw-Hill Education Applied Learning Science Team, p. 2).

Not so fast, says Jane Robbins (2018) of the American Principles Foundation in the YES article for this issue. Speaking before the U.S. House Committee on Education and the Workforce about protecting citizen's privacy, particularly in education. Robbins commented on student personal data, most of which would be collected through technology. Concern for student privacy and use of private data by the government (school) for purposes other than the reason for which it was originally collected, Robbins says, goes against, "personal dignity and autonomy every American Citizen is endowed with and is entitled to respect and deference when it comes to his or her own personal data" (p. 1). Herein, a debate is ensuing as to the protection of what is considered by many as student personal and private behavioral information/data. The impetus involves school children's information/data whether they be preschool or seniors in high school. Herold (2018, p. 1) notes that this is one example to use the great capabilities of technology to "measure, monitor, and modify students' emotions, mindsets, and ways of thinking."

Perhaps one of the strongest writings on this phenomena is found in Wattes' (2017) article *Education Technology and the New Behaviorism*. He notes that much is happening now with education, technology, and emotional health indicating that students are struggling, and students are more vulnerable regarding their emotional well-being. He calls for students to have more emotional intelligence, a term coined by Daniel Golman in the early 1990s with research and best practices being written in his very influential 1995 book of the same title, *Emotional Intelligence* (EI). EI is touted as more human capacity for empathy and care. Education technologists and education entrepreneurs are turning SEL policy mandates into products and have powerful advocates in powerful places who are investing millions of dollars into education products directly for SEL (Watters, 2017). The elements shared in these endeavors involve the "monitoring and measuring of student data, then measuring their emotions, sure, but more like, measuring their behavior" (p. 3). Behavior management products HERO K12, Neurocore, ClassDojo, Aperture Education, Kickboard, Emote, Panorama, Class Dojo, Bloomz, Tessera, and others "claim that they help develop correct behavior" (p. 3). Most of these companies are for profit enterprises. The main focus of these enterprises is on introducing and promoting growth mindsets and mindfulness to K–12 educators that are measurable and manageable. Some of the behavioral indicators of classroom conduct measured are "character, mindset, grit, malleability, and compliance" (p. 3). Watters (2017) notes this new *behaviorism* as behavior design, a term that derives from the work of Stanford psychologist B. J. Fogg and his Persuasive Technology Labs. The resulting data collected from the behavioral indicators are analyzed and used by teachers and schools to manage student behavior.

SEL is still an emerging field, particularly in regard to measurement and using the outcomes to improve student behavior and thus, student success in school. One huge barrier to SEL assessment is that SEL competencies are difficult to measure, yet to secure funding to improve programming as well as assessment tools, there must be a continuing effort to measure student SEL. In addition, many teachers are not prepared to take on the task of SEL assessment, analysis, and intervention. Many of these teachers still struggle on the front end to find effective ways to prioritize and teach SEL skills. Many schools and school districts still have not prioritized SEL in their strategic plans and/or budgeting process. Global education strategist at SMART Technologies, Giancarlo Brotto (2018, p. 3) provides a glimpse of the relevancy and urgency of implementing SEL stating, "we will forge a more well-rounded education system and produce more socially responsible and aware citizens who will be better prepared

to work together to create better communities, nations, and ultimately, a better world."

In a February 28, 2018, issue of District Administration (Author, 2018, p. 1), a partnership between two SEL companies, Kickboard and Aperture Education, were noted as "focusing on helping schools collect, monitor and analyze student social and emotional skill and behavior." The companies' merger allows schools the tools to assess behavior data on a daily basis and can support the schools PBIS programs and other initiatives directed toward positive behavior.

In the selections that follow, Jane Robbins is opposed to using technology to track student social–emotional learning stating, "It's just un-American. Sorry I don't want the government to know how my child's mind works" (Robbins, as quoted in Herold, 2018, p. 5). In regard to the assessment of student's feelings Robbins further states, "Some lines should not be crossed regardless of their supposed benefits, this is one of those lines (Robbins, 2018, p. 7). Benjamin Herold (2018) acknowledges Robbins position, but notes that real companies like Panorama Education is already working in over 500 school districts, including the 29,000-student school district in Spokane, Washington. Data collected from the students are analyzed by school counselors and principals. Herold concludes that if something needs to be done to curb this movement, it must be done now, "before the horse is all the way out of the barn" (p. 8).

Jane Robbins

Invited Testimony of Jane Robbins

American Principles Project Foundation before the U.S. House Committee on Education and the Workforce

Madam Chairman and members of the committee:

My name is Jane Robbins, and I'm with the American Principles Project Foundation, which works to restore our nation's founding principles. I appreciate the opportunity to speak to you today about protecting citizens' privacy when evaluating government programs, especially in the area of education.

The Commission on Evidence-Based Policymaking was created to pursue a laudable goal: to improve analysis of the effectiveness of federal programs.[1] We all certainly agree that public policy should be based on evidence, on facts, not on opinion or dogma. So unbiased scientific research, for example, is vital for policy-making.

But the problem arises when the subjects of the research and analysis are human beings. Each American citizen is endowed with personal dignity and autonomy and therefore is entitled to respect and deference when it comes to his or her own personal data. The idea that the government should be able to vacuum up mountains of personal data and employ it for whatever purposes it deems useful—without the citizen's consent, or in many cases even his knowledge—conflicts deeply with this truth about the dignity of persons.

Bear in mind that the analyses contemplated by the Commission go even further than merely sharing discrete data points among agencies. They involve creating new information about individuals, via matching data, drawing conclusions, and making predictions about those individuals. So in essence the government would have information about a citizen that even he or she doesn't have.

Our founding principles, which enshrine the consent of the governed, dictate that a citizen's data belongs to him, not to the government. If the government or its allied researchers want to use it for purposes other than those for which it was submitted, they should get the owner's consent (in the case of pre-K–12 students, parental consent). That's how things should work in a free society.

But according to well-funded organizations[2] with a vested interest in accessing citizen data for their own purposes, it's simply too limiting to have to get consent to use that data. Especially in the area of education data, they argue, important things could be done if the government were allowed to combine various repositories of data to track student outcomes. This consolidation of data need not be in one physical location—allowing or requiring agencies to link to each other's data will have the same effect.

In its wisdom, Congress has repeatedly prohibited the establishment of national education databases or other systems that would endanger student privacy. For example, section 9531 of the Elementary and Secondary Education Act (the No Child Left Behind iteration) prohibits "the development of a nationwide database of personally identifiable information" on students.[3] Section 182 of the Education Sciences Reform Act similarly prohibits "the establishment of a nationwide database of individually identifiable information on individuals involved in studies or other collections of data under this title."[4] And Section 134 of the Higher Education Act prohibits development, implementation, or maintenance of a federal student unit-record system (one that would allow the government to collect personally identifiable information (PII) on individual higher-education students and link education data to workforce data).[5]

This last prohibition is the focus of much of the current debate on use of education records. What's wrong with a unit-record system? For one thing, it's based on a faulty premise—that the "success" of a student's education is measured solely in terms of earning capacity. While a

Robbins, Jane. "Invited Testimony of Jane Robbins, American Principles Project Foundation" before the U.S. House Committee on Education and the Workforce, January 20, 2018, p. 1–7.

good education may increase earning power, that isn't and shouldn't be the sole or even the major point. Without exploring the question of the value of a liberal-arts education rather than simply workforce training, it's very dangerous to make policy on the assumption that a student who chooses to be a teacher or a minister or some other modestly compensated profession is less successful than one who makes more money.

The danger here is that government will look at this skewed data and conclude that students should be "nudged" in one direction or another regardless of their interests or indeed the unintended consequences for society. In fact, this social engineering is already happening in my state of Georgia, where last year the legislature changed the policy of subsidizing AP exam fees for low-income students.[6] Now, the subsidy will be limited to AP exams in STEM subjects. Low-income students interested in English or history or languages are out of luck. One legislator was quoted as saying, "The truth is that for employable skills . . . they need to be taking AP STEM courses in high school." So now the state government is decreeing what kinds of employment Georgia students should aspire to and what they should study to get there.

Our Founders would be surprised and, I think, alarmed, that government would be pushing students in *any* direction, much less away from the well-rounded liberal-arts education that enabled the Founders to create the most impressive political document ever written.

No government is equipped to make these kinds of decisions for individuals. No government can make better decisions than can the individual exercising his freedom. Human beings are not interchangeable. Our country has thrived for centuries without this kind of social engineering—by leaving these millions of small decisions to free citizens—and it's deeply dangerous to change that now.

Beyond this philosophical problem, a unit-record system violates the Fair Information Practice Principles[7] established in the Privacy Act of 1974,[8] and also rules of ethical research, in numerous ways. The same is true of other schemes designed to increase access to education data to accomplish other goals.

First, these envisioned structures would use and disclose students' PII without their consent—or even their knowledge that this is happening. It's one thing to collect and use data from a student who voluntarily participates in a government program and understands that participation will expose some of his PII to program administrators; it's quite another to forcibly suck every individual into a data-collection system simply because he enrolled in an institution of higher education or even in a public school at any level. Telling that student he must relinquish control over his personal data to promote a greater good as defined by bureaucrats and lobbyists—or even worse, just dragooning him without telling him anything—not only violates Fair Information Principles but is simply un-American.

As stated by Mr. Frank Balz of the National Association of Independent Colleges and Universities, "the act of enrolling in college, even for a single course, should not require permanent entry into a federal registry." But that's what all proposals for a unit-record system would require.

Mr. Balz also expressed concern about future expansion of such a system, which brings us to a second problem. Fair Information Principles also prohibit "repurposing" data for things not contemplated by the citizen owners when they turned it over. But the various program-evaluation schemes under consideration in Congress would do exactly that.

The problem is that literally everything can be linked to education. So why stop with employment data? Why not analyze the connection between one's education and his health? Or his participation in the military? Or his housing choices? Or the number of children he has? Or his political activity? Or whether his suspension from school in sixth grade might indicate a future life of crime? As education-technology companies brag, predictive algorithms can be created, and their conclusions could allow government to push students down certain paths or close off others. And every question can be justified by citing "transparency," "program effectiveness," or "better consumer information."

The chances of these data being "repurposed"— provided for one purpose but then used for something else entirely—are significant. Senator Warren very recently expressed concern about this issue in the context of whether the U.S. Department of Education is misusing federal earnings data to determine how much loan forgiveness should be allowed for defrauded students.[9] Regardless of how you come down on this particular question, the point illustrates that the government has a natural tendency to use this convenient data for other purposes, despite the lack of consent from the citizen who provided it.

Proof that the Big Data community wants to repurpose data in a multitude of ways comes from one witness from Booz Allen Hamilton (former employer of Edward Snowden), who testified before the Commission about the "predictive intelligence" possibilities of mining and sifting federal databases. "For example," he said, "eligibility and participation tracked by the Social Security Administration—when combined with taxpayer data and tax subsidies from the IRS, survey data from the U.S. Census Bureau, and data from other agencies, such as HHS and HUD—could exponentially . . . enhance our potential to draw insights that could not have been derived before."

This concept is simply chilling. This is what totalitarian countries like China do. It is not what free societies do.

Schemes that would connect all these distinct silos of data violate the Fair Information Principle requiring data minimization. Under this principle, the federal government should maintain as little data—not as much data—on each citizen as possible.

And will this dossier created on every citizen become permanent? Presumably so. If the goal of providing maximum consumer information is to be achieved, both historical and current data—constantly updated and expanded—must be compiled and preserved.

Perhaps this expansion won't happen. Perhaps the federal government, in stark contrast to its behavior over the last 100 years, will stay within its constitutional boundaries. But reality-based Americans know the government will push the envelope as far as it possibly can, as it always does. And they know that giving that government access to such a treasure trove of data is dangerous to privacy and to individual liberty.

A third concern is the inappropriateness of making this gold mine available for "research" without strict controls. Research is important and to be encouraged (at least when it's not of the biased type frequently funded by the federal government to produce evidence in support of a pre-ordained outcome[10]). But in a free society governed by consent, no identifiable citizen data held by the government should be made available to any researcher without the consent of the data owner—that is, the citizen from whom it was taken. Strict rules of ethics applicable to research require no less under the principle of "respect for persons."[11]

When it comes to pre-K–12 education data, this principle is even more important because the research subjects are children who can't give informed consent. If children's education records are to be used in research other than in the very limited applicable exemptions, it is critical that the parents be informed and allowed to control their children's participation. All legitimate research organizations, including applicable agencies within the Department of Health and Human Services, recognize the special protection due to children in research studies.[12]

When deciding how much access to allow to federal data repositories on children, it's critical to be aware of the enormously intrusive types of information that are being collected. The most sensitive is psychological data collected through the craze of so-called "social–emotional learning" (SEL). With SEL, the government (through the school) and corporate vendors can compile data about the most personal aspects of every child who is subjected to it, including (via sophisticated computer platforms) how his mind works and what attitudes, values, and dispositions

he holds.[13] In fact, the federal government is itself trying to "incentivize" this highly intrusive data collection through not only the Every Student Succeeds Act[14] but also through the Strengthening Education Through Research Act[15] (SETRA; which revises the Education Sciences Reform Act). Compiling this type of data is bad enough; allowing nonconsensual access to researchers and other agencies could create a nightmare for children and their families and should be unthinkable in a free society.

Fourth, the idea that this massive repository of sensitive PII (whether it exists physically or just through linkages of data systems) will be protected against unauthorized access and breaches is quite simply delusional. Merely two years ago, hearings of the House Committee on Government Oversight and Reform[16] revealed the shocking lack of student-data security throughout the U.S. Department of Education. The last few years have seen serious data breaches at other agencies including NSA,[17] DoD,[18] OPM,[19] and SEC.[20] The problems encompass both lax controls over the people allowed access to sensitive data, as well as outdated technology and inadequate security to prevent unauthorized access.

That the federal government should now consider ballooning the sensitive data contained in these insecure systems and opening it up to even more people is at best misguided and at worst, reckless. Given the difficulty or impossibility of truly securing data, ignoring the Fair Information Principle of data minimization can result in serious harm to American citizens.

This illustrates the difference between two concepts that are too often conflated in the discussion, and in fact in the Commission's report. "Data security" means whether the government can keep data systems from being breached. "Data privacy" refers to whether the government has any right to collect and maintain such data in the first place. The Fair Information Principle of data minimization is designed to increase security by increasing privacy. A hacker can't steal what isn't there.

Even if the data systems were secure, the regulatory gutting of the Family Educational Rights and Privacy Act (FERPA) in 2012 means that government education officials (federal, state, and local) now have enormous leeway to disclose PII on individual students without their consent. Pursuant to the recent FERPA regulations, these officials may share private PII with other government agencies, nonprofit entities, corporations, researchers, and literally anyone on the planet as long as the disclosure can be characterized as an audit or evaluation of a (broadly defined) "education program."[21] FERPA needs updating and strengthening, but that's a topic for another day.

Will the new conglomeration of student data be fair game for disclosure under these regulations? The danger is too real to dismiss.

As to the Commission's assurances that all these data would be disclosed only with "approval" to "authorized persons," we should ask: Approval of whom? Authorized by whom? There are myriad examples of government employees' violating statute or policy by misusing or wrongfully disclosing data. And even if bureaucrats have only good intentions, what they consider appropriate use or disclosure may conflict absolutely with what the affected citizen considers appropriate. Again, this illustrates the necessity for consent.

Two final points: much of what the government wants to accomplish through various so-called transparency bills can be accomplished through the free market. For example, any legitimate institution of higher education will be happy to provide statistics on graduation rates, alumni employment, and so on, to applicants who ask for it. If applicants aren't asking for it, that should tell us something about whether government should be mandating it. And the deeper problem here is that the government has taken over duties related to education and education financing that it manifestly has no constitutional right to be involved in. Having done so, it supposedly becomes necessary to add more layers of government control to ensure accountability for the results of this spending that never should have happened in the first place. I understand that this unconstitutional system won't be dismantled any time soon, but I do think it's critical for Congress to recognize this underlying problem and begin to address it.

In conclusion, we certainly recognize the value of unbiased research in pursuit of optimal policy-making. But we ask that Congress continue its protective policies when the subjects of such research are human beings. The goal of benefiting others in society, in vague and theoretical ways, or of "helping" citizens lead their own lives and make their own decisions, does not justify the federal government's collection and dissemination of millions of data points on individuals—without their consent. This should not be happening in a free country. Some lines should not be crossed regardless of their supposed benefits. This is one of those lines.

Notes

1. David B. Muhlhausen, "A Commission for Evidence-Based Policymaking: A Step in the Right Direction," Heritage.org (March 9, 2015), *available at* http://www.heritage.org/research/reports/2015/03/a-commission-on-evidence-based-policymaking-a-step-in-the-right-direction.

2. Kelly Field, "Rescind Ban on Federal Unit-Record System to Track Students, Report Says," The Chronicle of Higher Education (March 11, 2014), *available at* http://www.chronicle.com/article/ Rescind-Ban-on-Federal/145279/.

3. 20 U.S.C. § 7911.

4. 20 U.S.C. § 9572.

5. 20 U.S.C. §§ 1001 *et seq., available at* http://naicu.edu/docLib/20081030_HEA101-studentunit.pdf.

6. Ty Tagami, "Some Fear Change in AP Exam Subsidy Slights Low-Income Students," ajc.com (August 9, 2017), *available at* http://www.myajc.com/news/local-education/some-fear-change-exam-subsidy-slights-low-income-students/jMvPp7FznJQvZw936Jv6oM/.

7. See https://www.cippguide.org/2010/01/18/fair-information-practices-principles/.

8. 5 U.S.C. § 552a.

9. "Warren Seeks Inquiry of Education Dept. Use of Earnings Data to Judge Student Fraud Claims," politico.com (January 3, 2018), *available at* https://www.politico.com/newsletters/morning-education/ 2018/01/03/devos-considers-stricter-standard-for-student-fraud-claims-063595.

10. See Emmett McGroarty, Jane Robbins, and Erin Tuttle, *Deconstructing the Administrative State: The Fight for Liberty,* Manchester, NH: Sophia Institute Press (2017), pp. 113–134. In addition, research that reaches conclusions contrary to what the government wants is frequently ignored (see the multiplicity of studies showing the futility and perhaps harm of the Head Start program, to which the government responds by annually increasing funding for Head Start). Allowing the personal lives of millions of Americans to be studied under a microscope to benefit a political agenda is unconscionable.

11. See https://www.hhs.gov/ohrp/regulations-and-policy/guidance/faq/informed-consent/index.html.

12. See https://www.hhs.gov/ohrp/regulations-and-policy/guidance/faq/children-research/index.html.

13. Karen Effrem and Jane Robbins, "Schools Ditch Academics for Emotional Manipulation," thefederalist.com (October 19, 2016), *available at* http://thefederalist.com/2016/10/19/schools-ditch-academics-for-emotional-manipulation/.

14. "Funding for Social-Emotional Learning in ESSA," ASCD, *available at* http://www.ascd.org/ASCD/pdf/siteASCD/policy/ESSA-Resources_SEL-Funding.pdf.

15. See https://edworkforce.house.gov/education research/.

16. U.S. Department of Education: Information Security Review" (November 17, 2015), *available at*

https://oversight.house.gov/hearing/u-s-department-of-education-information-security-review/.

17. Scott Shane, "New N.S.A. Breach Linked to Popular Russian Antivirus Software," nytimes.com (October 5, 2017), *available at* https://www.nytimes.com/2017/10/05/us/politics/russia-nsa-hackers- kaspersky.html.

18. Elinor Mills, "Bad Flash Drive Caused Worst U.S. Military Breach," cnet.com (August 25, 2010), *available at* https://www.cnet.com/news/bad-flash-drive-caused-worst-u-s-military-breach/.

19. See "Congressional Report Slams OPM on Data Breach," krebsonsecurity.com (September 16, 2016), *available at* https://krebsonsecurity.com/2016/09/congressional-report-slams-opm-on-data-breach/.

20. Robert Hackett, "SEC Discloses Breach That May Have Enabled Insider Trading," fortune.com (September 21, 2017), *available at* http://fortune.com/2017/09/20/sec-breach-insider-trading/.

21. Letter from American Association of Collegiate Registrars and Admissions Officers to Regina Miles of U.S. Department of Education (May 23, 2011), *available at* https://aacrao web.s3.amazonaws.com/migrated/ FERPA-AACRAO Comments.sflb.ashx_520501ad842930.77008351.as

JANE ROBBINS is a senior fellow at American Principles Project, an attorney, and the coauthor of the book, *Deconstructing the Administrative State: The Fight for Liberty*.

Benjamin Herold

How (and Why) Ed-Tech Companies Are Tracking Student's Feelings

A push to use new technology to understand the "whole child" is sparking privacy fears.

All school year, Kaylee Carrell has been watching online math videos using a free software platform called Algebra Nation.

What the Florida eighth grader didn't know: the software was also watching her.

As part of her nightly homework, Carrell might start a video, watch an instructor explain a concept, rewind to review, press pause when she was ready to solve a problem, and post messages to the Facebook-style "wall" if she needed help. Occasionally, a brief survey might pop up.

Behind the scenes, the software was diligently tracking all that activity, anonymously logging the clicks and keystrokes of Carrell and more than 200,000 other students. As part of an $8.9 million federal grant project, researchers then used machine-learning techniques to search for patterns. Their ultimate goal: improve student learning by teaching the software to pinpoint when children are feeling happy, bored, or engaged. It's just one example of a growing push to use educational technology to measure, monitor, and modify students' emotions, mindsets, and ways of thinking.

> Eighth graders at Polo Park Middle School in Wellington, FL, were divided about the idea of using software that can identify and respond to their emotions.
>
> —Josh Ritchie for Education Week

The trend is provoking strong and conflicting reactions throughout the K–12 world.

"I can see how it could be really helpful," Carrell said after a reporter explained the mechanics of the Algebra Nation research in which she was unknowingly taking part.

"But home is also supposed to be a safe space. You don't want to feel like your computer is watching you."

Personalized Learning for the "Whole Child"

For years, there's been a movement to personalize student learning based on each child's academic strengths, weaknesses, and preferences. Now, some experts believe such efforts shouldn't be limited to determining how well individual kids spell or subtract. To be effective, the thinking goes, schools also need to know when students are distracted, whether they're willing to embrace new challenges, and if they can control their impulses and empathize with the emotions of those around them.

To describe this constellation of traits and abilities, education experts use a host of often-overlapping terms, **such as social–emotional skills**, noncognitive abilities, character traits, and executive functions.

For many parents and teachers, it's common sense: kids do well when they pay attention, work hard, and get along with others.

An emerging body of research backs that intuition, tying these nonacademic factors to improved school achievement, future workplace success, and long-term well-being. Learning scientists are also increasingly convinced these traits and abilities can be improved with practice.

The result has been a groundswell of interest. A major international test of students' social–emotional skills will be unveiled in 2019. The recently passed federal education law, known as the Every Student Succeeds Act, tried to push states and schools to broaden their definition of success. And major philanthropies and venture-capital firms are lining up to support the movement with hundreds of millions of dollars.

Sensing opportunity, a fresh crop of companies has sprouted up.

One of the most popular now administers online surveys to more than 7 million students a year, generating a massive database about children's "grit" and "growth mindset."

Others claim they can improve children's "impulse control" **through video games**; provide parents with a **"high-dimensional psychometric profile"** of their preschoolers; and allow school staffers to use smartphones to continually record their observations of students' feelings.

Meanwhile, cutting-edge researchers are also exploring facial recognition, eye-tracking, wearable devices, and even virtual reality as ways to better gauge what students are feeling.

Proponents view this push to understand and respond to the "whole child" as a promising path to dramatically improving student learning—and an antidote to the K–12 world's long-standing focus on standardized tests.

Critics fear an Orwellian surveillance state, in which government and corporations alike invade students' privacy, encroach on their individual liberty, and try to manipulate their behavior based on spurious measurements.

Recent fiascoes involving misuse of sensitive data harvested by consumer platforms such as Facebook have only amplified the stakes.

Add it all up, and the K–12 sector finds itself walking a tightrope.

"Social-emotional learning is really about building relationships and communities," said Jeremy Taylor, the director of assessment for the nonprofit Collaborative for Academic, Social, and Emotional Learning. "We hope ed tech can support that, but we have to make sure things are done in a way that is responsible and not outpacing people's comfort with what is happening in their schools,"

More Than Just a Test Score

Among the most prominent groups seeking to make sense of this new landscape is the Chan Zuckerberg Initiative.

A private venture-philanthropy organization founded by Facebook CEO Mark Zuckerberg and his wife, pediatrician Priscilla Chan, CZI plans to devote hundreds of millions of dollars per year to "whole-child personalized learning."

As part of that work, the group **teamed up in May with the Bill & Melinda Gates Foundation** to scour the field for the latest insights on how to measure and support

students' "executive functions," such as the ability to focus and filter out distractions.

Jim Shelton, who heads Chan Zuckerberg's education efforts, explained his thinking in an interview.

"Kids have physical development, mental-health development, identity development, cognitive-skills development, and social-emotional skills development, as well as academic-skill development," Shelton said. "Unless you understand how they are relating to each other, it is very difficult to optimize any of them."

Creating that kind of 360-degree view of each individual child is the key to reaching millions of students who have been failed by the existing education system, Shelton believes. Technology may eventually help make such a holistic understanding possible at scale, he said, but efforts to develop such tools are still in their infancy.

Nevertheless, real companies are already working to pursue various parts of what Shelton described.

Take **Panorama Education**. Founded in 2012, the data-analytics company has raised $32 million in venture capital (including multiple rounds from CZI).

It already works with 500 school systems, including the 29,000-student Spokane, Washington, district.

In addition to questions about school safety and their relationships with teachers, all of Spokane's 4th to 12th graders now take online surveys asking things like:

- In school, how possible is it for you to change how easily you give up?
- How often do you stay focused on the same goal for several months at a time?
- During the past 30 days, how carefully did you listen to other people's points of view?

"We have a bigger responsibility than just cranking out kids who can pass tests."
—Travis Schulhauser,
director of assessment and instructional technology, Spokane Public Schools

Panorama stores the responses in a central database, then feeds the information back to Spokane administrators and educators via customized dashboards.

As part of this year's pilot, a small group of Spokane teachers was able to see how each individual child in their classrooms scored on a 0–5 scale for the social–emotional domain corresponding to each question: grit, growth mindset, and social awareness.

Principals and counselors also analyzed the Panorama data alongside other information, such as class rosters, to identify students with an attitude that might help them thrive in Advanced Placement courses, even if they didn't have the highest PSAT scores. And district leaders examined how their schools compared with national benchmarks—which Panorama develops by analyzing the anonymized data of millions of students who take its surveys each year.

Spokane officials describe their multipronged use of Panorama data as key to making better decisions.

"As we get more and more information from kids, I think we'll respond to each student better and better," said Travis Schulhauser, the district's director of assessment and instructional technology.

Plenty of schools are embracing social–emotional learning without using technology or trying to measure individual students' development.

See Also: It remains an open question whether apps, online surveys, and other technology tools can reliably measure social–emotional skills at all. For an in-depth discussion of the challenges and concerns, read more here.

New research has raised questions about whether classroom-based interventions around concepts like growth mindset are likely to have a significant impact.

And some of the leading pioneers in the field have warned about the limits of using surveys and questionnaires to measure social–emotional skills. Even Shelton said CZI invested in the company primarily because of its surveys related to school climate and culture—and that he wasn't familiar enough with its "entire product suite" to say whether it provides "a valid and reliable measure of a developmental area."

Regardless, Spokane is just one of hundreds of districts embracing the digital tools and data they're currently being offered.

"We have a bigger responsibility than just cranking out kids who can pass tests," Schulhauser said. "We take seriously our responsibility to develop students who are well-rounded and able to achieve their hopes and dreams."

"Just Un-American"

Why wouldn't someone want schools to look beyond test scores, or use technology to encourage kids to persevere in class and build healthy relationships with peers?

"Sorry, but I don't want the government knowing how my child's mind works," said Jane Robbins, an attorney and senior fellow with the **American Principles Project Foundation**, a think tank that promotes individual liberty.

Like many conservative and libertarian parents and activists, Robbins is strongly opposed to using technology to track student emotions and mindsets.

An individual teacher encouraging students to try hard is one thing, she said. But surveys like Panorama's are "borderline mental-health assessments," she believes, and they encourage a view of children as potential patients in need of treatment.

In addition, Robbins argued, public schools are an extension of government. And government should not be trying to monitor and mold what individual citizens feel.

Plus, some critics on the right view the social–emotional learning movement as a thinly disguised effort to promote ostensibly left-wing causes, such as gay and transgender rights. ("Might a student's 'relationship skills' be deemed deficient if, in keeping with the influence of his family and faith, he rejects the LGBT agenda such as same-sex marriage and normalization of gender dysphoria?" asked conservative activist Karen Effrem in a 2016 essay, "Schools Ditch Academics for Emotional Manipulation.")

And all those concerns get amplified dramatically when large-scale digital data collection is added to the mix.

"You don't think these databases are going to be interesting down the line to employers, or prosecutors?" Robbins asked.

Given such opposition, it's not hard to imagine the reaction to newer entries into the social–emotional learning space, such as San Francisco-based startup **Emote**.

The company's core service is a mobile app that makes it easier for a wide range of school staff, from bus drivers to teachers, to record and share their observations of when students appear sad, anxious, angry, and frustrated.

Launched in 2016 with $120,000 in support from Y Combinator, one of the most high-profile "accelerators" in Silicon Valley, Emote is already used by 16 districts in more than a dozen states.

How does it work?

Imagine a student gets in an argument with his parent before school, said Julian Golder, the company's 32-year-old CEO. That morning, the boy stomps into the school building. A staff member at the front desk notices, so she enters the observation directly into the Emote app on her smartphone, selecting from a menu of keywords (sad) and a color-coded scale (blue).

That, in turn, prompts a notification to be sent to each of the student's teachers.

If those teachers then notice something similar—the student has his head down in first period, or seems disconnected in third period—they also record their observations in the app.

If a pattern emerges, Golder said, the student may be at risk of "escalation," such as getting into a fight or flunking his fifth period math test.

Despite their best efforts, he said, schools often miss these kinds of developments in the moment, leaving them to respond to the trouble after it happens.

But Emote helps adults notice and communicate about kids' feelings and behaviors in real time, Golder said. That way, they can respond before something bad happens.

> **"Sorry, but I don't want the government knowing how my child's mind works."**
> —Jane Robbins,
> *attorney and senior fellow, American Principles Project Foundation*

The company also allows schools to track students' feelings longitudinally: Maybe the student feels angry and disconnected every Monday morning because there's some underlying issue at home that needs to be addressed? Or perhaps the school's African American boys are consistently feeling disconnected after a particular class, and some observations of the teacher are warranted?

"I think this is a really exciting vision of what school can look like," Golder said.

"There's more interest than we can handle at this point."

Still, Robbins of the American Principles Project Foundation isn't buying it.

"The idea of telling children that even their feelings are not private, and that we're going to constantly surveil them and analyze them, is just un-American," Robbins said. "The only good thing I can see about this company is that they're not hooking kids up to wearables."

"Expand the Realm of the Possible"

Broadly speaking, however, that's exactly where the field appears to be heading.

In 2016, the World Economic Forum and the Boston Consulting Group issued a report on the future of ed tech and social–emotional learning. It highlighted wearable devices as a way to "expand the realm of the possible."

Among the companies trying to deliver on that promise: Cambridge, UK-based Tinylogics, which is currently testing a wearable it calls FOCI. When clipped to a waistband, the device will track users' breathing patterns, then tell them when they're feeling focused, relaxed, fatigued, or stressed. Tinylogics describes an accompanying app as a "focus-enhancing mind coach." A recent press release from the company billed the FOCI as a tool for managing digital distractions in the classroom.

Prominent ed-tech venture-capitalists are also touting virtual reality as an "empathy technology." A company called Mursion, for example, has been working with the Alexandria, VA, public schools to use immersive VR simulations as part of an effort to help students with autism develop their social–emotional learning skills.

And the World Economic Forum and the Boston Consulting Group also touted the field of "affective computing," in which machines are trained to recognize, interpret, and simulate human emotions.

Which brings the story back to West Palm Beach and Algebra Nation.

The effort to use clickstream data from the online platform in order to identify student emotions and engagement is being led by University of Colorado Boulder professor Sidney D'Mello, a national leader in the affective-computing field.

So far, all the information harvested by the team on the Algebra Nation project has been collected anonymously, in a way that is "intentionally insufficient to build affective profiles for individual students (which is not our goal at all)," D'Mello wrote in an e-mail.

Because of that approach, the institutional review board tasked with approving the project determined that no parental consent was yet needed.

But that could change soon.

Beginning in spring 2019, pending the review board's approval of a series of new consent

protocols, some students may interact with the current version of Algebra Nation. Others might interact with a version of the software that will analyze their individual click patterns in real time to identify when they're becoming bored or frustrated. If the predictions prove sufficiently accurate, it will respond in the moment with personalized prompts or supports. The researchers will see if the software that adapts to students' emotional states helps them learn algebra better.

At Conniston Middle School, Kaylee Carrell and her classmates had nuanced reactions, calling the idea both "cool" and "creepy."

The one place where students consistently drew a line: facial recognition.

"I would feel like I'm being watched, like someone is spying on me," said eighth grader Merlin Aguilar.

But even there, related technology is already being used in K–12.

Through the Emotive Computing Lab that D'Mello runs, for example, he's conducting a separate research project using eye-trackers and webcams to track consenting students' eye movements and facial expressions. Algorithms examine the resulting data to determine when kids' minds are wandering. If a student is zoning out, the software will intervene.

D'Mello acknowledged the privacy concerns associated with such technologies. But he said some level of risk is necessary in order to pursue a promising new vision of education.

"If I could always have teachers that are adapting to me, looking at my mistakes, giving me motivation and supports, and then backing away and giving me room, I think I'd be a much better learner," he said.

Clearly, that view has support from high places. The Algebra Nation project, for example, is being funded with an $8.9 million grant from the federal Institute of Education Sciences, the research arm of the U.S. Department of Education.

But recent controversies in other sectors have started to cast the use of technology to track student emotions in a critical new light.

Take the recent Facebook-Cambridge Analytica scandal, in which millions' of users had sensitive information about their preferences and personalities misused as part of an effort to influence their votes during the 2016 presidential election.

The resulting headlines and Congressional hearings have helped make the K–12 world more aware that similar technologies are already making their way into schools, said Ben Williamson, a lecturer at the University of Stirling in the United Kingdom.

That, in turn, is heightening awareness of the possibility of unintended consequences.

Data breaches are the most obvious potential downside, Williamson said, although he wasn't aware of any such incidents involving emotional or affective information collected from students.

But more pernicious, Williamson believes, is the potential for "psycho-compulsion and behavior modification."

"If you generate detailed information about students' feelings, then it becomes possible to target them in sophisticated ways in order to nudge them to behave in ways that conform with a particular, idealized model of a 'good student,'" Williamson said.

For supporters, that's part of the promise: the possibility that technology might help students develop grit and focus—and improve their grades, job prospects, and long-term health—is reason to invest millions now.

For critics, though, it's the wrong end of a slippery slope: government agencies and Silicon Valley companies deciding how students should be thinking and what they should be feeling—then collecting massive amounts of data and deploying invisible algorithms to enact that agenda—is something to be fought now, before the horse is all the way out of the barn.

The one thing both sides agree on?

"The technology is powerful," Williamson said, "and it could have real consequences."

An alternative version of this article appeared in the June 20, 2018, edition of Education Week.

Coverage of social and emotional learning is supported in part by a grant from the NoVo Foundation, at www.novofoundation.org. Education Week retains sole editorial control over the content of this coverage.

Benjamin Herold is a reporter covering educational technology for *Education Week*.

EXPLORING THE ISSUE

Is There Opposition to Using Technology to Track Student Social–Emotional Learning?

Critical Thinking and Reflection

1. Is it OK for technology to track student emotions, mindsets, and ways of thinking without prior written notice by parents, guardians, and/or students?
2. Should Every Student Succeeds Act (ESSA) support the social–emotional learning movement?
3. Do you see a real correlation to social–emotional learning to the overall standards in K–12 education?
4. Why are there so many concerns regarding the implementation of social–emotional learning measures?
5. What privacy issues, under what federal laws, are critical to understanding school measurement of student social–emotional learning?

Is There Common Ground?

Educators are hearing more and more about social–emotional learning (SEL) and in reviewing the literature on this topic, there is an emerging and resounding consensus from educators that they matter a lot. Educational leaders are looking for ways to use SEL research to identify and implement best practices that affect the following factors: "academic performance, behavioral problems, happiness, health, longevity, job performance, job satisfaction, and peer relationships" (Martin, n.d., p. 1). One example of measuring these traits has been prepared for the Collaborative for Academic, Social, and Emotional Learning by Marzano, that include a series of rubrics for K–12 schools aligning also with the Illinois state SEL standards. With an emphasis on multiple measures Wiggins and McTighe suggests that SEL sources of evidence include everything from surveys and focus groups to observations and assessments. The Association for Supervision and Curriculum Development identified this approach as multimetric accountability. SEL initiative like the ones just identified must include measurement as an essential elements for success of the program (Martin, n.d.). It is interesting to note that privacy issues are not addressed in most of the literature on SEL in schools, but as Jane Robbins testifies, the data being collected by SEL assessments could be wrongfully used by the government and that a very key issue is that students are providing their personal data without their consent or guarantees that their data won't be used for purposes other than those for which it was submitted.

Common ground appears very limited as the SEL movement continues to gain ground, noted by the quickly rising SEL curriculum updates being made in districts around the country and the push to assess SEL skills and daily behavior that are being pursued. Numerous school districts around the country are already measuring SEL and targeting intervention for students of all ages. The question for common ground is will the data being collected be used in the future against an individual for psychological profiling and or currently being used to label a child under a mental illness condition. Either one would result in the opposite rational for teaching and assessing SEL. Finally, SEL has a very strong base of support to continue growing as well as becoming more sophisticated in the design and use of measurement tools. Is there a breach in the Privacy Act of 1974, which includes conditions of disclosure to third parties, in collecting student behavior data without their consent? This question puts SEL at a crossroad that is ripe for continued debate.

Additional Resources

Author. (2018). Kickboard and aperture education partner to help schools use student behavior data to measure social emotional learning. *District Administrator*. Retrieved from https://www.districtadministration.com/content/kickboard-and-aperture-education-partner-help-schools-use-student-behavior-data-measure

Blad, E. (2016). States to partner on social–emotional learning standards. *Education Week*. 36:1.

Brotto, G. (2018). *Social emotional learning and the future of education*. Retrieved from http://www.

gettingsmart.com/2018/05/social-emotional-learning-and-the-future-of-education/

Elias, M., Zins, J., Weissberg, R., Frey, K., Greenberg, M., Haynes, N., Kessler, R., . . . Shriver, T. (1997). Promoting social and emotional learning for educators. *Association for Supervision and Curriculum Development*. Alexandria, VA.

CASEL. (2018). What is SEL? Retrieved from https://casel.org/what-is-sel/

Jones, S., & Doolittle, E. (2017). Social and emotional learning: Introducing the issue. *The Future of Children*. 27:1.

Martin, J. (n.d.). Eight steps for strengthening social emotional learning in your school district. *Act, Inc.* Retrieved from https://pages2.act.org/assessing-the-whole-child-ebook.html

Internet References . . .

Best Practices in Social–Emotional Learning Prepared for WASA School Information and Research Service

https://www.wasa-oly.org/WASA/images/WASA/1.0%20Who%20We%20Are/1.4.1.6%20SIRS/Download_Files/LI%202017/Sept%20-%20Best%20Practices%20in%20Social-Emotional%20Learning.pdf

Inside the Efforts to Measure Social Emotional Learning Progress

https://www.insidesources.com/social-emotional-learning-progress/

Is Social Emotional Learning Really Going to Work for Students of Color?

https://www.edweek.org/tm/articles/2017/06/07/we-need-to-redefine-social-emotional-learning-for.html

Learning How to Measure Social and Emotional Learning

https://www.rand.org/blog/2018/01/learning-how-to-measure-social-and-emotional-learning.html

The Psychological Approach to Educating Kids

https://www.theatlantic.com/education/archive/2017/03/the-social-emotional-learning-effect/521220/

Selected, Edited, and with Issue Framing Material by:
Glenn L. Koonce, *Regent University*

ISSUE

Should Electronic Textbooks Replace Print Textbooks?

YES: Ty Pierce, from "Electronic Textbooks for K12 Education: Lessons Learned from the Ohio as America Redesign," *Ohio History Connection* (2018)

NO: The Paper and Packaging Board, from "Paper and Productive Learning: The Fourth Annual Back-To-School Report," *The Paper and Packaging Board* (2018)

Learning Outcomes

After reading this issue, you will be able to:

- List some of the variables to be considered when creating websites and learning management systems (LMS).
- Give examples of the many benefits of reading a paper text rather than a tablet.
- Explain the advantages of addressing standardized testing and the use of K–12 digital content.
- Describe the differences between analog and digital lessons and how will this change the classroom in the future.
- Create a chart with the pros and cons of tablets versus textbooks.

ISSUE SUMMARY

YES: Ty Pierce, manager of Education and Multimedia Services at the Ohio History Connection, states that electronic textbooks are quickly becoming the norm for K12 education, and the use of myriad electronic resources is now standard practice in the modern classroom.

NO: The Paper and Packaging Board support print books noting that current research shows people are still more likely to have read a print book than a digital one.

McGraw-Hill, Pearson, and Houghton Mifflin Harcourt make up 85 percent of the $8 billion industry in publishing for the K–12 school market. No figure was found indicating the number or price tag for tablets in schools, but 42 percent of adults in the United States owns a tablet and overall it is a $72 billion industry (ProCon, 2017). Electronic textbooks may be the new norm now for K–12 schools. This is an interesting statement when one can see school children today on their way to school or returning from school who still have large and heavy backpacks. Are they not textbooks in those school bags? The weight of school bags has actually been scientifically studied and found that school going students should carry less than 15 percent of their own weight. Although no figure was given, it was noted that the weight of a sixth-grade student's backpack or a 10th-grade student's school bag with a day's load of books would certainly exceed far more than what is permissible. The logical conclusion to this dilemma of too much weight in schools bags would be for students to replace those textbooks with a tablet. Not only being less weight, it would be, according to some, cost-efficient and environmentally friendly. This is not the only advantage of tablets over textbooks. Some students feel dishearten and stressed when they find themselves continually behind in their studies. A tablet is much more interactive with multimedia learning for a high level of interest that helps students keep up and stay on task (CareerRide.com, n.d.).

Catalano (2018, p. 1) writes, "There's no question that tablets—and mobile computing devices of all kinds—remain on the rise in public schools." He notes that Futuresource Consulting conducted a market research project that showed "shipments of tablets and laptop computers to U.S. schools in the first quarter of 2018 were up 10 percent year-over-year" (p. 1). Academic year 2018 has also seen new tablet introductions and special pricing for schools from Apple.

Nearly 200 students from 15 elementary schools in Seattle, Washington, recently debated the topic, whether tablets or textbooks are better for students. The debated topic was, "Should Tablets replace textbooks in elementary schools? In a survey before the debate, 57 percent of students indicated tablets should replace elementary school textbooks, and 43 percent said they shouldn't" (p. 1). Parents, teachers, and administrators made up the audience for these energetic students, who were divided into teams of three to four students each who conducted their debate in 14 separate classrooms. These students identified pros and cons including topics such as backpack weight, the environment, transition of text for English Language Learners, costs for the initial buy and then to keep upgrades going, timelines of information in tablet versus print, higher grades for those who use a tablet, fewer distractions when using print material, eyestrain, quality of sleep, batteries in the tablet not lasting the whole day, Internet connectivity, and costly repairs. The debate was an opportunity for the students to see all sides of the issue being debated and how complex the issue really is. The final tally came at the conclusion of the debate, tablet votes dropped to 52 percent and printed textbooks up to 48 percent. Tablets won out, but the gap had closed. This seemingly minor debate with children in elementary school is an example of where the overall debate could be for the nation's educators. It is wise to have students who use the textbooks and tablets in school to have a voice in the ongoing debate.

The textbook is not extinct yet as there are disadvantages to a tablet driven textbook source. First, using a tablet provides students with numerous distractions and opportunities to veer away from reading the electronic textbook when they are supposed to be studying. Social network sites are very enticing and today's youth seem to be addicted to online games. There are sites that contain harmful content, as well as, age inappropriate websites. Many children's parents cannot afford purchasing a tablet

and there are times when a tablet needs repair. It could be stolen thus an interruption to required readings and studying which can result in students being behind and having to catch up. Likewise, not every parent can purchase the kind of Internet bandwidth for optimal online learning. Antivirus protection can be costly as well. Sometimes overlooked, but very insightful, is health concerns like Computer Vision Syndrome, eyestrain, headache, blurred vision, and dry and itchy eyes all from spending too much time using technology for textbooks (CareerRide.com, n.d.).

At the June 2018 International Society for Educational Technology (ISTE) conference in Chicago where 16,000 attended, a panel was convened with a posted description, "The Textbook Is Extinct! Now What?" (Cavanagh, 2018, p. 1). To sum it up, the panel indicated it was far too early for last rites and that the textbook is not dead. In addition, printed textbook are likely to be around for years to come even though many districts have moved to the digital textbook. The panel's comments were equally spread across textbooks versus tablets. As for textbooks, a weakness in lesson preparation make it more difficult for students to receive personalized instruction that includes more module-type resources. An example of a modular resource would be a collection of STEM learning modules to challenge students in middle school and above to use basic math and problem-solving skills. One panel member stated that, "Textbooks really deliver content in one way, and not every learner learns in one way" (p. 2). Relying on textbooks just does not meet every kids needs even though districts continue to rely on printed textbooks and publishing companies full-scale curricula across entire grade spans. The main argument against textbooks is that they deliver content in one way and that may not meet the needs of students who are not successful learning in the particular way being required. The movement to open educational resources has positively impacted electronic materials that allow teachers to pick and choose various content sources as they assemble their lessons. Even so, it is time consuming for a teacher to have ready all their lessons in electronic delivery form. In addition, not all districts have access to effective electronic materials or have the budget required for optimal access. A panel member stated, "Textbooks, for all their shortcomings, can 'level the playing field' and give districts with limited resources access to high-quality content" (p. 3). One other key point made by a panel member noted that textbooks go stale after a while, especially if the district does not pay to keep them up to date. Further, digital resources can be acquired in pieces that build a continuum of learning opportunities that provide flexibility and refresh the teaching learning environment (Cavanagh, 2018).

PreCon.org (n.d.) lists a number of pros (15) and cons (17) in their publication, *Should Tablets Replace Textbooks in K-12 Schools*. Some example are:

Pro: Tablets help students learn faster;

Con: People who read print text comprehend more, remember more, and learn more than those who read digital text;

Pro: Tablets can hold hundreds of textbooks on one device, plus homework, quizzes, and other files, eliminating the need for physical storage of books and classroom materials;

Con: Tablets help students better prepare for a world immersed in technology;

Pro: Tablet allow teachers to better customize student learning;

Con: Tablets enable students to cut corners or cheat on schoolwork;

Pro: Using a tablet is so intuitive that it makes learning fun; and

Con: Many textbooks are not available in digital format or on the specific tablet used in the school (pp. 1–4).

The YES and NO sections that follow this introduction, contrast the debate on "Should Electronic Textbooks Replace Print Textbooks?" Ty Pierce (2018) supports electronic textbooks and describes how the Ohio Connection's digital team redesigned the electronic textbook, *Ohio as America*. He is very convincing as he covers the following topics on this journey: (1) the website (Learning Management System, (2) do's and don'ts for teachers, (3) standards and tests, (4) interactivity and rich media, (5) digital versus analog, (6) accessibility and differentiation, and (7) projects or products?

The NO article derives its focus from the Paper and Packaging Board's (2018), *Paper and Product Learning: The Fourth Annual Back to School Report*. This report starts at the very beginning stating, "In today's fast paced, highly competitive classrooms, paper continues to be the preferred tool for productivity among students, teachers and parents" (p. 2). The main emphasis in this article is on reading print material everyday noting that, "Students tell us they remember more when reading in print" (p. 4). The *Paper and Product Learning: The Fourth Annual Back to School Report* affirms their earlier reports and continues with, "Experts say putting pen to paper has therapeutic value that can offer benefits similar to meditation. Ninety-four percent of college students say paper is essential to helping them achieve their academic goals, and 89 percent of students in grades 7th through 12th agree" (p. 3). This issue is close to many teachers, administrators, students, and parents who work within the confines of the district when it comes to textbooks, be they print or tablet.

YES

Ty Pierce

Electronic Textbooks for K12 Education: Lessons Learned from the Ohio as America Redesign

Introduction

In the past five years, the K12 classroom has experienced nothing less than a paradigm shift. While much has been made of K12's rapid adoption of technology, it underpins a much larger and more significant shift in pedagogy toward student-centric learning. More schools are adopting blended learning methodologies, the need for differentiation and extension has increased, and the efficient use of teachers' time has become even more paramount. Electronic textbooks are quickly becoming the norm for K12 education, and the use of myriad electronic resources is now standard practice in the modern classroom.

In 2015, a comprehensive evaluation showed that the Ohio History Connection's flagship education product, the *Ohio as America* electronic textbook, needed significant improvements to keep pace and continue to grow as a revenue generator. Our department embarked on a complete redesign that included the content, structure, and the platform itself. Less than a year later, we launched the "2.0 version" of *Ohio as America* in August 2016—an enormous undertaking that included more than 100 teacher-created lessons, hundreds of primary sources, and significant UX improvements.

The process of bringing this new product to market taught us countless lessons and involved many decisions and considerations applicable to any museum engaging K12 with digital content.

Project or Product?

Do you plan to make money from your project? The answer to that question will set your path down one of two development tracks. The project track is familiar to most of us. Choosing product, however, immediately mandates several considerations and leaves less room for error in others. A paid product will likely require a credential and access process for users, and that you protect your content from piracy, for example. Schools have very different expectations for functionality and support with paid products than the typical free museum-created resource. Functions like Single Sign On are becoming a necessity, and you will need to determine your team's capacity to manage subscriptions, process payments, and provide consistent and long-term technical support across the entire product.

This decision is also affected by how robust a resource you can deliver. With the plethora of free and open-source educational content, there is a dearth of material for teachers to incorporate into their lessons. There is a very real need for quality resources, however, and schools will pay for products that improve the quality of instruction and save their teachers' time. The more niche your resource may be, the smaller its potential audience and the less likely it will succeed as a paid product. Many times, museums may have high-quality collections that fit a particular subject area, but these may be better off as a free resource to supplement classroom instruction, rather than a paid one-off that fails to find an appreciable market. In addition, resources should be designed to be expansive, rather than restrictive, and allow teachers to adapt it to their own instruction methods as they see fit.

Teaching to Standards, Teaching to Tests

For better or worse, K12 right now is all about the *assessment*. Instruction at all levels and in all disciplines is focused on addressing standards and driving achievement on standardized tests; by and large, the success of our products depends on this reality. Rather than start with your institution's stories and content, you should start with the standards of your identified market. How many of their standards can you directly address? How many can you address in multiple ways? Art museums, for instance, may not have pieces that directly address the subject matter of a given standard, but they can create content to support skills-based standards or use art as a springboard for creative writing prompts. It's worth making an honest assessment of your content with standards in mind before starting any K12 project.

With *Ohio as America 2.0*, we created a pacing guide that aligned to the Ohio Department of Education's fourth-grade social studies standards. Every content statement has at least two activities that directly address it, resulting in more than 100 new activities; the standards drove all our content decisions. From image selection to video storyboarding and the way we incorporated outside education apps, the standards-aligned pacing guide formed the backbone of our entire project.

Website, Learning Management System (LMS), or Something Else?

A literal interpretation of the term "electronic textbook" leads many to think of popular e-book formats. Your digital team could simply create an e-book using one of the various methods available and put it up for sale. You could adapt text documents and images into a simple EPUB file, use iBooks Author to create a gorgeous and immersive digital experience, or anything in between. These options may work well for small- to medium-sized resources, but in our experience, e-book formats quickly begin to limit your development options in negative ways; iBooks don't work on Chromebooks, they are limited in overall file size, and Apple takes a cut of your revenue; EPUBs are limited in their ability to deliver multimedia and interactive experiences, and are typically utilized with a traditional approach to teaching.

Creating a website seems like a simple—and possibly obvious—place to start. The tools are familiar, the team can leverage existing infrastructure and hosting services, and it's accessible to anyone. But before you fire up Word-Press and go out for coffee, a few things to consider:

- You'll need a simple and reliable way to manage user credentials and access.
- The design and content must be fully compatible with multiple device and responsive to a wide variety of viewports.
- Its navigation and layout are optimized for the targeted grade level(s), as the students are the primary users in today's student-centric classroom.
- Any interactive components, functions, features, and so on will require additional development and therefore additional resources or dollars.

- Ongoing support is also a primary consideration. It's not enough just to run updates and answer the occasional e-mail. If teachers are expecting to use this as a daily part of their instruction, how quickly can you address and resolve issues that inevitably arise?

Another complicating factor is the adoption of LMSs to streamline instruction. This wasn't as important three years ago, when districts were testing the waters with various LMSs and might have several different systems in use. In Ohio, many districts have settled on widespread implementation of Schoology or Google Classroom, with Canvas also a major player. The more ingrained an LMS is in a particular district, the more that district will want your content to integrate with the LMS. For concise learning modules, this can be possible using compatibility protocols like SCORM or Tin Can API; however, for large-scale resources it becomes unwieldy and may undercut your ability to control your content. At the very least, LMS's have raised teachers' expectations for digital resources, and those expectations need to be factored into your planning.

Ohio as America was originally created as a website in Joomla with some additional modules and features. For the redesign, we kept it in Joomla but dramatically increased module development. These improvements included interactive pre- and post-assessments, an automatic Gradebook, and extensive improvements to the back-end management platform. In doing so, it has evolved to include many features of an LMS, and today it exists with a foot in both worlds. We have received additional requests from districts for deeper LMS integration, and over the course of this year we are exploring ways to make that a reality.

Working with Teachers: Pros and Cons

Tapping classroom teachers to create your content makes sense—they know the classroom better than we do, they're up on the latest methods, and they understand how to differentiate effectively for their students. For the redesign, we devised an activity framework, created templates and guides, and then contracted with around 15 Ohio teachers to create our activities.

While ultimately successful, the process was far from perfect. Some things to consider:

- There was a wide variety of expertise and knowledge, resulting in an equally wide variety of activity design styles.

- Even with template documents and specific guidelines, consistency was an enormous issue and required extensive staff time to clean things up.
- Fact-checking was imperative. While some teachers are excellent at research, much of the information we received was incorrect.
- Image citations and other references were rarely provided, resulting in quite a bit of primary source detective work to publish with the required bibliographies.
- Sensitive subject matter also raises concern. For our work, representations of American Indian history are rife with inaccuracy and cultural bias, and it's not realistic to expect the average K12 teacher to handle this with the same level of sensitivity as those working in our field.

That said, the pros far outweigh the cons. Our teachers generated some incredible lesson ideas that we would have never thought of. Teachers brought their own lists of favorite education apps, curating a list of tools that were already classroom tested, and found excellent sources outside OHC collections to incorporate. As we began marketing the new version, districts immediately responded to the fact our textbook was created by Ohio teachers, and the teachers themselves have become some of the product's strongest advocates.

Digital versus Analog: Designing Lessons with a Foot in Both Worlds

Despite all the tech talk, there's still a lot of analog happening in today's classrooms. For every teacher that's fully 1:1, there are easily several more who will print lessons for students to complete by hand. This continuum of tech in the classroom is a primary consideration; designing a digital-only product precludes a wide variety of use cases, but simple designs may fail to capitalize on the opportunity that blended learning and student-centric environments present. The broader your spectrum of use cases, the wider your possible range of adoption and impact.

An environmental scan is crucial to informing this aspect of decision-making. What percentage of districts are 1:1 or will be in two years? What percentage of classrooms have a SMART board or projector? Digital equity is also a concern; do a majority of students have reliable Internet access at home or have devices to engage with? Let the reality of your market's tech dictate your approach.

We designed *Ohio as America 2.0* to be easily adapted for classrooms with varying degrees of technological integration. Teachers are able to engage students as an entire class through SMART boards or other display systems,

1:1 through individual electronic devices, or a combination of both. Teachers can either print the student readings, activities, and other materials as PDFs, assign them as Google Docs, or have students work directly from the webpage. Although providing different formats added to development costs and the product's complexity, there are now very few barriers to entry, and subscriptions have increased by 24 percent in 2016.

Interactivity and Multimedia

Games, videos, and apps are all part of the daily curriculum and provide unparalleled opportunity to engage students with your content. Regardless of your approach, all of these elements increase development costs, so consider their implementation wisely. Compatibility is a top concern; some versions of Chromebooks, for instance, may have issues with video playback, and Flash-based content can create problems on Apple devices. All content should be optimized for fast page loads. The school may have blistering-fast Wi-Fi, but students may do their homework assignment on a phone while riding in a car.

Make sure video content is grade appropriate and, whenever possible, keep the runtime under three minutes. Have your production team work closely with your educators. Let the standards drive the script and design the entire production around that one piece of information students' need to glean from the video. Our students respond very well to first-person videos, and any documentary-style pieces are produced with an informal, informational style.

Interactive content elements cut both ways—they are certainly engaging but run the risk of taking instructional choice out of the teachers' hands. They can also present issues with compatibility and responsive design, which may limit their usefulness. As more states move toward digital assessments, however, developing interactive assessments may be well worth the effort. They can give students the content knowledge they need while also reinforcing the digital skills necessary to succeed on tests and providing teachers with a digital tool to assess their class will help save them precious time.

Interactivity is key to *Ohio as America*'s success. One of the most used features is an interactive map that allows students to select various informational overlays (railroads, major cities, American Indian tribes, etc.) to create custom maps for their own use. By far the largest improvement has been the creation of interactive assessments and an automatic Gradebook—these features have truly been a game changer for the product because they save educators time and also help prepare the students to perform on electronic assessments as part of state testing.

Accessibility and Differentiation

Differentiated instruction—providing different students with different ways to learn, often inside the same learning environment—has become a hallmark of the modern classroom. Teachers are expected to teach a wide range of student abilities at the same time, and the promise of educational technology is closely linked with individualized instruction. As you design an activity, build differentiation opportunities into the design. Include prompts and ideas on adapting the content for students with reading difficulty, or to extend the lesson and increase rigor for students with a higher aptitude. Incorporate multiple asset types to provide choice in how students obtain the information and also to allow teachers to pick and choose what will work best for a particular student. For activities that involve student-created content, it's important to incorporate both digital and analog methods to accommodate students more comfortable with a pen-and-paper approach.

Accessibility can also take many forms; some are technology-based, and others have their roots in content design. One key feature added to *Ohio as America* was a screen reader, which reads passages of text aloud to students, and a font selection tool, which lets students adjust the size and typeface of fonts. If your audience requires the product to support multiple languages, a combination of content and technology must be designed to meet that need. For *Ohio as America*, one improvement for next year is the creation of "social studies readers." These are versions of student readings that incorporate more images and reduce the length and rigor of the text to make information more accessible to students reading below grade level.

Conclusion

Whether you pursue the creation of an electronic textbook as a free resource or a paid product, the potential impact of these projects is truly incredible. We work hard to make *Ohio as America* a resource both teachers and students are excited to use, and we consider it a privilege to be part of daily instruction for thousands of Ohio students. When the bell rings at the end of the day, the knowledge those students have gained stands as the embodiment of our organization's mission.

Ty Pierce is a manager of Education and Multimedia Services at the Ohio History Connection.

The Paper and Packaging Board    **NO**

Paper and Productive Learning

The Fourth Annual Back-to-School Report

Introduction

In today's fast-paced, highly competitive classrooms, paper continues to be the preferred tool for productivity among students, teachers, and parents. Ninety-four percent of college students say paper is essential to helping them achieve their academic goals, and 89 percent of students in grades 7th through 12th agree.[1] Meanwhile, 92 percent of educators and 90 percent of parents agree that reading 15 pages a day on paper can benefit any student. Paper's enduring role in education comes as no surprise: 8 in 10 people say that paper and paper-based packaging are relevant in their daily lives. After all, paper is a versatile material that helps us ideate and create, accomplishing our objectives.[2] It also offers peace of mind as it secures our information and provides proof of our hard work.[3] Indeed, paper's many uses in the classroom—and beyond—help design our future.

"90 percent of parents agree that reading 15 pages a day on paper can benefit any student.[1]"

Building beneficial connections with paper is as simple as opening your favorite paperback and reading 15 Pages A Day or taking handwritten notes during a lecture or meeting. Paper has no flashing notifications that command us to respond immediately, so as we spend more time with paper, the more our senses are engaged. We can feel the texture of the page beneath our hand. We can hear the crinkle of a page turning. We can see the ink of our pen forming letters, our thoughts coming to life before our eyes. It is through this sensory contact that we absorb, comprehend, and retain information.[4] We're focused and undistracted. We are learning more deeply.[5] Because paper tools are so readily accessible, cultivating deeper-learning

techniques can easily begin at home with 15 Pages A Day, a sustained reading practice with a wealth of benefits. Nearly 90 percent of teachers and parents say reading 15 pages on paper each day can help improve a student's memory and language development.[1]

There's also the added bonus of extra parent–kid time: 81 percent of Millennial parents say they read with their child every night.[1] And time spent with paper is time not spent on the screen: 83 percent believe it's important to "unplug" from digital devices once in a while, and 59 percent are trying to limit their family's screen time.[3] In an always-on world where 59 percent say they're suffering from "digital overload," paper provides a welcome respite. That's why 73 percent say reading a printed book or magazine was more enjoyable than reading on a digital device.[6]

74 percent of parents believe that taking notes by hand should be encouraged in their child's education.[1]

94 percent of college students say paper is essential to helping them achieve their academic goals.[1]

91 percent of Millennial parents believe reading 15 pages on paper a day can help improve a student's memory and language development.[1]

92 percent of Millennial parents of K–12 students believe writing things down by hand has helped their child develop skills as hand–eye coordination.[1]

Paper and Productivity beyond the Classroom

Paper's positive effect on productivity doesn't end with reading and comprehension in the classroom, but rather it extends far beyond and into the professional workplace. Forty-five percent of college students agree that they learn things best when they write them down by hand—a practice that 85 percent of college educators encourage. Eighty-one percent of college students say they use paper materials such as flash cards, printouts, study sheets, and printed lecture notes to prepare for exam, a practice that makes learning easier and improves memory.[7] Writing on paper can also keep us on track in other ways. Experts say putting pen to paper has therapeutic value that can offer benefits similar to meditation.[7]

Expressive writing can even allow us to operate in the past, present, and future at the same time, which allows our brains to make sense of the recalled past, while choosing and shaping words at the moment of creating and, at the same time, imagining a person reading what is being written.[8]

Add to that the sensory engagement of the texture of each blank sheet, the weight of the writing instrument, and the visual and physical satisfaction of making marks on paper, and we understand why 45 percent of students in grades 7 through 12 say they learn best writing on paper.

"Experts say putting pen to paper has therapeutic value that can offer benefits similar to meditation.[7]"

81 percent% of college students say they use paper materials such as flash cards, printouts, study sheets and printed lecture notes to prepare for exams.[1]

85 percent% of college educators encourage taking notes by hand.[1]

62 percent% of adults agree paper-based products are an environmentally smart choice because they come from trees, a renewable resource.[3]

Such productivity habits will serve students well as they move from classroom to workforce, where 64 percent of employees say they prefer to distribute printed agendas and other documents at the workplace[3]—pieces of paper that are perfect for taking notes to be studied and referenced later.

It's also important to know that paper doesn't just make us smarter—it is a smart choice: 62 percent of adults agree paper-based products are an environmentally smart choice because they come from trees, a renewable resource.[3]

So, as the new school year approaches and new objectives are set, students, teachers, and parents will intuitively recognize the value of paper as the preferred learning tool—the smart tool that works hard to help keep us focused so we can achieve our goals. When it's time to jump-start your productivity by reading 15 Pages A Day or sketching out your next big idea in a favorite notebook, you can trust paper to help you make it happen.

"77% of students grades 7–12 believe that no matter their literacy level, any student can benefit from reading (or being read) 15 pages a day.[1]"

Research References for "The Productive Learning Report"

1. These are the findings from an Ipsos poll conducted March 25–April 6, 2018, on behalf of the Paper and Packaging Board. For the survey, a sample of 1,803 students and adults aged 13 and older from the United States was interviewed online, in English. The sample includes 400 college students, 501 students in grades 7 through 12, 602 parents with children in kindergarten through grade 12, and 300 educators.
2. Mueller, P. A., & Oppenheimer, D. M. 2014. "The Pen Is Mightier Than the Keyboard: Advantages of Longhand Over Laptop Note Taking." Psychological Science, 25(6), 1159–1168.
3. "Consumer Attitudes and Usage toward Paper and Packaging: Wave 7." Isobar survey conducted April 23–May 4, 2018, on behalf of the Paper and Packaging Board. For the survey, 904 men and women, ages 18–49, from the United States were interviewed online.
4. "Make Books a Daily Habit: Why Regular Reading Matters, Especially in Print." by Naomi S. Baron, 2017, Paper and Productive Learning: The Third Annual Back-to-School Report.
5. "Staying Productive with Paper: A Q&A With 2012 National Teacher of the Year Rebecca Mieliwocki." 2016, Paper and Productive Learning: The Second Annual Back-to-School Report.
6. "Print and Paper in a Digital World: Consumer Preferences, Attitudes & Trust." Toluna survey conducted in June 2017 on behalf of Two Sides North America. For the survey, 2,131 men and women, 18 and older, from the United States were interviewed.
7. "Pen, Paper, Power! Five Benefits of Journal Writing" by Kathleen Adams, LPC, The Center for Journal Therapy, for the Paper and Packaging Board. October 2016.
8. "Expressive Writing: A Path Forward for Your Health" by Jeremy Nobel, MD, MPH, for the Paper and Packaging Board. October 2016.

Research References for "All Hands on Books: The Power of Print"

1. Rowling, J.K., "Harry Potter and the Deathly Hallows," Scholastic: 2007.
2. Bureau of Labor Statistics, "American Time Use Survey."
3. Shusterman, Neal. "Arc of a Scythe," Simon & Schuster BFYR: 2016.
4. Mercola, Dr. Martin. "Read in a Quiet Place for a Better Life," April 18, 2016.
5. Zomorodi, Manoush. "Bored and Brilliant: How Spacing out Can Unlock Your Most Productive and Creative Self," St. Martin's Press: 2017.
6. "Scholastic Kids and Family Reading Report," 5th edition, Key Findings, p. 7. Scholastic: 2015.
7. Merle, Andrew. "If You Want to be Like Warren Buffett and Bill Gates, Adopt Their Voracious Reading Habits." Quartz: April 23, 2016.

THE PAPER AND PACKAGING BOARD is a commodity checkoff program overseen by the U.S. Department of Agriculture is self-funded through quarterly assessments paid by eligible manufacturers and importers of paper and paper-based packaging.

EXPLORING THE ISSUE

Should Electronic Textbooks Replace Print Textbooks?

Critical Thinking and Reflection

1. Is your district/area set up for electronic textbooks? Why or why not?
2. Do you believe the pros outweigh the cons when working with teachers to create activity framework, created templates and guides for classroom content in the digital world?
3. What does current research show about why people are more likely to use a printed text over a digital one?
4. Should students be involved in the decision-making process when choosing to phase out printed textbooks in K–12 classrooms?
5. Does having easy access to tablets in schools make differentiated instruction more feasible for all classrooms?

Is There Common Ground?

The common ground in the debate tablets versus printed textbooks lies in the school districts that have selected one over the other for presenting their curriculum to their students. It is likely that each district has spent time reviewing both entities and made their decisions per the procedure used in the district for textbook selection and purchase. Typically, these members of the selection committee include all stakeholders: parents, teachers, administration, school board, and in some cases students.

There appears to be more pressure to move to tablets in a review of the literature on the issue. Tablets have been in classrooms for a long period of time now, primarily because some parents can afford them and/or school districts who have taken the funding plunge providing tablets to their students. Once under the digital delivery of the curriculum, it is very difficult to move back. Knowing this, districts must weigh all the pros and cons giving particular attention to a comprehensive plan that includes infrastructure, apps that educators will need to use, and security. Of course, there are many other factors and processes to consider.

A data blog from 2015 gives a little more perspective, over time, how the digital education movement is predicted to grow. McKinsey and GAMA reported in 2014 that in a very short time, by 2020, the mEducation market globally could be worth $70 billion plus another $32 billion for mEducation devices, like smartphones and tablets (Rock, 2018). Today, schools continue to use technology in ways that can best meet their missions for continuous improvement and student success. Yet, there are countless school

districts who prefer a textbook over a tablet. For many years, printed textbooks have provided the foundation for student learning. Textbooks have been very successful as this foundation which provided students with a printed textbook to learn, to explore, and to discover the content found for the numerous subjects and grade levels in their K–12 education journey. "The most important part of the learning process is giving students the chance to connect ideas with what they see in front of them. Textbooks provide students a physical approach to learning and help them process information in a way that is easier than on a screen. Students also are able to see their progress right in front of them and understand what they're accomplishing as they learn" (Oxford Learning, 2016, p. 1). Will schools continue moving to electronic textbooks or will printed textbooks hold firm, or even come back?

Additional Resources

Catalano, F. 2018. *Tablets or textbooks: elementary students take on one of the great tech debates of our time.* Retrieved from https://www.geekwire.com/2018/tablets-textbooks-elementary-students-take-one-great-tech-debates-time/

Cavanagh, S. (2018). Is the textbook dead? Far too early for last rites, ISTE panel suggests. *EDWeek Market Brief.* Retrieved from https://marketbrief.edweek.org/marketplace-k-12/textbook-dead-far-early-last-rites-iste-panel-suggests/

Oxford Learning. (2016). *Should textbooks be replaced by notebook computers?* Retrieved from https://www.oxfordlearning.com/textbooks-vs-computers/

Paper and Packing Board. (2018). *Paper and product learning: The fourth annual back to school report.* Retrieved from http://www.howlifeunfolds.com/paper-productive-learning-fourth-annual-back-school-report/

ProCon. (2017). *Should tablets replace textbooks in K–12 schools?* ProCon.Org. Retrieved from https://tablets-textbooks.procon.org/view.answers.php?questionID=001874

Rock, M. (2015). Tablets versus textbooks. *Northwest Educational Recourse Association.* Retrieved from http://nwedresources.org/tablets-vs-textbooks/

Internet References . . .

Print Textbooks versus E-Textbooks

https://www.investopedia.com/financial-edge/0912/print-textbooks-vs.-e-textbooks.aspx

Printed Textbooks versus E-Text: Comparing the "Old School" Convention with "New School" Innovation

https://www.usma.edu/cfe/Literature/Haith-Rogers_15.pdf

Print versus Digital Textbooks and the Challenge of Meeting Student Needs

https://hub.wiley.com/community/exchanges/discover/blog/2015/07/31/print-vs-digital-textbooks-and-the-challenge-of-meeting-student-needs

Should Tablets Replace Textbooks in K–12 Schools?

https://tablets-textbooks.procon.org/

Students Prefer Print. Why Are Schools Pushing Digital Textbooks?

http://blogs.edweek.org/edweek/bookmarks/2016/03/students_prefer_print_schools_pushing_digital_textbooks.html